Dirk Mudge

All the way to an independent Namibia

Dirk Mudge

All the way to an independent Namibia

Protea Book House
Pretoria
2016

All the way to an independent Namibia – Dirk Mudge

First edition, first impression in 2016 by Protea Book House

PO Box 35110, Menlo Park, 0102
1067 Burnett Street, Hatfield, Pretoria
8 Minni Street, Clydesdale, Pretoria
protea@intekom.co.za
www.proteaboekhuis.com

Translator: Amy Schoeman
Editor: Danél Hanekom
Proofreader: Carmen Hansen-Kruger
Cover design: Hanli Deysel
Cover image: Street march, Katutura, November 1989
Typography: 10.5 on 14 pt ZapfCalligr BT by Ada Radford
Printed and bound: CTP Printers, Cape Town

© 2015 Dirk Mudge (Afrikaans text)
© 2016 Dirk Mudge (English translation)

ISBN: 978-1-4853-0456-2 (printed book)
ISBN: 978-1-4853-0457-9 (e-book)
ISBN: 978-1-4853-0458-6 (ePub)

If I tried to read, much less answer, all the criticisms made of me, and all the attacks leveled against me, this office would have to be closed for all other business. I do the best I know how, the very best I can. And I mean to keep doing this, down to the very end. If the end brings me out all wrong, ten angels swearing I had been right would make no difference. If the end brings me out all right, then what is said against me now will not amount to anything.

Abraham Lincoln

Contents

PREFACE Piet Croucamp   13

CHAPTER 1 Introduction   17

CHAPTER 2 The origin of the Territory Deutsch-Südwest-afrika   28
The 1914 Rebellion   31
South West Africa becomes a mandated territory   32
Politics between two World Wars (1920–1939)   35

CHAPTER 3 A new beginning in South West Africa   39
My ancestors   41
Rusthof, my birthplace   44
The Depression   45
Boskop, my father's first farm   47
Boetie goes to school   49
The Centenary of 1938   51
I visit Windhoek and Cape Town for the first time   52
The Second World War breaks out   54
Windhoek High School   55
Stellenbosch   57

CHAPTER 4 Farmer and South West African politician   60
Elandsvreugde   60
My brief sojourn in the world of business   62
I become a farmer   63
Our new farm, Lazy Spade   64
A new community and interesting experiences   65
My first taste of politics   66
Knee-deep in politics   68
Political turmoil   69
The National Party comes to power   72
The awakening of black nationalism   73

CHAPTER 5 My 20 years in the Legislative Assembly   77
Drought and foot-and-mouth disease   77
A newcomer in politics   78

The Odendaal Report of 1964   81
A "raised-hands" referendum and the expropriation of farms   84
Inauguration of the new Legislative Assembly building   87
My older colleagues in the Legislative Assembly   89
New role players in the National Party   90
On principles, policy, methods and approaches   91
The role of the UNSWP opposition   92
Once again the drought requires all our attention   95
The drought is over, but the political storm continues   95
I become a member of the Executive Committee in 1965   98
Adv. Percy Niehaus still a nuisance   98
Old friends leave us   101
A new team takes over   105

**CHAPTER 6   South West Africa becomes an international
problem**   108
South Africa versus the United Nations   108
The World Court case (1960–1966)   110
Ongulumbashe, the onset of the Border War   111
Local politics and South West Africa's affiliation with
     South Africa   115
South Africa says the people of South West must decide
     themselves   119
Reorganisation of administrative and financial functions   120
Back to politics   121
The first signs of distrust   122
The new administrative dispensation in operation   127
Fundamental differences rise to the surface   129

CHAPTER 7   My first experience of international politics   132
The South West Africa issue at the World Court for the
     sixth time   132
Differences about diversity and human dignity   133
Dr Waldheim and Dr Escher visit South West Africa   134
Our political differences intensify   138
The first meeting of the Prime Minister's Advisory Board, 1973   140
I attend the session of the UN General Assembly   141

CHAPTER 8   Internal political development from 1974 to 1977   147
Five years with John Vorster   147
The Turnhalle Conference takes shape   152

War and peace – strange bedfellows 154
The administration of the country is not neglected 157
The election campaign of 1974 159
New faces in the Legislative Assembly 161
I am expected to take the lead 162
Independence for Angola is announced 166
All options remain open, but to whom? 167
Were we playing for time? 170
The Turnhalle Conference – the first steps 171
The reaction of the National Party to the Conference 175
We travel abroad 177
The inner workings at the Conference 180
The division of functions 181
The bait of an interim government 183
The public must be informed 184
The playing field changes 186
A greater measure of public dialogue 188
The Turnhalle Conference grips the imagination 191
Rumours of discord within the National Party 193
The Prinsloo/Mey controversy 199
The international community and us 202
My Kamanjab speech 205
The Turnhalle Conference proposes an interim constitution 207
A referendum for the whites 208
The international community interferes, but we hold a
    referendum 211
My last lap in the National Party 216
Back to the drawing board 219
Discord in white ranks 222
The battle for leadership 231

**CHAPTER 9   The Republican Party and the Democratic
Turnhalle Alliance enter the scene, 1977** 233
A new party sees the light 233
Our task ahead 234
Our first public meeting 236
Minister P.W. Botha and I come to blows for the first time 238
Politics become dirty 240
The Turnhalle Conference comes to an end 242
The Democratic Turnhalle Alliance becomes a reality 244

Our own newspaper, *Republikein*, appears on 1 December 1977   246
Civilians and political leaders pay the highest price   252
My first experience as leader of the opposition   255
The final Western proposals   261
Cassinga, 4 May 1978   263
The political struggle remains intense   264
Diplomatic manoeuvres around the settlement plan   267
The general election of 1978   271

CHAPTER 10   An own government for South West Africa, 1978–1983   289
The first session of the Constituent Assembly   289
The status of the Constituent Assembly is confirmed   293
The National Party misses a golden opportunity   304
The Constituent Assembly has to take a stand   309
At a crossroad once again   314
A short political interlude   318
The interim government takes shape   323
The National Party hits the brakes   327
The National Assembly gains official status   330
Criticism from white ranks   331
The National Assembly takes off   335
The whites protest   337

CHAPTER 11   Between two fires, 1979–1983   343
P.W. Botha's dilemma   343
Dr Gerrit Viljoen becomes Administrator General   347
A new Legislative Assembly is elected   350
Danie Hough becomes Administrator General   353
A new American approach under Ronald Reagan   355
The Geneva Conference, 7–14 January 1981   356
P.W. Botha is seeking a "more representative" government   359
Constitutional principles are laid down   362
Conspiracy to push the DTA aside   363
Pik Botha tries to squeeze me out   366
I come to blows with the Prime Minister   369
The interim government is dissolved   371

CHAPTER 12   The steep road to independence, 1984–1989   373
P.W. Botha tries to justify his actions   373
New role players, new plans   374

The Multi-Party Conference 375
The last round: The TGNU, myself and Louis Pienaar 378
Meeting with Eben van Zijl again 382
The beginning of the end of the National Party 383
The home stretch to independence 385
The election is announced 386
The last election for whites 387
The establishment of UNTAG 388
I speak to Koevoet 389
An unnecessary human massacre on 1 April 1989 392
The Mount Etjo Conference 393
How does one fight an election without funds? 393
The election campaign and intimidation 398
The hour of reckoning arrives 400

CHAPTER 13 Writing the Constitution 403
A lost chapter in our history 403
The first meeting of the Constituent Assembly 404
The Standing Committee drafts its procedure 406
The first round: Surveying the terrain 407
Points of material dispute 410
The President's powers and competencies 411
A row over private schools 411
Land reform 415
The character of the State 415
Principles for government policy 415
The President's powers 415
The National Assembly (NA) 416
The Cabinet 416
A Second House of Parliament 416
Fundamental rights 417
Consolidation of our progress at the end of 1989 418
The role of Koos Pretorius during the deliberations 419
The second round: Meeting with our legal advisors 420
The Preamble 421
The capital, national anthem, flag and national symbols 423
Walvis Bay and the offshore islands 423
Official language 424
Citizenship 424
Fundamental rights and freedoms 425

Freedom of association   427
The right to own property   427
The right to political activity   428
Administrative justice   428
Cultural rights   428
The right to education   429
Affirmative action   430
Election and powers of the President   431
The transitional period   433
The powers and competencies of the Cabinet   437
The legislative authority   439
Regional and municipal councils   442
The judiciary   444
The Chairman becomes impatient   446
The position of the current bureaucracy   447
Do principles of government policy belong in the
    Constitution?   448
The third round: Resolving the differences   452
How to report back   452
Affirmative action on the table again   456
The President once again   458
Judicial authority   464
Outstanding points are settled   464
Did we reach consensus?   466
The Constituent Assembly considers the concept   467
A subcommittee hones the final product   472
The Constitution is officially ratified on 9 February 1990   477

CHAPTER 14   Independence and afterwards   481
The first National Assembly   481
My three years in the National Assembly   482
Party politics after independence   484
The Republican Party resurges   484

CHAPTER 15   Reflection   487

Epilogue   494
Selected source references   497
Index   499

Preface

Writing history is almost inevitably a pedantic and/or pedagogic exercise. Well, that is if you are doing it right. Conversely, autobiographies or memoirs are embedded in the subjectivity of personal experiences with an assumed, but relative, intellectual integrity. Henry Kissinger might well be the rare zoon politikon[1] to write personal history with scholarly veracity. Charles van Onselen[2] could have if he had wanted to. Chester Crocker[3] had the instincts of a historian, but his analytical compulsions too often fixated on the all too evident imbalances in power relations. Dirk Mudge has the raw, brilliant impulses of a grassroots politician and, in addition, his observations have the theoretical depth which provides for the conceptual overlay between a historical narrative and a memoir.

Often we have control over artefacts or observable phenomena which confirm or reject our historical postulations and extrapolations, but the interpretation of events is most likely to be filtered through a plethora of pampered narratives and/or ideological lenses. Historian Hermann Giliomee makes the point that all too often normative assumptions or judgements about events or observations beyond memory become invested with paradigms of the recent past. Autobiographies and memoirs are equally viewed with suspicion as sources of affirmation or confirmation. Larger-than-life-personalities romanticising historical events. Self-criticism being the only yardstick for truth and reality.

The nomenclature of reflection cannot escape the stigma of semantic variation, the natural determinism of change. It is here that Mudge's memoir displays an important insight into writing about a history by retaining the derogatory semantics of his historical discourse. Perhaps a thorough understanding of the complex nuances of historical events is dependent on the ability of the narrator to refrain from reinventing his or her memory and instead to collate experiences and observations within the comprehensive semantics and interpretative regalia of a specified era.

Mudge's memoir does not relive the past in times of modernity. The reader becomes displaced – in a way – to a familiar but awkward if not painful past. The narrative, conceived in stigma and shame, is presented with a "respectability" or even bizarre "reality" which once was "normal" to some and an abomination to others.

In being true to the past, Mudge not only demonstrates a remarkable sense of history, he also has a very intelligent interpretation of the relationship between the seemingly unrelated events of decades ago. He does not write from the perspective of an outsider or a "colonialist of a special kind"; he is an African, he had probably always been, but only realised it when he added political experience to his human and intellectual instincts. His aversion for the primitive political temperament of his own "tribe" is reflected upon with reason and the integrity of his "longing for justice for all Namibians" distinguishes him from his peers.

If history is to be written from a revolutionary disposition, the role of politicians such as Mudge could be and most likely will be scrutinised from a very critical perspective. But, if politics and the development of democratic rituals and practices are viewed as an evolutionary process, the role of visionary actors on the inside of the colonial or repressive state has to be valued for its constructiveness.

It is difficult, in retrospect, to imagine the resistance to change within the repressive state and the collective instincts of a colonial disposition; political agents such as Mudge might well have been the only transcending force with sufficient credibility to lead a white frontier society to the civility promised by an open society.

Mudge is his own man, but by comparison he never was the F.W. de Klerk of Namibia; he rather had the insights and political urges of a Van Zyl Slabbert[4]. He never sought the authority to negotiate on behalf of white Namibians, he worked towards a mandate from all Namibians; that is why the legitimacy of SWAPO to govern was contested, but never opposed by him.

Liberation struggles are rarely resolved by a military victory; almost inevitably the revolutionaries and the oppressors will settle into a compromise. The real question is about the extent to which civil society has been prepared to not only accept the compromise between elites, but to hold those elites to the compromise.

In that regard Namibia has done remarkably well.

Perhaps that is where Dirk Mudge finds a place in history; he contributed more than most to leading those on the inside into a brave new world called democracy.

Unfortunately, the codification of history is a neglected discipline in much of Africa and certainly also in Namibia. The complete history of Namibia still has to be written, but Dirk Mudge has made a remarkable contribution with a text which merits both literary and scholarly value. The work was not intended as a comprehensive history of Namibia – it is a memoir about the life and times of Dirk Mudge. However, the author certainly had the privilege to not only live during remarkable times, but to take the lead in changing a very complex society for the better. Dirk Mudge has been a political visionary in times of darkness.

Piet Croucamp
Published in The Namibian, *26 June 2015*

1. From the Greek; literally "political animal", or "political being".
2. Acclaimed South African historian and author.
3. Academic and diplomat; US assistant secretary of state for African Affairs (1981–1989).
4. Progressive South African political figure and analyst (1940–2010).

CHAPTER 1

Introduction

On 21 March 1990, we reached the end of the long and winding road from South West Africa to Namibia. The Republic of Namibia had come into being, and could take its rightful place among the more than 40 independent states in Africa. To reach this goal, which had been deferred several times, was not easy. I know, because for the last 30 years of that journey, I was personally involved as a politician. As we proceeded, my fellow travellers and I differed radically on which route we should take. I began to doubt whether we were even remotely heading in the same direction. Nevertheless, we eventually achieved our goal: a country that would no longer tolerate racists and terrorists, and where people could live together in peace and harmony.

For me the highlight of my long political career was the achievement of independence, and having been privileged to draft a democratic Constitution together with former militant enemies. It was an incredible experience. Since the Constitution had to be ratified by the elected Constituent Assembly by a two-thirds majority, and not one of the parties had been able to achieve this in the preceding election, we realised that this time around there could not be a sole winner. The constitutional proposals by the various parties differed fundamentally and would subject the participating parties to a stringent test of objectivity and fairness. Reaching consensus initially seemed impossible.

In the course of the 80 days during which the appointed Standing Committee of 21 members worked on the concept, a team spirit developed. All that was needed was for us to rise above our own personal prejudices, suspicions and outdated ideas. It was clear from the outset that the past was important only in so far as we could learn from it.

Dr Zedekia Ngavirue, a Namibian who achieved his doctorate at the University of Oxford and for whom I have the greatest respect, comments in the published version of his thesis, *Political Parties and Interest Groups in South West Africa*, on the past as follows: "We have a clear picture of the evils that have been perpetrated against us. We cannot and will not try to erase the record, yet we will not allow it to blur our vision." These wise words reflect exactly what we tried to do. They relate to our joint future, and future generations would judge us harshly if we failed to lay down a strong foundation.

On 9 February 1990, the Chairman of the Constituent Assembly, Dr Hage Geingob, announced that the Constitution had been ratified by consensus. The ACN, the name under which the National Party participated in the election, abstained from voting. Hage Geingob and I embraced each another; a black man and a white man who had opposed each other for so many years, had joined forces towards a new future for our country. A few days later Nelson Mandela was released from prison by President F.W. de Klerk of South Africa. On that day the democratisation process reached the final stage in Namibia while in South Africa it had just begun. F.W. de Klerk and Nelson Mandela had joined hands and started working on a new future for South Africa, as Clemens Kapuuo and I had done a decade earlier.

An unknown future lay ahead of us. Would all our lofty ideals become reality? What would the situation be in Namibia in 20 years' time? We had high hopes, but we couldn't know. We were, however, convinced of one thing: The future was in our own hands. Should we fail to realise our dream, we would have only ourselves to blame.

When the South African flag was finally struck on 21 March 1990, I had tears in my eyes, since I had forged strong emotional and cultural bonds with my language and cultural connections in South Africa in the course of my life. We had been jointly accused of being the architects of apartheid and racial discrimination, which was not true. It was a bitter inheritance, our mistake was that we had maintained it.

On 21 March 1990, we parted ways constitutionally, but historically we shared a past. Little did I realise then that what had transpired in South West Africa would also inevitably come to pass in South Africa. This process would unite me with my language and cultural associates again, not as citizens of the same country, but as Afrikaners, fellow-fighters for a peaceful and democratic future.

As the Namibian flag was hoisted, I was proud of what we had achieved. I was satisfied that we in Namibia could make a contribution towards rectifying the mistakes of the past and could start a process of reconciliation and democratisation in Southern Africa. I knew that much still had to change. Acceptance and reconciliation would have to be fostered and a nation would have to be built. To achieve this, we would have to anchor ourselves in the Great Commandment: That you must love the Lord your God, and your neighbour as yourself. This would probably take time, because the past does not let you go easily, and democracy does not work this way.

Now, 25 years after independence, many questions are still being asked and many reproaches are being thrown around. Know-it-alls who refused to walk the road with us tell us what we should or shouldn't have done. The questions raised and statements that are being made often demonstrate blatant ignorance of what had happened in the past, which leads to misunderstanding. But relevant questions are also being asked, questions to which I myself still do not have all the answers or explanations.

Examples of such questions are:

- Why did it take so long to achieve independence?
- To what can the intense interest and international involvement over a period of more than 50 years in the struggle for independence of a country with only 1,5 million inhabitants and 800 000 voters be ascribed? (Taking into account the small number of voters, it was one of the most expensive elections supervised by the United Nations that the world has ever seen.)
- Why had a bloody and expensive war of many years, in terms of human life and money, have to be waged?
- Was it in the first place a border war aimed at protecting the inhabitants of South West Africa, or was it meant to stop communist imperialism in Angola? Was it an unnecessary war? President P.W. Botha of South Africa described it as a *total onslaught* – was he right?
- While mutual deliberation and planning were required in finding alternative solutions, why then did a violent internal struggle ensue among the whites, especially the Afrikaners?
- Who took the lead to convene the Turnhalle Conference, which represented all population groups in the country? Was it a South African initiative, or was it ours? Why is it important to know this?
- Why were we allowed to consider our own future for the first time only at such a late stage?
- Could independence have been forced on South West Africa by South Africa without the consent of its inhabitants? Could South Africa afford it politically?

- What would have been the reaction of South African voters if their government were to hand over the territory to the Mandate Committee of the United Nations, or possibly to the South West African People's Organisation (SWAPO) itself?
- How did it happen that South Africa could finally state that independence had been achieved through the will of the people?
- Do the people who ask these questions realise how important it was for us and South Africa to gain the support of especially the white population of South West Africa to end the humiliating practices and eventually achieve independence?
- Why did John Vorster, Prime Minister of South Africa, call an election in 1978 in which SWAPO would not take part? Did he want to establish who could speak on behalf of the inhabitants of South West Africa? Did he mean to place South West Africa irrevocably on the road to independence?
- Why did President P.W. Botha, after he had agreed in principle that South West Africa would become independent, attempt to impose an ethnic form of government on the inhabitants of the country?
- Why did Minister Pik Botha try to marginalise me politically by discrediting me in the public media? Why did he try to create a split in the ranks of the Democratic Turnhalle Alliance (DTA) by influencing Peter Kalangula and Werner Neef to break away? Did he want to consolidate the proponents of an ethnic form of government?

Much has already been said and written about the Namibian independence struggle, primarily by people who were involved directly in the armed struggle, or who were sympathetic towards it. In most of these publications the impression is being created that Namibia's eventual political and constitutional destination was achieved only through an armed struggle, and that the peaceful inhabitants of the country had played no role in finding a democratic solution. There are South Africans who still maintain that we South West Africans were indulging in the luxury of fraternal disputes while South African youths were fighting on our border. Is this the truth?

We lived on the battlefield and were soft targets for terrorists. We were, after all, South African citizens who were entitled to protection. Our ancestors weren't illegal immigrants from South Africa, as was later alleged, but had come here in accordance with an internationally recognised mandate, encouraged by the South African Government. We not only depended on its protection, but were prepared to make a contribution towards ending the war by running political and related risks which South Africans themselves were not prepared to consider at that stage. We realised that once the war was over, we would still have to live here under a future dispensation. For us it was about our country and our future.

It was never clear why the South African Defence Force was deployed on our border or what the reasons were for their direct involvement in the civil war in Angola. The argument that the SADF had merely taken over the responsibility for the protection of the inhabitants of South West Africa from the police is false. The leadership of the National Party of South West Africa firmly believed that the involvement of the SADF in the armed struggle was mainly to maintain the political and diplomatic status quo. Sam Nujoma articulated SWAPO's objectives as follows: "The question of black majority rule is out. We are not fighting even for majority rule. We are fighting to seize power in Namibia for the benefit of the Namibian people. We are revolutionaries."

My DTA colleagues and I could obviously not identify with SWAPO's objectives, but we were also convinced that maintaining the status quo would not lead to lasting peace and that both SWAPO and the National Party would have to be convinced that only a democratic solution can lead to lasting peace.

While the South African Defence Force was involved in a military struggle, my DTA colleagues and I were involved in a political struggle. During the 13 years of armed conflict we addressed meetings in the operational area. Our struggle was not without loss of life. The lives of two DTA presidents, Clemens Kapuuo and Cornelius Ndjoba, were taken by SWAPO. Toivo Shiyagaya was assassinated while on the political stage. I was on SWAPO's death list with them, as was confirmed after the war by General Hamaambo of SWAPO. In the process the DTA often landed in the crossfire; we had to wage a political struggle against SWAPO on the one hand and the National Party on the other.

Because of a peaceful, negotiated settlement, the military struggle did not end conclusively, and both SWAPO and the South African Defence Force are still, 25 years later, claiming to have won the war. I still believe that the South African Defence Force was on the winning side and that it succeeded in saving our country from the ravages of war. I am also grateful for the ten years the Defence Force *bought* us to work out a peaceful solution. I have expressed my appreciation for this on several occasions.

A credible account of the decisions we South West Africans had to take, and the challenges we had to face to put an end to an international issue in which South Africa was involved for over 40 years, has yet to be published. War and violence remain popular topics for books and television programmes, while efforts to end them are regarded as signs of weakness and cowardice.

Nineteen years ago, on my birthday – 16 January 1995 – the late Jan Spies gave me a book, *Namibia's Liberation Struggle*, compiled by Colin Leys and John S. Saul. He wrote the following on the title page in Afrikaans: "Dirk. Wishing you a good year. This otherwise good book underlines the fact that its history is utterly one-sided without your voice. May you keep the strength and find the time to give it a voice and put it in writing. Jan Spies."

Relatives and friends also insisted that I should publish my memoirs, but I didn't feel up to it. I didn't think it was necessary and had no need or desire to blow my own trumpet or take revenge. Many of my harshest white political opponents had in the meantime become my friends and admitted that they had been wrong. Some of them had even apologised for their behaviour during meetings and personal encounters. I wanted to be left in peace to enjoy the rest of my life on the farm.

However, I allowed myself to be convinced that it was not about me, but that I owed it to those who had chosen to walk the road to freedom and reconciliation with me to record the hitherto unknown facts in writing. When I started writing this book in February 2012, I was 84 years old! Nine years had lapsed since my retirement from Parliament and nine years had passed since I handed over my leadership of the Republican Party to Pieter Boltman. What follows is based on my recollections and understanding of events and developments during my lifetime and in particular during my 48 years (1955–2003) in politics. The well-known Afrikaans author C.J. Langenhoven said that a given situation does not have only two sides. It has three: my side, your side, and the right side. My intention with this book is to present my side to the best of my ability.

The start of my political career – on 17 March 1960 – coincided with dramatic events in both South Africa and South West Africa. The awakening of black nationalism and active resistance led to violence and loss of life, as had happened at Sharpeville. International intervention became the inevitable outcome. The campaign against South Africa's administration of South West Africa entered a new phase when Ethiopia and Liberia lodged a complaint with the International Court in The Hague. During my first term as member of the Legislative Assembly, SWAPO started with acts of terrorism.

The leaders of the National Party were highly satisfied with the outcome of the preceding election and predicted that the end of the opposition was in sight. I wondered whether they underestimated the seriousness of the situation or whether they regarded it as a problem that had to be resolved by the South African Government.

I was thrown in at the deep end. I was barely 33 years old, completely unprepared for a political career, and I needed time to find my bearings in a confused world.

The change in my own political thinking did not happen overnight. It was by no means a Road to Damascus conversion. I learnt the hard way. I first had to get to know my black countrymen better. I first had to listen to their side of the story and then try to put myself in their position.

I realised that you have to put yourself in another person's shoes before judging anyone. I had to understand the concept of loving your fellowman before it became clear. You must not do to others as you would not have done to yourself. This might have been interpreted differently by some of my colleagues, but I had no intention of becoming involved in a theological debate. Early in my political career in the Legislative Assembly I had repeatedly emphasised that we as white people should change our attitude towards our black countrymen. In 1964 the Prime Minister of South Africa announced the so-called Odendaal Plan. At that stage I was still too inexperienced to express an independent opinion on future constitutional models. What made an impression on me, however, was Dr Verwoerd's undertaking that he would do everything for the black inhabitants of the country that he wished for himself. This corresponded with my interpretation of love thy neighbour. I could not foresee that it couldn't work in practice. As a loyal nationalist I was advocating the party policy without question.

Only after I had more international exposure and had become more senior, could I express my opinion on possible alternative political and constitutional solutions. Unfortunately, I often had to move slower than I wished, because I wanted to take my people, the whites, with me. This was not easy.

Independence was a foreign concept to many of my fellow country-men. On the basis of what had been stipulated in the mandate agree-ment reached with the League of Nations in 1920 – after the takeover of South West Africa – as well as repeated assurances by South Afri-ca regarding its responsibility towards South West Africa, they were convinced that South Africa would never relinquish its control over the Territory. Indeed, many people expected that South Africa would eventually incorporate the Territory. The recommendations of the Odendaal Plan, which made provision for the policy of separate devel-opment for the indigenous groups in South West Africa, as well as for a re-arrangement of administrative and financial functions between the Legislative Assembly of South West Africa and the South African Government, strengthened this perception.

The one-sided way in which South Africa made decisions regarding the future of South West Africa convinced local leaders that the final decision would also lie with South Africa. Opinions held by local lead-ers on political issues were probably never taken seriously by South Africa.

Seventeen years after I became a member of the Legislative Assem-bly, John Vorster created an opportunity for me in 1973 to initiate the process of self-determination. It was the beginning of our involvement in the determination of our own future. Up to that point all I could do was defend the South African policy of separate development and ap-peal for improved human relations and respect for the human dignity of our black countrymen. As from 1974, however, the ball was in our court. Until he relinquished his position as Prime Minister, John Vor-ster gave me his moral support.

The process to induce South West Africans to accept self-determina-tion, and hence independence, went hand in hand with serious differ-ences when it came to principles and policies. It also led to the eventual split in the National Party of South West Africa, and the establishment of the Republican Party and the Democratic Turnhalle Alliance (DTA). Former friends and even relatives labelled me and my RP colleagues as traitors of the white people and Afrikaners. I was suspended from Afrikaans cultural organisations, or resigned from them of my own accord. As an Afrikaner I was standing at a crossroads. I had to choose between right and wrong, between moral and immoral. Sentimental ties had to make way for rational thinking. I knew that this would have personal consequences for me, but I had to decide, and decide I did. I am sincerely grateful for the fact that our black countrymen in the DTA, and therefore also the representatives of SWAPO and other parties, accepted us during the writing of our Constitution. On 31 March 1990, 12 years after the split with the National Party and the establishment of the DTA, we had reached the end of the winding road from South West Africa to Namibia.

My country and its people had been good to me. As a result I owed my undivided faith in and loyalty to Namibia. Not only do I love this beautiful land of contrasts, I also have a special compassion for my countrymen with whom I, under difficult circumstances, walked the road of a lifetime.

I would like to pay tribute to someone who played an exceedingly important role in my life: Clemens Kapuuo, with whom I started walking the road to peace in 1973. He was the first black leader I would follow in my lifetime. His acceptance of the important office of President of the DTA cost him his life when he was assassinated in cold blood on 27 March 1978.

In the short period during which Clemens Kapuuo could fulfil a leadership role, he achieved the improbable – he united the Hereros and Boers to pursue a common goal. This was an improbability, because the Hereros, apart from the Namas, were the first population group to resist foreign oppression and colonisation by Germany during the 1890s and especially in 1904.

Following the establishment of the United Nations 40 years later, they continued the struggle by sending petitioners to the world body requesting the cessation of South Africa's administration of South West Africa. Was it mere coincidence that the Herero uprising took place only a few years after the Anglo-Boer War of 1899–1902. In both cases it was a resistance to colonial powers wanting to expand their empires into Africa.

It would be impossible for me to name all those who walked the road of peace and reconciliation with me. Even so, I would like to make an exception by mentioning six colleagues who deserve a special mention. On 31 August 1977 Appie Louw, Bertie Botha, Stefaans Malan, Werner Neef, Paul Smit and Paul Minnaar had only a few seconds to decide whether they would vote with me against a motion of confidence in the leader of the National Party, A.H. du Plessis. On 21 September 1977, the seven of us, with 78 other congress delegates, walked out of the National Party Congress. We all fell victim to character assassination, but 13 years later we could cross the finishing line together. I salute them.

And then there is Stienie, my life partner for 63 years, and our children. It still remains incomprehensible to me that civilised people implicated my family – often in a slanderous way – in the political smear campaign directed against me. The moral support and love I received from my family supported me through the most difficult years of my life. Without their encouragement I would certainly not have undertaken to write this book myself – on a computer with clumsy fingers.

Without the advice and assistance of Prof. Ernst Stals it would have been a cumbersome task to prepare the manuscript for publication. As I progressed, Ernst monitored the historical facts. My heartfelt thanks to Amy Schoeman for translating the book into English. It was not an easy assignment.

Much of the information contained in this book has been taken from documents, letters, declarations and speeches that I had at my disposal for many years, but subsequently donated to the University of South Africa. When writing my story I had to rely on my memory a great deal, which fortunately did not leave me in the lurch.

Since many of the events took place as far back as 70 years ago, I also needed to consult reference materials. When quoting politicians and other individuals, I steered clear of newspaper reports as far as possible, rather using authentic official documents, minutes and certified Hansard reports. In the list of references I list only those sources to which I had access.

Quotations come verbatim from the documents mentioned, inclusive of such grammatical errors as they contain, without indicating this with *sic*, as the repeated insertion could be an irritation to the reader. Through these citations I am allowing the individuals – especially the political leaders – to speak for themselves. This applies equally to myself. In this way readers of the book will get to know the important stakeholders better, as well as their often obsolete perspectives and how long it took to convince them that they would have to relinquish their unrealistic expectations.

While I would prefer not to mention the resentment and blows meted out to me by my own people while I was on my SWA to Namibia path, without these my account would not present the full picture, if not render it a superficial one. My objective was to record what I had experienced on my long and often uphill political career in as great detail as possible. Moreover, I had to present the course of events chronologically to explain the laborious evolutionary process that finally led to independence.

To put the exhaustive repetition of obsolete ideologies and unfeasible policy trends into perspective I resorted to citing from speeches, reactions to speeches, motions and amendments to motions. And I needed to elaborate on how attempts were made to justify policy trends on biblical grounds. For decades this course of events tried my patience to the limit. Those who come after us need to understand how exceptionally difficult it was for some people to let go of their set ideas, dogmatic approaches, prejudicial rejections and especially their unearned privileges.

Putting the speeches, motions and reactions on record, to my mind, not only has considerable historical value, but is first and foremost an authentic disclosure of the many political thought processes that frequently tended to bedevil the pursuit of independence in our country.

I would also like to point out that I used designations and terminology throughout the text as they were used in different periods and stages. For instance, in the beginning I refer to the indigenous population as natives, non-whites and non-Europeans. Later on the different racial groups are referred to as white, black and coloured and the ethnic groups as Herero, Damara, and so on. In the past the white inhabitants were referred to as whites; and they are still frequently referred to as whites. This is misleading, because in reality, due to the heterogeneous composition of the whites, they belong to a racial group.

I hope that in the process the reader will find answers to at least some questions. This is, needless to say, my side of the story. Whether it is the right side, I leave to the reader to decide.

CHAPTER 2

The origin of the Territory Deutsch-Südwestafrika

When I decided to publish an account of my experiences in this beautiful country of extremes, I had no idea where to begin. My friend, Ernst Stals, a historian with a good sense of humour, advised me: "Start at the beginning." But where is the beginning? We agreed that I should start with the declaration of a protectorate by the German Government in 1883 over large tracks of land in the south-western parts of the territory, later referred to as Deutsch-Südwestafrika, now Namibia. What transpired during that period and afterwards, had a significant influence on what my ancestors and I experienced subsequently. Historian A.L. Rowse expressed himself as follows on the importance of history: "How can we hope to understand the world of affairs around us if we do not know how it came to be what it is?"

During the Berlin Conference (1884–1885), the then colonial powers divided Africa amongst themselves by drawing borders arbitrarily. The demarcation of the eastern, southern and western borders of South West Africa (with the historical exclusion of the Walvis Bay enclave) caused no serious problems, but the northern border did. Portugal originally laid claim to an area that extended as far south as Cape Fria and would include Ovamboland. To give South West Africa access to the northern perennial rivers, an artificial border was drawn in 1893 by means of a treaty between Germany and Portugal. However, the exact location of this border was only finally agreed upon by South Africa and Portugal in 1926. The border was determined without considering traditional tribal areas, which resulted in seven of the Owambo tribes initially being subjected to German and, after 1925, to the South African authorities, and five to the Portuguese authorities. It also divided the Kwanyama tribal area, subsequently causing major problems, both for South Africa and for the inhabitants of the Territory.

The origin of the different population groups in the country – in total about eleven – is a long story that we do not know in full. What we do know is that the Bushmen (San) were here first, and the whites last. Fact is, we are now all here, and cannot wish one another away. Neither do we want to. Namibia is our common fatherland.

Britain was the forerunner of colonialisation in Africa. Cecil John Rhodes in particular played a major role in the southern portion of the continent. In his biography, *Rhodes, The Race for Africa*, Antony Thomas tells a fascinating story: Rhodes wanted to conquer Africa for the British Empire and nothing was going to stop him. He is quoted as follows: "I contend that we are the finest race in the world and the more of the world we inhabit the better it is for the human race ... Africa is still lying ready for us, it is our duty to take it."

It is further written about Rhodes:

> He laid the foundations of apartheid and drew Britain into the Boer War, the costliest and bloodiest war it was to fight between Waterloo and the First World War ... [If] anyone can be accused of laying the foundations of apartheid, it was that most English of Englishmen, Cecil John Rhodes. In 1887, 61 years before the Nationalists came to power in South Africa, he had stood before a packed House of Assembly in Cape Town and declared: "These are my politics on native affairs and these are the politics of South Africa ... The native is to be treated as a child and denied the franchise ... We must adopt a system of despotism, such as works so well in India, in our relations with the barbarians of Africa."

When Rhodes became involved in the race for Africa in 1872, only the Cape Colony and Port Natal, as far as the southern part of the continent was concerned, were under British rule. At the time of his death in 1902, the British flag was already waving as far north as the big lakes in Central Africa. This included the republics of both the Transvaal and the Free State, which had been occupied shortly before. The occupation of these two republics disrupted the lives of many families. Their houses were burnt down, their livestock was appropriated, and their wives and children were put into concentration camps, where they perished by the thousands.

It is important to know that Britain was reluctant to become involved in South West Africa. Although there were proponents of the annexation of the Territory, only the Walvis Bay enclave was proclaimed in 1878 as belonging to Britain, because – so it was thought – owning the only natural harbour along the coast would mean that access to the entire interior could be controlled. The Herero chief, Maharero, subsequently claimed that it was the Hereros who had ceded Walvis Bay to the British and that Britain had therefore let them down when Germany was allowed to take possession of their land. Cecil John Rhodes, who had no political status at that stage, remarked later: "If I had known at the time, England would not have lost that opportunity."

While Germany was the last country to become involved in the race for Africa, it was also the first to lose its colonies. There is no doubt that the role Germany played before and during its occupation of South West Africa had a direct influence on subsequent events and relationships within the Territory. The German colonial history has since become widely known and today pertinent literature is still available in bookshops. Besides, it is still part of present political debate, because the Hereros and Namas continue to claim reparation from the former colonial power. The Hereros' recollection of what happened to them a century ago is decidedly better than that of the Boers of the Anglo-Boer War, which took place at the same time.

On 7 August 1884, Germany proclaimed the area around Angra Pequena (later Lüderitzbucht) as a protectorate and subsequently entered into treaties with tribes in the interior, under which they were placed under the protection of the German Emperor. The main objective was to protect the interests of the missionaries and traders who had settled in South West Africa. As time went by, the Hereros and Namas built up a resistance against German occupation and only two years after the end of the Anglo-Boer War in South Africa, an armed conflict erupted in the German colony, with tragic consequences for the Hereros as a population group. After General von Trotha issued an *Extermination Order*, the Herero Rebellion was suppressed mercilessly. The German Colonial Government did not concern itself much with the northern groups and they were therefore, with the exception of the battle at Fort Namutoni, relatively uninvolved in the war.

Germany did, admittedly, spend a great deal of money on the development of the Territory during its short occupation of 31 years. However, it was definitely not done to further the interests of the local population. During the last years of German colonial rule, South West Africa experienced a period of economic growth, due primarily to the discovery of diamonds. However, the indigenous population benefited very little from this.

Four years before South Africa occupied South West Africa in 1914–1915, South Africa became a self-governing dominium within the British Empire, known as the Union of South Africa. As a result, the Union became involved in the First World War against Germany as part of the Allied Forces, and the Prime Minister, General Louis Botha, invaded South West Africa.

The 1914 Rebellion

With the Anglo-Boer War still fresh in their memories, many Afrikaners in South Africa and also here in South West Africa couldn't reconcile themselves with the idea of fighting on the side of Britain against the Germans. This led to another tragic event in our Afrikaner history: the Rebellion of 1914. Three Boer generals – Botha, Smuts and Hertzog – who together fought against Britain during the Anglo-Boer War, developed different political ideas after the formation of the Union. Botha and Smuts supported closer ties with Britain, and also reconciliation between the two white language groups in South Africa. Hertzog was not opposed to this, but was of the opinion that Botha and Smuts were prepared to put the Afrikaner in a subordinate position to the English. The differences revolved primarily around language equality and Afrikaner identity, and eventually led to a political split and the establishment of the National Party under Hertzog.

Following the declaration of war by Germany in 1914, protest meetings were organised, led by Generals De la Rey, De Wet, Beyers and Kemp. Protesting against the invasion of South West Africa, General Beyers resigned as Commander General of the Defence Force, and Colonel Manie Maritz, Commanding Officer of the Union Forces in the north-western Cape Province, joined the German forces. General Kemp, with 600 men, succeeded in joining up with General Maritz. Within a few weeks the Rebellion was over and its leaders behind bars. One of the rebels, Jopie Fourie, was found guilty of high treason by a military court and died in front of a firing squad.

To me it was incomprehensible that senior and respected military leaders made themselves guilty of disloyalty and even high treason. I accepted, though, that the Anglo-Boer War a mere twelve years before had left deep wounds. Most of the rebels had probably lost loved ones in this war against the mighty British Empire, if not on the battlefield, then most certainly in the concentration camps. Add to this the moral and material support that the Boers received from abroad during the war, and especially by the civilian population in Germany, for example Der Internationalen Burenliga, with an official publication titled *Der Burenfreund*. *Der Burenfreund* not only reported regularly on the war and associated atrocities, but also established a Buren Hilfs-fonds, which collected large contributions to provide assistance to the impoverished Boers. Furthermore, *Der Burenfreund* reported widely on the participation of German citizens in the war against England. This, amongst other things, must have influenced the rebels to support the German forces. German-speaking South West Africans and Afrikaners would often come into conflict in the ensuing decades.

Following the suppression of the rebels, the South African Defence Force continued its invasion of South West Africa. This led to the sur-render of the German Forces at Khorab near Otavi on 9 July 1915. The war in Europe, however, continued for another four years. During this period South West Africa was governed by an administrator, sup-ported by a military administration, until a mandate agreement was reached in 1920. This was the end of the German colonial period and the beginning of South Africa's administration of South West Africa.

What happened during the colonial period and afterwards is shock-ing and people do not easily forget the hurt. We, the white population of Namibia (Afrikaans-, English- and German-speaking) had to take the blame for what our ancestors had done, and later also for what we ourselves had done. The responsibility for what had happened in the past would come to rest on our shoulders.

South West Africa becomes a mandated territory

During the peace talks at Versailles at the end of the First World War, the Allied Forces needed to decide on the future of the former German colonies and certain parts of the Ottoman Empire. Except for South West Africa, which had been occupied by South Africa at the request of Britain, the following German colonies were at issue: New Guinea, which had been occupied by Australia; Samoa by New Zealand; cer-tain islands in the southern Pacific Ocean by Japan; and Togo, Cam-eroon and German East Africa (Tanganyika) by Great Britain. Some of these insisted on incorporating the colonies they had occupied into their countries. General J.C. Smuts was a strong supporter of the in-corporation of South West Africa into South Africa. He maintained this viewpoint throughout, and 25 years later, in 1946, he still continued his efforts to incorporate the Territory by making representations to the newly established United Nations Organisation. He was still pursuing this goal when his party – the United Party – was defeated in 1948 by the National Party under leadership of Dr D.F. Malan.

President Wilson of America, who played a major role at Versailles, was strongly opposed to incorporation and was a strong supporter of the principle of non-annexation. To keep both sides happy, the parties eventually agreed on a mandate system, one that had already been acknowledged by international law in the sixteenth century. In terms of the Covenant of the League of Nations, the former colonies and dependent areas would be entrusted to developed countries which, due to their resources, economic standing, experience and geographical location, were the most capable, and which were prepared to take on this responsibility.

In terms of Section 22 of the Covenant of the League of Nations, the former colonies were divided into three groups, namely A-, B- and C-mandated territories. According to this Section, the first of these groups, which included certain parts of the Ottoman Empire (Turkey) such as Syria, Palestine, Iraq and Lebanon, had already reached a state of development in which their existence as independent states could be recognised conditionally. In these instances, the mandatory (the country to which the mandate was given) would be responsible only for providing administrative advice and assistance until such time as the territories were able to rule themselves independently. According to Section 22 of the Covenant, the second group of former colonies, especially those in Central Africa, were not yet capable of governing themselves, and the mandatory had to, subject to certain conditions such as freedom of conscience and religion as well as a ban on the slave trade and militarisation, accept responsibility for the administration of those territories until such time as they were able to do it themselves. The third group of former colonies, the C-mandated territories (of which South West Africa was one), are described in Section 22 of the Covenant as follows:

> There are territories such as South West Africa and certain South
> Pacific Islands, which, owing to the sparseness of their popula-
> tion, or their small size, or their remoteness from the centres of
> civilization, or their geographical contiguity to the territory of

the mandatory, and other circumstances, can best be administered under the laws of the Mandatory as integral portions of
its territory, subject to the safeguards above mentioned in the
interests of the indigenous population.

Because the contents of the agreement played such an important role
in the struggle for independence, I have briefly summarised its terms
and conditions as follows:

- South Africa would have complete authority over the administration of South West Africa as an integral part of the Union and would
  be able to apply South African laws in the Territory;
- South Africa would have to promote the material, social and moral
  welfare of the inhabitants to the utmost;
- Practices such as slavery, forced labour, arms trafficking and supply-
  ing intoxicating liquor to the natives would be prohibited;
- Military training of the natives, except for the police force was prohibited and no military or naval bases could be established in the
  Territory;
- Freedom of conscience and religion had to be guaranteed.

The resettlement of farmers from South Africa and elsewhere will be
dealt with later, but I wish to quote a paragraph from a speech made
by the then British Prime Minister, Lloyd George, as recorded in the
minutes of the Permanent Mandate Commission. When he presented
the Peace Treaty of Versailles to the British Lower House on 3 July 1919,
he said the following:

> South West Africa, running as it does side by side with the Cape
> Colony, was felt so much a part, geographically, of that area that
> it would be quite impossible to treat it in the same way as you
> would a colony 2000 or 3000 miles away from the centre of ad-
> ministration. There is no doubt at all that South West Africa will
> become an integral part of the Federation of South Africa. It will
> be colonised by people from South Africa. You could not have
> done anything else. You could not have set customs barriers and
> have a different system of administration.

After the South African troops had conquered South West Africa, General Smuts decided not to repatriate all the German nationals, because
he – as he put it – wanted to establish a European civilisation here. In
addition to those who wanted to return to Germany of their own free

will, the Germans who had to leave the country consisted primarily of military personnel, public servants, police and undesirable individuals. Approximately half of the German population in South West Africa was repatriated. The remaining half, about 8000 settlers, were primarily ordinary citizens. At the same time Smuts, as was also envisioned by the British Prime Minister, encouraged South Africans to settle here for the same reason, namely the establishment of a "European civilisation".

My grandfathers, Dirk Frederik Mudge and Petrus Stefanus van Tonder, who were both involved in the South African troops that had conquered the German colony, were among the first South African farmers who settled in the Territory. Like the other South Africans who came to live here, they were not received with open arms by the German settlers. The reasons for this antagonism will be dealt with in the next chapter.

Politics between two World Wars (1920–1939)

Once the mandate agreement had been signed in December 1920, the military government under Administrator Howard Gorges came to an end. He was succeeded by Gys R. Hofmeyer. Hofmeyer was assisted by an appointed Advisory Board, initially consisting of six and subsequently of nine members, one of whom had to have expert knowledge of the indigenous population groups. The administration of the country was headed by the Secretary of South West Africa. The new farmers in the Mandated Territory had to find their feet under this administration.

A further important step in the development of the government of the Territory was the establishment of a representative authority for the Territory in terms of the South-West Africa Constitution Act (No. 42 of 1925). This law of the South African Parliament provided for an elected Legislative Assembly of 18 members and an Executive Committee of four members under the chairmanship of an Administrator. The establishment of a body of white elected representatives inevitably led to the formation of different political groupings and the holding of elections. As early as 1924, three political parties contested an election. These were the Deutsche Bund, the National Party of South West Africa, and the Union Party (subsequently called the South West

Party). All the German citizens had already been automatically natu-ralised and therefore had the right to vote, and although they were apparently not opposed to Smuts's ideal of a European civilisation, they were initially reluctant to accept South African citizenship, which would make them British subjects. They also did everything in their power to resist the immigration of South Africans. This attitude led to the white population being divided into two sections, namely the German Section and the Union Section. This division created a unique situation. The citizens of the conquered German Empire had the right to vote, but the indigenous population did not. The settlers from South Africa were referred to as imported voters (*Stimmvieh*) by the German settlers. The first election of members of the Legislative Assembly was held in accordance with the South-West Africa Constitution Act. The election took place on 25 May 1926, with the following result: Deutsche Bund 7 seats, National Party of South West Africa 3 seats, Independent candidates 2 seats, South West Party 0 seats.

Due to his view that no party would be allowed to dominate, the Administrator, A.J. Werth, used his right to nominate four additional members: two Germans and two Afrikaners. One of them was my grandfather's oldest brother, C.J. van Tonder.

In January 1927, Frikkie Jooste's National Party and B.J. Smit's South West Party amalgamated to form the United National South West Party (UNSWP), which united the political strength of the Afrikaners under one banner. This party defeated the Deutsche Bund in the elections of 1929 and ruled South West Africa at local level for the next 18 years. It is remarkable that in 1927, while their fellow cultural associates in South Africa remained severely divided, the Afrikaners in South West Africa were already united in one political party. In South West Africa, sup-porters of the South African political leaders, Smuts and Hertzog, were in the same political party. Both my grandfathers and my father were faithful supporters of Smuts and of the UNSWP.

Owing to the rise of Nazism in Germany during the 1930s, the un-realistic expectations of some German-speaking inhabitants that South West Africa would be re-occupied by Germany resurfaced. In 1933, in-spired by the emergence of Hitler and the Nazi Party in Germany, the National-Sozialistische Deutsche Arbeiter Partei (NSDAP) Südwestaf-rika Gruppe made its appearance as the local version of the NSDAP in their motherland.

On 2 August 1933, the UNSWP-controlled Legislative Assembly accepted a motion to ban the NSDAP and the Hitlerjugend. The leaders, H. Weigel and Erich von Lossnitzer, were deported. The German members left the Legislative Assembly in protest. There were small groups of German-speaking people who were opposed to the fascist attitude of the Hitler supporters, such as the Deutsche Afrikanische Partei and the Volksdeutsche Gruppe. One of the leaders of these moderate groups was the well-known Albert Voigts.

I was still at primary school in Otjiwarongo, and had no idea what was going on. I did experience an attitude of antagonism from the older German boys though. It was confirmed at a later stage through conversations I had with respected and reliable German-speaking leaders during my political career. One of them was Hans-Jürgen von Hase. He was not only a leader on several fronts, but was also a good friend of mine, a person for whom I had great respect. He was a like-minded supporter who wanted to promote the interests of all the population groups in our country.

In a document titled "Politik in meinem Leben" Von Hase relates how he experienced the attitudes and actions of the German population since his arrival in South West Africa in January 1933. The document is certainly worth reading, but I will only quote the sections relevant in this context. On his first impressions after his arrival he writes: *"[In] SWA war zur Zeit meiner Ankunft noch eine starke Abneigung gegen den 'Eroberer' Südafrika zu spüren."* During 1934–1935 he interrupted his stay in South West Africa to receive training as a *Pelzfachmann* (furrier) in Leipzig and London. Following his return to South West Africa he worked as farm manager and buyer of karakul pelts.

On his observations during this period he writes:

> "Ich lebte in einer ehemalig deutschen Kolonie, die von wieder-starken Deutschland sehr beeinflusst wurde. Die Hoffnung, dass Deutschland seine Kolonien zurückerhalten könnte bestand bei vielen Deutschen des Landes. Politisch machte sich das bemerkbar durch ein gespanntes Verhältnis der Deutschen zu den Südafrikanern, besonders den englischorientierten Teil der Bevölkerung."

The outbreak of the war in 1939 interrupted his career when he was interned with 2000 other internees in the Andalusia Internment Camp near Kimberley for six years. They kept up to date with what was hap-

pening on the war front by means of a hidden radio reception apparatus and rejoiced in Germany's initial successes. Von Hase writes on the
mood in the camp:

> Die Stimmung im Lager war fast immer diszipliniert und ge-
> fasst, voller Vertrauen auf die Kraft Deutschlands. Wir waren
> treue Deutsche und deshalb fast alle bereit uns durch Lernen
> und körperliche Ertüchtigung auf die Aufgaben der Nachkriegs-
> zeiten vorzubereiten … Ich wurde aus SWA ausgewiesen, mein
> Besitz wurde duch 'Custodian of Enemy Property' beschlag-
> nahmt. Der Tag der Kapitulation Deutschlands in Mai 1945 war
> der schwarzeste Tag meines Lebens.

After the end of the war the internees had to remain in the camp for
another year, and after that were still subjected to rigorous restrictions,
not knowing what their fate would be. Shortly after the National Party
came to power in South Africa in 1948, Hans-Jürgen became a free man
who could continue his farming career in South West Africa. He also
writes that the speedy manner in which the internees were freed illus-
trated the positive attitude the Afrikaans-speaking population had towards the German-speaking one. In the English media, however, they
were consistently labelled as "*Verbrecher*" and "*Abschaum*", according to
Von Hase.

CHAPTER 3

A new beginning in South West Africa

After the South African Government accepted responsibility for the administration of the former German colony Deutsch-Südwestafrika on 17 December 1920 in terms of a mandate agreement as "a sacred trust of civilisation", my two grandfathers, Dirk Frederik Mudge (Oupa Dick) and Petrus Stefanus van Tonder (Oupa Piet), settled with their families on the farms Omatjenne North and Omingondo in the Otjiwarongo District. As I have already mentioned, my grandfathers were both involved as volunteers in the South African forces that occupied the German colony in 1915. My Mudge grandfather transported supplies and equipment for the South African troops from Eendekuil in the Cape Province – at the time the end of the railway line to the north – to Keetmanshoop, and he decided to settle in the former German colony once the war was over.

Grandfather Dick Mudge, as he was called, was a sheep farmer on the Maskamberg Plateau near Vanrhynsdorp. To supplement his income, he was also a transport contractor. In those days a wagon with wooden wheels, drawn by donkeys, had to do the job. He was also an artisan who helped build the Dutch Reformed Church at Nieuwoudtville in 1906, as his father, Henry Mudge, had done 20 years earlier at Vanrhynsdorp.

During 1921 he embarked on the long road from Nieuwoudtville near Vanrhynsdorp to Otjiwarongo where a farm was allocated to him in accordance with a settlement plan. Like many other South Africans who went to settle in South West Africa, he couldn't use railway transport because there was no direct railway link between the Cape Province and South West Africa. They took to the road with as many of their earthly possessions as they could load onto the two wagons that were drawn by donkeys: a small number of sheep, their personal belongings and the money they received for assets sold before they left.

Reaching the border at the Orange River, they discovered that, due to veterinary regulations, he was not allowed to take any sheep across the border. He exchanged the sheep for 20 bags of corn, which provided for their personal needs for a long time, and also made the journey easier. My father Hendrik, then only 18 years old, drove one of the wagons, while grandmother Lyna and my father's two sisters, Dorothea and Helene, who were a few years younger than he was, were responsible for the day-to-day tending to the family.

The long trek – their journey to their new fatherland South West Africa – is a story of its own, to which I often listened dumbstruck. My father told us how he sometimes deliberately lagged behind with his wagon and then whipped the donkeys just to step up the pace a little. During one of these "speed sessions" the steel band of one of the wheels came off, causing serious damage to the wheel. Fortunately, grandfather Dick was an accomplished artisan and could fix it himself. He chopped wood, made spokes and rims, and put back the band over the wheel again. A day or two later, the journey was resumed.

I can no longer remember how long their trek lasted, probably six months, if not longer. They followed a double-track road for long distances and often stopped for the donkeys to rest and to service the wagons. Grandfather Dick knew the way to Keetmanshoop, but from there they simply had to find their way. To complicate matters, they didn't always know when next they would find water.

The farm Omatjenne North, situated just west of Otjiwarongo, was allocated to my grandfather. It is part of the experimental farm Omatjenne today. This farm where he and his family finally unharnessed the donkeys after their long trek, was not a farm as we know farms today. There were absolutely no improvements. It was just a bare patch of land without water, fences or buildings. The only visible structures were four pegs, propped up by stones, indicating the borders of the farm. They never managed to find water on Omatjenne North and my grandfather eventually succeeded in exchanging it for the neighbouring farm, Rusthof. It is important to note that it wasn't necessary to remove former occupants, because there weren't any. If there had been, they had probably been removed during the colonial period.

My mother, Magrieta Cornelia van Tonder, hails from a stalwart Afrikaner family from Western Transvaal. From 1915 to 1916, during the First World War, the seven Van Tonder brothers (my mother's father and his brothers) were also members of the Union troops tasked by General Louis Botha to occupy the German colony, Deutsch-Südwestafrika. After the occupation of the Territory, the Van Tonder brothers returned to the Transvaal. When South West Africa became a mandate of South Africa, some of them decided to settle in South West Africa. Commander C.J. van Tonder and his family settled on the farm Goede Hoop just outside Otjiwarongo, and my Van Tonder grandfather, Petrus Stefanus (Piet), and his family settled on Omingondo near Kalkfeld.

From 1920 onwards the history of South West Africa and that of my family were inextricably intertwined.

Their first two decades in the Territory coincided with political developments I described in the previous chapter. During the period between the two World Wars they were apparently so busy securing a livelihood for themselves in their new country that they didn't actively involve themselves in the political and governmental developments of the time. This happened only much later.

My ancestors

I always wondered how it happened that my grandfather could speak such good English. Why he was addressed as Dick and not as Dirk? And why all his sisters had English names: Jane, Mary and Susan. Towards the end of his life he sang a ditty, which – if I remember correctly – went as follows: "It's the blue, the navy blue, Britannia rules the waves." As a child I learnt that my great-grandfather, Richard Henry Mudge, was born in England. I never knew him, and even my father could tell me nothing about Oupa Harry (as they called him), because he died in 1902, the year my father was born.

I wasn't concerned about my origins during my childhood, and didn't know much about it anyway. My grandfather Dick was our hero, because he was different and interesting and our friend. He was everyone's friend and people liked him. I researched and learnt more about my English ancestors only many years later.

A friend of mine warned me that you shouldn't dig too deeply into your family history, because you never know what you might find. But I was curious. In a *Simon's Town Historical Society* bulletin a researcher wrote the following about the origin of South African families under the title "The Mudges at the Cape":

> A register in the church of Beckenham in Devonshire contains the entry: "Henry Mudge, a pirate at sea, was hanged in chains the 28th day of September in the Year of Our Lord 1581." Lat-

er the Mudges became more respectable, but they remained Devonshire men and they kept their love of the sea and of an active life. For more than two centuries the Mudges were involved in the British armed forces, a good many in the army and still more in the navy. Several of the latter specialised in the science of navigation and of marine surveying and made valuable contributions. There was for instance Thomas Mudge who designed and manufactured chronometers and other nautical instruments and wrote a number of books on the subject. A sailor expects to see the world, so during the eighteen-twenties no less than four of the naval Mudges spent some periods of service at the Cape.

My political opponents of the past would probably like to believe that I am a direct descendant of Henry Mudge, the pirate. I accepted this, because my great-grandfather was, after all, Richard Henry Mudge, my father was Henry Ferdinand Mudge, and my oldest son, Henk, was registered as Henry Ferdinand.

Later, during the negotiations with the Western Contact Group, I became acquainted with David Summerhayes, High Commissioner at the British Embassy in South Africa. Following a conversation about my Devonshire ancestors, he gave me a book titled *Devon Clocks and Clockmakers*, in which I was able to find the following information about our most likely forefathers:

> Thomas Mudge (1715–1794), pioneer of the lever escapement and one of the most brilliant watchmakers the world has ever seen, was a member of a remarkably talented Devonshire family. His father, the Reverend Prebendary Zachariah Mudge, was described by James Boswell as "that very eminent divine … who was idolised in the west, both for his excellence as a preacher and the uniform perfect proprietor of his private conduct." One brother, Dr John Mudge, was a fellow of the Royal Society and a winner, in 1777, of its prestigious Copley gold medal for his work on reflecting telescopes; another brother, the Reverend Richard Mudge, was a composer whose playing on the harpsichord impressed even the great Handel, who declared that he was second only to himself.

A clock that Thomas Mudge made for the wife of King George III of England in 1776 can still be seen at Windsor Castle, and a timepiece that was used with others to determine longitude at sea is preserved in the British Museum. Therefore, it is possible that my great-grandfather, Richard Henry, could be a descendant of Reverend Richard Mudge, the composer and pianist. It does seem that the Mudges, some 430 years later, have become more respectable!

The name Richard often appears among the descendants of my great-grandfather. My father's only brother, who died when he was 14 years old, was also called Richard. I don't know how or when my great-grandfather arrived in the Cape, but according to the researcher of the Simon's Town Historical Society, Richard Henry Mudge could have been attached to the British Naval Base in Simon's Town. Would this have been the origin of the song "Britannia rules the Waves" that my grandfather so loved to sing?

In the Cape Colony my great-grandfather, Richard Henry Mudge, married Susanna Johanna Maria Coetzee of Vredenburg. He was an artisan who built the Dutch Reformed Church in Vanrhynsdorp. According to the minutes of the Church Council in 1886: "De oude heer Hager van Stellenbosch was de architect, de heer Henry Mudge de hoofdmetselaar en de heer Heinrich Arp [my grandmother's father] zette het dak op en deed al het houtwerk." The family always referred to him (Heinrich Arp) as "the German".

My Mudge great-grandfather was known to his family and friends as Harry Mudge. He and his wife, Susanna Coetzee, had five children: Hendrik (probably registered as Richard Henry), my grandfather Dirk Frederik (he was probably named after his mother's father), and three daughters: Jane, Mary and Susan. Dirk Frederik (my grandfather) went on to marry Helene Ferendine Arp and was involved, among other things, in building the beautiful stone church in Nieuwoudtville. My grandfather Dick and grandmother Helene (Lyna) had four children: my father, Henry Ferdinand (Hendrik), his sister, Dorothea Wilhelmina, a younger brother, Richard Henry and an adopted daughter, Helene. So much then about the background of my half-English half-German ancestors.

The Van Tonder family in Namibia researched the origin of their ancestors and established that Andreas Corneliz van Tondern was born on 3 September 1676 in Tondern, Schleswig-Holstein. In 1700 he became an employee of the VOC (*Vereenigde Oostindische Compagnie* – Dutch East India Company) and worked as a miller in Stellenbosch. Van Tondern was probably derived from the name of a village on the German-Danish border, which was part of Friesland in The Nether-

lands and subsequently became part of Germany, but was incorporated into Denmark in 1920. The first name Cornelius (Neels) crops up in
many Van Tonder families in Namibia.

After the war, grandfather Piet van Tonder and most of the Van
Tonders and the Mudge's in Namibia became loyal Botha–Smuts supporters and members of the United Party of South Africa.

Subsequent to the occupation of the Territory, many other South
African families settled here. Some of them were poor, others not, but
they were farmers who were prepared to take on a new challenge,
and, as was apparent later, make a success of it, as did their successors
in years to come. In accordance with the terms of the Land Settlement
Law (Union Proclamation 310 of 1927), the farmers could, following
a trial period, buy the land they had settled on for a sum determined
by the then Administration. It is untrue that local inhabitants on the
allocated farms were driven off. The land was unoccupied, or if it had
been occupied previously, the inhabitants had been driven off during
the German regime.

Rusthof, my birthplace

My father was only 18 years old when he and his family arrived at
Rusthof. While my grandfather Dick was making the farm habitable,
the young Hendrik had to earn money to support the farming enterprise.

He started erecting fences for the few affluent farmers in the district.
His mode of transport was a donkey cart, which made going home in
the evenings not feasible. He slept where he had planted his last pole,
under a tarpaulin stretched across the shaft of the cart.

He sunk wells, and for a while, using a hand pump, drew water for
cattle belonging to other farmers at a *tiekie* (threepence, or two and a
half cents in today's currency) a head. His earnings were used to buy
livestock.

In those days no organised market for livestock and farm produce
existed. Otjiwarongo was a very small town with only a few inhabitants – primarily traders, policemen and a small number of railway
officials and civil servants. This was the only offset for meat and farm
products. There were only a few farmers in the entire district, because
the early settlers had established themselves mostly in the western

part of the country. Areas with a higher rainfall, such as Grootfontein, Otavi, Gobabis and even parts of the Otjiwarongo, Outjo and Oka-handja districts, were not suitable for livestock farming due to mineral deficiencies (phosphate) in the grazing, resulting in bovine parabotu-lism, which led to considerable livestock losses. Only later, once the necessary vaccines had become available, did these areas become ac-cessible for livestock farming.

In 1926 my father married Magrieta Cornelia van Tonder, daughter of Piet van Tonder, to whom I referred earlier. I was born on 16 January 1928 on Rusthof, the first Mudge to be born in South West Africa. My earliest memories take me back to Rusthof, to my grandfather Dick and dear grandmother Lyna, and to the small corner cupboard in which there was always something tasty for her first grandchild.

Shortly afterwards my father applied for the farm Goanab in the Outjo District, and with his small number of cattle moved there from Rusthof, but in less than a year he had lost so many animals to botulism that he moved back to my grandfather's farm with his few remaining animals. He told us how he had fed his cattle bone meal with a spoon. His problems were exacerbated by the drought and depression of the early 1930s. At the time I was just about old enough to understand what was going on around me.

The Depression

Few younger people are aware of the serious drought and worldwide economic depression experienced in the early thirties of the previous century. During those years farmers were facing financial ruin and the general economic situation reached an all-time low. This resulted in the South West African Administration of the time introducing support schemes to provide work and income to impoverished farmers.

The construction of the Omatjenne and Avis dams were two such schemes. This entailed whites walking behind a small dam scraper drawn by four donkeys. The dam builders were accommodated at Omatjenne in a tented town with very few amenities. There was a school for their children and Skolnick's shop, where basic necessities – mainly groceries and clothes – could be bought.

By then my father was leasing a farm that bordered on Omatjenne. He had good business sense and started selling fresh produce to the dam builders at Omatjenne. He found this both more acceptable and more lucrative than walking behind a scraper drawn by donkeys. By day he milked his cows, made butter, and slaughtered sheep until late in the night, and then prepared the meat for delivery early the next morning.

To keep the butter cold, my father made a small cooler with a wooden framework with double sides consisting of tin sheets on the inside and wire netting on the outside, with charcoal in-between, which was kept wet. Some of the dam builders were so impressed with these coolers that they asked my father to make some for them too. He added the making of coolers to his many other daily activities. At this stage I wasn't going to school yet. I attended the nightly slaughtering activities, and accompanied my father when he delivered his products. While the slaughtering was taking place, I grilled the *vetderm* (rectum stuffed with kidneys and liver) from the slaughtered sheep. I was very envious of the many children living in the tents whenever we visited the dam site.

Although my parents were poor during my childhood years, I cannot remember ever lacking for anything. However, there was never any money for luxuries, because buying cattle and sheep was the first priority. Many years later Ouboet Botha, a well-known farmer in our district, told me that he occasionally visited my parents on the farm Oslo, which my father leased before he owned a farm of his own. He told me that my mother was cooking over an open fire. When he asked her why my father hadn't bought her a decent stove, she replied that they first had to fill the kraal with cattle. It's probably hard for today's generation of farmers to understand how difficult it was for the pioneer farmers to survive in those early years.

Another memory from the depression years is that my grandfather's motorcar and farm engine ran on gas. I cannot fully recall how this worked, but I do remember there was a drum filled with charcoal and a bellows was used to fuel the charcoal, apparently to produce the gas. This gas was then led via a thin pipe to the carburettor of the engine. A smaller model of the same apparatus was mounted on my grandfather's car step. When the gas ran out along the road, the bellows had to be used again. As a result the journey of 25 miles (40 kilometres) from Rusthof to Otjiwarongo took several hours.

My father initially used a horse-drawn cart as a means of transport. He later upgraded to a Pedal Ford, a small vehicle with wooden spokes. He subsequently acquired a later model with wire rather than wooden spokes. The cap of the petrol tank was positioned on the bonnet in front of the windscreen, with the cap of the radiator right in the centre. Once, while playing in the car, I poured water into the petrol tank and sand into the radiator. The consequences of this I remember only too well.

My father was a hardworking man with – as already mentioned – a good business sense, and when an opportunity arose to make a little money, he made good use of it. At one stage the Administration asked for tenders to clear a road between Otjiwarongo and Kalkfeld. My father tendered £300 to do the work and even made a small profit in the end.

When tenders were asked again to clear a road between Otjiwarongo and Platveld on the Otavi route, other farmers tendered lower than my father and he wasn't awarded the tender, but the successful bidders never completed the work. My father's comment was that they weren't prepared to work alongside their labourers, other than go and check every now and then how the job was progressing. This was one of the lessons my father taught us – that you must work alongside your employees instead of just supervising them. He often bought cattle in the Grootfontein area and then trekked with them to Otjiwarongo. During such a cattle trek he wouldn't leave his workers on their own with the cattle, but accompanied them on foot over long distances.

Boskop, my father's first farm

After many years of moving around, the farm Boskop, 25 miles east of Otjiwarongo and close to the Waterberg, was allocated to my father in 1934. The conditions under which the farm was allocated were the same as those under which my grandfather obtained his land. This meant that he could lease the farm for a period of four years, after which he could apply to buy it. Approval to buy the land depended on what the applicant had achieved there during the lease period. Boskop extended over 5076 hectares and as in the case of Rusthof, was undeveloped land without water or any improvements whatsoever.

With the good news that he could now finally farm on his own land, came the "great rains" of 1934, ending a long and devastating drought. That year even the Omatjenne and Avis dams were full for the first time. Today, the high-water levels of 1934 are still indicated on signboards at river crossings in Klein Windhoek.

At Boskop there was a borehole that yielded virtually no water. The pump my father had installed yielded barely enough for human consumption. The large amount of rainwater that flowed over the farm in several rivers prompted him to build dams without further delay, applying the same methods used to build the Omatjenne and Avis dams. He got hold of scrapers, probably second-hand ones from the Administration, but had to look for donkeys. So he climbed into his little Ford and tackled the sodden road to Grootfontein, farm by farm, on virtually impassable roads. Even for today's modern four-wheel-drive vehicles it would have been a formidable challenge.

Assisted by a group of Hereros from the neighbouring reserve, my father finished the dam at Boskop in record time and the water problem was temporarily solved. Many years later I met some of these Hereros, and they invariably said "Oubaas Hendrik" was always in a hurry; everything had to happen fast, that he was strict but also fair and that they never went hungry. He always maintained that one could not work on an empty stomach.

After my father had finished the dam at Boskop, he decided that, with the equipment he had at his disposal, he could build dams for other farmers in order to earn money to supplement his cattle stock. One of his first projects was the town dam at Otjiwarongo, which is still visible from the crocodile farm in the town. While small by modern standards, it's big considering it was built with donkeys and scrapers.

Several dams followed, which meant that Pa Hendrik had to move from dam to dam with his entire household, including a wife and three young children. For accommodation they had a portable house consisting of a wooden frame covered with sheets made from cement drums cut open and flattened.

In those days cement was sold in metal drums and petrol in four-gallon tins, which were packed two-by-two in a petrol case. (A gallon was 4,5 litres.) Imagine asking your neighbour: "Please bring me a case of petrol and a drum of cement next time you go to town."

Boetie goes to school

I was called Boetie. I was the oldest son, the first grandson, and the first Mudge to be born in South West Africa. The extended family, my parents, grandfathers, grandmothers and aunts simply decided my name was Boetie, although I had formally been registered as Dirk Frederik Mudge. It took quite a while to get rid of the name, and it was, as I grew older, a great source of embarrassment to me.

But Boetie had to start school and I couldn't go to school from home, because home moved from dam to dam. There was no boarding school in Otjiwarongo. The solution presented itself when a farm school was established on the farm Omingonde, later called Renosterkloof, at the foot of Mount Etjo. The farm belonged to my mother's father, Piet van Tonder, but was occupied by my uncle, Eddie Mostert, who was married to my mother's younger sister, Bettie, at the time. I stayed with them. The school building was Uncle Eddie's garage, small and built with red bricks, and with petrol cases as benches. There were only a few pupils, and the first teacher, a Mr Nortjé, was succeeded by Mr Willem Marais of Outjo. We met few other people, and did not see many cars. Willem le Clus's Dodge truck with the wooden cabin was one of the few.

Over weekends I visited my grandparents on Die Fontein (The Fountain), which was part of Omingonde. The house was situated at the foot of the mountains and there was a spring surrounded by many fig and other trees. I always imagined the Garden of Eden to look like this. I played house with my mother's youngest sister Elsa, who was not much older than I was, with dolls we had cut out from *Die Huisgenoot*, making them stand up or sit down.

After less than a year Mr Marais was transferred, or possibly it was his own decision to move to another farm school on Schwarzenfels (the farm between Kalkfeld and Outjo). It was the end of the little school at Omingonde. It was then decided that I would move with him to Schwarzenfels, where we would both be accommodated in an outbuilding by the owner, Piet van der Westhuijzen. Once again the garage was the classroom. It was just big enough for the farmer's own children and those of the Hennings and Van der Merwes, who were living on the farm.

Although I didn't see much of my parents, I enjoyed school. I can't remember us studying much, but we rode donkeys and shot with catapults, and when Gert van der Merwe went to fetch wood from the Paresis Mountain with his donkey wagon, the school closed for the day and all the children went along to help, and to pick wild dates.

At a later stage Mr Willem Marais was succeeded by Jurie de Bruyn, who – as far as I know – had no teacher's qualifications. He subsequently farmed in the Outjo District and was, as a result of his mechanical aptitude, very much in demand when the farmers' pumps and engines needed repairing. Jurie de Bruyn later married one of his former learners, Bessie, a daughter of the farm owner, Piet van der Westhuijzen.

The farm Schwarzenfels was not very far – about 30 kilometres – from grandfather Dick's farm Rusthof. Every second weekend my grandmother sent old Wanga, an Owambo man, in a donkey cart to fetch me. The journey took several hours and we usually arrived at Rusthof only late on the Friday evening. Sunday afternoon after lunch we had to take the road back to Schwarzenfels. My grandmother loved her first grandchild very much and spoiled me a great deal. Even during the long holidays when I was with my parents on the farm, I used every possible opportunity to visit Rusthof, usually when my father and I went to town and met my grandfather. Our departure for Rusthof was often only after sunset because my grandfather had many friends and all of them were very fond of him. They met at the hotel, the only place to dally, have drinks and play *Knobel* to determine who should pay for the next round.

We usually arrived at Rusthof after dark, my grandfather announcing our arrival by singing "Where have you been Dicky boy, Dicky boy, where have you been charming Dicky?" Nobody could resist "Dicky Boy's" charms. In the meantime my grandmother would have gone to look for me in the horse cart where I often hid away. She never accepted that I hadn't come along until she had gone to check herself.

On 5 December 1935, my grandmother passed away at the young age of 54. This was a great loss to me, and life was never the same again for my grandfather and me. He had only his old Zenith short-wave radio that cackled, hissed and whistled. It was nearly impossible to tell what was broadcast. Time waits for nobody, and my farm-school days came to an end. I had to go to town school, but since there wasn't a hostel in Otjiwarongo, my sister Sannie and I had to board with Sergeant James Wright and his wife.

I had no idea what lay in store for me when I started town school at the beginning of 1937. I soon discovered that riding donkeys and shooting catapult were not requirements for admission to a normal school. Although I was regularly taken to task, I will always be grateful to the three teachers at the school at Otjiwarongo – Banie van der Merwe (renowned for his beautiful paintings), Mr Kilian and Miss Celliers – for getting me up to standard. In the next year, 1938, the new primary school was commissioned and the old school was converted into a hostel.

On 11 April 1938, my father received a letter from the Division of Lands in which he was informed that he met the necessary requirements and could therefore buy the farm Boskop for the price as set out in the attached account:

5076 hectares of land @ 2 shillings per ha	£507.12.–
Surveying fees	£79.15.10
Inspection fees	£20. –. –
Borehole (3200 gallons a day)	£100. – . –
TOTAL	£707. 7.10

Once the full purchase price had been paid, Receipt No. L 970867 to the tune of £726.12.11 was issued by the Department of Home Affairs. My father had to sell between 150 and 200 head of cattle to be able to pay this amount. In terms of cattle prices at the time, the price of an empty piece of land was extremely high.

The Centenary of 1938

On 16 December 1938, the centenary of the Battle of Blood River was celebrated all over South Africa and South West Africa. A symbolical Ox-Wagon Trek under leadership of Oom Henning Klopper was undertaken from the Cape to Natal, with big festivities all along the route. In Pretoria the cornerstone of the Voortrekker Monument was laid on 16 December 1938.

On that day festivities also took place in Otjiwarongo. I was only 10 years old – still too young to understand the real meaning of the symbolical Ox-Wagon Trek and the simultaneous revival of Afrikaner nationalism. Nevertheless, it made a deep impression on me. Men grew beards and wore corduroy suits, and women wore long dresses and *kappies* (sun bonnets). *Volkspele* (traditional Afrikaans folk dances) were performed and *jukskei* was played. We sang Afrikaans songs from the FAK (Federasie van Afrikaanse Kultuurverenigings – Federation of Afrikaans Cultural Associations) songbook and were told that that we should no longer use the English terms "tyres", "tubes" and "carburettors", but the correct Afrikaans ones: *buitebande, binnebande* and *vergassers*.

We were told how the Zulu chief had murdered our forefathers and how bravely our forefathers had fought; that the English had burnt down the Afrikaners' farms; and that the wives and children had been put into concentration camps. Afrikanerdom was impressed on our minds; also that we should speak our language purely and support Afrikaans enterprises to uplift the Afrikaner from economic inferiority.

Needless to say, this made a deep impression on me as a teenager. For many years afterwards we never went on holiday at the end of the year before we had attended the Dingaan Festival – later renamed the Day of the Covenant – on 16 December.

I joined the Voortrekker Youth Movement and remained a member until my matriculation year – an Afrikaner to the backbone. The fact that grandfather's father hailed from Britain and that my grandmother's mother was of German descent, could not change this.

I am still proud to be part of a group that, despite their European descent, developed an own identity here in Africa. We no longer have a "home" or *Heimat* to which we can return, nor do we want to. The name Afrikaner binds us irrevocably to Africa, and the language we speak is spoken only here on the southern tip of Africa.

I visit Windhoek and Cape Town for the first time

Once the centenary festivities were over, my father decided to show us where he had grown up and what it looked like in South Africa, the country we had heard so much about during the festivities. My first-hand knowledge of the world at this stage was limited to Otjiwarongo and neighbouring towns, and I couldn't wait to see and experience all the things my father had told me so much about. He told me about shops with huge glass windows through which you could see everything inside the shop. I actually couldn't imagine what this looked like, because the shops of Hans Langner and Julius Doll in Otjiwarongo had only small windows, and when the shop was closed, these were shut tight.

We left in my father's small 1938 Chevrolet truck on our long trip to Cape Town. My sister Sannie could sit in front with my parents but old Hans, one of our farmworkers, and I had to sit on top of the luggage behind the cab.

Windhoek with its large shop windows – though not nearly as big as they are nowadays – was my and Sannie's first experience of a city, although Windhoek was nothing like the size it is today. We didn't make progress very fast, because the road to South Africa was not tarred yet, and a motor vehicle had to be tough to make it all the way to Cape Town. Before reaching Vanrhynsdorp we crossed the Knersvlakte and my father told us that only the toughest of the tough could survive in this harsh and barren part of South Africa. Finally, covered in dust, we arrived at Vanrhynsdorp where my father was born, with Maskamberg in the background.

We visited Nieuwoudtville where my grandfather had harnessed his two donkey wagons a decade and a half earlier to venture forth to his new country. We also visited Vredendal, Koekenaap and Paternoster, meeting the descendants of old acquaintances. The men drank wine from the farmers' cellars – cooperative cellars did not yet exist in those days – and relived the past.

One evening we found our way to a family living in a *matjieshuis* (mat house) and my father decided to spend the night with them. My mother objected, because she couldn't believe that we could be accommodated in the tiny dwelling, to which my father replied: "These people always have space." Once again we were regaled with anecdotes from the past: How poor the people had been in that part of the world and how my father as a child had gone to fetch skimmed milk from a more prosperous neighbour.

The road from Vanrhynsdorp to Cape Town was very bad, but the Chevvie made it to Piketberg, from where I experienced a tarred road for the first time in my life.

In Cape Town we stayed with one of my father's nephews for a week. He was the Station Commander of the South African Police in Maitland – not exactly a posh residential area of Cape Town. My father's cousin's name was Richard – the name of one of our ancestors in England. Richard had children my age – between eight and 12 years old – and they showed Sannie and me the streets of Maitland. There were long rows of shops with lots of sweets and fruit displayed on the pavements.

We wanted to see more of Cape Town, but my father insisted on making a practice run by himself first. He returned in one piece and told us about a policeman who had insulted him, yelling: "Hey you, where the hell are you going?" when he mistakenly drove up a one-way street. My father stopped his vehicle right there, got out, walked up to the policeman and asked whether it was *him* he was talking to. The traffic piled up, but he wouldn't leave without an apology, which he got. He wouldn't be bullied.

We headed home, realising that it wasn't home any more. After 18 years, home was South West Africa. .

The Second World War breaks out

In 1939 we went to school in Swakopmund. I was 11 years old, Sannie nine and Piet six. We went by train, changing at Usakos in the middle of the night to arrive in Swakop in the foggy, ghostly early hours of the morning. From the station it was a long walk to the hostel, lugging our heavy baggage on our shoulders. My father was obviously convinced that I, at the age of 11, was big and strong enough to lead this little troop from Otjiwarongo to Swakopmund.

During the year in Swakopmund the Second World War broke out and I saw soldiers, fighter aircraft and warships for the first time. Canons were deployed between Swakopmund and Walvis Bay.

At the end of that year, as we returned to Otjiwarongo to continue our schooling there, I heard the grown-ups talking politics. At that time I knew nothing about the South African Party and the National Party, because – as far as I can remember – politics were never discussed at home. However, the adults were questioning whose war this actually was, and people started taking sides. Many people, especially Germans, sympathised with Germany and became suspect. Many Afrikaans-speaking people who still remembered the Anglo-Boer War couldn't make peace with the idea of fighting on the side of the English against Germany.

I understood very little about what was going on and collected cards of aeroplanes and warships that were distributed with cigarettes. Although I was still young, I knew that both my grandfathers and my father were members of the UNSWP (United National South West Party).

- It's never the "who" that is important.
  People are a summation of ideas

Shortly after the war broke out, my father joined the Defence Force as a volunteer. He told us it was his duty to make a contribution when his country was threatened. Because of knee injuries he had suffered in a car accident two years before, he was medically unfit, but kept quiet about this and was accepted as a member of the South West Division of the South African Defence Force, based in Windhoek. He was again classified medically unfit and was utilised in other auxiliary services.

My mother now had to take care of the farm all on her own which placed a tremendous responsibility on her shoulders. She had never been actively involved in the farming activities in the past, having given all her attention to taking care of her children. Besides, she couldn't drive a car. I became the designated driver on the farm over weekends, and took the family to town in our 1939 Chevrolet truck. I was 12 years old. One year later, I took my mother to Windhoek at her request, 250 kilometres on gravel. I remember it took four hours, at a speed of 50 mph.

After months of wasting time in the military camp in Windhoek, my father decided he could no longer neglect his farm to work in a kitchen peeling potatoes – a role in which I could hardly picture him. He had come to the conclusion that it wasn't our war, but a war between two major powers, both of whom we had faced in combat before. The South African Government subsequently decided that inhabitants of South West Africa could not be forced to take part in the war. From then on those who were willing and able, would be appointed on a permanent basis and identified by red tags on the shoulders of their shirts. Soon after this my father, based on medical disability, was discharged.

In South West Africa there was, as in South Africa, great confusion as to whose war it actually was. I can possibly illustrate this best with the following story I heard at the time. Two older men who had joined the "home guard" were listening to a corporal explaining combat position, referring to the Germans as the enemy, upon which one of them said: "Corporal, I think there's a misunderstanding here. You keep on talking about the Germans, but aren't we fighting against the English?"

Windhoek High School

In 1941 I started Standard 7 at Windhoek High School. At the time it was the only government school in South West Africa. During my high-school years I was inducted as a member of the Junior Ossewa Brand-wag (a right-wing Afrikaner movement). We went to camps and, using bamboo sticks, practised our drills in the Eros Mountains. As a demonstration of our Afrikaner patriotism, we wore little badges featuring the Transvaal and Free State flags. This, however, never amounted to much more than a demonstration.

Throughout my entire school career I was the youngest in the class because I had gone to school at such a young age. The Alte Feste, now a museum, was then the boys' hostel and I stayed in a tower room in one of the corners.

I remember a few boys who were at school with me, some who stand out in my memory. Jan and Wiks Tromp of Okahandja played rugby with me. They subsequently became successful farmers and were respected members of the Okahandja community until their death. There were also the Oberholzers of Outjo. Johanna Oberholzer married Ben van Zyl, who later became Commissioner of Native Affairs at Opuwo. Their son is currently working for NASA in America, where he made a name for himself. There was also Boebie Prinsloo of Outjo, who in the difficult political days to come stood by my side; Boesman van Niekerk, who became Secretary of South West Africa; and Hennie Brunette, who became a man of the cloth.

From the south there were the Van Lills, Willem and Piet de Lange, Jannie Steenkamp and Piet and Fanie Naudé. Those were good days for the karakul farmers of the south and I will never forget how I admired the tailored suits – with 24-inch trouser legs and double-breasted waistcoats – of Piet Naudé and Piet de Lange. We fellows from the north compared poorly, not to mention the cars their fathers drove – mostly Fords. When we went down to the primary-school hostel opposite the German Church for meals, we always checked whether it was a Ford or a Chev that could drive up the hill to the church in top gear.

Anna Jooste was one year ahead of me. She later married Simmy Frank and was the first and only woman to serve in the white Legislative Assembly. She represented the Republican Party. My girlfriend at school was Johanna Mouton. The Moutons, relatives of the well-known advocate and judge Chris Mouton, lived at Elisenheim – a farm a few kilometres outside Windhoek, which later belonged to A.H. du Plessis. Some Saturday afternoons I walked to Elisenheim. When it was time to return to the hostel in the evening, I chased the goods train coming from the north as it slowed down approaching Elisenheim, and jumped onto the last wagon to catch a lift to the station.

Because Windhoek High School was the only government high school in the country at the time, there were no other schools to compete against in rugby. As a result, WHS played in the second league against teams of senior clubs such as Wanderers, United and the Railways. Fortunately, this meant that teachers could also play for the school.

Stellenbosch

My father was adamant that his children should acquire tertiary education, probably because of his own lack of education. During the First World War when my grandfather transported supplies between Eendekuil and Keetmanshoop for the Union Troops, my father sometimes stayed away from school to assist him. When he returned after a long absence, he had outgrown the teacher. His school career ended when he wouldn't submit to the harsh treatment by the teacher. He later in life proved that book education on its own was not the only guarantee for achieving success in life. He left his mark in the history of this country, and many people who knew him bear testimony to this. He was amongst others Chairman of the SWA Agricultural Union, to be succeeded by Jan de Wet, and represented South West Africa in the South African Senate.

Hence, at the age of 17, after a three days' train journey, I arrived at Stellenbosch, with £5 in my pocket and my suitcase in hand, walking the streets looking for accommodation. I didn't have far to walk. I found accommodation with an English lady, Mrs Tawse in Alexander Street, less than a kilometre from the station, where I would stay for the next two years.

I registered the next day and obtained my BCom degree, majoring in Accountancy and Industrial Economics, three years later, together with 54 classmates. There were not many highlights during the three years at Stellenbosch. I was young and my pocket money was meagre, not really enough to provide me with much entertainment.

My first roommate in Alexander Street was Caswell Becker, also from Otjiwarongo, and after him Inno Leuvenink of Bonnievale, a

BMus student who shared a room with me in my final year in the newly completed university hostel, House Marais. He could never understand how I could sing all the popular songs of the time in tune from memory, while he had to play everything on the piano from sheet music.

I noticed Stienie Jacobs, the girl who was to become my wife, for the first time as far back as 1939 when we were at school together in Swakopmund. I was then 11 years old and she just over eight. Two years later, when I was in Windhoek High School and she in Emma Hoogenhout Primary School, I noticed her again, because you couldn't help but notice her, as it is still to this day.

We really got to know each other during the train journeys to and from Stellenbosch, she in Standard 9 at Bloemhof Girl's School and I a first-year student. The relationship was somewhat complicated, because of her staying in a hostel and a bicycle being my only mode of transport. After Stienie finished school, we saw very little of each other, since I was still at Stellenbosch, while she moved to a Bloemfontein teachers training college.

During my years as a student I didn't participate in politics and was also not a member of any party or student organisation, with the exception of the Students' Christian Association.

The Second World War came to an end in 1946, my second year at university, and many of the returning soldiers started or resumed their studies at Stellenbosch. In most cases they were tough soldiers sharing space in the lecture halls with us young students. They were also formidable contenders when it came to the girls. But it wasn't only soldiers who came back. During my first year I met Zacharias Eloff in my English Special class. He was noticeably older than I was, but we nevertheless became good friends. As conservative Afrikaners we agreed on many things that led to clashes with our English lecturer, Miss Marquard. After the first semester he didn't show up again and for many years I wondered what had become of him. Decades later Advocate Jan Strydom was appointed Judge in the Supreme Court in Windhoek. Through our children who were studying together at Stellenbosch, we became friends, and on occasion he and his wife Florrie visited us on the farm. While listening to an intervarsity rugby match on the radio, I realised I had met this man before. It struck me out of the blue: "Aren't you Zacharias Eloff?" He nodded and told me the story of how he had registered at the university under a pseudonym. At that time he had objected to fighting on the side of a former enemy of the Boer (Afrikaner) nation and consequently ended up in a concentration camp with, among others, John Vorster, later Prime Minister of South Africa. He escaped in 1945 and registered at the University of Stellenbosch under a pseudonym as a law student. He was detained again, and could only continue his studies after the war.

CHAPTER 4

Farmer and South West African politician

Elandsvreugde

From early childhood there had been consensus in the family that I would never be a farmer. I showed great aptitude for mechanics, taking apart everything that could be taken apart, although I couldn't always put it back together again. I disappointed the family by deciding I would rather obtain a degree in economics. Becoming a farmer was the last option I would ever consider. When, towards the middle of 1947, a few months before the final examination for my degree, my father asked me to consider assisting him on the farm, I was completely taken by surprise. At that stage he was only 45 years old, in the prime of his life and certainly not ready to relinquish his authority yet. He already owned four farms and 2000 head of cattle. He probably needed assistance, especially with his bookkeeping and income tax returns. I joined him on the farm after graduation, with the hope that this partnership between father and a newly graduated student would work.

Professor Schumann, Dean of the Faculty of Commerce, was taken aback when I told him I was planning to take up farming, since he had already secured a position for me with a large financial concern in Cape Town, but my mind was made up. I was not keen on settling outside of my country, South West Africa. And so I became a farmer, the one thing I had always said I would never be.

Unfortunately, it was a recipe for failure. My father was used to doing things his way and I was inexperienced, although quite convinced that I knew how to run a business. After a short while we decided I should farm on my own on Elandsvreugde, one of his farms. This was anything but the kind of life I had envisaged for myself during my student years. My father gave me a number of cattle to manage for my brother Piet and myself. Piet, always seen as the farmer in the family, was to join me at a later stage.

There was only one borehole on the farm which yielded little water. I had to stand watch over the old Lister engine many a night. If it stopped during the night, there would be no water for our cattle the next day. Sitting next to a small fire to keep me warm, I wrote letters to Stienie, my girlfriend in Bloemfontein, telling her about my life on the farm and how I was looking forward to the day she would join me. There was a small somewhat dilapidated house on the farm and fortunately grandfather Dick, who by then had given up farming some years ago, came to live with me on Elandsvreugde with his second wife. I have fond memories of the time we spent there together.

On 30 June 1949, I typed my first income tax return on an old Remington typewriter. The Mudge Brothers' income for the year was £915.1.8 and the expenses £500.3.8. This left us with a taxable income of £325.18.5. Divided proportionately with 55% for myself and 45% for Piet, I had earned a taxable income of £179 for the year.

Plans to get married had to wait, but fortunately both Stienie and I were still very young. The following year Stienie secured a teaching position in Otjiwarongo and I had high hopes for a future on the farm. We decided to get married early the next year. My grandfather whose health had deteriorated in the meantime, moved to town. On 15 January 1951, Stienie and I got married, and since then Stienie has walked alongside me through good and sometimes difficult times.

I had already started restoring the house on Elandsvreugde before our wedding. The walls were painted light cream, with a narrow brown line where normally there would be a picture rail. We spent £500, a wedding gift from my father, on furniture. Most of it – a dining-room suite; a small sofa and two chairs for the living room; a small green Jewel wood stove; and a bed and one or two mattresses – could be loaded onto our Chevrolet truck in which we had travelled to the Cape for our honeymoon. There was no water for a garden, except for a gardenia next to the front door. This was only the beginning and we hoped that it would all improve soon. But it didn't.

Soon our firstborn was on the way and the prospects for a larger income were slim. Our needs had increased, and our small farm could not provide adequately. I was too proud to ask my father's assistance and our circumstances led to tension between my father and myself, barely a few months after we had moved into the small house on Elandsvreugde. My father was a hard taskmaster and not particularly impressed with my education. I, on the other hand, believed that many of my father's ideas were outdated. I only realised several years later how little I had actually learned at university and how important practical experience is. Stienie and I then decided to apply my qualifications elsewhere to provide us with a decent living.

A brief sojourn in the world of business

My father was highly upset by our decision to quit farming and move to Windhoek. There wasn't time to be too selective, so I accepted the first offer made to me, namely as accountant at a car dealer, Malherbe & Kiesewetter.

We hadn't taken into consideration that accommodation was virtually unobtainable in Windhoek, and at a salary of £50 a month, it was unaffordable anyway. We had no choice but to rent a room in the old Hotel Stadt Windhuk, diagonally across from the current municipal building in Kaiser Street, today's Independence Avenue. The hotel couldn't accommodate us for longer than a week. After that we moved to the Hansa Hotel on the corner of Kaiser and today's Dr A.B. May streets, but they could also not accommodate us for long. Fortunately, Koot and Anna Hurter took pity on us and put us up until we found a single garage and servant's room in the vicinity of the current municipal swimming pool. It was summer and very hot in the garage with its corrugated-iron roof without a ceiling. Moreover, Stienie was expecting our firstborn. However, we put on a brave face until Stienie's father loaned me £5000 to buy a house in Eros Road. There is a price to be paid for stubbornness.

We have fond memories of our life in Windhoek, although it would only be for a short while. We met Boet and Pickles Viljoen, with whom we established a friendship which still exists more than half a century later. They would not only share this short period in our lives with us, but also virtually everything else that happened to us after that. It included the use of their refrigerator in the early days! They lived in the same street in Eros as we did.

Boet and I were both young, he a few years older, and both of us faced an unknown future. Boet held a junior position at Old Mutual, but years later became Managing Director of the Permanent Building Society in South Africa, where he subsequently served on several councils and boards. My path went into a different direction; I became involved in politics.

We didn't stay in Eros for long, because my employers offered me the position of branch manager in Otjiwarongo, with a salary of £60 a month. In January 1952, we arrived in Otjiwarongo where we were fortunate to find a house to rent. In the meantime I managed to sell our house in Windhoek and repay my loan to my father-in-law. Shortly afterwards, on 18 February 1952, our firstborn, Henk (Henry Ferdinand), was born.

Soon after our arrival in Otjiwarongo, grandfather Dick fell seriously ill. While he was in hospital, my father contracted Malta fever and ended up in the same hospital room as my grandfather, who died a few days later. Having recovered, my father decided to live in town in future. He needed his sons to become involved in the farming activities, and regarded it essential for me to move to the farm. However, I still had to manage the business in town until a replacement was found.

I become a farmer

My father, brothers, sister and I managed his farms Boskop, Bynadaar, Elandsvreugde and Otjenga in the partnership Mudge & Sons. Piet was then living with Stienie and me on Boskop, and Sannie and her husband, Nico Oelofse, on Bynadaar, while Henry was still at school. This arrangement continued until Henry returned to the farm. Piet and Henry had the advantage that they both attended agricultural college, and there was never any doubt that they would farm one day, and that Henry would ultimately inherit Boskop.

New arrangements had to be made, and since I was the oldest and also married, my father and I decided that Stienie and I should settle somewhere else. The first opportunity to acquire our own farm came when the farm Rietfontein near Otavi was offered for sale by public auction. The farm reached the unprecedented price of £4 per hectare. I could not match this, so we had to continue our search.

Gertjie Meyer – a well-known farmer in the Outjo District who also attended the auction – informed me that the farm Lazy Spade, bordering his farm Meyerton, was for sale. On 23 March 1954, I bought the farm Lazy Spade, 6500 hectares in size, for £19 500. To be able to pay the purchase price I borrowed £8000 from the Land Bank (agricultural bank) while my father undertook to pay the balance. The cattle and other assets of the partnership were divided equally between the partners after which the partnership Mudge & Sons was dissolved and I could farm on my own for the first time.

Our new farm, Lazy Spade

Stienie had to leave the comfortable house and lovely garden of Boskop behind, to start from scratch again on a drab lime ridge in a dilapidated two-roomed shack. Although there was a strong borehole about 500 metres away, the water had not been laid on to the house and had to be brought in cans from the borehole.

Stienie didn't complain about any of this. We both felt that Lazy Spade was the place where we would be able to master our own destiny. Henk and Chrisna were then two and one years old respectively, and owing to a shortage of funds, we had to make do with very little. There was no bathroom, just a portable zinc bath in our bedroom. The toilet was an outside pit latrine, and the kitchen was in a small outbuilding.

The town and district of Outjo were unfamiliar to us. Stienie and I had grown up in the Otjiwarongo and Kalkfeld environment. We had to adapt to new surroundings and to a new community.

I played rugby against Outjo when I was still at school. One of the boys from Outjo against whom I played rugby was Jan de Wet, who was to become our neighbour in later years. Jan's younger brother Blok was our immediate neighbour. Although my family was long-time friends with the two De Wet families our involvement in politics later resulted in Jan and I having serious political differences. Nevertheless, we have maintained a friendly relationship in spite of this. Blok de Wet and I worked together in the political arena for many years and I remember him with great appreciation for his friendship, assistance and loyal support.

Our other neighbour was Gertjie Meyer, one of the most practical and successful farmers I have ever met. For him there was no middle way; something was either right or wrong, and he never beat about the bush. This did not make him popular with everybody, as will presently emerge. When I wanted to know how to put up a wire fence, I went to Meyerton to see how it was done, and when I needed advice on how to sink a borehole or which equipment to use, I always felt free to phone Gertjie Meyer – he would unfailingly give me guidance.

Other neighbours were: the Immelmans, originally from Halfmanshof in the Southern Cape; the Van Heerdens from Victoria West; and the Louws, children of the well-known Dr M.S. Louw. They were all considerably older and wiser than Stienie and I. Although we didn't visit one another frequently, they always welcomed us with open arms.

A new community and interesting experiences

Living in the Outjo District was pleasant. The people there were friendly and hospitable, and they included us in the many different activities of the community. I served on the church council of the Dutch Reformed congregation, was recruited for the Rapportryers and Broederbond, and at one time was captain of Outjo's rugby team.

Henk, our oldest, had to go to school at the beginning of the 1959 academic year and, of course, also to boarding school. This was not a pleasant prospect for Henk, and also not for Stienie and me. But then something happened that made his going to school a little easier for both him and his mother, at least in the beginning, and which saved many tears.

A few days before school was due to start, Mr Mynhardt of the local high school telephoned me from Reitz in the Orange Free State, where he was spending his long leave. The person scheduled to relieve him during his leave had pulled out, which meant that he – if he couldn't find anyone to relieve him – would have to head back for Outjo that very same day. He asked whether I would be prepared to relieve him for the first term. He was responsible primarily for commercial subjects such as Accountancy and Typing. I pointed out that although I had a BCom degree, I didn't have a teacher's diploma. I would also have to discuss it with Stienie first. Mynhardt had a good ally in her. Her immediate reaction was that Henk would then be able to go to school from home. After I had discussed the matter with Mr Rossouw, the principal, I agreed to become a teacher for a term. Another interesting experience lay ahead.

Bookkeeping and other commercial subjects were not a problem for me, but the closest I had ever come to typing was typing my income tax returns with two fingers on my old Remington. Mr Rossouw then suggested that the classes that already had a year or two of typing instruction should practise what they had already learned, and that

I would have to keep the Standard 7 typing class busy in some way or another. After a few days I decided that I couldn't keep a class occupied with trifles for an entire term. So I took the Pitman typing textbook home and studied it thoroughly. The next morning I informed the class that we would begin typing and that they should follow my instructions closely. So I taught a beginners' class how to type. When Mynhardt returned, he was entirely satisfied with how the class had progressed. Where there's a will, there's a way.

Our life in Outjo was far from boring. Apart from rugby, Rapportryer get-togethers and Broederbond meetings, I joined the rifle commando, or Skietkommando as it was called in those days. With the assistance of Steve Vermaak and Blok de Wet, we built a new shooting range. The range was named after me until I became involved in political controversy later, when the signboard disappeared and was never put back.

In November 1956, I attended a non-commissioned officer's course in Windhoek, after which I was promoted to the rank of sergeant. Three years later, in July 1959, I attended an officer's course at Tempe near Bloemfontein and was awarded the rank of lieutenant. This was my first real experience of the army and how it felt to be ordered around by a young sergeant major, who on occasion swore at me. Although we were given relatively intensive training in warfare, at the time there wasn't a war in our country yet.

My first taste of politics

My time in the Outjo District also led to my becoming involved in politics – something that Stienie and I had never foreseen.

I was 26 years old, had just started farming on my own, and was, as far as politics was concerned, living in my father's shadow. I rejoiced with him about the outcome of the 1948 election in South Africa and the 1950 election in South West Africa. In the 1950 election campaign he worked hard for the National Party and the remark was made that when Hendrik Mudge was not working for the Church or the Cooperation, he was working for the National Party. It's probably unnecessary to say that my two grandfathers, especially grandfather Dick, were shocked by my father's decision to support the National Party. My father wasn't the only one who left the UNSWP in those years, which for many years had been both my grandfathers' and my father's only political home, but now they had a choice of parties. I transported wood and tables and chairs to National Party functions, but otherwise I remained in the background.

Shortly before and after our arrival at Lazy Spade in March 1954, events came to pass that turned our plans for the future upside down and gave new direction to our lives.

The previous year, in 1953, two people made themselves available as candidates for the National Party in a by-election for the Outjo Constituency to elect a member for South West Africa's Legislative Assembly. They were Coeries Theunissen, a local attorney, and Gertjie Meyer, to whom I referred earlier. Theunissen won the by-election, and represented the constituency until the next election a year later.

The dust had not yet settled after the previous year's members' vote and the Meyer supporters were determined to have Gertjie Meyer nominated as candidate for the general election. It was my first contact with the inner workings of a political party. To gain sufficient votes for your candidate in the Constituency Council, not only did the party had to gain the support of the existing branches; new branches also had to be established. Accordingly, Nico Lemmer was elected Chairman, and I Secretary of the newly established Outjo East Branch, which – as can be expected – were Meyer supporters. Gertjie Meyer was nominated as candidate for the Outjo Constituency, and to my great surprise, I was asked to be his Party Organiser for the 1955 election.

The constituency was large, extending from Kamanjab in the west to north of Grootfontein in the east. At age 27 I was young and politically inexperienced. I didn't ask questions about policy, because I was in good company – the Broederbond, Rapportryers and Dutch Reformed Church, which all supported apartheid and approved of the National Party policy. I advocated the policy contained in the election manifesto and spent a lot of time away from home – which certainly did not help my farming activities. Indeed, in the years to come, I found that politics was not exactly a lucrative business (nowadays this is probably different), but I regarded it as a new challenge. This was the beginning of my political career, something which I also never considered before. Gertjie Meyer was elected and represented the constituency for the next five years in the Legislative Assembly. During this time I served as Chairman of the Constituency Council of the Party, with Blok de Wet as my Secretary. We worked diligently together with our representative, but discovered some people in the constituency didn't like Gertjie Meyer and that the wounds of the nomination battle had still not healed. The fact that he excelled at farming and was outspoken made him unpopular in certain circles. He wouldn't promote any cause unless it had merit. While I did everything in my power to defend him against unfair criticism, there were other committee members who pretended to be his friends, but who chose to side with the discontented. Hence, I had my first taste of the ugly side of politics already in the first five years of my political life.

Knee-deep in politics

The next general election for the Legislative Assembly took place in 1961. In the meantime, there had been a re-demarcation of constituencies, which resulted in the disappearance of the Outjo Constituency and sections of it being added to neighbouring constituencies. These developments had far-reaching implications for Gertjie Meyer, as well as for me. Our constituency disappeared and a few of our branches, of which Outjo East was one, became part of the Otjiwarongo Constituency. Up to that stage Pieter Pretorius, father of Koos Pretorius, was the MLA (Member of the Legislative Assembly) for the Otjiwarongo Constituency, but he indicated that he was no longer interested.

Some of the Outjo representatives on the Constituency Council, of which I was one, wanted "Oom Gertjie" to be the candidate for Otjiwarongo, while others sided with the Otjiwarongo representatives, who maintained that it could not automatically be assumed that Gertjie Meyer should now represent the newly demarcated Otjiwarongo Constituency. I was asked by the Otjiwarongo committee members to make myself available as candidate. They maintained that I knew them and their circumstances and problems best, since I had grown up in Otjiwarongo. I flatly refused.

At the nomination meeting, of which I was Chairman, a group of committee members refused to accept Gertjie Meyer's candidature as automatic and accused me of defeating the democratic process out of loyalty towards him. They demanded that I leave the meeting while the nomination of a candidate was being discussed. I refused to leave and tried for hours to unite the two factions behind Meyer without success. Meyer, who was present throughout, then asked to me to join him outside, suggesting we leave the decision to the meeting and accept whatever it turned out to be.

The two of us were sitting on the veranda of the hotel when they came outside to inform us that the meeting had nominated me as candidate. Meyer was the first to congratulate me and said afterwards that I reminded him of someone who had become the father of twins, I sincerely appreciated his attitude. Putting the interests of the country above personal ambitions underscored his integrity. Later that evening when I informed Stienie, her first reaction was: "But you refused consistently to make yourself available for election and I always told you that I was glad I hadn't married a politician." I can't remember what I replied, but I can imagine it didn't make sense.

A few days later I learned that a petition had been signed by three prominent committee members (Jan de Wet, Adolf Wenhold and Maritz Laubscher) in which it was alleged that I had been nominated unconstitutionally. They demanded a vote by the members of the Party in the constituency. I had no objection to this, as I was of the opinion that the complainants had a valid argument. I had also objected during the nomination meeting to the way the nomination had been handled. However, as to the motives of the three protestors, I can only speculate. I accept that years of friendship and business relationships played a role. I was a newcomer in Outjo, while it was Jan de Wet's hometown and he probably felt entitled to succeed Meyer.

In the members' vote I was again elected as candidate, after which the dust settled. I can gratefully say that these events did not harm the relationship between the Meyer family and myself. We remained good neighbours and lifelong friends. Through his unselfish action, Gertjie Meyer had proved once again that he was a true friend. Shortly after this he was nominated as the candidate for the Swakopmund Constituency. The friendly relationship between the De Wet family and ourselves did also not suffer in the process.

Political turmoil

My opponent in the 1961 election was Brian Thompson for the UNSWP. I won the election by an absolute majority and represented the

Otjiwarongo Constituency in the Legislative Assembly for the next 20 years. During this long period there were, apart from my family, two people who supported me faithfully and loyally, namely Blok de Wet and Engela Maritz, who were my organisers during elections for more than 20 years. No candidate could have wished for more. Nothing was ever too much trouble for Blok. He was always available and prepared to sacrifice his personal interests for the cause and the principles we stood for. Engela was a formidable woman who could be stopped by nothing or no one, and for whom everyone had great respect. When a dispute arose at a ballot box, no polling officer stood a chance. She didn't easily concede an argument. I experienced this personally. Many years later during the turmoil within the National Party, Blok and Engela stood by me throughout.

I cannot imagine a more dramatic time for me to become involved in active politics. On 10 December 1959, Windhoek – and indeed the whole of South West Africa – was shaken to the core when 11 black residents of the old location were shot and killed by police, and another 44 wounded. This was a result of the forced relocation of the residents of the old location to a new black suburb, which subsequently became known as Katutura. This shocking incident, following decades of oppressing black people, led to the emergence of black solidarity and nationalism in South West Africa.

Shortly afterwards, in January of the following year, nine policemen lost their lives during a police raid in the Cato Manor residential area in the Natal Province in South Africa.

On 3 February 1960, the same year in which I was elected as a candidate for the Legislative Assembly of South West Africa, Harold Macmillan, the British Prime Minister, delivered his "Winds of Change" speech during his visit to South Africa. This was followed on 21 March by the rebellion in Sharpeville near Vereeniging in the Transvaal when 69 black people were shot dead and 180 were wounded. It was probably one of the most tragic events in the history of South Africa. This episode set the world on fire and rioting increased, with the battle cry "Verwoerd must go"! Shortly after this, Verwoerd was seriously wounded by David Pratt when he opened the Rand Easter Show.

On 5 October 1960, the referendum, with a view to South Africa becoming a republic, took place. It was ratified with a majority of 74 480 votes, and 31 May 1961 was announced as the day on which South Africa would become a republic. As requested by A.H. du Plessis, leader of the National Party of South West Africa, inhabitants of Namibia who had the right to vote, participated in the referendum. The year 1961 was a year of uprisings and bloodshed in Angola. The MPLA (*Movimento Popular de Libertação de Angola*) was at the forefront of armed resistance against the Angolan regime.

On Friday 17 March 1961, with 17 other re-elected and newly elected members, I was sworn in as a member of the Legislative Assembly. The proclamation that constituted the Assembly, indicating that South Africa was still a member of the British Commonwealth, concluded with the words:

> *GOD SAVE THE QUEEN*
> *given under my Hand and Seal*
> *D.T. DU P. VILJOEN*

I had been thrown in at the deep end, but soon discovered that my older colleagues were not unduly perturbed by the developments in South Africa. They were very pleased with the outcome of the 1961 election and predicted that the end of the UNSWP was in sight. Not much was said about the incident in the old location and the events in South Africa. I wondered whether they were underestimating the gravity of what had happened, or whether they regarded it as not our problem.

It soon became clear to me that they were not impressed by the warnings and admonitions of the opposition and that they were dismissing them as negative and alarmist politicians. I sensed that the society in our country was severely divided. Not only was there discord between white and black, but also still discernible prejudices between the Afrikaans-, German- and English-speaking inhabitants.

I have already referred to my observations during the war years. Because I was then still in primary school, I didn't know enough to determine the origin of the deep-rooted antipathy. What was clear to me was that something had to be done to improve the relationships between the different racial and cultural groups, and that the future could not be built on hatred. Only after I learned more about the past, could I understand and make a contribution.

The National Party comes to power

After the outbreak of the Second World War in 1939, the old divide among Afrikaners in South Africa and in South West Africa widened. The decision by the Union Parliament in 1939 to side with Britain in the World War resulted in a split between Generals Smuts and Hertzog. Many Hertzog supporters eventually found an affinity towards Dr Malan's National Party, while the supporters of Smuts remained with him in the United Party. In South West Africa they felt drawn to the UNSWP, while the conservative Afrikaners and German speakers supported the National Party.

In 1939, more or less at the same time as General Hertzog's resignation from the South African Cabinet, Frikkie Jooste founded the National Party of South West Africa.

By the end of the war in December 1944, the National Party of South West Africa, under leadership of Henning Klopper, was re-organised. In May 1948 the National Party of South Africa, under leadership of Dr D.F. Malan, defeated General Smuts's United Party, and the new direction taken would also have repercussions on South West Africa.

In August 1949 the National Party of South West Africa and the UNSWP convened under chairmanship of Administrator P.I. Hoogenhout, and reached a nine-point agreement regarding the representation of South West Africa in the South African Parliament, as well as financial arrangements between the two countries. The two parties announced that they accepted South Africa's absolute internal and external sovereignty over the Territory, and agreed furthermore that decisions in respect of the indigenous (black) population should be taken in consultation with the Executive Committee of South West Africa. In the course of a visit to Windhoek, Dr Malan, the new Prime Minister of South Africa, accepted these points of agreement and stated that giving the right to vote to non-whites was not an option. However, he remained silent about consultation with the Executive Committee on the non-white policy.

In 1949 South Africa placed the South West Africa Affairs Amendment Act on the statute book, with the approval of the two South West Parties, and South West Africa was granted ten representatives in the South African Parliament: six in Parliament and four in the Senate. In 1950, in the next election, the National Party secured 15 of the 18 seats in the Legislative Assembly and accordingly took over the responsibility for the administration of the Territory. Within a decade of National Party rule, resistance emerged from black ranks.

The awakening of black nationalism

The awakening of black (African) nationalism after the Second World War played a decisive role in the political and constitutional development of Namibia. For much of the information in this regard I am grateful to Dr Zedekia Ngavirue, whose doctoral study at the University of Oxford bears testimony to a great deal of research, as well as his objectivity. His personal involvement in the birth of black nationalism and the formation of black political parties in South West Africa makes this source highly credible.

Paramount Chief Hosea Kutako of the Hereros, assisted by Chief David Witbooi of the Namas, was undoubtedly the leader of the post-war liberation movement. Between December 1945 and April 1946, the Smuts Government solicited the advice of the non-white population of the Territory regarding the integration into South Africa by means of a referendum. Consultation was done primarily through the traditional leaders, and the total vote would be calculated according to the number of followers of the different leaders. Chief Kutako was sceptical and insisted that five big powers be involved in such an opinion poll. He formulated his viewpoint as follows:

> I will not answer you at present. I will answer you when the five great powers have sent their representatives: the Americans, the British, the Russians, the Chinese and the French. I should very much like to have the representatives of the five powers here when I give you the answer of my people to this question of incorporation … [O]ur fathers made a pact with the Germans when they were in this country. Because there were no witnesses, the pact broke down.

South Africa dismissed the proposal about witnesses and continued with the referendum. Chief Phillipus van Waterberg expressed himself as follows on possible incorporation: "Yesterday we heard that our flag was part of the British flag, but we are not treated like other people under the British flag. We want our country to be returned to us and want to be under the protection of the Trusteeship Council."

The result of the referendum was as follows: 208 850 in favour of incorporation and 33 520 – primarily Hereros – against. However, based on the argument that the black population had not yet reached the level of political development that would enable them to make such a weighty decision, General Smuts's request for incorporation was not sanctioned by the UN.

Kutako started sending petitions to the United Nations through Reverend Michael Scott, who had been sent to him by Frederick Maharero, son of the old Paramount Chief Samuel Maharero from Botswana. The objective was primarily to stop any attempts by South Africa to incorporate the Territory, and to ask the UN to act with the view to achieving freedom for South West Africa under trusteeship of the United Nations. Two of the petitioners representing the chiefs with Michael Scott at the time were Fanuel Kozonguizi and Mburumba Kerina (previously known as Eric Getzen). The status quo was maintained, and likewise South Africa's battle against the international community. This process would continue for years, with the Hereros at the forefront, while other groups – as alleged by the Hereros – were relatively uninvolved.

Therefore, the League of Nations' old policy of retaining trusteeship over former German colonies until they were ready for independence, had ceased to exist. At the same time membership of the UN increased dramatically, due primarily to the large number of new independent states in Africa and Asia. These states did not concede that the lack of political, economic, social and educational preparedness could be used as an excuse to delay independence. It was in sharp contrast to the view taken by the UN in respect of the 1946 referendum in the Territory. The result was that all the former mandated territories in Africa, with the exception of South West Africa, attained their independence by 1962. There were still a few other subordinate regions, such as Portuguese colonies and Rhodesia.

A further development in the international arena was the fact that decisions taken by the International Court in 1955 and 1956 formally opened the door for international intervention in the South West African issue, and also for the UN to receive petitions and listen to petitioners. The result was that black (African) nationalism started playing a decisive role in Namibia's political and constitutional development.

The first fully fledged black political party in South West Africa was SWANU (South West Africa National Union), which was established in 1959 following the uprisings in the old Windhoek location caused by the forced relocation of its residents to Katutura. This happened shortly before my election as member of the Legislative Assembly. Well-known individuals present at this event were Clemens Kapuuo, who would succeed Kutako as Paramount Chief of the Hereros, Zedekia Ngavirue, Sam Nujoma, Mburumba Kerina, John Muundjua, Reverend Karuaera and Erwin Tjirimuje. Before the foundation of the party, problems surfaced between the traditional leaders under Kapuuo and the young radicals, who mostly had studied at teacher's training institutions (also in South Africa). The Chief's Council wanted an organisation they could control, while the young radicals wanted an organisation that operated beyond traditional borders, using new symbols. At the founding meeting Fanuel Kozonguizi was chosen as its first President, as proposed by Kapuuo.

Kapuuo and his supporters were not satisfied with the new organisation Kapuuo himself had started, and the traditional leaders could not control the young radicals due to their lack of political experience and formal education. Chief Kutako's Chiefs' Council subsequently requested the Hereros to resign as members of SWANU. This pursuit of control over political organisations by traditional leaders continued, especially among the Hereros, for many more years. In the election of the Constitutional Committee 30 years later, the traditional leaders featured strongly through the DTA, while SWANU played a relatively negligible role. However, the secret of the success of the younger generation was the fact that, although initially unwilling, they had later become, through their political organisation NUDO, a member of the wider umbrella organisation, the Democratic Turnhalle Alliance (DTA).

The other important black political organisation that appeared on the scene at more or less the same time as SWANU was what eventually became known as SWAPO (South West Africa People's Organisation). As a result of objections to the system of contract labour to which Owambo workers had already been subjected for many years, the Ovamboland People's Organisation (OPO) was established in 1958 by Owambo workers, under the leadership of Herman Toivo ya Toivo. Sam Nujoma was to become the leader of this organisation. Although

Nujoma and a large group of Owambo supporters attended the founding meeting of SWANU in Windhoek, they did not join it, since they wanted to continue as an independent organisation. Subsequent attempts by Kozonguizi and Nujoma to merge OPO and SWANU were unsuccessful. During June 1960 Mburumba Kerina recommended that the name Ovamboland People's Organisation (OPO) be changed to South West Africa People's Organisation (SWAPO). During this period many political organisations were established – it is estimated that there were more than 40 political and related organisations.

CHAPTER 5

My 20 years in the Legislative Assembly

Drought and foot-and-mouth disease

On my way to Windhoek to be sworn in, my thoughts weren't about politics. We were struggling with a prolonged drought since as far back as the fifties, and it was becoming critical. On Lazy Spade we had reason for concern.

There were big cattle losses, and farmers had to go to great expense to save their livestock. Aid schemes were implemented, as well as a rehabilitation scheme to help farmers who found themselves on the verge of bankruptcy. Fortunately, farmers were still able to sell marketable animals for reasonable prices, and there was a definite increase in the price of karakul pelts. The communal areas did not escape the effects of the drought, and the inhabitants were also subjected to hardship. Assisted by the Railway Services, subsidised maize and maize products were sent to the northern areas and food and vitamin supplements were delivered to schools and hospitals at no charge. Rations and supplementary feeding were also provided to farms in the south.

While farmers were still battling the drought, foot-and-mouth disease broke out on four farms in the Windhoek District on 12 July 1961. Despite strict control measures, it spread rapidly across large sections of the country, resulting in the introduction of restrictions on the movement and marketing of livestock. This, added to the drought, caused many farmers to be faced with financial ruin.

Hundreds of kilometres of game-proof fencing were put up immediately – 368 kilometres from north to south and 608 kilometres from east to west. A large number of farmers signed up as volunteers to help put up the fences in their surroundings. I also signed up and helped put up the east-west fence in the Etjo-Omatako region. Typical farmers' optimism reigned around campfires in the evenings rather than pessimism, which reminded me of the Langenhoven proverb: "*Dat jy jou swaarkry met lekkerkry moet klaarkry.*" (That you must put an end to hardship by enjoying yourself.)

Vaccination against the dreaded disease was administered on a large scale for the first time in history. Dr Herbert Schneider, a senior official in the Department of Veterinary Services, said afterwards that this achievement had been acknowledged worldwide.

The drought and foot-and-mouth disease lasted for a few years and affected me personally as a farmer. I now also had a civic responsibility towards my voters, and had to contend with the problems of individuals daily. Some farmers managed to find grazing for their livestock elsewhere, but due to the control measures could not move their animals there. Tension between farmers and the Department of Veterinary Services often ran high. The importance of a meat-processing factory became evident during this time when Damara Meat Packers was able to export tinned meat when there were no other means of marketing animal products. Even an attempt to export refrigerated or frozen meat was unsuccessful.

A Farmers Assistance Board with Hans-Jürgen von Hase, Charl Marais, the Secretary of South West Africa, and myself as members, was subsequently appointed to rehabilitate farmers who were experiencing financial difficulties. My appointment by the Executive Committee as a member and Chairman of this Board, led me to believe that even as an ordinary member of the Legislative Assembly I could also make a positive contribution towards the wellbeing of my countrymen. To the great dismay of Charl Marais, a public servant with many years of experience, Von Hase and I ignored many of the rules that were usually applicable to government assistance, and in this way rehabilitated many farmers.

A lifelong friendship developed between Von Hase and myself while serving on the Board. I never addressed him by his first name, because he was much older than I was and I had far too much respect for him. We subsequently also worked together in other areas, especially in the political arena. To me he was proof that there is no substitute for experience. He started out as a farm manager and ended up as a successful farmer and leader in agriculture. Later in life the example he and my father had set, resulted in my disapproval of people who depended too much on theories and philosophies they had learned at university.

A newcomer in politics

What I failed to realise as a newcomer to politics was that politically, socially and culturally we dealt with an exceptionally fragmented society. There was no common goal or aspirations, since we had no say in our future. The National Party of SWA and the UNSWP were subordinate to the mother parties in South Africa and could therefore not offer a solution independently and unilaterally. We could, moreover, maintain that this was also not our responsibility. Long and futile debates on constitutional matters were subsequently conducted in the Legislative Assembly but did not in any way give rise to the development of a common goal.

During the session of the Legislative Assembly in 1961, Adv. Percy Niehaus of the UNSWP asked the Administrator, Daan Viljoen, how far the development of native areas – as they were referred to in those days – had progressed. The Administrator answered that this was the responsibility of the Department of Bantu Administration of the Republic of South Africa (RSA); the Legislative Assembly therefore had no jurisdiction over it. However, he informed the Assembly that active steps were being taken towards the establishment of modern towns for the coloured people. During the first year of my political career it was clear to me that the black inhabitants of the Territory – as South West Africa was referred to officially – were the responsibility of the South African Government; a responsibility that had been conferred on them in accordance with the mandate agreement. The other two matters over which the Legislative Assembly also had no authority were Defence and Foreign Affairs.

The first school for Owambo children was opened in Katutura in that same year. This was the result of the large number of detribalised Owambos (about 1500 adults and children) who lived in Windhoek. The South African Government further announced that a military training camp would be established in Walvis Bay, which was then still part of South Africa.

Because there wasn't a transcription service (Hansard) yet, and I never collected newspaper clippings, I cannot remember much about the political speeches given during this session. However, they did not amount to much more than arguments about a policy over which, in truth, we had no say. It had to do primarily with the retention or winning of seats in the Legislative Assembly and defending the South African policy as regards South West Africa.

During this session Niehaus asked further difficult albeit relevant questions concerning the progress regarding the implementation of the South African Government's homeland policy. The Administrator answered without fail that this resorted under the South African Department of Bantu Administration and Development, and that he could not answer these questions. In the ensuing years Adv. Niehaus remained a thorn in the flesh of the National Party.

On 20 May 1963, Adv. Niehaus proposed that the House refuse to enter the Budget Committee stage before receiving the following assurances from the Administrator (in the Executive Committee): In the first place they had to assure the House that the establishment of towns, schools, hospitals, hostels and other facilities for natives and coloureds within the so-called white areas would be of a permanent nature. The South West Administration had plans to spend millions on this. With a view to ultimately accommodating each of the indigenous groups in its own area, Niehaus wanted the assurance that these facilities, in accordance with the so-called Bantustan policy, would not merely be of a temporary nature. The objective had to be the creation of permanent facilities for members of the indigenous groups that were permanently established in the so-called white areas. Secondly, he asked for assurance that the control over Native Affairs would be handed over to the Administration of South West Africa, instead of the Legislative Assembly merely being a stamp on the allocation of state funds for this purpose, which was, in effect, the case at that stage.

Adv. Niehaus's proposal was put to the vote and, as could be expected, only two members of the opposition voted for it. As usual, the 16 members of the National Party stood by the South African policy, over which they had no authority in any case. In later years, when in my capacity as Member of the Executive Committee entrusted with Works I pleaded for the improvement and expansion of amenities for the non-white population, I was regularly given the answer that this was not necessary, since the numbers of non-whites in the white areas would gradually diminish. I never took this seriously. When the material and personal interests of the inhabitants were at stake, the two parties often cooperated – although not always.

By mid-March 1963 the country was still in the throes of the serious drought that had started in the late 1950s. The Administrator summarised the situation as follows:

> After that we were exposed to years of drought such as we had
> seldom or ever experienced before; the worst outbreak of foot-

and-mouth disease in history; and rabies and less serious diseases that even affected the population. Sometimes the cloud was so black that we could hardly see that it still had a silver lining, if at all. A recession developed in the building industry, in trade and industry, and in a large section of the farming community. The property market regularly threatened to collapse.

On the positive side he pointed out that during this difficult time the Administration had constructed buildings to the tune of over R30 million and that the country already had a road network of almost 60 000 kilometres, 460 kilometres of which were tarred, while Hardap Dam had been opened on 16 March.

The Administrator mentioned the following medical care/health projects: a new hospital in Windhoek; institutions for psychiatric patients and lepers; a tuberculosis and general hospital complex at Okatana (Oshakati) in Ovamboland, as well as other projects in Kaokoland. In conclusion, he pointed to strict control measures to prevent a further outbreak of foot-and-mouth disease.

From the above you can deduce that the Legislative Assembly of the time had important responsibilities, which were put into practice in a competent manner to the advantage of the entire population.

The Odendaal Report of 1964

On 11 September 1962, the State President of South Africa appointed a Commission of Enquiry into the Affairs of South West Africa under chairmanship of the then Administrator of the Transvaal, F.H. (Fox) Odendaal. The Commission had an extensive directive, which also included the political future of the Territory. After the Commission completed the report in 1963, and its proclamation in 1964, it was referred to as the Odendaal Report. At no stage were the political leaders in South West Africa consulted about the report. On 18 March 1964, in answer to a question by Adv. Niehaus, the Administrator confirmed that we had neither been consulted, nor had we given any evidence before the Commission.

In 1946 the South African Government under General Smuts conducted an opinion poll among the population groups of South West Africa on the issue of whether the Territory should be incorporated into the Union of South Africa, but the consultative process had serious shortcomings. It is therefore true that until the middle of the 1960s the inhabitants of the Territory were never involved in or properly consulted about the administrative or political policy that the South African Government implemented here. It is also true that the white political leaders, especially those in the National Party, accepted this actual situation without protest.

Although the position of the UNSWP as regards our relationship with South Africa changed from election to election and from individual to individual, the members were nevertheless at times adamant that we should have a say in our own affairs and that we should accept responsibility for them. However, the position of the South African Government regarding the political position of South West Africa remained unchanged. Although the mandate agreement of 1920 had lapsed, South Africa would continue administering the Territory in the spirit of the mandate and as an integral part of South Africa. Moreover, South Africa's laws would be applied in the Territory, with slight adjustments to make provision for local conditions.

In the introduction of the Odendaal Report it is implied that not much had been done to uplift the black population of South West Africa until that stage. This contention is not entirely fair, but it is true that more could have been done. The report contained 470 recommendations, of which I shall refer to only a few, such as the Ruacana Hydroelectric Scheme, which would supply electricity to the entire country, as well as a canal system that would provide water to large parts of Ovamboland. Furthermore, a comprehensive network of tarred roads, airports and other communication systems were proposed, which would put the Territory in a position far better than that of most of its neighbouring countries, probably with the exception of South Africa. Education and health were also high on the list of priorities and, according to the plan, there would be a comprehensive expansion of health care and educational facilities such as clinics, hospitals, schools and colleges. The economic injection that the strategy could provide for the Territory impressed me as a young politician.

The Commission recommended furthermore that approximately 400 commercial farms be expropriated at an estimated cost of R20 million for the expansion of the communal areas, which made this the biggest land reformation to date. When taken into account that the Commission at that stage estimated the total population of the Territory to be 526 000, of whom 86% were black, it is even more remarkable. Despite the anger and sorrow this would cause the affected farmers, to me it seemed to be in the best interests of the country.

With these ambitious development plans, a new political dispensation was also envisaged, namely the creation and separate development of self-ruling homelands. At that early stage of my political career this made sense to me, especially seen against the background of the unequivocal assurance of the Prime Minister, Dr Verwoerd, that he would do everything for the black inhabitants that he accorded the whites. This did not seem immoral to me and was also not incompatible with the Christian principle of loving thy neighbour. I took it for granted that, in accordance with South Africa's stated policy, the proposals also had to be acceptable to the other population groups. The astronomical sums of money which would be spent in pursuance of the Odendaal Report towards the development of the homelands, making over 400 farms available to black farmers, led me to believe that the proposals would also be acceptable to them.

It was difficult for me to accept that, in accordance with the recommendations of the Odendaal Commission, a rearrangement of the administrative and financial functions would have to take place, which would result in many of the functions of the Legislative Assembly being transferred to ministries in South Africa. The Legislative Assembly was responsible for all state functions except Defence, Native Affairs and Foreign Affairs, which were the responsibility of the ministries concerned in South Africa. Many important functions would now, in accordance with the recommendations, be transferred to the Government of the Republic of South Africa. As far as the white inhabitants were concerned, it would come down to a de facto incorporation with South Africa, with the downscaling of the Legislative Assembly to the status of a Provincial Board, responsible only for education and health services for whites, roads, nature conservation, local management, public works, and a few less important functions. That this would subsequently turn out differently, I could not foresee at that stage.

Since the founding of the United Nations there had already been strong international pressure on South Africa to place South West Africa under the control of the United Nations. The Herero group had already been sending petitions to the United Nations for several years asking for this, and at the same time there had been a revival of black political parties. The white population group felt threatened, but consistently placed their hopes on South Africa to resolve these problems. It was also clear to me that it was up to South Africa to find solutions, since South Africa had to assume the consequences of its presence in South West Africa. This, more than anything else, unfortunately resulted in a lack of development towards a common goal among the different population groups in terms of the future of our country. Every group was concerned only with its own interests. In any case, the inhabitants of the Territory had virtually never been consulted about their future before.

A "raised-hands" referendum and the expropriation of farms

In February 1964, the leader of the National Party, A.H. du Plessis, and I had to explain the Odendaal Report to the voters in my constituency in Outjo, and had to solicit their approval for it. The opposition referred to this series of meetings as the "raised-hands referendum"– which is exactly what it was.

We were expected to explain and gain approval for a plan that had been devised without the involvement of the Legislative Assembly or the National Party of South West Africa or the non-white inhabitants.

Before the meeting I proposed to Du Plessis that I would make a few general observations at the beginning of the meeting and would then leave it to him to explain the contents and recommendations contained in the report. To my shock and surprise he responded: "To tell you the truth, I've not yet read the report properly, but I understand you have, so you go ahead and explain the contents and recommendations, after which I will pick up the loose ends and expand on them." He expected from a newcomer and junior in politics to explain the most comprehensive and ambitious development plan my country had ever seen. I put on a brave face, hoping that the saying "In the kingdom of the blind, the one-eyed man is king" would save me.

During question time most of the questions centred on the expropriation of land according to which the plan would be implemented in the following years. It was the main concern. At a follow-up meeting Tom Potgieter, who subsequently became one of my most passionate supporters, became emotional about a farm that he had "built up with blood and sweat", and which we "now wanted to give to the blacks". My answer was that he would probably be able to buy himself a better farm closer to town for the price that he could get for the farm. At the end of the meeting the Plan was approved by a show of hands.

When the Administrator, Wennie du Plessis, opened the Legislative Assembly on 17 March 1964, he emphasised that the House had been assembled primarily to deliberate on two matters, namely the approval of the Supplementary Budget of Expenses, and to consider the Report of the Commission of Enquiry on Matters pertaining to South West Africa. The in-depth report with its far-reaching implications would be submitted to the Assembly for deliberation and to formulate its conclusions, which would then be presented to the South African Government for further consideration.

In his address the Administrator made no further mention of the Report of the Odendaal Commission, but confined himself primarily to the achievements of the Administration over the previous decades, with special reference to services rendered in the field of health, education, roads and water affairs. This overview was impressive, but difficult to assess realistically so many years later. Because it is consistently alleged that the previous Administration had done so little to develop the country in the interests of all its inhabitants, I would like to mention a few facts to the contrary, although it does not compensate for the many things the Administration did wrong.

The Administrator quoted figures that had already been cited by his predecessors regarding the building of hospitals and clinics – also for black people – in various towns, for example Walvis Bay, Outjo, Omaruru, Okatana (Oshakati) and Tsumeb. He pointed out that the number of beds and nursing units in proportion to the population – with one nursing unit per 650 and 8,2 beds per 1000 of the population – compared well with figures in other regions. According to him the annual population growth of 2,1% compared to an annual world average of 1,7% indicated a favourable state of affairs regarding matters of health.

In respect of education, the Administrator revealed the following details about the facilities that existed in the country at that stage:

- Whites had 61 state schools, with 15 956 pupils and 670 teachers. In addition there were 13 private schools with 2165 pupils and 123 teaching staff.

- For coloureds there were 52 recognised state and mission schools, with altogether 7271 pupils and 268 teaching staff.
- For black people the figures were 311 schools, 49 297 pupils and 1294 teaching staff.

As far as roads were concerned, considerable progress had been made in the preceding decades. Main roads had increased from 3003 to 3320 kilometres; secondary roads from 7314 to 9078 kilometres; and district roads from 14 333 to 20 344 kilometres. Where there had formerly been no tarred roads in the country, during this period 643 kilometres of gravel roads were provided with a tarred surface.

In the field of water affairs great progress had been made to keep up with the increasing consumption of water. Two developments worth mentioning during this period are the completion of the dam and irrigation scheme at Hardap and two canals of 96 kilometres each in Ovamboland. The canals were planned in such a way that they would subsequently become part of the water supply for Ovamboland from the Kunene River.

With regard to agriculture, the Administrator revealed livestock figures in accordance with the agricultural census of 1963, namely 2,3 million cattle and 2,9 million karakul sheep. He also mentioned that the number of meat-processing factories had increased to three, which represented a major safety factor to the industry.

The figures above are important in as far as they reflected the achievements of the Administration before it commenced with the projects arising from the Odendaal Plan.

During this session the much-discussed if not controversial Odendaal Report was accepted. It was, in reality, a mere formality because, as in the past, we once again found ourselves faced by a *fait accompli*. During April of the same year the South African Government also approved the report. There wasn't clarity about who would pay for it, but as I understood it then, South Africa would finance the scheme by means of a loan at 5% interest, with the understanding that the loan could eventually be written off. This arrangement was described by our opposition as "charity at five per cent".

After this the Executive Committee appointed me as chairperson of a committee which, when there was a dispute, had to negotiate with the farmers whose farms had been expropriated. The other members of the committee were two senior officials of the Division of Agricultural Credit and Landownership, Tienie Erasmus and Joos van Zyl. When evaluating farms, aspects such as grazing and the land value of the farm, improvements, moving costs, and loss of income were taken into account. Compensation for the trauma the dispossessed farmers experienced when they had to leave behind the land they had inherited or the graves of their loved ones were also provided for. The interviews we had with the dispossessed farmers elicited different reactions. Some of them were highly upset and made no bones about it. Others were emotional and sad about having to give up the farms, some of which had been inherited. There were of course also those who accepted the expropriation, but were contemplating every possible way to negotiate the best prices for their farms.

The owner of the farm De Riet, a Mr Fourie, asked for a meeting with the committee to lodge his dissatisfaction with the price offered. Meeting us in Windhoek, he asked that the meeting be opened with a prayer. I invited him to go ahead. He then accused us before God of stealing his farm and not paying him enough money for it, and went on to ask God to punish us for the injustice we had committed against him. We refrained from reacting and eventually agreed on a price.

This all happened during the first five years of my political career. I had to rely on common sense and the experience of those who walked the road with me. I learnt that some things happened over which you had no control and the consequences could therefore not be avoided.

Inauguration of the new Legislative Assembly building

By coincidence the Odendaal Report was released in the same year we moved into a new Legislative Assembly Council Chamber and office block. It was also the year speeches in the Assembly were recorded for the first time and the transcriptions were bound in volumes referred to as Hansard. The building was inaugurated on 14 May 1964 by President C.R. Swart of South Africa, followed by a speech by the new Administrator, Wennie du Plessis, who succeeded Daan Viljoen, and after him party leaders were given the opportunity to make speeches to celebrate the joyous occasion.

During the inaugural ceremony, the leader of the National Party, A.H. du Plessis, confirmed South West Africa's commitment to and dependency on South Africa as follows in the Legislative Assembly: "We know how it came about that South West Africa landed in the international maelstrom. For this reason I would like to give our friends in South Africa the assurance that we appreciate the fact that we have South Africa's word that it will hold South West Africa's hand."

The leader of the UNSWP, Percy Niehaus, had the following request:

> I should like him [referring to the State President] to carry the message back to the Republic that no matter how much we differ here in this House, or how much it may seem that we are disunited, we are in fact united; our hearts beat as one in our determination to preserve what has been built up in this country, to preserve our standard of living, our standard of civilisation and all the good things that our being in this country has brought to this country. We are determined not to bow before the winds of change.

The Administrator presented his budget speech during the next session, and as can be expected, paid a great deal of attention to the Odendaal Report. Previous commissions reported that South West Africa could meet its expenses by itself only in unusually good years. The Commission therefore recommended that a system be implemented by which development in South West Africa could be financed interest free from a separate account. The Administrator emphasised South West Africa's dependency on South Africa and welcomed the development schemes proposed in the Odendaal Report. The Administrator noticeably refrained from mentioning the constitutional recommendations in the plan. Most of the members were probably having visions of future prosperity, with little concern for the winds of change that were awaiting us.

One would have expected the members to have used the budget debate as an opportunity to clearly present their policy views for inclusion in the first Hansard, particularly in terms of the Odendaal Report. However, the speeches that followed were mainly election speeches. Bobby MacDonald, one of the two representatives of the UNSWP, had passed away shortly before and although an election date had not even been set, speeches were clearly aimed at the coming by-election. The debate followed the usual pattern of two parties accusing each other of ambiguity. In the absence of a Hansard, excerpts from newspapers were used. "Annihilate the opposition," was A.H. du Plessis and Koos Pretorius's appeal to the voters.

My older colleagues in the Legislative Assembly

During my first term in the Legislative Assembly I depended to a large extent on the members of the Executive Committee, most of who were much older and more experienced than I was.

A.H. du Plessis, the senior member of the Executive Committee and Leader of the Legislative Assembly, became involved in politics at a relatively young age and, based on his intense interest in this field, and his undeniably strong personality and leadership qualities, he was promoted to Secretary of the National Party in South West Africa. In 1948 he was elected as member of the Legislative Assembly, and with Johannes van der Wath and two other National Party members represented the opposition in the House.

The political philosophy of A.H. du Plessis was grounded in separate development and social apartheid and were non-negotiable. It would remain like this until the end of his life. The leaders of his party understood this and followed him blindly.

A.H. du Plessis's three colleagues in the Executive Committee were Sartorius von Bach, Dr J.W. (Grammie) Brandt and P.A.S. le Roux. Von Bach was a dignified and respected individual who managed the departments under his control efficiently and responsibly, and I will always remember him for the tremendous contribution he made in Water Affairs and Nature Conservation. He was never mean-spirited in politics and had no time for frivolity. He was often indignant about the jokes that Eben van Zijl and I made during Executive Committee meetings. He later admitted that he as a German-speaking person didn't understand our Afrikaans jokes. He was a true gentleman and everyone treated him with the greatest respect.

Dr Grammie Brandt was a scientist (geologist) – unique in his field – and a valuable member of the Executive Committee when it came to technical matters. He was never a true politician: he was too straightforward and outspoken – which is probably why he was called Grammie. We were good friends, although he was considerably older than I was. We played rugby against each other, where I came to know him as a bit of a bully. When confronted with this, he responded with a big smile. He was also a farmer in the Grootfontein District, although he always said his wife Kotie was the farmer, which was probably true.

I never really knew P.A.S. (or *Pas* as we used to call him) le Roux because he represented a constituency in the south and we saw each other only during sessions. His resignation resulted in my becoming a member of the Executive Committee in 1965 when Dr Grammie asked me to stand for the election.

New role players in the National Party

During my first term as a member of the Legislative Assembly, a new generation of leaders appeared in the political arena. The first was J.W.F. (Koos) Pretorius, who was elected shortly after me in 1961 as representative of the Gobabis Constituency. Three years later Jan de Wet was elected as one of South West Africa's representatives in the South African Parliament, and in the same year Eben van Zijl became a member of the Legislative Assembly. Between the four of us we had the potential to play a determining role in the future politics of our country. Although we initially as a team supported the policy of the National Party, this team also had the potential to dig a grave for the National Party. No one could foresee the differences that would develop among party members and it took a long time for it to surface, and eventually led to all four of us moving into different political directions.

At the age of 25 Koos Pretorius was the youngest. Immediately after he had completed his studies at the University of the Orange Free State he accepted the position of Deputy Secretary of the National Party of South West Africa. Because of his academic background and field of study, he was ideally suited for the job. He admitted that he had chosen politics as a profession, and speculations were rife that he would become the future leader of the party. As Party Secretary and organiser it was Koos's task to lobby for votes, and his speeches bore witness to this. He initially wanted to enter the clergy, but subsequently decided against it. It could therefore be expected that his MA dissertation and religious convictions would become a characteristic of his political views.

Eben van Zijl had studied law and was a practising advocate. In addition, he was a successful farmer in the Summerdown area. He was intelligent and eloquent, but was unfortunately not popular with everyone due to his somewhat obstinate and haughty behaviour. Nevertheless, we maintained a pleasant and friendly relationship.

Jan and Lesinda de Wet were our neighbours on Lazy Spade and we became family friends. We often discussed the role we could play in politics and I encouraged Jan to make himself available for election as a member of the South African Parliament, which came to pass in 1964.

In 1970, following the discontinuation of South West Africa's representation in the South African Parliament, Jan de Wet was appointed by the South African Parliament to the important and influential position of Commissioner General of the Indigenous Peoples of South West Africa with the responsibility to implement South Africa's policy regarding the "indigenous peoples" of the country. We, too, remained lifelong friends.

The four of us could have become a formidable team, but this did not happen.

On principles, policy, methods and approaches

During my first two terms, nobody could have foreseen that a split would occur in the Party 17 years later. After only four years as a member of the Legislative Assembly, I was elected unanimously as a member of the Executive Committee, and after nine years became the senior member of the Executive Committee and leader of the National Party in the Legislative Assembly. In the latter capacity I often acted as Administrator. This was still my position when I left the Party 17 years later. During that period I endeavoured to promote unity within the party. When I eventually realised that change was necessary, I approached it with care. I tried to avoid a split until the last day, which explains why my resignation came as a shock and a surprise and was regarded by many as an impulsive decision.

Was there possibly an element of disunity from the beginning? If there was, I was not aware of it. There could not have been policy differences in the beginning. Did it concern principles, methods or approaches? In order to reach a conclusion, I needed to follow my track record during my first two terms as a member of the Legislative Assembly. It was a long-drawn-out and often frustrating process, reconciling ideals with reality. We also had to contend with human failures and limitations.

Koos had said early on during his first term in the Legislative Assembly that we would have to reflect a Christian philosophy of life in all areas, but specifically in our political policy; and that our Christian principles could come into conflict with what was happening in practice, that principles should never change, although there could be changes in the way they were being applied.

I still agree with this, but he was vague about and even remained silent on which principles were relevant and could not change. Separate development, just like apartheid, is to my mind a policy, not a principle. At that early stage I didn't doubt his intentions. I was, due to my background and education, also not obsessed with terminology and philosophical principles.

In spite of our initial differences in approach and subsequent policy differences, I respected Koos as a person and still do. I never regarded my political opponents as enemies. Many of them, such as Jan de Wet, remained our friends, and Jan's death affected both Stienie and myself deeply.

The role of the UNSWP opposition

Although the opposition consisted of only two members, they played a role that cannot be ignored. Adv. Niehaus asked difficult and intelligent questions, and never hesitated to criticise the policy of the National Party. This obviously elicited fierce reaction, as could be expected.

During the session of the Legislative Assembly in May 1964, Adv. Niehaus expressed his displeasure with the political and governmental recommendations contained in the Odendaal Report. His speech on this occasion was, in retrospect, on target and had members of the National Party up in arms. He made the statement that should he come to power "... his first step ... (would) be to consult with the conservative and responsible elements of the non-white population groups to try and reach a basis for fruitful cooperation with them." It is ironic that the National Party did exactly this ten years later in the Turnhalle where we deliberated on our political future with the conservative and responsible elements of the black population.

Koos, in a lengthy speech, disagreed strongly with Adv. Niehaus and reprimanded him in no uncertain terms. Niehaus made it even more difficult when he said that he was relieved about the implementation of the political recommendations of the Odendaal Report being postponed, and expressed the hope that we would not hear of it again. He referred to the speech made by Pretorius and continued:

> I honestly believe that the honourable member Mr Pretorius mistook his forum. He forgot for a moment that he was address-ing the Legislative Assembly of the Territory. He delivered a very learned dissertation on philosophy, which I think would have been more appropriate in an adult education class... [But] I think he has gone a little too far when he attributes to the people of my party – who may I say to him now, are as good Christians as he is – the things he does.

Adv. Niehaus was furthermore concerned about what would become of the expropriated farms and how they would be maintained. He pointed out that in the first place the criticism against South Africa was not directed at economic issues but at the disregard of human rights, and that he welcomed the acceleration of the tempo of development, especially in the black areas. He was also pleased that the takeover of certain powers of the Legislative Assembly by South Africa, including financial control as conditional to development programmes, would not be continued.

He added that the South African Government had already decided not to take any further steps in this respect until after the pending judgement by the World Court in The Hague concerning South Af-rica's status regarding South West Africa. He was pleased that the pro-posal of the Odendaal Commission to create a number of homelands would also be kept back until after the court decision. It was his opin-ion that the sword of Damocles would hang over us as long as there was any possibility that such homelands would be created. These were undoubtedly prophetic words.

I would like to say that debates about budget details as well as other administrative matters were never the same again once Adv. Niehaus and the UNSWP were no longer in the House.

On 24 May 1964 in the Legislative Assembly I also referred to cer-tain recommendations in the Odendaal Report. In my view this was of greater importance than an imminent by-election, but apparently other members of the Assembly did not share this view. Although the Odendaal Report had already been accepted during the previous ses-sion, an additional amount of R20 million had to be approved to defray certain expenses arising from the plan – more specifically the cost of expropriating farms. I welcomed the plan and referred to the recommendations in respect of industrial development in black and white areas. I also expressed my satisfaction with the fact that there would be an immediate execution of the recommendations in question. The reason for delaying the implementation of the political recommendations was not known to me, but I believed it to be due to the legal proceedings that had been instituted by Liberia and Ethiopia at the International Court.

Just like my colleagues, I had accepted the policy of the National Party of South Africa as provided for in the Odendaal Plan. Likewise I accepted Dr Verwoerd's clear undertaking that he granted the other groups everything he claimed for himself. I was, however, as will emerge later, unsure of whether the Odendaal Plan would be acceptable to the black inhabitants and whether there was enough goodwill and mutual understanding to bridge possible differences. Hence, I made the following appeal, which I would subsequently repeat regularly, to the white inhabitants:

> The solution to our problem lies – and this is Dr Verwoerd's policy – in a policy that is satisfactory to the inhabitants of this country, white and non-white. It is not a policy designed to comply with world opinion. If all the racial groups in this country live here happy and satisfied, we do not have to fear what the world thinks, and they would then also not have a case. A happy population living here in peace and harmony will be the best trump card against the United Nations Organisation with its policy of interference in our domestic affairs. With an honest policy that allows the non-white everything in accordance with his nature and capabilities that we claim for ourselves, we can and will achieve that harmony, despite the efforts of those ill-disposed people who are trying to sour our relations … The task to accomplish this goodwill rests not only with Government, but with each and every white inhabitant of this country. With our higher level of development and civilisation, we must set an example of showing mutual respect to the non-whites. Each white citizen must behave in such a way that the non-whites never doubt the honest intentions of the whites.

It is clear from the above citation that I was harbouring false expectations in terms of Dr Verwoerd's policy. A dispensation that would make the peaceful cohabitation and coexistence of white and black possible was still a long way off.

Once again the drought requires all our attention

On 10 March 1965, the Legislative Assembly convened for what we referred to as the "short session". It so happened that practically the entire country was in the throes of a serious drought since I had become a member of the Legislative Assembly in 1961. There was not much time for politics, because both the white and black inhabitants were reeling under the drought that had set in as far back as the late 1950s, and for a long time ran concurrently with an outbreak of foot-and-mouth disease.

Thousands of head of cattle were driven across our farm, which was situated between Outjo and Otavi on the way to Grootfontein, where the Administration had allocated emergency grazing at boreholes that had been sunk in the Horabe Block. It wasn't ever necessary for me to move my livestock, but when we left for Windhoek for the short session on 9 March 1965, our prospects on Lazy Spade did not look too rosy. The entire country had by then been declared a drought-stricken area.

Considerable livestock losses and a new outbreak of foot-and-mouth disease were reported. The Administration immediately implemented different kinds of relief measures, such as the emergency grazing in the Horabe Block and Diamond Area No. 1; the feeding and transportation of animals; investments in commercial banks to bring money in circulation; loans to the FCU (Farmers' Cooperative Union) and BSB (Boere Saambou Beperk – Farming CC cooperations), enabling them to render assistance to farmers; loan accounts; an advance to the Farmers' Assistance Board for the rehabilitation of farmers; and lastly a subsidy on maize products and food assistance in communal areas. The amount of R20 million doesn't sound like much in today's terms, but compared to the total income budget of that year, it was phenomenal.

The drought is over, but the political storm continues

Although the Legislative Assembly did not have jurisdiction over the black and coloured section of the population, and were concerned only with the practical application of the policy, the interests of the black inhabitants were not ignored.

In his budget speech during the session in March 1965, the Administrator emphasised the development of human resources by means of education, training and social services. Bursaries and loans were made available to deserving pupils wanting to qualify in different professions. He said, among other things: "Deserving pupils of all ethnic groups who wish to prepare themselves for professions may make use of liberal loans and bursaries made available through the education branch for higher education at universities and colleges in South Africa. These facilities are also available for non-white students who have attained the requisite educational qualifications." He continued by pointing out that provision was made at the Augustinium Training School not only for secondary education and teachers training but also for training black pupils in different professions. The Augustinium would eventually accommodate 700 students. He also referred to the new secondary school that was to be established in Ongwediva.

Koos Pretorius would not leave the opposition in peace. It was his contention that South West Africa was being accused of moving towards a one-party state due to the opposition slowly but surely disintegrating. He had problems with the fact that voters were being asked to vote for the UNSWP for the sake of creating an opposition and thereby avoiding a dictatorship. In addition, he warned Adv. Niehaus that he would once again bore him with a little bit of adult education. This time it was about "civic freedom" instead of a "political voice". He contended that "freedom without the vote does not necessarily signify suppression". If this principle were to be applied in general, it would mean that black people, while enjoying civic freedom, did not necessarily need the right to vote. He repeated this view at a later stage.

Adv. Niehaus responded by making a statement with which you would expect the National Party to concur wholeheartedly, but this did not happen. He said inter alia:

> I also feel that now that we are embarking on this large-scale spending on the non-Europeans and the natives, we are running a grave risk of depriving them of that very feeling that they are contributing something towards it; that we are exposing them to the same danger as the parent who is over-generous and who showers his children with presents. They do not appreciate it; they are not thankful, because they have never worked for it and, in fact, you will soon find that those presents are just thrown away. I think that it would be fatal for the non-European

> and the natives to gain the belief that, because he is black, and
> because there are certain privileges that he does not have, and
> that the white man has, that therefore the white man must just
> go on giving him everything free, without any contribution
> from his side.

Some members of the National Party were highly sensitive to the criticism that we were doing too much for the black people. They were apprehensive that this would cause the party to lose the support of the white people. In response to a question by Adv. Niehaus, the Administrator confirmed that the Administration had indeed spent large amounts of money in the interests of the black people, while the Department of Native Affairs, as it was referred to then, was the responsibility of the South African Government. In this instance both parties were seesawing on the question of whether too little or too much was being done for black people. This was to continue for many years.

According to Adv. Niehaus it was significant that the constitutional recommendations by the Odendaal Commission were not discussed during the session. He believed that these plans would never be implemented and avowed that should this happen, he and his party would fight it tooth and nail. He presented a very sober and realistic analysis of the proposed plan. When looking back on it today, one has to agree with him, because in most cases what he predicted came to pass. One statement that he made – and which I subsequently repeated – was that black and coloured inhabitants were not in the first instance seeking constitutional reform, but the acknowledgement of their basic human rights.

In response to a question by Adv. Niehaus, the Administrator also divulged interesting figures concerning the expropriation of farms owned by white farmers. By May 1965, a total of 195 farms had already been purchased to the value of R10 684 151.

I had the responsibility to report on the activities of the Farmers' Assistance Board of which I was Chairman. I reported that it was the policy of the Board to consolidate the farmers' short-term liabilities in the form of long-term loans, to be repaid while continuing to farm, albeit with less livestock. During the previous year, 519 applications had been received, of which 210 were successful. In 11 cases arrangements were made with the creditors of the farmers concerned. A total of R1 600 000 was advanced to farmers of which R412 000 was used to purchase livestock, and the balance to consolidate debt. I also expressed my concern about providing the farmers with financial assistance without the necessary training and guidance.

I become a member of the Executive Committee in 1965

In 1965 one of my colleagues in the Legislative Assembly, Dr Grammie Brandt, informed me that one of the members of the Executive Committee, Pas le Roux, had resigned and that some of my colleagues felt I should make myself available for election. To me this was an unexpected development and a difficult decision to make, because it meant that we would no longer be able to live on the farm. Members of the Executive Council had to fill their positions on a full-time basis and therefore had to live in Windhoek.

My farming activities had not been fully established yet, we had recently renovated our home, and our children were at school in Outjo. Moving to Windhoek without knowing when we would return to the farm was not an easy decision to make. I had set so many ideals for our farm, and things were just beginning to improve when we were confronted with this decision. After lying awake for a night or two we decided that I should stand for election. That our children would be able to go to school from home was a point in favour of the move.

A few weeks later, at a National Executive meeting of the Party, I was unanimously appointed a member of the Executive Committee of the Legislative Assembly, and in October 1965 we moved to Windhoek. To enable me to continue my farming activities, I acquired a private pilot licence and bought my first aircraft, a Piper Cherokee 235. For the next 20-plus years I was able to travel to the farm regularly and comfortably. My farming activities progressed so well that I could even purchase more land – first Nissan (3000 hectares) and subsequently Langgeleë (4900 hectares).

Adv. Percy Niehaus still a nuisance

When the Legislative Assembly convened in February 1966, the Administrator pointed out in his opening address that it would be the last session of the eighth Legislative Assembly and that the dissolution of the Assembly would coincide with the publication of a proclamation in terms of which the House of Assembly of the Republic of South Africa would be dissolved. The future simultaneous election of the Legislative Assembly of South West Africa and the House of Assembly of South Africa would take place in accordance with an amendment of the Constitution of South West Africa Act of the South African Parliament. This was yet another confirmation of the gradual linking of the white Legislative Assembly to the Republic of South Africa.

The Administrator announced furthermore that the campaign that had been launched to recruit personnel for the Territory from overseas had been successful, and that 42 people had been recruited in West Germany to supplement the acute shortage, especially of technicians. He indicated that the drought which had ravaged the country since the late 1950s was still ongoing and that the churches in the country would organise a day of prayer for rain on 19 March of that year.

There had been a considerable rise in the average price for Grade 1 beef in the previous year, while the market for karakul pelts remained robust. As usual, the Administrator paid a great deal of attention to health services and informed the House that the new state hospital at Oshakati in Ovamboland, which had been so long overdue, would be inaugurated later in the year. The hospital would have beds for 200 general patients and 250 patients suffering from tuberculosis, and would be equipped with all modern treatment facilities. A part-time service by specialists would be provided from Windhoek.

The construction of a 92-bed hospital at Rundu in the Kavango Region was progressing well, while a new settlement for 120 lepers and 140 tuberculosis patients at Masari was being planned. At that stage the total number of hospital beds and mats available in the Territory was 4149, in other words 8,6 for every 1000 of the population. The Administrator emphasised that it was the task of the Administration to raise the standard of the health services provided to the non-whites.

Although I had already been elected to the Executive Committee the previous year, I was officially elected and instated by the Legislative Assembly as MEC during this first session of the year on 18 February 1966. The functions initially allocated to me were roads, airports, transport services, works, agricultural credit and landownership, as well as a few less important support functions, which were mostly the responsibility of the junior member of the Executive Committee.

In his speech on the Supplementary Budget, the Administrator referred to a few additional expenses that had to be financed such as: the purchase of vehicles for use by officials responsible for the different projects recommended in the Odendaal Report; two rent-free loans to the Rhenish Mission Society to construct two hostels for "native and Coloured pupils"; a loan to the Dairy Board to subsidise the cheese factory in Outjo; a loan to South West Air for the expansion of essential services; an additional loan to the *Schülerheim* in Otjiwarongo; a loan to the Dutch Reformed Church for equipping hostels for coloured pupils; and a loan to the Finnish Mission Society for overhauling its health facilities in Ovamboland and Kavango.

During this session Adv. Niehaus posed many questions to the Administrator, especially regarding the Odendaal farms, as the expropriated farms were referred to. In answer to a question whether there was any truth in rumours that the Administration intended leasing the farms for ten years and then offering them for sale, the Administrator replied: "Of course not. It surprises me that the Honourable Member finds it necessary to ask the question formally."

One of the reasons for leasing the expropriated farms was that the final decision on how to utilise the land in the interests of the different population groups had not yet been taken by South Africa. I am convinced there were also other reasons, but because we never knew what was going on in the minds of the South African Government, I can only speculate on this. In the meantime the South West African Administration and the Division of Lands and Resettlement – which was my department – were responsible for the maintenance of the farms, the collection of rental fees, and the fulfilment of all the other stipulations in the lease contracts. The problem was complicated when beginner farmers started leasing the unoccupied farms. Initially I welcomed this, because at least there would be supervision over the farms until such time as the South African government departments took transfer of the farms. However, a problem later arose when the lease contracts of these tenants were terminated, but I will elaborate more on this matter later.

Adv. Niehaus made a remark then that, almost half a century later, is now an embarrassment. I quote him here:

> I am concerned about the increase in vehicle traffic within this Administration, and about the lack of control that is exercised over such vehicle traffic by this Administration. Those of us who drive around in the country have noticed that the Administration vehicles now have Administration numbers by which they

can be identified. However, you notice cases where it is abundantly clear that that the vehicle is not being used for Administration purposes. You see them over the weekends transporting women and children. You see them at drive-in theatres with women and children inside. You see them at all kinds of events and in all sorts of places in the country. You would probably have to stretch imagination considerably to find a connection between that place and that event and the duties of this Administration.

What can one say about this today? There is nothing new under the sun; history repeats itself.

Old friends leave us

We came to the end of the eighth Legislative Assembly. Seven of the sitting members announced their retirement. Koos Lombard and Rev. Van Jaarsveld had started with me in the Legislative Assembly five years earlier, and although they were considerably older than I was, we were good friends. They were Nationalists from the old school and had many tales to tell from the distant past. They believed so firmly that they were on the right path that it was infectious. But they were leaving and I listened to their farewell speeches with a lump in my throat.

Gertjie Meyer spoke next. He was my neighbour and responsible for launching my political career, a logical thinker with an outstanding sense of humour. Dr Grammie's farewell speech bore testimony to the fine man he had always been. After replying fittingly to questions, criticism and expressions of thanks concerning the departments under his control, he referred to his entrance into politics in May 1958. He thanked the Chairman for the patience he had shown towards someone who was used to the wide-open spaces of the Kalahari and whose living space during assemblies had been limited "to the horseshoe-shaped table of this Honourable House". He also thanked his colleagues for listening so attentively to his speeches when he explained issues or sometimes made them even more incomprehensible. Meyer once again came with his interjections: "The Honourable Member just thought we were listening: we were actually fast asleep." Dr Grammie could, as is often the case with intelligent people, become so lost in his thoughts that he would start rambling. His profession as a geologist lay very close to his heart. In this respect he told us how his daughter – when she was asked at school what her father did for a living – replied: "He's a stone doctor." He very appropriately concluded his farewell speech by referring to the variety of rock formations that are found on this earth, linking it to the diversity of our population.

This would also be the last session of the Legislative Assembly that Adv. Niehaus attended, since shortly after this he lost his seat in the general election. During debates he was often subjected to interjections. He started his address by saying that, in view of the coming election, he had initially intended making a political speech, but that he had decided against this and was intending to make a kind of "I remember" speech. However, he proceeded to make a political speech:

> In dealing with those problems I would have traced the developments and the evolution of the Nationalist Party native policy until it has reached this final addition – the concept of Bantustan or self-determination – which has now been put into cold storage so as to leave the Government Party in this most invidious, unfortunate position that it goes into an election – and such a vital election – without a policy on the major problem facing this country. I intended in that speech showing that even if this policy were taken out of the cold storage and an attempt were made to put it into effect, it could not have worked in practice, and if such an attempt had been made, to take it to its logical conclusion, it would have been disastrous to our economy, to our standard of living, to our safety and security ... and it would have destroyed South West Africa as we know it now.

Later on in his speech he elaborated further, saying the following with regard to the future and our calling:

> I do not believe that that great future and that great destiny will be realised if we become afraid, if we fear for the future, if we abdicate our position of leadership and our responsibilities, if we start surrendering portions of our country, if we start fragmenting our population, if we develop a defence mentality and retire into the innermost bastion.

With this he had the members of the National Party up in arms. A.H. du Plessis reacted as follows to the allegation that the National Party's Bantustan Policy had been put on the back burner:

> The Honourable Member cannot produce a single piece of evidence that would convince any unbiased person with the ap-

propriate powers of distinction that the Bantustan Policy of the National Party has been placed on the back burner; not a single shred of evidence. In the White Paper it is stated very clearly why, for the time being, the creation of homelands will not be implemented." He continued: "Unless I am totally misinformed – the National Party of South Africa that is ruling South West Africa has not departed a jot or tittle from its policy of creating homelands as the solution to our colour problem.

On petty apartheid, against which Adv. Niehaus had also cautioned, A.H. du Plessis expressed himself as follows:

> I believe it is written in the Big Book that you must beware of the little foxes that ruin the vineyard. You must guard against small cracks appearing in the wall that will threaten your safety and continued survival. Like the Dutch have to guard against small leakages appearing in one of their dykes, this is how the National Party sees this matter (petty apartheid) … he must watch out for those small leakages that eventually can only mean that everything we stand for will be destroyed.

After this Du Plessis agreed that for the black people a great deal of inconvenience was associated with petty apartheid. If that inconvenience were to be calculated, it would probably appear – seen especially from a financial point of view – that the major inconvenience was on the part of the white people. The latter had been prepared to accept this inconvenience for a period of over 15 years, for the sake of wanting to emerge at the other end as master over themselves.

However, a general election was imminent and I would have to answer questions. I was prepared for the implementation of the Odendaal Plan, because I was impressed with the extensive economic development that had been envisaged. Making 400 farms that had formerly belonged to whites available to other population groups I could not fault. I accepted Dr Verwoerd's position that everything he asked for the whites he granted equally to the blacks. I was prepared to deal with whatever the questioners put to me, but I also knew that I wouldn't have all the answers, especially as regards the viability of independent homelands.

Fortunately, the implementation of the Plan was postponed. Nonetheless, I trusted that South Africa would come with the final solutions, because my leader had stated clearly in his speech that the National Party Government of South Africa would make the decisions and that we would govern by delegated powers. I was still feeling somewhat peeved about some of our functions being transferred to ministries in South Africa in due course and that our Legislative Assembly would have the same status as the four Provincial Councils in South Africa. We South Westers had always regarded ourselves as somewhat different, rather more special. Let's call it a *Wir lieben Südwest* mentality.

Against the background of a world threat, however, I felt deeply dependent on South Africa and connected to my language community. With this conviction I approached the election. I wouldn't be the only candidate to be apprehensive about questions, and fortunately we would have our own chairperson at meetings, which, in line with standard practice at the time, did not exactly give questioners a fair chance. How many times did questioners not have to subject themselves to restrictions such as: "Don't make a speech, ask your question", or "You've said enough now; give someone else a chance," or "This is our meeting; if you want to make speeches, organise your own meetings."

I did not feel comfortable about my leader's remarks regarding petty apartheid, especially after my speech the previous year when I appealed for better relations and a change of attitude. That, more than anything else, would be an important pointer in my political career. At that stage I could not have imagined that later in my life I would agree with the perspective of Adv. Niehaus, that we, or (may I try to evade my responsibility a little here) South Africa, came with constitutional development for which the population was not yet prepared, while that which can never come fast enough, namely the acknowledgement of the human dignity of your fellow human beings regardless of race or colour, had been left behind.

Besides, I wasn't at all impressed with the UNSWP's policy and also not with their newspaper, *Die Suidwes-Afrikaner*. The editor, Angel Engelbrecht, had the gift of driving us Nationalists up the wall. One day the National Party would be accused of doing too little for the non-whites, and the next day of doing too much. While the UNSWP was placing a great deal of emphasis on a unitary state, members often let it slip that they feared domination by the northern groups. This in turn led to their subsequent federal policy, the basis on which Adv. Bryan O'Linn would run the 1974 election.

A new team takes over

Once the general election had run its course, the elected members of the new Legislative Assembly were instated on Friday 15 April 1966. Since Adv. Niehaus had lost his seat in the election, all 18 members represented the National Party. The Executive Committee was subsequently elected, consisting of Messrs A.H. du Plessis, S. von Bach, D.F. Mudge, and Adv. E van Zijl, who succeeded Dr Grammie Brandt.

During this session Koos Pretorius elaborated further on his political philosophies. On 19 April he explained to us what a political party was: in effect a group of people who had the same political creed and principles in respect of their politics, with principles that remained the same on all terrains. He continued talking about South Africa, saying that it made no sense for the National Party to strive for a republic, since they already had a Republic. He continued: "We can, therefore, accept that the future political differences in the Republic of South Africa will crystallise as state philosophical differences – principles will drive the people apart." According to him, there are therefore still two major determining factors, namely world opinion and the old problem of race relations. The National Party believed it should continue along the old traditional route, striving towards what he had always regarded as Christian guardianship, that he should do this in spite of the world opinion and that he should not give way to the world.

Pretorius referred to a press statement Adv. Niehaus had released after the election, with the following gist: that time alone would tell whether the unmitigated victory of the National Party would strengthen the Party, or whether – on the other hand – this would just lead to greater pressure due to the black population in South West having no representation in the legislative authority of the country. Pretorius contended that it was not essential to be represented in the authority that ruled over you, justifying it as follows:

> From a Christian philosophical approach, the right to vote is therefore not an issue of authority, but one of responsibility, namely: who is sufficiently responsible to exercise that right ... The Humanist, on the other hand, believes exactly the opposite. He believes that he will have certain inherent human rights at his disposal, among other things that he has the authority to delegate to someone to rule over him. When you take this reasoning to its logical conclusion, you come to the conclusion that all people without the vote are suppressed.

So you need to have something, to have the responsibility

He wraps up his speech with the words:

> I regard the results of this election as a stance taken by the whites
> of South West to prove to the world out there, where we know
> a process of equalisation is taking place … while our Christian
> faith, in fact, teaches of a diversity that exists in creation, which
> says beyond all doubt, no, it is our viewpoint that we would like
> our Christian traditions to be maintained and that we are pre-
> pared to prove to you that we are right.

This theoretical approach to politics and the fanaticism in respect of
principles bothered me, and I wasn't the only one. It often filtered
through in discussions among the other members that it bothered
them too. This was probably why, after Pretorius had concluded his
speech, there was no loud applause. I never argued with him in public
debates, although I did speak about our different approaches in private conversations with him. The conversations, as he later confirmed,
took place in a good spirit.

Van Zijl's first speech after he had been elected MEC was outstanding, and demonstrated that he had already established himself firmly
in the areas for which he was responsible.

The representatives from the south of the country painted a dark
picture of the critical situation in which farmers in those parts found
themselves. Where circumstances in the north had since improved, the
drought in the south had persisted for the past seven years. Many of
the farmers had already been forced to decrease their livestock drastically, while others had to find alternative grazing in the north – many
on appropriated Odendaal farms. During the budget debate I could
reveal that the Administration had already provided emergency grazing for large numbers of animals.

The Odendaal Plan inevitably led to a new problem for the National Party, namely accusations that too much was now being done
for the black people. Reference was made to the large number of farms
that were being bought for them, while there were many landless
white farmers who didn't qualify for land under one of the settlement
schemes. The opposition newspaper *Die Suidwes-Afrikaner* also fuelled
these misgivings. In the meantime many of the Odendaal farms, due
to the delay in the execution of the constitutional proposals of the
Commission, were leased to landless and part-time farmers. Some of
these farmers regularly addressed presentations to me in my capacity
as MEC tasked with state settlement.

I reacted to this in my budget speech, referring to the unrealistic expectations by potential farmers as regards the profitability of farming. False expectations were the downfall of many a farmer and lead to the extensive squandering of farmland, one of our most valuable natural resources. I warned against inflated land prices, because land prices were determined by several subjective factors, such as family sentiments and the love of land, and against the easily accessible and sometimes excessive loans that were available, as well as the fact that land was attractive to investors from outside the agricultural sector. Land therefore became a popular means of speculation, because when treated well, it was indestructible. I warned that vacant state land was something of the past, which meant that over-capitalised farms fetched high prices, leading to too little working capital and experience, and a lack of proper planning. An important fact to be taken into account was that we were farming in a country with a low and erratic rainfall.

Taking this stand didn't go down well with potential farmers. Nowadays, caution that farming is not the easiest way to make money is interpreted as an effort to deter black farmers or potential farmers against land reform.

In June 1966 A.H. du Plessis referred to world opinion and warned against an exaggerated fear of "foreign elements":

> I can now say this to South West Africa: If we want to lose our foothold in this country, we should start by attaching too much value to it. We must not start doubting and become irresolute. This will be the surest way to ensure that we lose our foothold. If we want to keep our footing here, we must keep the faith, faith in ourselves, and faith in our community; and we must not become fearful and allow ourselves to be influenced by talk that is directed at striking alarm and fear. If we let this happen, we will lose. In other words, the formula for South West Africa to emerge unscathed at the other end is the hackneyed expression: 'business as usual'.

Easy for Mr Du Plessis to talk about "business as usual", since our future was totally in the hands of the South African Government at that stage.

CHAPTER 6

South West Africa becomes an international problem

South Africa versus the United Nations

Since the establishment of the United Nations Organisation in 1945, South Africa was at loggerheads with the international community about its presence in and administration of South West Africa. Because Foreign Affairs was not a responsibility of the Executive Committee and Legislative Assembly of South West, we were not concerned about this. To be honest, we didn't take the UN seriously. Indeed, for us it was "business as usual", as A.H. du Plessis had said. However, for South Africa it was anything but "business as usual". Not in the least.

As with the First World War, the end of the Second World War had far-reaching implications for the global community, also for South Africa. To better understand what followed on the international front, I would like to take a brief look at the role played by the international community and the UN since its establishment in 1945, and how South West Africa was drawn into the international maelstrom. It was only in the early sixties that any of this became apparent from the speeches and statements made by local politicians. As we saw it, this was South Africa's problem, and South Africa assured us regularly that it would not hand Namibia over to the UN. But matters could not continue like this.

The United Nations, of which South Africa was one of the 50 founding members, was established on 24 October 1945, while the League of Nations dissolved only in April 1946. For many years afterwards the question of whether the UN was the legal successor to the League of Nations, and whether the control and supervision over the mandated territories had been transferred to the newly established world organisation would remain a bone of contention between South Africa and the UN. It could be argued that the UN had not been established for this purpose. Provision had, in fact, been made in the Charter of the United Nations for such territories to be placed under the supervision and control of the UN.

Some mandatories requested that the territories under their control be placed under UN trusteeship immediately, but the South African Government under leadership of Gen. J.C. Smuts requested that South West Africa be incorporated as part of South Africa. During the discussion of this matter in the UN, Smuts declared emphatically that South Africa was under no obligation to the UN to assume trusteeship of South West Africa, and that if his application for incorporation were not granted, the Union would continue to administer South West Africa as an integral part of South Africa. He indicated that South Africa would do this in the spirit of the original mandate.

In the ensuing years the UN repeatedly requested South Africa to enter into a trusteeship agreement, but this was denied consistently. During this period the United Party in South Africa and the UNSWP under leadership of Percy Niehaus in South West Africa were in office. Indeed, General Smuts still continued his efforts to incorporate South West Africa when his Party was defeated in 1948 by Dr Malan's National Party; and Adv. Eric Louw, the new Minister of Foreign Affairs, had to continue the battle in the UN.

After this the South West Africa issue was referred to the International Court three times. In 1950 the court, in an advisory capacity, ruled as follows: Firstly, that the original mandate in terms of which South Africa administered the Territory was still in existence; secondly, that the UN was the legal successor of the League of Nations and was responsible for supervising the implementation of the mandate; and thirdly, that the South African Government was obliged to report on its administration of the Territory. In addition, the court was of the opinion that South Africa was not legally bound to assume a trusteeship agreement with the UN in respect of South West Africa. Six of the 14 judges did not support this view. The court case of 1955 concerned itself with voting procedures when considering reports, while the 1956 court dealt with the admissibility of oral hearings of petitioners. Since the rulings were advisory in both cases, they were not binding.

In February 1957, the UN's General Assembly requested its Committee on South West Africa to review the steps that could be taken to ensure that South Africa honoured the obligations to which it had consented in terms of the mandate, until such time as South West Africa was placed under international trusteeship.

The World Court case (1960–1966)

The international campaign against South Africa's control over South West Africa entered a new phase when Ethiopia and Liberia lodged a complaint at the International Court in The Hague on 4 November 1960. The court case, which would continue for a full six years, dealt primarily with South Africa's international accountability and the furtherance of the wellbeing of the population of the Territory. The applicants alleged that the UN was the legal successor to the old League of Nations and that South Africa's refusal to report to the UN was a breach of the mandate agreement. The second charge was that South Africa had implemented its apartheid policy in South West Africa to the detriment of the indigenous population.

South Africa's legal team, if I remember correctly, consisted of about ten legal minds, one of whom was Adv. Pik Botha. Before and during the court case, the advocates representing South Africa visited the Territory several times, but at no stage did they consult with my colleagues or me. In fact, we weren't informed at any stage as to whom had been consulted.

The South African Government called 14 witnesses, mostly academics and other experts from South Africa and the United States of America. Only one witness from South West Africa was called, namely Mr Kurt Dahlmann, the editor of the *Allgemeine Zeitung*. The pleas of the South African Government consisted of just over 4000 pages, in which the Government essentially took the position that the mandate no longer existed and that the UN was not the legal successor to the League of Nations.

On 18 July 1966 the court, with the Chairman's deciding vote, delivered the following judgment: "The court rejects the claims of the Empire of Ethiopia and the Republic of Liberia." This first part of the ruling was widely regarded as a victory for South Africa, which in fact was not the case at all, as appears from the second part of the ruling: "The Court finds that the Applicants cannot be considered to have established any legal right or interest appertaining to them in the subject matter of the present claims, and that, accordingly, the court must decline to give effect to them." This meant that the plaintiffs, Ethiopia and Liberia, had no direct interest in the case. But on the merits of their complaints, no ruling was made and at least South Africa could relax again.

The court case and the 1966 ruling probably impacted fundamentally on beliefs and eventualities in South West Africa for the first time. What had happened before was unknown to most South Westers, while those who were aware of these factors, such as the political leaders, took little notice. National Party leaders uniformly took the viewpoint that we should not allow ourselves to be influenced by world opinion. I did, nonetheless, caution from time to time that we were part of a wider global community and that we could not ignore its opinion.

During the court case I became aware for the first time of the young Adv. Pik Botha, with whom I would become better acquainted over the next 20 years. Although we were kindred spirits in many respects, it gradually emerged that when it came to South West Africa, we had different agendas.

Ongulumbashe, the onset of the Border War

Politicians in South West Africa were never informed about the activities of the SA Defence Force, and at the end of the war even researchers confirmed that the SA Defence Force consistently handled military activities with great secrecy. For the information I have at my disposal I was dependent on books such as *Operasie Savannah* by F.J. Du Toit Spies, *Namibia's Liberation Struggle* compiled by Colin Leys and John S. Saul, *Dié wat gewen het* by Jannie Geldenhuys, *Die Buffel Struikel* by L.J. Bothma, and *The SADF in the Border War* by Leopold Scholtz.

According to information from these sources, the first six SWAPO terrorists left their base at Kongwa, Tanzania, under leadership of Johny Otto Nankudu in March 1965, with the directive to report to Herman Toivo and Eliazer Tuhandele, the local SWAPO organisers in Ovamboland. They were armed with submachine guns and Russian Tokarev pistols, and arrived in Lusaka on 16 May 1965, where Sam Nujoma wished them a successful journey. From Lusaka they proceeded first by Jeep, then by bicycle and ultimately on foot, across the Zambezi and Kwando rivers, and through the sparsely populated south-eastern extremity of Angola, to eventually arrive in Ondangwa in August 1965. In 1966 a second group of ten followed the same route to Ovamboland, but were tracked down by the police virtually right away. In the meantime, the first group dispersed in Ovamboland, signed up recruits and settled at a training camp at Ongulumbashe.

During this period South West Africa experienced acts of terrorism for the first time. These consisted of farm attacks, the murder of two Angolan shopkeepers, attacks on traditional chiefs, and the vandalism of government buildings at Oshikango on the border of Angola. These attacks were aimed at soft targets. At this early stage it was not clear what SWAPO wanted to achieve with these acts. In due course we would gain greater clarity about this from SWAPO ranks and other reliable sources.

According to Susan Brown, co-author of the book *Namibia's Liberation Struggle*, the establishment of the training camp at Ongulumbashe was preceded by a process of international diplomacy by SWAPO, which was directed primarily at UN and the already independent African states. At that stage no Western country (with the exception of the Nordic countries) wanted to support anti-colonial movements, and it was left to the Soviet Block and China, which were competing with each other to win the favour of the anti-colonial movements. It was eventually accepted that only an armed struggle would give credibility to the anti-colonial activities. In 1962 the first SWAPO fighters were trained in Egypt and in the following year both SWAPO and SWANU became members of the OAU (Organisation of African Unity). But first SWAPO had to develop its image as a fully fledged freedom movement to enable it to gain international acceptance and support.

At that stage the SWAPO members who had received military training were few, and SWAPO was still hoping that the International Court, which by then was already in session, would declare the presence of South Africa in South West Africa illegal. The SWAPO leadership was waiting for a favourable ruling before they commenced with armed resistance. The rejection by the court of Ethiopia and Liberia's application was met with great bitterness, and SWAPO decided to start an armed struggle. The following passage from *Namibia's Liberation Struggle* is illuminating:

> The SWAPO leadership in exile seems to have had a clear awareness that undertaking an armed struggle was a diplomatic necessity with few military prospects though it was seldom publically stated at the time. According to a hostile account accompanying the 1968 resignation from SWAPO of a small group of exiles, propelled by selfish ambitions, some SWAPO leaders ... tried to make SWAPO appear to be a revolutionary movement wag-

ing an armed struggle. The motive behind this was and still is to seek more money and more recognition. Another reason is to instigate the UN to action. In one of the SWAPO papers it is plainly put: SWAPO also accepted the fact that we could not possibly win a decisive victory against South Africa. However, we realised that we could create certain conditions within the country, which would activate the United Nations to intervene on our behalf. Thus SWAPO launched an armed struggle on the 26th of August 1966.

Without realising it I became personally involved in the Ongulum-bashe incident and the onset of the Border War. Early in the morning of 25 August 1966, I received a telephone call from Pretoria. The person who spoke to me was somewhat secretive about the purpose of his call, but I gathered it was someone from a state department in South Africa who wanted to know whether the new airfield at Ruacana was ready for use by a large aircraft. He had probably contacted me because as MEC I was responsible for airfields, among other things. Although the airfield was virtually completed, at places there were obstructions on the landing strip where smaller finishing touches still had to be done. He requested me to make arrangements urgently for the obstructions to be removed.

The chief roads inspector, Lewis, and I departed by air to Ruacana to do the necessary. Upon our arrival I noticed a Ford truck parked under a tree. It had the name of some or other engineering firm on its door. I assumed it had something to do with the construction of the air-port, but recognised one of the people standing there as Commandant Blaauw of the South African Police. He was responsible for the safety of the UN delegates Carpio and De Alva, who had been sent to Nami-bia on a fact-finding mission in 1962. I accepted that he was probably waiting for the aircraft from Pretoria, and that a follow-up operation or some or other armed action was being planned. I was curious and de-cided to wait for the arrival of the aircraft. When it eventually landed, I was surprised when only a small number of uniformed people, prob-ably policemen, disembarked. It didn't appear to me as if a large battle was being planned, and Lewis and I returned to Windhoek.

I learnt subsequently that there had been a clash in which two of SWAPO's fighters had died and nine had been captured. With the meagre information at my disposal, I could never understand why the incident at Ongulumbashe had been so significant to the SWAPO government that 26 August was proclaimed a public holiday, Heroes' Day. I had to wait many years for an explanation.

On the significance of this incident and what followed, Susan Brown wrote the following: "Two of the guerrillas who made the long trek from southern Zambia through south-east Angola to the Owambo Region in Northern Namibia, were killed; nine were captured, together with 45 of their recruits from the surrounding areas."

In the book *The SADF and the Border* War by Leopold Scholtz, more is written on the Ongulumbashe incident.

> The Border War is generally assumed to have started on 26 August 1966, when a force of 130 men – 121 policemen and 9 members of 1 Parachute Battalion hastily attested as policemen in Alouette 111 helicopters – under command of Captain (later Colonel) Jan Breytenbach, attacked a base of the People's Liberation Army of Namibia (PLAN), SWAPO's armed force base at Ongulumbashe in Owambo.

Therefore, we had to accept that the attack on Ongulumbashe was intended to wipe out a SWAPO training base, or at least one that was in the making. The battle at Ongulumbashe is generally regarded as the beginning of the Border War. So you can understand why 26 August is of such great historical importance to SWAPO, in spite of the fact that PLAN lost the battle.

After this the police started an intensive campaign against the infiltrators and SWAPO's internal leaders. (In those days SWAPO was not a banned organisation.) On 27 April 1967, there were already more than 200 SWAPO members being detained in Pretoria, among others Andimba Toivo ya Toivo, Eliaser Tuhadeleni, Nathaniel Maxuilili and John ya Otto. In terms of the Law on Terrorism and the Law on the Suppression of Terrorism, 37 of them were charged and sentenced to imprisonment of up to 20 years on Robben Island.

Not much came from SWAPO's declaration of war after Ongulumbashe. The next seven years would still be characterised by isolated incidents of terrorism, periodic clashes and police action. The coup d'état in Portugal, the attainment of independence by Angola and the establishment of the South African Defence Force on our northern border in 1974, when other countries also became involved, subsequently led to conventional warfare.

Local politics and South West Africa's affiliation with South Africa

The UN and its threats were still not being taken seriously. The debates in the Legislative Assembly were still being characterised by an ongoing election battle between the National Party and the UNSWP. It was about votes and not solutions, and we were being bombarded with newspaper clippings from *Die Suidwes-Afrikaner*. We were not unduly concerned about matters concerning the political future of our country, probably also because the political recommendations contained in the Odendaal Report had not been implemented immediately. I, as well as some of my colleagues, was finding it challenging to provide convincing answers when we were being cross-examined by opposition leaders during meetings. But then we always took the view that this was actually South Africa's problem and that the parliamentarians would have the answers.

This reminds me of one evening at Karasburg when I was addressing a meeting with the late Hendrik Schoeman, Minister of Agriculture in the South African Cabinet. Kerneels van den Bergh of the UNSWP was asking the questions and wanted to know from Schoeman whether Tswanaland would eventually also become independent, to which Schoeman, stalwart Nationalist that he was, answered with a loud *"Ja!"* Needless to say, the audience burst out laughing, because there is and never was a Tswanaland in South West Africa. In fact, a number of farms bordering the Botswana border were put aside for the Tswanas who had formerly lived in the communal area at Aminuis. I cannot recall the exact number, but it couldn't have been more than 20.

I, too, often had to answer this same question, and the closest I came to an acceptable answer, was that the different groups in our country had communal land at their disposal; that the territories would be expanded and developed in terms of the Odendaal Report; that the authorities of the different groups would have a say over the utilisation of the land; and furthermore, that all options would be open to them.

On 6 September 1966, Dr Verwoerd was assassinated and was therefore never given the opportunity to prove that his policy, according to which he wanted to give everything to the black people he wished for himself, could succeed in South West Africa. After this the responsibility of interpreting and implementing what he had envisaged rested on the shoulders of his successor, John Vorster.

On 13 March 1967, the Administrator alluded to the ruling of the World Court – especially the storm of protest that had emanated from UN member countries. He referred to a resolution made by the General Assembly of the United Nations on 27 October 1966, which amounted to the termination of South Africa's mandate and that South Africa had no right to administer the Territory, which from then on would be the direct responsibility of the United Nations. In addition, an ad hoc committee was appointed by the UN to make recommendations on how South West Africa should be administered, whereby the people of the Territory would be in the position to exercise their right to self-determination and independence. As already mentioned, the ruling of the World Court was locally regarded incorrectly as a convincing victory for South Africa, which led to our local politicians taking even less notice of the UN's resolutions, and of world opinion.

The drought was broken during the preceding rainy season, marking the end of seven lean years. Combined with the economic revival resulting from the implementation of the Odendaal Plan, this created a spirit of optimism. But as ironical as this might seem, a major problem was created during the drought as a result of the temporary availability of grazing on the acquired Odendaal farms.

In my budget speech I referred to different categories of farmers who were given emergency grazing on these farms, and warned that we should not lose sight of the fact that these farms had actually been bought to settle black farmers. The categories to which I referred were: previous owners; drought-stricken landowners; landowners who saw this as an opportunity for them to increase their livestock; farmers without land; and lastly, "chancers" (as I called them), who saw an opportunity in the temporary availability of these farms to start farming. I cautioned people against being so foolish as to resign from their positions to go farm on a temporary basis with a small number of animals. Both the Administration and I would have many problems with this later on. Since most of the members of the Legislative Assembly were farmers, farming was often discussed.

The political *boeresport* [traditional Afrikaner games such as *jukskei* and *kennetjie*] between the National Party and the UNSWP continued, and since there was no longer a representative of the UNSWP in the Legislative Assembly, *Die Suidwes-Afrikaner* was for all practical purposes elevated to the position of official opposition party. While reams of clippings from this newspaper were being used by the National Party speakers and especially by Koos Pretorius, to their discomfort the editor of the newspaper, Angel Engelbrecht, was sitting in the press gallery with a smile on his face, knowing that his newspaper would gain a special place in the history of South West Africa through the Hansard reports.

In an attempt to dispute the accusation that too much was being done for black people, Pretorius delivered a long speech in the Legislative Assembly on Monday 22 May 1967, saying inter alia:

> Thus I believe that all voters, and in my view especially the voters of Gobabis (his constituency), have the right to pose the question why I gave my vote for the expenditure of a good portion of this contribution ... and whether or not I did this in accordance with promises and policies adhered to by my party in earlier years. [...] In this respect I would much rather take a stand based on principles and then test the National Party against this background.

Pretorius pointed out that, according to the South West Africa Constitution Act of 1925, the say over policy in respect of black people was in the hands of the Administrator and therefore the South African Government. He even went as far as to say that should the UNSWP govern in South West, it would change nothing, and quoted members of the opposition who had also expressed themselves in favour of apartheid. Then he stated the principle against which, in his view, the policy of the National Party should be tested, namely "Christian guardianship", and repeated, for the umpteenth time, that while principles could never change, methods and policy could.

According to Pretorius, the Party, that is to say the South African National Party, only put forward the principles, but it was then up to the executive authority to determine the policy. He elaborated at length on the fact that money was being spent on black people in execution of the NP's policy of separate development and apartheid. To make the large expenditure on black people somewhat more acceptable, he added the following:

> I therefore want to emphasise that money can be spent on the non-whites only in so far as it is within the capabilities of that non-white to absorb it ... He (the non-white) must realise that he must ultimately increasingly accept responsibility ... We can therefore not bestow a political status on him that is above his

capabilities if he has not yet also developed in other areas – the economy, education and so on – and precisely for this very reason we must help him to develop more rapidly in these fields, especially in respect of education, so that we can enable him to take over the reins on his own behalf.

The next ten years would continue to be characterised by a local election battle that dragged on and on. When not reflecting on the past election, arguments were presented to substantiate why the voters should vote for the National Party in the next election, and this while the UNSWP no longer had a single seat in the Legislative Assembly.

The responsible and efficient way in which the members of the Executive Committee of the Legislative Assembly cooperated with the senior officials of the Administration to handle the different departments under its control was praiseworthy. Extensive reports on the activities of the Administration and reports from the Auditor General bear testimony to sound administration and strict financial control. Surpluses were built up in the Territorial Development Fund and loans were kept to a minimum. During sessions of the Legislative Assembly, members of the Executive Committee reported extensively on the departments under their control and all members took care of the interests of their constituencies in a responsible way.

Following the implementation of the recommendations of the Odendaal Report, deficits did, however, occur in South West Africa's account for the projects that had to be financed in line with these recommendations. While the original arrangement had been that South Africa would accept the full financial responsibility for these projects, in the end they made good only for the shortfalls.

As a result of the recommendations of the report by a commission of enquiry into the fishing industry, an additional quota of 9600 tons of pilchards was awarded to each of the five existing pilchard concession holders, subject to a special levy for research on fish resources.

With a view to the development of a harbour, airfield and roads on the north-western coast, two pilchard concessions of 90 000 tons each were granted to the Sarusas Development Corporation to build a fishing harbour at Cape Fria on the northern coast. Apart from the fact that this concession entailed great financial benefits to a few people, it is doubtful whether the fishing industry derived any benefits worth mentioning. The plans to build a harbour also did not materialise.

The role that the meat-canning factories played to save the farmers from ruin during the periods of drought and foot-and-mouth disease cannot be over-emphasised. While tinned meat could be exported in unlimited quantities, this was not the case with frozen or refrigerated meat. However, the increase in the price of meat on the controlled markets in South Africa and the decrease in the price of tinned products caused serious financial difficulties for the meat-processing factories. In the past the Administration had given financial support to these factories. At this point a committee was once again appointed to conduct a survey into this possibility. A further milestone was reached when the Mangetti Quarantine Station was completed, which made it possible for animals from the northern areas to be marketed.

To promote the marketing of karakul pelts, a successful mission under leadership of the Assistant Director of Agriculture visited 11 countries, while an official from the Division of Agriculture attended the World Karakul Symposium in Vienna in Austria and a karakul auction in London.

The installation of a microwave telephone communication system between Okahandja, Windhoek and Keetmanshoop was commenced; radio-telephones were installed at various hospitals and clinics in the Kavango Region; and two fully fledged post offices were opened in Ovamboland.

Until this stage 1000 miles (1600 kilometres) of tarred roads had been completed. As MEC responsible for roads, it was my privilege to open the new bridge at Okahandja in 1966. Good progress was made with the planning of the dam and water scheme at Naute, and also the Swakop Dam. Various other water schemes, such as the Kunene Scheme, and those at Henties Bay, Karibib, Otavi, Karasburg, Omaruru, Lüderitz and Rosh Pinah also showed progress. In addition, the first pension scheme for black teachers was established.

The above progress in various fields reflects only a few of the development projects that were already underway, and many more would follow.

South Africa says the people of South West must decide themselves

In 1967 the Ministry of Foreign Affairs of South Africa published a bulky volume under the title *South West Africa Survey 1967*. This document was undoubtedly meant for the overseas market and contained a great deal of information, especially on everything that was being done for the inhabitants of South West Africa. It was clearly a continuation of the arguments that had been presented at the International Court where South Africa had been accused by Ethiopia and Liberia of not fulfilling its obligations in terms of the Mandate. Apparently the Ministry of Foreign Affairs had realised that the charge was still supported worldwide, although the "favourable" court ruling had temporarily taken them off the hook.

Reference was made in the document to a future political dispensation for South West Africa, giving the reassurance that population groups (peoples) would be able to decide their future themselves. I'm sure that many people did not notice that reference was made to "peoples", and not "people". The South-African position at that stage was therefore that the different population groups could decide about their future themselves, and it was subsequently confirmed that no population group would be forced into a dispensation against its will. The document was not taken seriously by political leaders; it was rather regarded as a chess game that South Africa was playing with the international community.

Reorganisation of administrative and financial functions

In his budget speech on 11 March 1968, the Administrator referred to the steps that would gradually be required to reorganise the administrative and financial functions between the Republic of South Africa and South West Africa. On 26 April he elaborated further, stating that 1968 would be written in the financial annals of the Territory of South West Africa as the year in which the new financial dispensation was announced.

He continued that where the old would have to give way for the new, the question arose: What were the most important characteristics of the old financial dispensation? In his view the most important attribute was the sound estate that had been passed on to the next generation. He pointed out that during the previous decade the income of the Territory had far exceeded its expenditure, and although it might be good practice to let the next generation repay the debts incurred by the present generation for development projects, it nevertheless remained our moral obligation to leave a better world behind than the one we had inherited.

He then referred to the impressive list of assets that had been created in the old dispensation from current income in the form of loans to municipalities, town management councils, hospital boards, private schools, mission and church societies, meat-processing factories, the South West Airways, the Land Bank, the South African Railways, the Farmers' Assistance Board, and many more. Cash assets that had accumulated over the years and had been invested in financial institutions amounted to over R60 million, which equalled the total annual income of the Administration.

In the previous decade, R128 million had been spent on roads, telecommunications, buildings and state water schemes. During the same period the Territory had to contend with a protracted drought and the simultaneous outbreak of foot-and-mouth disease, which made major demands on the Administration. All this was possible only because of healthy financial practices and strict financial control. The state income, which increased year on year, was derived from sources such as taxes on individuals, companies, foreign investment, diamond mines, and a diamond levy.

Back to politics

During the ensuing debate, Koos Pretorius once again ventured into the field of statesmanship and paged back in the House documents as far as 1926. He referred especially to the position in which the Administrator and members of the Executive Committee and Legislative Assembly would find themselves once the new administrative dispensation was instated. According to him the Administration of South West Africa would find itself in the same position as the Provincial Administrations of South Africa. This would require adaptations from both officials and voters. With regard to government functions, which would resort directly under the South African ministries, voters would have to approach either officials of the South African Government or their representatives in the South African Parliament, while in the current dispensation they could make contact with their representatives in the Legislative Assembly and officials of the SWA Administration.

Although he was probably not alone in this respect, it was understandable that Pretorius, who had stated earlier that he had chosen politics as a career, was concerned about the future status of the members of the Legislative Assembly. However, he was realistic in his expectation that the new dispensation would require adjustments and that South African officials in the new dispensation would play a more important role. In future the Legislative Assembly and members of the Executive Committee would be responsible only for roads, education for whites, local authorities, nature conservation, health services, public works and other support services. Important functions, some of which had formerly already resorted under the South African Government and others that had now been entrusted to them, would include matters such as defence, foreign and home affairs, Bantu administration and education, justice, agriculture, fisheries, water affairs and economic affairs. Hence, there could no longer be any doubt that all important policy decisions would henceforth be taken in South Africa.

As it happened in the years to come, South Africa came with another surprise by granting a limited form of self-government to the Owambo population group, with its own Legislative Board, Chief Minister and Executive Council in October 1968. The ultimate objective was not clear to me, and – I was convinced – neither to my colleagues. The opportunity the Owambos now had to gain experience in government, and even the creation of a federation, was already being discussed in private conversations. When Adv. Bryan O'Linn announced his federal policy a few years later, Pretorius accused him of stealing our policy. If there was such a policy, I was not aware of it. The National Party of South West Africa was never consulted about this new arrangement for Ovamboland. In my address during the budget debate, I played devil's advocate and asked: "If Ovamboland can become independent, why not us (the whites) too?"

The first signs of distrust

While the South African Government was in the process of systematically taking over the administration of South West Africa, the resolution of the General Assembly of the UN to terminate the mandate in terms of which South Africa administered the Territory was ratified by the Security Council in 1969. A few months earlier the General Assembly decided to change the name South West Africa to Namibia. I was most unhappy about this, and like most South Westers I refused to accept the new name.

The Administrator Wennie du Plessis's term came to an end, and for the first time in history, a South West African was appointed to the position, namely J.G.H. van der Wath. He was a teacher and the principal of the school in the water-rich Stampriet area where he subsequently bought land and became a successful farmer. He was intimately involved in public life and at one stage President of the Agricultural Union. Since 1950 he represented South West Africa in the South African Parliament.

After his appointment as Administrator, Van der Wath could obviously no longer stand for election as a member of the House of Assembly in South Africa. He also had to stand down as leader of the National Party of South West Africa – a position he had held for many years. It was accepted by everyone as logical and self-evident that A.H. du Plessis, who was Deputy Leader and Chairman, would be assigned as Van der Wath's successor – as member of the House of Assembly and as Leader of the National Party of South West Africa – and that a new deputy leader would have to be elected at the next congress.

Despite his reticent nature, A.H. du Plessis was a formidable leader and speaker, and few people ever had the courage to oppose him. In several respects he had a great deal in common with P.W. Botha. To clash with either of them was no joke. I had experienced this for many years. His position was clear and unequivocal: apartheid all the way. He was never prepared to make any concessions about this, not even in respect of "petty apartheid". Right until the end he took a stand against any dispensation that would result in a cessation of ties between South Africa and Namibia. Just like P.W. Botha, he did not tolerate opposition. Despite our difference in age we were good friends, and although I did not agree with his unapproachable attitude regarding petty apartheid and human relations, I fully supported his policy of separate development and continued ties with South Africa.

In the years that followed, this difference in approach towards and relations with our black countrymen also came clearly to the fore between myself and my other colleagues in the Executive Committee. One would have expected that a party that stood for Christian principles would place a great deal more emphasis on respect for human dignity.

I had no intention of pursuing a political career any further. The rearrangement of administrative functions limited the role of South

West politicians substantially, and I would rather devote myself to my farming enterprise on a full-time basis. However, one morning shortly before A.H. du Plessis was to bow out as MEC, he summoned me to his office where I also found Eben van Zijl. A.H. du Plessis started the discussion by saying that once Van der Wath had assumed his duties as Administrator, Du Plessis would in all probability be elected as leader of the National Party. Up to that point it was customary that the deputy leader be elected from the ranks of the Legislative Assembly if the leader of the Party represented South West Africa in the House of Assembly in South Africa. He then asked me to make myself available for election in his place as deputy leader and chairman of the party; in short, that I should abandon my plans to withdraw from politics.

Although I regarded it as a great honour to be identified by the leader of the Party as his probable successor, I also realised that if I were to accept the invitation, there could be no more talk of my withdrawing from politics. I put it to him that I was still young – just 40 years old – and had a farming concern that I still needed to develop, and that it was therefore an extremely difficult decision, but that I would nonetheless give it my serious consideration.

A few days later when I was on my way to my office, Van Zijl stopped me to inform me that I no longer needed to make myself available as deputy leader, since they had decided to propose at the next congress, that the Constitution of the Party be amended to do away with the position of deputy leader. The leader of the Party would then also be chairperson of the Party, to be assisted by two deputy chairpersons, in all probability him and me. My immediate reaction was to ask who the "they" were who had made the decision, since, after all, it also involved me. It surprised me that I had not been consulted. While I was considering one of the most important decisions of my life, "they" had decided to do away with the position of deputy leader without consulting me. His reply was that the decision had been made during a conversation he and Pretorius had had with Du Plessis.

I was flabbergasted, because over the years I had come to know A.H. du Plessis as someone who didn't allow people to mess with his mind and who didn't easily rescind on his decisions. I called him immediately and asked him to arrange a meeting with Van Zijl and myself. Du Plessis, who appeared exceedingly uncomfortable, then explained that

Eben van Zijl had tested the feeling of party members and had come to the conclusion that I didn't stand a chance of defeating Dr Brandt in the election for the position of deputy leader. To eliminate any possibility of Dr Brandt being elected, they had decided to do away with the position of deputy leader. I was shocked on two accounts: firstly, because they wanted to use me to eliminate Dr Brandt, who was a friend of mine and who had asked me four years earlier to stand for election as MEC, and secondly, because they had done this behind my back and without my knowledge.

Although I mistrusted their motives and also disagreed with the desirability of such a change, I decided not to oppose their plan. I also decided to refrain from participating in the discussion when the issue was discussed at Congress. However, I did caution that a party should not change its constitution to deal with a specific situation. I was in any case convinced that the entire scheme was Van Zijl's brainchild and that he and Pretorius wanted to prevent me from becoming the future leader of the party.

Before the congress of 1969, Van Zijl informed me once again that he was of the opinion that in terms of the proposed new provisions of the Constitution, A.H. du Plessis would be elected as leader and chairman and that he (Van Zijl) and I would be elected as deputy chairmen. It was ridiculous in the extreme, so I asked him the following: If he was so convinced that I couldn't win an election as deputy leader against Dr Brandt, how did he think the two of us could oust Dr Brandt from the position of vice-chairman, a position that he had already been occupying for some time. His plan became ever more transparent to me. I had to be prevented from rising in seniority.

The congress accepted the proposal to change the Constitution of the Party without knowing the real reason behind it. Because of their faith in A.H. du Plessis, the delegates had no problem in giving so much power to one person. However, the election of the two vice-chairmen proved how wrong Van Zijl's so-called opinion polls were. There were six proposals for the two positions of vice-chairmen, namely Dr Brandt, Eben van Zijl, Jan de Wet, E.T. Meyer, P. Roux and myself. In the first vote I achieved an absolute majority. Du Plessis showed me the slip of paper on which the counters had written the result before announcing my election. He was noticeably amused about Van Zijl's "opinion poll".

I didn't comment. After a further process of elimination, Dr Brandt was elected as the other vice-chairman. The two of us subsequently worked together for many years, inter alia because my constituency in the Legislative Assembly, Otjiwarongo, was part of his constituency, Etosha, in the House of Assembly. The fact that our political paths split eight years later had no bearing on our personal relationship.

The question can rightfully be asked: What makes this somewhat idiotic interaction worth mentioning at all? At that stage there could be no question of my loyalty towards the Party, because I had whole-heartedly supported the policy of separate development. My position on policy could not be a reason for the mistrust that some of my colleagues clearly harboured towards me already at that stage. What might have been a possibility was that my outspoken stance on human relations and the acknowledgement of the human dignity of our fellow human beings had by then cast suspicion on me with certain colleagues. They had possibly already interpreted the speech I had made five years earlier in the Legislative Assembly as a first step towards the humanism and pragmatism of which I was openly accused years later.

I fully supported separate development, as I understood it. However, a system based on universal suffrage was unacceptable to the vast majority of the members of both the National Party and the UNSWP, because the whites – of whom I was one – were a small minority group. We were aware of how other countries in Africa were governed, of which the reign of terror of Idi Amin of Uganda was but one example. It was obvious that SWAPO would form the government under a system of universal suffrage, while at that stage it was intensifying its terrorist activities and killing innocent people. We had to face up to reality and adapt our political route accordingly. At that time separate development seemed to be the best option, especially since we believed that South Africa with its enormous economic and military power could implement it, and to all intents and purposes on the acceptable moral basis that you must treat your fellow man as you would expect him to treat you. Exactly how this would work in practice was still not clear to me. However, I accepted that in exercising the right to self-determination, no group could act unilaterally. The granting of limited self-government to the inhabitants of Owambo gave me the impression that in the case of the departments of Foreign Affairs and

Bantu Affairs and Development, the proverbial left hand did not know what the right hand was doing.

The new administrative dispensation in operation

On 7 March 1969, J.G.H. van der Wath, who succeeded Wennie du Plessis as Administrator, opened the fourth session of the ninth Legislative Assembly. On the same occasion Koos Pretorius was elected as member of the Executive Committee to replace A.H. du Plessis, who succeeded Van der Wath in the South African Parliament, and was eventually promoted to Deputy Minister. At that stage South West Africa was represented by a strong team in the South African Parliament – six members in the House of Assembly and four members in the Senate. I had every reason to believe that the future of South West Africa was in safe hands.

The following members of the Legislative Assembly, in order of seniority, were then elected as members of the Executive Committee of South West Africa: S. von Bach, D.F. Mudge, E. van Zijl and J.W.F. Pretorius. From then on it was our responsibility to manage local administration, which would have limited functions in terms of the new dispensation.

In his budget speech, the Administrator confirmed that the White Paper, in which the details of the rearrangement of the financial and administrative functions were set out, had been published by the South African Government. The required legislation had already been accepted by the Government to empower the different state departments in South Africa to expand their activities in South West Africa, and steps were taken to expedite the takeover of functions on 1 April. In his survey of events of the previous year he referred inter alia to the crash of a South African Airways Boeing shortly after takeoff from Windhoek Airport. The major development was, however, the acceptance by the leaders in Owambo of the offer of self-rule for that area and the establishment of an own Legislative Assembly and Executive Committee. He also mentioned that during the previous year the Farmers' Assistance Board had dealt with 425 applications for settlement and 643 applications for assistance. In the meantime the relocation of the inhabitants of the Old Location to Katutura, which had commenced in December 1959 and had caused such a major upheaval, had been concluded.

The Administrator reported extensively on the activities of the Administration. Regarding education, the number of pupils in the country had increased by 52% over the previous five years, so that in 1968 there were in total 113 495 children in school, of whom 81 809 were "natives" (in other words blacks), 21 114 whites, and 10 572 coloureds. Other signs of progress were a decision by SWAWEK (SWA Water and Electricity Commission) to construct a power station on the outskirts of Windhoek, and the planning of a canal to provide water to large areas of Ovamboland. In the ensuing years we would no longer have any say in many of the functions the Administrator had mentioned. At the end of the session he presented details about the progress that had been made over the past five years in the execution of the recommendations of the Odendaal Report.

During this first session of the Legislative Assembly under the new administrative dispensation and for the rest of 1969, members of the Executive Committee reported extensively on the activities of the departments under their control. They would henceforth handle the departments falling under their control in an equally responsible and competent manner as they had in the past. In my speech during the budget debate I referred to the criticism by the opposition that the Administration had built up large reserves by collecting unnecessary millions from taxpayers. They referred specifically to the Territory Development and Reserve Fund. It had always been the policy of the Administration to transfer surpluses to the fund during good years for utilisation during less good years. This enabled us not only to combat crisis situations but also to undertake large capital expenditures without having to resort to loans. Hence, it was not necessary for South Africa to take over a bankrupt estate. The first "loan" we had to take due to the rearrangement of financial and administrative matters was the R20 million to purchase the expropriated farms, a loan that was supposed to be written off by South Africa.

Members had little to say about politics during this session, and when they did, it was still the same old story. The opposition and its newspaper exploited the large expenditure in the communal areas to prove that too much was being done for the black people and that the white people were being neglected. The National Party Representatives were still extremely sensitive to these accusations and denied it vehemently.

Fundamental differences rise to the surface

During this and the next session of the Legislative Assembly, it became increasingly clear to me that Pretorius and I disagreed fundamentally on important issues.

When Pretorius said he would be quoting from the Bible and specifically from Luke 14, Stony Steenkamp interrupted: "Ecclesiastes would have been the appropriate Book." Everyone knew what Steenkamp meant. The passage from Luke 14 reads as follows: "For which of you, desiring to build a tower, does not first sit down and count the cost, whether he has enough to complete it? Otherwise, when he has laid a foundation and is not able to finish, all who see it begin to mock him, saying, 'This man began to build and was not able to finish.'" He used this quotation when referring to road construction, but said that in future he would also make it applicable to the political views expressed in the Legislative Assembly.

On 9 March 1970, the Legislative Assembly convened for its last meeting before the general election, which was to take place a month later. My first ten years as member of the Legislative Assembly were behind me. No one could foresee with certainty what would happen during the next term. Dramatic changes lay ahead, which would steer the political ship in a completely different direction. In my case it would lead to reflection, as well as to new ideas that would subsequently bring me in conflict with some of my colleagues and later on with the Party. No one could have thought it possible to turn the entire political process on its head so soon after the implementation of the administrative reorganisation, which in reality boiled down to a de facto incorporation of the Territory into South Africa.

We were still building the Tower of Babel, firmly convinced that it would be completed, absolutely sure that the planning had been done well, and that the expenditure had been calculated to the finest detail.

Adolf Brinkman said we did not need an opposition; E.T. Meyer struggled with the Reconstituted National Party (Herstigte Nasionale Party), which wanted to tackle the National Party from the right; and A.P. Steyn said his goodbyes, promising that he would continue supporting the Party. The highly regarded Von Bach also bade the Party farewell. While he would not be remembered as a politician, he was the only German-speaking member of the Assembly for many years, thus opening the political arena also for German participation in politics. He was a child of the land – someone who left indelible footprints in the fields of agriculture, nature conservation and water affairs. At an early stage he was Chairman of the Parks Board and could speak enthusiastically about the country's natural resources. He launched both the Nature Conservation Ordinance (1967) and the Accommodation Establishments and Tourism Ordinance (1967) through the Assembly. His enormous contribution in the field of water affairs led the Executive Committee to name the Von Bach Dam outside Okahandja after him. I was moved when I bade him farewell.

During the election campaign Pretorius continued, as always, to build the political Tower of Babel based on Christian principles, which according to him could never change. He started by saying there were two dominant issues or aspects of political life in South West Africa that required attention, namely the political status of the Territory and the problems relating to colour issues. He wasn't talking about ethnic issues, but about colour issues. According to Pretorius, the voters expected his Party to execute what it had undertaken. The Party had to be capable of completing the Tower of Babel.

He maintained that the National Party of South Africa and in South West Africa was in fact one. When it comes to policy, the five parties of the four provinces and South West Africa stood together and decided together. When it came to the colour policy, he demonstrated by means of many cuttings – primarily from *Die Suidwes-Afrikaner* – that the UNSWP and the United Party in South Africa were not speaking the same language and that they would not be able to implement their colour policy. As to his interpretation of the National Party's colour policy he remained silent.

On 11 March 1970, Pretorius alleged that the Administration could only maintain the economic and financial position of our country because the National Party could uphold its policy on South West Africa's political position and colour relations. By doing so the Party could promote order, peace, security and confidence in the country. He ascribed the favourable situation in South West Africa to the fact that the National Party in South West Africa was linked to the National Party of South Africa on a federal basis, while in this respect the UNSWP had tried to formulate its own policy. He continued on 27 May, quoting A.H. du Plessis, who had said at one stage: "Our ideal for South West Africa is total apartheid. When apartheid comes to its logical conclusion, we will have a total division of territory and we will be living in separate areas."

In the preceding four years we'd had to contend with increasing acts of terrorism and farmers had already started constructing safety fences around their homesteads.

CHAPTER 7

My first experience of international politics

The South West Africa issue at the World Court for the sixth time

On 29 July 1970, the Security Council of the United Nations approached the International Court for an advisory opinion regarding South Africa's presence in South West Africa. Their question was: "What are the legal consequences for States of the continued presence of South Africa in Namibia (i.e., South West Africa) notwithstanding Security Council Resolution 276 (1970)." This was the sixth time the South West Africa issue had come up before the International Court in one form or another, but this time it would have serious consequences.

By 1971 circumstances were beginning to catch up with us. I opened the session of the Legislative Assembly in February 1971 as Acting Administrator since the Administrator, Van der Wath, was indisposed. I referred to the large degree of uncertainty that was prevailing in the Territory due to the pending court case, but since the matter was sub judice I indicated that I wouldn't comment on it. However, I emphasised that we had the assurance of the South African Government that we would not be left in the lurch. Combined with the dark political clouds – figuratively speaking – that were hanging over us, rainclouds were fortunately also building up, bringing an end to the drought of so many years.

While the court case was still underway, the National Party of South West Africa continued as if global opinion were not a factor. We were misled by South Africa's position that the ruling of the court was only advisory and was therefore not enforceable. It serves no purpose to elaborate on all the arguments brought forward by the South Africans to justify their view. The ruling of the court would be followed by a resolution of the United Nations which would have serious consequences for South Africa.

A mere month earlier Pretorius had referred to a statement by the well-known heart surgeon, Dr Chris Barnard, who warned that: "If the youth of South African do not want to be accused of inhumanity towards those who are less privileged, they have to start working towards giving equal opportunities to every member of the community." Pretorius had a problem with this.

> What Dr Barnard and so many others fail to see, whether in good faith or deliberately I do not know, namely that in our moral laws there are two elements: self-love and love for your neighbour. We must first define self-love before we can decide for ourselves what kind of neighbourly love we grant our neighbours. I must first decide what is right for me, what is good for me, what is precious to me, what my self-love is, before I can decide how I am going to behave towards my neighbour.

He based his problem with our countrymen having equal opportunities on his basic Christian principles. He concluded his argument as follows: "Equal opportunities in our country with its problems will mean no opportunities; it will mean that the one group will obliterate the other. We also believe in equal opportunities, but separately and with the provisos that we have set."

On 21 June 1971, the International Court gave its ruling, which reads as follows:

1. that South Africa was in illegal occupation of South West Africa and under an obligation to withdraw its administration from the Territory immediately;
2. that States members of the United Nations were obliged:
   (i) to recognize the illegality of South Africa's presence in the Territory and the invalidity of its acts on behalf of or concerning the territory;
   (ii) to refrain from any acts or dealings which would imply recognition of the legality of, or lend support or assistance to, the South African presence or administration;
3. that it was incumbent on States not members of the United Nations, to give assistance in the action taken by the United Nations with regard to the territory.

If I remember correctly, the British and French judges voted against the ruling, which led to both Britain and France announcing subsequently that they rejected the court ruling.

Differences about diversity and human dignity

The differences in approach between Koos Pretorius and myself became increasingly obvious. Although members of the National Party

of South West Africa could not play a meaningful role in the determination of the constitutional future of our country we could at least
create the right climate for a peaceful solution by simply changing our
attitude towards our black countrymen/-women and to refrain from
making public statements which might create suspicion and spoil human relations.

On 25 February 1972, during a discussion of a motion on education
proposed by Pretorius, I decided to make my views on the diversity
of our population, racism and respect for the human dignity abundantly clear. I repeated what I had said before that you cannot ignore
ethnic and religious differences when looking for peaceful solutions.
It is a given fact that must be acknowledged. The mistake often made
in countries with a heterogeneous population is to ignore these differences for the sake of simple solutions while in South Africa and in
South West Africa it was over-emphasised with separation as the proposed solution.

> It is also essential that you acknowledge the human dignity of all
> groups; that you will not regard them merely as separate groups
> and will not simply accept that they are different, but that you
> also respect them for what they are. The white people in this
> country must not make the mistake of regarding the non-whites
> as an inferior group. If and when we are prepared to acknowl-
> edge their human dignity and through our actions behave in
> such a way that we earn their respect, we will have taken an im-
> portant step towards better human relations, and this will also
> be an important step in the execution of our policy ... [T]here
> are still too many people who have become accustomed to the
> old dispensation where (when) they were regarded as nothing
> more than unskilled workers. We must accept one thing: no po-
> litical agreement that can result in peace and prosperity would
> be feasible or successful if it does not carry the approval of the
> non-whites ... It is also important that they – the non-whites –
> realise that their actions in this respect are equally important. It
> cannot be one-sided if it is to succeed.

Dr Waldheim and Dr Escher visit South West Africa

In pursuance of the advisory opinion of the World Court on 21 June
1971, the Security Council of the United Nations took a most important decision on 4 February 1972, which amounted to South Africa's
presence in South West Africa being illegal. The Council furthermore

reaffirmed its position regarding the principle of national unity and territorial integrity for the Territory and gave the Secretary General instructions to create, in consultation with certain parties, conditions that would make it possible for the people of South West Africa to exercise their right to self-determination and independence. They called on the South African Government to cooperate with the Secretary General to implement this directive.

On the same day the Prime Minister of South Africa, John Vorster, said in the House of Assembly:

> If the Secretary General of the United Nations Organisation wants to come to South Africa to discuss, among other matters, the self-determination of the non-white nations with the Government, he would find us willing partners in the discussions, since it is our policy to lead the nations towards self-determination. However, if he wants to come to serve as a mouthpiece for extremists of the OAU (Organisation of African Unity) and others, and to take decisions in this regard, he would still be welcome and be received courteously, but I can tell him in advance that he would be wasting his time.

What is important here is the willingness of the Prime Minister to discuss self-determination, even though it concerned only the non-whites.

On 7 March 1972, Dr Kurt Waldheim, the Secretary General of the United Nations, visited South Africa in an effort to avoid a confrontation between the United Nations and South Africa. He unexpectedly also visited Windhoek, and for the first time in history, local politicians were given the opportunity to have discussions with a representative of the international community. The visit was nothing more than a courtesy visit, but for us – the members of the Executive Committee under the leadership of our new Administrator – it was a historical event.

I would just like to mention a meaningful exchange between myself and A.H. du Plessis shortly after Waldheim's visit. Ben van der Walt succeeded Johannes van der Wath, who was the first South Wester to occupy the position of Administrator. When Van der Wath indicated that he was no longer available, speculation about whether his successor would again be a South Wester, and who it could be, started. Since I had acted as Administrator on several occasions in the past and since there was a strong sentiment towards the practice of appointing a South Wester in the position, I was – as Du Plessis informed me – considered for the position by John Vorster.

Du Plessis and I discussed the issue during a visit to Pretoria and agreed that it was more important for me to remain active in politics so that I could assist him as leader. If I were to accept the position as Administrator, I would probably not be able to participate in the important political developments that would follow Dr Waldheim's visit. Moreover, I would be working for the South African Government, which was unacceptable to me.

According to Dr Waldheim's report to the Security Council as relayed to me by Pik Botha, the Prime Minister confirmed that his policy for South West Africa was self-determination and independence. They further agreed that the Secretary General would appoint a personal representative to reach the objectives they had agreed upon, and to consult accordingly with all parties concerned. Hence, a Swiss diplomat, Dr Alfred Escher, was assigned to make a follow-up visit to the Territory, which would take place in October 1972.

Until this point the white political leaders in South West Africa had played a negligible role in the international political struggle relating to South West Africa, regardless of the fact that the declared policy of the South African Government since 1967 had been that the inhabitants of South West Africa should decide about their political future themselves.

When Dr Escher visited South West Africa I was asked by the South African Government to accompany him on his tour through the southern part of the Territory, while Jan de Wet, Commissioner General for the indigenous groups, would escort him through the homelands. Although other UN committees had already visited South Africa, such as the Good Offices Committee under chairmanship of Charles Arden-Clarke in 1958, and the Carpio and De Alva Committee in 1962, this was the first time that a white political leader was directly involved in the visit of a representative of the UN to South West Africa.

During our tour through the south, Dr Escher, to my mind, overstepped his mandate by propagating certain constitutional models – in particular the federal system, while he had been sent purely on a fact-finding mission and was supposed to listen to the people and to familiarise himself with the circumstances in the country. Tension between Dr Escher and myself increased to such an extent that the then Minister of Foreign Affairs, Dr Hilgard Muller, and the Secretary of his Department, Brand Fourie, had to fly to Oranjemund to salvage the tour.

During my tour with Dr Escher I was embarrassed by the racial prejudice in our white community. Dr Escher's party included a Togolese and an Indian man. I asked a friend who owned a smallholding outside Otjiwarongo whether we could entertain the party there. To my surprise he refused on the grounds that it would not be good for his business if he entertained a mixed group on his land. I tried to persuade the hotel owners to accommodate the group and to arrange a reception for them on the premises. It was at that stage still illegal for accommodation establishments to accommodate non-whites. I invited several German-speaking people to meet with Dr Escher (who was German-speaking) and fortunately the evening progressed smoothly. However, this would not be the last embarrassing situation. In Windhoek I experienced no problems, but in the south no hotel was prepared to accommodate us. I kept this from Escher, and on our way back from Oranjemund, we spent the night in the half-completed Hardap Rest Camp.

After his visit to South West Africa, Dr Escher had a meeting with Prime Minister John Vorster, the Minister of Foreign Affairs, Dr Muller, and the Secretary of Foreign Affairs, Brand Fourie. A.H. du Plessis, Eben van Zijl, Jan de Wet and I were invited to the meeting in Pretoria. During the discussions, the Prime Minister and Dr Escher reached a ten-point agreement. In response to questions by Dr Escher, the Prime Minister emphasised that experience in self-rule was an essential component for the ultimate implementation of self-determination, and that this could best be achieved on a regional basis. This was acceptable to Escher, on condition that an authority was introduced for the Territory as a whole. The Prime Minister agreed to set up an Advisory Board for South West Africa to advise him on matters pertaining to South West Africa. He himself would exercise control over all the South African state departments operating in South West Africa, and an office would be established in Windhoek to facilitate this.

The Prime Minister also declared himself willing to investigate all restrictions on freedom of movement, as long as this did not frustrate measures to combat influx control. In addition, he agreed that there would be freedom of speech and political activities in the Territory, including having public meetings. Dr Escher in his report to the Secretary General proposed that "Within the framework of the above it is felt that contact between the Secretary General and the South African Government should be continued."

This agreement was generally regarded as a triumph for John Vorster, especially since it contradicted the position held by the United Nations until that stage that South Africa's position in South West Africa was not and would not be recognised. The Department of Bantu Administration and Development, and the Commissioner General for the indigenous peoples of South West Africa, Jan de Wet, were instructed to invite the leaders of the different population groups to serve on the Advisory Board. Billy Marais was appointed as the Representative of the Prime Minister in South West Africa, based in Windhoek. Dr Escher himself was apparently not received well on his return to New York, and we never heard of him again.

Our political differences intensify

In spite of clearly discernible signs that a clash between South Africa and the international community over the South West Africa issue was unavoidable, our local political leaders were still living in a fool's paradise. On 17 February 1973, Koos Pretorius proposed the following motion in the Legislative Assembly:

"That this House wants to emphasise that if a political party professes Christian principles, those principles would gain stature in his political household, especially as regards the norms that apply to giving people the right to vote." On Christian principles Pretorius said:

> It is a generally accepted fact that those who want to see the South African philosophy of life destroyed, who want to mix and integrate the white and black nations who live here, never tire of accusing the whites of South Africa of being unchristian … [T]the point of departure of these people is apparently the commandment that you must love your neighbour as you love yourself … This is the so-called Social Gospel …

Regarding the concepts of neighbourly love and self-love, he went somewhat further: "Modern humanism, however, emphasises not only the freedom but also the equality of all people … You cannot use

Christian terminology to try and Christianise a philosophy of your own." He asserted that humanists were tagging on the term neighbourly love not in the Christian sense but to justify their policy.

However, Pretorius was guilty of exactly this in trying to justify the racial policy of the National Party on Biblical and Christian grounds, alleging that to love God you must love what He had created, in other words, love the rich diversity of His creation. To use the diversity of creation as an argument to discriminate against man who had been created equally and to deny him his human dignity concerned me. This surely did not reflect Dr Verwoerd's clear point of view that he granted his neighbour (the non-white) everything that he (the white) asked for himself. Pretorius's emphasis on the diversity of creation, which I have never disputed, does not justify disparaging human dignity. My colleagues still failed to support my repeated appeals to my white countrymen to change their attitude towards our black countrymen.

Pretorius even alleged that not everyone living together in the same country could lay claim to the right to vote. He based it on circumstances and level of civilisation, with the assumption that all whites were civilised and therefore had the right to vote and that all blacks were uncivilised and could therefore not claim the right to vote. He somehow reached the conclusion that it is not necessary for an individual to have the right to vote, since there are other political freedoms that enable him to take part in the actions of Government politically.

He again reiterated his view that in the moral code you must distinguish between two equal elements, namely self-love and love of your neighbour, proclaiming that self-preservation as a realisation of your vocation was probably not wrong. However, he came to the conclusion that "… although all men had been created in the image of God and were therefore equal before God in terms of their personal dignity, they had not been created equal." This he based on his belief that different nations and races were not created equal and differed from one another. On these grounds Pretorius rejected the Charter of Human Rights and presented arguments in an attempt to justify apartheid in its crudest form, as well as his disparagement of human dignity.

Although no one denies the rich diversity of creation (and even admires it), no one can accept on Christian grounds that God created inferior beings. If differences in civilisation and experience developed,

God should not be held responsible for this too. If anybody were to be held responsible for the black inhabitants of our country not progressing more rapidly, it was the National Party of which I was a member.

Pretorius even objected to the principle of equal opportunities for all. They had to wait, so it was said, for total apartheid to materialise, which never happened and which remained a political dream – or was it a nightmare? – until the end. While the non-whites (to differentiate from population groups) had to wait for the implementation of the National Party's policy of separate development, they were deprived of opportunities and subjected to humiliation and discrimination.

The first meeting of the Prime Minister's Advisory Board, 1973

Following Escher's visit, the Advisory Board held its first meeting under chairmanship of the Prime Minister in Windhoek in 1973. Eben van Zijl and I represented the whites. It was clear to me that those representing other population groups were primarily sympathetic leaders and not really representative leaders. I had my doubts about the Herero, Nama, and Damara representatives, while no Tswana representative had been invited. The deliberations were generally superficial and dealt more with the local interests of the different groups.

In order to involve more of the actual leaders of the ethnic groups in the activities of the Board, Billy Marais and I immediately started making contact with the Hereros and Namas, and later also with the Damara leaders. Our first target was Clemens Kapuuo, who had not been invited by Jan de Wet. De Wet alleged that Kapuuo was not a recognised traditional Herero leader. It was common knowledge that Kapuuo was one of the most influential black leaders in South West Africa. Initially he was often referred to disparagingly as the "shopkeeper of Katutura". Even the then Minister of Bantu Administration of South Africa made degrading remarks about Kapuuo. I succeed in making contact with him, albeit in a clandestine manner due to the considerable risks that he as a black leader would be running by communicating with leaders of the National Party with whom he had always been in conflict.

It is important to note that the Hereros until that stage consistently refused to cooperate with the authorities. They declined any form of economic or political development, or at the least accepted it under protest. It was only the so-called "Small Group" that cooperated, largely because they were opposed to Kapuuo's leadership. However, they were maligned as "stooges" or "white feet" by most of the Hereros.

During the second half of 1973, Kapuuo revealed in a press interview that he and Johannes Karuaihe were to meet with me. We agreed that we should strive for a peaceful solution and that violence and war were not an option. His anti-Owambo attitude, his fear of Owambo domination, and his reservations about the UN became very apparent. However, I was unsuccessful in persuading him to participate in the Advisory Board. He repeatedly mentioned that he did not trust the South African Government and that it was difficult for him to accept my bona fides as a white man. It took more than two years to convince him otherwise. Both of us realised that we would have to proceed with care. Our people were not yet ready for such a fraternisation between white and black.

I attend the session of the UN General Assembly

Following the visit of the Secretary General Dr Kurt Waldheim in the previous year and the subsequent visit by his special representative Dr Alfred Escher, I realised how uninformed I was in respect of international affairs. By means of mediation by Billy Marais, who in the meantime had been manning the Office of the Prime Minister in Windhoek, I succeeded in attending a session of the UN for the first time.

In October 1973 Billy Marais and I, invited by Dr Hilgard Muller, departed to attend the session of the General Assembly of the UN as observers. This was one of the most frustrating experiences of my life. It is difficult to imagine such animosity, prejudice and ignorance. The General Assembly tried to prevent Dr Muller from delivering his speech, again referring South Africa's membership to the UN Credentials Committee. When the President of the Assembly, after a long and emotional debate about South Africa's credentials, ruled that Dr Muller may deliver his speech, most of the members of the General Assembly left the conference hall. The only African state that stayed was Malawi.

I realised for the first time the extent of the struggle that South Africa was waging, also on behalf of South West Africa, and the many humiliations South Africa's representatives had to endure at the UN to enable the white inhabitants of South West Africa to live in peace and prosperity, without us even being aware of the dangers we were facing. The white inhabitants of South West Africa regarded the UN as a joke. John Vorster once remarked to me that it seemed as if everyone was concerned about the future of South West Africa except the inhabitants of the Territory themselves; especially the whites.

By coincidence Clemens Kapuuo was also in New York to address the Fourth Committee (the Trusteeship Committee) of the UN. Kuaima Riruako, who was a student in America at the time, had arranged the appointment for him. In his speech Kapuuo pointed out that his group had been appealing to the UN for very long to put an end to South Africa's occupation of South West Africa, but that the world organisation had now apparently turned its back on them. In my view he delivered a good speech, but at the end of it he was only thanked for his contribution, and there was no further discussion or commentary by members of the Committee. I was in the conference hall when he was speaking, and felt very sorry for him. Later in the evening when I visited him, he opened his heart to me, telling me how the Hereros, under leadership of Paramount Chief Hosea Kutako, were the first to campaign for the independence of South West Africa by sending petitioners to the UN. While the other groups were cooperating with the South African Government and being given benefits, the Hereros refused to accept any favours from the South African Government, and in the process lost out when it came to development. He found it incomprehensible that the UN was now recognising SWAPO and turning its back on him, just because he did not support violence.

That evening I finally understood the dilemma of black leaders in South West Africa. Kapuuo had been rejected by the United Nations because he denounced violence and was also prepared to speak to a white leader. I put it to him that I would probably find myself in the same position in the near future, and that we should continue the conversation we had started earlier in the year. I also informed him of the impressions I had gained at the UN and my serious reservations about South Africa ever winning the battle.

After the humiliating experience by Dr Hilgard Muller in the General Assembly, Pik Botha, Carl von Hirschberg – South Africa's Representative at the UN – and I agreed that events were rapidly building up to a confrontation between South Africa and the world organisation, which subsequently happened when South Africa withdrew from the UN proceedings the following year (1974).

I expressed the opinion that the time had come for the inhabitants of South West Africa to be given the opportunity to exercise their right to self-determination, as had been undertaken in the *South West Africa Survey 1967*. I also pointed out that, contrary to how it had been stated in the survey, it was the right of the "people" and not of the "peoples" to decide about their collective future.

I offered to repeat my proposal to John Vorster personally. Both Pik and Carl insisted that I present it as my personal opinion, as confirmed on page 484 of Pik's biography, *Pik Botha and His Times*. Carl von Hirschberg described it as a milestone, which indeed it was.

I wondered why Carl and Pik had felt so strongly that I should act in my personal capacity in my discussion with the Prime Minister. I had to wait many years for clarification. In an interview with Theresa Papenfus, the author of *Pik Botha en sy tyd*, Carl relates an incident about which I recently learnt for the first time – 40 years after my discussion with the Prime Minister. He tells of a meeting that took place in February 1973 – six months before my visit to the UN and my discussion with him and Pik in New York. On this occasion he informed the Prime Minister on South Africa's position at the UN as follows: "Our position at the UN is becoming less and less tenable and we might be able to buy time and lessen the pressure on us in one area if Government could proceed to apply the policy the Prime Minister has announced." According to Carl, John Vorster said he was not convinced that the leaders of South West Africa were prepared to, and capable of exercising their right to self-determination. He spoke about the people of South West Africa not seeing eye to eye on this. If they were allowed to decide on their future themselves, they would probably resort to violence. Carl agreed: "It is doubtful whether the internal leadership was politically ready to engage the SWAPO leadership in serious negotiations."

I would have felt less assured of myself on my way to John Vorster, had I been aware of the views taken by the Prime Minister and Carl six months earlier. I would, however, have understood why Pik and Carl requested that I act in my personal capacity.

I informed the Prime Minister about my observations at the UN. It was the first time I had a personal discussion with a South African Prime Minister. He received me courteously, offered me a comfortable chair, asked whether I preferred tea or coffee, and enquired about my welfare and that of my wife and children. I soon felt sufficiently at ease and confident enough to speak candidly about my impressions at the UN as a newcomer to the field of international politics. Among other things I expressed my concern about the role the different South African government departments were playing in the Territory, and the confusion that often arose as a result.

The Department of Bantu Administration and Development, under leadership of the Minister responsible, M.C. Botha, and the Commissioner General of the indigenous people, Jan de Wet, regarded the future of the black population groups as their exclusive responsibility. The Legislative Assembly of South West Africa and the Executive Committee were expected to limit themselves to the administration of the white population group, and no interference was tolerated.

In the meantime the South African Defence Force did not confine itself to military matters, but started to apply what it referred to as "psychological warfare". A special committee was established for this purpose, referred to as the *Bronskomitee* (Brass Committee). Meetings were arranged with commando members and municipalities to discuss matters that related directly to policy. The objective was supposedly to win the hearts and minds of the black people. My view was that the role of the Defence Force was to guarantee our safety, while political parties were to work on administrative and political solutions. The current situation could lead to equivocation, and besides, it was being done in an uncoordinated way.

I also admitted to the Prime Minister that he had been correct in saying it seemed to him that everyone was concerned about the future of South West Africa except the South Westers themselves. I offered my assistance in involving the inhabitants of the Territory in the search to find a lasting solution to the administrative problem. I suggested that the inhabitants of South West Africa should be allowed to take the initiative to determine the future of our country.

The Prime Minister suggested that a discussion be scheduled to take place in January 1974 to give me the opportunity to formulate my proposal thoroughly, with suggestions as to how to put it into practice.

I left his office with the conviction that I had shared my thoughts with a reasonable and sympathetic man. Although he was probably very well informed about the tension between the whites in South West, he made no mention of it. In the course of the next five years a position of trust would develop between us.

At the November session of the Legislative Assembly in 1973, I reported on my visit to the UN and my discussions with Clemens Kapuuo. I emphasised that I wouldn't do or say anything that would cause the dialogue between myself, Kapuuo and the other black leaders to come to grief. I stressed once again that South West Africa's problems could not be solved by the international community, but only by the people of South West Africa themselves, in cooperation with the former mandatory, South Africa. I referred to the fact that the UN recognised SWAPO as the only true and authentic representative of the people of South West Africa; that the UN was interested solely in the handover of the Territory to SWAPO and nothing else; and related how badly Kapuuo had been received by the Fourth Committee.

The Hereros under leadership of their traditional leader, Hosea Kutako, were the first campaigners against colonial rule, and Kapuuo himself was an outspoken proponent of independence, which made it incomprehensible that the UN recognised SWAPO purely because Kapuuo did not favour violence. Although Kapuuo and I did not necessarily agree on everything, we both rejected violence as a solution, and believed that solutions should be sought through dialogue. I asked that understanding be shown when Kapuuo were to say things with which we did not agree, since he as a black leader was under great pressure.

I emphasised that the white and black inhabitants had an equal right to be in the country, and that we should desist from undermining anyone's human dignity, or deceiving anyone. I concluded:

> But it depends on the Government. It depends on every one of you in this meeting, and it depends on the whites of South West Africa whether or not the non-whites will believe us, and whether they will be prepared to accept us. We will have to act wisely, not only in our daily dealings, but also in the execution of our governmental policy ... We must not allow ourselves to be thrown off course by persons and elements in our country who want to turn everything into politics. We must not allow ourselves to be intimidated by the HNP and the United Party. We as whites, and the Government, must have the courage of our

convictions to continue on this road … When the Prime Minister opened Congress here in Windhoek, he said that it was up to South West Africa to decide on its own future, and that he would see to it that we would be able to exercise our right to self-determination. He said that a decision would be made here, in the building on top of the hill (the government office) about the future of the whites in South West Africa … Are we then afraid to take on this responsibility? … If an election is on its way, I will surely be affected. Yet I am prepared to state here today, unequivocally, that I do not have any objection to having a conversation with a non-white person in the street. I would invite him into my office. And if there are people who are interested in knowing this, I would offer him tea. If I were to have a meal with him, I would invite all the newspapers to come and take photographs. If people think that it poses a threat to white civilisation, they are making a big mistake. In the days that lie ahead we will have to separate the important from the unimportant; we will have to do away with the little things that are just a nuisance and concentrate on principles. You can adapt your methods, and you can adapt your policy, without sacrificing principles. When it comes to the future of South West Africa, we must be a dynamic party, a party with confidence in ourselves and a party with only one objective in mind, and that is to work out a prosperous future for this country.

CHAPTER 8

Internal political development from 1974 to 1977

Five years with John Vorster

The meeting which the Prime Minister and I had agreed upon following my return from New York took place in Cape Town on 31 January 1974. The following dignitaries were present: Prime Minister John Vorster; Minister of Bantu Administration and Development, M.C. Botha; Minister of Foreign Affairs, Dr H. Muller; Pik Botha, member of the House of Assembly; Administrator B.J. van der Walt; General Hendrik van den Bergh of the State Security Council; A.H. du Plessis; Jan de Wet, Commissioner General of Indigenous People; and Carl von Hirschberg and David Totthill of Foreign Affairs.

When the Prime Minister gave me the opportunity to inform the meeting of the proposals I had discussed with him, I had a moment of doubt, wondering whether I wasn't perhaps being, as my father had often said, "too big for my boots". I knew I would be stepping on the toes of people who were older than I was and had many years of experience in international affairs. I didn't expect them to welcome my proposals, as they would no doubt see this as interference in their separate domains. Coming from a young politician of whose existence many of them were probably not even aware, it was to be expected that some of them might take offence. I knew I would have to choose my words carefully, since I was depending on support from the Prime Minister. He didn't disappoint me, also not in the years to come.

As could be expected, Pik and Carl didn't have much to say. They were probably waiting for the Prime Minister's reaction before supporting my proposal. As they had indicated in New York, they wanted me to present the proposals as my personal views.

The meeting was adjourned to give me the opportunity to formulate my proposal more comprehensively and to come forward with a suggestion on how to proceed. I was not sure whether I would hear from the Prime Minister again, and had already accepted that my well-meant attempt had failed when two months later, in the first week of April 1974, I received a letter from Prime Minister Vorster's secretary informing me that he was waiting for my proposals regarding the composition and terms of reference in order for a committee to consider my proposals.

On 11 April I replied:

> I don't think I need to elaborate on the necessity of coordination except to emphasise once again that the actions of departments that currently have a responsibility in South West Africa are often inconsistent. The constitutional position and political development in South West Africa are extremely delicate issues, which – according to the Prime Minister – cannot be tackled in a clumsy way. It is therefore not the responsibility of only one department, namely the Department of Bantu Administration and Development, but of all who fulfil a function here … I believe that a coordinating body under the personal leadership of the Prime Minister should be established and that the following institutions should be represented: the Office of the Prime Minister; the Executive Committee of South West Africa; Bantu Administration and Development; Foreign Affairs; the South African Defence Force; the Police; and the Bureau for State Security. The purpose of the committee should be to implement policy decisions in a coordinated manner.

I subsequently realised that I had accidentally omitted Coloured Affairs from the list, but they did come on board.

In the seven months after the committee, referred to as the Quo Vadis Committee, had been established, various issues pertaining to South West Africa were discussed. The situation in Owambo was so precarious that, despite the opinion of Jan de Wet to the contrary, I had little hope that an acceptable compromise with the Owambos could be reached. During this period strikes and threats of strikes caused much unrest. Secession of the northern areas and closer ties between the south of the country and South Africa were mentioned as possible solutions, although it was still too early to be talking about constitutional models. First we had to decide how to go about giving the inhabitants of the Territory the opportunity to determine their own future and, more importantly, which groups, parties or leaders should be involved in the process.

During the deliberations, the discussion I had with Clemens Kapuuo in New York kept coming back to me. Among other things, he had said that cooperation between the Hereros and Owambos would be impossible, because while the Herero nation was virtually being decimated during the war of 1904, the Owambos were multiplying. He was not prepared to submit to Owambo domination. Although it would have been unwise for me with my limited knowledge to express an opinion at that stage on a future constitutional dispensation, I had understanding for the fact that Kapuuo was in favour of cessation for the northern areas. My attitude was based less on conviction than on sympathy for my newfound friend. I had to be careful not to over-play Kapuuo in this company, as he was considered just as dangerous as SWAPO by the Department of Bantu Administration, as well as by its Minister, M.C. Botha, and the Commissioner General, Jan de Wet. From the outset it was obvious to me that, as in the case of the Advisory Council, they again wanted to fall back on the traditional and sympa-thetic leaders who were recognised by them.

General Hendrik van den Bergh (State Security) alleged that he had reliable information at his disposal about various black leaders in South West Africa and cited as an example that Fanuel Kozonguizi had been on the Bureau's pay sheet for a long time. He suggested that Ko-zonguizi's image be promoted so that he could become leader of the black groups and assured the meeting that he could control Kozon-guizi. I have never been able to establish the truth of Van den Bergh's allegations. In later years I would often clash with this short-sighted strategy. However, Kapuuo was my man and I would stand by him until his death in 1978. For me he was the epitome of a black national-ist, who, unlike SWAPO, was opposed to any form of violence.

During the deliberations of the Committee several proposals about a possible future strategy regarding South West Africa were tabled. There were many random discussions and ludicrous suggestions were sometimes made. I often had to act as devil's advocate. All that was important to me at that stage was that a platform should be created to give the people of South West Africa an opportunity to determine their own future. In my opinion thoughts expressed in the Committee were in most cases wishful thinking. I realised from the outset that each of the members had to protect their wickets by not batting too wildly.

To my surprise a proposal that was in line with the position I took on 30 January 1974 and which received strong support from the rep-resentatives of Foreign Affairs, was tabled by A.H. du Plessis. What it amounted to was that the Legislative Assembly of South West Africa under control of the National Party of South Africa should invite the leaders of the other population groups to participate in discussions on the future of South West Africa. The proposal eventually had the full support of all members of the Committee. I was especially pleased that the proposal had been tabled by Du Plessis, because it committed the National Party irrevocably to the principle of self-determination through deliberation.

During the second week of September 1974, Du Plessis undertook to submit the Committee's decision to the Prime Minister for approval. While he was briefing the Prime Minister in his office, Jan de Wet and I waited in the corridors of Parliament. Du Plessis joined us later with the following information: "I suffered a setback in the Prime Minister's office, but it's a long story."

When we met that evening, to my surprise, Du Plessis referred to an article in the magazine *To the Point* in which prominence had been given to the role I was playing in South West Africa. Du Plessis alleged that people were questioning the prominence I was receiving, feeling it was at his expense. I realised for the first time that Du Plessis saw me as a threat to his leadership. His fears were totally unfounded and I assured him of my absolute loyalty to him as my leader. "What I'm doing, I'm doing with conviction, and in the interests of the Party and the country. Any credit I receive in the process, I regard as a gain for the party," I explained. However, I also realised that the new initiative I had taken could founder due to Du Plessis's unsubstantiated fears. That was exactly what was happening.

Most of the evening's discussions centred on the Prime Minister's reaction to the Committee's proposal regarding a political conference. Du Plessis alleged that the Prime Minister had dismissed the plan. Later that evening, he said: "The more I listen to you two fellows, the more I am convinced that the Prime Minister is correct." With this he rejected the idea of a political conference, which he himself had proposed. Jan de Wet and I were both deeply disappointed. I could simply not believe that the Prime Minister would repudiate the plan, because it was not in line with his views about South West Africa as discussed in the Committee. I subsequently wondered why Jan de Wet and I had not been invited to accompany Du Plessis to inform the Prime Minister.

Jan de Wet had an appointment with the Prime Minister the next day about another matter. We decided to use this appointment to air our disappointment to the Prime Minister about his decision as conveyed to us by Du Plessis and to gain more clarity. The Prime Minister listened to us, assuring us throughout that he did not disagree with us. He instructed his Secretary to arrange a meeting with Du Plessis and Dr Hilgard Muller that same afternoon. Jan de Wet and I returned to Windhoek.

Upon our arrival I received a message at J.G. Strijdom Airport that I should phone Eben van Zijl. He informed me that Du Plessis requested that Jan de Wet and I return to Cape Town on the first available flight. I invited Van Zijl, who until that point had not been involved in the Committee, to accompany us.

The meeting took place in the Prime Minister's office the next morning. He immediately gave me the opportunity to state my case and I met with no resistance from him. He reiterated his support for the idea of a Conference. In reaction, Du Plessis said he had reconsidered the matter and that he supported the idea of a Conference. To this day I don't know exactly what was discussed between him and the Prime Minister, but I was so relieved that the plan had been salvaged that I no longer cared. I had every reason to doubt whether Du Plessis had conveyed the decision of the Committee to the Prime Minister at all. After the meeting, Du Plessis wanted to know from Jan de Wet and me: "What did you guys tell the 'Prime' that I couldn't?" My reply was that we probably looked so utterly disappointed that the Prime Minister felt sorry for us!

Jan de Wet, Eben Van Zijl and I returned to Windhoek that same afternoon. We agreed that a wonderful challenge lay ahead of us and I expressed the hope that the three of us would cooperate to make the plan a success. Unfortunately, Jan de Wet almost derailed the entire plan when he, shortly after his return, said in an exclusive interview with a journalist from the *Sunday Times*, Caroline Clark, that a confederal system was envisaged for South West Africa, whereas the intention was that the leaders of the various population groups decide jointly on a form of government. The Prime Minister repudiated him immediately, while I had no choice but to repudiate him in public as well, which made him very unhappy. I don't think he ever forgave me for this. This interlude was, in fact, the first indication that although he and I agreed in principle, Jan de Wet lost sight of the fact that it would be for the proposed conference to agree on a future constitutional dispensation.

The Turnhalle Conference takes shape

The next step was to formalise and execute the decisions taken in Cape Town. We had agreed in the Prime Minister's office that the Legislative Assembly should be the institution to extend the invitation to the leaders of the other population groups. However, since the Legislative Assembly would convene only in February 1975, it was suggested that the National Party's Top Executive Committee should meet as soon as possible to approve in principle and to request the Legislative Assembly to extend the invitations. I immediately started drafting a proposal. After discussing it with Van Zijl, I called A.H. du Plessis in Cape Town to read the draft to him. However, he informed me that he had already drafted a document, which was approved by the Prime Minister. Van Zijl and I were appointed to continue negotiations. Du Plessis would join us later if deemed necessary.

In the meantime our first task, pending approval by the Legislative Assembly, was to make contact with recognised leaders of the various population groups. The reason for not contacting political parties was that there were about 40 political parties in the country at that stage and no indication of their level of support, since none had ever participated in elections. In this respect the National Party was probably the only exception. Most of the parties, just like the National Party, had an ethnic support base. In some instances there was more than one political party in an ethnic group, mostly as a result of internal differences about tribal issues and leadership. SWAPO, whose existence had been the result of the inhumane contract labour system, had at no stage indicated an interest in collaborating with any of the internal parties over the future of the Territory, and was simply demanding that control of South West Africa be handed over to it.

The Owambos, Kavangos and Caprivians indicated through their leadership that they wanted to participate in the deliberations. In the case of the Hereros, I insisted that the true leaders under the leadership of Mr Clemens Kapuuo should be involved. Initially my colleagues didn't agree and rather wanted to involve the chiefs who had cooperated with the Government in the past. When this didn't happen, those leaders, amongst others Munjuku of the Mbanderus, joined SWAPO. Although the Namas were predominantly in favour of participation, leaders needed to be identified. The largest group among the Damaras, under leadership of Chief Justus //Garoëb, as would happen so often afterwards, kept a back door open and laid down conditions that were unacceptable.

The three groups to be focused on were therefore the Hereros, Damaras and Namas. Though Billy Marais and I had already made contact with these groups and had made great progress with the Hereros, I asked Van Zijl to take responsibility for the Namas and at the same time to maintain contact with the Basters and coloureds, although we didn't expect problems from the latter two. I would devote all my attention to the Hereros and Damaras, while both of us, when the time came, would extend formal invitations to the Owambos, Kavangos, Caprivians and Bushmen.

On his cooperation with the whites, Kapuuo declared that I had convinced him that I could be trusted. The two years of discussion between Kapuuo and myself resulted in not only him, but also the vast majority of the Herero nation being willing to cooperate with the white and the other groups to fight against SWAPO. Kapuuo's explanation to foreign journalists who questioned his change of opinion was: "I have always strived for independence for my country and its people. Now the South African Government, which never wanted to grant us independence, has offered it to us, while the UN always regarded SWAPO as the true leader of the people of South West Africa." As a result, he said, he had no option other than, in the interests of his people, to accept the word of the South African Government.

The fact that I was successful in gaining the cooperation of Kapuuo and the Hereros had a great influence on the other black and coloured inhabitants of our country. Van Zijl managed to involve the Namas. I made no headway with the leaders of the Damaras under Justus //Garoëb. Billy Marais and I spent many hours and even nights attempting to accomplish an agreement among the Damaras on their participation, without any real success. //Garoëb and his clan insisted that the conference be held under leadership of South Africa and the UN. The other leaders did not agree on this. It soon became evident that the Damara Council, due to lack of strong traditional leadership, as well as a plethora of political organisations without any support worth mentioning, was critically divided.

On 20 November 1974, Billy and I addressed the Damaras on participation in the planned conference. When we arrived, a few hundred people were waiting for us in the community hall. Our excitement did not last long, as it soon became evident that Simon Gobbs, a supporter of //Garoëb, had organised the meeting. Gobbs was intelligent and well spoken, and I knew I had a difficult day ahead of me. The meeting started at about ten that morning and by five in the afternoon we were still arguing. I had compared the planned conference to a building we were constructing with different bricks, and that we wanted to include a Damara brick. Mrs Mutenga, who participated from the floor, had scant interest in the building I wanted to construct. She said: "There is a big rift and debate alone will not help. First the whites must come into our houses, so that we can then go into their houses. That will be the first step to give us the right feeling."

The message was clear to me once again: For the Damaras it was about apartheid; about the disregard of their human dignity, not about constitutions and independence. Although I had often spoken about this in the previous ten years, it was again confirmed that the actual problem was about apartheid at a social level, and not apartheid at governmental level. Unfortunately, I had to end the meeting without having made any progress.

Although we had consistently referred to the "population groups" who were to be invited, it is important to note that political parties would in fact eventually represent the groups at the Conference. It was therefore necessary, as in the case with the whites, to identify and involve the majority party. In the case of the Damaras, we never succeeded. Justus //Garoëb, leader of the Damara Council who would later be crowned king of the Damaras, chose to walk the road on his own to the very end. Many considered him to be sitting on the fence and keeping his options open. It could be that this characteristic of //Garoëb and the Damaras had a historic base, but this is a subject for historians. I did, however, manage to involve the party of Engelhardt Christie (SWAPDUF) in the Conference, although there were doubts about its support among the Damaras.

War and peace – strange bedfellows

In 1974, the year in which the National Party of South West Africa would invite leaders of other population groups to jointly exercise their right to self-determination, other important events occurred that would have a fundamental influence on the future. Most important was undoubtedly the coup d'état in Portugal, which overthrew the government of Marcello Caetano on 25 April 1974. António de Spínola, who had published a book entitled *Portugal e o Futuro* (Portugal and the future) the previous year, was appointed leader of a military government. (Said book undoubtedly gave rise to the coup d'état.) The coup d'état would obviously have far-reaching consequences for the Portuguese colony Angola, and therefore also for South West Africa and South Africa. In Angola a full-scale armed rebellion had already been waging against the Portuguese government for over a decade. There were three rebel groups – the MPLA, the FNLA and UNITA – and thousands of Portuguese soldiers had lost their lives in the process.

I have already indicated that our local politicians were never informed about the activities of the South African Defence Force on the border and their involvement in Angola. Most of the information about this I gathered only years later from books written by military leaders. We were brought under the impression that the South African Defence Force took over the responsibility to protect the inhabitants on our northern border from the South African Police only because, so they alleged, the police could no longer handle it properly. During the armed struggle P.W. Botha as Minister of Defence often visited the operational area, but seldom stopped over in Windhoek. He often referred to a "total onslaught" against South Africa by communist-minded forces in Angola and elsewhere. However, it soon became common knowledge that the South African troops had crossed the border and had become involved in a power struggle among the rebel groups. Rumour had it that the attack on Calueque by Unita rebels was an excuse for the presence of South African troops in Angola. A soldier doing military service once told me that while he was stationed deep in Angola, he heard government representatives giving the assurance on the radio that there were no South African troops in Angola.

I was and am still not in a position to judge what the main consideration was for South Africa's involvement on our border and in Angola, but I am prepared to accept that both South Africa and America had reason to be concerned about the presence of, among others, Russian and Cuban forces in Angola. I am also prepared to accept that South Africa chose to defend the northern border of South West Africa rather than falling back to the Orange River. Reproaches by South Africans that the Border War was solely in the interests of South West Africa and

A true different opinion

for the protection of its inhabitants are therefore unjust. I would also be extremely unfair and ungrateful if I did not acknowledge that the South African Government and Defence Force prevented Russian- and Cuban-supported militant organisations from taking over our country by force and unilaterally imposing a governmental system on us. On occasion I have expressed my appreciation and gratitude to the parents of boys who fought on our border, as they gave us ten years to develop political and constitutional solutions and forced SWAPO to participate in them. I am also grateful that the South African Defence Force prevented our infrastructure from being destroyed, as happened in Angola.

Another important event in 1974 was the announcement by John Vorster of his détente policy to make contact and to establish friendly relations with African countries. President Kaunda of Zambia reacted positively to this, calling it "a voice of reason". Vorster followed it up with visits to various African states, and a meeting with Kaunda on the bridge at the Victoria Falls.

What I could never understand was that while we, with John Vorster's approval and support, were in the process of organising a constitutional conference and he had announced his détente policy, the South African Defence Force became involved in the civil war in Angola. This didn't make sense. Did John Vorster and his Minister of Defence agree on the military operations in Angola?

In the book *The SADF in the Border War* written by Leopold Scholtz, you will find possible explanations. The author claimed to have had access to sources that other authors writing on the war did not have. He refers to acts of terrorism, even as far south as Windhoek, Gobabis and Swakopmund, and continues as follows:

> This in itself was probably enough for the hawks in the SADF to eye the Angolan border, hot with desire to cross it and clobber SWAPO on the other side. But although P.W. Botha sympathised, Prime Minister John Vorster was a very cautious man and held back. He relented only when the governments of the United States, Zambia, Zaire and Liberia implored him to move in and stop the Marxist MPLA taking over in Angola … In fact, the Cabinet was deeply divided. Prime Minister Vorster, who had just invested a great deal of political capital in a détente policy with black African States – and even had some modest success – was unwilling to jeopardise it. He was supported by the influential head of the Bureau of State Security (popularly

known as BOSS), Hendrik van den Bergh, who felt that securing
the Angolan Border would be enough to keep SWAPO out. General Constant Viljoen wrote to P.W. Botha that Van den Bergh
saw Angola solely as a political matter ... Botha and his generals,
therefore, told Vorster that South Africa needed to take the initiative if it wanted to win the war. In the end, Vorster was won
over, although his misgivings remained.

Scholtz, like so many other researchers, remained silent about the
fact that John Vorster had already given his full support to a peaceful
process in South West Africa (Turnhalle Conference), and it would be
difficult to reconcile this with military action in Angola. Up until his
retirement as Prime Minister in 1978, John Vorster supported the peace
process in South West Africa. The announcement of the election based
on universal suffrage is proof of this. As Ongulumbashe is celebrated
every year as the beginning of the war, the Turnhalle Conference (with
the support of John Vorster) should be remembered as the beginning
of the peace and independence process.

The administration of the country is not neglected

While everything possible was being done to organise a constitutional
conference and the situation on the border was deteriorating, the work
of the Legislative Assembly continued unabated in Windhoek.

On 25 February 1974, in his opening speech at the last meeting of
the fourth session of the tenth Legislative Assembly, the Administrator
referred to various important issues. He started by congratulating the
Owambos and Kavangos on gaining self-governing status, each with
an elected legislative authority, executive committee, flag, anthem and
official language, and also on the establishment of a High Court. This
development took place in accordance with the Development of Self-
Government for Native Nations in South West Africa Act (No. 54 of
1968), which was being implemented by the Department of Bantu Administration of South Africa.

This strange action by a South African state department, about
which the South African Government should surely have been informed, was once again proof of the existence of different agendas
within the South African Government. Although it was agreed that
the inhabitants of South West Africa would have to determine their

own future by means of a constitutional conference, a government department was continuing to implement a policy of segregated political development. Even if separate development, and even independence for the northern territories, were among the possible options for the envisaged Conference, this presumptuous step by the South African Government was unacceptable. It would be argued later that this was intended to be an opportunity for the groups to gain experience in local government. Even if this was the intension, it was difficult to explain, and doubts arose about the Government's motives. As would happen several times in future, the prospect of status, salaries and black cars predominated responsible thinking. This obviously led the conservative white leaders and their supporters to believe that when all was said and done their policy would win the day. However, it was noticeable that the southern groups, especially the Namas, accepted this development in silence, while the Hereros themselves were not prepared to consider self-governance. Self-governance for the northern groups and possibly secession later on would eliminate their fear of Owambo dominance.

The Administrator took note of the impasse in the dialogue between South Africa and the Security Council of the UN, especially after the discussions over the previous two years between South Africa and the Secretary General and his personal representative. He mentioned the progress made in the development of the Kunene Hydro-electric Scheme (one of the positive recommendations of the Odendaal Report) and reported that since January the pump station at Calueque had been delivering six cubic metres of water per second to Ovamboland via a canal system. He also referred to the completion of the Van Eck Power Station on the outskirts of Windhoek, which had three generators, each with a capacity of 30 megawatts, while the Ruacana Project, which would cost R121 million once completed, would have a capacity of 320 megawatts.

The Administrator also presented a long list of impressive projects that had been completed over the previous years, or that were in the process of being completed. Among these he singled out the teachers training college under construction in Windhoek, as well as the new hospitals in Okakarara, Hereroland and Windhoek. There is no doubt that the South West African Administration carried out the responsibilities assigned to it very successfully.

The election campaign of 1974

The election of a new Legislative Assembly in 1974 took place against a background of a few conspicuous controversies in South Africa's handling of the South West situation, to which I have already referred.

During the election campaign, my leader A.H. du Plessis and I addressed a meeting in the school hall in Outjo, where I said:

> Peaceful solutions require concessions, giving up privileges, and making compromises, but unfortunately those who subscribe to this are regarded as cowards, pragmatists and even traitors, while those who opt for military solutions are glorified as heroes. It is incredible that many people would rather sacrifice their lives than their privileges. While we profess to upholding Christian principles, our Christian principles mostly carry apartheid signs proclaiming: Whites only. We teach our children to respect old people and to acknowledge the human dignity of others, but this often applies only to whites.

While I appealed for a change in attitudes and the acceptance that selfish privileges needed to be relinquished, my leader once again assured the white voters that apartheid had come to stay and would be enforced to the letter. He said to rowdy applause: "We promised you apartheid and gave it to you, right down to the benches at stations." Three years before the National Party would eventually split, our different approaches became blatantly obvious.

The National Party's opposition in this election was the Federal Party under leadership of Adv. Bryan O'Linn. The Federal Party succeeded Percy Niehaus's old United National South West Party (UNSWP). Du Plessis accordingly focused the greatest part of his speech in Outjo on that Party's election manifesto. The Party's election pamphlet was a short summary of a book, *The Future of South West Africa built on Reality*, published by Advocate O'Linn early in 1974. This book reflected O'Linn's personal view unequivocally; nowhere was it mentioned that the Federal Party had played any role in the compilation of the book. Likewise, this applied also to the election pamphlet. For that matter, it was relatively well known that within the Party there was no unanimity on the policy. Members of the Party told me that O'Linn acted autocratically and was not taking his people with him; and that this would mean the end of the Federal Party. This is what came to pass. When you objectively examine the proposals that followed, you would have expected O'Linn to gain lots of support (also from National Party ranks), because his proposals were conservative with a great deal of emphasis on group and ethnic interests, and with the South African Government and white Legislative Assembly playing a key role. What more could the conservative whites wish for?

The election pamphlet stated that South Africa has committed itself to a separate international status, as well as to self-determination and independence for South West Africa. Decisions about the realisation of this would be taken in cooperation with the UN Secretary General and in consultation with the population of the Territory. The expectation was that the population would have gained sufficient experience in self-governance to be ready for such a decision within ten years. On this basis, O'Linn came to the conclusion that the interests of the population groups in South West Africa could be managed and secured only by a federal system of government. You get the impression that he was worried about South Africa's concessions to the international community.

O'Linn was of the opinion that the South African Parliament and not the UN was the proper entity to set up a federal system for South West Africa. Since the Legislative Assembly had the required experience at its disposal, all legislative and administrative powers should be transferred to this body, and the Legislative Assembly was also to play a key role in the establishment of the federal structures. During the developmental process to achieve self-determination and independence, the Legislative Assembly would be responsible for the protection of minority rights, including the powers regarding local and ethnic matters that it would eventually transfer to the legislative assemblies of the different federal units. In the completed federal structures, the white Legislative Assembly would retain all its powers relating to the white population group. In the Central Legislative Assembly, each ethnic body would have equal representation. To conclude, O'Linn's plan made provision for a population group to withdraw from the Federation at independence, and even after that.

At the last session of the Legislative Assembly before the election, I emphasised that those who disagreed with our policy for whatever reason, should never doubt the sincerity of our objectives; that it was not our intention to serve the interests of only certain groups; and that each group was entitled at one stage or another to exercise its right to self-determination in such a way that no minority group would be dominated by majority groups. I criticised the Federal Party for coming up with an already-devised plan, while the majority of the population had not yet reached the stage where they could evaluate whether the plan was good or bad.

Already after my visit to the UN, my discussions with Kapuuo and the first meeting of the Committee in Cape Town, it was clear to me that the time that systems and solutions could be forced down the throats of our countrymen had passed. Self-governance for the various population groups made sense only in so far as it would give the groups the necessary experience to govern, as well as the opportunity to identify leaders and train them. By then it was also clear to me that if we wanted to succeed in involving our countrymen on the route to self-determination, we needed to leave all options open. At that stage neither the Federal Party nor the National Party was prepared to go that far, and I had to choose my words carefully not to derail the process that I had started with Kapuuo.

Bryan O'Linn's policy and proposals did not appeal to the white voters, and the Federal Party did not secure a single seat in the election. I had the greatest respect for Bryan as a jurist and a human being, and at one stage I defended him when he was unjustly criticised. It is, however, a fact that in spite of his knowledge and competence, he never succeeded in inspiring and mobilising people. He simply never was a leader, and was as such never relevant. He was clinical, obstinate, opinionated, and one can even suggest that he was somewhat conceited. Few people were enthused by his proposals; likewise a few hated him for his liberal views. In the political process he was never sufficiently contentious to play a decisive role.

Several years later and after a final settlement plan (Resolution 435) had been agreed upon by South Africa and the UN on the future of South West Africa, and had been accepted by the DTA and the National Party, Adv. O'Linn again climbed onto the political bandwagon with a new endeavour. He founded a new organisation, NPP 435, and published a book in which he detailed the aims of the organisation.

New faces in the Legislative Assembly

My third term was behind me and on 20 May 1974, four new members were sworn in, namely Bertie Botha, Paul Smit, Nico Jansen and Fanie

Vilonel. The elected members of the Executive Committee were Eben van Zijl, J.W.F. Pretorius, A. Brinkman and me.

In the meantime the members of the Executive Committee attended the opening ceremony of the Legislative Assemblies of the northern areas, and decided forthwith to reciprocate by inviting the members of their Executive Committees to the opening of our Legislative Assembly. The members informed the Assembly about abundant rain received in the northern and central parts of the country, between 100% and 150% above the average, while in the south the rainfall was up to three or four times the normal annual average. In the south lakes had formed between the dunes, while farmers on the South West side of the Orange River had suffered heavy losses. Harvests had been devastated, water furrows had been destroyed and valuable topsoil had washed away. As if this were not bad enough, a locust plague hit the south, which could fortunately be brought under control.

The Administrator provided figures on marketing, local processing and local consumption of beef in the previous year. The bad news was that cattle numbers were declining. He reported that there were about half a dozen farmers who were exclusively practising game farming, with market prices of R30 for ostriches and springbok, R225 for eland and R350 for giraffe. The budget he tabled projected an income of R85 229 000, which – added to the surplus of the previous year – would make R90 619 885 available for the new financial year.

I am expected to take the lead

As the senior member of the Executive Committee and in my capacity as leader of the House, I was expected to take the lead with regard to the political situation in the country. I emphasised that the population groups of South West Africa would have to put their heads together to plan for the future, since they were all entitled to exercise their right to self-determination in one way or another. I added that I believed that none of these groups would be able to exercise their right to self-determination without taking into consideration how this would affect the other groups in the Territory. I further pointed out that the whites still supported the policy of separate development, but that the non-white groups found it unacceptable and would rather support a unitary state – an undivided South West Africa.

It was already evident that in reality the policy of separate development was aimed only at development and gaining experience, and that the road to independence would be determined by consultation and negotiation. I emphasised that no one could deny that different population groups lived in South West Africa. To deny this would be fatal. I still held the view that each one of the groups concerned should be represented by their recognised leaders, and that the previous elections had shown that the Federal Party did not represent the whites.

Eben van Zijl pointed out that the National Party's policy of separate development had already been approved in nine elections, but he didn't clarify what the status of the policy was at that stage. He referred to the "chaotic situation" the National Party had inherited in 1948. Van Zijl contended that what had become known as "apartheid" had to be cleaned up first; after that came the positive part, namely separate development; and that we have reached the third phase, in which the signs of separate states are already visible.

He referred to the Transkei, spoke of a "historical day for us in South Africa" and indicated that South West Africa "had now been placed on the same path; that we would not curb the population groups' freedom; and would empower them to exercise their right to self-determination and develop sovereign independent states." Once that stage had been reached, according to him, contact with the non-whites would take place on inter-state and inter-nation levels. He stressed further that the representatives of these homeland governments should be received with the greatest respect as our guests. He concluded with the following words: "I want to emphasise again, Mr Chairman, that when contact is made on this basis, then it is contact on an inter-state level, or contact on an inter-nation level. Then it is not contact on an integration level and that is the big difference."

When you compare this explicit explanation of the National Party policy – essentially that of the National Party of South Africa – with the vague and careful manner in which I dealt with the policy of separate development, you can understand why I was viewed with suspicion in certain quarters. Nonetheless, in spite of this I was elected unanimously into all the senior positions I held in the National Party. My insistence on respect for the human dignity of my black countrymen was unequivocal throughout and I never tried to apologise for it. For this position I did, in fact, frequently receive appreciation and even praise from many people, including some colleagues in the Legislative Assembly. This encouraged me not to throw in the towel. It would, however, still take a long time to convince my colleagues that one needed to keep one's options open when entering a process of negotiations and that lines should not be drawn too soon. As mentioned before, I had to tread carefully, because I always said that I, in whatever I did, wanted to take my people with me.

On 20 November 1974, I tabled a proposal in the Legislative Assembly in which an invitation was extended to the different population groups to deliberate on political solutions for South West Africa. I stressed that all the population groups who lived in Namibia had a right to be here, including the white inhabitants, and that we would like to be accepted as such. We did not want to stay here as guests of Sam Nujoma; we wanted to be full and equal citizens of our common motherland. Likewise we could not expect the black inhabitants to be satisfied if they had no say in the future of their own country. I warned that complicated formulae to protect us against each other would not work as long as our attitudes towards each other did not change. In the past the whites had appropriated the right for themselves to develop the formulae on their own and expected the blacks to accept it. I continued:

> Today, on behalf of this Legislative Assembly and speaking for the whites in this country, I would like to extend a hand of friendship and cooperation to the non-whites, and invite them to cooperate with us towards a political solution that will make it possible for us to live together and in peace in this country – a country in which there must be a place for all of us. In this process, we need to free ourselves from prejudice and hatred. Hatred brings no resolution … any reasonable person will understand that when someone else works out a future for you, or makes plans for you, it can lead to suspicion. I want to appeal to every man and every woman in Namibia. Go home with the thoughts that I have repeatedly left with you. Go home and reflect on what you can do – not what the Government should do. What every person in South West Africa can do to improve relations in our country. There will have to be visible proof of our honesty and good intentions. If we approach the future in this spirit, we will succeed. If, above all, we have faith in God who controls the destiny of populations and nations, we have nothing to fear.

Van Zijl seconded the motion and cautioned that we should refrain from making unfair, unreasonable or irresponsible comments when discussing it. He summarised the early history of South West Africa, referring to the various options we had had in the past and explained why this proposal tabled in the Assembly was the best. He also elaborated on how the Conference should be set up and emphasised the necessity of the members being representative of the different population groups. On the subject of apartheid he said:

> On previous occasions I argued in this house that for me there
> is no principle involved in differentiating between the concepts
> "apartheid" and "separate development". In my view, apartheid
> is simply a practical and historical arrangement, and because
> there is no principle attached, I see no reason why apartheid
> measures that cause irritation and friction can't be done away
> with. When I say this I want to express myself very clearly. To-
> day I am not pleading to throw overboard and abolish the exist-
> ing order to which we have become accustomed. All I'm appeal-
> ing for is that we remove the dead wood from our social system.

He went further, saying that we first had to find a political solution, and asked that we should not blind ourselves with other issues. Once the main issue was solved and the Constitution written, these little side issues would sort themselves out. What he meant was that chopping away the dead wood should wait until the key problem, namely the political future, had been finalised.

I realised once again that the two of us were on different wavelengths. What was important to me was for my motion to be adopted. If there were certain reservations, the members would have the opportunity to debate these later.

Koos Pretorius reacted to my motion with a long speech and once again dug far back into history. He referred again to his Master's degree thesis, the Peace Conference of 1919, and also to the Mandate Agreement that had been agreed upon between South Africa and the League of Nations on the future of South West Africa. He explained that this agreement had been interpreted by the then Prime Minister, General Smuts, in such a way that independence of the C-mandate (in respect of South West Africa) was not the ultimate objective. Moreover, he tried to prove that only the holder of the mandate, South Africa, could request that the mandate be terminated and that the inhabitants could not make such an appeal.

It was clear from his speech that Pretorius did not object to the proposed deliberations, but that in his opinion whatever was decided, had to be based on South Africa's viewpoint, namely that the "peoples" of South West Africa should decide for themselves. He cited from the *South West Africa Survey 1967,* namely that "democracy means that people should have a say in their own affairs, and not in those of others." While he again maintained that the extension of the right to vote should keep pace with the growth of political awareness and competence of the voters, he stated that it was "… the policy of the South African Government to … limit the powers of an electorate to the group to which they belonged". It is therefore clear that Pretorius did not accept that all options were open for the envisaged conference, but that the National Party's principles should be the basis of any possible agreement.

A considerable number of members of the Assembly took part in the discussion. All of them supported the motion, albeit not all with the same enthusiasm. What was especially noticeable was the emphasis on the diversity of the population, the role of the white population group, and the importance that decisions be taken by consensus – probably because that would give the whites the right of veto.

I closed the debate with the following words: "You can never determine exactly which road you will follow to reach your destination, and only a fool, when he encounters mud pools, ditches and ridges on this road, would simply barge ahead stubbornly, and not adapt and seek alternative or better routes." It was already clear that all possible options had to be open and that a future dispensation would not be bound by any existing political framework. Nevertheless, the Legislative Assembly approved the motion and our journey towards a political conference and independence had commenced. But from here on the road became an uphill battle. However, turning back was no longer an option. We had taken the initiative to start deliberations, and now we had to walk the talk.

Independence for Angola is announced

While we continued looking for the road ahead, events in our neighbouring country, Angola, came to pass that would inevitably impact on our political future. We not only heard about this, but were eyewitnesses to a dispensation coming to an end as a result of short-sightedness.

On 15 January 1975, Portugal and the three Angolan independence movements – the MPLA, FNLA and UNITA – signed an agreement stating that Angola would become an independent country on 11 November 1975. The prospects of an independent Angola and a democratic election of a government inevitably resulted in the three rebel groups, which until then had been united against the Portuguese regime, engaging in a civil war. As usually happens in circumstances such as these, other powers, for different reasons, sided with the different rebel groups.

It was during this period that about 135 000 Portuguese fled Angola. Many of them, at a rate of about 1500 per week, crossed the border into South West Africa at Oshikango, travelling in fully loaded trucks, tractors, trailers and overloaded sedan vehicles. It was clear that they had left Angola in great haste with as many of their earthly possessions as they could possibly take with them. Many were accommodated temporarily in camps at Grootfontein where the townspeople took care of them. They sold many of their belongings to the local people. Those who wanted to return to Portugal sold virtually everything to pay for their flight tickets. The refugees spoke of foreign powers operating in Angola that were supporting the different rebel groups with heavy equipment and even tanks. They referred specifically to the Russians.

All options remain open, but to whom?

On 13 March 1975, the Administrator announced: "As the representative of the Government of South Africa, I declare unequivocally that all options regarding the future political and constitutional setup of the Territory are open and every conceivable option or options can be raised and discussed." He emphasised that SWAPO could not claim to represent all the inhabitants of South West Africa. He also referred to developments in Southern Africa resulting from the coup in Portugal, and to the negotiations between the Rhodesian Government and black political parties of that country, as well as the prospects of Mozambique attaining independence in that same year. The Administrator further mentioned the role the South African Prime Minister had played to relieve tension in Africa, for which he had received praise worldwide.

As mentioned earlier, in all their declarations and documents South Africa referred to the inhabitants of SWA as "peoples" (population groups), and not as "people" (population). It is surprising that many people never picked up on this. Clarification was needed on this count, and I explained it as follows:

> The inhabitants of the country consist of different population groups that live together within the borders of the country, all of them contributing towards the development of the country. These people have no other home and provision will have to be made to accommodate them within the borders of the country and for their rights and entitlements to be respected. But then it must not be forgotten that the white inhabitants also have an inherent right to be here, especially in view of the contribution they have made towards developing the country, and that the whites are not prepared to live here as guests of any government.

I emphasised that we had to accept the existence of the different groups in the country as a fact, and should not try and find any other reasons for this. The South African Government had implemented its policy of separate development in the Territory because it believed that this was the best way to promote the interests of the different groups. Unfortunately, this policy was developed and implemented only by whites. For this reason and also because in practice the policy had not achieved the lofty objectives that had been envisaged, the other population groups regarded it with great suspicion. This meant that we now had to grant them the opportunity to deliberate on the future with the whites. I again stressed that we had to approach the deliberations with an open mind, because if we were to come to the conference table with preconceived ideas and inflexible viewpoints, the discussions would not succeed. The exchange of viewpoints would concern not only the constitutional future of the country, but also a future social and economic pattern. I believed firmly throughout that as far as possible each population group had to be represented by democratically elected representatives, and that a large number of small dissident parties mushrooming to take part in the deliberations would only lead to confusion.

In his contribution to the debate Eben van Zijl referred to the difficulties of bringing the Basters, Namas and coloureds to the conference table, emphasising that groups would not be represented by political parties. However, this is not how the process eventually developed. The National Party majority in the Legislative Assembly extended an invitation to the other groups, and although they took their seats at the

Conference according to their groups, in most cases the representatives were leaders of political parties. Van Zijl and I, who were supposed to represent the whites in the Conference, could do nothing without the approval of the National Party.

Frans van Zyl tabled an important motion during the session, in which he promised the support of the Legislative Assembly to the Executive Committee in its endeavours to promote good relations among the people of South West Africa. The Executive Committee was requested to pay attention to measures and practices that could impede the process of attaining better relations. In my opinion this was an outstanding speech and it received wide support from the Assembly. Frans van Zyl, Eben van Zijl's brother, had always impressed me as a logical thinker and a moderate politician. Needless to say, I was elated about the motion, as I had been appealing in the Assembly for better human relations since 1964.

I accepted the directive on behalf of the Executive Committee, but warned that the problem could not be solved by removing a few signboards. To my mind too many people expected Government to make or do away with laws to improve dispositions within the country. The responsibility to live according to Christian principles and maintain good human relations lies with each and every Christian. I emphasised that it was a difficult directive, that it covered a wide range of issues, and that it would have to be implemented in great haste.

A committee under chairmanship of Van Zyl then made proposals that were discussed in a caucus meeting, but which led to serious differences of opinion. It soon became apparent that most of my colleagues were not prepared to go all the way. Their only concession was to allow hotels that had applied for international status to accommodate non-white guests, whereas the theatre – under the management of the South West African Performing Arts Council (SWAPAC) – would still be open only to whites.

I simply could not accept that a man like Dr Ben Africa of Rehoboth, who was to be one of the participants in the deliberations, would not be allowed to attend a performance in the theatre. He was not only a medical practitioner, but also a music lover who could play more than one musical instrument. When I asked – as a concession – whether non-whites could be allowed to attend dress rehearsals, the objection was that they would then use the toilet facilities and that this would have serious ramifications for the National Party. It became clear that the National Party was prepared to accept only cosmetic changes, which in my opinion would have been an insult to my future conference delegates. I realised that the road ahead would not be easy, and that it would require a great deal of self-discipline on my part.

Were we playing for time?

In reply to a frequently asked question, namely whether we were playing for time, my answer was that uncertainty about the future for an indefinite period had never been in the interests of any country. We in South West Africa could also not afford to live in uncertainty about what exactly the future held in store for us. I further appealed to all the people of South West Africa not to become embroiled in petty politics. I gave assurances to the Assembly that Van Zijl and I would be going to the Conference with open minds, believing that we would reach consensus. About the National Party's policy of separate development, I said it contained all the elements that could lead to a peaceful solution, especially since it did not stipulate a final dispensation. This was stated explicitly by South Africa in the *South West Africa Survey 1967*. Separate development, however, gave all the groups the opportunity to gain experience in all facets of governance. In conclusion, I called on all the other population groups to choose sides for what they believed was right without fear, and not to allow themselves to be intimidated.

Within a few days after this positive discussion in the Assembly, Koos Pretorius tabled a draft ordinance for the summary and consolidation of certain legislation on education. At one stage during his explanation of the draft, he deviated so much from the actual topic under discussion that the Chairman had to call him to order. Again he harped repeatedly on liberal thinking, socialism and humanism, and the right of every ethnic group to be entitled to claiming certain rights as a nation or as an ethnic group. He referred to an equalisation process that was taking place globally and that, in the endeavour to avoid conflict, people must be seen as individuals and not as members of a nation or ethnic group. He stated furthermore: "The fundamental principle for South Africa is the Christian national principle, with its point of departure that in the eyes of God all creatures are equal, but that there is a rich diversity that we must accept not only among nations but also among races."

For me it was about the acknowledgement of human dignity and the elimination of discrimination based merely on race and colour. For me the human being has always been more important than the group. The individual remains the smallest possible minority that needs to be protected, which is why I supported The Charter of Fundamental Rights from the outset. The individual can be suppressed for various reasons, even by his group, his family or his party. I personally experienced this in the National Party and in the Dutch Reformed Church.

The Turnhalle Conference – the first steps

On 1 September 1975, the Constitutional Conference officially convened in the historic Turnhalle (gymnastics hall) building, which had been renovated into a worthy venue for an equally worthy historical event. To succeed in bringing the leaders of the 11 population groups together to deliberate on the future of South West Africa was no mean feat. It was not only a case of gaining the cooperation of the leaders, but also of overcoming distrust and creating enthusiasm for the task at hand. However, the biggest challenge still lay ahead, and this was to maintain and strengthen cooperation among the leaders. Although they were willing to give the Turnhalle Conference a try, there was still a high degree of scepticism and mistrust towards the whites.

At the beginning of the Constitutional Conference the leaders agreed to appoint a Credentials Committee to decide on the representation of the various population groups in the Conference. From the very beginning this led to serious problems. Initially it was decided that each delegation would consist of four members, but when the doors of the Turnhalle opened that morning, there were hordes of people. The Hereros arrived with more than 70 prospective candidates, while the Caprivians showed up with two chiefs – Chief Mamili and Chief Moraliswani – who represented the two main tribes in the Caprivi, each tribe having its own entourage. Neither of these was willing to accept the leadership of the other. The Herero delegation, under leadership of Clemens Kapuuo, included two Mbanderu chiefs who insisted on taking part as Herero/Banderu. The coloureds and the Basters were divided into different political parties, making it difficult to convince them to work as one team. And so I can continue. It took wisdom and patience to sort out these problems, but fortunately we managed to achieve this and could move on to other problems, of which there were many.

We had to decide next on the chairmanship of the Conference, and again this was not an easy task. Should it be someone from outside or one of the representatives within the ranks of the Conference? After long deliberations, it was decided that each delegation would nominate a person to serve on the Chairman's Committee and that the chairmanship would then rotate on a daily basis. After a few days it became clear that this was not a good plan. The Committee then recommended that I act as Chairperson on a full-time basis. The General Assembly accepted the proposal. I considered it a privilege to chair the Conference to the end. I found it a wonderful opportunity to gain experience in upholding impartiality, fairness and patience. This sometimes required me to make rulings that my own delegation did not always understand. Nonetheless, in this way I won the trust and confidence of the representatives.

One of the first decisions of the General Assembly of the Constitutional Conference was to adopt a Declaration of Intent. I first contemplated the idea of such a declaration when a foreign journalist told me that there were African countries that did not necessarily expect the situation in South West Africa to change overnight, but that they would like to see a definite declaration of intent from our side. I raised the idea with my colleagues, who found it acceptable. My white colleague, Van Zijl, initially proposed that a draft constitution be drawn up as a basis for the discussions. It wasn't clear who should draft such a document and how long it would take. In any case, drafting a constitution was one of the tasks the Conference had to accomplish. We then agreed that the Conference should draft a Declaration of Intent. The process, however, turned out to be more difficult than I had expected, especially when you anticipated decisions in the process that could limit future options. That, in fact, is exactly what happened, but we realised this only much later.

In the meantime the Herero delegation had employed the services of an American lawyer, Stuart Schwartz, who submitted a draft to me that made provision inter alia for the immediate establishment of an interim government. This interim government would then be responsible for drafting a constitution. This did not make sense to me and I found it unacceptable. I gained the impression that these agents from abroad, and especially from the USA, wanted a government with whom they could conduct business as soon as possible. My supposition was subsequently confirmed when they were prepared to spend large amounts of money to entertain conference delegates locally and abroad.

After long deliberations, the Conference succeeded in reaching consensus on the following Declaration of Intent:

- That in the execution of our right to self-determination and independence we are voluntarily meeting in this Conference to deliberate on the constitutional future of South West Africa.
- That we condemn and reject in the strongest terms the use of violence or any form of improper interference with a view to overthrowing the existing order or to imposing a new dispensation.
- That we are determined to resolve our future ourselves by means of peaceful negotiation and cooperation.
- That, bearing in mind the particular circumstances of each of the population groups, it is our set intention to serve and honour their wishes and interests in the execution of this task.
- That, bearing in mind the inter-dependence of the different population groups and the interests of South West Africa as a whole, we therefore intend to create a form of government that will guarantee population groups having the greatest possible say in their own affairs as well as the greatest possible say in national affairs, and which will protect the rights of minorities and ensure that law and justice is upheld for all.

The draft, proposed by Eben van Zijl, initially read that each population group would have the greatest possible say in their own affairs without clearly defining their say in public affairs. The delegates were vehemently opposed to this formulation and Van Zijl then changed the wording to read as it was eventually accepted. Even the modified version of this clause would later result in vital differences of opinion in the Standing Committee on Standing Rules and Orders.

With the acceptance of the Declaration of Intent, independence for the Territory was at least agreed to in principle, which diametrically contradicted the policy that the National Party had been propagating for decades. Secondly, the principle of power-sharing was accepted

once it was agreed that population groups would also have the greatest possible degree of authority in national affairs. Thirdly, it was spelt
out more clearly than ever before that discrimination on the basis of
race or colour had to be eliminated.

After the approval of the Declaration by the Conference, I urged
Eben van Zijl that the National Party's Excecutive be informed at all
times about important decisions made. I was concerned about speakers in the Legislative Assembly making statements that could be contradictory to the principles already accepted in the Declaration of Intent. I discussed this with the leader, A.H. du Plessis, but his opinion
was that the time was not yet ripe to inform the Party. This approach
would create serious problems for the party later.

The Conference then decided to establish the following Advisory
Committees:

- The First Committee, which had to investigate discriminatory practices regarding salaries, wages and general conditions of services at
all levels, as well as the implementation of the principle of equal pay
for equal work, qualifications and productivity.
- The Second Committee, which had to draft an economic development plan for South West Africa.
- The Third Committee, which had to investigate social practices that
discriminated on the basis of race and colour.
- The Fourth Committee, which had to make recommendations on
educational matters, in particular equal standards regarding syllabi,
teaching facilities, obligatory education, and tertiary educational institutions.
- The Standing Committee or Constituent Committee, of which I was
Chairman, which was tasked with developing a draft constitution
for South West Africa.

Except for the approval of the Declaration of Intent, progress on the
development of a constitutional model was initially slow. However,
it must be taken into account that the Turnhalle Conference was the
first joint effort by white and black inhabitants to work out a future
and generally acceptable dispensation for our country. It must also be
borne in mind that when such a large group of people – most of whom
had little or no administrative experience – had to work on such a complicated process they needed sufficient time to orient themselves in
respect of political, economic, social and governmental issues.

I realised from the outset that a favourable atmosphere and disposition had to be created for the constitutional deliberations to succeed. Distrust had to disappear first. The other groups also had to be convinced that freedom and independence would carry some responsibilities, and that the highest form of freedom could be found in the submission to self-imposed laws. Freedom does not mean dissipation and lawlessness, and may also not mean curbing the freedom of other people or groups.

In our initial discussions great emphasis was placed on these values. Events in Angola opened the eyes of the participants in the Conference to become realistic. For all of us this was the best example of how not to exercise your right to self-determination. It was evident right from the outset that the delegates had no intention of repeating the mistakes that had been made elsewhere in Africa where constitutions were drafted too hastily and were then equally rapidly disregarded and violated. I was prepared to make concessions to appease the black and coloured inhabitants of the country in economic and social fields and did not feel threatened in these areas.

Although we couldn't afford to drag our feet indefinitely regarding progress on constitutional and political issues, we had to accept that it would be an evolutionary process and that it would be in nobody's interest to do it any other way. I expressed the conviction that if we could convince the international community of our sincere intentions and in the meantime did not hesitate to do the things we had undertaken to do in our Declaration of Intent, we would be afforded the time to do it.

The reaction of the National Party to the Conference

Since I was the Vice-Chairman of the National Party, Party leader in the Legislative Assembly, and Chairman of the National Party Caucus at that stage, it was a matter of course that I would also act as leader of the white delegation at the Constitutional Conference. However, Van Zijl had a different opinion, alleging that the Legislative Assembly had not appointed a leader for the delegation. This attitude was not the first manifestation of his pettiness – a characteristic that would cause serious misunderstanding among the leaders of the National Party.

Each delegation at the Constitutional Conference had a specific leader and the other leaders generally accepted me as the leader of the white delegation, for reasons already mentioned. The fact that the

Legislative Assembly had not taken a definite decision about this also holds no water, because when A.H. du Plessis joined the delegation later, he automatically – on the basis of his seniority – became its leader, without the Legislative Assembly having taken such a decision.

I realised that, should differences of opinion arise, a two-man delegation would soon lead to serious difficulties, so I suggested to Van Zijl that all the members of the Legislative Assembly should be members of the white delegation. This would not necessarily mean that they would all have to attend the Conference full time. It would, however, result in them continually being informed on decisions taken in the Conference and prevent contradictory statements being made in public. I decided to submit my proposal at the next meeting of the Party Caucus.

When I suggested to the National Party Caucus in the Legislative Assembly on 15 September 1975, just two weeks after the first session of the Conference, that the white delegation be extended to include all the members of the Assembly, Frans van Zyl immediately suggested that the leader of the Party, Du Plessis, be asked to join the delegation full time. It would later surface that the decision for Du Plessis to become a member of the white delegation had already been taken behind my back before the caucus. This was undoubtedly done because members of the caucus did not trust me – for reasons I could not fathom. I learnt later that I was apparently too liberal in their opinion and needed to be neutralised by Du Plessis.

During this same period I had an appointment with Prime Minister John Vorster. He told me that he had already been informed by a journalist that Du Plessis would be joining the white delegation at the Conference. John Vorster was not too pleased with Du Plessis's decision, saying that Du Plessis would have to resign as member of the House of Assembly and as a Minister of the South African Parliament.

I also had serious objections to Du Plessis's participation in the Conference. In my view, he as leader of the Party could continue playing a leading role in the process without joining the delegation permanently, and that membership of the House of Assembly and the Cabinet was of great importance to us at that stage, since the South African Cabinet had very important decisions to take with regard to South West Africa. However, he was apparently of the opinion that he would not have to resign as Minister until the Prime Minister explicitly told him to do so.

I felt that in view of the prevailing sentiments in South West Africa, Du Plessis's return would be a contentious issue. I knew that a substantial section of the population that was highly enthusiastic about progress made by the Conference would raise questions about the reasons for his return and would have reservations about the wisdom of such a step.

I remembered the discussion we had in Du Plessis's apartment in Cape Town when he had expressed his concern about the prominence I had been receiving from the media and other quarters. I tried my best to influence him not to accept the invitation and to convince him that my proposal of members of the Legislative Assembly joining the conference team was a better option. However, he was determined to return to Windhoek.

His decision caused consternation in South West Africa. There was great dissatisfaction among all the population groups, especially among the whites – more specifically the German-speaking whites. For the first time A.H. du Plessis became a controversial figure – exactly what I wanted to avoid. All the questions I expected would be asked were indeed asked. Predictions were already being made that A.H. du Plessis and Eben van Zijl would cause the Turnhalle Conference to fail. To my mind the fears were unfounded, but I nevertheless expected the negative reaction. It was a pity that Du Plessis had allowed himself to be forced into this position.

We travel abroad

Shortly after these developments, 33 representatives of the Turnhalle Conference departed on an extended trip to the United States of America, Great Britain and Germany. For most of them this was their first visit abroad. In contrast to their SWAPO counterparts, who had lived and studied overseas for long periods, this was the first time they would be exposed to an alien and foreign world. In America we visited Indian reservations, each with its own tribal office. We were taken to a modern school that had been built for them [the Indians] by some or other organisation. Peter Kalangula of the Owambos wanted to know if they could read the Bible in their own language, boasting that he could do so in his country.

We visited Washington where we were entertained by Pik Botha, then South Africa's Ambassador to America, in his official residence.

Many important guests had been invited, but the problem was that some of the people in our group were not that conversant in English. This, however, was not too much of a problem, as the waiters were plying us with drinks and the men soon felt at home. I did not enjoy the evening, and left the serious discussions to Kapuuo, Kalangula, Eben, Billy and others who spoke the language well. My responsibility was to make sure that my colleagues did not overdo the drinks that were being offered so readily. One of our team, Sylvester Mootseng, who was a member of a men's choir back in Windhoek, had the habit of breaking into song at the top of his voice when he was slightly inebriated. This I had heard from Gregor Tibinyane – almost too late. I asked Billy to give me a hand by keeping an eye on Sylvester, and to take him outside immediately to the bus parked in front of the residence should he start singing. After a while I saw Billy and Mootseng descending the long staircase; but it was too late. Mootseng started singing *Bearing the Cross of Jesus* at the top of his voice. In front of the building Billy and Mootseng encountered a long queue of SWAPO protestors holding candles. Mootseng refused to stay in the bus and promised not to sing again. Later that evening when we asked one of the protestors what they were demonstrating against, he had no idea; he was probably only earning a little pocket money.

In New York we were accommodated in a very luxurious hotel, and the men dropped in at a nightclub. Afterwards Kashe, the Bushman, had little to say about the fact that the dancer was half-naked, but was very firm about the fact that she couldn't dance. Johannes Karuaihe, Kapuuo's secretary, related how surprised he had been when, looking out of his bedroom window, he saw white homeless people sleeping under cardboard boxes on the pavement. Later, when we were in London, the men became acquainted with white prostitutes who cornered them in the lifts. In Berlin a taxi driver came to get me in the middle of the night to fetch one of my colleagues from a nightclub, where his tab for the evening was running too high. I didn't judge them too harshly, because for them this was a whole new world, and they were only doing what many more experienced people had done before.

A new experience was in store for Alfons Majavero. He was from Kavango and was musically gifted, the accordion being his instrument. I invited him to visit the Berlin Opera House with me. I didn't know which opera was being performed that evening, and unfortunately for us, it turned out to be a very modern German one. Even I couldn't make much sense of it, but when the lights went on at interval, Alfons was clearly relieved that it was over. When he realised that the performance wasn't over yet, he wasn't that enthusiastic about his first visit to an opera house.

While our visit abroad couldn't exactly be described as a political breakthrough, we did use the various press conferences organised for us to state our case. At these conferences most of the questions were addressed to Clemens Kapuuo and myself. It was obvious that Van Zijl did not like this. At our last press conference I asked him to give a general introduction, which I think he handled well.

After the press conference he asked a group of coloureds what it was they saw in the man Dirk Mudge, because he, Van Zijl, was after all the person with the knowledge and brains. According to him it was just his human relations that weren't as good as mine. As proof [of his intellect] he then argued that I had asked him to do the introduction at the news conference, because – according to him – I was unable to do it myself. Van Zijl would subsequently deny categorically that he had said this.

This incident gave me even greater clarity about the reason for Du Plessis's return to Windhoek. Indeed, following our return from abroad, Du Plessis summoned me to his farm to ask me what my objections against and problems with him and Van Zijl actually were. I replied that I had no objections against him as a person and that I accepted him as a friend and a leader, but that I was convinced he had made a mistake returning to South West Africa with the purpose of participating in the Conference full time. Although he didn't agree with me, he intimated that he accepted my bona fides. I reminded Du Plessis of the incident in 1969 when Van Zijl and Koos Pretorius had changed the Constitution of the Party to prevent me from becoming deputy leader of the Party. It was now six years later, and Van Zijl and Fanie Vilonel were still playing the same game. In my opinion Van Zijl had once again succeeded in getting someone else, this time the leader of the Party, to do his work for him – and with tragic consequences for the leader!

The inner workings at the Conference

When the Conference resumed its sessions in 1976, we initially concentrated on the business of the various committees. Du Plessis joined
the Committee on social issues. It was clear from the outset that he did
not easily connect with the black leaders. During teatimes he and Van
Zijl would mostly sit alone at a small table. His explanation was that
he would rather maintain his position by not mixing with the other
leaders on an informal level. Van Zijl, who prior to Du Plessis's return
mixed easily with the black leaders, now also stopped doing this.

Anyone who knows anything about the art of persuasion should
know that it was not always achieved in conference halls, but mostly
in private conversations. After Du Plessis's return, this responsibility,
as far as the white delegation was concerned, rested squarely on Billy's
and my shoulders. Although our delegation was now larger, our work
had increased. This meant that Billy and I now had to work late into
the night to maintain a good spirit and attitude in the Conference. After adjournment of the meetings and during weekends my two white
colleagues were simply not available. Every delegation at the Conference can attest to this.

Later that year when we started the activities of the Standing Committee, I often had to use my position as Chairman to prevent decisions
from being forced onto inexperienced delegates. I never put unnecessary pressure on the other leaders to make quick decisions, because I
firmly believed that they should know and understand exactly what
they were deciding on, otherwise the issue would simply reappear on
the agenda.

A characteristic of our black and coloured colleagues that we whites
do not always understand is the fact that for them a matter is not easily
finalised. The Basters often, when making a statement, would add that
they "were speaking under correction", meaning that they could possibly change their point of view later. The question was not whether
a decision had been made, but whether the decision had been understood and accepted – hence my statement that a constitution for our
country should not be written on paper alone, but also in the hearts of
the people.

Van Zijl and other leaders were often irritated because I didn't finalise issues more rapidly. However, I believed firmly that if we wanted
to succeed, we needed to gain consensus on important issues step by

step. To use an example, the Standing Committee agreed fairly soon on the principle of a three-tier governmental system, but it was clear to me from the outset that there were major differences of opinion on the areas of authority of the second-tier authorities, and that this was the crux of our problem, which, if not handled correctly, could derail the entire process.

As Chairman it was vital that I understand from the outset how my black and coloured colleagues thought and reasoned. I soon realised that they, due to their background and experience, considered problems from a different angle than we did. I hadn't come to know the delegates in conference rooms, but through long and incisive personal discussions, which took up a great deal of time and energy. My white colleagues had never had these experiences; it seemed they were under the impression that at a meeting you could sell any clever plan to the black leaders. With the exception of one or two, such as Billy Marais, few people are aware of how much time we had spent to get the other leaders to understand certain concepts, and how difficult it was to convince them of the sincerity of the whites. At the same time the team had to be kept together. At times there was tension not only among the groups, but also within the groups. On occasion, Billy and I were summoned to help solve an internal problem. This was how I got to know the delegates well, every one of them. I frequently responded not to what they had said, but to what I knew they were trying to say.

There were one or two delegates who on occasion tried to undermine my position, but I usually knew about this within a few hours. However, on the whole I can say that the loyalty of these people was unprecedented once they had accepted you. To win their trust, however, required much more than clever arguments. This begs, more than anything else, an approach that is tangible. In that respect my white colleagues, to say the least, were amateurs. Their attitude left much to be desired. With all the will in the world, they could not buy goodwill.

The division of functions

Before I proceed to examine the governmental system we had devised in the Turnhalle, I first want to focus on the actual situation in South West Africa for which we had to find a solution. Only an exceedingly uninformed person would deny the fact that South West Africa has a heterogeneous population. The population consists of different population groups that differ significantly from one another in terms of language, culture and tradition. It must be borne in mind that in most cases members of the different population groups are not confined to specific geographical areas. In some cases they live mainly outside the areas regarded as their homelands, while the coloureds have no specific geographical homeland. Another significant fact is that the population groups actually accept that they differ from one another, but never that they are inferior to any other group.

It must also be accepted that segregation among people based on their population group is acceptable to the greater section of the population, but that segregation on the basis of colour or race is demeaning and cannot be defended. This created the impression that protection was only for the white groups. The fact that some public amenities were reserved for whites only, while all the other groups had to share amenities that were reserved for "non-whites" is indefensible.

After a three-tier government system, which implied a Representative Authority for each ethnic group, was accepted in principle (this did not take long), differences of opinion arose regarding the area of authority and the division of functions between the different levels of government. The draft constitution drawn up by the Standing Committee reads as follows (on this issue):

> 3. Area of authority of a Representative Authority.
>> (i) A Representative Authority has personal authority over all those persons who, according to legislation of the Representative Authority concerned, are members of the population group over which this particular Authority was established and in effect regarding the matters that have been allocated to the Authority in question.
>> (ii) When the powers and functions of the Representative Authorities also involve territory and landownership, this relates only to the land (except in certain local authority municipal areas) that is part of traditional territories and land that is owned by members of the Representative Authority concerned that resorts under the jurisdiction of the authority in question.

The remaining functions would then be the responsibility of the Central Government.

It is my contention that very few voters who voted in the referendum for the Turnhalle Constitution really understood it, because it was, in fact, unintelligible, and my colleagues – not only my white colleagues – and I differed about its interpretation from the outset. I, for instance, emphasised the principle that no inhabitant of our country may be subjected to laws and regulations that apply to the area in which he or she normally resides without him or her having been represented in the authority that made the law.

In the different traditional areas, for example Caprivi, Kavango, Ovamboland, Hereroland, Damaraland, Namaland, Bushmanland and Rehoboth, the authority concerned would be responsible for roads, traffic control, administration of nature conservation, economic development, agricultural credit, landownership and surface rights, to mention but a few. But what about the whites and coloureds? In which areas must they build roads and conserve nature; and control traffic, landownership and surface rights? In terms of the draft constitution, the area of authority where the white representative authority would execute its functions was described as "the land that belongs to the white population group". This implied that the total southern farming area as well as the urban areas owned by the whites, would resort under the white representative authority. Black and coloured people who happened to be living in these areas would therefore be subject to the laws and regulations of the white authority.

Indeed, the Conference was extremely divided on the idea of geographical areas of authority, while some of the delegates would consider this only if excessive land claims were considered. The black and coloured delegates consistently objected to the idea that members of their population group living in the so-called white areas had to – in terms of second-tier functions – be subjected to an authority in which they had no say. This was not the only unacceptable component of the draft constitution. Already at this early stage a deadlock seemed unavoidable to me. • See the demographics as they are

The bait of an interim government

I mentioned earlier that the white delegation did not favour an interim government, but rather wanted to draft a constitution. However, while we were struggling in the Standing Committee with the division of functions and the land issue was still pending, Van Zijl unexpectedly came with the proposal that an interim government be established as soon as possible and that South West Africa become independent on 31 December 1978. The fact that Van Zijl and Du Plessis had so unexpectedly changed their views on an interim government and were in such a hurry to have it finalised made me suspicious. My suspicions were soon confirmed.

partial incorporation

They knew that an interim government with all the privileges associated with it would be an attractive prospect for the representatives, and that it would render them less critical as regards the proposals of the white delegation. It would also suit the foreign advisers of some of the delegations extremely well. Immediately after tabling the proposal, my white colleagues emphasised the fact that, if we wanted to introduce an interim government soon, we would have to move fast on the decisions regarding the division of functions. They added that the delegates would be given the opportunity to make changes at a later stage, should they not be completely satisfied with the division initially.

Despite my misgivings about the secretive way in which this proposal had come about, I thought the plan had some merit. Putting it into practice would be the best way to demonstrate which functions belonged where. There was talk about salaries for ministers, official residences and black cars, and arguments about the division of functions became fewer. However, I could not make peace with the plan to introduce an interim government in terms of a half-completed constitution, but realised that the necessary legislation would have to be drafted by South Africa before we could proceed with the formal inception of the planned interim government. Experienced legal drafters would no doubt be aware of the impracticability of the Turnhalle Constitution and refer it back to the Conference. Things could therefore not happen overnight and we would have enough time to find solutions. Events on other levels contributed to the fact that the planned interim government never became a reality, but more about this later.

The public must be informed

While we in the Standing Committee were trying to find solutions in camera, I realised that the people whom we were representing were totally uninformed about what was happening in the Conference. Because the meetings of the Committee were not open to the media, the information to the general public was limited to leaks to the press by members of the Conference. Even members of the National Party and the Legislative Assembly were not informed, because Du Plessis felt the time was not yet ripe to inform them. In the Legislative Assembly Koos Pretorius was still fighting against the division of powers, while his leader had already accepted it.

I suggested to my colleagues that an information committee be established and that meetings be held countrywide to inform the population about our plans and decisions. I was convinced that it was not enough to reach consensus among the leaders, but that the greatest possible level of acceptance should also be reached among the population. At these meetings we would also be able to determine the views of the wider public.

My white colleagues did not agree, being of the opinion that each leader should inform his own population group. Because there were pockets of members of all the population groups in virtually every small town in South West Africa, it would mean that 11 meetings would have to be held in every town. The same objective could be reached at a much lower cost and in far less time if the leaders were to address the inhabitants from the same stage at the same meeting.

A.H. du Plessis refused point blank to address meetings together with black and coloured leaders. He believed that if one of the black leaders were to attack or insult the whites, it would lead to a confrontation on stage. He was also concerned about the reaction from the whites should anything happen to a white speaker at such a meeting. I was shocked and disappointed about this viewpoint and suspected that there had to be another reason for his objection to joint meetings. When I insisted on addressing such joint meetings, Du Plessis gave me permission, provided I didn't act in my capacity as a member of the National Party or as a member of the white delegation, but only in my capacity as Chairperson of the Conference.

After this we organised meetings throughout the country, achieving incredibly positive results. The population increasingly supported the Turnhalle Conference. Unfortunately, the issues on which we disagreed in the Conference were seldom discussed. We spoke to thousands of people all over the country without any protection, despite the danger that we could set off landmines in the northern areas where SWAPO terrorists were active. When I used my aeroplane, I was cautioned to fly as low as possible because of the possibility of missiles being fired by SWAPO.

Although the Turnhalle leaders were prepared to address meetings as far away as Caprivi at our own expense, we had to organise transport for the people who were not living within walking distance from the meetings. My white colleagues refused to have the costs of the meetings covered from funds budgeted for by the Administration. A good friend, Piet Malherbe, offered to collect funds for this purpose from well-disposed businessmen, and made contact with A.P. du Preez, who was involved in the fishing industry. Piet Malherbe's auditing firm offered to manage the funds, which led to the founding of the SWAMEX Trust.

In the meantime my two colleagues did little to inform the white group, and Pretorius continued to disregard world opinion and rejected power-sharing. He was still propagating principles that clashed with what his leader had accepted in the Conference.

The playing field changes

While the different committees of the Conference continued doing their work, the Standing Committee had still not reached the stage where we could present a petition for the institution of an interim government to the Prime Minister of South Africa. It was a question of one step forward and two steps back, while in the meantime battles ensued on several fronts. In the Committee we were struggling to paraphrase an area of authority; in the Legislative Assembly we were discussing principles, especially Christian principles; and meanwhile South Africa and the UN were wrestling with each other about the international status of South West Africa.

At the same time the Defence Force was involved in an armed struggle in the north against SWAPO freedom fighters, who in turn were being supported by foreign powers. The man on the street had no idea what was going on, and whom to trust. However, the Turnhalle had captured the imagination, both internally and abroad. The moderate and peaceful inhabitants of the Territory placed their hopes and aspirations on the Turnhalle Conference, but the UN and SWAPO dismissed it as nothing more than a South African scheme.

On 30 January 1976, the Security Council of the United Nations had already made a decision that augured a new chapter in the history of our country. Resolution 385 of the Security Council contains a long introductory paragraph that refers inter alia to declarations by the President of the Council for Namibia and the Administrative Secretary of SWAPO, Moses //Garoëb. A long list of previous decisions by the Security Council and rulings by the International Court were pointed out. The responsibility of the UN to end South Africa's illegal occupation of Namibia and its implementation of repressive and other measures in the Territory, was re-affirmed. The Security Council then announced: "... that in order that the people of Namibia be enabled to freely determine their own future, it is imperative that free elections under the supervision and control of the United Nations be held for the whole of Namibia as one political entity."

There was no doubt in my mind that the Turnhalle initiative and the decisions taken there had elicited this reaction from the world body, and later also gave rise to the proposals by the five Western countries.

While we in the Turnhalle were focusing all our attention on a possible peaceful solution to the problems of our country, events were taking place elsewhere, but we were dependent on the media and other sources for information on it. For instance, there was the involvement of the South African Police in Rhodesia, then the declaration on 1 August 1975 that South Africa was to withdraw its policemen from that country. At the same time, the Defence Force became embroiled in the civil war among the three liberation groups in Angola, and indeed, from what we learnt later, was supported by the USA.

On 19 December 1975, the tide turned again against South Africa when the American Senate voted against any support to the Angolan manoeuvres with an overwhelming majority. This resulted in South Africa withdrawing its troops from Angola. However, there were a series of contradictions. The South African Government was still justifying its involvement in Rhodesia and Angola, explaining why it would now withdraw from the two areas, when the Security Council made the decision to which I referred above.

We never had any say in military matters and, in addition, were never informed about it. International negotiations were South Africa's responsibility and although we took note of it, we were not sufficiently informed to express an opinion. I could not simply ignore what was happening on these other fronts. I was worried and felt that more frankness should be forthcoming if South Africa was serious about allowing us to determine our own future.

A greater measure of public dialogue

On the home front white politics were still being conducted as though there were no outside factors that could complicate matters. It was the same old story of inappropriate interference and pressure from outside not being allowed. The Legislative Assembly's first session of the year took place a mere two months after the resolution by the Security Council.

On 17 February 1976, it became clear that Koos Pretorius was not happy about the tempo at which we were progressing on the constitutional front. This came as no surprise to me, because it wasn't the first time that he mentioned how far the non-white population was lagging behind in terms of civilisation, experience, education and development; a shortfall that could only be overcome through a longer, evolutionary process. He gave two reasons why we should not move faster than would be good for the maintenance and benefit of our own civilisation: "Firstly, the post-war ideological trends, and secondly, the instigated and fomented impatience of the non-whites." About the Conference he said: "There are those who apparently take the greatest pleasure in announcing day after day that things are not changing fast enough." He added: "To go and rip everything out of the folds into which it has been moulded over decades and even centuries, can cause as much, if not more, chaos than if you were to do nothing."

In the same debate Frans van Zyl spoke about different forms of terrorism, and besides armed terrorism, referred to another form – psychological terrorism: people who wanted us to open the floodgates and cast aside the existing practices much faster. "Give the Conference a chance!" was his appeal to the inhabitants of South West Africa. However, during this session no attention was paid to the decision by the Security Council. In the meantime welcome rain fell over the entire country, but the optimism that came with it was ruined by intensified terrorist activities on the Angolan border.

On 25 February 1976, Clemens Kapuuo delivered a speech "The Future of South West Africa" at a symposium presented in Windhoek. Other speakers included Prof. Tjaart van der Walt of the Potchefstroom

University and Adv. Bryan O'Linn, leader of the Federal Party of South West Africa. Afterwards Kapuuo gave me the handwritten notes he had used on the occasion. I am quoting a few sentences from these notes: "If a constitutional conference was held in the fifties or sixties, I am sure a peaceful solution would have been found. Unfortunately the people in authority always thought that the situation in Africa and the world would always remain the same." He warned that foreign investors wanted the assurance that South West Africa would have a stable government, and then continued:

> Although we are not yet independent and are being adminis-
> tered by South Africa, we have been watching developments in
> Africa and other parts of the world where governments were
> formed and then collapsed after a short time when military gov-
> ernments were formed. Many governments were overthrown
> because the countries introduced a constitution from other
> countries that did not suit their own country, or forced a consti-
> tution, wanted by one ethnic group, onto the country without
> considering whether the constitution suited the situation in the
> country as a whole.

He was, without a doubt, referring to SWAPO's attempts to enforce a constitution onto our country by means of violence. He added that although we appreciated the advice of the UN, its members should respect our right to elect our own representatives. "The Charter of the League of Nations and the United Nations ... did not say that the world organisation would promote the wellbeing of one tribe or ethnic group. If they cannot work in accordance with their own charter, will they be able to maintain their reputation?" About the Turnhalle he said the following: "We have a valuable opportunity in the Turnhalle Conference where people of different languages, different cultures and different historical backgrounds now sit together to work out a peaceful solution."

In his speech Adv. O'Linn emphasised the increasing pressure that was being put on South Africa by various countries and referred to the Turnhalle as follows: "This new initiative recognises an old truth expounded for many years by the United Party without success in white elections." Referring to the northern part of South West Africa, he indicated that Ovamboland, due to its large and homogenous population, could perhaps be in a position to accept separate independence.

However, he pointed to the interdependence of Ovamboland on the rest of South West Africa and referred to an interview *Rapport* had with me, in which I strongly criticised Jan de Wet for his proposal that the southern part of South West Africa be incorporated into South Africa.

Bryan O'Linn didn't rule out the possibility of independence for the northern areas, but a reasonable basis for such a step needed to be negotiated, he said. On the possibility of a unitary state, he expanded as follows:

> A unitary form of constitution as propagated by SWAPO and other organisations within and outside the country would be totally unacceptable to the powerful white population group, primarily because it would put the black and brown people in a dominant position, at a time when there is insufficient development in depth in the whole of the country to guarantee stability, security and civilised standards and the basic rights of minorities. In such circumstances it is feared that the present system will merely make place for a black racialist dictatorship. Furthermore, there is a real fear among many minority groups, black, brown and white, that in such a constitution one population group, the Owambo, would dominate.

It was obvious that Clemens Kapuuo and Bryan O'Linn were both concerned about possible domination by the Owambo in a future dispensation. Where O'Linn offered the Federal Party's federal concept as a solution, Kapuuo kept to the Turnhalle's viewpoint that all options must remain open and that preconceived plans, especially when coming from a white party such as the FP (Federal Party), would create suspicion. In summary, however, it can be said that there were areas of agreement between the FP's federal plan and the Turnhalle's suggested plan. The most important difference was probably that the Turnhalle Constitution, as I interpret it, did not make provision for separate geographical areas, but only for representative authorities that would take care of the interests of the respective population groups. I must point out that it is precisely around this interpretation of the Turnhalle Constitution that the fight within the National Party would later ensue.

During the symposium O'Linn also made a strong statement regarding the protection of minorities: "I believe, however, that any solution which provides only for unity without recognising diversity and the necessity to protect minorities and the basic rights of the individual would not ensure justice, happiness, prosperity and reasonable civilised standards." However, he was treading on thin ice in that he wanted to implement a qualitative norm based on the contribution of the various federal regions to the national income as a whole when it came to representation in the central authority. I was convinced that he would not be able to sell this proposal.

Adv. O'Linn felt the FP should also be allowed to participate in the Conference and we corresponded on this matter. My viewpoint throughout was that within each of the 11 groups participating in the Conference there were different political parties. The existence of these parties within a group could mostly be traced to personal differences and the struggle for leadership. In cases where we had tried to accommodate more than one party in a group, it had led to endless complications. The inclusion of the FP as a participant to the Conference would probably not cause the same problems, and I didn't underestimate the contribution that O'Linn could make. Unfortunately, it was a matter of principle. If we made an exception in the case of the whites, it would immediately elicit negative reaction. It would have been really interesting though to see Adv. O'Linn and Van Zijl in the same conference.

Prof. Tjaart van der Walt's speech at the symposium elaborated on the role of Christians in the creation of a new dispensation in the relationships among nations. I would like to quote his introductory paragraph:

> Your problems are in fact also our problems, except that you are way ahead of us in some respects. You have already started with a necessary step, which with us in South Africa is still in the preparatory phase: open-hearted deliberations among representatives of all the population groups in your country about your joint future. If you here in South West Africa were to manage to organise your relationships among nations successfully – in law and justice, peace and to the good of all nations and groups – you would be offering the utmost example, a model or blueprint even, to the RSA, and indeed to the rest of the world.

The Turnhalle Conference grips the imagination

The Turnhalle Conference gripped not only the imagination of the people in South West Africa, but also elicited keen interest in South Africa among South Africans. The fact that there was dialogue between blacks and whites in South West Africa on the political and constitutional future of our country was news, and the people of South Africa clearly wanted to know more about it. During and after the Turnhalle Conference I received more invitations to inform various institutions in South Africa about our activities than I could accept. I wanted to elicit as much insight and understanding as possible about what we were doing. It was definitely not my intention to influence political and constitutional development in South Africa. I never for one moment thought that I could possibly achieve this. For me it was solely about my country and its people.

While interest came from all quarters, student organisations at universities were among the first to invite me. Among other things I was asked to deliver a paper at an Autumn School presented by the University of Stellenbosch; to speak at a Winter School at the University of Cape Town; and to address a gathering of student leaders from various universities on an island in the Vaal River in which Prof. Sampie Terblanche also participated. I also accepted invitations from the business sector such as the Chambers of Commerce of Cape Town, Johannesburg, Durban and Pietersburg, while the De Beers Company asked me to present a paper with Van Zyl Slabbert and other speakers to their middle-management personnel. I also received invitations from cultural organisations, service clubs such as Toastmasters International, the Broederbond (a conservative Afrikaner fraternity), and branches of the National Party. I was even asked to inform supporters of the HNP (Herstigte Nasionale Party – a far-right group in South Africa) about events in South West Africa. A women's club also invited me to address their concerns about their sons on the border.

It was still too early to talk about constitutional models. I repeatedly stressed the importance of dialogue with our black and coloured compatriots, but added that such discussion could only be meaningful if we recognised and respected the human dignity of our countrymen. We could not expect moderate inhabitants to join us in taking a stand against a militant organisation as long as they were being treated like second-class citizens. What I did venture to say was that if we in South West Africa were to find a peaceful solution, it could mean the end of the war, and would relieve South Africa of the "South West Africa problem". I could point out that although SWAPO was not participating in the Conference, it was the most representative forum that had ever deliberated on the political future of South West Africa.

My meetings in South Africa were no concert tour and I was not a political entertainer. For me it was about our future. Wherever I spoke in South Africa, I was consistently well received and congratulated on what we were doing in South West Africa and the Turnhalle. The message from my audiences was loud and clear: Something like this was not going to happen in South Africa. On several occasions I was asked why South African boys had to fight on our border. I found it especially remarkable that people in South Africa seemed to have lost sight of the fact that we were still South African citizens; that we had accepted independence – with all the risks involved – to solve a problem with which the country had already been struggling for decades at great expense and loss of life, also in the interests of South Africa. I added that we were prepared to accept all the risks, but expected South Africa to prevent revolutionary powers from taking over our country. If this were to happen, South Africa would be very vulnerable. The war would then only move from the Kunene and Okavango rivers south to the Orange River.

I could also tell them that upon my return to South West Africa, my colleagues and I would – unarmed – continue our deliberations with black and white across the entire country – also in war-torn Owambo. I could furthermore not neglect to tell them about the discord among the white Namibians.

Rumours of discord within the National Party

Owing to the resignation of A.H. du Plessis from the South African Parliament a by-election had to take place in the Windhoek Constituency. When the Legislative Assembly resumed proceedings on 4 September 1976, Koos Pretorius fought a newspaper-clipping war against the Federal Party which wasn't even contesting the election. Again, no mention was made about the sword hanging over our heads.

I also participated in the debate, but refrained from focusing on the election, but rather concentrated on the discord in the party. It was alleged later that the split in the National Party had been planned long before the time. I want to state most emphatically that I had never planned to leave the Party. I wanted to change the Party. I believed that if I could succeed in doing so, the whites would be able to speak with one voice and walk the road in unity with the other population groups, all the way. I always had the feeling that the members of the National Party relied on me to find a solution to our recurring problems. I simply could not allow personal and sometimes differences regarding principles between myself and the other leaders of the Party to shock and drive our supporters apart. I tried everything in my power to bring about change. The problem was that dialogue took place only among our leaders and that the man in the street had to rely on slanderous rumours. To me this was not acceptable and I wanted to set their minds at ease by saying:

> We are living in a time to which I have referred several times as decisive, a time in which a great deal of level-headedness and self-control is required. It is usually under circumstances such as these that people like to sow confusion. Therefore it is not strange that precisely at times like these, the so-called panic merchants become active … [T]here has never been a time in our history that it is so vital for us to stand together. I have always taken the view that we should ignore rumours, but I think it is necessary to point this out before it reaches a stage where it can cause damage. If there is absolute certainty about policy, it is not that important if there are sometimes doubts about leadership, but if you have doubts about where you're going, there has to be absolute trust in your leaders to take charge and find the right way … There is talk of a leadership conflict … I am not aware of a leadership conflict and I am not aware that Mr Du Plessis is being challenged by anyone in the Party. I am also not aware that he has plans to withdraw, and if he is not planning to withdraw, then I cannot understand why there should be a leadership conflict, because there can surely only be a conflict if there is a vacancy.

I referred to my viewpoint concerning Du Plessis's participation in the Conference and indicated that there was a difference of opinion regarding the wisdom and desirability of his decision, but that I never questioned his motives; that the composition of our delegation was finalised; that great responsibility rested on our shoulders; and that we should now dedicate our strength and energy to this. I once again pointed out that we have accepted the existence of different population groups in our country, as well as the importance of the maintenance and protection of an own identity.

It often worried me that we referred to the whites as an ethnic or population group as if they were a homogenous group with a common language and culture, which is not the case. Language groups such as the Afrikaans-, German- and English-speakers, to mention only three of many, are probably just as different from one another, or even more so, than the Damaras and the Namas – who speak the same language. The description "whites" refers to skin colour and therefore to a racial rather than an ethnic group. The fact that the German-speakers in South West Africa regarded themselves as a separate cultural group, came to the fore pertinently when, shortly following the commencement of the Turnhalle Conference, I received a letter from Carl H. Frey in which he requested that the German-speaking group wants to participate in the deliberations as separate group. I assured him that the white delegation would promote the interests of the German-speaking people at all times. It would not be the last time the German- and English-speakers would insist on participating in the political and constitutional process as specific separate groups.

I stressed the fact that the existence of different groups did not mean that they could be discriminated against or considered inferior. I stated it clearly that although we accepted that the different groups could develop separately, this was not necessarily their final destination; that with the realisation of the Turnhalle Conference we had accepted a common right to self-determination, that each of the participating parties would have full say in the process. I stressed that we have recognised how many common interests there actually were and how little there was that separated us from each other. I reminded the Assembly of the undertaking given by Prime Minister John Vorster to Dr Escher: "With regard to the question whether individual population groups may suddenly become independent as separate entities, the South African Government states that it does not envisage such an eventuality."

I concluded my contribution with the following appeal:

> Perhaps it is true that what I am going to say now I deem too important. Perhaps it is true that I am giving it too much priority – I don't know; time will tell – but I want to appeal to the people of South West Africa, no matter which language we speak, no matter our colour or the ethnic group to which we belong: Let's stop hurting each other. Let's tackle the real problems and resolve them. For this our descendants will be most grateful.

Not all the members of the Legislative Assembly were happy with my reassurances. Some remarks I had made probably raised misgivings among them regarding the direction in which I was moving.

It was unfortunately not the end of speculations about the differences between my white colleagues and myself. I suspected that most of the allegations originated from delegates to the Conference. It was inevitable that they would notice during sessions that there were differences between my white colleagues and myself. A journalist later said that some of them would regularly furnish them with information from the Conference in exchange for a drink. In fact, it was ultimately the media that kept the rumours alive.

On 10 August 1976, I opened a National Party Youth Congress in Windhoek and made statements that were afterwards interpreted by the newspapers as clear indications of conflict within the Party. I started by discussing in detail the origin of the Conference and the progress that had been made with the development of a constitution and other related issues. I expressed my conviction about the possibility of representatives of the Conference talking to representatives of SWAPO at a later stage. They would be regarded as political opposition with an ideology that differed from the views of the people who were participating in the Conference.

I wanted to test the congress on whether they would, for the sake of a peaceful and permanent solution, be prepared to make adjustments, even if this would mean the sacrifice of privileges and elimination of prejudices. I said the following:

> We will have to adapt our views of the past and not take the stance that we may never change what we inherited because the older generation will take exception to it. If you consider it your responsibility to maintain what was prescribed to you over the years, you will not be the masters of your own destiny. We need to correct many injustices before we can finalise a constitution. A constitution must reflect the wishes, aims and ideals of all the inhabitants of the country. If we cannot succeed in cultivating mutual understanding for this, a constitution would be nothing more than a contract or agreement between enemies. We must judge our real problem against the background of our past. It is not a technical problem; it is not a problem of international law. The problem in South West Africa is a human problem, a relationship problem, and this can be solved only with goodwill, mutual esteem and respect, and with honesty and sincerity. You

cannot correct anything by writing it into a constitution. This is what I meant when I said previously that a constitution must also be written onto the hearts of people. If you don't see your way clear to do this, go clean your guns and choose revolution; choose a war that no-one can ever win. Because cooperation doesn't mean that one side give up everything, but that we join hands and work on the relationship problem from all sides. The road will not be easy and we will need a great deal of leniency. We will simply have to prove to our countrymen that we are not trying to cheat and force them into a dispensation for our interests alone. Like us, they too have no other country, and many of the things we will have to do are in fact not that difficult. All we have to do is show a little more understanding in our daily dealings with people. I have never received anything but respect in return for treating others with respect. Friends, this is what I want to ask of you. Go sit together in groups, form a think tank, and then come back to us with suggestions about what must be done, and how. I am going to tell you what I am prepared to do. I am prepared to make certain compromises in economic and social areas, even if this may not be to my liking. I am also human and none of us gladly give up comfort and privileges. I want to stay in this country, I cannot think of another country where I would like to live, but black and coloured people live in this country too, they also have no other country. We will simply have to live here together. I don't fear for my identity because I live with black and coloured people in the same country. We should not be scared of being labelled as progressives or even as liberals. I have been labelled a pragmatist and even a humanist. I am not going to bore you with definitions. There are things that you know are wrong. Let's fix them. Let's do it while a constitution is being hammered out in the Conference. But I know that we cannot depend only on a written constitution; this Africa has taught us.

The young congress delegates gathered in small groups and came back with positive suggestions. I left the congress inspired and with hope for the future. However, it soon became evident that I had seriously rocked the boat by some of the things I had said. In their reports the newspapers presented this as a clear indication of differences within the National Party.

Under the headline "Talks with SWAPO indeed possible – Mudge on the future" *Die Suidwester* drew the attention to the issue about which there was of course no clarity yet within the Party. The next day

The Windhoek Advertiser reported under the headline "Mudge flings gauntlet" as follows: "The *verligte* [enlightened] Deputy-Chairman of the National Party in South West Africa, Mr Dirk Mudge, threw down the gauntlet here last night to right-wing elements inside and outside his own Party." This was, however, how the newspapers interpreted my speech and what they emphasised. It was definitely not my intention to challenge my National Party colleagues. Our white politicians are often more concerned about votes than about solutions. I wanted to test what was brewing in my mind among a group of young people, those things that kept me awake at night but which I was not emphasising strongly enough for the sake of Party unity. What I said at the Youth Congress was, when all is said and done, not that radical. These were things that had to happen and which, in fact, did happen.

My reference to the possibility of a discussion with SWAPO elicited a mixed reaction not only from the whites, but also from other leaders of the Constitutional Conference. My good friend and ally, Clemens Kapuuo, was known for his anti-Owambo and anti-SWAPO sentiments, and the Owambo delegation and the Government of Owambo could have interpreted it as a motion of no confidence. I also didn't expect such a possibility to be embraced in the Turnhalle ranks. There was no denying that the fact that SWAPO was not part of the Conference detracted considerably from the credibility of the Conference internationally. To come to a peaceful solution, SWAPO would have to be involved in the non-violent process of achieving independence. Fortunately, we could use the fact that SWAPO had refused to participate in any discussion with internal leaders as an excuse for their absence, but I knew then already that ultimately they would have to be involved. I wanted to test the Youth Congress on this.

The statement in the *Windhoek Advertiser* that I had challenged my colleagues to take on the struggle was not true. I never referred to the National Party or its leaders in a negative way. My objective with what I had said was to smooth the road ahead for them. I was simply doing what I had stated before, namely to inform our followers about what we were doing and what they could expect in the future so that it would not come as a shock at a later stage.

The annual congress of the National Party took place two weeks after the Youth Congress. Rumours that there was going to be a clash at the congress were already doing the rounds. I was oblivious to this, hearing only much later about talk of "unharnessing" or "changing the horses" when referring to the usual election of leaders. Although I didn't exclude the possibility that the activities of the Conference would be discussed during the congress, I didn't have the slightest intention of doing anything that could split the Party. I was intent all along on changing it, not splitting it. I was prepared to state my views openly, as I had done at the Youth Congress.

The election of officials would, however, give an indication of whether there were serious problems. This was avoided at the congress by a motion of order tabled by Dr Paul van der Merwe, proposing that nominations for office bearers be done orally – as had been decided previously – and not in writing. He then proposed that A.H. du Plessis be re-elected as leader and Chairman and Van Zijl and myself as deputy chairmen. It was accepted unanimously.

A year later Paul showed me a letter he had written to the Prime Minister in which he alleged that without his proposal, other candidates would have been nominated for the different positions. It had never been discussed with me and I would definitely not have supported it. He alleged in his letter to the Prime Minister that he had been attacked by his constituency for having averted the election.

The Prinsloo/Mey controversy

The information department of the Turnhalle Conference, with Johan de Waal and Theo Mey as the responsible officials, accomplished a gigantic task with limited resources. With his pleasant disposition, Johan de Waal, who had been with us from the outset, soon won the confidence of the other leaders, and was always prepared to perform the most humble tasks. He travelled long distances to organise meetings, put up tents and set up the loudspeakers.

Theo Mey – I discovered much later that he had been a Brigadier in the South African Defence Force – became involved with the Turnhalle Secretariat in a way that I cannot explain to this day. He had special talents and applied himself heart and soul to our cause. He was keen to learn and wanted to familiarise himself with the affairs of South West politics as soon as possible. He asked to be present when I explained the South West issue to visitors, and usually recorded these discussions on tape. This caused another unpleasant incident, which contributed to the rumours about discord in the party.

On 15 September 1976, Dr Daan Prinsloo of the Association International Organisation requested an interview with me to, as he put it, obtain more background on the South West Africa issue. He informed me that he often had to write articles about South West Africa and had to rely only on the cold facts as reported in the media. The interview took place at my home. I had invited Billy, my good friend and confidant, to attend the discussion, and Theo Mey was present with his tape recorder. I spoke openly about my plans, problems and fears, probably like anyone speaking to a good friend. It had been agreed beforehand that the discussions would be off the record.

Theo Mey had the tape transcribed by the typists at the Turnhalle. They recognised my and Billy Marais's voices, but indicated Dr Daan Prinsloo as Mr X. The document landed on the desk of Marius Maree together with other minutes of the Conference. Mr Maree was responsible for preparing the agenda and the minutes for meetings of the Conference. He later handed the transcription to Billy with the explanation that it had landed on his table probably by mistake. Billy in turn handed it to Theo Mey. A few days later Du Plessis confronted me with a photocopy of the transcription (which had apparently been made in great haste, since sections of it were missing) and demanded to have the original. In reply to my question of how he got hold of a photocopy of the transcription of a private discussion at my house, he replied evasively. I insisted that this had been a private conversation held in my house, but Du Plessis insisted on the original transcription. After some consideration, I sent him a copy that was still available.

Marais and I were then summoned to Du Plessis's office, where we found him and Van Zijl. Du Plessis's tape recorder was in front of him on the table. Marais and I were cross-examined very formally about certain statements we had made in the discussion with Dr Prinsloo. Du Plessis was particularly interested in my remark about the need for ties between the National Party of South West Africa and the National Party in South Africa to be severed due to the fact that we no longer had the same policy, as well as the possibility, if not necessity, of a "political union" between the parties represented in the Conference. I had already mentioned the latter possibility at a meeting, but as had happened so often in the past when Du Plessis did not agree with something, he had ignored and probably forgotten about it.

He wanted to know from me what I had in mind and I explained that, although the delegates participated in the Conference as representatives of population groups, a stage would probably be reached when an election would have to be forthcoming. In the process political parties or alliances would have to be formed. There was a possibility that, although the groups in the Conference would agree on a constitution and a form of government, they would differ on policy. I did not expect Du Plessis to agree with this, since it was still the policy of the National Party that the different ethnic groups would exercise their right to vote only within their own group. It is interesting that such alliances – of which the DTA and AKTUR are examples – were in fact later formed.

Regarding my view on ties with the National Party of South Africa, he accused me of disloyalty towards South Africa. When the ties with the NP of South Africa were eventually cut, Du Plessis explained that it was done on insistence of the Prime Minister of South Africa.

There were other less important points about which Du Plessis was upset, and he made no secret of it. However, not once during my interview with Dr Prinsloo had I launched a personal attack on any of my white colleagues. The conversation with Du Plessis ended without him announcing any further action. I think he found himself in a weak position because of the manner in which he had obtained the transcription. I was particularly upset and even shocked by precisely that. The idea that I was being spied on and that files were being compiled about me, despite the fact that I was trying to keep the team together often without his support, upset me greatly.

Whenever there was the threat of a split occurring among the delegates at the Conference, it was my responsibility to prevent it. On one occasion, after an unpleasant incident, some of the delegates walked out of the Standing Committee. Clemens Kapuuo, Gregor Tibinyane, Ben Africa and I were tasked to mediate between the disgruntled. It took us two days of intense discussions. Two of their objections arose from an interview the white delegation had had with the Prime Minister shortly before, that had been reported in the press. It was alleged that the white delegation, because of its ties with the NP of South Africa, was receiving instructions from South Africa, which was not true. It was also alleged that we were prevented by the NP of South Africa to abolish discriminatory measures. I assured the malcontents that this was not the case, but they argued that Van Zijl and Du Plessis, following our visit to South Africa, had adopted a more intolerant attitude. They challenged me to declare publicly that this was not the case. After this incident I realised that our ties with the National Party of South Africa was turning into a serious problem and that a position had to be taken about it as soon as possible.

The international community and us

During the session of the Legislative Assembly that resumed on 20 September, Koos Pretorius again had problems with foreign interference. I doubted whether he understood what it was about. When he said we shouldn't give way to international pressure, who were the "we" to whom he was referring? It was, after all, South Africa that was in the dock, that was being threatened with sanctions, boycotts and isolation, and that had to decide to what extent it should take notice of world opinion. In the end only South Africa could decide up until which point it could ignore the world's opinion; that would be prepared, at great cost and loss of lives, to give us in South West Africa the opportunity to exercise our right to self-determination. That which had started in 1966 with the infiltration by a small group of SWAPO terrorists, had in the meantime developed into a full-scale war.

While listening to Koos, I made up my mind not to react to his views again. For the sake of party unity I would again just state the other side of the issue without making it look like a confrontation. I was tired of listening to his sermons. I had had enough of his citations from his MA thesis and of what his professors had told him. His one-sided interpretations of Christian principles went against my grain. The members of the Legislative Assembly were all adults and surely no longer had a need for "adult education", as Percy Niehaus had put it years ago.

Van Zijl referred to the peace offensive undertaken by America and I assumed that he was referring to the visit by the Secretary of State, Henry Kissinger, to South Africa. I don't know whether Pretorius saw this as foreign intervention, but it was generally welcomed. Van Zijl spoke of a possible settlement. If this couldn't be reached, the alternative would be too frightening to contemplate. With this he indicated clearly that he wasn't as opposed to intervention as his colleague. He then pointed out the negative role the media, namely *Die Suidwes-Afrikaner*, played by discrediting members of the Conference, of which he was one. He was disturbed about information being leaked from the Conference, while all delegates had signed a declaration of secrecy.

Van Zijl outlined the position of the white delegation in the Standing Committee and the viewpoint they were representing:

> Mr Du Plessis, the Honourable Member Mr Mudge, and I myself are the flag bearers, but as far as the Honourable Member Mr Mudge and myself are concerned, we are also representatives elected on the basis of the policy of the National Party, and there is only one viewpoint that we can state if we want to be honest and ethical. We can state only one because we have only one directive and therefore there may be no doubt in the minds of anyone in South West Africa.

He acceded that additional points of view could be stated in the conference and that a common point of view could develop. "It will take a bit of compromising here and there, and from different opinions one common South West African viewpoint will grow." He continued: "If I am not prepared to settle, then I go to court or to the battlefield. If I want to settle, if I want to investigate the possibility of a settlement, then I am immediately saying by implication that I am prepared to compromise." About our relationship with South Africa, Van Zijl took a strong and responsible stand: "The point of view that we should maintain all the ties we now have with South Africa is unrealistic." Then he made an important statement, which I would like to cite verbatim: "As difficult as it will be for me who knows no other anthem and no other flag – to name only two things – to part ways on 31 December 1978, I realise that I will have to make a choice, and with me every white South Wester ... In my mind I have already made the choice, as difficult as it was, and I have chosen South West Africa." Van Zijl also mentioned that the existence of SWAPO was a fact that couldn't be wished away, and that from our side we had to consider every reasonable proposal to involve SWAPO.

I fully agreed with what he had said. Although we had not agreed on everything in the past, we did agree on many things. In my opinion it was a brilliant speech, and as far as I was concerned, Eben had crossed the Rubicon. I often wondered why there had been tension between us over the years. It's a pity, because we could have become a strong team. Later his path inevitably also split from that of the National Party, but first we had to go through the political melting pot.

During the debate I spoke about the world opinion – not in reaction to Koos's speech, but in reference to Dr Kissinger's visit to Africa. I pointed out that we were part of the global society; that we did not want to be isolated; that no country could survive without good business relations with other countries; and that we wanted to establish good sports relations and cooperate with different countries at different levels. If it were possible for us to achieve international recognition for our efforts, we would be happy, because no country wants to be regarded as the enemy by the international community.

I welcomed Dr Kissinger's peace mission to Africa and wished him success in his deliberations with African leaders. I expressed the hope that he would convince them that we did not want to see a repetition of what had happened in our neighbouring countries; that in this country we wanted true peace and a true democracy. While I pertinently acknowledged and accepted the importance of world opinion and furthermore welcomed advice and support by other countries such as America, I maintained that in our efforts to achieve an international understanding the interests of the people of South West Africa can never be ignored.

I discussed the principle of a majority or representative government and pointed out that in Africa there was often a misconception about what this meant. We believed in true democracy and that after independence all the inhabitants of the country would be better off, not only a small privileged group.

Once again I dared to stick my neck out about the possibility of political development and that groups in the Conference, after completing the task of writing a constitution, would organise themselves into a political party or alliance. I knew that my colleagues were not yet ready for multiracial politics, so I refrained from using the word "multiracial". The formation of political parties was something that would have to be decided on in future, which, in fact, happened within a year.

I mentioned that the chances of SWAPO ever participating in the Conference were unlikely due to the stance of the organisation that it was prepared to talk only to South Africa. This was indicated by the party's many statements. The furthest SWAPO was prepared to go was stated as follows by Sam Nujoma when he referred to putting a SWAPO delegation together to negotiate with South Africa: "Some of them [the Turnhalle leaders] have been demanding independence for South West Africa for many years and would be welcomed in a Namibian delegation. If the Boer government brought the traitors they would have to sit on the South African side."

My Kamanjab speech

Following the adjournment of the last session of the Legislative Assembly of the year, and especially due to the increasing tension in the Standing Committee, I pondered the possibility of also testing the ideas I had shared with the Youth Congress on another occasion. Such an event presented itself when, on the invitation of Bertie Botha, I addressed a public meeting at Kamanjab on 5 November 1976. Bertie and I often discussed the problems within the party, and what we could do about them. He was young and well-read and had a particular interest in politics. The Kamanjab community consisted mainly of farmers, in most cases younger farmers who had to build up from nothing the farms allocated to them. One could expect that they would generally be conservative and that this would probably be the right place to test my "liberal" ideas.

In my speech I repeated that the day would come when the National Party of South West Africa would have to sever its ties with its counterpart in South Africa; also that a firmer basis needed to be developed for cooperation among the political parties in the Turnhalle Conference; and lastly, that I did not need the Immorality Act or the Mixed Marriages Act to protect my identity.

Although it was not a closed meeting, I didn't anticipate that the media would be there in large numbers. I had probably mentioned to a confidant that I was planning to call a spade a spade and this had been leaked to the journalists. My speech appeared in the South African newspaper *Rapport* on Sunday 7 November 1976, under a big bold headline, "Mudge Breaks Out". In addition, it was carried into the world by various other newspapers and news media. This was not what I had had in mind. What I had said there was still in accordance with what I had said on various other occasions in the Legislative Assembly and at the Youth Congress.

However, this time my specific reference to the Immorality Act and the Mixed Marriages Act probably stirred the emotions. What was gratifying to me was that the people of Kamanjab – who had listened to the entire speech and not only learnt of it in the media, reacted to it very positively. The farmers of Kamanjab had joined me in identifying a new direction, and in the years to come a strong alliance would develop between them and me, which meant a lot to me. They were not what one would describe as liberalists; they were realists who knew how to deal with the hard realities of life. I will always remember them. Besides Bertie Botha, there were Jan Steyn, Faan Labuschagne, Rob Robberts, Ernst von Bach, Niel Greeff, and others.

The media had, as one could expect, used mainly the contentious aspects of my speech. I don't know to what extent the reporters' articles were influenced by events earlier that day. The mischievous Paul Robberts had received and entertained them lavishly, but I was totally unaware of this ... until later that evening, when the meeting was already in progress. The reporter from the South West African Broadcasting Corporation (SWABC) sat behind me with his big tape recorder. It was one of those old models that worked with big round reels. At one stage I heard strange sounds behind me and when I looked around, saw that his reels had become entwined. He was busy pulling out the tape and winding it around his hand and elbow. Probably due to the events earlier that day. The result was that the journalist had to use the Security Police's tape to do his story. When I heard about this later, I wondered what the Security Police had been doing there.

Du Plessis reacted strongly to my remarks in a speech he made in Maltahöhe. He objected particularly to my saying it in public and not through formal party channels. I could have answered that the party channels were blocked because the party machine had seldom been taken into consideration throughout the entire process. The party machine had repeatedly been confronted with a *fait accompli* that had already been dealt with by Du Plessis and Van Zijl. My statements in Kamanjab would often be thrown back at me. Nevertheless, the National Party of South West Africa would later decide to sever its ties with South Africa, and to agree to the repeal of the Immorality Act and the Mixed Marriages Act. But, as happened so often in the past, it was again too little too late.

The Turnhalle Conference proposes an interim constitution

The Standing Committee of the Turnhalle Conference met with the South African Prime Minister on 25 November 1976. The Committee had informed him on the progress made in the Conference, and that consensus had already been reached on the most important aspects regarding the different levels of government. However, the Conference was not yet ready to present a specific proposal to the Government of South Africa. The reason for this was that during the last stages of the Conference, controversial issues were simply put on the backburner and other issues adopted provisionally, while important issues – such as the division of funds among the different second-tier authorities – had not even been discussed. The Standing Committee, however, was keen to hand a petition to the South African Government as soon as possible with a view to the establishment of an interim government. The interim government would then be given the opportunity to identify and consider all remaining points of difference. After all, assurance on this had been given over and over again.

The General Assembly of the Constitutional Conference met afterwards to approve the final draft of the petition for an interim government to be submitted to the South African Government. However, Du Plessis notified the Conference of the intention of the white population group to consult their members by calling a referendum on the draft constitution for an interim government.

This provoked a strong reaction from the other delegates. They wanted to know why only the whites would be consulted and not the other groups. They felt that an opportunity should rather be created at a later stage for all the inhabitants of the country to express their approval or non-approval. Willie Maasdorp of the Baster delegation raised an important point: "If the whites were to approve the draft constitution now and suggestions for changes to it were made at a later stage, including during the period of the interim government, the whites could refuse to accept the changes, because they would be able to argue that they couldn't change a constitution that had been approved by the whites in a referendum." Du Plessis gave the assurance that this would not be the case, using the following words: "You are not being bound at all. You will be given all the choices you want."

However, the General Assembly was not prepared to support the motion and it fell by the wayside.

The Standing Committee had access to the services of several legal advisers and instructed them on 8 December 1976 to work on the proposed constitution during the recess, especially on the aspects about which consensus had not yet been reached. This included issues such as property rights and certain remaining aspects of the division of functions. The group included advocates Piet Henning, Rit van Rooyen, Chris de Jager and A.P. Steenkamp, Professors Verloren van Themaat and Marinus Wiechers.

On 18 January 1977, the Standing Committee considered the draft constitution prepared by the legal advisors. Then followed the task of finalising a few unresolved issues, which was delegated to a small committee under my chairmanship. This again led to an intense debate over points on which I could not agree with Van Zijl, especially concerning the issue of areas of authority. The Committee had accepted the proposals of the legal advisors as set out in the draft, but it was clear to me that Van Zijl and I had different interpretations of the section on areas of authority and the division of functions. About these we would still argue long and vociferously in the days to come.

On 16 February 1977, Eben van Zijl wrote a letter to Piet Roux, one of South West Africa's representatives in the House of Assembly and a very good friend of Van Zijl's, attaching the draft the Committee had finalised. I was subsequently given a copy of the letter by one of Piet Roux's colleagues in the House of Assembly. Eben closed his letter with the following sentence: "At the Standing Committee and the Conference problems can still be expected, because for certain people, things did not go as they wanted them to go." This clearly referred to me, which once again indicted that the rumours started by Fanie Vilonel, another friend of Eben's, had not yet been laid to rest.

A referendum for the whites

At the session of the Legislative Assembly on 22 February 1977, Eben van Zijl referred to the mistrust that was being spread, saying that although consensus had been reached in the Turnhalle on most issues, it could still take weeks for a final decision to be taken. I knew to whom he was referring.

My white colleagues were in a hurry to have the draft constitution approved and were impatient when delegates posed questions or expressed reservations, which I allowed them to do. I didn't allow myself to be influenced and never cut a discussion short before I was convinced that everyone understood what the decision was about. I knew that there were many things that my black and coloured colleagues did not understand yet. My main concern, however, was about the broader population out there and the possibility that the product we were devising might not meet their expectations. If we, who were supposed to be the leaders, were slandering and running each other down, the people out there could certainly doubt the product. I was determined to put an end to this later.

On 24 February 1977, Van Zijl tabled a draft ordinance providing for a referendum to determine whether the white voters in the Territory of South West Africa were in favour of the establishment of an interim government and independence for the Territory of South West Africa in accordance with the principles accepted by the Constitutional Conference. I can't recall whether I had been informed about the exact wording of the draft beforehand. If so, I had probably not paid enough attention to it, since I was not particularly excited about the referendum. Nevertheless, it is no excuse, because the draft contained words that were open to different interpretations. The conclusion that could reasonably be drawn from this was that not only would the interim government be instituted in accordance with the provisions of the Turnhalle Constitution, but that ultimately independence would be cast in the same mould.

In explaining the draft ordinance, Van Zijl didn't pay much attention to its wording, explaining that "… this was not an ordinance that would be valid indefinitely". What he said was important, yet it was contrary to the wording of the draft. He then continued to explain why only the whites were being consulted and the same was not being envisaged for the other ethnic groups. His explanation was that it was tradition among the whites to consult their members in this way; and that it would be presumptuous to prescribe to other groups how they should test their people.

In hindsight this did not make sense, since it had been our viewpoint throughout that a final solution had to be acceptable to all the inhabitants of our country. It could be argued that there would be another test by means of a referendum or election before independence through which, as Du Plessis put it, "they would have all the choices they wished for". At the end of his speech, however, Van Zijl created doubt as to whether there would be such an opportunity again when he said the following: "If the voter were then to answer yes to the question and if the majority of the votes were to be yes, then according to my interpretation it would mean that we need not have another referendum before independence." Van Zijl then announced that the Constitution as accepted by the Conference and the proposal about a referendum would be referred to a special National Party Congress for ratification, and that the Executive Committee would determine a date for the referendum.

In my contribution to the ensuing debate, prompted by what a friend had told me on my way to the Assembly, I said that black people stand together when they feel threatened, whereas white people fight with each other when they are threatened. I said that I wouldn't mention names or try to establish who the guilty parties were, but that a turbid atmosphere was prevalent in the Conference and that I would be neglecting my duty if I didn't point this out. I made a long speech and was somewhat emotional. I wish to quote a single paragraph verbatim:

> Mr Chairman, I have consistently refrained from talking about my problems and myself. I leave that to others who apparently find pleasure in doing this. None other than I has ever been the victim of a countrywide smear campaign by the media before. It does not only happen out of criticism, but also because of opportunistic people who want to use you to suit their own agendas, to present you as they want you to be seen, to draw you into a caricature. The methods that they use are legion, and I have long experience of this. Has the time not come for us to make our personal differences secondary to that which is in the interests of the country? The easiest way to discredit a fellow white is to accuse him of not being loyal to the whites, of wanting to sell him out, and of calling him a traitor. We shouldn't be apprehensive about it. Let us do what we believe is right and accept responsibility for it. Let us work towards a future that will be fair and just for all our people, and that will not discriminate on the basis of race and colour.

While writing this, I realise that I had said this more than 30 years ago. At the time whites in Southern Africa were not exactly receptive to it.

The draft constitution was accepted by the Conference on 18 March 1977. It was not perfect and also did not cover the whole spectrum. The provisions on areas of authority and the division of functions were still being interpreted differently, and on the allocation of state income and the division of state assets there was no consensus. However, there was a clear understanding that it would be the responsibility of the interim government to resolve these problems. For me it was a memorable day. I was satisfied that for the first time we had succeeded in building a team that could tackle future problems as a united front. It was also a pleasant prospect that we would for the first time be able to decide on issues over which we had no control in the past.

A special congress of the National Party was convened on 29 March 1977 to approve the Turnhalle Constitution and the holding of a referendum. The members of the congress and the whites would not have much of a choice. The whole process had progressed too far to be reversed. Legislation providing for a referendum for the whites had already been accepted by the Legislative Assembly, and the Executive Committee had determined 17 May 1977 as the date on which the referendum would take place. Apparently the time to consult the whites was now. When I, during the early stages of the Conference, suggested that members of the Party should be informed about decisions taken by the Conference, Du Plessis was of the opinion that the time was not right. They were now being faced with a *fait accompli*. I had to use the Youth Congress and my speech at Kamanjab to convince the leaders of the party.

The international community interferes, but we hold a referendum

Before all the formalities referred to above could be concluded, five Western countries – the United States of America, Great Britain, Germany, France and Canada – appeared on the scene and steered the ship in a totally different direction. Was it international interference in our domestic affairs in the hope that we and South Africa would give way under pressure? The opportunity had now arrived for my colleagues who were so concerned about principles, to take a firm stand.

Probably as a result of the plan to establish an interim government in South West Africa, representatives of the five Western countries arrived in Cape Town during the first half of April 1977 to propose a possible solution to the South West African question to the South African Government. Donald F. McHenry, who represented the USA in the group, started the talks with a speech from which I would like to quote briefly. He began by expressing his appreciation for the fact that his group had been received by the South African Government and for the willingness to exchange opinions about – as he put it – the problem of South West Africa. To him an incident that had occurred in Ovamboland shortly before, when SWAPO had abducted 121 pupils and staff from the Catholic Mission School at Anamulenge, was a sign that a peaceful solution had to be sought urgently. Among other things, he said the following:

> We believe that a peaceful settlement will be found acceptable to Namibia and the international community through the concerted efforts of all parties … We recognise that South Africa has made the right decision in treating the international territory of Namibia as entitled to an independent nationhood as a single political unit. The South African Government has an important role to play in the process of bringing Namibia to independence and we see the following as the objectives of our discussions in Cape Town:
> - South Africa's agreement that the purpose of future negotiations should be to develop an internationally acceptable settlement on the question of Namibia consistent with Resolution 385 (of 30 January 1976).
> - We look to South Africa's cooperation in developing a negotiating process in which the parties primarily concerned will be provided an opportunity to participate in the development of any settlement.
> - South Africa's agreement that all parties must avoid any steps that will foreclose possibilities for arranging an internationally acceptable solution. It must emphasise the serious consequences, which we believe will follow from the implementation of the Turnhalle Constitution.

From this one thing was clear: If the three conditions above were to be accepted, the planned interim government with constitution and all would be provisionally abandoned and from then on the international community would be involved in the process. But equally important was that the handing over of South West Africa summarily to the Trusteeship Committee of the UN or to SWAPO was ruled out. The South

African Government had now been accepted as a party to the talks, with an intrinsic interest in the future of the Territory and its people.

In the light of the talks with the "Five", the members of the Standing Committee were summoned to Cape Town by the Prime Minister. John Vorster and the Minister of Foreign Affairs conveyed the proposals of the Five to us. They were of the opinion that these had to be examined thoroughly. They expected the deliberations to last a week and the Prime Minister proposed that five members of the Conference be designated to stay in Cape Town to be consulted on a continuous basis. A.H. du Plessis suggested that 11 leaders be designated – one by each population group. Dr Ben Africa probably realised that this would mean Du Plessis would be the white representative and proposed that I, in my capacity as Chairman of the Standing Committee, should also remain in Cape Town. The Prime Minister agreed and as he adjourned the meeting for lunch, he requested me to give him the names of the persons who will remain during the talks with the Five.

In the bus on the way to the hotel a fairly upset Du Plessis wanted to know from me how I could consider remaining in Cape Town for a week when I was scheduled to address three referendum meetings in South West during this period. My reply was that I hadn't offered myself and that I didn't consider it necessary to remain in Cape Town. I had planned to return to Windhoek later that week after a commemorative exhibition of paintings by the late Arnfried Blatt, which would be opened by Prime Minister Vorster. As Arnfried had been a good friend of mine, his widow Cathy had asked me to introduce the Prime Minister.

After opening the exhibition, the Prime Minister remarked that we would still see each other during the following week. I informed him that Du Plessis and I had decided that it was more important for me to return to Windhoek. John Vorster was visibly irked and remarked: "You guys must get your priorities straight." I nevertheless decided to return to Windhoek.

After the meeting at Leonardville I received a call from Minister Pik Botha, who informed me that the Prime Minister was most annoyed because I hadn't been present at the talks, and that he insisted that I join the delegation immediately. I departed to Cape Town that same evening in the private plane with which I had flown to Leonardville. We took off in the early hours of the morning – at 02:30 – by the light of car headlamps, landed at Upington to refuel, and at 09:00 I joined the group in the Office of the Prime Minister and attended the rest of the discussions.

There I learnt that the delegation, including Du Plessis, had the previous day accepted a one-person-one-vote-election under UN supervision in principle. Issues that still needed to be clarified had to do mostly with the conditions under which the election would take place, and with a different form of interim authority than the planned interim government. These matters were then further discussed. I left the discussions at about 15:30 and flew back to address the meeting in Windhoek. Despite the fact that it was becoming dark when we approached Mariental and that we had to dodge a number of thundershowers, I was only about an hour late for the meeting. Du Plessis subsequently expressed his dissatisfaction to me about the Prime Minister's insistence that I attend the consultations.

One of the first decisions that had to be taken during the talks with the Five was the composition of an interim authority that would have to administer South West Africa until the envisaged election. The Five were prepared to consider a Central Administrative Authority, which would consist of 23 members, of which the Conference could nominate 11, hence a minority. The Chairman would then probably be an impartial person nominated by South Africa. This proposal was not acceptable to us. After a long discussion in our hotel among the members of our delegation, I suggested that an Administrator General be appointed by the South African Government to rule as a one-man-government during the interim period. I telephoned Pik Botha from the hotel to convey our decision to him. He found it acceptable and it was also accepted by the Western representatives. After that the meeting discussed the modalities of the election.

In terms of our internal politics, the year 1977 was an eventful one. After our return from Cape Town, the white leaders had to focus on the referendum campaign. It could probably be argued that the referendum should have been cancelled, since the question to be put to the electorate after the agreement in Cape Town was no longer relevant. In terms of our agreement in Cape Town, the interim government had been swept off the table and South West Africa would become independent on the basis of a constitution drafted by a constitutional conference that would be elected in a one-person-one-vote election.

A.H. du Plessis was adamant that the referendum should take place. You cannot come to any conclusion other than that he wanted to use the outcome of the white vote in the referendum as a political platform. I must admit that it would have caused great confusion if the referendum were to be called off at this stage.

It was difficult for us – who knew what had happened in Cape Town and what had been agreed upon – to address meetings during the referendum campaign, because we had been requested not to anticipate future events. Some of our colleagues did not feel as strongly about the sensitive nature of our talks with the Five and questions about this would soon arise. The three members of the white delegation did not always tell the same story.

The responsibility of explaining to the electorate what had been agreed on with the Five rested on the shoulders of the leader of the Party. On 5 May – in a speech at Karasburg – Du Plessis replied to a question as to whether the details of the negotiations in Cape Town would be made known to the public "that it is not common practice for details of negotiations to be released before they had been concluded". A few days later, on 9 May, he said in Mariental: "In the last few weeks there has been speculation about the deliberations between the South African Government and the Western Five in Cape Town. Let there be speculation; what was discussed will eventually be made known. Now is not the appropriate time to reveal it."

In an interview with *Die Suidwester* on 11 May, Du Plessis said that even if the modus operandi as provided by the Turnhalle were to be modified in certain respects, this by no means meant that the programmes and principles that had been agreed upon would be affected. And so we plodded on. We were asking for a "yes" for the implementation of the Turnhalle principles, but had already said "yes" to the Western proposals in principle. If it weren't such a serious matter, you would feel inclined to compare it to a man with two girlfriends who don't know about each other. The problem comes when they learn about each other. This obviously also had to happen in our case.

The referendum took place on 17 May 1977 and the whites voted "yes" with an overwhelming majority. Hence they accepted independence on the basis of the Turnhalle Constitution. Later on, in the Legislative Assembly, appreciation was expressed for the role played by advocates O'Linn and Niehaus to encourage supporters of the Federal

Party to vote for an interim government and independence. As motivation for their unexpected attitude, Adv. O'Linn said on occasion that the interim government would be able to amend the Turnhalle Constitution, as was, in fact, also suggested by the delegates to the Conference shortly afterwards. The Federal Party could hardly vote against independence.

In the meantime the discussions between South Africa and the Western countries had progressed so far that, more or less a month after the referendum, they agreed on the broad principles of the Western settlement proposals. With a view to the planned election, agreement was reached on the appointment of an Administrator General and a special representative of the Secretary General of the UN. The rules of the game had changed overnight. The product of the Turnhalle, which had at least been accepted by the whites, would have to be sold on a different market and under different circumstances. If SWAPO were also to accept the Western settlement plan, it would mean that they would have to participate in the planned election. The new challenge was to beat them in such an election. If SWAPO were to win the election, we would have no other choice than to accept the result, in other words to accept a SWAPO constitution.

Important questions surfaced immediately. Would the Turnhalle Constitution in its current form be able to pass the test of a country-wide one-person-one-vote election, or would we have to amend it? Could the Conference as such in its present form participate in the election, or should the creation of a political organisation rather be considered, as I had already suggested on several occasions? Would we be able to keep all participants in the Conference in the fold, considering the differences that had been set aside temporarily, because an interim government without the prospect of an election was being envisaged? Time would tell that these were not easy questions to answer.

My last lap in the National Party

On 23 May 1977, in my capacity as Acting Administrator, the highest position that a politician could attain in the country, I opened the fifth session of the eleventh Legislative Assembly. It was, without it having been planned or expected as such, my last session as NP representative in the Legislative Assembly. Exactly four months later I would resume my political career as leader of the opposition. But first a lot of political water would have to flow into the sea.

In my budget speech I spoke mostly about the general economic conditions in the Territory and the different budgetary allocations. I concluded by expressing my absolute confidence in the future of our country. The speakers given the floor after me, spoke jubilantly about the result of the referendum, thanked everyone who had voted "yes" (also the Federal Party) and denounced the right-wing elements such as the HNP (Herstigte Nasionale Party), which so unpatriotically voted "no".

In the meantime conservative attitudes were still filtering through among the National Party leaders. Christo de Jager said it was clear that in terms of the Turnhalle Constitution the political battle would be fought at second-tier level, and that "more confusion than anything else would result from the possible cooperation with the so-called Turnhalle Party". From speeches it became increasingly clear that members of the Assembly were still opposed to a multiracial or non-racial political organisation. Paul Smit was talking about liaison between different ethnic parties and Bertie Botha was calling the envisaged government system an ethnic federation, while complaining that there were people who linked ethnicity to racism.

Koos Pretorius said that since the referendum was behind us, we could sit back, relax, and look at certain deficiencies and shortcomings. He continued that where we were dealing with a large diversity of people, different languages and, what's more, with an outside world that was hostile towards us, there could not be ambiguities about the use of words and terminology. He spoke for over an hour on the meaning of the concepts discrimination, race, people, cultural community, nation, tribe, ethnicity and democracy, and told us how different persons and explanatory dictionaries defined and explained these terminology and concepts. He rejected the system of one-person-one-vote that had already been accepted by his leader in the negotiations with the Western Contact Group. According to him the Turnhalle was not a multiracial, but a multinational gathering. He compared it to when a coloured [rugby] team played against a white team; then it was not a multiracial but a multinational competition. In conclusion he pointed out that when a community is involved, a multinational basis is the

only lasting basis for contact arrangements and methods of cooperation.

While Koos continued expanding on multinationalism and multi-
racialism, some members started making interjections and I suggested
that in future we should all carry a pocket dictionary around with us.
Once again we were dealing with "adult education". It almost seemed
as if Koos hadn't heard of the negotiations with the Western Contact
Group yet. In my reply I referred particularly to countries that were
well disposed towards us, and had used their right to veto in the Security Council on various occasions to prevent far-reaching measures
against South Africa. I cautioned that we should not expect other countries to jeopardise their positions out of sympathy with us or South
Africa. We should not rely on sentiment or sympathy, but rather look
for common interests.

Because this was the last session of the Legislative Assembly in
which I participated as leader of the National Party, I would like to
clarify some of the viewpoints I had taken in the debate. In reaction
to a motion by Willem Odendaal that "note be taken with appreciation of the constitutional foundation that had been worked out by the
Constitutional Conference and also thank everyone who had made
a contribution to this", I referred to the negotiations with the contact
group and apologised for the delay caused by their intervention, but
stated that in my opinion it would be worthwhile to wait longer and,
in doing so, gain the approval of at least the Western countries. I also
expressed the opinion that we should not fear the proposed election
of a Constituent Assembly, because the rules and regulations in terms
of which the proposed election will be conducted would be drafted in
cooperation with and to the satisfaction of the Administrator General.
I emphasised further that South Africa in the person of the Administrator General would remain in effective control until independence and
that the existing authoritative bodies would not be affected.

As far as the continued existence of the Turnhalle Conference and
the future role of this body was concerned, I asked that we should
disappoint neither our own people, nor the black and coloured people
who had come with us all this way. As Chairman of the Conference I
knew that the building of trust up until that stage had been a laborious
process and that we needed to strengthen it further.

Koos used his turn to speak on this motion to elaborate in length on the right of population groups to take care of their own education. My colleagues apparently did not understand that the work we had done in the preceding years would be in vain if we were unsuccessful in winning the planned election under UN supervision. The Western settlement proposals were once again not taken seriously. Van Zijl, however, apparently did realise that the possibility of an election in accordance with the Western settlement plan could not be ruled out, because he announced in the Legislative Assembly that a fund under the name TUFEK was to be created to spread the Turnhalle message. He appealed to well-disposed persons and institutions, internally and abroad, to support the fund.

It was clear that with TUFEK Van Zijl wanted to gain control of the information activities of the Turnhalle instead of supporting the initiative already in place. When TUFEK was founded, I was left in the dark for the umpteenth time. Although this had been discussed and decided upon beforehand by my white colleagues, I would hear about it for the first time only when Van Zijl announced the plan in the Legislative Assembly. Because my two white colleagues were not available for joint meetings, it was not clear to me how they wanted to convey the message of the Turnhalle. At a much later stage and only after the Turnhalle Conference had split, were Du Plessis and Van Zijl prepared to address meetings with black and coloured leaders. However, it was again a case of too little too late.

Back to the drawing board

Shortly after the result of the referendum and the agreement in principle with the five Western countries, the Standing Committee of the Turnhalle Conference met to discuss the consequences of the Cape Town agreement. The majority of the members of the Committee were of the opinion that since an interim government was off the table, the Turnhalle Constitution, which was meant specifically for such a government, would have to be adapted. They argued that the interim constitution was not acceptable as the final constitution, and that they could not see how we could win a democratic election with it. They did, however, agree that the basic constitutional principles of the Turnhalle Constitution had to be retained. Du Plessis and Eben van Zijl were, nonetheless, only prepared to accept "consequential" changes and had proposed that the Constitution that had been approved by the whites in the referendum should be accepted virtually unchanged as the final proposal.

The black and coloured delegates reminded Du Plessis of the promise he had made at the Constitutional Conference when he gave notice of a white referendum, namely that the other groups would in no way be bound and that they would have all the choices they wanted, subject only to the basic constitutional principles of the constitution. Apparently, Du Plessis and Van Zijl considered all the provisions contained in the original constitution as principles, yet the other delegates emphasised that during the discussions they had clearly indicated which provisions they had accepted provisionally and conditionally.

The Standing Committee then discussed the original constitution point by point. The third-tier governmental system, which made provision for a central government; representative authorities for the different ethnic groups; as well as local authorities for the different towns in our country, was adopted unanimously, although there were still strong differences on two aspects, namely the areas of jurisdiction of representative authorities, and the division of functions among the different tiers of government.

Some of the groups vehemently opposed the idea that a representative authority, for example the whites, would have control over a geographic area. This would mean, for instance, that if functions such as roads, traffic control, nature conservation, health or agriculture were to be allocated to the white authority in so-called white areas, members of other groups who lived in that area would be subject to laws and regulations that had been drafted without them participating in any way.

In the Declaration of Intent that had been adopted by all delegates right at the beginning of the Conference, it had been agreed that each population group would have the maximum say in its own affairs. The problem was: What are own affairs? Own affairs were afterwards described as issues that are of particular importance to an ethnic group. If you take into account that the National Party placed a lot of emphasis on ethnicity and cultural values, then the question could be asked: What do roads, traffic control or nature conservation have to do with culture? Or was the motive behind all of this, as Du Plessis put it, that "the Central Government must only have functions that have no teeth?"

In the case of areas with homogeneous populations it was simpler, but in the case of the proposed white area there was a problem. About this I had already argued with Van Zijl in the early stages of the Turnhalle Conference, but he always maintained that I was not interpreting the provision correctly. As proven later, this system could not work in practice. Where it was self-evident to have separate schools for the different population groups (not racial groups) wherever they were living, it was, however, absurd to think the same pattern could be followed in the case of roads, traffic control and nature conservation, to mention only a few.

After much reflection and many attempts to reach a compromise, I came to the conclusion that there were in reality only two functions that affected a population group specifically, namely cultural affairs, which included education, and traditional affairs, which included communal land. Intense clashes were to follow on these issues. What was making the problem even more complicated was the eagerness of some leaders of the white as well as of the other groups to gain control over as many functions as possible, mainly because of the importance and status of the particular representative authority.

In the case of each of these differences, Du Plessis balked, indicating that he would only be prepared to accept a few consequential amendments. This resulted in some of the delegates having to ask him pertinently if he was prepared in any way whatsoever to consider changes – yes or no. They argued that if he were not prepared to accept any amendments, arguments about specific differences would serve no purpose. To this he couldn't or wouldn't give a clear reply. He said later that the other delegates had confronted him with a *fait accompli*, namely to accept or reject their proposals. But actually it was he who confronted them with a *fait accompli*. He and Van Zijl simply refused to accept any amendments.

When it seemed that an impasse had been reached, Van Zijl suggested that a smaller working committee consider the points of difference and then report back to the Standing Committee at the next session. The legal representatives of the different groups would also serve on the committee.

Because I believed that the viewpoints of the other groups were valid, and also that on the basis of Du Plessis's promise they were entitled to propose changes to the original constitution, there were now differences of opinion within the ranks of the white delegation, which reignited the already existing mistrust. The credibility of the whites was now at stake. In my opinion the advice and leadership of the whites were necessary, with the proviso that their credibility would not be questioned. With this in mind I decided that an open-hearted discussion needed to take place among the white members as soon as possible – in any case before the next session of the Standing Committee.

Discord in white ranks

Attempts from my side to convene an Executive Committee meeting to discuss the points of discord were unsuccessful. In response to a formal letter to Du Plessis by Appie Louw, the Secretary of the Party, in which he proposed that a meeting be arranged to discuss the matter, Du Plessis maintained that this was unnecessary, since an ordinary meeting of the Executive would take place during the annual congress. The differences of opinion between me and my colleagues, and Du Plessis's unwillingness or inability to do something about this, must have come to the attention of the Prime Minister and some of his colleagues. It was common knowledge that Fanie Vilonel was zealously spreading rumours about me in the south of the country.

During the first week of August 1977, I was informed by the Administrator that two ministers from South Africa, P.W. Botha and Pik Botha, as instructed by Prime Minister John Vorster, would be visiting Windhoek to talk to the leaders of the National Party. A.H. du Plessis, Eben van Zijl, Jan de Wet and I were requested to be in attendance. The talks took place a few days later in a small room under the control tower at Eros Airport. I wondered why two senior Cabinet ministers were being received in such an uncomfortable place, but the reasons soon became clear. They had arrived in a South African Air Force aircraft and would depart immediately after the meeting. We were asked to keep their visit a secret, because if it were to leak out that two senior ministers from South Africa were visiting South West Africa unexpectedly, speculation would ensue on all fronts.

P.W. Botha put it to us that they were speaking on behalf of the

Prime Minister, being the leader of the National Party in South Africa, and that they wanted to convey his concern and displeasure over the discord among the leaders of the National Party of South West Africa. The Prime Minister suggested that Du Plessis should resign as leader of the National Party in South West Africa and that the Party could bestow lifelong honorary membership on him, as they had done in the case of Senator Paul Sauer in South Africa. I was totally dumbstruck and taken aback. I knew Du Plessis well and realised that it must be a humiliating experience for him to be given such a choice in front of all of us. He was adamant that he was not interested in any honorary position and that he had no intention of resigning because he could not disappoint the people who had faith in him. P.W. Botha's reaction to this was a clear instruction to Du Plessis that should this be his decision, he must restore unity in his Party. He suggested that Du Plessis arrange a meeting with all the South West African members of the Senate and House of Assembly in South Africa, the members of the Legislative Assembly including Jan de Wet, and that their personal and policy differences be resolved. Du Plessis agreed to convene such a meeting.

On 10 August Jan Joubert, Assistant Secretary to the Party, directed a circular to all the parties concerned, requesting them to attend a meeting to be held on Thursday 18 August at 14:30 in the caucus room of the Legislative Assembly. Dr Paul van der Merwe was assigned Chairman of the meeting, which proceeded without an agenda. Except for the four of us who had met Ministers P.W. and Pik Botha two weeks earlier at Eros Airport, no one knew what the reasons for and the purpose of the meeting was. They didn't know that the meeting was called at the request of Minister P.W. Botha with an explicit instruction to Du Plessis to restore unity in the Party.

It was clear right from the outset that Du Plessis was on the war path, and that he wanted to neutralise me by insinuating that I was responsible for the disunity in the Party. Pretorius handed out a document to those present. The document of two typed pages, which had been drafted very formally, referred to differences that exist within the National Party and to persons who had expressed themselves publically against the policies of the National Party. Other "facts" that I can no longer recall were also mentioned. In the second part of the document a motion of full confidence in the National Party and its leader

was proposed. In conclusion it was proposed that the white delegation formalise cooperation agreements with the other delegations in
the Constitutional Conference. It was accordingly accepted that there
were unbridgeable differences within the Conference that would make
a "Turnhalle Party" impossible should there be an election, so that only
a cooperation agreement could be considered.

It was clear to me that a multiracial party was unacceptable to my
colleagues, and that the Turnhalle Conference was still seen by them as
a multinational gathering. The different delegations could therefore,
while retaining their different policy standpoints, enter into a cooperation or election agreement, should there be an election. To me this
proposal was totally unacceptable and I had no doubt that it would be
rejected by our colleagues in the Conference. I was also convinced that
the black inhabitants of our country would never vote for a dispensation that in terms of certain important functions would subject them
to a white second-tier government in the greatest part of the country.
I suspected that Eben van Zijl had drafted this "clever" proposal. (He
was also responsible for drawing up the Turnhalle's interim constitution, to which the National Party was clinging so fiercely.) After independence this was confirmed by Koos Pretorius.

After reading the proposal by Pretorius, Dr Van der Merwe arranged
that all the documents that had been handed out were returned to
him, because they – as he had put it – contained dynamite. Until late
that night the meeting's time was taken up with reproaches, accusations and denials being slung to and fro, without any progress being
made. Nothing came of the request by the two ministers.

Because I realised how important it was that we reach consensus
on policy and the interpretation of policy, I moved that we put our
personal differences aside and, should there be any bad feelings, offered my hand as a gesture of friendship to everyone at the meeting.
My condition was, however, that another meeting be scheduled within
two weeks, that an agenda be compiled with all the policy issues on
which there were differences of opinion, and that during that meeting, time not be wasted again on personal matters. It wasn't easy for
me to make such a proposal, because the stories that had been spread
were not only untrue, but in some cases even libellous. However, I
also knew that my conscience was clear and that my case was strong
enough to survive these cowardly attempts.

At the meeting on 18 August I held out my hand to Fanie Vilonel, Koos Pretorius, A.H. du Plessis and Eben van Zijl. Initially, Du Plessis and Van Zijl were not prepared to shake my hand, but eventually they did. After the meeting there was great satisfaction among at least the majority of the members present about these developments, and after that they looked forward to achieving unanimity on policy matters in the white ranks before the next session of the Committee under my chairmanship was to resume. It was, after all, the instruction given by the two ministers that peace be made and unity in the party restored. I was satisfied that I had played my part. However, it was soon obvious that Du Plessis regarded the interview with the ministers as a serious setback to his leadership and that he would not use the coming meeting to make peace, but rather to enforce his authority as leader.

The proposed meeting was set for 30 and 31 August 1977, and Appie Louw, the Secretary-in-Chief of the Party, was requested to wait until he had received the discussion points before drafting an agenda, which was to be made available to the members before the time. When the meeting opened under the chairmanship of Dr Paul van der Merwe, there were 14 points on the agenda. To give an idea of the questions and reservations that concerned the leaders of the National Party at the time, I have reproduced the complete agenda below:

1. Evaluation of the position locally as well as abroad – Adv. C.J. Mouton MP.
2. Adaptations of the interim constitution with a view to independence – D.F. Mudge MEC.
3. Political cooperation – D.F. Mudge MEC.
4. Irritating regulations and human relations – D.F. Mudge MEC.
5. Mining policy– Dr W.J. Brandt MP.
6. (a) Defining the National Party policy for the future.
   (b) Uniform policy statement by the leaders corps at the pending congress.
7. Regular meetings of
   (a) the full white delegation,
   (b) elected representatives,
   (c) the Executive Committee – M.C. Botma MP.
8. Informal settlements in towns – A. Brinkman MEC.
9. Landownership in rural areas – A. Brinkman MEC.
10. Schools – A. Brinkman MEC.
11. Political parties – A. Brinkman MEC.
12. Information and propaganda – S.F. Malan MLA.

13. Outreach for foreign recognition and acceptance by African states.
14. Unification of the ethnic groups within SWA following independence.

The first point on the agenda, proposed by Adv. Chris Mouton, requested the leaders to inform the meeting about the latest political and constitutional developments. A.H. du Plessis started the discussion of this point in a very negative way by saying that there was nothing he could say to the leaders that they did not already know or should know. He spoke for about 45 minutes, after which first Eben van Zijl and then I made contributions. Adv. Mouton then expressed his appreciation and the entire meeting was very pleased with the information, to which the members, due to lack of communication, had definitely not had access before.

The second point on the agenda dealt with the amendment of the interim constitution with a view to independence. This was without any doubt the most important point on the agenda, because, together with the issue of the areas of authority, it listed the differences that still had to be dealt with by the Standing Committee, and about which there was a difference of opinion between myself and my white colleagues on the Committee. I reiterated my already well-known position and especially emphasised the promise that Du Plessis had made on more than one occasion, namely that the Conference would be given the opportunity to propose amendments with a view to a UN-controlled election. Messrs Du Plessis, Van Zijl, Pretorius and Brinkman refused to accept any amendments – probably because they thought nothing would come of the Western settlement plan.

After a long-drawn-out discussion, which lasted for hours without us making any progress, Du Plessis proposed that we move on to the next point on the agenda, as he was of the opinion that the majority in the Assembly did not support my view. I was not prepared to accept his proposal, because the majority of the members had not yet expressed an opinion on this sensitive issue. To me it was so important that absolute clarity be reached on these points that I appealed for another hour to be devoted to it at the resumption of the Assembly the next day. The Committee of the Conference was to resume its business on the following Tuesday and I would then have to convey the viewpoint of the National Party to them. I could just imagine how the other members of the Committee would react if I were to inform them that Du Plessis's guarantee that they would be given the opportunity to make amendments to the Turnhalle Constitution before independence, was no longer valid.

The credibility of the whites was at stake. I was determined to not simply throw in the towel. I couldn't accept that the National Party, after everything we had done to gain goodwill and trust, would now go back on its word. While I was crisscrossing the country with my black and coloured colleagues to gain support for the Turnhalle Conference, my white colleagues did not even see their way clear to convince their white supporters that changes, even compromises, would have to be made.

Besides the possibility of an election under UN supervision, in which we would need the support of all the moderates in the country, there were also still the increasing terrorist activities to which the civilian population was being subjected. The murder of white families, among them the Walther couple who had been murdered in front of their children on their farm 20 kilometres north-west of Okahandja, was still fresh in our memories. But it wasn't only the whites who were victims of SWAPO's terrorism.

I have already mentioned the abduction of 121 pupils and a number of teachers from the Catholic School at Anamulenge on the night of 20 April. This school was situated 18 kilometres from the Angolan border and the abduction was carried out by 40 members of SWAPO's armed wing. Russian aircraft were bringing in 200 fully equipped Cuban soldiers per day from Havana to Luanda. It was established that there were already thousands of Cuban soldiers and a large number of Russian advisers in Angola. But here in Windhoek ramparts were being erected to protect whites against moderate and well-disposed inhabitants.

Du Plessis agreed very reluctantly that we could continue the discussion of this point the next morning, but it was abundantly clear to me that he saw my opposition as a challenge to his authority as leader. Over the years he had become used to having the last word and few people had the courage to oppose him. When the caucus started the next morning, it was clear to me from his appearance and hoarse voice that he'd had a bad night. He asked to speak immediately and according to notes kept by the Chairman, Dr Paul van der Merwe, said the following: "I stand here as an accused man. The last session of the caucus was futile and now it is like this again. We keep walking into a brick wall. I am directing the question personally to Mr Mudge: What's going on in this Party? I planned to resign as leader of the Party during the coming congress, but now I'm going to stand for re-election. I remained silent at first but I won't run away." He said that he had spent a long time the previous evening looking for two recent statements I had made that had been published prominently in *Die Suidwester* and that he had found them. I knew then that nothing would come of the appeal by the two ministers to Du Plessis to restore unity; that a further discussion of the policy would not take place; and that we were back to personal attacks.

Du Plessis referred to a report in *Die Suidwester* under the headline "Mudge says he will not be dictated to". The report covered an interview I had with the editor of the newspaper in reaction to certain remarks that Werner Neef, MLA, had made to Kurt Dahlmann, editor of the *Allgemeine Zeitung*, and Dahlmann's persistent attempts to prescribe to me regarding my political future. I reacted to this by saying that I would not let Mr Dahlmann or anyone else dictate to me, but would be led by my convictions and conscience. Apparently this was seen once again by Du Plessis as a challenge to his leadership, although in that specific article it was about Mr Dahlmann's attempts to prescribe to me. Du Plessis launched a venomous attack on me and asked whether it was right that a loyal party member say such a thing. I was not prepared to accept that the Party leader could deprive me of my right to place this very sensitive issue on the agenda of the meeting in such a dictorial manner.

Du Plessis then produced a second newspaper report, which featured a speech I had made at the annual dinner of the Chamber of Commerce in Windhoek. The members of this organisation included many members of the English and German language groups and it was especially from the ranks of these two groups that tremendous pressure was being exerted on me to break away from the National Party of South West Africa. I maintained that since I was consistently trying to bring the different language and colour groups together, I could not be expected to divide them by splitting my party. Du Plessis apparently interpreted my words as meaning that I was claiming that

I alone had brought the different population groups together, and that I was therefore trying to diminish the role he and Van Zijl had played.

No objective person could have interpreted the report like this, and I could draw no other conclusion than that Du Plessis was trying to render me suspect. Immediately after this E.T. Meyer, MLA, proposed a motion of full confidence in the leader, Du Plessis. As a loyal supporter of the National Party and someone who had great faith in Du Plessis, you could probably expect this from him. He was a conservative Afrikaner and disloyalty and fickleness were not qualities that characterised him. He probably felt sorry for Du Plessis and was not sure whether I was on the right track. I had no reason to suspect that he had anything against me as a person, but he had to choose between a long-standing leader and a younger man whose political views were still regarded with suspicion by many party members. He probably wanted to put an end to an unpleasant debate with his motion, hoping the problem could be resolved later. He also had every reason to believe that I had no or little support among Party ranks for my viewpoint, as it eventually became evident.

Furthermore, like the other members of the caucus, he had also not been informed about the real objective of the meeting. Du Plessis had not told his colleagues about the visit of Ministers Pik and P.W. Botha, so they did not know that the main purpose of the meeting was to solve the Party's internal problems. Even though this information would have put me in a better light, I also kept quiet about it, because I didn't want to cause him embarrassment. I, as well as other members, objected to E.T. Meyer's proposal because we could not understand why it was necessary. It had nothing to do with confidence or distrust in the leader, but was about differences on certain policy issues. The motion could only have been aimed at enabling the leader to cut the discussions short and impose his personal opinion. Despite my objections and pleas, the motion was put to the vote and six members of the Assembly had no other choice than to vote with me against the motion of confidence in their leader. They were Appie Louw, Paul Smit, Stefaans Malan, Paul Minnaar, Bertie Botha and Werner Neef – all members of the Legislative Assembly.

A tense silence prevailed in the meeting. None of us – including myself – had ever thought that anything like this could happen in the mighty National Party. Everybody expected Du Plessis to react first, which he did. He was brief and to the point, saying only that the events would be discussed by the pending congress where decisions would be taken, and that all Party members would then have to subject themselves to the decision of the congress.

I realised immediately that from then on my position in the Party would be untenable, but I didn't for a moment consider resigning. That decision, so I believed, I could not take on my own. I accepted the proposal to refer the events to the caucus at the annual congress of the Party as the correct course of action. I did, however, realise that reconciliation was not possible and that the congress would have to vote on viewpoints, and what's more, that they would have to choose between the proponents of those different viewpoints. With this in mind, I stated that, if requested to do so, I would make myself available as candidate for the leadership position. Dr Paul van der Merwe then, without there being any further discussion, adjourned the meeting.

Few people were aware of the tremendous pressure I was subjected to during the preceding months to break away from the National Party. Prominent Germans such as Dr Herbert Halenke, Conrad Lilienthal, Albi Brückner, Volker Rodenwoldt and many others, were – due to impatience – already forming an organisation of German-speakers. The Steering Committee of the to-be-founded Interessengemeinschaft Deutschsprachiger Südwester (IG) had already handed a memorandum to the representatives of the Western countries on 17 June. In fact, the founding congress of the IG took place on 11 August, only a few days before our meeting of 18 August.

My white colleagues, however, could not see that the writing was on the wall. The German-speakers, who had been loyal supporters of the National Party for many years, had lost faith in the Party, especially after Du Plessis joined the Conference, and now they were fast losing faith in me. It was under circumstances such as these that I felt inclined to say like John Vorster: "Lord, where to now?" I subsequently wondered why Du Plessis hadn't proposed that the disagreements between the two of us be referred to the congress instead of allowing a stalemate to be reached at a secondary committee meeting. We were, after all, the two most senior office-bearers of the Party, him being leader of the Party and me being leader of the Legislative Assembly of South West Africa.

The battle for leadership

During the next four weeks supporters of Du Plessis and those who backed me started canvassing support for their respective candidates. It wasn't done on an organised level and I didn't participate. I urged my supporters to act responsibly. In spite of everything, we were all still members of the same party, and if I were elected leader, I would obviously still need the support of those who had voted against me. The only organised meeting I attended was in Gobabis. Koos Pretorius had invited me to accompany him to meet the Constituency Council of the Party in his constituency. At this meeting it became clear to me once again that the ordinary members of the Party were completely uninformed about what was happening in the Conference and what the differences were. As a result of our information meetings, the population groups were much better informed.

Amid this political discord, Judge M.T. Steyn arrived in Windhoek on 1 September 1977. He had already been appointed as Administrator General in June, following the discussions with the contact group, to administer the Territory in terms of the settlement agreement during the transitional period. In accordance with his assignment, he also had to supervise the planned election of a Constituent Assembly in cooperation with the representative of the UN Secretary General.

The National Party Congress was opened by Du Plessis on 27 September 1977 in the Safari Motel just outside Windhoek. Unlike normal procedure, the election of office-bearers was first on the agenda. Van Zijl, who acted as Chairman, had arranged that Du Plessis and I, as nominees for the leadership, would each have an opportunity to address the congress – something that was not customary when electing office-bearers. This underlined the fact that this was not about a choice between two individuals, but a choice between two points of view. Du Plessis, who was first to speak, launched a sharp attack on me, trying to link certain rumours about him to me. In addition, he tried to cast suspicion on my actions in the preceding period. I can no longer remember everything he said, but it must have been clear to everyone that for him it was not about a conflict of viewpoints, but a challenge of his authority. I am convinced that because of this he had lost a great deal of the support he had at that stage.

In my speech I didn't launch a personal attack on Du Plessis or anyone else. I didn't have a written speech. In fact, throughout my political career I seldom used pre-written speeches. I expressed my appreciation to Du Plessis for the role he had played over the years and furthermore stated only my views on policy issues. I had planned to compare our points of view systematically so that the congress could make a choice. If I then lost the leadership election, it would mean that my point of view had been rejected. Then I would have no other choice but to leave the congress and the Party. I didn't say this to the congress, because I didn't want to create the impression that I wanted to blackmail them, while Du Plessis had, in fact, indicated that if he were to lose, he would go back to his farm. I realised afterwards that I had made a mistake. Many delegates later admitted that had they known what would happen, they would have voted for me. They knew that Du Plessis would resign if he lost, but were hoping that I would remain in the Party if I were to lose. To maintain unity in the Party, they then voted for Du Plessis.

The voting resulted in a narrow victory of 141 votes versus 135 in favour of Du Plessis, with three spoilt ballot papers. After this I announced that I was going to leave the congress, but urged my supporters to remain in the Party and to make right what was wrong. It was an unreasonable request and contradicted my sustained conviction that, whatever I did or decided, I would take my supporters with me. A total of 78 delegates, including the Secretary, Appie Louw, the Assistant Secretary, Jan Joubert, Blok de Wet and Diana Anthonissen who were responsible for keeping the minutes, followed me out of the hall.

As can be expected, for many years after this, the question was asked whether I had made the right decision. Many wondered whether, as a result of my good performance at the congress, I wouldn't then have been in a better position to bring my views home within the Party. I knew, however, that if I had subjected myself, I would have lost the initiative of cooperation that we had with the other population groups. I had to decide whether I would go under with the Party. I also realised that if I were to stay on, it would not be the end of the infighting. Today I am more convinced than ever that I made the right decision. I did, however, hope that I wouldn't have to fight against the National Party of South West Africa in the first place, but rather against SWAPO.

The Republican Party and the Democratic Turnhalle Alliance enter the scene, 1977

I could not really foresee how the situation surrounding South West Africa's attainment of freedom would develop over the next few years, but I was convinced that a new political and governmental dispensation was an absolute prerequisite for the creation of a just and peaceful society. When I left the National Party Congress on 27 September 1977, there was perhaps clarity in my mind on the general direction in which we should move, but at the same time I had great uncertainty about the practical steps that were required.

A new party sees the light

Outside the meeting hall the delegates who had walked out gathered around me. They wanted to know where we should go from here. In the meantime journalists were constantly bothering me for more information. Because nothing had been planned before the time, there was absolute chaos outside the hall. Someone suggested that we meet in the hall of the SKW (Sportklub Windhoek) at eight that evening.

When we arrived at the hall that evening, over 200 supporters had gathered there. Although I knew beforehand that if I lost I wouldn't be able to remain a member of the National Party and would also not be able to leave politics, I hadn't planned any action prior to the time. A split was never considered before it actually happened; it was the natural outcome of the series of events that had preceded it. Up until that point I was still entertaining the hope that I would be able to convince the Party of my viewpoints. There was the possibility of a political union with other parties, but not that it would be preceded by a split. There were probably some of my supporters who were thinking of a new party; indeed, this was strongly advocated, especially from the German side.

The mood of the meeting was strongly in favour of establishing a new party. However, I was of the opinion that final decisions should not be taken; that we should first allow emotions to calm down so that we could decide calmly and unemotionally. Consequently, the meeting appointed a convener for each constituency, which in turn would have to assemble steering committees for those constituencies. The steering committees then would have to test the feelings in their respective constituencies.

On 28 September 1977, the newly appointed Administrator General, Judge M.T. (Theunie) Steyn, promulgated Proclamation R.429, thereby ending South West Africa's representation of 27 years in the South African Parliament. Things were starting to happen and the establishment of a new party could no longer be delayed since the now dynamic developing situation around South West Africa required setting up structures and developing policy viewpoints.

The Inaugural Congress of the new Party took place on 5 October 1977. Congress decided on the name Republican Party of South West Africa, since there was no longer the slightest doubt that an independent republic would be our ultimate goal. We didn't know exactly how we would get there, because we could not decide this on our own. We knew, however, that we would have to reflect on this with our black and coloured countrymen, as we had attempted to do in the Turnhalle.

I was subsequently chosen as leader of the new Party, with Werner Neef as Chairman and Appie Louw as Secretary. I was filled with dreams and ideals and believed in the justice of our cause, but could fortunately at that stage not foresee what lay ahead for me on the road to independence. I couldn't foresee that it would take another decade to reach our destination; that we would frequently be brought to a standstill and would have to make U-turns to seek new alternative routes. It came down to taking two steps forward and one back. I would not have believed that on more than one occasion we would be tripped by people and organisations that were supposed to join us in the fight against a common enemy.

Our task ahead

At the conference already we realised that we would have to fight on several fronts. For starters, the majority of the white inhabitants disagreed with us on the most fundamental principles and objectives. Then there was SWAPO, which was not interested in a democratic solution. There was also a critical, and in some instances even a hostile, international community. The worst was the decisions that were taken about our future over which we had little or no say, despite all the fine promises that we would be the ones to make decisions about our future. This young Party, born in controversy, had to find answers to the following questions: Do we have a role to play? If so, what will it be? And where are we going to start?

Six of the 18 leaders of the white Legislative Assembly left the National Party with me, but we were still members of the Legislative Assembly of South West Africa. I was not prepared to hand this important platform over to the National Party by resigning from it. If we were to remain there, we could not only influence the decisions taken by this important government institution, but could take over the Legislative Assembly by winning two more seats. To be able to achieve this we had to win over and enrol persons who would be eligible to vote in an election of the Legislative Assembly of South West Africa as members of the Party. In view of the fact that non-white persons at that stage did not have the right to vote it made no sense enrolling them as members of the Republican Party – making the party for all intents and purposes a white party. I knew that South African leaders, due to the problems within their own ranks, would not risk opposing a white majority in South West Africa. I also knew that when an alliance was formed at a later stage, our new partners would want to know what the support of the Republican Party was among the whites, just as we would want to know what their support was among their respective population groups.

In the short term it was therefore necessary for us to prove two things: Firstly, that we were prepared to stand by our stated convictions despite threats and vilification; and secondly, that we did indeed have noteworthy support among the whites. My black colleagues said to me on more than one occasion: "Mr Mudge, you must get the whites on board; we will bring our people." The message was clear: It should not be the RP's objective to keep the whites apart, but to make them part of a comprehensive political alliance in due course. First, however, we had to do some house-cleaning of our own. Our black and coloured countrymen agreed: Get those whites who were obstacles to cooperation on board. It would not be that simple. A hefty fraternal quarrel would first have to be resolved.

Ethnicity reared its head also in the Republican Party. The German-speakers, under leadership of Conrad Lilienthal, and the English-speakers, under leadership of Louise Van Wyngaarden, asked for guaranteed representation on the Executive Committee of the Party. Kurt

Böhme, a Navy captain in the German fleet during the Second World War and a valued friend until he passed away, did not agree with this. He saw no reason why we could not trust one another with our language, culture and traditions. But I opposed him, because I was of the opinion that there were certain factors that you could not ignore and that solutions had to be found for these. Three language committees were established. In spite of criticism opposing this, we could at least prove to our countrymen that ethnicity was not based on colour.

Therefore, the next step would have to be to accomplish political cooperation, for which I had been fighting for so long. To achieve this, we had to go to the people.

Our first public meeting

On the Wednesday evening after the adjournment of the Inaugural Congress of the Republican Party, I addressed my first public meeting in the Windhoek High School. About 1200 people filled the hall and the tension was tangible. Werner Neef acted as Chairman and Appie Louw, Paul Smit, Stefaans Malan, Bertie Botha and Paul Minnaar joined me on stage. In my speech I said that confusion had probably arisen after what had happened in the preceding days, and that I would attempt to bring clarity. I gave the assurance that, although the temptation was great, I had no relish for mudslinging, and appealed to all those supporting me not to sink to that level. I pointed out that political parties were not holy cows, but a means to an end, and that it was not a sin to differ from one another, but a fundamental right. I supported the Prime Minister's plea that we would not do anything to make a difficult situation worse.

I addressed the German-speaking members in the audience, who had placed their hopes in me and had applied pressure on me over a long time to break away from the National Party. I addressed them in their own language (as I had consistently done in the past). I closed my introduction with the following words:

> The political phase now lies ahead, and the time has come for political orientation aimed at the important changes now inevitable. Sentimental considerations will have to make way for practical, realistic and sober thinking. The time has come for us to get our priorities straight. Organisations and people – including myself and my colleagues – can no longer be more important

than the objective we wish to achieve and the country and its
people that we want to serve.

I then recalled the events on the international front over the past few
decades in chronological order. I referred to the Turnhalle Conference
and the decisions taken there; and reassured the audience that the Defence Force was fully competent in ensuring our safety, and that the
events on the political front would change nothing in this respect. On
the implications of an election under United Nations supervision and
its possible consequences, I did not beat about the bush, emphasising
that it did not only concern the future of the whites. For this reason
the Republican Party would not walk this road alone, but would seek
alliance with other parties and groups, especially those that had been
involved in the Turnhalle Conference.

With reference to the National Party I merely reiterated what I had
often discussed in closed meetings of the Party and the Standing Committee: the lack of communication, credibility, realism and the clinging
to dogmatic concepts within the Party.

Towards the end of my speech I referred to important policy matters, especially in relation to discriminatory legislation and the disregard of the human rights of our countrymen and -women and that we
should immediately terminate these unfair practices. Concerning the
sensitive issue of education, I emphasised that the cultural (not racial)
diversity of the population should be accommodated. With reference
to land reform, I suggested that black farmers should have the right to
buy agricultural land in the commercial agricultural areas. I envisaged
a properly drafted, comprehensive policy document on this matter in
due course.

I was happy with the course of the meeting. There was no bitterness or malice, neither on my part nor from the audience. However, I
did not bargain for what lay ahead for me as well as for my family in
the months ahead. Obviously my position as member of the Executive
Committee and member of the white delegation to the Standing Committee were now compromised. I had to vacate my official residence
and return my official vehicle within a month, while my salary was
reduced to that of an ordinary member of the Legislative Assembly.
I didn't own a private home and had to buy a house immediately. It
would not be the last time in my political career that I would end up in
such a situation as a result of my convictions.

Minister P.W. Botha and I come to blows for the first time

On 8 October 1977, less than two weeks after the split, I happened to bump into P.W. Botha, then Minister of Defence, in Port Elizabeth. Quite some time before the fatal congress and my resignation from the National Party, I was invited by the Toastmasters organisation in Port Elizabeth to address them on the importance of communication and the advancement of human relations. That same evening Minister Botha was addressing a public meeting of the National Party in town, but we were unaware of each other's presence. I was invited afterwards by my hosts to have a drink with them at the hotel where I was staying.

While enjoying ourselves, someone tapped me on the shoulder and introduced himself as Minister P.W. Botha's private secretary. He invited me on behalf of the Minister to visit Botha in his suite later that evening, since the Minister wished to speak to me. I accepted the invitation and later knocked on the Minister's door. I had barely entered the room when he started berating me for having caused discord among the white people of South West Africa. He said he had a good mind to "*donner*" (wallop) me there and then, to which I replied laughingly: "It takes two to tango!" It was clearly not an evening for jokes. In the presence of Elize Botha and the editor of *Die Oosterlig*, Louis Oosthuizen, I was accused of many things.

This was my first clash with P.W. Botha, but not the last. Over the following decade we regularly came to blows. He was totally obsessed with white unity and could never understand that white unity would inevitably lead to black unity.

My relationship with P.W. Botha was very different to the one I had with John Vorster. A month before the split I consulted with Vorster in Pretoria. Upon leaving the Union Building, he asked me if his information was correct about my intention to contest the leadership of Du Plessis at the next congress. Upon confirmation from me, he asked: "What are you going to do if you lose?" My answer was that I would have no other choice but to resign from the Party, to which he replied briefly: "That would be a pity." Just that. No reproaches, no threats. His reaction came as no surprise, since it was he who had sent P.W. and Pik to Windhoek shortly before to ask Du Plessis to resign as leader of the Party, the result of which, must surely have been brought to his attention. I still remember the conversation I had with him and Jan de

Wet when our leader wanted to thwart the plan for a constitutional conference.

On my way back to Windhoek, I felt assured that Mr Vorster and I were friends and that we would form a strong bond in future. I was not concerned about his political past – such as his Ossewa Brandwag years and internment in the Koffiefontein Camp – since I am not too proud of my own political past. Whenever I met with him, he never spoke to me from behind his desk, but always invited me to talk to him from a comfortable chair at his coffee table. He was always prepared to listen, which P.W. never was, and regularly enquired after the well-being of my wife and family. He liked to talk about his children and grandchildren. I remember him saying once that a grandchild was a gift from God to an old man. He could also talk passionately about rugby. I hoped that we would be able to walk the road to independence together. However, we would first have to cross deep waters in the course of the next year.

I am digressing. The morning after my altercation with P.W. Botha in Port Elizabeth, we found ourselves on the same aeroplane to Cape Town. I sat right in front on the left side, and he right in front on the right. Our meeting was jovial and us ending up in a boxing match seemed unlikely. After a while he asked the person sitting next to me to swop seats with him. He didn't mention the split again, but wanted to know more about my plans for the future. I assured him that I would act only in the best interests of South West Africa, but that the National Party of South West Africa, which in any case had already decided to sever its ties with the Party in South Africa, was not prepared to come out of its trenches. He indicated that the English press was using the split in the National Party of South West Africa at the expense of the National Party in South Africa. It was clear to me that he was concerned about the effect of what was happening in South West Africa on the politics in South Africa.

At that point I couldn't foresee that what was happening with us should have any influence on the political climate in South Africa. Time, however, proved that it was indeed the case, although South African political leaders and writers were not prepared to admit it. Pik Botha and his Department of Foreign Affairs even claimed at one stage that everything that was happening in South West Africa was the result of an initiative taken by them. In a speech at the Rand Afrikaans University my reaction to this was that Pik wanted to be the bridegroom at every wedding and the corpse at every funeral. Needless to say, he did not like this and reacted in his customary way.

When I bade P.W. Botha farewell at Cape Town Airport, I mentioned that I would be staying over in Stellenbosch for an appointment with the Cape Town Cultural Board on Monday evening. He clearly didn't like this at all, saying curtly: "You mustn't confuse my people," to which I replied: "I won't."

Politics become dirty

The next few months were characterised by the dirtiest politics ever in the history of South West Africa. It was clear that I would be the main target of the smear campaign by the National Party, and in the process nothing would be spared to discredit me. Notwithstanding, the Republican Party grew from strength to strength and it became clear to all that A.H. du Plessis had completely underestimated the ability of the young Party. During the next two and a half months I addressed 45 meetings – from Noordoewer on the banks of the Orange River to Katima Mulilo on the banks of the Zambezi River. The RP did not yet have branches in many of these places. Coen Brand, an attorney, offered to be my travelling Chairman. We sometimes landed my aircraft at small places and had to walk to the meeting because no one was prepared to stick his neck out to fetch us. At most of the meetings we were met by a wall of resistance. The National Party supporters were rebellious, I was accused of treason and of "licking the boots of the kaffirs". Eben van Zijl called me the "darling of the leftists". Nevertheless, I succeeded at getting my message across at most of the meetings, albeit it with numerous interjections.

Occasionally things became rather unruly. At Grootfontein the school hall was packed with members of the National Party. It was organised beforehand by Gernot Schaaf, a local farmer. The organisers had even filled the gallery with schoolchildren. There was chaos from the outset and never a moment's silence. When Coen Brand and I took our seats on stage with Jurie Opperman, who ironically had HNP (Herstigte Nasionale Party) connections, tomatoes and eggs were hurled at us. It would have been inappropriate to open the meeting with a prayer, which was normally the procedure. I spoke for about an hour – without there being a moment's silence – but I didn't allow myself to be distracted.

The real confrontation came during question time. The racket was at such a pitch that even the questioners, Gernot Schaaf and Grammie Brandt, couldn't be heard. Referring to a newspaper report, Gernot wanted to know from me whether I thought I was the Messiah. He insisted that I hand the microphone to them so that they could make themselves heard. Fortunately, I had been involved in politics far too long to do such a stupid thing, and advised them to restrain their supporters, in which case neither them nor I would need a microphone. Some of their supporters leapt onto the stage and tried to take the microphone away from me. They managed to get away with the stand, but I held onto the headpiece – it was one of the older models, nice and heavy – and threatened to hit the next fellow to jump on stage over the head with it. Before someone switched off the lights to restore order, I heard my old colleague Grammie yell (which he had to do to make himself heard): "You said this evening that we Grootfonteiners gossip about you behind your back. Last night at Mr Du Plessis's meeting I said that you are a political coward. Tonight I am saying it to your face!"

Back at our hotel Coen, Jurie and I discussed the events of the evening. I asked Jurie, who was known for his extremely conservative approach, why he had agreed to act as chairman, since it exposed him to being insulted and having eggs hurled at him. He answered frankly that he didn't like the direction things were heading, but that his common sense told him the RP policy was the only one that could work. I didn't entirely understand it, but I appreciated his support. *Die Suidwester*, the mouthpiece of the National Party, reported the next morning: "Mudge disappears into the dark."

On 6 December in Gobabis it did not go any better. This was Koos Pretorius's constituency and we couldn't manage to put together a committee. I telephoned a friend with whom we had worked in the National Party in the good old days. I heard via the grapevine that she was kindly disposed towards us, but that her husband did not share her sentiments. She offered to organise the hall for us, but wanted nothing more to do with the meeting, since it would – she said – cause tension in her family. The large show hall was packed with NP supporters, and a few – according to eyewitnesses – were armed with horsewhips and even pistols. A group of Herero supporters under the leadership of Bishop Kamburona attended the meeting. That evening

I didn't feel particularly proud of my white countrymen, but I came off best.

With the next RP meeting at Gobabis things did not go well at all. Dr Paul van der Merwe, a member of the House of Assembly in the South African Parliament, and now member of the Republican Party, was the main speaker, and the dear, mild-tempered Oom Jan Wiese was Chairman. There was absolute chaos right from the outset. Oom Jan was unsuccessful in getting the audience under control. Dr Paul, formerly Deputy Speaker of the House of Assembly in South Africa and a seasoned politician, realised that Oom Jan would not be able to bring the audience under control. Relying on the Christian principles so often professed by members of the National Party, he appealed for a moment of silence for the opening prayer and continued to pray starting with the well-known passage, "I lift up my eyes to the mountains – where does my help come from?" when he was interrupted from the audience by someone shouting: "Paul van der Merwe, tonight you're going to sh-t your pants!" This was not only the end of the prayer but also the end of the meeting. Because of the mayhem Oom Jan simply had to adjourn the meeting.

It was the same story with the meetings of my other colleagues Appie Louw and Michael Meyer in Pionierspark and Outjo, among others, but the story is so unpleasant that I'll leave it at that. It carried on like this until the general election in 1980. Today many of the agitators of those days are prosperous businessmen and farmers in the new Namibia.

The Turnhalle Conference comes to an end

As a result of the events on the white political front, the activities of the Standing Committee of the Turnhalle Conference temporarily came to a standstill. Needless to say, it was not my resignation from the National Party that brought the Conference to an end. I was just no longer a member of the white delegation. When the Standing Committee was convened again, I attended the meeting as serving Chairman, and it was proposed that I stay on as impartial Chairperson. There was no objection – to my surprise also not by the white delegation. Jan de Wet took my position as member of the white delegation.

The Committee immediately continued discussing the points of dissent that stood over from the previous meeting. Emotions ran high and a deadlock was averted when Van Zijl proposed that a conciliation committee be appointed in an attempt to reach a solution. It is tragic that the National Party first had to split before a compromise could be considered by the white delegation. Although some delegates had serious doubts about such a committee, I appealed to them to give it a chance. A committee under my chairmanship was then appointed, with Van Zijl and Jan de Wet as the representatives of the white delegation, and Barney Barnes and Fanuel Kozonguizi for the other groups.

The Conciliation Committee convened on 3 November and started its deliberations by identifying the differences between the two groups. The representatives of the National Party then argued that it would probably be difficult to reach agreement on these differences. They proposed that we accept that we disagreed on the interpretation of the areas of authority and the division of functions, but that we, in spite of the differences and with a view to a future election, draw up an agreement of cooperation. The attitude of the NP representatives was difficult to explain, especially since they had decided at the National Party Executive meeting shortly before to make concessions in respect of six important points of disparity. At the congress where the split had occurred, the National Party also decided in favour of repealing the Immorality Act and the Mixed Marriages Act, and to sever its ties with the National Party of South Africa.

An exceedingly long discussion then followed on the practical implementation of an electoral agreement while there were still such serious policy differences. Barnes pointed out that it would be untenable if two speakers advocated conflicting policies from the same stage. And how would such differences be accommodated if such an electoral front were to win an election?

The majority of the members of the Standing Committee were not prepared to make further concessions, and it was clear to me that we were on a collision course. Ten delegations intimated that they wanted to meet separately – that is to say without the white delegation – to formulate their final stance, after which they would come back to the full Standing Committee with their final decision. This put me in an uncomfortable position. Although I was still accepted as Chairman of the Committee, I was no longer a member of the white delegation and could also no longer convene with the others unless they invited me. In the meantime Administrator General Judge M.T. Steyn had already decided that the Constitutional Conference should conclude its activities and then dissolve.

The ten delegations, which were subsequently referred to as the "Black Caucus" by the National Party, met during the first week of November under the chairmanship of Barnes in the Grand Hotel in Windhoek. I was invited to attend the meeting as an observer. The proceedings were recorded and is still in my possession. The first few speakers took the view that there was no possibility for reconciliation or for an agreement, and that a political alliance, as I had envisaged on several occasions, should be established. The Republican Party, with the other ten parties, should then become members of it.

After several speakers had taken part in the discussions, I was asked for my opinion. Although I felt strongly about political cooperation and the realisation of an alliance, I reminded the meeting that the gathering had been convened to consider a final proposal about a possible electoral agreement, and then to report back to the Standing Committee, which was still in existence. This was what we had undertaken to do, and for the sake of credibility, this is what I felt we should do. After this we could proceed to establish an alliance. My proposal was accepted as such.

Following a long and sometimes stormy session, the caucus decided that if the National Party were not prepared to make concessions relating to the differences in respect of the draft constitution, an electoral agreement would not be possible. The decision was conveyed to the white delegation in writing. This was, as could be expected, not acceptable to the National Party.

That was the end of the historical Turnhalle Conference, which was able to reach consensus on so many principles over a period of two years, but stumbled over a few remaining points. A.H. du Plessis and Eben van Zijl will go down in history as the people who, due to their unyielding attitude regarding the remaining points of difference, were responsible for the split – not only in the National Party, but also in the Turnhalle Conference. Van Zijl even ignored the decision taken by the National Party Executive to make certain concessions.

The Democratic Turnhalle Alliance becomes a reality

On 6 November 1977, the ten black and coloured delegations met with the Republican Party, and the Democratic Turnhalle Alliance (DTA) was founded. The fact that the Republican Party would become a member of an organisation such as the DTA was actually a matter of course. Clemens Kapuuo was elected as the first President, with Pastor Cornelius Ndjoba of Owambo as Vice-President, I as Chairman and Dr Ben Africa as Deputy Chairman. This heralded the birth of a strong political alliance that grew from strength to strength in the years to come.

We immediately started organising public meetings to introduce the DTA throughout the country. This had to be scheduled between the meetings already organised by the Republican Party, but it caused no problems. I could not imagine that whites would be interested in attending a political meeting on a Saturday or Sunday. On Saturdays they watched rugby or some other sport, or hunt or fish, and on Sundays they go to church. I could also not imagine that whites would be prepared to attend DTA meetings, which sometimes lasted from two o'clock in the afternoon until sundown, because as many as four speeches were translated into three or four other languages.

For the other population groups, understandably, weekends were the only opportunity they had for political meetings, cultural get-togethers and funerals. During the week, for example, they could not travel long distances to attend meetings because their working hours didn't allow it. There are numerous other reasons. This, however, made it easy for us to organise meetings. During the week we addressed meetings mainly for whites, and over weekends we were in the black towns and communal areas.

As I paged through my diary of 1977, it occurred to me how often the names of Appie Louw and Michael Meyer appeared in it. They were simply always available, also for DTA meetings. My other colleagues in the Legislative Assembly were equally diligent in their respective constituencies. This way we reached thousands of people in two and a half months. During this period whites attended our meetings in large numbers, sometimes as many as over a thousand at a time. Never in the course of my political career was there so much interest in politics as during this period. Even the people who were mobilised to disrupt RP meetings got the message. I must admit that it was often an embarrassment to me to explain why so few whites attended the meetings in black towns where I was sometimes the only white face. Fortunately, my explanation about the habits of different communities was accepted.

Our own newspaper, *Republikein*, appears on 1 December 1977

During the first two months of the Republican Party's existence we were fighting against a formidable and well-organised opponent. *Die Suidwester*, the mouthpiece of the National Party, spread the message – and the backbiting of the National Party – throughout the country and trashed the Republican Party in every edition, while we had to rely on meetings to spread our message. What happened and what was said at our meetings was reported by *Die Suidwester* selectively and negatively. We simply had no choice – we had to have a mouthpiece.

How does one start a newspaper without funds, which we simply did not have? Nonetheless, we decided in principle to start a newspaper. A prominent businessman offered us a floor in his business building free of charge, which could be shared by the Republican Party and the newspaper. The next problem was to find an editor. I considered Dirk Richard, who was involved in the Perskor newspapers, and met him in Johannesburg. I knew that while working for a newspaper that promoted the National Party, he often irked the NP with his criticism. Another problem was: How do you negotiate remuneration with a senior journalist when you have no money? In the end we agreed that it couldn't work, but we nevertheless remained friends for many years after that.

The next possibility was Dr Jan Spies – known to most people for his humorous anecdotes. But Jan Spies was more than a storyteller. Someone dropped the hint that Jan, coming from a well-known SAP (South African Party) family from Maltahöhe, had at one time considered accepting the position of editor of the SAP-newspaper *Die Suidwes-Afrikaner*. I decided then and there that he was the right man for the job. I had no idea how to get hold of him, since I was unable to reach him at any of the telephone numbers I had at my disposal. I found out later that he was somewhere in Kaokoland making a documentary film and that I could reach him by radio-telephone. I reached him via the radio station at Walvis Bay and there I started, in full hearing of everyone who had two-direction radios and were tuned in on the same frequency, to persuade him to come to Windhoek immediately to become the editor of our new newspaper. We decided to discuss his salary at a later stage – if, of course, there was any money by that time. We recruited Johan Britz of *Die Suidwester* as our first journalist.

Bill Hulme, my daughter Riéth, and son-in-law to be, Paul van Schalkwyk, also joined us. In the meantime volunteers canvassed advertisements for us from door to door, walking the streets for a newspaper that didn't yet exist. We were surprised by the positive response.

But, as was to happen often from then on, I received assistance from a source I least expected. Duimpie Opperman of the Perskor newspaper group in Johannesburg telephoned me one morning to say that his boss, Marius Jooste, wanted to make me a proposal and that I must come to Johannesburg immediately for a meeting – he would pay the travelling expenses. I had heard from people who knew him that Marius Jooste was a difficult man, but I experienced him in a different way. He offered his assistance in publishing our newspaper and suggested that we put together the newspaper and make the plates in Windhoek, after which he would print it in Johannesburg. Printing technology had not yet developed to the stage where everything could be done by computer. The plates were flown to Johannesburg by South African Airways, and the printed newspapers transported back to Windhoek by the same means. Needless to say this cost a great deal of money, but how else could we do it?

Thanks to the assistance of Marius Jooste and Duimpie Opperman, we succeeded in having the *Republikein* on the streets for the first time on 1 December 1977, and every Thursday after that. We invited our DTA colleagues to the launch of the newspaper. We discussed politics and boasted with our new partner, but our black colleagues were mostly impressed with the large number of whites present. One of them said to me: "We didn't realise that you had so many whites supporting you!"

It will probably not be taken amiss if I say a bit more about our new newspaper. We chose the name *Republikein* because we, just as in the case of the Republican Party, knew that this would be our ultimate destination: a free, independent and democratic Republic of South West Africa. Under the heading "*Dagsê Suidwes*" (Good day South West), Jan Spies made valuable remarks about the future of the newspaper. He wrote inter alia: "From the word go and shaking hands we want to say that we've not come to chit-chat or giggle. Also not to whisper from behind cupped hands. We have come to work, to create something big and worthy from the opportunities this country offers." On the subject of democracy Jan said: "The democrat's most indispensable friend is the opponent who comes critically (but honestly) to cross swords for the sake of the truth. Not one person or another person's truth, but the truth. Langenhoven said in days of yore that a matter does not only have two sides but three: my side, your side and the right side." Jan worked on the assumption that you rarely stop thinking and stop speaking. He continued:

> [...] the transience of many so-called solutions ... [can] be sub-
> scribed to half-baked thinking, not only as a result of over-hasti-
> ness or unilateralism, but also because the reality of man's exist-
> ence is so endlessly difficult to fathom ... The free press must
> assist in securing its community against any form of absolutism.
> The surest form of heresy is to absolutise a principle, dogma,
> tradition or any power or ideology that can take hold of a lot
> of people. Big nations have been cast into the abyss by such a
> clouding of the senses, and if you were to delve into their histo-
> ry, you would find that the press did not yet exist, or was asleep,
> or took part in the heresy.

In years to come, I got to know Jan Spies well and had great apprecia-
tion for him. He was someone who could speak authoritatively about theology, archaeology, astronomy, literature, history, philosophy and more. The stories he told made people laugh, albeit it often a laugh with a tear. Behind each anecdote was a message. Many years later at his funeral on 12 January 1996 when I gave a eulogy, I read a passage from his story, *Oubaas en Mankoeraan*. I did this with reference to the black child who was present when Jan had the fatal accident. Many wiped away their tears, as I did.

The lead story in the first edition of the *Republikein* was about Proc-
lamation 12 announced by the Administrator General (AG), which stipulated that the "natives" (black and coloured) could now obtain propriety rights over land in urban native suburbs without permis-
sion. The AG stated further that he did not intend doing anything in respect of mixed residential areas, "because these, according to the old rule, were regarded as part of the white area". As the South African representative, the AG only had authority over black and coloured towns.

I said in my introduction to this memoir that I would not depend too much on newspaper reports, but since this first edition of the *Republikein* was a historical event and voters who did not attend meet-
ings could now for the first time learn about what the RP stood for, I am making an exception.

When compiling the first edition, Jan Spies attempted to give background on the origin of the RP and the DTA and to enable voters, who until that stage had been exposed to one-sided propaganda, to catch up on the political chain of events of the preceding years. Hence, I have briefly summarised a few of the reports that appeared in the first edition.

The *Republikein* reported on a captaincy crisis in Rehoboth – an occurrence that repeated itself with regular intervals – and on Daniel Luipert of the Namas who took on Eben van Zijl because the National Party had not honoured its promise that the Turnhalle Constitution could be amended. I myself was quoted on what I had said at a meeting in Ariamsvlei, namely that "a peaceful solution would not be forthcoming without pain".

The newspaper revealed that several coloured families had been living in "white" residential areas for many years without causing any problems. Cases made known included that of a Lutheran pastor who lived in Church Street opposite the German private school. Two coloured families, the Samuels and the Cupidos, had been living in Planck Street for many years, and some of the neighbours commented that they had not experienced any problems with them. Coloured men and women were living near the Grand Hotel in several apartment buildings without causing any problems.

In another report Eben van Zijl was quoted as follows: "Whites joining a political alliance means the death sentence for the Whites … the fact that Mr Mudge now suddenly sees a difference between the internal and external wings of SWAPO amounts to 'if you can't beat them, join them'." And on the issue of residential areas, Van Zijl expressed himself as follows: "The sum total of Mr Mudge's incorrect actions and the fact of open residential areas and open hospitals spell only one thing: 'Angola'."

Following Du Plessis's assertion that he didn't know about the difference of policy existing between myself and the National Party, the *Republikein* reported on him as saying the following on 26 October: "The first time I became aware that the current leader of the Republican Party differs from us was about two or three weeks before the National Party Congress, when he proposed certain changes to the second-tier functions at a caucus meeting of members of the Legislative Assembly and members of Parliament." However, Van Zijl said the exact opposite on 19 October at Koës: "When the Standing Committee convened for the last session, we walked into a torrent of demands. Then there were also other viewpoints, viewpoints that were not new to us, but that Mr Mudge had already mentioned on several occasions within the National Party."

Van Zijl admitted therefore that the National Party had been aware of the differences for more than three weeks before the Congress. What neither *Die Suidwester* nor the *Republikein* knew was that the differences had existed for so long that by then they were already known to the Cabinet in South Africa, and that the Prime Minister, two months before the Congress, had sent two ministers to Windhoek to resolve them. However, Du Plessis maintained that the first time he had become aware that I differed from him was only two or three weeks before the Congress.

Because it is one of my fondest memories, I have to mention a reader's letter. It was from Bokkie Louw, wife of Senator W.P. Louw and mother of Appie Louw, which was published in the first edition of the *Republikein*. The Louws were stalwart Nationalists and family friends of the Du Plessis's, but had left the National Party Congress with me, following their convictions. Bokkie Louw's rational mind, realism and support were of great value to me. After the establishment of the Republican Party, it was not only important for me to know how many people would support us, but also who they would be. I expected that many of my German- and English-speaking countrymen would support us, but there was speculation that the "conservative" Afrikaners who were traditionally supporters of the National Party, were not yet ready for my "liberal" viewpoints. The delegates who left the congress of the National Party with me were respected and valued people from all the language groups, but I was not sure about the support of the Afrikaans-speakers out there. For instance, the reaction we elicited at Grootfontein and Gobabis obviously made me uneasy, although I knew that it was organised opposition. Tant Bokkie's letter, which encouraged people to think clearly, was important to me, not only because of the message it conveyed, but also because it came from an Afrikaner mother who was not a political disciple or a political hitchhiker.

The *Republikein* rapidly gained ground, not only because of an increase in circulation but also in its influence, although the Nationalists referred to the newspaper disparagingly as the "*Blou Bollie*". It didn't take long before Van Zijl tried to discredit the newspaper. He wouldn't let off, asking where the money came from and alleging that our newspaper was under the influence and control of some or other clandestine money power. Firstly, there wasn't a lot of money; and secondly, the money came from loyal party supporters. Supporters among the farming community for example decided that farm owners would contribute a certain amount per hectare of land they owned. Businessmen, also from South Africa, donated generously. On several occasions I addressed chambers of commerce and other associations in South Africa on invitation, and although I hadn't accepted the invitations with fundraising as the objective, this nevertheless helped gain support for our Party and newspaper. It was encouraging to me to experience so much interest in the new political developments in South West Africa from South Africa and later also from abroad.

The National Party and its newspaper *Die Suidwester* did not take kindly to our success. The scandal mongering about a secret money power would stay with us for years. During a meeting on the Neudamm Experimental Farm a young man accused me of being under the influence of the Illuminati and that I was possibly a member of the order. I was caught somewhat off guard because I wasn't aware of the existence of such an organisation. I asked him who and what the Illuminati were, to which he answered that he was shocked that I did not even realise that I was being controlled by a dangerous organisation. Shortly after this the Herstigte Nasionale Party (Reconstituted National Party) distributed a pamphlet with a photograph of me on it, in which the same allegations were made.

With 40 meetings already under our belt – following the excitement of launching the *Republikein* on 1 December – and four more meetings still to come, namely in Gobabis, Windhoek, Rundu in the Kavango, and Katima Mulilo in the Caprivi on 15 December, we all deserved a holiday and I departed to Hermanus with my family to escape from the political battlefield for a few weeks. I knew that if we were to go to our beloved holiday resort, Swakopmund, I would be running into political friends or foes from early until late. Of this I'd had enough for the time being. Ovamboland would have to wait for the next year, which I knew was going to be a difficult one. We had already decided to tackle SWAPO from the outset in its stronghold, Ovamboland, and we arranged a series of meetings from 6 to 11 February 1978.

Civilians and political leaders pay the highest price

It wasn't only soldiers who died in the war on our borders. In the northern districts of our country white farmers became soft targets to be murdered by SWAPO terrorists, while a disturbing number of Owambo chiefs lost their lives. General Jannie Geldenhuys writes in his book *Dié wat gewen het* (Those who won), that 28 chiefs were murdered over a period of two years. While we were busy making our arrangements for the series of meetings in Ovamboland, a SWAPO supporter informed Billy Marais that there was a plot to murder DTA leaders. I didn't take this seriously, regarding it as an effort to prevent us from holding meetings in Ovamboland, so we continued with our preparations. Billy didn't agree with me and arranged for protection at our houses, and armed guards for the leaders. For Stienie and me this was an uncomfortable situation. We had lost our privacy.

At our last meeting in Katutura before our departure to Ovamboland, steel plates had been placed in front of the stage where the speakers were seated, and bulletproof vests had been issued to them before the time. I flatly refused to wear the vest, saying that it would change my entire personality. I pointed out to the organisers of the meeting that steel plates could not protect anyone's life, since the speaker's entire torso was exposed. This was the last of the steel plates and for most of us, also of the bulletproof vests. At a later stage, however, I would blame myself for not encouraging the wearing of bulletproof vests.

Our first meeting in Ovamboland took place at Okahao farm. I was unable to attend because I still had a meeting to address that same evening at Kalkfeld, after which I would join my colleagues in Ovamboland. Shortly before my meeting was to start at Kalkfeld, Bertie Botha brought me bad news. Billy had telephoned him from Ovamboland to inform him that Toivo Shiyagaya, one of our speakers, had been shot and killed by a SWAPO terrorist during the meeting at Okahao. The terrorist had then sped off on a bicycle, but had been shot and killed by a member of the Territorial Force. I wasn't only shocked, but blamed myself for not being there to support my colleagues at this tragic moment.

Early the next morning I flew to Ovamboland to join my colleagues, among others Clemens Kapuuo. The next evening our meeting took place at Ombalantu. It was raining and the community hall was in semi-darkness. There were many people in and outside the hall, and many of them were wearing coats. No one would have been able to recognise a terrorist among them. My colleagues were uneasy and I have to admit that I wasn't entirely at ease myself. I was blissfully unaware that Kapuuo, Pastor Ndjoba and I were already on SWAPO's hit list. Nevertheless, I was impressed with the large number of people who had shown up despite the events of the previous evening. The meeting proceeded smoothly and without any incidents, as did all the other meetings that followed. We didn't have Defence Force protection during the campaign and could move around freely. However, I did have one or two security guards accompanying me at all times.

We gained the impression that the inhabitants of Ovamboland had already become used to living in a battlefield. We spoke to them in a language that they could understand: We sought peace, not war. Our message was that the members and supporters of SWAPO were our brothers and that they should come home and work with us towards a new Namibia. But SWAPO did not want peace. They were not interested in democratic elections and wanted to take over the country with military force. We warned the people that they should not believe all SWAPO's promises, because "after a SWAPO victory, the thorn trees would not carry fruit, and milk would not come out of the cows' udders on its own".

From the audience came questions and complaints. They could no longer discern between friend and foe. SWAPO was shooting and killing their leaders and the Defence Force was driving their Casspirs through their *mahangu* (pearl millet) fields. When their own brothers came to their kraals, they had no way of knowing whether they were friend or foe, because both sides were exerting improper pressure on them to gain information. One of them said: "If my own brother were to come and hide in my house tonight, what am I to do? Must I chase him away or inform the police?" In the same way that others were concerned about the fraternal quarrels among the whites, I was gripped by this fraternal quarrelling among the Owambos, and wondered: Do our white people know about this, and if they do, do they care?

The rest of the meetings ran smoothly and were concluded with a successful gathering at Oshakati. I felt satisfied that the people of Owambo preferred peace to war. But Sam Nujoma did not seek peace; he wanted war. This became abundantly clear when a week later, on 26 February 1978, he announced to the press: "The question of black majority rule is out. We are not fighting even for majority rule. We are fighting to seize power in Namibia, for the benefit of the Namibian people. We are revolutionaries. You can talk to Kapuuo, Kerina and all those reactionaries about majority rule, but not to SWAPO."

A month later, on 27 March 1978, the President of the DTA, Clemens Kapuuo, was shot and killed in the backyard of his shop in Katutura. The first I heard of this was when a group of weeping Herero chiefs arrived at my house in Pasteur Street in Windhoek. They simply barged in past the security guards and knocked on the front door. When I saw their faces I knew that something terrible had happened. They were speaking so incoherently that all I could make out was that Kapuuo was dead. It took a while to find out exactly what had happened, because they were so traumatised they could barely speak. I later realised that the fact that they had first come to me – a white Afrikaner – for advice and assistance, was proof of mutual trust. I invited them in and there, around my dining-room table, allowed them to vent some of their emotions. As we started talking about our immediate plan of action, they threatened to kill every Owambo they came across if they were to return to Katutura at that point.

It took me a long time to convince them that this would not be the proper way to go about it. I reminded them of the goodwill we had experienced in Ovamboland. We parted an hour or two later, with the understanding that we should convene an Executive Committee meeting of the DTA as soon as possible to discuss further action. But what further action could there be? The police never succeeded in tracking down the murderer, while SWAPO maintained that they had killed the "puppet" Kapuuo. Shortly after this, the Defence Force discovered indisputable evidence that I appeared with Kapuuo and Pastor Ndjoba on SWAPO's hit list. But more about this later. We were sure about one thing though, which was that we had to fight SWAPO politically, at all costs and with all the power at our disposal.

At Kapuuo's funeral in the Herero Heroes' Acre at Okahandja where I was to pay tribute to the deceased leader together with the Administrator General, Judge Theunie Steyn, and senior Herero chiefs, I felt extremely sad and depressed. Not only had I lost a friend, but also a leader in whom I had placed my trust. He was a man of few words, each of which had been considered carefully. I knew that it would not be easy to replace him. Unfortunately, SWAPO also knew this. After the assassination of Kapuuo, I realised that it would not be easy to be involved in politics in my country, and that political leaders would have to fight without arms against an armed enemy. It was difficult to understand that while my colleagues and I were prepared to resume this struggle, we would have to spend more time and energy on the National Party and its supporters, who regarded undermining and slandering the Republican Party and the DTA as their only objective.

My first experience as leader of the opposition

The National Party's most favourite topics were the secret money power with clandestine financial resources behind the RP and the DTA, and Dirk Mudge's bulletproof vehicle. As absurd as this might be, I nevertheless want to tell the story about the bulletproof vehicle. Unaware of the risks associated with our new kind of politics, I was informed by a customs official that a bulletproof vehicle, a gift from the Prime Minister of the Free State of Bavaria in Germany, Franz Josef Strauss, had arrived at the airport.

Before pursuing the matter any further, I called Franz Josef, a long-time friend of mine. It was a friendship that lasted until his death. I asked about the vehicle, to which he replied briefly and succinctly that I apparently did not realise that a politician who was fighting against a militant organisation such as SWAPO ran the risk of being eliminated and that he had been informed that I was on SWAPO's hit list. I was still unaware of any such plans aimed at me specifically and I obviously did not realise that we had entered a new era in politics.

I thanked him for his concern about my safety and for the vehicle that had been delivered to Windhoek at such great expense. What I didn't tell him was that a heavy sedan vehicle was useless and impractical in most parts of South West Africa, especially in Ovamboland. The car, of which the windows couldn't open, was exceedingly impractical, especially when the air-conditioning was not functioning properly, even when driving in Windhoek and on tarred roads. I later swopped the bulletproof Mercedes with Kuaima Riruako, Kapuuo's successor, in exchange for an ordinary vehicle. In the meantime the vehicle gave leaders of the National Party and their newspaper something to gossip about. It was easy for them to talk, because they had never come anywhere close to danger.

With the murder of our DTA colleague Toivo Shiyagaya still fresh in our memories (this was before Kapuuo's murder), the white Legislative Assembly met for the first session of 1978. This was a historical session in more than one respect. For the first time in years there was an opposition again. When Nico Jansen, Member of the Legislative Assembly for Keetmanshoop, also joined the Republican Party, we had eight members in the Legislative Assembly as opposed to the ten representing the National Party.

I had reason to believe that Christo de Jager was also going to join us, and the representation of the parties would then have been equal. From personal discussions I had with Christo before the Congress, I knew that he also had serious differences with the National Party and doubts about Du Plessis's leadership. He had probably voted for me, but – like many others – had not left Congress with us. Subsequently Christo, due to the special status of Walvis Bay, represented this constituency for the National Party in the Cape Provincial Council and subsequently in the South African Parliament.

Before the session commenced, the RP Caucus decided that we would not propose the customary motion of no confidence in the governing party, but instead a motion aimed at a discussion on the political future of South West Africa. The motion read as follows:

That this House declares itself:

1. in favour of an independent Republic of South West Africa while retaining the territorial integrity of the Territory as defined in Section 1 of the Mandate Agreement of 17 December 1920, with a constitution that provides –
   (i) for a democratic form of government that satisfies the reasonable and just political aspirations of its inhabitants, which will protect the rights of the population groups without detracting from the status of the independent state, and that will promote common trust and loyalty and guarantee a stable government;
   (ii) for a free economic system with equal economic opportunities and prospects for all its inhabitants that leads to an increased standard of living and the largest possible degree of economic prosperity and self-sufficiency;
   (iii) for a social system that will recognise the human dignity of all the inhabitants of the country;
   (iv) for the safety of the individual and the state as a whole by maintaining law and order and protection of the boundaries of the country.

2. for the maintenance of law and order and the protection of the country's borders during the interim period without which the attainment of the above objectives will not be possible.

The day before the session commenced, the mouthpiece of the National Party, *Die Suidwester*, stated that it was expected from an opposition party to bring a motion providing for a broad discussion of policy. This is exactly what the motion in question provided for, but then soon afterwards *Die Suidwester* sang a different tune, writing that "the motion was as meaningful as a message on a birthday card, and on face value alone could offer little that could reflect the content and ideas expressed in the motion."

Since this was my first speech as leader of the opposition, it was expected that I would probably delve into the past, be reproachful and make accusations. I decided against this, stating clearly that I wanted to talk about the future of our country. I pointed out that the envisaged election would be different to that which we were accustomed to. We would not be fighting a white opposition in the Legislative Assembly, but SWAPO in a one-person-one-vote election. I argued further that, while the National Party were previously fighting against independence and power-sharing, they now accepted it as a *fait accompli* and that we found ourselves in a whole new situation. I myself had already accepted this a long time ago, as well as that it would be senseless to tackle this new challenge with old, obsolete concepts and policies.

Too many people were still under the impression that the Turnhalle Constitution would be the final constitution for an independent South West Africa, while it had been intended purely as an interim constitution. The National Party, in the words of its leader Du Plessis, had promised that the Turnhalle Constitution could be amended prior to independence, a promise he wouldn't keep and which ultimately led to the split in the Party. In my address I paid a great deal of attention to the shortcomings of the Turnhalle Constitution, wrong interpretations and the need for a new approach. In my closing remarks I reiterated my well-known viewpoint on political cooperation, namely that all moderate inhabitants of our country should form a united political organisation. The National Party recognised the need for this and founded the organisation AKTUR – Aksiefront vir die Behoud van die Turnhallebeginsels (Action Front for the Retention of the Turnhalle Principles).

In his reaction to the motion, Koos Pretorius said for him it did not revolve around personal squabbles, but rather "deep-rooted differences about principles". He continued: "The Honourable Leader of the Opposition and I have often discussed our views in the past. There was a time when we agreed and could find common ground, but it became clear later that we could no longer agree with each other. I must say, however, that these discussions always took place in a very good spirit."

Koos Pretorius said he openly disagreed with me for the first time more or less a month before the NP Congress (when the split occurred) "... when the Honourable Member took the floor speaking on the topic: Amendments to the interim constitution with the view to independence". Pretorius said I had devised a new doctrine and continued as follows:

> Mr Mudge said he was not satisfied that the proposed system of government is based on sound principles, because it would subject thousands of disenfranchised people to a government in which they had no say. During that caucus meeting I sided with the other members whose objections were of a practical nature and announced that I object in principle to the Honourable Member's (Mr Mudge's) point of view. I said among other things that I felt the viewpoint of the Honourable Member, Mr Mudge, clashed directly with our Christian view of authority and that it revealed a strong humanitarian tendency.

Pretorius aired his views on authority as follows:

> The Christian view is that God is the origin of all authority of man over his fellow man and also of man over what is sub-human. Therefore, any person in a position of power has that position due to the origin of all authority and is responsible to that origin for his deeds ... Humanists, on the other hand, seek the origin of authority in the cosmos here on earth and one of the ramifications of humanitarian thought finds its origin in man, in the individual himself ... and without that individual having given his permission, and delegating his original powers to an authority, the authority does not have the legitimate power and he may not make laws that affect the particular individual.

What he meant was that since God is the origin of all authority, the white representative authority is responsible only to God for his deeds, and that this authority could therefore enforce laws on disfranchised black inhabitants living in so-called white areas.

Pretorius admitted that there were indeed differences between his interpretation of "authority" and those of his NP colleagues, and although he agreed with those who had practical objections to my viewpoints, he also had objections in principle. When I later in the debate questioned Van Zijl about the principles of the National Party, he replied that I should rather discuss principles with Pretorius. I realised once again that Pretorius's colleagues did not always agree with, or understood his dogmatic viewpoints. For me it made no sense whatsoever.

At the end of his speech Pretorius proposed an amendment to my motion, which amounted to my proposal being scrapped and replaced by the following motion:

> That the Honourable House take cognisance of the fact that the voters through whom this meeting was constituted gave their overwhelming support to a draft constitution that had been accepted by the Constitutional Conference of South West Africa on 18 March 1977 and therefore identified itself unambiguously with the principles of the above constitution and the maintenance thereof.

The above amounts to a constitution that would be used for an interim government and would be subjected to no other democratic test other than a white referendum, and would be offered as a political platform in a countrywide election under United Nations supervision. The only explanation I could find for this unrealistic and short-sighted amendment proposed by Pretorius was that the National Party was more concerned with soliciting white votes in the 1980 white election than support in a UN-controlled election against SWAPO. The prolonged negotiations between South Africa and the Secretary General of the United Nations obviously suited the National Party in the short term. Although it would still take another decade, it ended up costing them dearly.

Van Zijl seconded Pretorius's proposal. First he had a problem with the fact that the DTA, following the murder of Mr Shiyagaya, had organised a march protesting against SWAPO's murder of politicians and civilians. According to him we had used the murder on Shiyagaya inappropriately to gain political advantage. He took great exception to my observation that this man, who had sacrificed his life for all our interests, was not allowed to have a cool drink with Billy Marais in a café on their way to the meeting. He then referred to the proposal that Pretorius had tabled at the disastrous caucus meeting of the National Party shortly before the "split congress" and confirmed that he (Van Zijl) had drafted it. He accused me of rejecting his attempt to bring about a political ceasefire by refusing to accept his proposal regarding a cooperation agreement among the Turnhalle delegations.

While the Republican Party and the DTA were being severely criticised by National Party members in the Legislative Assembly, the formation of the RP and DTA had created expectations with many people, also South Africans, that we might possibly free ourselves from the checkmate position in which we had found ourselves for decades. For us it was about a peaceful solution and ending the armed struggle. SWAPO had to be coerced into taking part in a democratic process and we, the internal parties, had to broaden our power base to enable us to oppose SWAPO in an election. But Gen. Jannie Geldenhuys saw it differently, stating in his book *Dié wat gewen het* (Those who won), that the whites of South West Africa were involved in an internal struggle because "they did not understand what it was all about".

We knew exactly "what it was all about". It was about our and our children's future. It was about gaining support for a political confrontation with SWAPO. It was actually simultaneously a political fight and an armed struggle. We never denied the important role the Defence Force played in giving us political space and time. However, the Defence Force underestimated the role we had to play. They were in the fortunate position that they could return to South Africa. We had to stay here. We had to become involved in an internal struggle to convince those whites who did not understand "what it was all about".

The military leaders were probably so convinced that our problem would be solved on the battlefield that they completely underestimated the role of political parties, and the inevitability of an internal political confrontation. I was aware all along that, since a large number of people had been recruited by the South African Defence Force in the north of our country, brothers, literally brothers, were involved in a war amongst themselves, shooting and killing each other. Nevertheless, I admit once again, that had it not been for the South African Defence Force, the political parties would have had neither the time nor the opportunity to find political solutions.

The final Western proposals

While the Republican Party and the Democratic Turnhalle Alliance were fighting a fierce political battle against the National Party and SWAPO, the five Western countries submitted their final settlement proposals to the Security Council. These proposals, which made provision for the election of a constituent assembly under United Nations supervision, in essence agreed with the provisional proposals as accepted in principle by the Turnhalle leaders a year earlier in Cape Town, albeit in greater detail. The proposals were far-reaching and entailed serious risks for South West Africa.

Although my colleagues and I had already accepted the Western settlement plan in principle the previous year, the Security Council still had to prove that the UN would be impartial when it came to its implementation. The recognition of SWAPO by the General Assembly of the UN as "the true and authentic representatives of the people of Namibia" had given rise to serious reservations about the impartiality of the United Nations. Although the contact group often pointed out to us that it was the General Assembly that had given this recognition to SWAPO and not the Security Council, this problem would delay implementation of the settlement plan for a long time to come.

A cessation of all hostilities before the proposed election was agreed upon by all parties, but the proposal that most of the South African troops had to be repatriated to South Africa twelve weeks before the election, and that all commandos, the citizen forces, ethnic units and their command structures had to be disbanded, remained a point of dispute.

The proposals determined furthermore that SWAPO's armed units had to be confined to their bases, but there was no clarity on where these bases were. According to the South African Defence Force, SWAPO had no bases in South West Africa at any stage. SWAPO, however, claimed that they had. What would happen if SWAPO were to continue the war after the South African Defence Force had withdrawn? The presence of a United Nations Peace Force was no acceptable alternative since their presence could – and in fact did – benefit SWAPO psychologically because the Peace Force was already regarded by the population as SWAPO allies. It took several months of protracted discussions to settle this dispute between South Africa and the Security Council.

The National Party (SWA), through its leaders and mouthpiece, *Die Suidwester*, immediately rejected the proposals, without stating clearly on what grounds. After certain obscurities regarding the proposals had been clarified by South Africa, I convened a meeting of the DTA's Executive Committee to consider this. It wasn't easy. I was convinced that we, despite all the risks involved, had no other option than to accept the Western proposals. My DTA colleagues were extremely suspicious, some of them even thought that South Africa was in the process of handing over our country to SWAPO.

It was clear to me that my colleagues, just like the National Party supporters, still believed that South Africa would not withdraw its military operations. I was of the opinion that, from a military and economic perspective, South Africa would not be able to hold off the rest of the world indefinitely, since the price in terms of money and human life would become too high. I recommended that we rather concentrate our full attention and energy on strengthening the DTA in view of an election against SWAPO. I stood firm, and after hours of arguing, the Committee agreed to accept the proposals, but made it very clear that they would hold me responsible should things go wrong. Our decision was subsequently conveyed to the Administrator General.

On 25 April 1978, Pik Botha informed the Ambassadors of the five Western countries that South Africa, after consultation with the Administrator General, had decided to accept the Western proposals in their "final and definitive form". Shortly after South Africa formally accepted the settlement plan, it was also accepted by the National Party, and even Koos Pretorius had to acknowledge that sometimes you had to face realities head on, despite all your self-imposed principles. At the same time the proposals forced SWAPO to relinquish its plans to take control of South West Africa by force, since they had not been prepared to accept it up to that stage and have consistently refused to achieve independence by means of a democratic process. SWAPO flatly refused to meet with the internal parties and to discuss the future of our country, because, as one of their leaders explained it to me, these parties did not have a military component. At a later stage they described the internal leaders as puppets of South Africa.

SWAPO was obviously not that sure of their chances in the envisaged election. Therefore, it came as no surprise when SWAPO tried to derail the democratic process. On 4 May 1978, the General Assembly of the United Nations, which – compared to the Security Council – had taken a more irresponsible stance throughout, took a lethal decision. The Assembly totally ignored the Western settlement plan, as well as the fact that South Africa and the internal parties had accepted it. The major part of the decision amounted to the recognition of SWAPO as "the sole and authentic representative of the people of Namibia". The Assembly also supported the escalation of SWAPO's armed struggle and expressed the conviction that the armed struggle would play a decisive role in setting the inhabitants of Namibia free. All countries that did not yet recognise SWAPO as the authentic representatives of the people of Namibia were requested to do so immediately. In addition, an appeal was made to countries to coerce all international corporations under their authority not to invest in South West Africa. The efforts by the internal political parties to cooperate in finding solutions for the country, were questioned and condemned in the strongest possible terms, and demands were made that Walvis Bay, which was constitutionally part of South Africa, be handed over to Namibia.

Such irresponsible rulings did not make it easy for me to reassure my DTA and RP colleagues that the settlement plan was the best solution to our problems. Representatives of the Western Contact Group regularly pointed out to me that the Security Council itself had never, at any stage, given recognition to SWAPO, and that the General Assembly did not have the final say. In my view this was an underestimation of the influence of the General Assembly. Most of my countrymen only knew about the UN and never understood the difference between the Security Council and the General Assembly.

Cassinga, 4 May 1978

On the same day – Ascension Day, 4 May 1978 – when the resolution of the General Assembly to which I referred earlier was accepted, an event took place that reverberated throughout the world, namely the devastating attack by the South African Defence Force on the SWAPO base at Cassinga in Angola. I would have thought it to be a case of the left hand not knowing what the right hand was doing, and that the Defence Force was once again on its own mission. Subsequent conversations with Pik Botha and information from Gen. Jannie Geldenhuys's memoir however confirmed that this decision had been taken by a seriously divided Cabinet. General Geldenhuys wrote about the operation as follows:

> Nearly a thousand insurgents died and 200 were captured, while only six members of the Security Forces lost their lives. A great deal of equipment and many supplies were destroyed and valuable documents were seized. The loss of trained personnel and the result of the information that had been gained by the Security Forces was a great setback to SWAPO – one from which it never fully recovered.

I now no longer knew what to believe. Less than two weeks earlier South Africa had formally accepted the Western proposals for a peaceful and democratic solution, and now this, on the same day the General Assembly of the United Nations took a decision in which SWAPO was encouraged to continue with the armed struggle. (The Assembly was probably unaware of what had happened at Cassinga.) Among the documents seized by the Defence Force was one in which Gen. Dimo Hamaambo gave the instruction that Kapuuo, Ndjoba and Mudge be assassinated. After independence this was confirmed by the General himself during a hunting trip on our farm.

The inevitable consequence of these actions of the South African Government, the United Nations and SWAPO was that the inhabitants of South West Africa no longer took the possibility of an election under United Nations supervision seriously. Instead of preparing ourselves for an election aimed at independence, we once again found ourselves locked in intense battles among the internal political parties, especially in view of ethnic elections. Even member parties of the DTA were more interested in winning elections within their own group than in defeating SWAPO.

The political struggle remains intense

Before the commencement of the session of the Legislative Assembly – on 16 May 1978 – the RP Caucus decided to pay specific attention to the uncertainty prevailing in the country as a result of SWAPO's continued terrorist acts and delaying tactics. The attack by the South African Defence Force on Cassinga was also thoroughly examined, especially in view of SWAPO's allegation that an unknown number of civilians had lost their lives in the attack. We couldn't establish the truth, since the Defence Force was denying it. If SWAPO had allowed civilians in a military stronghold, they should have been aware of the dangers involved. We also had to bear in mind the large number of civilians, including political and traditional leaders, who had been deliberately murdered by SWAPO. When all was said and done, SWAPO had chosen the military option and we who inhabited the battlefield were the soft targets – totally dependent on the protection of the South African Security Forces. Against this background we decided to table a motion in the Legislative Assembly not to encourage armed conflict, but to insist on the finalisation of the Western proposals.

In motivating the motion, I pointed out the prevailing uncertainty in the country, and emphasised that finality should be reached as soon as possible. I mentioned the remarkable progress we had made compared to the situation a year ago. With the acceptance of Resolution 385 of the United Nations a year earlier, South Africa's presence in South West Africa had been declared illegal and the UN was adamant that South Africa should terminate its administration of the Territory immediately and withdraw its Defence Force. It was now a year later and the Western proposals had been accepted, the South African Administrator General was still in full control of the administration, and South Africa was still accepted as a fully fledged partner in the independence and election process. This was in accordance with the conditions set by the DTA when we accepted the Western settlement plan.

However, I stated that it was unacceptable to us that SWAPO was in the privileged position of participating freely in the political process in the Territory while continuing its terrorist acts of violence. SWAPO had to decide whether it wanted to be a militant organisation or a political party. It was not possible to be both. Neither could the DTA be both, because we had to and wanted to uphold the laws of the country. The DTA was not prepared to take the lives of political opponents, although it was not easy to convince the Hereros not to resort to violence following the murder of their leader, Clemens Kapuuo. It was not generally known that SWAPO was not a banned organisation domestically. This certainly was an exceptional situation that would not have been accepted anywhere else in the world.

I had every reason to expect that the National Party would support my motion in the Legislative Assembly, but it didn't. A.H. du Plessis reacted very negatively. He wondered about the objective of the motion and hinted that I merely wanted "to show off my oratory skills in some way or another". According to him I had given a historical review that was well known to everyone in the Honourable House and in South West Africa and which could hardly be elaborated on and that he wished to see the "genius who could still add something new". This was an attempt to ridicule the motion introduced by me. This was vintage A.H. du Plessis: Your opponent had to be humiliated, as he had humiliated the leader of the UNSWP, Percy Niehaus, in the past. He maintained that no one knew the objective of my motion. If it was a political manoeuvre, he maintained it was a very clumsy one. He reminded the opposition of an old song: "Do what you do, do well, boy." He did not see himself as having a tendency to be derogatory, but could not help thinking about what Langenhoven had said, namely: "Empty vessel keep your tap closed, lest you be regarded as one that is full."

There was a noticeable lack of reaction from his colleagues to these witty remarks. There was no laughter, and no "Hear, hear!". My former leader for whom I had always had respect, appeared pathetic. I could not bring myself to take pleasure in this, realising that he would no longer play a role under these new circumstances. He continued by proposing an amendment to my motion, explaining it step by step. I listened attentively and tried to establish how it differed from my motion. He questioned SWAPO's claim that it represented the inhabitants of South West Africa and pointed out the organisation's unwillingness to subject itself to a democratic test, and also how SWAPO was obstructing efforts to find a peaceful solution. He then expressed his appreciation for the South African Government's efforts to ensure safety and law and order, and requested South Africa to continue doing so. He confirmed the conditions under which the South African Government had accepted the proposals; AKTUR had accepted the proposals under the same conditions. Du Plessis expressed the conviction that any deviation from the final Western proposals, which had been held up as final and decisive, would undermine the trust of the people of South West Africa in further negotiations.

Up to this point the amendment was essentially the same as my motion and I could therefore not fault it. The operative paragraph of the amendment, however, differed from my motion. It reads as follows: "That this House recommends to the South African Government that, should there be any deviation from the accepted proposals, alternative peaceful ways to achieve independence for South West Africa will have to be considered." On the "alternative ways", Du Plessis chose not to elaborate, other than saying that "any realistic person could think of alternatives".

With there being no other speakers in the debate on the motion, I had to respond forthwith. I was not prepared to engage in the old outdated way of playing political games; the situation was far too serious for this. The fact that the amendment did not differ much from my motion made me contemplate the possibility of a unanimous decision. "Why vote against the amendment simply because it had been proposed by the other side of the House?", I asked, and Du Plessis's amendment was then accepted unanimously.

It serves no purpose to go into details of arguments during the rest of the session, since most of them were irrelevant under the prevailing circumstances.

The speakers of the National Party remained unrelenting regarding the Turnhalle Constitution, which had been intended as an interim constitution, and had become obsolete in view of the election of a Constitutional Assembly. They were still referring to the whites as an ethnic group, while in reality it was a racial group that could be distinguished from other groups purely on the basis of skin colour. Moreover, reference was still being made to a white area of authority where all other inhabitants would be subjected to the white authority, as well as to a central government in which the whites would have a right of veto.

Diplomatic manoeuvres around the settlement plan

On 12 July 1978, the five Western countries – Canada, France, Germany, the USA and Britain – issued a joint statement after a meeting they had with SWAPO in which they announced the following: "… the two delegations … agreed to proceed to the United Nations Security Council, thus opening the way to an early internationally acceptable settlement of the question of Namibia". Martti Ahtisaari was appointed by the Security Council as the Special Representative of the Secretary General to administer the Territory during the envisaged election under UN supervision and control, in cooperation with the Administrator General of South West Africa. Over the years I had become accustomed to this kind of diplomatic language, and to me this declaration was meaningless. It wasn't even an acceptance of the settlement plan by implication, but at least it wasn't a rejection of it either.

As if the situation was not complicated enough already, on the same date, 27 July, the Security Council of the United Nations made a decision that Walvis Bay, which had constitutionally never been part of South West Africa, was to be integrated into our Territory. Walvis Bay has never been part of the original German colony, but belonged to the original British-controlled Cape Colony. This is a long story, which I will leave at that, other than saying that for strategic reasons South Africa would not easily give up its control over Walvis Bay.

On the same day – 27 July – Pik Botha, the South African Minister of Foreign Affairs, addressed the 282nd session of the Security Council. Although I didn't always understand the political and diplomatic manoeuvres of the South African Government, I was nevertheless impressed with the skilful way in which Pik Botha kept the discourse with the Security Council going for many years without reaching an impasse. The delaying tactics employed by his Department and the South African Government was frequently mentioned. Was this to South West Africa's advantage or disadvantage?

In his speech Pik Botha addressed various matters concerning the settlement proposals that still needed to be discussed. He referred to a paragraph in the South West Africa Survey of 1967, stating that it had always been the South African Government's viewpoint that the peoples of South West Africa must decide about their future themselves. What he did not say was that in 1967 and beyond, South Africa was engaged in implementing the recommendations of the Odendaal Commission without having consulted properly with the people of South West Africa. He continued that the leaders of South West Africa (the Turnhalle leaders) had already stated that they were ready for independence and furthermore that they had insisted on it two years before. He admitted by implication that the inhabitants had only been involved in the determination of their future for the first time two years before.

Pik Botha went on to state that he welcomed the Western initiative, but then accused SWAPO of obstruction and for not having accepted the Western proposals yet. He especially emphasised the size and deployment of the military component of the envisaged United Nations Transition Assistance Group (UNTAG) and the gradual demobilisation of the South African Defence Force in the Territory. I agreed with him on this point. We as politicians were not responsible for the safety of the inhabitants, but we had to fight an election, and we knew what the consequences of losing would be. We understood the enormity of the challenge and the importance of preventing the deployment of the military component of UNTAG and the demobilisation of the Defence Force from giving SWAPO a psychological advantage. Pik concluded his speech with the threat that South Africa would no longer cooperate in the implementation of the settlement plan if the Security Council, with the support of the Western countries, decides in favour of the incorporation of Walvis Bay.

Short-sighted decisions by the South African Government often left Pik to pull the chestnuts out of the fire at the United Nations, and although he and I often had our differences in the years to come, I give him full credit for being a diplomat par excellence. For those who saw a communist around every corner, and those who never realised that there was indeed such a thing as communist involvement in Africa, I quote a paragraph from Pik's address to the Russian delegation to the Security Council:

> We all know what is going on in the world today. We all know about the struggle for the balance of power. And we all know that the Soviet Union lusts after world domination. The Soviet Union's concern for Africa and the welfare of the African people is hypocritical and contrived. I want to ask the representative of the Soviet Union: What has your country done to improve the quality of life on the African continent? ... Instead of using every inappropriate opportunity to engage in unsubstantiated attacks on my Government, I urge the United Nations and in particular the Security Council to devote attention to the plight of millions of human beings who must live a life without hope of receiving proper training and education, of enjoying a balanced diet, of living under conditions of personal safety and security – in short, of exercising in any meaningful sense a choice between alternatives for the improvement of their lives.

Pik must have known that he couldn't win, because although he was right about what was happening in the rest of the world, he was burdened with the baggage of the past like the rest of us. The withdrawal of the Russian-supported Cuban troops as the last hurdle to overcome in order to achieve independence – with the approval and cooperation of the Western countries – confirmed that Pik was right.

The dispute between South Africa and the Security Council over the size and deployment of the military component of UNTAG was brought to a head on 27 August 1978 with the report by the Secretary General to the Security Council. The ratio of a small population of 1,5 million, with 700 000 registered voters, to the proposed extent of the United Nation's involvement in the envisaged election was frightening. In accordance with Mr Ahtisaari's proposal, the peace force (UNTAG) would consist of 70 infantry battalions with 5000 members, 200 monitors and 2300 other personnel – a total of 7500 people at an estimated cost of US$300 million.

On 6 September Pik Botha reacted to the Secretary General's report in a very long letter in which he objected to the deviations from the original proposals as contained in Resolution 385. He pointed out that SWAPO was still committing its acts of terrorism and that there was still no indication that the organisation had accepted the settlement proposals. He warned that South Africa was not prepared to decrease the number of South African troops to less than 4000 – not even after the implementation of the settlement plan. He further reminded the Secretary General that there should be consultations over the composition, size and functions of UNTAG, making comparisons to the nature and extent of the UN presence in other parts of the world. From his letter it became obvious that the number of South African troops in the Territory and the size and extent of UNTAG were still a matter of serious dispute: "My Government for its part accepted the proposal on 25 April in its final and definitive form – nothing more, nothing less. We are prepared to adhere to that decision but not to go along with interpretations inconsistent with the proposal."

Two days after Minister Botha's letter – on 8 September – the President of SWAPO wrote a letter to the Secretary General in which the organisation accepted the Secretary General's report to the Security Council. However, SWAPO did not accept it unconditionally and expressed reservations about certain aspects. These were mainly about the registration of voters: the SWAPO President was concerned that persons who were not Namibians would be registered. He also insisted on the complete cessation of hostilities, but accused the South African Defence Force of continuing to murder women and children, as was the case at Cassinga.

It was often alleged that both SWAPO and South Africa deliberately delayed the implementation of the settlement plan. For those of us not directly involved, it was difficult to judge whether this was the case, but our future was at stake and we were living in a state of uncertainty. With an election as its main focus, the DTA was actively involved in preparing for one without knowing when it would take place. This is reminiscent of a race in which the winning post is being moved time and time again. For some political leaders, especially those who realised that they would not play a role in such an election, the delays strengthened their hopes that it wouldn't take place.

In its negotiations with the Western Contact Group and the Security Council, the South African Government regularly referred to the people of South West Africa. But who were the people of South West Africa and what were their wishes and aspirations? There could be no doubt that South Africa could not make any decision without the approval and cooperation of the people of South West Africa. Politically they could not afford to accept any dispensation that could be regarded by South African voters as treason, or selling out of fellow whites, or even fellow Afrikaners. It was therefore important that South Africa could lay claim, in everything it did, to having the full support and cooperation of the inhabitants of South West Africa. It had, after all, been the Government's viewpoint all along that the people of South West Africa should decide about their future themselves. Had these people been consulted at any stage in a credible way?

When South Africa accepted the Western settlement plan on 25 April 1978, Minister Pik Botha put it as follows in a letter to the Western Contact Group:

"Having now being advised by the Administrator General that he has consulted the various political parties and church organisations in the Territory and that he is satisfied that the proposals are acceptable to the majority, he has recommended acceptance by the South African Government." Does this amount to adequate consultation? Were his conclusions trustworthy when he said "… the people of South West Africa are anxiously and impatiently awaiting their independence, which has been promised them not later than the end of this year"?

The general election of 1978

I had no doubt that independence based on the settlement plan was the best option for South West Africa, but, for reasons already mentioned, I did have doubts about the impartiality of the United Nations and whether the Secretary General's Special Representative and UNTAG wanted to, or were able to guarantee a fair election. I was relying on South Africa being able to address shortcomings regarding arrangements for the election. I also knew that the white inhabitants, as well as many of the black inhabitants of the Territory were by no means looking forward to independence. After the acceptance of the settlement plan, a large number of whites, especially farmers, sold their land and moved to South Africa. Those who remained still believed that the settlement plan would never be implemented, and the National Party did nothing to convince them otherwise.

In the Legislative Assembly the National Party continued referring to principles that could never change while some of my colleagues in the DTA still had their hopes pinned on independence without SWAPO. Many inhabitants relied on the South African Defence Force to defeat SWAPO, while SWAPO was merely paying lip service to a democratic solution. An enormous task of persuasion was lying ahead, and I was prepared to do it, but I was still not sure of my power base. On whose behalf would I speak? The Republican Party was in the minority in the Legislative Assembly with eight members as opposed to the National Party's ten. No election had taken place since my resignation from the National Party, and the motion on independence that I had tabled in the Legislative Assembly had been rejected. Although the DTA had clearly gained considerable support, it had not stood the test of a democratic election yet. South Africa still had no way of determining who could speak on behalf of the people of South West Africa, and could only rely on superficial observations.

On 20 September 1978, Prime Minister John Vorster unexpectedly invited the former members of the Standing Committee of the Turnhalle Conference to a meeting in Pretoria. This happened not long after Vorster had suffered a serious health setback and had spent considerable time in hospital. We had no idea what the meeting would be about; I expected another attempt to put an end to the infighting among the internal parties. President Vorster, after welcoming us, announced his intension to speed up the process by providing for the election of a constituent assembly in South West Africa. This announcement came as a great surprise to some of us, and a great shock to others. There were much speculation afterwards about the reason for and motivation behind this decision of the South African Government.

In a press release issued by the Prime Minister immediately after the meeting, many of our questions were answered, but for further clarity we had to wait a while longer. In his statement Vorster briefly repeated the views on South West Africa held over decades by the South African Government, with special reference to the right of the inhabitants to eventually decide on their future themselves. He then referred to the discussions with the Western countries and the fact that South Africa had accepted their final proposals. He did, however, express his disapproval of certain substantial deviations in the agreement as contained in the Secretary General's report to the Security Council. He mentioned that long-drawn-out deliberations had taken place shortly before between the South African Minister of Foreign Affairs and the five Western countries, but that no progress had been made towards finding a solution. Therefore, said John Vorster, the Cabinet had given serious consideration to the different alternatives and had taken the following decision: "... that the people of South West Africa in accordance with their wishes would have to be given the opportunity to elect their own representatives. This will be done on the basis of universal adult suffrage in countrywide elections in order to establish unequivocally who has the right to speak for the people of South West Africa."

Although I had not expected this, I immediately grasped what it was about. John Vorster and the South African Government found themselves in a difficult position. While on the one hand South Africa was being put under pressure by the United Nations, on the other hand the inhabitants of the Territory were divided. SWAPO continued its military struggle, while the so-called moderate and peaceful inhabitants of the country were fighting each other, and the National Party clung frantically to certain constitutional principles and attempted to influence South African members of Parliament. This was placing the Prime Minister in an untenable position. An election in which all the inhabitants of the Territory could participate would be the obvious way to determine who could speak on behalf of the people of South West Africa. I agreed with him wholeheartedly. It struck me that John Vorster had referred to the "people of Namibia" and not to the "peoples of Namibia".

At a press conference after the meeting and in the presence of the Turnhalle leaders, the Prime Minister issued a press release, which due to its importance I quote here in broad terms. In his introduction he

confirms South Africa's commitment to the following principles regarding the future of South West Africa and the election process that
must lead to the country's independence:

- South West Africa to be a unitary state;
- All forms of discrimination on the basis of colour to be termi-
  nated;
- Free and fair elections to be held;
- The urgency of the achievement of independence;
- The return of all South West Africans to take part in the elec-
  tion;
- The return of all political refugees.

The Prime Minister also drew attention to the fact that the Secretary
General's report to the Security Council contained certain substantial
deviations from the original Western proposals, amongst others:

- The size of the UN's military contingent;
- The addition of a further UN police contingent;
- The lack of consultation with the Administrator General;
- The election date.

He elaborated extensively on these deviations. I would like to quote
one paragraph verbatim, as it contains one of the objections that I personally raised at subsequent events. John Vorster formulated it as follows:

> During the lengthy negotiations the Five were repeatedly re-
> minded of the political and psychological effect of such a large
> number of United Nations personnel on the people of South
> West Africa. The impartiality of the United Nations is rendered
> suspect by the continued and sustained assistance to SWAPO to
> the exclusion of all other political parties in South West Africa.
> Thus, for example, SWAPO is recognised by the United Nations
> General Assembly as 'the sole and authentic representative' of
> the people of South West Africa and receives considerable finan-
> cial assistance. Furthermore, it enjoys extensive facilities to beam
> propaganda to the Territory and elsewhere. Indeed, the United
> Nations' whole information system itself supports SWAPO.

This was a valid point of view with which I fully concurred. What's
more, it stands to reason that an election held in accordance with the
Western settlement plan and under supervision of the UN which were
not fair in all respects and where SWAPO were to enjoy a decisive psychological advantage would amount to political suicide for the opposi-

tion parties. All it would have come down to is that our participation in the election would have given legitimacy to a constitution that would be written solely by SWAPO. In the years to come there would be a great deal of debate about this.

The rest of the Prime Minister's announcement caused quizzical looks and was interpreted in different ways. I was concerned that the powers to be bestowed on the yet-to-be chosen entity as suggested by John Vorster could be interpreted as a rejection of the settlement plan, and hence create the impression that a unilateral declaration of independence, as in the case of the former Rhodesia, was being planned. This was far from the truth, the intention undoubtedly being the following: firstly, to establish who could speak on behalf of the people of South West Africa; secondly, to delegate certain important decisions about the future of the Territory to this elected body. This was stated clearly in the announcement of the Government's decision.

In his statement the Prime Minister pointed out that 85% of the inhabitants of the Territory who were entitled to vote, had registered, despite intimidation during the registration process. He also elaborated on the options to the to-be-elected body:

> All options remain open to them. We will not prescribe to them.
> The body to be elected may –
> • decide to draw up a constitution or postpone the drafting thereof;
> • decide to proceed with the implementation of the proposal of the Western Five;
> • decide to accept the Secretary General's Report.
> They will, of course, also be free to express themselves on numerous other matters, which will be dealt with in the relevant proclamation to be issued shortly.

The fact that John Vorster was not prescriptive in any way, and that he even considered leaving the possibility of further cooperation on the basis of the Secretary General's report open, convinced me that he wanted to establish who could speak on behalf of the inhabitants of South West Africa. It was subsequently confirmed by his successor P.W. Botha.

After the meeting and the subsequent press conference, still in the presence of our delegation, Vorster announced his intention to resign as Prime Minister. This was bad news to me, since I had a good relationship with him. He at no stage criticised me about what I was doing or saying. Although he never openly took sides, I was convinced that we understood each other, that he had strong sentiments about the solution of the international dispute about South West Africa, as well as more relaxed relations in Africa. I also suspected that he often had to make compromises among state departments and individuals, for example Foreign Affairs, which had accepted the Western settlement plan; P.W. Botha, who was never in favour of the plan and referred to it afterwards as "Vorster's plan"; and Bantu Administration, which still wanted to implement the Odendaal Plan. The relationship between John Vorster and Gen. Van den Bergh also deteriorated, because of the General's opinion that South Africa could no longer afford South West Africa and that the Territory should be handed over to the United Nations. General Van den Bergh himself confirmed this viewpoint to me. There is no doubt that John Vorster had to lead South Africa through a very tumultuous period.

Although John Vorster's departure was sad news to me, I was elated about the announcement of an election. As I understood it, an election would provide us with different options. I immediately realised that an opportunity had now been created for the DTA and the RP to prove their support and to stake a political claim, as well as give direction to the political and constitutional development in the Territory.

The question that begs an answer is: Why would John Vorster make this contentious decision at the end of his career? Why not leave it to his successor to take over the responsibility for South West Africa? For me the decision was in accordance with the understanding John Vorster and I had reached after my visit to the United Nations five years before, albeit with one important difference. The election would take place on the basis of universal suffrage and therefore made provision for a multiracial-elected Assembly. The decision left little manoeuvring space for his successor P.W. Botha, and for the proponents of an ethnically constituted government. It created opportunities for the DTA to bring about meaningful changes in our country. The National Party would for the first time find itself in a minority position.

The announcement of the one-person-one-vote election added to the unabated continuation of diplomatic conflict between the South African Government on the one hand and the five Western countries on the other. A few days before the announcement of the election by the Prime Minister, the South African representative at the United Nations directed a letter to the Secretary General in which he once again insisted that SWAPO cease all further hostilities. He also repeated that a ceasefire agreement was a necessary prerequisite for the implementation of the settlement plan.

On 27 September 1978, Pik Botha once again reminded the Secretary General of the Prime Minister's announcement of the election to be held in South West Africa, and that his Government was still committed to its acceptance of the settlement plan, but that South Africa could not be expected to accept deviations from it. He, however, gave the assurance that the door was not closed for further negotiations. Despite still unresolved problems, the Security Council on 29 September ratified the Secretary General's report, which made provision for the election of a constituent assembly under UN supervision. Resolution 435, as it was known, stated that any unilateral decision by the "illegal" administration in respect of the electoral process, the registration of voters, or the transfer of authority conflicting with Resolution 435, would be regarded as null and void.

In an effort to avoid an impasse, a conference was scheduled for 16 October 1978 between the South African Government and the Western countries, to – as they termed it – find common ground for the implementation of Resolution 435. P.W. Botha, who had shortly before succeeded John Vorster as Prime Minister, gave a welcoming address at the opening of the conference, which created great interest and anticipation, both internally and abroad.

There was, however, a question in everybody's mind: To what extent would the Prime Minister regard himself bound to the commitments of his predecessor, and what would his attitude be in terms of the envisaged internal election? I knew that he wasn't exactly impressed by the Western settlement plan, since he on occasion had referred to it as "John Vorster's plan". It was to be expected that he, as the former Minister of Defence, still believed that the Defence Force was capable of defeating SWAPO and its allies. Since I'd had a very good relationship with the former Prime Minister, I could only hope that my relationship with P.W. Botha would be the same.

In his welcoming address Botha expressed the hope that the visit of the Western representatives would not be limited to the conference room, but that they would use the opportunity to see more of the country, and that the necessary arrangements had been made. He expressed his satisfaction with the visit to Windhoek by some of the delegates, as well as their discussions with representatives of the people who were directly involved in the future of South West Africa. He then stated his intention to point out to the Western world certain unresolved salient features that were pertinent to the strategic situation in Southern Africa. P.W. Botha emphasised South Africa's rejection of the communist ideology and although it was prepared to uphold democratic ideals, it was also prepared to actively fight communism. He reminded those present that the current dispute (the South West Africa problem) could be traced back to where the South African troops, on behalf of and in cooperation with Great Britain, had taken possession of the German Colony of South West Africa and that this went hand in hand with a rebellion. The Prime Minister proceeded to reveal the numbers of South African troops that had fought on the side of the Allied Forces during the different wars and indicated that South Africa's contribution was in the interests of the West. He then elaborated extensively on the possible impacts that a Russian and Cuban presence could have on Southern Africa. According to him the implementation of the Western proposals was possibly the best way to avoid such an eventuality; that is why his government had negotiated with the five Western countries during the preceding 18 months on the subject of an internationally acceptable solution, but that this could not be done at the expense of internal security.

To conclude, P.W. Botha referred to the envisaged December election:

> We have reached a critical juncture, and the results of the present discussions might affect the whole of Southern Africa for many years to come. It is my government's hope that we can avoid running over-hastily into a tragic confrontation. The present situation is delicately poised and we have to move with caution. In this framework, the envisaged December elections in South West Africa should be seen neither as a final step nor a South African challenge to the international community. All options will be open to the elected representatives and they will, therefore, also be free to accept the Secretary General's report. South Africa will at that time point out to them the various alternatives and their likely consequences, both internally and externally. South Africa will also bring to their attention the views of the Five in regard to the requirements for international recognition of an independent South West Africa.

I carefully read the Prime Minister's speech. His fear that an escalation of long-term Russian presence in Africa could also become a security threat for South Africa made sense. The fact that the Western countries were also concerned about this became evident with America's initial involvement in the Angolan civil war between the rebel groups – MPLA, FNLA and UNITA – by giving support to FNLA and later to UNITA. America even participated in clandestine paramilitary operations organised by the CIA and led by John Stockwell in Angola. According to the Prime Minister it was to "stabilise matters and effect a balance so that an unfettered government, free from Russian influence, could take control." France was not involved in the Angolan civil war to the same extent as America and Russia, but did deliver arms to the FNLA at some stage, because the French government was worried about the Russian-supported MPLA becoming the future government of Angola. American involvement in the armed conflict in Angola only ceased when the so-called Clark Amendment, which put an end to further assistance to the Angolan rebel movements, was ratified by the American Senate. These events probably caused subsequent allegations that P.W. Botha was disproportionately fixated on the communist threat and the "total onslaught".

After the cessation of America's support to the rebel movements, Dr Kissinger sent the following message to South Africa:

1. The United States shares the concern of the RSA over the danger of the provocative role of the Russians and the Cubans in Angola.
2. The United States deplores the support of the MPLA by the Russians in its rejection of political settlement and in pursuit of military conquest.
3. The United States will regard the imposition by force of a Soviet/Cuban/MPLA regime in Angola with great concern.
4. The United States, however, believes the FNLA and UNITA have received enough and adequate arms for their own protection, including ack-ack [anti-aircraft equipment].
5. The United States believes the only solution to be a political settlement in which no one group is to dominate the others.
6. We have made our deep concern about the Angola situation known to all concerned, including Russia.

Although there was a considerable measure of unanimity between South Africa and the Western countries on the Russian/Cuban presence in Southern Africa, and they agreed that a cessation of hostilities and a peaceful and democratic solution would be the ideal, the primary object of their involvement differed. The Western countries were there because they clashed worldwide with the communist ideology, and moreover, had economic objectives. South Africa was there because of an international dispute about the administration of the Territory and its policy of racial discrimination. Consequently, South Africa had an additional motivation to get rid of the Russian/Cuban presence – the support given by these powers to SWAPO. There wasn't unanimity on the reasons for their presence other than an agreement in principle on the implementation of the Western proposals. At that stage the actual extent of the Russian and Cuban presence was not generally known.

The second part of P.W. Botha's speech made me uneasy. I could not foresee what the "alternatives and their possible after-effects" were that he would put to the elected leaders. According to John Vorster, in his announcement of the election, all options would be open to us.

Following discussions that lasted three days, South Africa and the Ministers of Foreign Affairs of the five Western countries issued a joint statement on 19 October 1978 in which they announced that they had once again discussed the remaining issues, especially regarding the UN's military and police components. They recommended that the Secretary General's Special Representative, Ahtisaari, visit South West Africa as soon as possible for negotiations with the Administrator General on the modalities of the proposed election, as well as on the date of the election.

In the announcement of the December election it was confirmed that the election should be seen as an internal process to elect leaders, and that the South African Government would do its best to convince the elected leaders to find ways and means of gaining international recognition by means of "the good offices" of the Special Representative and the Administrator General. It states further that the South African representatives had stated clearly during the discussions that the number of South African troops would not be decreased until there was a complete cessation of all hostilities; furthermore that an election date should be determined, and that this date would be adhered to, regardless of whether there was an end to hostilities and a decrease in South African troops or not.

The joint statement of 19 October elicited many questions from visiting members of the press – especially Nicholas Ashford of the *London Times* – to which the Prime Minister responded satisfactorily. At no stage did he lose his temper. This was certainly not the same P.W.

Botha who had washed the floor with journalists in the white political struggle. It was clear that in his new capacity as Prime Minister he was determined to act responsibly and retain his self-control. Ashford attempted unsuccessfully to drive him into a corner. Many of the questions were about the domestic election in December. Ashford asked whether the to-be-elected constituent assembly would be entitled to draw up a constitution, to which Botha replied that while this was a possibility, the South African Government would have the last say.

For consumption abroad this was the right answer, because the concern in those circles did not revolve in the first instance around drawing up a draft constitution, but about its possible unilateral implementation. We had already drawn up a draft constitution in the Turnhalle and in my opinion there would be another opportunity to work on drafts in the future. Regarding the final Constitution, the work we had done before the time would put us in a good position to put our stamp on it. There could be no doubt that whatever the proposals of the to-be-elected assembly in 1978 were to be, the final decision about a constitution would be taken by a constituent assembly that had to be elected in terms of Resolution 435. The discussions that had taken place were an attempt to eliminate the last points of difference, not about principles but about specific matters. In this respect, South Africa's approval was also necessary.

In terms of the Prime Minister's undertaking that, after the December election, he would try to convince the elected representatives to cooperate on the basis of Resolution 435, Ashford asked him whether he could give a guarantee to the Five that he would be successful, to which Botha answered wittily: "How can I give anyone a guarantee that I can persuade another person? I cannot guarantee that I can persuade you." Ashford also wanted to know what the status of the body that would be elected in December would be should the Secretary General want to continue negotiations, since the body would be recognised neither by the West nor by the United Nations. To this the Prime Minister gave a most valid reply: "The South African Government for its part says that we believe that there are recognised leaders other than SWAPO representing the majority of the people. So what is now better than to allow these political parties to put their cases to the 90% already registered voters and to allow the voters to decide who their leaders are." Ashford asked many more questions, to which the

Prime Minister replied without hesitation, but it was clear to me that the last word on the implementation of the Western settlement plan was yet to be spoken.

While the discussions with the Five were still ongoing, representatives of the internal parties that would possibly want to participate in the envisaged election, were hastily summoned to Pretoria. Dr Ben Africa and I were in Ovamboland for a series of meetings when a military aircraft was sent to Ondangwa to fly us to Pretoria. After our arrival at the Waterkloof Air Force base, we were taken to the International Guesthouse. Apart from the DTA leaders, we were also met among others by A.H. du Plessis and Jan de Wet of AKTUR, Ian Kirkpatrick and Vekuii Rukoro of the Namibia National Front, Andreas Shipanga of the SWAPO Democrats, Hans Diergaardt of the Liberation Front and someone from the Namibia Christian Democratic Party. Sarel Becker of the HNP was not present.

After dinner, the Prime Minister and Pik Botha informed us of the discussions they had had with the representatives of the Western countries, the contents of his opening address, as well as the joint and separate statement by South Africa. After the representatives of the NNF and SWAPO–D had posed questions, Du Plessis raised his objection to the election, saying that "he did not understand the election". He objected to it especially on the grounds that it would be taking place on a one-person-one-vote basis. Apparently the Prime Minister failed to understand Du Plessis's reservations, because he appeared to be annoyed and reacted brusquely to the latter's words. He said inter alia that he, as Minister of Defence, had always taken care of South West Africa's interests, but that Du Plessis should understand that he as Prime Minister also had a responsibility towards South Africa. From then on Du Plessis refrained from taking part in the discussion. When it was subsequently reported in the South African press that there had been a clash between him and the Prime Minister, he commented that he "had not clashed back".

The DTA delegation, agreeing with the Prime Minister's views, had little to say. Upon leaving, I mentioned to P.W. Botha that I would like to have a personal conversation with him at some stage. He suggested that I arrange a meeting with him when next I went to Cape Town. Shortly after this, when Stienie and I found ourselves in Mossel Bay for a family event, I had the opportunity to visit him at his holiday home in Wildernis. We received a friendly welcome and I felt at liberty to candidly share my views on the negotiations with the UN and the internal political situation. But, as I would experience many times in future, P.W. Botha wasn't a willing listener. He complained that the South West Africa issue had now landed in his lap, and I got the impression that he wasn't exactly overjoyed by it.

As regards the controversial issues between South Africa and the Security Council, he took a strong stance, especially in respect of the security situation before and during the implementation phase of the settlement plan and, more specific, the extent of the involvement of the South African Defence Force during this period. Although, according to the settlement plan there had to be a total cessation of hostilities, P.W.'s fears were, as would subsequently be proven, not unfounded. He once again expressed his concern about the discord among the whites in South West Africa.

I informed him that we were trying to split the votes among the black inhabitants in the election campaign currently underway in South West Africa. White unity could possibly lead to black unity. It was obvious that he was not convinced by this. Nevertheless, referring to the South African situation, he did remark that something would have to be done about the situation of the coloureds in South Africa and – if I understood him correctly – he alluded to the coloured people possibly being put back onto the common voters' roll. This gave me the opportunity to remark that we in South West Africa would also have to be prepared to make adjustments that could divide the whites even further.

As he accompanied me to my car, he expressed the hope that the election would run smoothly. Just that. I left with the feeling that although his attitude was not the same as it had been a year ago when we met in Port Elizabeth, we were not entirely on the same page. My perception was correct, because in the years to come, we had frequent disagreements, and at times opposed each other vehemently.

The UN team led by the Secretary General, Dr Kurt Waldheim, and his Special Representative, Martti Ahtisaari, visited Windhoek to discuss the practical implementation of the proposals with the Administrator General, but it contributed nothing towards the solution of the remaining obstacles. Gen. Philipp, who would head the UN Peace Force, made a very good impression with his sober and objective approach. Unfortunately, the same could not be said for Martti Ahtisaari and the rest of the team.

Although Ahtisaari tried his best to maintain an appearance of impartiality, he did not succeed entirely. His association with SWAPO over many years because of his association with the Council of Namibia and his investiture as Commissioner for Namibia, probably made this impossible. After their visit to Windhoek, the team held deliberations with the South African Government in Pretoria. Only a few days after these deliberations, the Secretary General, in his report to the Security Council, alluded to the results that had been achieved. He concluded with the following meaningless words: "I and my Special Representative are continuing with our endeavours in regard to the issues concerned, within the competence prescribed in the relevant Security Council decisions."

Although the Secretary General and the Western countries still attempted to keep the discussion going, the Security Council started taking a more unapproachable attitude by accepting Resolution 439, a highly drastic and far-reaching proposal, on 13 November 1978. The resolution stated that the Board:

- censures the decision of South Africa to, contrary to Resolution 435, proceed unilaterally in holding an election in South West Africa;
- regards it as a clear challenge to the United Nations and the authority of the Security Council;
- declares the election and its results null and void, and that no recognition, either by the UN or by any member country or entity elected in the process, would be given;
- requests South Africa to cancel the planned election with immediate effect;
- demands that South Africa cooperate with the Security Council with a view to implementing the different Security Council resolutions;
- warns that, should South Africa fail to do this, the Security Council would be obliged to convene immediately to activate effective measures in accordance with the Manifest of the United Nations, inclusive of Chapter VII; and
- requests the Secretary General to report to the Security Council before 25 November 1978 on the progress made with the implementation of the decision.

The five Western members of the Security Council, namely Canada, France, Germany, Britain and America, abstained from voting.

After this the Secretary General passed on the Resolution to Brand Fourie, South Africa's Secretary of Foreign Affairs. He urgently requested Pik Botha to come to New York for deliberations with him before 25 November, when he (the Secretary General) had to report back to the Security Council. In his usual hard-boiled way Pik replied that he could not be there before the 25th; only at a later stage.

On 2 December the Secretary General reported to the Security Council that South Africa had reaffirmed its willingness to cooperate on the basis of Resolution 435. South Africa had already given this assurance repeatedly, but always subject to certain conditions. This assurance would be given repeatedly in the years to come. The Secretary General was clearly not prepared to throw in the towel; his reputation was at stake. So they continued their game of chess; both dogs barking, but not biting. In the meantime, the war was intensifying at great cost in terms of money and human lives.

Also in his report the Secretary General wrote that South Africa was willing to conclude its consultation with the parties concerned over the implementation of Resolution 435 during December and to report back. He did not say who the parties concerned were. Was he possibly referring to the parties who would be elected in the December election and who would not be acknowledged by him? He reported further that South Africa, up until implementation of Resolution 435, would retain authority over the Territory. This, too, South Africa had already undertaken repeatedly. Waldheim concluded his report by assuring the Security Council that consultation about the remaining points would continue in an effort to resolve them. This did not look like progress at all, because after all the threats, they were back to the unresolved points. Since the Secretary General was not prepared to commit himself to a fixed election date – as proposed by South Africa – the winning post was being moved again.

Despite the drastic decision taken by the Security Council, the preparations for the 1978 election went ahead and the following parties and organisations registered to take part in the election: the DTA – an alliance of 11 political parties of which the Republican Party was one; AKTUR (Aksiefront vir die behoud van die Turnhallebeginsels – Action Front for the Retention of the Turnhalle Principles), which had been created by the National Party together with a few splinter groups and individuals (they were still not prepared to establish a multiracial party); the HNP (Herstigte Nasionale Party – Reconstituted National Party); the Liberation Front of Baster Captain Hans Diergaardt; and the NCDP (Namibia Christian Democratic Party). As could be expected, SWAPO did not take part in the elections. Since SWAPO was not a banned organisation, its members could vote or participate indirectly by influencing voters not to register or vote in the election.

For many of the inhabitants of the country this was the first time they were allowed to vote, making it different to any previous election. We held meetings across the country. Amenities reserved for whites were not available to us, and in black towns and the communal areas we addressed our supporters under trees and in some cases in the open countryside from the back of a truck. Unfortunately, white voters attended the DTA meetings only in small numbers and my RP colleagues and I had to organise separate meetings for them. In the north, which was frequented by SWAPO infiltrators, the inhabitants were still hesitant to attend the meetings.

It often happened that by the time speakers arrived at a venue, there was no audience. They would then trickle in cautiously like antelope on their way to a waterhole where a lion could possibly be lying in wait. Only once a reasonable number of people had gathered, would they feel safer and show up in larger numbers. Many of the inhabitants of the communal areas had no transport, and had to rely on us to make it available to them, and sometimes also provide food for those who had travelled long distances on foot. National Party speakers referred to our meetings as "pap-en-wors-vergaderings" (porridge and sausage meetings). In the four months before the election we reached tens of thousands of voters, black and white.

To boost their confidence and rouse their enthusiasm, colourful processions with flags, T-shirts and multicoloured dresses were organised. We used microphones to announce our meetings. I can't recall who came up with the interesting suggestion that we broadcast our announcements through a loudspeaker from an aircraft. A recording of the DTA song "This is the voice of Namibia! This is the voice of the DTA!" sung by Gé Korsten were also broadcasted from the aeroplane. This upset many of our opponents, who alleged that we were trying to create the impression that it was God talking to the people. This was ludicrous, to say the least.

AKTUR, and especially Eben van Zijl, still wanted to know where the DTA was getting its funding from. I was obviously not prepared to reveal the names of our donors, and rejected the insinuation that we were being controlled by some or other foreign money power with the contempt that it deserved. My colleagues and I accepted invitations to address various chambers of commerce in South Africa from which we received substantial donations. We also received funding and equipment from foundations, especially in Germany. The DTA received financial support because what we stood for captured people's imaginations.

Not much was said about constitutional models at our meetings, and our differences with the National Party did not really come up for discussion. We spoke mainly about SWAPO and what could be expected if SWAPO were to take over the country. We had to address this issue, because we knew that sooner or later we would have to fight an election against SWAPO.

I spoke in very plain language, using metaphorical language that the people could understand, and made comparisons to situations and matters with which they were familiar. For example, I warned that they must not think that if SWAPO comes into power, thorn trees will bear fruit or milk will automatically run out of cows' udders. They should therefore not believe everything SWAPO promised them. I spoke frequently about the distribution of wealth – and this was a difficult one to explain. I again compared the situation to a cow, saying that you could do one of two things with a cow. You could slaughter the cow, divide the meat and the family would have meat for a week, or you could keep the cow alive so that she could produce milk for the family for an indefinite period of time. I compared this to the natural resources in the country, namely land, minerals and fish resources, which weren't produced by us but which had been given to us by the Creator. If these resources were to be divided, it had to be done carefully and responsibly, so that it would not be "slaughtered" but that its produce could feed the nation. To this day I use the same comparison.

We also spoke about a peaceful solution, saying that you couldn't bring about peace by killing people. That we had asked that SWAPO speak to us about a peaceful solution and free and fair elections. I spoke about apartheid and racial discrimination, saying that these things had to be abolished. This upset the leaders of the National Party, who accused us of promoting an anti-white attitude.

We advocated these things in 1978, more than 30 years ago, when the whites were still trying to defend apartheid on biblical grounds, and Koos Pretorius was postulating that you first needed to determine your love for yourself before you could decide how much you could love your neighbour.

At the time of the election a large number of observers, journalists, TV teams and politicians from the Western countries visited the Territory and I received piles of condemnatory telegrams, but also some of support. Despite the intimidation by SWAPO, 80% of the voters cast their votes and the DTA achieved an overwhelming victory. The result of the election was announced by the chief electoral officer as follows: DTA 268 130 votes (41 seats); AKTUR 38 716 votes (6 seats); NCDP 9073 votes (1 seat); HNP 5781 votes (1 seat); LF 4564 votes (1 seat). Total number of seats: 50.

The outcome of the election was a triumph for the DTA. In the run-up to the election many so-called informed people predicted that the voting percentage would be very low. SWAPO did everything in its power to keep voters away from the ballot boxes, even attempting in the northern areas to do this with the assistance of armed terrorists. The voting percentage of 80% and the number of votes that the DTA managed to get, came as a surprise even to me. A joint effort by white, black and coloured was therefore rewarded with great success.

My English great-grandfather, Richard Henry Mudge, shortly before he passed
away on 23 September 1902, and his wife, Susanna Coetzee. They had five
children: Henry, Jane, Dirk Frederik (Oupa Dick), Susan and Mary.

Dirk Frederik (Oupa Dick) Mudge and his wife, Helene (née Arp), with their three children (from left to right) Richard Henry, Dorothea Wilhelmina and Henry Ferdinand (my father).

The seven Van Tonder brothers who were part of the South African troops that conquered South West Africa in 1915. Oupa Piet is at the back on the right.

The first elected Legislative Assembly of South West Africa (1925). It consisted of seven members of the Deutsche Bund, three of the National Party, two independents and four appointed members. My grandfather's oldest brother, C.J. van Tonder, is at the back, second from the right.

My sister Sannie and I (the first Mudge to be born in South West Africa),
with my father's Pedal Ford in the background.

My father Hendrik (Henry Ferdinand) Mudge, my mother Grieta
(Magrieta Cornelia), and the five of us (from left to right),
Lyna, Sannie, me and Piet, with Henry in front.

The Constitution Committee of the Turnhalle Constitutional Conference
with me as Chairman, 1975.

The Herero leader Clemens Kapuuo.

Clemens Kapuuo's funeral in March 1978.

Demonstrations by the National Party after I had introduced the Abolition of Racial Discrimination Act in 1979. My son, Henk, was jeered at by demonstrators when he attempted to come and listen to my speech.

Addressing the Geneva Conference organised by the Western Contact Group under chairmanship of Brian Urquhart, Assistant Secretary General, in January 1981.

A meeting with Sam Nujoma and other SWAPO leaders in Lusaka with President Kenneth Kaunda and Administrator General Willie van Niekerk, May 1984.

With Jonas Savimbi in Angola, 1979.

Members of the Multi-Party Conference (MPC) visiting the Ivory Coast
and President Fëlix Houphouët-Boigny, May 1984.

An interview with CNN in Washington, May 1984.

The members of the Multi-Party Conference meet Chester Crocker,
second from the left, in 1984.

A DTA election meeting in Katutura, Windhoek, 1989.

A DTA meeting in Rundu, 1989.

A DTA meeting in Katima, 1989.

I meet Queen Elizabeth II of England at the
Windhoek Agricultural Show, October 1991.

Me with my champion cow.

The highlight of my political career: This photograph was taken moments after the Constitution Committee accepted the draft constitution unanimously.

Christmas 2014 at Cape Cross. In the middle row next to me on my right is my wife Stienie. We are surrounded by our five children, their spouses and our sixteen grandchildren and seventeen great-grandchildren.

CHAPTER 10

An own government for South West Africa, 1978–1983

The first session of the Constituent Assembly

The first meeting of the newly elected Constituent Assembly took place on 21 December 1978 with Johannes Skrywer elected as the first President (Speaker) of the Assembly. The South African Prime Minister, P.W. Botha, accompanied by Pik Botha, came to Windhoek to give effect to his undertaking to his Western counterparts that South Africa would point out to the elected Assembly the various alternatives and their likely consequences, both internally and externally. South Africa would also bring to their attention the views of the Five in regard to the requirements for international recognition of an independent South West Africa. Since the announcement of the election, South Africa had repeatedly undertaken not to prescribe to the elected representatives but to leave all options open to them. They would even have the right to accept the report by the Secretary General, should they so prefer.

The meeting adjourned to give the different parties the opportunity to reflect in their various caucuses on the matters raised.

While the DTA supporters were lighting celebratory fires throughout the country and harbouring great expectations, we now had to decide whether we should simply continue as before; and should we indeed decide to go ahead on this basis, would it mean that the election was a futile exercise? Our caucus meeting was a long one, and many reservations were expressed. It was expected of me as Chairman to take the lead. Although I had appreciation for the trust my colleagues had consistently placed in me, this nevertheless placed an almost impossible responsibility on my shoulders.

Since I had followed the negotiations between South Africa and the Western Powers closely, I was in a better position than some of my colleagues to pass judgement in this complicated situation. I realised that any effort towards unilateral steps would be futile, and that the implementation of the settlement plan was the only option. I was also well aware of the fact that South Africa would not easily agree to an election that was not free and fair and that the South African

Government could not afford to be seen as having sold out South African citizens, especially whites in South West Africa. I never underestimated P.W. Botha's determination to fend off a total onslaught, and I knew that the presence of the Russians and Cubans in Southern Africa was unacceptable to him. The capability of the South African Defence Force gave him confidence. I tried to convince my colleagues that no one could prevent us from working on constitutional models, and that by means of the elected assembly we were able not only to advise the Administrator General on important matters, but would also have a greater say in the constitutional future of our country.

Nevertheless, the caucus was still deeply divided and we continued until late that night before we could agree on a motion to be tabled the next day. The first part of the rather long motion stated that the Assembly:

- wanted to thank the inhabitants of South West Africa for the peaceful and orderly way in which the election had been conducted and for the confidence they had placed in the elected leaders;
- was aware of the great responsibility resting on the shoulders of the elected assembly;
- confirmed that it commits itself to execute the clear finding of the inhabitants in favour of the attainment of peace and security by means of a constitutional process;
- endorsed the importance of international recognition of an independent South West Africa;
- supported the initiative of the five Western countries to achieve an internationally acceptable settlement;
- after the explanation by the Prime Minister of South Africa, decided to work together towards a speedy implementation of the Security Council's Resolution 435, provided that there would be no withdrawal of South African troops before a complete cessation of hostilities; a fixed date for the election would be determined; unresolved problems, such as the size of the UN's military component and the monitoring of SWAPO bases in neighbouring countries, with specific reference to paragraph 12 of the Settlement Plan, would be cleared with the Administrator General; the South African Police would remain responsible for maintaining law and order; and that the administrative responsibility for the Territory would rest with the Administrator General until independence.

In the second part of the motion were the following points which we regarded as unacceptable and might complicate the independence process:

- The recognition by the UN of SWAPO as the only true leaders of the inhabitants of South West Africa.
- The financial support that was given to SWAPO by the UN.
- The encouragement and moral support the UN was giving to SWAPO to continue its acts of violence and terror.
- Neighbouring countries making their territory available to SWAPO for establishing bases there.

The motion demanded the elimination of the above injustices and that absolute impartiality be maintained during the election process. Other countries favourably disposed towards the democratic parties would be lobbied for support, should the UN or its member states continue favouring SWAPO. All parties that wanted to participate in the election would be required to declare beforehand that they would do so peacefully and would desist from violence. The UN was requested to denounce all acts of violence and to commit to severing its ties with SWAPO. In conclusion, the hope was expressed that South Africa and South West Africa would reach an agreement regarding Walvis Bay.

This long motion was concluded with a proposal that the Constituent Assembly insists on a final decision by the Security Council on the implementation of Resolution 435 before 31 January 1979.

After I had tabled the motion in the Constituent Assembly on behalf of the DTA, it was seconded by Dr Ben Africa, after which the other parties were given the opportunity to comment. For the DTA the decision to proceed by cooperating with the Security Council and South Africa on the basis of Resolution 435 was not – as I have already indicated – an easy one, but for AKTUR, and especially the National Party, anything other than the continued existence of this one-person-one-vote elected assembly that had been dominated by the DTA was more acceptable to them. It came as no surprise to me when AKTUR objected to determining a deadline. Du Plessis, as well as Van Zijl, took part in the debate and argued that the deadline was unnecessarily tight. However, putting the Security Council under pressure was precisely what we intended. AKTUR then proposed a motion which was rejected by the Assembly; my motion was accepted.

The Assembly had averted a confrontation with the international community by taking this responsible decision. On 23 December 1978, the decision made by the Constituent Assembly was communicated to the Secretary General in New York. Although his reply on 2 January 1979 made no mention of the Constituent Assembly, Dr Waldheim took cognisance of the fact that South Africa was in favour of a speedy implementation of Resolution 435. Without naming them, he confirmed that the "parties" had given him the assurance separately that they would honour the terms of a comprehensive ceasefire agreement. (Since the internal parties never took part in the armed struggle, the reference was probably made to SWAPO's armed wing and the South African Defence Force.)

As far as the election date was concerned, the Secretary General, after consultation with the Administrator General, was of the opinion that it should be determined as soon as possible. UNTAG would then be deployed before the end of February. In his view an election on 30 September 1979, for example, would be reconcilable with the settlement plan. He also referred specifically to paragraph 12 of the proposals, stating that he had the undertaking of the neighbouring states that they would cooperate with the UN in ensuring that UNTAG was effecting its mandate. Paragraph 12 made provision for the total cessation and monitoring of hostilities. He proposed that his Special Representative, Ahtisaari, depart for Windhoek on 8 January 1979 for discussions on the final deployment of UNTAG. He ended his letter expressing the sincere hope that a solution would be reached regarding the Namibian question in the new year and added that this would be a crucial contribution to the attainment of peace in Southern Africa.

Unfortunately, Dr Waldheim did not react in his letter to the demands made by the Constituent Assembly relating to impartiality and the recognition, support and preferential treatment by the UN of SWAPO. Until this was resolved, the political playing field would not be level.

Those of us who were in favour of a peaceful and democratic solution could not foresee that it would take another ten years for independence to become a reality by means of a democratic process. Had I known this, and that the decade lying ahead would be the most difficult period of my road to independence, I would probably have considered throwing in the towel. But I didn't, and for the next ten years my colleagues and I fought on three fronts – against SWAPO under Sam Nujoma; the South African Government under P.W. Botha; and the rightist parties in South West Africa. We learnt by experience that war mongers did not make peace easily, and that some people would apparently sooner give up their lives than their privileges – as I had said five years before in the school hall at Outjo.

The status of the Constituent Assembly is confirmed

When the Constituent Assembly resumed its activities on 22 January 1979, the President of the Assembly, Johannes Skrywer, introduced rules of procedure that had been compiled by a committee during the recess. Appie Louw, the Chairman of the Committee, explained the necessity of such a procedure, and briefly sketched its content. He countered arguments that the Constituent Assembly no longer had a function and that procedural rules were therefore unnecessary due to the motion that had been accepted during its first session. According to Appie, the allegations that the elected body no longer had a function were based on the most dubious misconceptions possible and that this Assembly had important functions to perform in accordance with a mandate that had been bestowed on it by the electorate. Dr Africa proposed an amendment that further strengthened Appie's motion. It read: "… that the importance of this Assembly, in the search for an acceptable solution to the South West Africa problem, cannot be underestimated and that this Assembly still retained its authority in terms of Proclamation AG 63 with reference specifically to paragraph 2."

Directly after this the President read the following letter he had received from the Administrator General:

Highly esteemed Mr President,

In view of the possibility of a second election that might be held this year to elect a Constituent Assembly in terms of Resolution 435 of 1978, I am of the opinion that it would be in the public interest to confirm that notwithstanding such an election this Honourable Assembly is still a legal body consisting of appropriately elected real leaders of the population of the Territory and that it will continue to play a necessary role to assist me in the execution of my duties as government authority of the Territory. I trust accordingly that the Honourable Assembly will orchestrate its activities in such a way that a consistent effective interaction between us is promoted and will continue to, as mentioned above, maintain its important objective as envisaged in Section 2(2) of the Proclamation.

The President proceeded by requesting notification of motions to be tabled. From the long list of motions that were introduced by the DTA, it became clear what the Alliance wanted to achieve. Through different leaders, the DTA proposed a number of motions that were so important that I am presenting them below as comprehensively as possible:

- That the AG be requested to pay attention to the following matters immediately:
  1. An institute for the training of the inhabitants of Namibia as public servants.
  2. The in-service training of the inhabitants of SWA/Namibia as public servants.
  3. The development of a diplomatic service by the training of diplomatic representatives.
- That the Constituent Assembly insists in the strongest terms that the following discriminatory measures be abolished immediately:
  1. The reservation of certain tourist resorts, guesthouses, hotels, restaurants, bioscopes and residential areas for members of certain population groups.
  2. Other such discriminatory measures that may be brought to his attention by the Constituent Assembly from time to time.
- That, due to the necessity of an effective Public Service for the administration of South West Africa; and due to the limited funds and shortage of local manpower available to the State; and seen in the light of the necessity for coordinated action regarding the activities of the State; and considering the necessity of a South West African/Namibian-oriented control and management of the Public Service; and since the Public Service had to fulfil the common needs of all population groups, it was decided:
  1. that attention be given immediately to the establishment of a fully fledged and independent Public Service for the Government of South West Africa/Namibia;
  2. that the existing state departments and state institutions in and for South West Africa/Namibia be reorganised in view of the requirements of an effective service delivery;
  3. that appropriate provision be made in the new Public Service for the coordination of the activities of state departments and state institutions at all levels of government;
  4. that the responsibility for control and management of the state departments be transferred to the departments in South West Africa/Namibia without delay, including accountability for and control of personnel matters;

5. that it be indicated to civil servants who currently resorted under the Public Service Act (No. 54 of 1957) of the Republic of South Africa or under any other existing law or proclamation or ordinance in South West Africa/Namibia exactly where they stood in terms of their continued service in the Territory and what the associated service conditions were;

6. that the Constituent Assembly appoint a committee to assist His Excellency the Administrator General to determine the needs of a Public Service for the country; and

7. that His Excellency the Administrator General be requested to report back to this Assembly as soon as possible on which steps had been taken regarding the implementation of paragraphs 1–6.

- That the Constituent Assembly appoint a committee with the authority to look into the matter of citizenship and to make recommendations in this regard;

- That the Constituent Assembly appoint a committee with the authority to call and listen to witnesses to initiate negotiations with the Government of the Republic of South Africa on the situation with Walvis Bay.

As could be expected, there was much speculation as to what this newly elected Assembly had up its sleeve. After independence, SWAPO leaders told me that they were convinced that we (the DTA) were planning a unilateral declaration of independence. We never considered such a possibility, because barely a month earlier we had committed ourselves irrevocably to cooperate on the basis of Resolution 435. To act in contradiction to this commitment would have been immoral and irresponsible. I was totally convinced that none of the motions we had introduced contradicted what would in any case be considered and, in all likelihood, be accepted by a constituent assembly elected in terms of Resolution 435.

More importantly, the elected leaders had now committed themselves to independence more than ever before and were planning to prepare the inhabitants of the country accordingly for such an eventuality. We were aware that SWAPO, assisted by its allies, had established an institution for the training of public servants in Lusaka and that they had already been working on a constitution for our country for several years. Why couldn't we do the same?

Although we could not have anticipated that it would take another ten years for the UN-supervised election to take place, we learnt from previous experience that the winning post might still be moved forward several times. Why then did we have to wait for SWAPO to effect the necessary changes? We had the opportunity to do so ourselves, although the Constituent Assembly itself had no original powers.

Therefore, with the few powers we had, and in spite of a great deal of resistance, also from the side of the South African Government, we began to pave the way for a new and independent Republic.

The AKTUR leaders, A.H. du Plessis, Eben van Zijl, Jan de Wet and Percy Niehaus, took a different view. Van Zijl tabled the following motion:

> In compliance with its decision on 22 December 1978 to cooperate for the speedy implementation of Security Council Resolution 435 (1978) in order to call an election for a Constituent Assembly under UN supervision, this Assembly is of the opinion that:
> (i) This Assembly had renounced its power to draw up a constitution for South West Africa; and
> (ii) All associated powers as set out in Section 2(2)(a) and (b) of Proclamation AG 63/1978 had been terminated.

When Van Zijl introduced his motion the next day, he based his argument, as one would expect from a jurist, on legal grounds. He cited the article in the Institutional Proclamation that vested the authority to draw up a constitution in the Assembly and to communicate with the Administrator General with regard to matters pertaining to the independence process. He took the view that, since the Assembly had relinquished its authority to write a constitution, the additional powers relating to requests to the Administrator General in respect of an independence process had also lapsed and could no longer be exercised by the Assembly. He further maintained that the Assembly could also not make recommendations to the Administrator General nor advise him on his administration of the judicial system that resorted under him.

Appie Louw, with a legal background himself, in reaction to Van Zijl's arguments, pointed out flagrant inaccuracies, substantiating this with quotations from authoritative textbooks. However, it was clear from the remainder of Van Zijl's speech that he was not concerned with the legal status of the newly elected Assembly but rather with the proposals tabled by the DTA leaders. He commented: "They are on record … but you can analyse each one of those motions, every one of them, and you will come to the same conclusion and this is that the purpose and intention of each of these motions is to write a Constitution piecemeal." He elaborated, arguing that these motions were in conflict with the objectives of the Western nations and those of the United Nations "… and that this could give rise to a confrontation with South Africa and a confrontation with the Western nations and could have absolutely catastrophic consequences for this country."

I was stunned. A party that had for such a long time been opposed to cooperation with the Western nations or with the UN, now entered a plea that nothing should be done that could lead to a confrontation with them. For the life of me I could not understand Van Zijl's arguments. The motions tabled by the duly elected internal leaders were recommendations to the legal authority over the Territory, namely the Administrator General. One of the demands from the Security Council was to do away with all discriminatory measures immediately. This was the objective with most of the motions, and was even in line with many of the principles contained in the Turnhalle Constitution. Why would any rational thinking person wish to delay changes and preparations for independence until the Constituent Assembly had been elected in terms of Resolution 435?

There were other speakers, such as Adv. Niehaus and Jan de Wet, who seconded Van Zijl's motion. Sarel Becker of the HNP spoke incoherently and contradicted himself several times. The HNP and the National Party fully agreed that they had to get rid of this Assembly as soon as possible, because the DTA was in the process of slaughtering sacred cows. Appie Louw closed his contribution to this debate as follows:

> The DTA agrees that we want no discrimination and this is what our Party says. So what are the members on the other side saying? They don't want to tell us whether they are for or against this. They say they won't participate when these motions are being discussed. The Honourable Members on the other side of the House want us to allow the illegal representative of South West, SWAPO, to do the things that we now want to do.

Du Plessis felt beleaguered because it had been alleged that he and the National Party wanted to block the abolition of discriminatory practices, which according to him was precisely what the National Party was doing already. Once again I failed to understand why the opposition parties had a problem with our motion. Du Plessis continued that the DTA was gate-crashing and asked: "Why are they going about it in this manner when they know that some of the things they want to do here will cause profound unrest and deep concern with, for instance, the white population group?" His question confirmed my suspicion that the Assembly was seen as a threat to the whites, while it was in fact the opposite.

I was not aware of any objections made by South Africa against the continued existence of the elected Assembly. As a matter of fact, in an interview with the DTA leaders a few days before the Assembly commenced its activities, the Minister of Foreign Affairs, Pik Botha, stated unequivocally that "... as far as the Government is concerned, ... this body was created in terms of a legal, existing Proclamation and as far as the Government is concerned, that body has an important role to play." Although Ahtisaari had expressed misgivings about the continued existence and functions of the Assembly during his visit, the arrangements for its implementation had gone ahead and no "catastrophic results" had ensued.

Van Zijl reminded the Assembly that the Prime Minister, prompted by Ahtisaari's criticism, had said that after a constituent assembly had been elected in terms of Resolution 435, it would be the only legal assembly. I concurred with this wholeheartedly. I had said earlier that two constituent assemblies could not exist simultaneously, but that the current body would continue to exist until the final one had been elected.

Following a debate of over four days, the motion I had introduced and which had been amended by Werner Neef was accepted by a majority vote. The Assembly then continued the discussion of the motions that had been put forward at the beginning of the session. AKTUR members maintained the position they had taken during the discussion of my motion, namely that they would not participate in deliberations on matters that, in their view, fell outside the jurisdiction and powers of the Assembly, but that they would consider participating in the discussions of matters on the agenda on an ad hoc basis and on merit.

On 6 February 1979, Pik Botha wrote to the Secretary General expressing his disappointment that no progress had been made with regard to the outstanding points. He pointed out once again that it was his Government's wish that the deployment of UNTAG forces start no later than the end of February and that any postponement of the election – to after 30 September – could derail the entire settlement plan. As a practical step the Minister proposed that the date for the ending of hostilities be set for no later than 20 February 1979. He could not foresee that any of the parties involved would object to this, adding that the South African Government had gone out of its way to remove the obstacles hampering the implementation of Resolution 435.

Matters were further obscured by a revelation by Ottilie Abrahams of SWAPO-D that SWAPO deserters were being held in inhumane conditions in holes in Zambia. P.W. Botha accused Ahtisaari of insensitivity towards these detainees who were being threatened with abolition and appealed to him and the UN to take cognisance of these circumstances instead of making derogatory remarks about his (Botha's) objections. He questioned Ahtisaari's position as the Representative of the Secretary General.

Following an interview that a SWAPO delegation under leadership of its President, Sam Nujoma, had with Ahtisaari in Luanda on 11 February 1979, the organisation issued a statement in which South Africa was accused of having set new conditions for the implementation of the Western settlement plan. It was based on the following: Firstly, South Africa's proposal that SWAPO fighters be restricted to bases outside Namibia, and that they would be monitored there; secondly, that concentration camps referred to as "reception centres" be established where SWAPO fugitives, following their return, would be held for an indefinite period; and thirdly, that South Africa proposed a complete departure from the timetable for the withdrawal of South African troops before the election. SWAPO declared further that the deviations from the settlement plan changed it in essence, and that they rejected it as a matter of course.

SWAPO maintained throughout that it had bases within the Territory, something that had been denied by the Defence Force and inhabitants of the country. My colleagues and I criss-crossed Ovamboland during the election campaign where we only encountered SWAPO infiltrators who were responsible for hit-and-run incidents. For SWAPO it was important to prove that they had a military presence in the Territory before the election. Their return, therefore, had to take on the appearance of a military operation. At the same time the South African Defence Force was to withdraw and the territorial forces demobilised.

Were it to happen like this, it would give SWAPO a major psychological advantage in the election, especially if their military component were to return in large numbers.

After this Pik Botha reiterated South Africa's position that SWAPO terrorists be confined to their bases where they would be monitored, and that they would only be allowed to return to South West Africa to take part in the election if they did so peacefully and unarmed. Furthermore, they had to enter the Territory via pre-arranged entry points, that no intimidation by SWAPO would be tolerated and that not a single South African soldier would be allowed to leave the Territory before there were visible signs that peace had been achieved. SWAPO would not be allowed to enter the Territory from Walvis Bay and would not receive any preferential treatment, but would take part in the election on the same conditions as everyone else. This, said Pik, would put an end to the absurd claim by SWAPO that it was the only representative of the people of South West Africa.

On the same day that Pik Botha released this statement, 250 insurgents attacked the Nkongo SADF base 15 km south of the border, and shortly after that they bombarded the base at Elundu. SWAPO later announced that they had killed more than 300 South African soldiers; destroyed two military bases; shot down two reconnaissance aircraft; had taken out 40 military vehicles; and had taken a large number of weapons and ammunition as booty in the previous three months. In *Dié wat gewen het*, General Jannie Geldenhuys writes that if only a quarter of what SWAPO claimed were true, it would have been a national disaster for South Africa. It was subsequently confirmed that this propaganda by SWAPO was a total farce and that only seven members of the South African troops had been wounded.

We as political leaders had not been informed about the military situation and had to rely on the media for information. I learnt many of the facts in books which appeared only after the war and after independence. I read in Geldenhuys's book that the operations following this attack on their bases were "… of the most important turning points in the war. The long-term statistics indicated subsequently that as from July 1979 we fared ever better and the insurgents ever worse."

Minister Pik Botha's reaction to the incident at the Nkongo base was important to me and my colleagues. He condemned SWAPO for taking this action so close to the envisaged deployment of the UN Peace Corps. I wondered at the time whether it was realistic to expect either of the two fighting parties to cease their operations before a truce cessation of hostilities had been announced formally. I was more interested in finding out to what extent an agreement about a fair election could be reached. The only point raised by Minister Botha in his follow-up statement was that Sam Nujoma in his Lusaka statement objected to points about which consensus had already been reached.

And so the political and diplomatic war raged on concurrently with the military battle. Diplomats on more than one occasion remarked to me that Pik Botha was a formidable negotiator. He often got away with murder, but, as I have mentioned before, he had to pull the chestnuts out of the fire for South Africa over a long period of time. I would like to illustrate his ability to exploit a lack of judgement with the following incident. On 15 February 1979, Secretary General Dr Kurt Waldheim remarked as follows in an interview with Voice of America: "But the basic issue here is that the South African Government is in the Territory illegally and this has to be stressed. I have to say this. You know that the United Nations decided long ago on the basis of decisions by the International Court of Justice that the presence of South Africa in Namibia is illegal." The same evening Pik responded as follows:

> After two years of negotiations with the South African Government Dr Waldheim has suddenly discovered that South Africa is in South West Africa illegally. The decisive factor in the two-year negotiation, which held so much promise, has been that the parties would not insist on basing themselves upon their technical-juridical positions. But now Dr Waldheim declares, after two years of negotiations, that South Africa's illegal presence in South West Africa is a basic issue. We cannot rely on a single binding decision of the International Court in support of such an allegation. There is no juridical base for this position. However, if South Africa were to be illegally in South West Africa as suggested by Dr Waldheim, the question would arise as to whether he should continue to concern himself with illegalities. In terms of his own assessment of South Africa's position, the question arises as to whether we have anything further to say to one another. The most important question according to Dr Waldheim's own view of the situation is whether he should not henceforth conduct his negotiations with the authority that he considers legal. The South African Government would concede him that privilege.

I did not think that this little tête-a-tête would have any influence on further negotiations, but due to my own experiences with haughty representatives of the Western countries and the UN, I enjoyed reading it. Dr Waldheim did in fact react to it briefly, expressing the hope that all the parties concerned would refrain from steps and comments that could jeopardise the negotiations.

A letter from Dr Waldheim to Pik Botha after this resulted in more questions being raised than answered. Since the entire settlement plan would be turned upside down during the following weeks, I would like to go into further details in this regard. Dr Waldheim did indeed condemn the continuance of hostilities and said that at an appropriate time he would announce a procedure for setting up a ceasefire. He went on to explain why more rapid progress could not be made with the implementation of the settlement plan. However, Pik Botha was not satisfied with this explanation and in his reply to Waldheim's letter confirmed that the remaining issues were not so important that they should delay the implementation of the settlement plan. In his view these points of difference were of secondary importance and could easily be resolved once South Africa had been given answers on certain questions he had posed. P.W. Botha pointed out that the South African Government was highly disturbed by a statement the leader of SWAPO had issued in Luanda in which he made certain outrageous demands, among others that upon their return SWAPO fighters (members of PLAN) would be established in five different bases within South West Africa, and also that in neighbouring countries they would no longer be subjected to monitoring. Minister Botha quoted several paragraphs from the original proposals to verify the unacceptability of Sam Nujoma's demands.

On 26 February 1979, the Secretary General submitted a report to the Security Council that would inevitably lead to a confrontation between South Africa and the Security Council, and would also involve the elected leaders of South West Africa. Waldheim referred to the visits made by his Special Representative Martti Ahtisaari to South Africa, Tanzania, Mozambique, Zambia, Botswana, Angola and, on special request, also to Nigeria. He reported that he had also consulted with the leader of SWAPO, Sam Nujoma, and that it had emerged clearly that the two parties, South Africa and SWAPO, interpreted certain paragraphs of the settlement plan differently.

Dr Waldheim stated that in view of information he had received and after he had listened to the arguments of the parties directly involved, he would like to propose how the remaining points could be resolved. In general terms his proposals were in line with the original proposals, but in respect of paragraph 11 there was a serious departure, which had apparently been proposed by SWAPO and some of the neighbouring states. It boiled down to the fact that SWAPO forces in the Territory at the time a ceasefire came into effect, would be restricted to bases within the Territory. Bases would be established as determined by the Special Representative in consultation with the Administrator General, and that the movement of SWAPO units to these bases would not be regarded as a tactical move.

I often had to answer the question why this deviation was so important to us as a political organisation. I'll answer it once again. When the internal parties accepted an election under UN supervision, I knew that in many respects it would be an uneven contest. SWAPO would undoubtedly be the favourite since it had already been pronounced by the arbitrator – the UN – as the true and sole representative of the inhabitants of South West Africa. As a result of its military wing, SWAPO had a strong-man image and could use this to its advantage during the election. Added to this was the fact that SWAPO had already enjoyed the moral, material and military support of the world for a considerable period of time. We were prepared to accept the risk to participate in an uneven contest. We could, however, not accept a military presence in the Territory after a ceasefire, a presence SWAPO never had at any stage during the war. The fact that SWAPO could never establish a military presence in South West Africa was one of SWAPO's biggest problems throughout. It was therefore important for them to use this opportunity to get some of their units across the border just before the ceasefire, if not simultaneously.

If there was ever any doubt about this, SWAPO proved it to be the case when, on 1 April 1989, the day on which the ceasefire finally became a reality, it crossed the border in large numbers and fully armed with heavy equipment, at the cost of many lives. It was without a doubt important for SWAPO to create the impression amongst the voting public that they had won the war. In this respect the internal parties were in a weak position. Although we were dependent on the South African Defence Force for our safety, it was politically of little benefit to us. The SADF carried the insignia of a colonial power and had to withdraw before the election. Our electorate was easily impressed by military display and had lived in fear for so many years that it could easily be intimidated. Any tactical move by armed units would undoubtedly influence the voters.

In respect of paragraph 12 of the settlement plan, the Secretary General reported that SWAPO's armed forces in neighbouring states would be restricted to bases in those countries. He announced, however, that although paragraph 12 did not specifically make provision for the monitoring of these bases by UNTAG, neighbouring states would be requested to ensure that the conditions regarding the temporary measures and the result of the election were respected. What it actually boiled down to was that SWAPO bases in neighbouring states would not be monitored, which was definitely not in line with the understanding that had been reached. In a letter to South Africa and SWAPO, the Secretary General suggested that the ceasefire take effect at midnight on 15 March 1979, and that both parties indicate whether they accepted the proposals no later than 5 March.

Even before the Secretary General's letter reached the South African Government – as a matter of fact, while it was still in draft form – Prime Minister P.W. Botha reacted to the report in Parliament. He announced that a serious situation had arisen in respect of the implementation of the settlement plan. He continued that there were no longer any guarantees that the bases across the border would be monitored and, even more alarmingly, that bases for armed SWAPO fighters within the Territory were going to be established. He added that he was also aware of outrageous and unacceptable demands by SWAPO which had not been spelt out in the report, but which, reading between the lines, SWAPO had not yet relinquished. The Prime Minister announced that he would consult with the Constituent Assembly in South West Africa as soon as possible, after which he would, in turn, inform Parliament.

The National Party misses a golden opportunity

The Constituent Assembly was in the meanwhile engaged in debating and approving the motions that had been tabled by the DTA leaders. The four members of the National Party (affiliated member of AKTUR) reiterated that they would not participate in the discussion of the motions and, moreover, they stopped attending the Assembly. Andrew

Kloppers of AKTUR did attend the meetings, but with instructions not to take part in the discussions. One of the members remarked by way of an interjection that old Kloppie was only there every day to collect his allowance. On 8 February the President, that is, the Speaker, announced that in view of the unauthorised absence of the members of the National Party, there were now four vacancies in the Constituent Assembly.

The argument put forward by AKTUR and the National Party that they would not take part in the discussions because this would amount to a constitution being written piecemeal, can best be judged by considering the motions which had been accepted during their absence. The most important of these were about the repeal of discriminatory regulations, the training of public servants, the establishment of an own public service (since the Administrator General had now taken over the executive powers in the Territory), the shortage of teaching educational facilities, an independent radio service, the establishment of a university for all the inhabitants, equal remuneration for equal work, short- and long-term economic planning, citizenship and the status of Walvis Bay.

All these motions contained recommendations to the Administrator General, who was the legal executive authority in South West Africa; he could consider and implement them. There was no reason to delay dealing with these matters until after the election of a Constituent Assembly in terms of Resolution 435. There could, therefore, only be one reason for the attitude of the National Party's objection in principle to a body which had been elected on the basis of universal suffrage, and in which they had only four representatives.

The absence of the four representatives of the National Party and the two abstaining members of AKTUR (Andrew Kloppers and Pieter Diergaardt) resulted in the three other parties – the HNP represented by Sarel Becker, the Liberation Front represented by Hans Diergaardt, and the NCDP, represented by Hans Röhr – taking over the role of opposition.

Sarel Becker was intelligent, consistent and openly opposed to the Western settlement plan, opening up residential areas and domination by blacks. He accused South Africa of abandoning us and demanded that SWAPO immediately be declared a forbidden organisation internally. On his involvement in an assembly that he condemned in every respect, his premise was that he had decided to "fight the devil with his own fork". As could be expected, he could find no one to second any of his many motions.

After this the Assembly was adjourned until 1 April 1979 without us having any information about when the South African Government intended informing us about the Secretary General's report and the serious deviations it contained. But while a sword was hanging over our heads and important decisions had to be made, the Legislative Assembly for Whites convened from 13 to 16 February 1979, and political issues pertaining mainly to white interests were discussed as if the implementation of the settlement plan and the election concerned were nothing but a daydream. Matters that could be discussed fruitfully in the Constituent Assembly were now being scrutinised in detail in the Legislative Assembly for Whites.

When the session commenced, the Chairman of the Executive Committee and leader of the National Party, A.H. du Plessis, proposed that since the term of the Legislative Assembly would come to an end on 19 May 1979, the South African Government be requested to proclaim an election, or to prolong the term of the Legislative Assembly for Whites. It is clear from the motivation of his motion that he was concerned about the continued existence of the Legislative Assembly. The fact that the request was directed at the South African Government and not the Administrator General supported my suspicion. While I had no objection to the motion in principle, I did object to holding a white election before the envisaged election of a Constituent Assembly.

In virtually all cases the speeches made during the session dealt with the same matters that had been discussed in the Constituent Assembly the previous week. They missed out on a golden opportunity to present their position on sensitive matters such as education, open residential areas, discrimination and Christian principles in the presence of black and coloured delegates. In the Legislative Assembly, however, where the National Party was in control and where they could get their motions passed with a majority vote, they were prepared to discuss these issues.

Koos Pretorius postulated his Christian principles yet again, saying that in reality the Republican Party and the DTA were offering a humanist ideology as an alternative to communism. He maintained that we had decided to adhere to a new principle, namely that no one should be subjected to legislation in the making of which he had no say and that for all practical purposes it had to culminate in the concept of general universal suffrage, a concept the National Party vehemently opposed ever since the establishment of the interim government. They were apparently still under the illusion that a body in which the black and coloured inhabitants were the majority (as in the existing Constituent Assembly) would accept a system under which black inhabitants (non-whites) within a so-called white area could be subjected to an authority they had not chosen. Once again he based his argument on the view that a person had no innate rights and powers, but that God decides on governments and that all persons should subject themselves to that authority.

Pretorius proceeded to present a lengthy argument on education that actually boiled down to each population group having control over its own education. Although I had understanding for this aspiration, I pointed out that as long as standards and facilities differed, no black man could be expected to accept such a system.

After this Van Zijl attempted to justify separate residential areas for white and black people by pointing out that in London special residential areas had been set aside for Bengalese people and that this was not regarded as discriminatory. He pointed out that he was not insulting anyone when he expressed his desire to spend evenings and weekends in his own house with his family. He maintained that he had no objection to sharing amenities at his workplace, in the street and in the post office, but when it came to residential areas, he regarded it as his fundamental right to say: "I want to live among my own people." What he neglected to say was that there were thousands of black people who were part of daily households living in servants' rooms in urban areas, probably also in his own yard.

It was clear to me that the time for beating around the bush was over and that realistic thought needed to prevail. By then I knew from experience that by far the majority of whites at that stage preferred residential areas that were exclusively white. On the strength of the National Party's propaganda, many whites accepted that there would be a white area where the whites would rule. I also realised that if a white election were to take place later that year, the policy of the Republican Party on residential areas and other discriminatory rules would cost it votes. More was at stake for us than merely winning a white election; it focused on the future of our country. As much as I wanted to prove that whites supported the Republican Party, I decided it would not prevent me from putting our viewpoint across in no uncertain terms.

I indicated that I would like to address a few matters that were close to my heart, and particularly discriminatory practices. I referred to a case where a respected black man was asked to go drink his cool drink outside on the veranda because blacks were not allowed in the café. In my opinion an appeal would have to be made to all hotels, restaurants and cafés to make their facilities available to all races. If they were to refuse, we would have to force them to comply. I pointed out that we would in all probability have a black government in future, or at least black ministers. Would a black minister then be refused entry to a hotel for whites? How long were we still going to cling to selfish privileges and endanger our future?

I maintained that the fact that independence had been postponed frequently should not create false expectations, warning that we have to make our public amenities available to all and not wait until we have a knife at our throats. I repeated that it had nothing to do with a threat to anyone's language and cultural heritage; that we were totally inconsistent when wanting exclusive facilities for whites, while all the other groups were classified as "non-whites" and had to share facilities.

If language and cultural differences between groups justified social separation, the 11 black and coloured groups with their different languages and cultures could not be forced to share public amenities. It was, after all, not fair that a residential area or beach and other facilities had to be shared by ten ethnic groups, while the eleventh one, the whites, remains exclusive; the division would then be based on race and not on ethnicity. The National Party's policy and Koos Pretorius's Christian principles, according to which there would be a white area where the black majority would be subjected to the laws of a white minority, bordered on the absurd.

Ever since the Constitution drafted by the Turnhalle Conference was approved there were different interpretations of the clause pertaining to the areas of jurisdiction and functions of the different representative authorities. The communal areas previously set aside for groups such as Kavango, Ovambo, Damaraland etc. were clearly demarcated in terms of the Odendaal Plan, but in the case of the white and coloured groups there were no geographical areas which could be considered as their areas of jurisdiction, and the land belonging to and occupied by them were privately owned. Based on this the National Party claimed that the entire area outside the "homelands" be proclaimed as their area of jurisdiction and that all members of other groups residing in this area will be subjected to the laws of the white representative authority. Moreover, the white inhabitants of this "white area" were by far in the minority and it was unrealistic to accept that the white minority, solely because they owned the agricultural land, could regard this as their area of authority. It was indefensible to expect any black owner of land not to have the right to vote in the area where he was born. It would completely negate the fact that no policy or no dispensation could succeed in South West Africa unless it was acceptable to the majority of the population.

Not even the moderate representatives in the Constituent Assembly accepted the Turnhalle Constitution as the final one for an interim government. For the National Party it remained a holy cow to which they would cling until it was buried in the political cemetery together with the Party. The NP was primarily concerned with group interests and group rights. When the Republican Party and I over the years appealed for the recognition of the human dignity of our fellow men or women, we were accused, especially by Koos Pretorius, as humanists. My contention throughout was that the individual was the smallest conceivable minority that needed protection and that groups were a voluntary association of individuals that could jointly be resolute about the protection of their fundamental rights.

The Constituent Assembly has to take a stand

On 1 March 1979, during the recess, the members of the Constituent Assembly were summoned by the Administrator General in order to give the Prime Minister the opportunity to discuss the Secretary General's most recent and dissenting views with us. The four representatives, who had withdrawn from the sessions earlier, showed up at the Assembly after they had again been nominated by AKTUR to fill the vacancies caused by their absence. The Speaker read the Administrator General's letter in which the purpose of the meeting was explained. The Assembly decided to comply with the Prime Minister's request that the session be held in camera.

It was apparent from the discussions that the relationship between South Africa and the Security Council had become strained and it seemed that an agreement, in the light of the dissenting proposals by the Secretary General had become highly unlikely. P.W. Botha requested the Assembly to take a stand on the dissenting proposals. He recommended that the Western countries be requested to inform the Constituent Assembly of their viewpoint.

The countries denied the request because they did not recognise the Assembly. However, an understanding was reached that the parties – should they so decide – have separate discussions with the Western countries. AKTUR refused the opportunity to have discussions with the Western representatives. As it turned out, the DTA's interview with the Western countries did not have a positive outcome either.

In response to the Prime Minister's request, the Constituent Assembly decided to clearly state their views on the matter: That since we were not aware of SWAPO ever having had bases in the Territory, the new proposal that SWAPO be allowed to establish bases within the Territory after the ceasefire was unacceptable. The new provision that SWAPO bases in neighbouring states would not be monitored by UNTAG was equally unacceptable and we expressed our shock about the inability of the Western countries to defend and honour the understandings they themselves had reached with the parties concerned. We requested the South African Government not to allow any further concessions in respect of paragraphs 11 and 12. Moreover, we insisted in the motion that the envisaged election takes place no later than 30 September 1979 and that, should the settlement plan not be put into operation on 15 March 1979, the Assembly be convened on 2 April to consider taking alternative measures to lead South West Africa to independence.

The DTA's cooperation in reaching an internationally acceptable settlement for the South West Africa issue was well known. At that time we had accepted the Western proposals as is, and we subsequently also decided to cooperate on the basis of Resolution 435, albeit with certain reservations. We made it clear that the withdrawal of South African troops until such time as total peace and an end to hostilities had been attained, was unacceptable. Accordingly, we insisted on a definite date for the election, and were resolute that the finishing line should not be moved repeatedly. The date 30 September 1979 was set by both the

Secretary General and his Special Representative as a target date and was accepted by the South African Government.

Our request that we abide by the set date and that the implementation of the settlement plan be adapted accordingly, was therefore not unreasonable. However, after the Special Representative met with the frontline states and SWAPO leaders, they moved away from the original proposals, and requested that certain stipulations be reconsidered, which inevitably affected the target date once again. According to Waldheim, his Special Representative also had a discussion with the five Western countries. You would expect that these drafters of the original proposals would adhere to these dates, but they did not.

We lost faith in the Western countries, since they were unable to provide answers to simple questions. One of the questions we put to them was: Supposing hundreds of armed SWAPO soldiers were to cross the border shortly before the election and after the ceasefire, would it be accepted that SWAPO had a military base in the Territory? This was a claim that we, as well as the SADF, denied categorically. It would be regarded as a tactical move to give SWAPO a psychological advantage. Their reply was: "You can counter any moves at that time." Our reservations were confirmed on 1 April 1989.

During the debate, Van Zijl proposed an amendment on behalf of AKTUR, which was completely contrary to views they had held in the past. While he condemned the departure from the original proposals, he was "… still keen to find an internationally acceptable solution to the South West Africa issue that would result in international recognition". He "… requested the South African Government to bring about a speedy implementation of Resolution 435 by means of further negotiations with the parties concerned …" He had reservations about the DTA expressing its shock in respect of the position of the Western states and asked if it was tactically correct to do so at that stage.

Although he agreed that the deviations in the amended proposals held serious threats for the internal parties, he was of the opinion that the Western countries would again have to take the initiative and show leadership to salvage the plan. Van Zijl came to the conclusion that my motion would amount to contact with the Western countries being ended abruptly, which was not at all what I had proposed. He then warned against the possibility of oil boycotts and sanctions being imposed on us and expressed the hope that the Western countries would come to our aid in such an eventuality. He proposed that a panel of jurists be appointed to decide who was right and who was wrong.

This was not coming from the Eben van Zijl I knew. He appeared uncomfortable and I wondered about the reason behind AKTUR's sudden change of attitude. They had never been committed to the Western settlement plan and Resolution 435. Why now suddenly be concerned about a possible stalemate merely because we had set a deadline for the implementation of the settlement plan? AKTUR's fear was clearly (as subsequently became evident) that the Constituent Assembly would consider alternative solutions in its session on 2 April should the Security Council not adhere to the deadline.

As his speech progressed, it became clear why Van Zijl did not want a stalemate with the Security Council. He believed that the DTA was aiming for an election of a National Assembly on 2 April and that the Assembly would be elected on the basis of proportional representation rather than the constituency system. (Apparently someone had suggested this possibility to him, although he did not reveal the identity of this person.) He made a skilful attempt to gain the support of the other ethnic leaders, including DTA members, by pointing out that according to the system proposed in the Turnhalle Constitution, ethnic groups would no longer have the right to appoint their own representatives in Central Government. Once again I found the argument confusing. In the first part of his speech he pleaded that nothing be done to jeopardise the implementation of Resolution 435, which provided for a one-person-one-vote election; then, in the second part of his speech, he made a case for setting up a government with representatives appointed by ethnic groups. After this confusing argument, Van Zijl came to his actual problem. He said, according to his information, the thought was being entertained that parties currently represented in the Assembly would be involved in an interim government. He warned that if parties which were yet to prove their support through democratic means were to be involved, it could cause much dissatisfaction and would amount to a coup d'état. Van Zijl concluded his speech by appealing to us not to do anything in terms of the settlement plan for which we and South Africa would be blamed later and that we should put the blame on the shoulders of the people where it actually belonged. It became apparent that AKTUR feared a government in which the DTA had the majority and in which I might play an important role. Jan de Wet devoted a large part of his speech to SWAPO's hesitation to take part in a democratic process, continuing their acts of terror and murdering other political leaders. He argued that we had to accept that South Africa would conduct the negotiations on our behalf, since the Constituent Assembly was not recognised by the international community. He appealed for greater unanimity among internal political parties, forgetting that the National Party's refusal to make any concessions in respect of the Turnhalle Constitution had caused the party to split mainly as a result of the inflexibility of the National Party and its leader.

Hans Diergaardt, leader of the Federal Convention of Namibia (FCN), who had often agreed with AKTUR in the past, disagreed with them. He suggested that we go ahead with a second election with or without SWAPO. DTA leaders such as Julius, Tibinyane, Christy, Haraseb, Tjingaete and Africa supported my motion and made valuable contributions. In my reply I referred to the fact that AKTUR in the past had accused the DTA of selling out South West Africa to the UN and of putting too much value on international recognition, after which their members said: "This is enough"; and "Don't push us too far." It seemed there had been a change in their attitude; something which the people of South West Africa must no doubt have noticed. The DTA had done everything in its power in the past to gain international recognition, and accepted the criticism. Now suddenly, at this late stage, AKTUR was trying to be more liberal than we were. AKTUR, refusing to talk to the Western countries the previous weekend, suddenly wanted South Africa to continue its negotiations with them.

During the Turnhalle Conference I had realised that my playing a prominent role as a white man holding a prominent position in a primarily black organisation could easily be exploited by malicious people. However, during my long association with the Alliance, I was at no stage the leader of the DTA; as Chairman I was only third in the ranks. Yet I was the leader of the Republican Party, a member party of the Alliance. Since the Turnhalle Conference, set up on my initiative and of which I was Chairperson, I succeeded in gaining the trust of the black and coloured delegates. The fact that I was white never played a role with my black colleagues. They accepted my greater political experience and leadership as Chairman.

At DTA meetings, local leaders regularly insisted that I take the stage as one of the speakers, preferably the main speaker. I realised that this was a unique situation, which political opponents could exploit by suggesting to the primarily black DTA members that they were being led by the nose by a white man. I would expect such an eventuality to come from the black ranks. However, it never happened. The first attempt to exploit the situation came from Van Zijl when he insinuated in his reaction to my speech that Billy Marais, Chief Secretary of the Constituent Assembly, and I – both white – was prescribing to the DTA members of the Assembly as far as policy and planning were concerned. While Eben van Zijl did not succeed, I realised that colour prejudice could be a powerful weapon.

At a crossroad once again

The Constituent Assembly accepted my motion in which the amended proposals of the Security Council were rejected, and it was communicated to the South African Government as such on 5 March 1979. Thereby, we once again found ourselves at a political crossroad.

Prime Minister P.W. Botha in a speech in Parliament on 6 March reminded the Secretary General that he and his Minister of Foreign Affairs had flown to Windhoek on 21 December 1978 to convince the newly elected leaders of Namibia to cooperate towards the speedy implementation of the Security Council's Resolution 435: "[It] was no easy assignment. On the contrary, it was awkward, especially when viewed against the background of SWAPO's public statements to the effect that the terrorist organisation would continue with its campaign of violence and terror against the people of South West Africa. Furthermore, it was embarrassing because the members of the Constituent Assembly had just been elected in an election in which 80,3% of the registered voters supported them." The remainder of his speech described the process of negotiations up until that point, on which I have already elaborated extensively. He proceeded to refer to various acts of terrorism that had been committed in the previous months and to the violation of agreements by Western countries and the Security Council. He continued:

> Where do we go from here? Our position remains unchanged. We stand by our expressed undertakings. We stand by the settlement proposal we accepted on 25 April 1978. We stand by our undertakings to the people of South West Africa that we will not allow a political solution to be forced on them from outside. We stand by the provisions of the settlement proposals, which clear-

ly stipulate that SWAPO personnel be restricted to their existing bases and that SWAPO's restriction to those bases be monitored. We stand by the settlement proposal which contains no stipulation, directly or indirectly, expressly or implied, that SWAPO personnel who may, either fortuitously or for a short duration, be in the Territory for the purpose of sabotage are suddenly entitled to come forward on the date of the cease-fire with a claim to be assigned to camps which do not exist and in so doing achieve the establishment of bases in South West Africa they could not succeed in establishing through force of arms.

It begs the question here on whether the SWAPO bases were so important that failure to reach consensus could derail the settlement plan and put an end to further negotiations with the Security Council. It was probably not as important to South Africa as it was to the internal political parties – including SWAPO. For SWAPO it was important throughout to create the impression that it had won the war and conquered South West Africa militarily. Politically speaking, it would have been an embarrassment to them to admit that after years of warfare they had still not succeeded in establishing a single base in the Territory. If the amended proposal were to be accepted, SWAPO would have to move armed personnel to designated locations as far south as Mariental. The psychological effect of something that had been referred to in the original agreement as a "tactical move" would have been extremely detrimental to the internal parties.

Probably only a few people in South Africa realised that the playing field in the election we had accepted in the interests of peace in South West Africa was not level. SWAPO had an armed wing, while we depended on the defence force of a colonial power for our security. Politically speaking, cooperation with the defence force of the country from which we wanted to be liberated counted against us. Discriminatory legislation was still applicable in our country. We were powerless to do anything about it, other than condemn it and make recommendations to the Administrator General – the first-tier one-man ruler. The white Constituent Assembly, in which the National Party had a majority – still applied the policy of apartheid, especially in terms of education. Public facilities, hotels, restaurants, the theatre and many other amenities were still not accessible to black and coloured people. The South African Government was still trying to accommodate the rightist elements in our country and frustrated all our attempts to change the situation. When the DTA accepted an election under UN supervision, we knew that it would cost large amounts of money and we had not the faintest idea where it would come from. We suspected that if SWAPO were to win the election with an overwhelming majority, there would be no true democracy and protection of fundamental rights to speak of. Despite all these handicaps, we accepted the original settlement plan. To expect us to accept unilateral amendments to the plan was really asking too much. We therefore had great appreciation for the strong viewpoints taken by the Prime Minister in his speech.

On other deviations from the original plan he had the following to say:

> There was the undertaking that was given on the question of Walvis Bay. During our negotiations with the Five they undertook to keep the question of Walvis Bay out of the Security Council and declared that if the question should arise, they would take the view that it was a matter which could be settled between the new government of South West Africa and the South African Government at a later stage. The Five openly breached this undertaking when they sponsored and voted for a Security Council Resolution which declared that Walvis Bay must be reintegrated into South West Africa. The resolution further supported the initiation of steps necessary to ensure early achievement of the decision.

Another example of the breach of the undertaking that P.W. Botha had mentioned was the Secretary General's unilateral increase of the number of troops of the UN Task Force to 7500. It was unacceptable to the internal parties as well. The mere fact that UN troops were to be deployed in the country was detrimental to the parties because the inhabitants of the country regarded the UN as allies of SWAPO – especially when taken into consideration that South Africa had already undertaken to decrease the number of South African troops which had to remain in the country until independence was achieved. There were also other cases in point where agreements and understandings were negated. The Prime Minister concluded his speech with the following warning: "Even now South Africa stands by its undertaking. We insist on the implementation of the settlement proposal as presented to us and accepted by us. If there are others who deviate from it, they must bear the consequences."

It was clear to me that South Africa would not concede easily and Dr Waldheim's evasive response to P.W. Botha's speech left me with no doubt that we had reached the end of the negotiation process for the time being. In an attempt to salvage their settlement plan, Cyrus Vance, the Minister of Foreign Affairs in the USA, arranged a meeting in New York on 19 to 20 March, to which South Africa and the internal parties (the DTA, NNF, AKTUR, SWAPO-D, NPLF, LF and the HNP) were invited. Besides these, the frontline states (Angola, Botswana, Mozambique, Tanzania and Zambia), as well as the UN's Secretary General, Nigeria and SWAPO were also invited. The meeting would take the form of proximity talks.

The South African Government reacted positively to the invitation, with the understanding that the objective of the meeting would be deliberations on the implementation of Resolution 435 and not to re-negotiate the issue. The attempt was doomed when a session of the Security Council was convened at practically the same time as the proximity talks. In a letter to the President of the Security Council Pik Botha reacted sharply to this, since the expectation was that the session had been convened especially to condemn South Africa. He informed him of SWAPO's sustained acts of terrorism and confirmed that the security forces were exercising utmost restraint. He then accused the Security Council of failing to do anything to put an end to this and suggested the following: that during the scheduled session, the Council take a decision in which SWAPO was condemned for its acts of violence, and that it appeal to SWAPO to cooperate towards the immediate implementation of Resolution 435.

The planned session of the Security Council took place on 28 March 1979. Despite pleas by the South African Government, a far-reaching resolution (Resolution 447) was accepted. It started with the already well-known declarations about the acts of violence by the SADF, the violation of the sovereignty of Angola, the continued illegal occupa-tion of South West Africa by South Africa, etc. The neighbouring states were thanked for their continued assistance to and support of SWAPO, and all member countries of the UN were requested to support Angola and the other frontline states in their struggle to protect their sover-eignty. As it subsequently transpired, this inopportune decision by the UN delayed independence for South West Africa by ten years.

A short political interlude

I have already mentioned that the South African Government as well as the DTA warned that should the differences in opinion with the Security Council not be resolved, alternative plans to lead South West Africa to independence would be considered. Although I was not always informed of what was going on in the minds of the South African leaders, I can attest that the possibility of a unilateral declaration of independence as in the case of the former Rhodesia was never mentioned. I would never have supported such a notion. I will not deny that some of my colleagues in the DTA would have found such a possibility acceptable. Nevertheless, decisions had to be made about the future of the Constituent Assembly, which had been elected at great expense and much hard work. I was strongly in favour of the elected body being vested with powers that would enable the internal parties to bring about changes, which up until then had been blocked by the National Party. I could not accept that doing away with unfair and discriminating practices would have to wait until after independence.

Therefore, when the Constituent Assembly convened on 3 April 1979, we had to reflect on (as had been decided during the March session) the future status of the Assembly. The decision had to be conveyed to the South African Government as soon as possible. Immediately after the session began, I proposed on behalf of the DTA that the Assembly be adjourned for a week to give the different political parties, including those not represented in the Assembly, the opportunity to deliberate on the future status and composition of the Assembly. I pointed out that I could introduce a final proposal immediately and have it carried through with the majority vote of the DTA, but that the DTA wanted to involve the other parties in order to reach the highest possible degree of consensus.

The Assembly took off on a false note once again. Du Plessis of AKTUR contended that I had not acted in accordance with the standing orders, because I had not given prior notice of my proposal to adjourn the House. I failed to understand what his problem was. It emerged later that AKTUR had prepared a motion to introduce immediately, which in this case would have to wait until the Assembly convened again after the adjournment. He called it a "distasteful incident", saying that he had considered leaving the Assembly, but then reconsidered and decided to abstain from voting. He indicated further that I motivated my adjournment proposal for "the drama effect". When the Speaker subsequently cited the relevant stipulation in the standing orders, it appeared that when a motion for the adjournment of the Assembly is proposed, it is not required to give prior notice. When the session was resumed on 17 April, I introduced a long motion in which I quote only the pertinent clauses:

1. That the Waldheim proposal as contained in Security Council Document S/13120 be rejected;
2. That the doors for further contact with the international community remain open, but that this may not happen at the expense of internal constitutional development;
3. That an interim authority with legislative and executive powers be established as soon as possible, with 15 May as the target date;
4. That a committee consisting of members of this Assembly be appointed to make recommendations to this Assembly on 30 April 1979 in respect of the form, compilation and functions of such an interim power and that the committee would also have the right to deliberate with political parties outside the Legislative Assembly in an attempt to gain their cooperation;
5. That the status of the Legislative Assembly remain unchanged until the Assembly itself decided otherwise;
6. That South Africa be requested to do everything in its power to ensure the safety of the inhabitants of South West Africa.

In my motivation of the motion the following day, I pointed out that discussions with the Five had already been ongoing for more than two years without finality being reached, and that uncertainty and frustration had a negative impact. I furthermore expressed my doubts as to whether cooperation with the Western countries and the international community was really in the best interests of South West Africa/Namibia, contending that the Western countries would continue to serve their own interests. It was no secret that the Western countries were concerned about the presence of communist forces in Africa. They were, however, naïve to believe that these foreign forces would withdraw if the struggle for freedom in Africa could be brought to an end, even if a SWAPO government in South West Africa, a Frelimo government in Mozambique and an MPLA government in Angola were in power.

The inhabitants of South West Africa, who had been looking forward to having a share in the Government towards creating a new and fair dispensation in their country for a very long time, were in the meantime being disappointed again. The deviation from the original proposals, which was indisputably meant to give SWAPO a psychological advantage in an election, was unacceptable to the internal political parties. Even parties outside the Constituent Assembly, among others the NNF, rejected it as unacceptable. I spelt out very clearly in my speech that the DTA was not in favour of a unilateral declaration of independence and that we wanted to keep the doors open for further negotiation.

I tried once again to bring about some understanding of the black and coloured inhabitants of the country by asking the whites to put themselves in the position of the black inhabitants in order to understand their aspirations. The black and coloured people yearned for self-determination and independence, for which many people in Africa were prepared to not only sacrifice their lives, but also ravage their countries. The decision of whether it would be a peaceful or violent process in our country was ours. An interim government could only be a temporary solution, but for the first time the black and coloured inhabitants of our country would have the opportunity to free themselves, with us, from oppressive and discriminatory practices and to reflect with us on the future of our common fatherland. The greatest obstacle we had to overcome was to set up a representative legislative body, in consultation with other political parties.

We were once again surprised by Du Plessis's reaction to my motion. He insisted that doors be kept open for further negotiations and maintained that the ball was now in the court of the Western countries and that South Africa had to continue negotiating a solution. This came despite the National Party never being enthusiastic about the Western settlement plan at any stage. We nevertheless agreed that doors should remain open for further negotiations. However, it became increasingly clear that AKTUR, although it had agreed in principle with the establishment of an interim government, had serious concerns about the powers and composition of the intended body. This was understandable, since the National Party of South West Africa now suddenly found itself in a minority position after it had dominated the political scene for 27 years. Whenever reference was made to the 1978 election and the DTA's 80% support, members of the National Party were notably embarrassed.

While listening to speeches from both sides of the house, it became evident that the representatives of AKTUR seriously believed that the Turnhalle Constitution, which provided for a government based purely on ethnicity, would be acceptable to the majority of the population. Were they really convinced that a constitution providing for a white territory in which non-white persons would be subjected to the laws of a white representative authority could be justified on any grounds? What about the coloureds? Where would their area of jurisdiction be? AKTUR members were concerned about us antagonising the international community by establishing an interim government. But what was the struggle really about? It was about discrimination based on race and colour; it was about apartheid. AKTUR (in essence the National Party) had nothing to say about this. An interim government would at least be able to do something about this fundamental problem, but according to Du Plessis they didn't want any of the holy cows to be slaughtered, since great unrest and frustration prevailed among the whites. He even insinuated that anything and everything could happen if the whites were pushed too far. He remained silent about the other population groups; about their frustration about laws in the making in which they had played no role. They had the opportunity for the first time in history, but were prevented from doing so. Cooperation with the Western countries was suddenly more important, and I was cautioned not to set target dates unnecessarily.

Jan de Wet spoke about a total strategy to achieve international as well as local acceptance, and asked that we combine forces against a common enemy. My question to him was: How will you unite people in a fight against terrorism and communism while, among other things, the rest camp at Swakopmund had not yet been made accessible to all races? I asked him by way of an interjection whether he intended making an announcement that the rest camp was going to be opened to all races. He expressed his surprise that I could refer to something like this while we were discussing a matter as momentous as international recognition. Advocate Niehaus sided unequivocally with Jan de Wet. I reminded Niehaus of something he had said many years ago when he was still leader of the United Party: "Either we share everything with the non-whites in all aspects of life, or we lose everything." I asked him whether he still stood by this. Neither he nor Jan de Wet reacted to my questions; they just paged through the notes in front of them.

I pertinently directed my next question to Jan de Wet: "Can we expect cooperation from the black people while they are being denied entry to tourist resorts because they are black? Do we say to the black man you are welcome to join the fight against terrorism, you are welcome to sacrifice your life for the country, but you are not welcome here, this is reserved for whites only?" Pointing to the two coloured members of the AKTUR delegation, I said they could not be bribed with a seat in Government or the Legislative Assembly to relinquish their right to having their human dignity acknowledged. I failed to understand how the right to visit a rest camp could be a threat to anyone's identity. While I was speaking I noticed that Andrew Kloppers and Piet Diergaardt sat staring in front of them in obvious embarrassment.

Listening to other speakers taking part in the debate, many questions entered my mind. Percy Niehaus being part of the AKTUR delegation was beyond my comprehension. While he was leader of the UNSWP, he was often the target of attacks by National Party leaders, especially Koos Pretorius, for his "humanistic" and "non-Christian" views. At the time I, as member of the National Party, often accused him and the UNSWP of being inconsistent, but I had to admit at a later stage that he was right in more than one respect. And now only a few years later he was a member of the National Party delegation.

During the 1978 election campaign Adv. Niehaus invited me to his house in Klein Windhoek for a cup of tea. Angel Engelbrecht commented afterwards that I had been privileged, because Percy didn't invite just anybody to his house. To my surprise he began the conversation by reprimanding me for going too far and making concessions for which the blacks were not ready yet. I could hardly believe my ears. I came to the conclusion that his views of the past were nothing more than party political opportunism; and that he and the UNSWP still stood for white supremacy. Needless to say, our conversation could not exactly be described as fruitful.

Hans Diergaardt, leader of the Liberation Front and captain of the Basters, was a personality of his own. I completely failed to understand "oompie Hans". He and his people had been victims of apartheid and racial discrimination over a very long period of time, but as a result of Hans's strong feelings about self-government for Rehoboth and absolute control over the land that belonged to the Basters, he often sided with AKTUR. The position of Pieter Diergaardt, also a Baster, and Andrew Kloppers, a Coloured, in the AKTUR delegation was equally difficult to comprehend. They had also been victims of racial discrimination in the past. How could they feel welcome in AKTUR while their white colleagues never even mentioned these discriminatory measures or the importance of the acknowledgement of human dignity in debates?

I remember with great appreciation the contributions made by the non-white representatives of the DTA, and the subdued and responsible way in which they expressed their views. The trust they had in me as a white man to play a leading role, touched me deeply. They rejected with contempt the insinuations by Eben van Zijl and Jan de Wet that they were being led by the nose by a white person and that their speeches were being written by whites. I could never understand the National Party's reprehensible attempts to exploit racial prejudice for political gain. It would have made sense to me if SWAPO did this, but coming from fellow whites it was beyond my comprehension.

When I now read the minutes of the Constituent Assembly, I can only have deep appreciation for what Ben Africa, pastor Cornelius Ndjoba, Daniel Luipert, Max Haraseb, Engelhardt Christy, Gregor Tibinyane, Jeremia Jagger, Willie Maasdorp, Kuaima Riruako, Elifas Tjingaete and Gabriel Siseho had said in that debate. They were prepared to give their full cooperation for a peaceful solution despite the discriminatory system to which they had been subjected.

After a long debate my motion, slightly amended, was accepted by majority vote. We tried to allay AKTUR's fears by giving the different political parties the opportunity to continue debating the functions and compilation of the envisaged National Assembly, with the understanding that it was done in a coordinated and orderly way. With this objective in mind, the Assembly was adjourned until 30 April 1979.

The interim government takes shape

Nothing came of these envisioned coordinated and orderly negotiations. AKTUR immediately started negotiating with parties inside and outside the Constituent Assembly, with exclusion of the DTA, which definitely had not been the intention. We expected them to cooperate with the DTA, instead of forming a pressure group, and confronting us with a plan already agreed upon. After several attempts to discuss the envisaged legislative body with them, their answer was that they were not ready to talk yet.

When the Constituent Assembly convened on 30 April, we were informed of a blueprint that had been drafted by them and which contained unacceptable and outrageous proposals. What it basically boiled down to was that the membership of the envisaged legislative body be increased to 60 and that the DTA sacrifice 20 of its 41 seats, meaning the DTA would retain a mere 21 seats out of the 60 seats. The remaining seats would then be allocated to the representative authorities and political parties inside and outside the existing Constituent Assembly. Since these proposals were never discussed with us, we were unable to determine with certainty what areas they actually covered. It was clear, however, that there had been an attempt to ignore the result of the 1978 election and to wangle an arbitrary division of seats that would place the DTA in a weak minority position.

The only two relevant parties outside the Assembly to which seats could possibly be allocated, namely the NNF and SWAPO-D, had indicated in the meanwhile that they were not interested. In a long press release issued on 2 April 1979, the NNF rejected the Secretary General's divergent report, in particular the proposals regarding the establishment of armed SWAPO personnel in bases within Namibia, and the proposal that SWAPO bases in neighbouring states would not be monitored by UNTAG. The NNF proposed further that a National Convention be convened, instead of the envisaged National Assembly, to deliberate on the subject of an "all-party responsible government". The NNF further stated clearly that it was not considering a unilateral declaration of independence. On 17 April 1979, SWAPO-D issued a press release in which its members, in spite of their reservations, accepted – in the interests of progress – the Secretary General's controversial report. SWAPO-D was also not interested in participation in an interim government.

When the Constituent Assembly met on 30 April 1979, I introduced the following motion on behalf of the DTA:

> The Assembly
> - draws attention to the inhabitants' wish for and unalienable right to self-determination and independence;
> - confirms the decision of the Assembly to cooperate towards the speedy execution of Security Council Resolution 435;
> - rejects the latest Waldheim proposals, which will affect the fairness of the election in terms of Resolution 435 gravely;
> - also rejects a unilateral declaration of independence for South West Africa;

- is of the opinion that the doors for further negotiation with the Security Council must be kept open;
- is convinced that the inhabitants of South West Africa must be awarded a greater share in the government of the country as soon as possible.

It is thus proposed
- that the name of the Legislative Assembly be changed to the National Assembly of South West Africa/Namibia;
- that provision be made to increase the membership of the Assembly to 65 by nominating members from the political parties that are not yet represented in the Assembly;
- that the Assembly be awarded the authority to make laws and to amend existing laws and ordinances; however, all legislation must be signed by the Administrator General, and the Assembly will not have the authority to make a law that would regulate the status, authority and compilation of the National Assembly;
- that provision be made for the appointment of members of the National Assembly to assist the Administrator General in the execution of his powers; and
- that provision be made for identification documents to be issued to all the inhabitants of South West Africa/Namibia.

It begs the question whether prior discussions were held with the South African Government with a view to avoiding conflicting opinions on the idea of an interim government. It must be borne in mind that there was regular communication with the Administrator General on a number of relevant matters.

Pastor Njoba seconded my motion and made wise remarks in his speech. He said that we had wanted to establish an interim government in 1977 but desisted for the sake of cooperation with the Western countries. In December 1978 we participated in a countrywide election for a Legislative Assembly. Once again the DTA majority was prepared to cooperate with the plan devised by the Western countries, and to relinquish its plans to draw up a constitution. But, said Pastor Ndjoba, still the UN and West did not cooperate. He said:

> The black man in Africa has lots of time. When your friend tells you he is going to visit you on Sunday, he might come on Monday or Tuesday, it doesn't matter, and then you may talk for the entire day, or for two or more. The white man always tries to rush the black man. The first word that the white farmer on the farm in my country learns is 'hendelela' or 'hakahana' in the

> Herero language, which means 'hurry up'. But our leaders must now take care. In other countries in Africa people's time and patience have run out and we must take care that our people's patience does not also run out.

After a few customary snide remarks in my direction, A.H. du Plessis accepted the establishment of an authority that "in one way or another" could speak on behalf of the people of South West Africa. He expressed the wish that the greatest possible degree of consensus be reached between the parties in the Assembly, but failed to mention the "blueprint" that was drawn up during the recess without consulting with the DTA and that was clearly meant to nullify the results of the countrywide election. I wondered afterwards whether he had even been informed about the blueprint, which was in all probability an Eben van Zijl product.

Another important amendment proposed by Du Plessis pertained to the laws that, in terms of my proposal, the National Assembly were not allowed to make, namely to change the status, powers and structure of the Assembly. He maintained that this stipulation should also apply to the other existing authorities, such as representative authorities. He further proposed that decisions by the National Assembly be taken by a three-quarter majority – something which was unheard of in any democratic system. He warned further that, should my motion be passed in its existing form, a shock wave that we could not afford would reverberate through the white community. Although he included other second-tier authorities in his argument, primarily to win their support, I knew it was all about the powers and competencies of the white Legislative Assembly that controlled white education (including the teacher's training college), residential areas, hotels and rest camps, hospitals, homes for the aged, the arts theatre, and tax on individuals.

Although these functions could not all be regarded as the most important functions in a normal state household, it was important to the National Party, because this was where discrimination between races – not ethnic groups – was applied in its crudest form. Although there could be no doubt that apartheid could not survive independence, the current privileged position had to be maintained for short-term political advantage.

The National Party's reluctance to abolish petty apartheid was sim-

likely to lose, but we all realised our chances of winning were extremely slim – more so because the white Legislative Assembly refused to share public facilities with people of colour. At this late stage Pretorius still refused to open the teachers training college to all races.

Despair overwhelmed me. If the whites of South West Africa could not, or would not understand and have sympathy for the hopes and aspirations of our black and coloured countrymen, they should at least be prepared to make concessions – in their own interests. I tried my best to bring this hard reality home. On 17 May 1979, the last day of the session, I warned that foreign powers were using, if not abusing, the aspirations of our countrymen to gain a foothold in our country and that only a fool would ignore the need for change to be affected here. Circumstances prevailed in our country that were unacceptable to the vast majority of the population. "Although there is a considerable degree of understanding for culturally bound education, it will never be accepted as long as there are differences in the standards and facilities," I cautioned. As regards the teachers training college, which at last opened its doors to all in January 1979, I rejected the argument that it was financed by the whites. I argued that South West Africa's money financed the facilities and could not be kept exclusive for whites. In conclusion, I again stated my view of residential areas and public conveniences. It cannot be left to the owners of public facilities such as rest camps, hotels and cafés to decide who they will allow entry to their facilities. For the umpteenth time I stated that our future could not be secured by laws, but by the extent to which we could succeed in living together in peace and mutual respect. People > laws

The leader of the National Party painted a rather negative picture of the economic situation in the country, confirming my suspicion that he didn't understand what it was all about. He said: "... It will be short-sighted to create a situation during this process by promoting goodwill and reconciliation only. The concessions we make will take us nowhere if those concessions are not acceptable to the white population group."

Du Plessis reaffirmed that the whites, as represented in the House, had never committed themselves to a one-person-one-vote election. He added that there were many influential people in the world who realised that a one-person-one-vote election in South West Africa would not work. He warned several times during his speech that a stage could be reached where the whites would say: "We are not prepared to run any more risks." He continued: "When that stage will be reached, I do not know. No one knows, but that will be the deadline the Honourable Member Mr Mudge spoke about. Not the line that my colleagues or I draw for them; that line will be where and how they draw it themselves. This is simply a matter of logic."

It was unclear to me what Du Plessis meant, but what it boiled down to was that the whites would put their foot down if they were pushed too far. I once again realised I was wasting my breath. It was obvious that for the National Party it was about apartheid, social segregation and maintaining and protecting a privileged position, not principles. And so another session of the Legislative Assembly came to an end.

One can accept that the National Party also tried to influence the South African Government in an attempt to gain support for their viewpoints. However, in all likelihood the liaison was not with the Government as such, but rather with individual ministers and members of Parliament.

The National Assembly gains official status

Proclamation AG 21, which was approved by the State President on 14 May 1979, made provision for the "… establishment of a Legislative Authority for South West Africa." In short this amounted to a National Assembly having the authority to administer the Territory and to make, amend and repeal laws. This power was comprehensive in so far as the National Assembly could also amend or repeal laws and rules of law of the Parliament of South Africa that had bearing on the Territory or its administration. There were certain limitations to the power of the National Assembly. The Assembly would not have the power to make a law that changed the international status of the Territory. This provision ruled out the possibility of a unilateral declaration of independence. The Assembly could also not amend Section 38 of the South West Africa Constitution Act (No. 39 of 1968) or affect the status and powers of the Administrator General or amend the law that had established the National Assembly.

An important power given to the Assembly was to submit requests, recommendations or proposals to the Administrator General regarding the code of conduct to be followed or the measures that needed to be taken in connection with any matter relating to the Territory. In addition, the Assembly could at its request or of its own accord advise the Administrator General or make recommendations to him in respect of any law as intended in the Proclamation. Included here were matters concerning the execution by the Administrator General of government activities pertaining to the Territory or inclusive of another authority. The Administrator General was not obliged to act on any requests, rec-ommendations, proposals or advice. The Proclamation also provided for a body consisting of members of the Assembly who could make proposals and recommendations to the Administrator General on be-half of the Assembly.

The National Assembly would consist of 65 members, comprising the 50 existing members of the Constituent Assembly and 15 seats that could be allocated to political parties by the Assembly.

Criticism from white ranks

Proclamation AG 21 undoubtedly gave far-reaching powers to the Na-tional Assembly and the objective was surely that the Assembly should put these powers to use. This is what the National Party was afraid of and wanted to prevent at all costs. Speeches by leaders of the Party, especially Messrs Du Plessis and Pretorius, again provoked white re-sistance. Now, for the first time, Afrikaans churches and ministers of religion became involved in politics. On the same day that Proclama-tion 21 was issued, an article appeared in *Die Hervormer*, published by the Reformed Church of South Africa. The author was Rev. J.A. Viljoen, a minister of the Reformed Congregation in Windhoek. The five-page article was placed in *Die Hervormer* with my face prominently on the cover. The editor of *Die Hervormer* wrote by way of introduction the following under the heading "Bitterness among the whites in South West":

> What's going on in South West? To what extent have the promis-es made over the years regarding the future of the Territory been kept? Rev. J.A. Viljoen, who has been a minister in Windhoek since 1951, knows this country and its people. In this article Rev. Viljoen puts forward a series of facts and questions that give rise to concern. The accusation could be made that an article with a strong political angle does not belong in a church bulletin. How-ever, when it affects the truth about the future of a country, its people and the churches in that country, no questions or facts may be concealed, least of all by the Church. If any matter put forward here is untrue, it should be indicated as such. The ten-

dencies that prevail in South West, also prevail in South Africa.
The Church has a right to be given clear, straight answers when
it comes to the credibility of actions taken by the authorities.

Rev. Viljoen began his article as follows: "In all the years I've been in
South West, I've never experienced so much confusion among the
church members, if not among a large section of the whites, as in the
last year or two. There is uncertainty, there is unrest, there is despair
and there is bitterness."

I can't recall that Rev. Viljoen ever spoke to me about politics. I
learnt at a later stage that he was married to a sister of Boet Botma,
who represented Walvis Bay in the South African Volksraad (House
of Assembly) and was definitely not one of my political supporters. I
initially thought that Rev. Viljoen gained most of his information from
Mr Botma, but once I had read the article carefully, I was convinced
that he had close contacts with the National Party and probably with
Koos Pretorius. If this was the case, it confirms the close relationship
that existed in those days between the National Party and the Afrikaans
churches. Without the editor of *Die Hervormer* necessarily realising it,
the newspaper was indeed carrying and distributing one of the National Party of South West Africa's longest and most comprehensive
political pamphlets in South Africa. The objective was undoubtedly to
promote a protest action in South Africa against the policy of the South
African Government regarding South West Africa.

What Rev. Viljoen as well as the National Party failed to understand
was that both the South African Government and the South African
people had misgivings about their involvement in the South West
Africa issue. At various meetings I had addressed by invitation in South
Africa, I was frequently questioned by parents – especially mothers – on
how long their sons would still have to fight on our border. I knew that
the price of the war in terms of money and human lives could become
too high for South Africa, and that we should make a contribution
towards finding a solution to the South West Africa problem and help
bring an end the war too. Fact is, we were all South African citizens
and could therefore rightfully look to South Africa for assistance and
protection. It would, however, have been unrealistic to expect South
Africa to compromise its own position by maintaining the status quo
in South West Africa.

The Dutch Reformed Church, of which I was a member, also took sides. I was being criticised and denounced by most ministers and church council members. I was appointed deacon in the church council in 1954, shortly after our arrival at Lazy Spade, and for the next 23 years, with short intervals, I served as church council member – initially in Outjo and subsequently in Windhoek. After leaving the National Party in 1977, I was regarded undesirable as a member of the church council for the next 12 years, not because of my involvement in politics – my former political colleagues were still serving on church councils – but because I was seen as a traitor of the whites. The minister of the Hochland congregation to which our family belonged accused me of conspiring with heathens.

I was also denounced by the leadership of the Dutch Reformed Church, as became apparent at meetings of the Broederbond and Rapportryers where many ministers of the Dutch Reformed Church were members. Attempts were made to have me banned from these organisations – mainly on the initiative of my previous white colleagues, Du Plessis and Van Zijl. But my RP colleagues, also members of these organisations at the time, and I decided to stay on as long as possible to prevent the Afrikaner Broederbond from actively and formally supporting the National Party. For all practical purposes this made the Afrikaner Broederbond irrelevant in South West Africa. I was ultimately banned from the Rapportryers movement, and in 1983 I resigned as a member of the Broederbond on own accord. I will elaborate in due course.

It was not only in closed meetings and private conversations that I experienced opposition from ministers of the church. At the official opening of the white teachers training college in 1979, the moderator of the Dutch Reformed Church, Rev. Paul du Toit, also packed his punch. He was Chairman of the Board of the new college. After he had welcomed all the dignitaries, he pointed out that "dissidents" were also present, referring to me and a few of my RP colleagues. Dr Daan Gresse, Rector of the college, who subsequently became one of my loyal supporters, could also not resist the temptation to refer to the "dissidents" in his speech. He thanked us for our presence and added that the fact that someone thinks differently is at least an indication that he thinks. Daan Gresse was subsequently never very popular with the Executive Committee and education authorities. My involvement, as a former member of the Executive Committee responsible for public works in the planning and building of the college, was not mentioned by Rev. Du Toit. I had worked closely with the architects, Taljaart and Carter, during construction of the impressive complex. Two other members of the College Board, E.T. Meyer and Danie Opperman, prominent figures in education, subsequently became involved in politics and supported the National Party and its policy to the end. They, however, never sunk to the banal level of some of the other politicians. Dr Thys Nieuwoudt – of the Dutch Reformed Church – also openly opposed me, but at a personal level we were friends for many years.

I won't elaborate on the policy and actions of the different churches. As far as the Reformed Church (another Afrikaans church) is concerned, my contact was limited to prominent members. I also had the privilege of becoming acquainted with two prominent leaders of this church in South Africa, namely Drs Wimpie de Klerk and Tjaart van der Walt, who both showed great understanding for what we were trying to achieve in South West Africa. I was aware of the fact that black churches sided mainly with SWAPO, but did not really experience any antagonism. The goodwill I received from the Spade Reën organisation was incredible.

There was occasional tension in the German church circles as well. This mostly concerned the presence and influence of ministers of the German Evangelical Lutheran Church (GELC), an organisation that was not always accepted locally. Paolo Doll of Outjo informed me of his intention to establish an organisation called SOS Notgemeinschaft with, among others, Thea Hälbich of Karibib. He objected vehemently to the conduct of some of the German ministers and threatened to support a split in the church. My advice to him was to rather try and resolve their differences within the church and that a split should be the last option. Paolo was a former friend who didn't follow me when the National Party split. Afterwards he denounced me in a strongly worded letter. His sons, on the other hand, subsequently became my most loyal supporters and co-workers.

Before and after the split in the National Party it became evident that the majority of the German- and English-speaking voters supported me, which was definitely not the case with the majority of the Afrikaans-speaking electorate. It was difficult for me to accept this, and it caused me considerable sorrow. These were my people with whom I had come a long way, and for whom I had such high ideals. It always upsets me when members of other groups belittle the Afrikaners, sometimes even accuse them of being backwards. It hurt me when the Afrikaners, the Boers, were held responsible for everything that was wrong in the country. I wanted to prove them wrong and show that there was a time when the Afrikaners had also been the victims of discrimination. I wanted to prove that we were willing to rectify our mistakes of the past; that we were prepared to take the lead in this process. To that end I had tried so hard in the decade before the split to bring about a change in attitude within the National Party.

The National Assembly takes off

The process of converting the Constituent Assembly into the National Assembly was inevitably more or less a repetition of the one a year ago. When the National Assembly convened for the first time on 21 May, in accordance with Administrator General M.T. Steyn's Proclamation (AG 24 of 1979), my DTA colleagues and I found ourselves fighting on two fronts: on the one side the National Party with its policy of racial discrimination, and on the other SWAPO, which had never been a forbidden organisation and had the same rights and privileges as the other local parties. While SWAPO infiltrators were murdering and kidnapping innocent people, local SWAPO leaders could participate in politics freely. SWAPO leaders refused to speak to the DTA and merely paid lip service to the idea of a democratic election. On the other hand, the DTA had to fight the National Party, which was striving towards the continuation of the practice of racial discrimination at all costs.

I realised that the National Assembly had to use its newly acquired powers to address these two problems as soon as possible, but the proceedings of the Assembly had to be organised appropriately. The Administrator General, as representative of the South African Government, stated this clearly at the opening of the first session:

> With the formation of this National Assembly the community of nations of South West Africa enters the promised land with a bona fide right to be heard on its own affairs. The legislative powers vested in this Assembly include the cardinal authority to determine domestic policy. The administration of domestic affairs by means of social and fiscal policy therefore falls within the framework of the jurisdiction of this large body, enabling it to give practical execution to the wishes of the inhabitants.

Johannes Skrywer was then elected the first President of the National Assembly. As proposed by Appie Louw, a Representative Committee was appointed to draw up the rules of procedure and regulations of the House, following which the Assembly adjourned until 5 June to give the Committee sufficient time to carry out its mandate. When Appie Louw submitted the report by the Committee on 6 June 1979, AKTUR objected vehemently to the provision in the Proclamation that decisions by the Assembly be approved by majority vote, and proposed a three-quarter majority vote for all decisions. Eben van Zijl, Jan de Wet and Percy Niehaus referred back to decisions made by the Turnhalle Conference under completely different circumstances. However, level-headed and logical, Gregor Tibinyane and Willie Maasdorp of the DTA pointed out the unacceptability and unenforceability of their proposal. Obviously AKTUR would never manage to have any proposal accepted by the Assembly. Their only objective was to block decisions with the possible support of the additional 15 members. This would amount to the wishes and aspirations of the population being ignored.

The rules of procedure were accepted with a majority of votes, while Jan de Wet on behalf of AKTUR and Sarel Becker on behalf of the HNP demanded that the counter-votes of their parties be minuted. How they managed to gain the support of Andrew Kloppers and Joey Junius, both victims of racial discrimination in the past, was beyond my comprehension. I suspect they had never been consulted.

On 7 June 1979, I proposed in the National Assembly that effective steps be taken to put an end to SWAPO's privileged position as political and terrorist organisation. I pointed out that there was no longer a need for any party to fight for independence – especially not with arms – since independence and self-determination had already been accepted in principle, the implementation of which were delayed only by SWAPO and the Security Council.

The question arose: Could SWAPO be allowed to continue its political activities unimpeded while fighting, murdering and kidnapping people and causing damage? I referred to recent incidents, among others things the umpteenth attack on the Ruacana Project in which an employee lost his life; the kidnapping of Headman Silas; the kidnapping and murder of Hisleiti; as well as many other civilians. The murder of our two DTA colleagues, Clemens Kapuuo and Toivo Shiyagaya, was still fresh in our memories. This inequitable situation could not be allowed to continue. The Assembly accepted the proposal unanimously.

It was necessary for steps to be taken to gain the support of the majority of the population to be able to fight SWAPO effectively. It was often propagated by, among others, the Defence Force that the hearts and minds of the population needed to be conquered. I have said repeatedly this was not feasible as long as the black population was expected to participate in an armed struggle together with the whites against SWAPO, while they were subjected to humiliating rules and regulations at the same time. Various politicians and traditional leaders had already lost their lives because they sided with the whites against SWAPO. The hour of truth had arrived for the whites – as well as for me personally, and for my colleagues in the DTA.

The whites protest

When I proposed the first reading of the Bill on the Abolition of Racial Discrimination (Urban Residential Areas and Public Amenities), I knew that there would be a negative reaction. For my black colleagues and their supporters the enforcement of this legislation would be a joyous occasion, but for the few whites in the DTA and for our families and supporters hatred and condemnation lay ahead.

Sarel Becker of the HNP was the first to react, calling the envisaged Act a dagger in the heart of the social, economic and political life of the country. He said he wanted nothing to do with "this act of treason". A.H. du Plessis said AKTUR was going to oppose every stage and every facet of this bill with every legitimate means at its disposal, since it was aimed at attacking white identity. He warned that if the Administrator General were to approve this draft and it became law, it would not be the end of the story; there would be a gradual build-up of repercussions. The legislation would create tension; not remove it. He referred repeatedly to the "good relations" that had now been disturbed.

I listened in speechless amazement to Du Plessis's reference to good relations. What was he talking about? During the Turnhalle Conference where black and coloured delegates accepted certain interim arrangements under duress, there had already been tension between him and other delegates. Generally, calm prevailed among the whites because they believed the National Party was engaged in negotiations that would favour them. Nothing was said about the thousands of black inhabitants who had left the country in large numbers and the even larger numbers who supported SWAPO in its struggle against an unjust system.

The fact that black and coloured people were still prepared to fight against SWAPO under these circumstances came as a surprise. We were often accused of overstating the SWAPO threat. Reference was regularly made to a "total onslaught" and a "total strategy". Much was made of the possible results should the draft bill be accepted, but about what would happen if it were not accepted, nothing was said. Although all rational people must have realised that separate residential areas and public amenities could only be temporary, they nevertheless clung to these practices. If AKTUR, as already mentioned, in essence the National Party, could not support the legislation on the basis of moral and humanitarian considerations, one would at least expect that they would do so on practical and political grounds. Once again this was too much to expect.

Van Zijl began his speech as follows: "When it suits the circumstances the SWAPO ghost is taken off the shelf without fail, dusted and polished, and used to strike fear in us." He said that the blacks could also not win the struggle against SWAPO without the whites, and that with the legislation currently being considered, the indispensable co-operation of the whites would be forfeited.

The first reading of the draft bill was approved with 37 votes to seven, after which AKTUR and the HNP requested that their counter-votes be minuted. Whether the two coloured members of AKTUR, Kloppers and Diergaardt, supported AKTUR's stance, was not known.

At this stage the debate on the draft bill on racial discrimination was interrupted by Fanuel Tjingaete of the DTA with a motion requesting the establishment of an independent land and agriculture bank for South West Africa, since the existing Land Bank made loans available only to white farmers. But Jan de Wet had bad news for Tjingaete. He said the Land and Agricultural Bank was a financial institution that loaned money only when it was backed by security; in other words, only to owners of farms. Under the existing legislation the farmers Tjingaete was concerned about would therefore not qualify. Tjingaete said that he could not see this legislation changing. Under these circumstances loans to settlers or farmers who rented land, or to farmers on communal land, could not be granted. He recommended that black farmers in communal areas be supported through the establishment of a Department of Agricultural Development and Settlement. By implication he excluded the possibility of black farmers buying white-owned farms through the Land and Agricultural Bank. He was vigorously supported by Sarel Becker. According to Ernst Kuhlmann of the DTA, not all black farmers would qualify for Land Bank loans, just as all white farmers would not qualify for them. He accepted that loans would be granted only on merit; race and colour should therefore not play a role when it came to granting loans.

When I parked my vehicle behind the conference hall at 14:15 on Monday 11 June, I knew that my colleagues and I were in for a hard day. What I didn't know or expect was the large group of whites protesting in the street in front of the building. Some of my colleagues informed me about this in the conference hall, saying that Du Plessis and his colleagues had been applauded by the protestors. The posters they were brandishing read, among other things: "Dirk Mudge, who do you think you are to renounce the birth right of the whites?"; "Chase the betrayers of the whites into the sea"; "Take Mudge, Neef, Louw, Botha, Marais and Spies to court as reactionaries"; "*Weisse bekämpft erzwungene Rassenmischung gnadenlos*"; "Apartheid is by God, integration by the devil." There were other slogans which I won't quote here, it was a disgrace to us whites.

I was determined not to be influenced by the protest when I later explained the contents and implications of the bill during the second-reading debate. I assured the members that I approached the legislation in all seriousness, and that I was well aware of its implications. I expected opposition, since I knew people do not like change (especially not drastic change as envisaged in the bill). I had my doubts about it happening, but admitted the price of residential plots could drop when black and coloured people moved in. It would be temporary, though. The passing of the legislation could lead to claims being laid to other facilities, such as schools, in which case we would have to take clear-headed and realistic decisions. I once again stressed the inevitable implications of not doing away with racial discrimination.

Referring to the demonstration by white radicals in front of the building, I said the black and coloured representatives who shared the benches with us in the Assembly and who were still being subjected to discriminatory practices every day, had never considered taking this kind of action, and never would. Hence, I gave them the assurance that we would continue to voice our policy fearlessly. The bill determined that every inhabitant of the country, irrespective of race or colour, would henceforth have the right to buy a residential plot in a proclaimed urban area. I acknowledged that there were still shortcomings in the bill. These would have to be addressed at a later stage. I was referring to the lack of clarity in respect of non-proclaimed towns and business premises, and promised to attend to this forth-with.

As to the opening up of public amenities, I explained that this applied mainly to public accommodation establishments, hotels, res-taurants, cafés and recreational areas, and also other facilities that had not been included previously. My colleagues could confirm that this bill was merely the first step, and that other changes that had nothing to do with the identity of an individual or group would be attended to in due course.

As far as schools and education were concerned, our contention was that, although we rejected any form of racial divide, for the time being the control over education should remain with the different representative authorities. As to the issue of education, there wasn't agreement, even within DTA ranks. It was understandable when aspects such as ethnic heterogeneity – as represented by the DTA – were taken into consideration. Although I felt strongly about the com-plete abolition of racial discrimination, I could never ignore the exist-ence of different ethnic groups. Today, more than two decades after independence, it can still not be ignored. Chief Kuaima Riruako was recently recognised by the SWAPO government as Paramount Chief of the Hereros, and different tribes still have their kings. The DTA later realised that in spite of the language and cultural differences, the integration of schools was unavoidable, but had to be done in an orderly, practical and realistic way.

I was expecting the penal clause in the bill that provided for a fine or prison sentence to be strongly opposed. This was subsequently amended to provide for a fine or loss of licence only. To conclude, I gave the assurance on behalf of the DTA that standards would be upheld, and that owners of public amenities would be entitled to refuse entry in cases of unseemly and irresponsible behaviour.

Daniel Luipert of the DTA, who seconded my proposal, reminded us that the invitation to the other groups to work together on a future form of government "… so that we could make laws together" had been extended by the whites. Now, the very people who had extended the invitation opposed the drafting of the first legislation. It was well known that it was Van Zijl who convinced Mr Luipert and the Namas to take part in the Turnhalle Conference.

A.H. du Plessis made good on his promise to fight the bill with every means at his disposal. He read a telegram he had received from the Municipal Association requesting that local authorities be given the opportunity to consult its voters and/or property owners. He argued that this was democracy; either we accept this or reject democracy.

We had to, yet again, deal with the National Party's view on democracy. As was the case with the white referendum on the Turnhalle Constitution, the whites had to be consulted yet again. Once again the National Party wanted the right to veto and prevent change. Yet they did not regard the 1978 election, in which the vast majority of the population had indicated they were opposed to racial discrimination, as a democratic process.

The last AKTUR speaker to take part in the discussion on the bill was Jan de Wet. He referred mainly to the rights of the whites and to the contribution they had made towards developing the Territory. No one could dispute this, except that it was irrelevant to the debate. The Speaker requested that Jan de Wet confine himself to the motion under discussion. In his speech, one of the Damara representatives asked whether he could become a Nationalist as well, to which Jan de Wet replied that he could become a Damara Nationalist. Jan de Wet regarded the legislation as an impairment to the entrenched rights of the whites.

What he apparently failed to understand was that it was about exclusive rights of the whites. Whites were regarded as a uniform ethnic group, which they were not. White people had only one common feature, namely the colour of their skin, but included people with different languages and cultures. Segregation in residential areas and public amenities was therefore based on race. Ethnicity was not the issue, since all the other ethnic groups, regardless of ethnic differences, had to share amenities. Jan de Wet concluded by objecting vehemently to the dismantling of the powers of representative authorities.

Following the acceptance of the Act on racial discrimination, AKTUR indicated that they would for the time being no longer participate in the activities of the National Assembly. As could be expected, the National Party and AKTUR decided to take the matter further. They asked the court to have the National Assembly declared illegal, but lost the case.

It was clearly a turbulent process that for the first time in the history of South West Africa led to a National Government representative of all its population groups. Old alliances crumbled by the wayside and new ones were formed. However, the end of the road was not yet in sight. The big hurdle towards achieving international recognition still lay ahead.

CHAPTER 11

Between two fires, 1979–1983

The interim government that came into being when the National Assembly was established in 1979 represented an important milestone in the political and constitutional development of South West Africa. It formally transformed the administration of the Territory from a primarily ethnically based system to a central government with extensive legislative powers. For all intents and purposes, institutionalised apartheid now belonged to the past. This development must therefore be seen as an important step towards a free and independent unitary state as demanded by the international community. The final lap to our envisaged constitutional destination would however prove to be strewn with serious obstacles:

- The lack of sufficient trained and experienced manpower;
- SWAPO's refusal to participate in the interim government; and
- South Africa consistently preventing the interim government from bringing about meaningful changes to ensure that the road ahead was conducive towards eventually achieving independence.

P.W. Botha's dilemma

Besides the satisfaction of at least achieving self-government, the ensuing years were traumatic and frustrating to me. The road for the DTA as the governing party was hardly strewn with roses. In addition to having to prepare for a confrontation with SWAPO in the unforeseen future, we had to work towards a dispensation that would be best for the entire population of the country. All indications were that there would be opposition, especially on the part of the whites. We also experienced opposition from another quarter, to be exact from the person responsible for giving legislative powers to the Constituent Assembly elected in 1978, namely P.W. Botha. He summoned me to Cape Town.

I did not exactly receive a warm welcome, and I could see from P.W.'s attitude that I could expect trouble. He expressed his indignation at the abolition of legislation relating to racial discrimination (in urban residential areas and with public amenities) and especially the penal clause providing inter alia for prison sentences imposed for violating the law. He asked me how I could do this to the whites. He threatened to dissolve the National Assembly if the penal clause were not amended. P.W. Botha had the power to do it and I could not ignore his threat. To reach my objective I would have to compromise, and offered to propose at our next caucus meeting that the penal clause be amended in such a way that, should the owner or manager of an accommodation establishment (a hotel, restaurant, café or public recreational area) deny entry to any person on the basis of race or colour, such an owner or manager, if found guilty, would lose his or her licence. My proposal was accepted by the caucus.

P.W. Botha addressed me at length on the necessity of unity among the whites. He could not and simply would not understand that any attempt towards white unity would unavoidably lead to black solidarity. I gained the impression that the decisions he had taken on South West Africa since becoming Prime Minister resulted in political repercussions for South Africa. At meetings I addressed on invitation in South Africa, appreciation was regularly expressed for what we were doing locally to resolve the South West Africa issue, as well as for the effect it would have on South Africa. At the same time the opinion that what was happening in South West Africa would never happen in South Africa, was expressed consistently. I often wondered how long it would take before P.W. Botha would have to explain his policy on South West Africa to his electorate, and especially how it would influence policy in South Africa. He was in a predicament from which he would have to disentangle himself. As it happened, this took place on 28 July 1979.

In a speech he gave at an NP meeting in Upington, he announced that he "regarded it as crucially imperative to provide clarity on South West Africa". What he actually tried to explain and justify was the change of policy that had set in after he had become Prime Minister. After this his remarks were directed primarily at AKTUR (including the National Party of South West Africa) and the right-wing elements in South Africa. I think it's important to refer to the content of his explanation in greater detail.

He started by citing the following paragraph from the publication, *South West Africa Survey 1967*:

> However, at this stage it is impossible to foresee with any degree
> of accuracy the ultimate interactions of the various population

> groups. Circumstances will alter radically. What is considered
> anathema today may well become sound practical politics to-
> morrow, and vice versa. Nor is it necessary to embark on specu-
> lation as to what the ultimate future political pattern will be – i.e.
> whether and to what extent there may be amalgamations or un-
> ions of some kind, federations, commonwealth or common mar-
> ket arrangements, etc. The peoples themselves will ultimately
> decide.

Botha called these words prophetic, since the future of the Territory
was now in the hands of its inhabitants and all options were now open
to them. What he refrained from saying was that in the piece quoted
above, reference was made to groups and not to inhabitants.

The National Party (SWA) retained its position that this meant that
each ethnic group would decide on its own future and to what extent
it wanted to cooperate with other groups. The possibility was raised
that the southern part of South West Africa could eventually become
part of South Africa. It was abundantly clear that the policy accepted
by the South African Government in 1979 differed in essence to that
which had been envisaged in 1967.

P.W. Botha was expected to explain, especially since objections were
raised by the NP (SWA). He did this most skilfully. He referred to the
Constitutional Conference (Turnhalle Conference), which in his view
was a logical outcome of the 1967 policy. Factually P.W. Botha was correct, because the Turnhalle Conference was an attempt by the non-
violent inhabitants of South West Africa to start working towards their
future themselves. I have already dealt with the origin of the Turnhalle
Conference. Botha confirmed that the South African Government's
discussions with the five Western members of the Security Council
since April 1977 were intended to achieve international recognition. It
has always been my conviction that the proposals from the five Western countries came because they feared that the Turnhalle Conference
could be the first step towards a unilateral declaration of independence. SWAPO leaders subsequently confirmed this to me.

P.W. Botha subsequently raised a very important point, namely that
the Turnhalle leaders had committed themselves to the following principles:

- South West Africa would become independent as soon as possible.
- The Territory as a whole would become independent.

- Countrywide elections to elect a Legislative Assembly would be held on a one-person-one-vote basis under supervision of the UN.
- An Administrator General, appointed by the South African Government, would administer the Territory until independence.
- Discrimination on the basis of race and colour would be eliminated.

He further confirmed that the Turnhalle leaders had already in June 1977 agreed to relinquish the establishment of an interim government based on the constitutional proposals of the Turnhalle Conference, and that Justice M.T. Steyn had been appointed Administrator General as from 1 September 1977. Additional issues raised were the position of Walvis Bay; the gradual withdrawal of South African troops; and the termination of South West Africa's representation in the South African Parliament on 29 September.

P.W. Botha confirmed that the National Party of South West Africa had decided on 28 September 1977 to conclude its association with the National Party of South Africa. According to his information, the National Party of South West Africa had decided on 5 October 1977 to do away with certain discriminatory laws.

In my speech at Kamanajab the previous year I had proposed that the federal connection with the National Party of South Africa be severed, and discrimination on the basis of race and colour be abolished. I also contended that political cooperation with the black and coloured inhabitants of South West Africa was essential. I was duly accused of disloyalty, cross-examined by Du Plessis and Van Zijl, and subsequently repudiated in the press.

Why was it necessary to wait until a split in the party before doing what I had recommended?

In his long speech in Upington, P.W Botha once again referred to the necessity of white cooperation:

> On more than one occasion my predecessor, Mr B.J. Vorster, attempted to prevent the people of South West Africa from losing the opportunity of exercising their right to self-determination due to mutual suspicion and strife. Since August 1977 and October 1978, both the Minister of Foreign Affairs and I have made concerted efforts to persuade the leaders of South West Africa not to give priority to their differences in favour of essential matters about which they should agree. On several occasions these discussions lasted for many hours.

Botha was not referring here to the conversation that had taken place at Eros Airport as insisted on by John Vorster, during the course of which he had requested Du Plessis to act as leader, with his replacement by me probably at the back of his mind. I would like to repeat: I had no aspirations of being leader of the National Party, but I had no other choice but to make myself available as a candidate in September 1977. The issue was above all conviction, not leadership.

Up to this point P.W. Botha's speech and the position he had taken were acceptable, but then he concluded his speech with a statement that filled me with serious misgivings. Although he consistently emphasised that the people of South West Africa should make decisions about their future themselves, he became prescriptive. "The identity and territorialism of the different nations of South West Africa are an important component in the future governmental framework of South West Africa and should be taken into consideration when writing the constitution." Had he meant this purely as his personal opinion and advice, he was probably entitled to it, but he continued by saying that second-tier governments for the population groups wishing to have them, should be set up and acknowledged, while an effective first-tier government should be maintained. It would become clear later that he meant for this to take place before the envisaged election under UN supervision. The result of this "instruction" was that the division between the people of the Territory deepened, and since the period of interim government lasted longer than we had anticipated, there were a number of clashes between P.W. Botha and myself. The fact that he referred to the right of nations for self-determination in his speech did not augur well for us.

The DTA had no problem with P.W. Botha's policy at that stage. What was becoming increasingly clear was that he was set on exonerating himself from the responsibility for his political change of course by placing it on the shoulders of the people of South West Africa. It suited the DTA, because it was exactly what we wanted. However, among the AKTUR ranks his speech was not received favourably. For the National Party of South West Africa his pronouncements were bad news.

Dr Gerrit Viljoen becomes Administrator General

On 2 August 1979, a mere two days after the Upington speech, Dr Gerrit Viljoen was appointed to succeed Justice M.T. Steyn as Administrator General. We heard through the grapevine that his mission was to set up second-tier authorities for all the population groups. I was highly upset, since my understanding was that it would be done according to the constitutional proposals as set out by the Turnhalle Conference. In his Upington speech P.W. Botha had, after all, emphasised that the National Party of South West Africa had given up the idea of an interim government on the basis of the Turnhalle proposals. What happened to the South African Government's undertaking that the people of South West Africa must decide about their future themselves? After being accused in South Africa of leaving the whites in South West Africa in the lurch, P.W. Botha was finding himself in an impossible situation. Similar allegations were made about what was happening in Zimbabwe where Mugabe was set to win an election and come into power the following year. It was clear to me that the DTA was moving too fast for his liking.

I visited Viljoen in Johannesburg before he took office in Windhoek. I had great respect and appreciation for him as an academic, but I wanted to establish to what extent our political views corresponded. I put it to him that since we had no idea when the envisaged election in terms of the Western settlement plan would take place, we should use the time we had available to address the wrongs in our country. If we should lose the election because of a desire to please the right-wing elements among us, it would cost all of us dearly. I warned that the establishment of second-tier authorities based on the Turnhalle Constitution would be an unmarketable political product in that election. By the end of the interview I was satisfied that there was good rapport between Viljoen and myself, and that he valued my viewpoints.

After his arrival in Windhoek, Viljoen immediately began preparing for the establishment of a central authority. It would consist of a National Assembly and a Ministers' Council while provision would be made for the establishment of representative authorities. The DTA tried its best to limit the functions allocated to the second-tier authorities to that which would affect population groups in particular. Viljoen showed sympathy for our viewpoints, but it was obvious he had been given specific instructions. We did, however, manage to have a few functions transferred from second-tier to central government. My biggest problem was that many of my DTA colleagues were tied to specific ethnic groups and did not want their ethnic authorities to be dismantled.

Proclamation AG 8 was announced on 1 June 1980. It provided for a National Assembly and Ministers' Council and approved the members who had been elected in the 1978 elections as members of these bodies. The DTA was pleased about the enhanced status of the National Assembly, but the extended powers that had been allocated to the representative authorities were still unacceptable to us. The provisions of AG 8 that allocated by far the major portion of the country's tax revenue, including individual tax, to the white representative authority, was a recipe for failure. In the years to follow it became obvious that the other authorities, due to their limited sources of income, would not be able to balance their budgets. The argument that the whites were making the biggest contribution as regards individual tax did not hold water. The white authority had built up huge reserves which enabled them to allocate funds to, amongst others, Cultura 2000, a trust that would support only whites and especially the Afrikaners at a cultural level, enabling them to, inter alia, privatise facilities such as the teachers training college, the Conservatorium, old-age homes and the children's home in Windhoek. Cultura 2000 would also be in a position to buy properties from white owners in mixed areas when requested. The privileged position of the white representative authority would remain a cause of annoyance and would result in the failure of the system.

The fact that I had to make concessions under pressure to keep the National Assembly relevant, bothered me. The fact that I had to fight against white people to change their perceptions also caused me considerable grief. I was after all one of them, and I so badly wanted them to walk alongside me.

In the early hours of 27 April 1980, a month before the proclamation of AG 8, as it became known, I wrote a long letter to Viljoen from a foggy Swakopmund, where I had gone to address a Republican Party Youth Congress. I was still deeply aware of the trust that 200 young white people had placed in me the previous evening, and of the enthusiasm with which they were facing a new future. I also contemplated the new political direction I had taken when I resigned from the National Party in 1977 and founded the Republican Party, and of all the decisions I had made after that. I wrote to Viljoen that in recent years I had led people in this country – even coerced them, into a direction they did not want to go – because of my conviction that it was the only way we could serve the interests of South West Africa and also

South Africa. I also expressed the fear that my desire to be accepted by my own people could possibly supersede my convictions of what was in their best interests. I expressed my doubts about my chances of success, especially taking into account what was happening with re-gard to the introduction of representative authorities for the different ethnic groups with far-reaching powers. I wrote that the DTA, for the sake of credibility and a strong-man image, should withdraw from all government institutions.

I hoped that Viljoen would understand my position and would bear it in mind when he made his final decisions. His reaction was always sympathetic, but it was obvious that he had been given a direc-tive which he was obliged to carry out and that I could not expect too many concessions from him. On 1 July 1980, the interim government was sworn in officially and I was nominated unanimously by the DTA as Chairman of the Ministers' Council. The fact that I had been chosen as Chairperson of a predominantly black organisation was proof that racial prejudice did not play a role. When the Ministers' Council was inaugurated I made special mention of this.

A new Legislative Assembly is elected

This eventful year – 1980 – had still not come to an end. The term of the white Legislative Assembly – which had been converted into the white representative authority in terms of AG 8 – had expired and an election was announced for 13 November 1980. After the split in 1977, the Republican Party was regularly accused of occupying eight seats that were not representative of our support. We would now have the opportunity to prove our support. I decided not to make myself avail-able as candidate in order to give my full support to the activities of the National Assembly.

The election campaign was characterised by emotions and accusa-tions that I had split the whites and was in the process of sacrificing them for the sake of black support. Koos Pretorius used the last ses-sion of the Legislative Assembly in May to explain why white schools should have the exclusive use of their school halls and sports facilities. He evaded his responsibility, saying that parental opinion in this re-gard must not be overlooked, referring throughout to the utilisation of facilities by "outsiders", while all of us knew full well that he was talk-ing about black and coloured children and their parents.

The decision whether the school facilities could be made available to "outsiders" was left to the headmaster and school committee. He used this occasion to try and explain the difference between "multinational" sports, which would be acceptable and permissible, and "multiracial" sports, which would be unacceptable. I failed to understand how this principle would be applied to our society.

During the debate the Chairperson of the Executive Committee and leader of the National Party took a strong stand on any deviation from the Turnhalle principles, and accused me of being responsible for breaching consensus. It was clear that he had already been informed about the intended proposals by the Administrator General. He declared his dissatisfaction with these, and reiterated that the members of the National Party would continue fighting for their beliefs. Should they fail to achieve their goals, they could at least say that they had tried their best.

During the same debate, other National Party speakers attacked me personally and made typical election speeches. I listened closely to the speech made by E.T. Meyer, an NP member of the Legislative Assembly. He was a respected member of the community, who had made his mark in the field of education in South West Africa. I respected him and still believe, as was the case with Gerrit Viljoen, that he should never have involved himself in politics. I told them so on occasion. His speech confirmed this. He neither attacked nor insulted anyone personally and did not waste time playing political games. For him it was about education, a subject he knew and about which he could speak with authority. He pointed out that the future was uncertain, and that he was concerned about the forthcoming availability of adequate facilities and teachers to prepare the youth for the future. He emphasised the importance of mother-tongue education, as well as the desirability of children being taught by teachers from their own population group, since he regarded schools as an extension of the parental home. He also expressed his concern about the decrease in the number of white teachers and children.

While I did not react to what he said in my speech, I shared his concerns. In my communications with Dr Viljoen I expressed the opinion that education was the one function that should resort under these representative authorities, although I realised that other representative authorities might not share my view in this regard, and that a large section of the population possibly preferred integrated education. For this reason the DTA's policy was that there should be culturally bound as well as open schools. To initiate a move in this direction I – in my capacity as Chairman of the Ministers' Council – negotiated with CDM (Consolidated Diamond Mines) of the De Beers Group about the establishment of such an open school. The company made available R5 million to establish Concordia College on the western outskirts of Windhoek.

I had no idea how long this dispensation could continue. Nobody had. When the internal parties, including the National Party, accepted independence in terms of the Western proposals, the road ahead was, to use E.T. Meyer's word, unpredictable. Much would depend on the performance of the internal parties in the envisaged election. The most important question was still whether these parties could offer an acceptable alternative to SWAPO's policy. If not, we would lose the election and with it everything we felt so strongly about, including culturally bound education. A large number of whites and teachers left the country following the acceptance of the Western settlement plan, about which I can only comment how regrettable it is that they lost faith in the future at such an early stage. It is well known that many of them wanted to return at a later stage, but were unable to do so due to financial constraints.

The election campaign began in all earnest after the Legislative Assembly adjourned on 13 May 1980 for an indefinite period. I have no desire to repeat everything that transpired and was said during this campaign, other than that it was a political duel that spared nobody and nothing. Although I was not a candidate in the election, it was probably inevitable that during the campaign, I and the policy I supported were part of the discussions. I was, after all, the leader of the Republican Party and Chairman of the DTA, and both these organisations were in the direct firing line.

In June 1980, three weeks after the instatement of the new Government in accordance with AG 8, Koos Pretorius said the following in an election speech: "… if the leader of the Republican Party, Mr Mudge or whoever, wants to imply that the National Party of South West voluntarily accepted the political dispensation that currently exists, then he and his party should know that they are engaged in proclaiming untruths …" He pointed out that he was obliged to reserve his position until such time as all misunderstandings had been resolved, and stated that he would no longer associate himself with the envisaged one-per-son-one-vote election in South West. He continued as follows: "[T]here is such a thing as integrity. I, and especially the whites in South West, are shocked when it comes to the integrity of some people."

On the same occasion Jan de Wet said the following:

> It is tragic that the whites have been forced into a situation where they have to make a case for their birth right … to pro-tect their rights, people now have to engage in demonstrations, while in essence demonstrating goes against their grain. The whites, however, have to make use of such methods because they have been deprived of their democratic right. They are no longer given the right to elect their own leaders. To the contrary, they are bullied by a voting power in the National Assembly. Their minority rights and fundamental rights have been thrown overboard. If they continue on this road, white unity will have to be consolidated in such a way that they can still perform ef-fectively.

However, exactly ten years later, Koos and Jan – with other members of the Constituent Assembly – reached consensus over a constitution that made provision for everything against which, ten years ago, they had mobilised white unity and organised demonstrations. Another 20 years later Jan was a guest of honour at an event organised by Theo-Ben Gurirab to commemorate the acceptance of the Namibian Consti-tution.

The result of the 1980 election proved that the Republican Party was here to stay, contrary to the National Party's announcement after the split. The RP won eight of the 18 seats, exactly the same number we had at the time of the split. It terms of actual votes, the NP won only 48% of the votes, the RP 42% and the HNP 10%. It was arguably better than could be expected. The RP was only three years old, while the National Party had ruled for several decades.

Danie Hough becomes Administrator General

Gerrit Viljoen was replaced as Administrator General by Danie Hough on 2 October 1980. Dr Viljoen became Minister of National Education in the South African Cabinet and later the Minister tasked with the administration and development of black people. I had great regard and admiration for Viljoen. The role and responsibilities of his successor Hough would differ from those of his predecessors. According to my information, P.W. Botha was of the opinion that once the new Government had been instated, the Administrator General would no longer play an active role in the Government but would merely act as Representative of the South African Government, although he was still tasked with ratifying the laws of the National Assembly. When At van Wyk, author of my biography *Reënmaker van die Namib* (Rainmaker of the Namib) asked Pik Botha how it had come about that Danie Hough was appointed as Administrator General, he explained it as follows: "Danie Hough knew all the cabinet members. He and a few friends owned the farm Bergtop in the Soutpansberg, and P.W. and all these guys … went to Bergtop every winter on a hunting trip. Every winter … So they knew one another. Knew, knew, knew."

After the official inauguration of the new Government, with Danie Hough as Administrator General, a new era began in the history of the country. While the new dispensation could be regarded as a creation of the South African Government and more specifically of the Prime Minister, P.W. Botha, it was characterised by clashing viewpoints between myself and P.W. Botha and his Administrator General, Hough. As had already been revealed clearly in his Upington speech, the Prime Minister was becoming ever more prescriptive. He was also becoming increasingly preoccupied with white unity and the recognition and institutionalisation of ethnicity. Koos Pretorius and I were summoned to Pretoria or Cape Town on more than one occasion.

I clearly remember what transpired on one such occasion in the Castle in Cape Town. Pik Botha and Gen. Magnus Malan were also present. After an initially jovial conversation, P.W. Botha accused us of making his position in South Africa impossible. He said that people in South Africa were beginning to ask questions. They wanted to know if it was fair that South Africa spend millions on South West Africa, inter alia to defend us, while the whites afforded themselves the luxury of fighting each other. I tried my best to explain that the situation was not that simple; that unity could not be cosmetic but had to be based on communal points of view and policy. He himself, in the company of Pik Botha at Eros Airport, had made an appeal to Du Plessis to resolve the differences within the National Party at the time. This did not happen. I pointed out that all the other population groups were politically divided as well, and that white unity would inevitably lead to black unity.

The Prime Minister assumed a threatening attitude, asking Pik Botha how long it would take to recall seconded South African public servants in South West Africa. He asked Magnus Malan how much time was needed to withdraw South African troops from the Territory. As could be expected, they both played along, saying that they could do it within two weeks, to which the Prime Minister replied: "Do it." I did not take this cheap threat seriously. During a tea break he came to me, saying: "Dirk, don't think I'm joking here. I'm serious." He could probably see I was not taking him seriously. I assured him I did, but it must have been obvious that we both knew his threats were ridiculous. Similar conversations were to follow, and clashes between me and P.W. Botha would become more intense. These discussions led nowhere, but I had no doubt that he recognised the threat of his own creation and that he would try and leave an imprint while he was still in control of South West Africa.

A new American approach under Ronald Reagan

The election of Ronald Reagan as President of the USA in November 1980 was good news for South Africa and to some extent also for us in South West Africa. We hoped that this more conservative American president would have a more sympathetic attitude towards the internal parties. This did not happen. It soon became apparent that President Reagan had his own agenda for South West Africa and Angola. Peter Kalangula, President of the DTA, and I decided to make contact with the Reagan administration at a high level, and with this objective in mind we travelled to America. We succeeded in getting an appointment with Jeane Kirkpatrick, the UN's Permanent Representative at the United Nations. However, she was more interested in the welfare of Jonas Savimbi, the US's ally in Angola, and knew very little about our internal politics. We managed to set up a few appointments with senators and members of Congress, but were shocked by their ignorance. In most cases the officials who assisted the members of Congress were better informed than they were themselves. The visit was not particularly productive.

Reagan's election as President gave a new twist to the internal developments, as well as to the international negotiations about South

West Africa. The American President shared P.W. Botha's concern over the Cuban presence in Angola. Although the Americans were not prepared to become involved in Angola on a military basis yet again, they were prepared to exert pressure to have the Cuban troops removed from Angola. In this process Chester Crocker, who had been appointed by Reagan as Deputy Chairman of Foreign Affairs, played an important role. At the time Reagan's policy in respect of South West Africa and Angola was referred to as "constructive engagement", and Crocker's role as "shuttle diplomacy". The latter was a fitting description, because Crocker flew backwards and forwards to conduct discussions with the different role players.

I had a few meetings with him and was impressed by his practical approach. I gained the impression that he, unlike the Western Contact Group, believed that the Cubans had to be removed from Angola before the South African Government could agree to the implementation of Resolution 435. This process took approximately eight years. I was not expecting it to take this long, and was primarily intent on strengthening the position of the DTA with a view to the anticipated election. We were subsequently glad that we had been given so much time, but unfortunately this delay also gave P.W. Botha the opportunity to complicate my life. Rather than allow the DTA to gain support, he continually tried to derail us. I often wondered whether he really intended allowing the implementation of Resolution 435, or whether he was merely playing politics. I could simply not understand why he was still adamant to force an interim dispensation on us at this critical stage in the run-up to an election where we were to fight a formidable opponent, simply to please the right-wing elements in South West Africa and South Africa. We were aware of his problems within the Party regarding the conservative Treurnicht faction which split from the National Party a year later, yet he had already stated his position on South West Africa unequivocally in his Upington speech.

The Geneva Conference, 7–14 January 1981

As if the drama we experienced during the year was not enough, 1980 ended with yet another drama. The Administrator General moved his office to Swakopmund for the holiday season, as usual. The Swakopmunders were particularly proud of the executive authority of the Territory moving to their town for a month at the end of the year, and each time organised a large dinner party to which the townspeople were invited.

I happened to be in Swakopmund – where we had a holiday home – and was looking forward to relaxing with my family for a few weeks after a difficult year. But, as a friend of mine always used to say, "hier beneden is het niet", or to use my grandmother's words, "there's no rest for the wicked". Danie Hough invited me to his office to inform me that a conference was being held in Switzerland early in the New Year, to which all the internal parties, including SWAPO, had been invited. The internal parties would attend under his leadership. He also informed me that a former vice president of SWAPO, Mishake Muyongo, who had left the organisation, would accompany the delegation. He arranged for me to meet with Muyongo and his group later that same day. I subsequently learnt that Muyongo and his entourage had been transported to Swakopmund by aircraft. Among them was the deputy president of CANU, Siseho Simasiku, who had recently left SWAPO with Muyongo. I was also subsequently informed that the conference had been arranged by the Western Contact Group and the UN, and would take place under chairmanship of Mr Brian Urquhart, Assistant Secretary General of the UN.

I was infuriated by these developments. How could the DTA be expected to confront SWAPO, which was still structured on an ethnic and even racial basis, at such an informal and casual get-together? We had little in common. To top it all, we would have to sacrifice our credibility in Geneva by meeting our political enemy under leadership of a South African Governor General surrounded by a number of South African officials. I told Danie Hough that I was not prepared to participate in this ridiculous political game, but would, however, discuss it with my DTA colleagues. Alas, as was the case in the past and would be in future, they had different considerations. The temptation to embark on a free trip overseas and the lack of understanding of the implications of participating in such a naïve endeavour made them decide differently. Once again I had to subject myself to a majority decision with which I did not agree. Fanuel Kozonguizi, a colleague of mine who had a great deal of international experience, calmed me with the suggestion: "Let's go, but then we do our own thing."

Hence we departed, flying to Geneva via Frankfurt, without Muyongo, who in the meantime had withdrawn. I developed a kidney-stone infection and suffered a great deal of pain during the overnight flight.

Billy Marais gave advice: Drink lots of beer to flush out the kidney stone. I took his advice, with the result that by the time we reached Geneva the next morning, I was somewhat intoxicated. Moreover, the advice had not done the trick and the hotel doctor was summoned. He gave me an injection and recommended I drink water rather than beer. Fortunately, this improved the situation and, for the first time since we'd landed, I could admire the view of the snow-covered landscape from the windows of my hotel room.

The conference took place from 7 to 14 January in a large hall of the Palace of Nations. Our delegation sat on one side of tables arranged as a square and Sam Nujoma and his people on the other side, with the Administrator General at the top. I can hardly remember anything that was said that first day. To be precise, I can remember only one sentence, something said by Sam Nujoma. He was probably hinting at the structure of our delegation when he, with his fist in the air, shouted: "SWAPO is one!" I understood what he meant and realised once again that the DTA now found itself in the wrong company.

The conference did not take place only in the council chamber. Cocktail receptions and excursions were arranged "so that we could get to know each other better". Amateurish efforts were made especially for the DTA and SWAPO leaders to be introduced to one another. A train journey to Glion near Montreux on 11 January had been arranged for the 140 delegates and we were treated to lunch at a beautiful hotel school. Nothing much came of personal conversations, however. At one of the receptions I was introduced to Theo-Ben Gurirab, SWAPO's representative at the UN. I pretended not to know him and asked: "Who the hell is Mr Gurirab?" This was not very polite of me, but I was highly agitated about these counter-productive attempts to resolve serious issues. At one stage Peter Kalangula came to me, saying: "Mr Mudge, tonight I was forced to greet my brother's murderer [this was Nujoma]." On the same occasion the French Ambassador, who was also the representative of the Contact Group, asked me to follow him because he wanted to show me something. When we entered one of the adjoining rooms, we found Sam Nujoma there. This had obviously been a prior arrangement. What could we possibly say to one another, other than enquire after each other's health?

During the conference the DTA confronted the UN with a list of conditions we regarded as prerequisites for a fair election. One of these prerequisites was that the UN withdraw its recognition of SWAPO as "the sole and authentic representative of the people of Namibia". It was later alleged that these prerequisites had resulted in the failure of the conference. However, it is my contention that the conference had failed before it started.

When it became obvious that the conference was leading nowhere, Kozo – as we referred to Kozonguizi – and I decided that we should utilise the presence of a horde of pressmen to present our case, so we convened a press conference. Whether this served any useful purpose, I do not know, but what it most certainly accomplished was to bring us into even greater disfavour with the Administrator General and the South African representatives. Perhaps they suspected us of attempting to derail the conference. This suspicion was confirmed when Billy Marais came across members of the press fiddling with bugging devices in the room where the DTA convened regularly.

The representatives of the Western Contact Group probably also realised that the conference would not achieve the intended objective. One evening the German Minister of Foreign Affairs, Hans-Dietrich Genscher, and his colleagues in the Contact Group unexpectedly invited me to join them for a drink in their hotel. When I arrived it was obvious they already had a head start on me. Genscher and Donald McHenry of the USA couldn't understand why I was so concerned about the UN's acknowledgement of SWAPO. They tried their best to convince me that it was not important, since the decision had been taken by the UN's General Assembly and not by the Security Council.

As I had done on previous occasions, I upheld my contention that the voters of South West Africa did not understand the difference and were convinced that the UN, under whose supervision the election was to take place, was not and could not be impartial. Genscher and McHenry then alleged that the time had run out for routing a decision like the one we had asked for through the General Assembly, since the election would take place shortly. I disagreed with them. None of us knew that evening that it would still take almost nine years before the election would eventually take place. This was yet another unsuccessful attempt of theirs to indoctrinate me.

P.W. Botha is seeking a "more representative" government

Back at home the dogfight continued unabated. The National Party was satisfied with the dispensation that had been introduced by Dr

Viljoen by means of AG 8. Although I was grateful for the few adaptations Dr Viljoen had made at my request, I was not happy with AG 8. Representative authorities had become a reality and the National Party with their surpluses and adequate annual income promoted the interests of the whites on various terrains. That the other authorities would battle to keep afloat was of little concern to them. It soon emerged that their next target would be the structure and powers of the National Assembly. On 6 February I asked for more powers to be given to the Assembly, but P.W. Botha set the involvement of the other parties in the Assembly as a condition for broadening the Government's base. He cautioned further that we were compromising the future should the DTA and AKTUR not come to grips with each other.

In the course of the year the chain of events on the local political scene was dominated by the increase of Cuban and other foreign powers in Angola. However, the local population knew little about it, because local leaders were not involved in military affairs at any stage, while the Defence Force, under the banner of security, regularly interfered in local matters. Prime Minister Botha announced emphatically that a "total onslaught" was being planned against South West Africa and South Africa and the USA under President Reagan shared his concern over the Cuban presence in Angola. This resulted in the SADF launching several military operations in Angola in the early 1980s to combat this total onslaught.

In the meantime, at meetings I was addressing on invitation in South Africa I was again consistently being asked whether it was fair that young South African boys had to fight on our border. I was also targeted by accusations and anonymous letters containing phrases such as: "You are murdering our young boys"; "SA babies are dying for you, Mudge"; "We believe your daughter married a pitch-black man. How can she stand the smell of him?"; and "… we want to shoot you so that your brains stick to the DTA's contemptible board …, you Dog". P.W. Botha's statement that we were dealing with a "total onslaught" was apparently not accepted. Perhaps we should forgive South Africans for their ignorance, because even we, who lived on the front, heard of these operations in Angola only after independence.

The American initiative of "constructive engagement" and the increasing role that Chester Crocker was playing in its implementation were gradually side-tracking the Western Contact Group. The Contact Group believed that the Namibian issue should be resolved before an Angolan solution could follow. Crocker's conviction, on the other hand, was that the South African Government would be more inclined to accept the implementation of Resolution 435 if the threat represented by the Cuban presence in Angola to South Africa could be removed. Crocker's viewpoint eventually won the day, but took many years to accomplish. Local politicians were never involved in these negotiations.

The indefinite delay of the independence process inevitably led to the structure and functions of the National Assembly and Representative Councils being high on the agenda once again. The points of view within the DTA on how this period could be applied were worlds apart from the plans of the National Party and P.W. Botha. The DTA was convinced that we had to do everything in our power to promote the chances of the internal parties winning an election against SWAPO – especially by removing all vestiges of discriminatory practices. Among these were the unfair and indefensible division of assets and financial resources between the white representative authority and the other authorities. Jan de Wet warned in the National Assembly: "If you meddle with AG 8, it will create a storm in this country." Did he mean that the whites would rise up in protest? He apparently did not consider the same possibility among the majority of the population when the National Party wanted to "meddle" with the National Assembly.

In the years that followed, P.W. Botha made sustained efforts to make the National Assembly "more representative". It was his contention that the National Assembly was not representative because it had been chosen on a one-person-one-vote basis. He alleged that a government could be representative only if all the ethnic groups were represented. Efforts to achieve this goal led to hefty clashes between him and me. It became ever more evident that he, supported by Pik Botha, would resort to underhand methods to reach his goal. One such goal was to get me out of the way. In February 1982, Werner Neef and Peter Kalangula announced that they were resigning from the DTA to form a new party, the Christian Democratic Action. The reasons they put forward for their resignation made no sense. However, it was clear that they had access to funding. I was convinced that this party was a South African creation engineered by Pik Botha.

These developments must probably be seen against the background of the political situation in South Africa. On 24 February 1981, Dr Andries Treurnicht and his supporters left the National Party of South

Africa. This threat from the right definitely contributed towards P.W. Botha's compulsion to please the right-wing elements in South Africa. Kalangula's image as a black nationalist and ethnic leader of the Owambos had to be promoted because it was believed that he was the only black leader who could gain Owambo support. I was the stumbling block that had to be removed, and they had to find a reason for doing so. One of the reasons put forward – I learnt in a roundabout way – was that I as a white man should not play a role in the intended election and that my involvement would undermine the chances of defeating SWAPO in an election. The real reason, however, was that I was obstructing the way towards ethnicity.

To my mind, P.W. Botha was having difficulty reconciling the basis of an interim government with that of a future elected government. I wondered if he and the leaders of the National Party of South West Africa really believed that the system they wanted to enforce in the interim could survive the test of an election under UN supervision. When the Contact Group decided in June 1982 that the withdrawal of Cuban troops from Angola was a prerequisite for the implementation of Resolution 435, it should have been obvious that independence was a reality that had to be reckoned with. The South African Government's attitude therefore did not make sense. We had to "hunt with the hounds and run with the hares".

Constitutional principles are laid down

On 12 July 1982, yet another hurdle was cleared when the Security Council ratified an agreement reached by the Contact Group following long discussions with the internal parties, including SWAPO. This subsequently became known as the "1982 principles" and set out certain prerequisites for the future Constitution of an independent Namibia. This, together with the earlier decision on the withdrawal of Cuban troops from Angola, levelled the playing field for a democratic election and independence. The document was entitled *Principles concerning the Constituent Assembly and the Constitution for an Independent Namibia*. It set out all the democratic principles to be contained in a Constitution for an independent Namibia. It determined that the Constitution had to be accepted by a two-thirds majority of the total chosen members of the Constituent Assembly.

I would like to quote the following sections from the 1982 principles, because it would play such a vital role in the eventual writing of the Constitution:

1. Namibia will be a unitary, sovereign and democratic state.
2. The Constitution will be the supreme law of the State ...
3. The Constitution will determine the organisation and powers of all levels of Government ...
4. The electoral system will be in accordance with the principles cited in 1 above.
5. There will be a Declaration of Human Rights which will include the right to life, personal liberty and freedom of movement; to freedom of conscience; to freedom of expression, including freedom of speech and a free press; freedom of assembly and association, including political parties and trade unions; to due process and equality before the law; to protection from arbitrary deprivation without just compensation; and to freedom from racial, ethnic, religious or sexual discrimination.
6. It will be forbidden to create criminal offences with retrospective effect ...
7. Provision will be made for the more balanced structuring of the public service, the police service and the defence services ...
8. Provision will be made for the establishment of elected councils for local and/or regional administration.

Conspiracy to push the DTA aside

Through all of this P.W. Botha carried on as if there was no likelihood of an election and independence. On 11 August, while I was conducting a series of meetings in Ovamboland, I received a message that the Prime Minister had sent a military jet to fly me from Ondangwa to Pretoria for urgent discussions. I had not the faintest idea what it was about. Since I was holding election meetings, I assumed it had something to do with the intended election. At the Waterkloof Air Force base I was met by an officer in uniform, and taken to a military base at the old Observatory in Pretoria. The aroma of braaivleis and the sound of merry voices, among others that of Barney Barnes, greeted me as I entered the building. I was surprised to see P.W. Botha and Brig. Theo Mey together with Koos Pretorius, Justus //Garoëb, Hans Diergaardt and Peter Kalangula.

I realised immediately what the purpose of the get-together was. It was the old story of broadening the base of the central authority, to render it "more representative" by giving representation to ethnic groups. I had no idea how long the group had been convening there and what matters they had discussed, but it soon turned out that my assumption was correct. I received a hearty welcome from the Prime Minister and was offered a drink, supposedly to put me in the right frame of mind.

P.W. Botha addressed us at length. I made comprehensive notes and want to refer to a few statements he made here. He started by saying that the gathering was informal, that we were friends – this was his usual softening-up technique. I knew it was directed at me personally. He had tried this several times in the past and I had never fallen for it. He alluded to the international problem we had to contend with, saying that final decisions would have to be made. I was curious to know what important decisions these could be. First we had to hear how interdependent our two countries were, as well as what the inhabitants of South West and South Africa had in common and what bound us together. He expressed his disappointment about the distrust between the eleven population groups in South West Africa. Referring to the negotiations on the withdrawal of Cuban troops from Angola, he said that the hour of truth would arrive within the next four weeks and that we – he probably meant South Africa – would have to make a decision. If the Cubans withdrew, a new South Africa would come into existence and the negotiations would assume a new shape. If the Cubans did not withdraw, the struggle would intensify, he said.

Appearing satisfied that he had impressed on us, especially on me, the severe gravity of the situation, he directed the following three requests at us: Go sit around a table and draw up a list of the things on which you agree; see if you can put a National Assembly together that will also take care of economic concerns; assemble a better Ministers' Council than the current one, representative of all your people.

He ended his request by saying: "If you don't help me, I wash my hands of you, and will have to take drastic steps." He added that the DTA would have to make concessions.

I wondered whether this was the final decision we would have to make in the face of serious threats. I failed to understand how ethnic representation in the Government would contribute to the solution of an international issue and be in the economic interests of South West Africa. I wondered once again whether South Africa was really interested in a peaceful solution and if its leaders didn't, in fact, prefer an armed struggle. It was also unacceptable that the Prime Minister of South Africa was now prescribing to us how we should elect and set up our Government after he had announced repeatedly that we must decide on our constitutional future ourselves.

Eventually the Prime Minister left the gathering, indicating that he would return the next morning, expecting our response. He arranged for Brig. Mey to stay behind to act as facilitator. It was already very late in the evening and I was exhausted after an extremely long day and week, and was not in the mood for nonsense. I wanted to know why only I of the DTA had been invited. I wasn't the President of the DTA; merely the Chairman. I could surely not be expected to take final decisions on behalf of the party. From questions and opinions expressed by other leaders during the rest of the night, it was clear that they wanted to make drastic changes in the Government. Peter Kalangula put it like this: "How are we going to reorganise the Ministers' Council and the National Assembly? The Ministers' Council is not representative in the democratic sense of the word. The whole thing must be undone, dismantled. I will not be part of a DTA government. The new government must not even smell of the DTA."

I suspected that they had already gained the Prime Minister's support for their plans prior to my arrival. My reaction to the proposals of the "Gang of Five", as I referred to them from then on, was that I had always been prepared to cooperate with them and had already offered two seats in the Ministers' Council to the opposition, which they turned down. I pointed out that 75% of the voters had supported the current system in an election, and that there could be no suggestion that the composition of the Government was not democratic in the true sense of the word. I continued to emphasise that the DTA believed that we should scale down the powers of the Representative Councils and move away from ethnicity. To conclude, I pointed out that the cooperation of the DTA should not be accepted as a given; they were welcome to seek confirmation of my version of the Alliance's points of view from the other DTA leaders. It is probably unnecessary to say that the Prime Minister was not particularly impressed when Brig. Mey informed him the next morning that no agreement could be reached. His reaction was that he was washing his hands in innocence. I knew that he wouldn't leave it at that.

In the meantime I had encountered another problem. Before I could inform my colleagues in the DTA of the outcome of the negotiations, Theo Mey nailed me to the post, telling them that I had accepted a restructuring of the National Assembly and the Ministers' Council in principle. He then asked them to accept a more ethnically based government. Needless to say this was not true. When I made the offer of having my viewpoints confirmed by my colleagues during my discussions in Pretoria I, as an experienced politician, should have known that I was dealing with a shrewd member of the SADF. He had gained my trust at an earlier stage; I was even prepared to give him the benefit of the doubt after he had leaked the contents of a confidential conversation we'd had at my house. It was not difficult for me to set my colleagues' minds at rest that the information given to them by Mey was incorrect. I seriously reprimanded Theo Mey about his behaviour and requested him to refrain from interfering in the affairs of the DTA.

I realised once again how easily my colleagues could be influenced when ethnicity came up for discussion. After all, they were all ethnic leaders and it was *that*, not merit, which had been the basis on which they had been appointed members of the Ministers' Council. For that matter, most of them did not have the skills to manage the departments to which they had been allocated. Kashe, the Bushman representative in the Ministers' Council, could neither write nor read, and the Secretariat had to write speeches even for those who could read and write. This placed an impossible workload on some of us. I must, however, admit that most of them had enough common sense and knew full well what they stood for. In the DTA, fortunately, we had a considerable degree of consensus and, assisted by competent officials, we fared surprisingly well.

Pik Botha tries to squeeze me out

I knew that the consultations we'd had in Pretoria were not the end of the story and that we could not ignore the threats made there. I realised I was the biggest stumbling block in the way if the Prime Minister wanted to carry out his plans.

This was first borne out a month later when, on invitation, I opened an agricultural show in Standerton on 8 September. The evening before the show I received a telephone call from an unknown individual. He said that he had highly important information he wanted to convey to me personally, but that this should be done in secret as he did not want to put his career in jeopardy. He was prepared to meet me very early the next morning in the hotel where I was staying with my wife. He then told me that he was a journalist at the *Sunday Express* in Johannesburg and that something shocking had happened about which he could not keep silent. The previous day Pik Botha had held a confidential session with all the newspapers and the broadcasting corporation during which he had written me off as a factor in South West African politics. The journalist warned me that I was going to be portrayed in a very bad light by all the media the next morning; he was most unhappy that his editor was prepared to play along.

It all came to pass exactly as he had predicted. Not only did the newspaper *Beeld* of Thursday 9 September 1982 publish a report in which the so-called division in South West Africa was denounced, but also an editorial that probably gave the best summary of what Pik Botha had deluded them into believing. In the editorial it was stated:

> It is an indisputable fact that since the election of 1978 Mr Mudge has lost a great deal of support, in the sense that the Government would probably like to see the establishment of a more widely representative and more effective government structure. If Mr Mudge is creating the impression under these circumstances that he wants to hang on to his position too much, he would, above all, prejudice the matter for which he had fought so long and hard.

Rapport, which belonged to the same stable as *Beeld*, reported on Sunday 12 September as follows: "It is general knowledge for anyone who is remotely interested in South West Africa that the DTA no longer has the same following as in 1978 when it took control of the first-tier government." In the *Sunday Times* of the same day, the following appeared:

> Mr Dirk Mudge is a gentle man with the noblest of political intentions, which were often obstructed when others blocked his plans to make Namibia a more visible non-racial place. However, he has been unable to construct a viable power base and, quite simply, he is clearly not the man to take on SWAPO in post-independence elections, hence the complex manoeuvrings to construct a new moderate coalition. Pretoria, it seems, may wish to back a horse (quite literally) of a different colour, Mr Peter Kalangula.

The Star, The Citizen and the *Sunday Express*, as well as the SABC's daily column "*Sake van die Dag*" (Matters of the Day) had the same drift, having swallowed everything that Pik Botha had told them as the gospel truth. This was not the first time that the media was manipulated to put me in an unfavourable light.

At van Wyk refers in his book, *Reënmaker van die Namib* (1999), to the scandalmongering of those days. Afterwards, in a review of the book, H.L. Grosskopf wrote the following on this aspect:

> Shortly after the Turnhalle – I was then still Editor of *Beeld* – a piece was submitted to me for publication with the message that it had already been sent to Piet Cillié of *Die Burger*, that it had been shown to P.W. Botha, and that he had said we should publish it. It consisted of a whole lot of defamation about Dirk Mudge. I had a great deal of sympathy with what Mudge wanted to achieve and it was not my function to publish slander. Cillié also refused to print the story. It is unnecessary to ask why.

Grosskopf also wrote some favourable comments about me in his review, which I will not repeat here since I decided that in these memoirs I would not reproduce any complimentary comments made by whomsoever.

It surprised me that intelligent people could not see right through P.W. Botha's schemes. I still wonder what the authors of these articles said after the results of the 1989 election when the DTA robbed SWAPO of a two-thirds majority. In the same election Peter Kalangula's Party did not win a single seat – this despite the generous financial contributions made by Pik Botha's Department. Mr Kalangula ended up with a considerable number of unused T-shirts.

Directly after Pik's amateurish attempts to undermine my and the DTA's status, I invited the very same newspapers to which he had given the wrong information, to a press conference where I expressed my shock and disappointment in respect of their unethical conduct. I addressed Tertius Myburgh, Editor of the *Sunday Times*, in particular, accusing him of playing a dual role and asking him whether he was well informed about the envisaged "moderate coalition" he and Pik Botha wanted to initiate – actually nothing less than a conspiracy to strengthen ethnic authorities at the expense of Central Government.

After this, I addressed students of the Rand Afrikaans University on invitation, where I also accused Pik Botha of playing a dual role. My remark that Pik wants to be bridegroom at every wedding and the corpse at every funeral was possibly a trifle harsh, and I later admitted this. Pik was most definitely not impressed by my remark.

By that time I knew Prime Minister Botha well enough to know that he was not a graceful loser and that I would hear from him again. However, I was not prepared to take this lying down and presented my views to the Johannesburg Press Club in no uncertain terms. P.W. Botha retaliated by attacking me once again at the Transvaal Congress of the National Party, labelling the DTA as unrepresentative and ineffectual. At a press conference in Windhoek I reacted, as the Windhoek Observer subsequently put it, "with barely concealed emotion and bitterness". I confirmed once again that I was not prepared to accept a purely ethnic government. Referring to the issue of broadening of the Government base, I pointed out that the opposition in the National Assembly had opted not to accept my offer of two seats in the Ministers' Council.

I come to blows with the Prime Minister

P.W. Botha, as it subsequently came to light, was looking for an opportunity to land a knock-out blow and was given the chance two months later on 19 November 1982. Without my being aware of it, he – accompanied by Pik Botha and Gen. Magnus Malan – paid a visit to Windhoek. I was in the middle of a DTA Executive Committee meeting when I received a call from the Administrator General, Danie Hough, informing me that the Prime Minister and his entourage were with him and that P.W. Botha wanted to speak to me. I immediately objected to being summoned on my own again and suggested that he should meet the National Executive of the DTA. My colleagues persuaded me to go there and to fill them in afterwards on what had taken place there.

Pik was waiting for me at the entrance of the Administrator General's residence and suggested that he and I have a brief discussion before joining the Prime Minister. He warned me that there was something I needed to put right; if not, a conversation between the Prime Minister and myself would reach a deadlock. He informed me that the Prime Minister was going to insist on an apology because I had rebutted him. I didn't know what he was referring to. Pik then reminded me that I, following the Prime Minister's allegation that South Africa contributed R600 million to South West Africa's budget annually, had pointed out that about R200 million represented our share from the customs pool and that this was our own money. My immediate reaction was that I had provided the correct figures and that it had not been my intention to offend anyone. Pik tried his best to persuade me to apologise, but I refused. He then warned me that I would have to accept the consequences of my stubbornness, after which we walked towards the Administrator General's office. P.W. Botha, Gen. Magnus Malan and Danie Hough were waiting for us there.

I really did not expect the apology Pik had mentioned to be first on the agenda, but it was. P.W. was sitting with a file on his lap and immediately began by reading a section in which I was clarifying the facts about South Africa's contribution to our budget. He demanded that I apologise for repudiating him. I was resolute that all I had done was allude to the correct figures and that I had had no ulterior motives when doing so. To this he reacted angrily, demanding again that I apologise unconditionally. Since I had nothing more to say, I looked up at the ceiling. P.W. also cited other matters from documents and newspapers on which I differed with him, which had more to do with my refusal to agree with five ethnic leaders on a new system of government.

It was clear that he was looking for a confrontation. Meanwhile Pik had written on the back of a red Life cigarette box: "Is it asking too much of you to just say you are sorry?" I wrote back: "Sorry for what?" and sent the box back to him. Pik then jumped up and reprimanded me for not being sufficiently grateful for everything P.W. had done for South West Africa. He said the least I could do was cooperate in broadening the Government's base. I also rose to my feet, and cautioned him that he was not talking to a child; that I was older and had been involved in politics longer than he had, and that they were welcome to take the five ethnic leaders and see how far they could get with them. On that note I left the office, probably slamming the door somewhat louder than was necessary. After that incident one of the South African newspapers published a cartoon portraying me leaving the room with Pik busy filling the cracks in the wall, the rest of the group looking on in surprise.

After I left the office, Danie Hough followed and tried to persuade me to return. I flatly refused, telling him in no uncertain terms out there on the lawn what I thought of the exchange with and the attitude of the Prime Minister and Pik Botha. I can no longer recall all the things I said to him; what the exchange amounted to was that I was no longer prepared to allow myself to be intimidated. What I did not realise was that our conversation out there had taken place within earshot of security men and possibly also journalists. There were also members of the DTA waiting outside to be informed of the outcome of my meeting with the Prime Minister. The whole to-do ended up in the newspapers.

The interim government is dissolved

The following morning the parties represented in the National Assembly were summoned and informed that the interim government would be dissolved three months later, on 28 February 1983. P.W. Botha had taken revenge and also achieved his objective of dispensing with the DTA-controlled government. About his plans for the future he had nothing to say. I was concerned that my colleagues in the DTA would blame me for the situation that had now developed, which would result in them losing their salaries and other privileges. The fact is, they were not well-off people, and most of them would barely manage to survive financially. While naturally shocked and disappointed, they supported me wholeheartedly. At least they would still be receiving their salaries for the next three months, which they could use among other things to celebrate Christmas with their families. In my case this was not the first time I would be without work as a result of my political convictions.

Since it was so close to the December holidays, I considered the possibility of arranging a last meeting of the National Assembly for February 1983 to give us the opportunity to present our points of view on the intended dissolution of the National Assembly. Once again I underestimated P.W. Botha's determination to block us.

While on holiday in Swakopmund, I was informed on 10 January 1983 that the Administrator General had refused to ratify the Public Holidays Act and had referred it back to the National Assembly. This came as an additional shock, although under the prevailing circumstances we should probably have anticipated it. During the discussion of the bill the previous year I had received many letters from church councils, cultural associations and individuals objecting to the fact that the Day of the Covenant would no longer be a public holiday. They had lost sight of the fact that anyone who wanted to could still organise and attend Day of the Covenant festivals; as well as the fact that the biggest section of the population had no interest in celebrating the Day of the Covenant. The only objective with the bill was that we should have our own public holidays to commemorate those things that were relevant to our country. Representatives of the National Party repeatedly accused me of betraying the fundamental sentiments of the Afrikaner.

In refusing to sign the bill, the Administrator General was probably carrying out the Prime Minister's instructions. Whether it was out of fear of the rightist elements in South Africa or simply out of recalcitrance, I would never know. On 18 January I resigned as Chairman of the Ministers' Council out of protest, although a session of the National Assembly had already been arranged. In terms of the institutional proclamation of the National Assembly, my resignation meant that the Ministers' Council as such had resigned. The proclamation also stipulated that in such a case the Speaker was to call for a special session to elect a new Ministers' Council. The Administrator General pre-empted us by dissolving the National Assembly with immediate effect – probably after consultation with the Prime Minister – and took over Government for an indefinite period. At that stage the National Party of South West Africa was no longer part of the National Assembly, since it had withdrawn from the body in March of the previous year.

AKTUR's candle was also snuffed when Koos Pretorius, leader of the National Party, announced on 28 January 1983, two weeks after the dissolution of Government, that "the AKTUR National Executive had convened for the last time to confer in particular about its objectives, constitution and organisation", and had decided that "new goals had to be created". In reality AKTUR as an election front – which implied participation in a one-person-one-vote election – had disbanded. According to the announcement, AKTUR's main purpose from then on would be "to promote attitudes and conduct propaganda by means of negotiation, rather than to try and win votes in competition with others". The truth was that after Andrew Kloppers resigned from the National Party due to its opposition to opening up residential areas and public facilities, AKTUR existed in name only. The moderate coloured leaders had been involved only to oppose the DTA in the one-person-one-vote election in 1978. Moreover, it was clear that the National Party was no longer expecting such an election and had already been informed by the South African Government about its future plans. After this the National Party would continue the political struggle under different names.

CHAPTER 12

The steep road to independence, 1984–1989

P.W. Botha tries to justify his actions

When the South African Government took the unusual step of dissolving the National Assembly, it did not go unnoticed and elicited reaction by the press, even from abroad (Japan and France). The opposition in the South African Parliament accused the Prime Minister of treating me unfairly, to which he responded on 1 February 1984 – two weeks after the summary dissolution of the National Assembly – as follows: "[I] do not want to choose political leaders for the people of South West. It is their business." But in the meantime he had dissolved our Government because we wouldn't cooperate when he was trying to do exactly that. He continued: "The South West African Government must accept my advice because I have a responsibility towards the taxpayers of South Africa. My advice to the Government is that they should stop this wanton behaviour if they expect the taxpayers of South Africa not to become negative." If we didn't accept his "advice", he would dissolve Government!

As was the case in the little tête-à-tête we had in the Administrator General's office, South Africa's contributions to our budget, not to mention the millions that had been spent on military operations in Angola, were once again raked up from the past. When it suited him, he maintained that the South African Defence Force was in Angola to fend off a "total onslaught on Southern Africa", but then we were also told how South Africa was involved in a border war to protect *us*.

P.W. Botha continued informing Parliament as follows: "After all, I didn't rob Mr Mudge of his followers. I didn't tell Peter Kalangula that he had to go. Neither did I tell the gentleman Justus //Garoëb that he had to go. I was not the one who created these problems." However, he was apparently not aware of the fact that Justus //Garoëb had never been a member of the DTA, but only one of the "Gang of Five", who played along with him to make the interim government more "representative". As far as Kalangula was concerned, he refrained from mentioning his and Pik's role in engineering Kalangula's resignation from the DTA.

On the same day that P.W. Botha made this speech, Dr Willie van Niekerk took over the role of a one-man government from Danie Hough. This dispensation would continue for the next two years. Without further ado he stated that the people of South West Africa would decide for themselves what form of government they wanted. We were hearing this for the umpteenth time, but whenever we made an attempt to do just that, our efforts were ignored.

New role players, new plans

I accepted that Dr Van Niekerk had not been appointed without a specific brief. While he did state that the people of South West Africa had to decide about their future themselves, he did not indicate exactly who was to make these decisions. I assumed that in all likelihood it was to be arranged on a "more representative" basis. Van Niekerk was a member of the Broederbond, an organisation from which I had resigned after a charge was brought against me with its Executive Council for expressing views that were not in line with the Broederbond's ideals for the white Afrikaner. (My reaction to this was that what I advocated was exactly in the interests of the Afrikaner.) I was not suspended as was the case with the Rapportryers, but resigned as a member of my own accord. In fact, following my resignation from the National Party in 1977, I stopped participating in any of the activities of the organisation.

During a private conversation, Dr Willie, as I called him, informed me that he intended establishing a State Council similar to the State Council of South Africa, of which he had been Chairman before. I warned him that it would be a mistake to transfer the same initiatives taken in South Africa onto SWA/Namibia. The name "State Council" in itself would render such an effort dubious.

However, things have a way of taking a different route to the one we expect. South Africa simply continued interfering in local politics, as if a United Nations-supervised election or independence for Namibia was not part of the future. It became increasingly clear that, for them, the DTA's dominance on the political playing field had to be stopped at all costs. I could simply not comprehend the unrealistic expectation that the Botha government would be able to establish a constitutional dispensation in Namibia that would outlive independence. Did its principals still believe that a military solution was possible?

Unbeknown to me, Dr Willie started having discussions with two members of the DTA, as well as with two new role players in local politics, Andreas Shipanga of the SWAPO-Democrats and Moses Katjiuongua of SWANU. Moses came up with the idea of a multi-party conference, but getting the team together would be no easy task; neither was reaching an agreement on how it should be constituted. It was decided initially that SWAPO should be invited to participate, but nothing came of this. There were many different opinions on the number of participants that each participating party would have in the conference, but all the parties (with the exception of the DTA) agreed on one point: the DTA must not have an absolute majority. I was sceptical about this new initiative right from the start, but decided to let my colleagues have their way. I made it very clear, however, that I was not in favour of yet another interim government.

The Multi-Party Conference

The Multi-Party Conference (MPC) convened on 12 November 1983 for its first session. It remained active for a considerable period of time and did, in fact, achieve positive results. During January 1984, members were given the opportunity to have discussions with Chester Crocker in Cape Town, and afterwards issued a statement in Windhoek on 24 February that reflected certain basic constitutional principles on which consensus had been reached. A Declaration of Human Rights was released on 14 April 1984.

In the meantime Pik Botha, without consulting the MPC, announced that a meeting had been arranged in Lusaka, Zambia for us to meet the SWAPO leaders. The meeting took place from 10 to 13 May 1984. The Prime Minister and his Minister of Foreign Affairs were enthusiastic about this new initiative – something I could not explain. When Shipanga of SWAPO-D and Katjiuongua of SWANU – two fierce opponents of ethnicity – joined in, the chances of the proponents of ethnicity succeeding in their objective seemed to have become exceedingly small. The South African leaders were probably satisfied that the DTA's position, which they had written off as a factor to be reckoned with in future elections, were by now sufficiently weakened. The eventual result of the election in 1989 proved the opposite. I will deal with that delight later.

In their enthusiasm for the visit to Lusaka to be extended to further destinations, the South African Government made a Boeing available for our trip. This was no doubt less expensive than transporting this large delegation on scheduled flights. Upon arrival in Lusaka, we were entertained by President Kaunda at a reception with Sam Nujoma and other SWAPO leaders. While watching traditional dances, a concerted effort was made to photograph me in the company of Nujoma and Kaunda. However, the next morning when seated in the conference hall, Eben van Zijl and I were insulted and made scapegoats. Sam Nujoma accused us of taking advantage of black labour in order to become millionaires, and that we had blood on our hands and would pay with blood. I was on the point of telling him in no uncertain terms what I thought of his remarks when Andreas Shipanga stopped me, imploring me to calm down. This was how a second amateurish attempt to engineer reconciliation with SWAPO came to an end. During a break, Libertine Amadhila let it slip that she wished to return to her country. This made me realise that personal and private conversations with SWAPO members could be more fruitful than exchanges at such formal gatherings.

We departed from Lusaka to various other African countries – Gabon, Togo, the Ivory Coast and Senegal – where we had deliberations with presidents Houphouët-Boigny of the Ivory Coast and Eyadéma of Togo. We then flew to the USA where we arranged meetings with the Secretary General of the UN, Dr Javier Pérez de Cuéllar, the American Minister of Foreign Affairs, George Schultz, Chester Crocker and a few other senators and members of Congress. We then flew to London where nothing much happened, and then on to Germany. We were well received there and were granted an interview with Hans-Dietrich Genscher, the Minister of Foreign Affairs. We were also given the opportunity to shake hands with Chancellor Helmut Kohl.

When we arrived back in Windhoek, a large number of supporters were waiting to welcome us. At a well-attended meeting in Katutura, the MPC leaders were given the opportunity to report on their "successful trip" and their various deliberations. Unfortunately, my colleagues did not realise that we had been well received because we were a group of local political leaders and not an interim government. Previously, and also afterwards, no foreign government was prepared to have talks with any "illegal government" of South West Africa.

The MPC leaders, however, were under the impression that the events had paved the road towards an interim government and insisted on the establishment of such a government. Dr Van Niekerk accordingly departed to Cape Town to convey this wish to the Prime Minister. I was apparently once again the stumbling block. Dr Van Niekerk telephoned me the next day to inform me that the Prime Minister was prepared to grant an audience to the MPC leaders on condition that I apologise to the Prime Minister for having repudiated him. I thought that Dr Willie was joking, but he assured me that P.W. Botha insisted on an apology. I wanted to know what this had to do with the formation of an interim government, that surely it was a personal matter between myself and the Prime Minister, a matter in which my colleagues were not involved. I was simply not prepared to accept this condition.

Dr Willie ended the conversation with words to the effect that I knew what I had to do. I informed my colleagues about the appointment, telling them about the condition and commenting that I found it difficult to believe that the Prime Minister of a country could be so petty. I persisted in my refusal to apologise. As could have been expected, they pleaded with me not to jeopardise the possibility of our achieving self-rule. They were aware of the fact that I was not that enthusiastic about another interim government. I still remember Andreas Shipanga saying: "I have never ruled a fly in my life and now you want to bugger up my first opportunity to rule." Hence we departed for South Africa to ask for an interim government. I was convinced an interim government was exactly what P.W. Botha wanted, albeit on a constitutional basis that he would dictate.

When we arrived at the Prime Minister's office we formed a long line to greet him. I was right at the back. Dr Willie did the introductions and when it was my turn, took me by the arm, saying to the Prime Minister that I "had something to say to him", expecting that I would apologise. I was not prepared to be intimidated, but realised I had to say something. Because I couldn't think of anything quickly, I apologised for our having arrived so late. I will never forget the expression on P.W.'s face. It was one of shock and surprise. A political youngster had dared challenge him for the third time. I looked at my colleagues, Pik Botha, and the other high-ranking officials watching us. The expressions on their faces, which amounted to shock and disbelief and fear that I would once again be the cause of a deadlock, were almost beyond description. They were all looking at me pleadingly, as if imploring me not to be so stubborn – which I was, to be honest.

P.W. started the negotiations on a challenging note, saying that he didn't have much time. I cannot recall everything he said. I had to quickly find a way out of this current predicament. Without referring to the so-called repudiation, I merely said that there had apparently been a few misunderstandings which were now delaying our progress, and if I were to blame for them, I was sorry. P.W. Botha responded immediately by saying: "Since Mr Mudge has now apologised ... we (can) continue with our deliberations." I could see the relief on my colleagues' faces. And so the road to the next interim government was back on track.

The last round: The TGNU, myself and Louis Pienaar

The new Transitional Government of National Unity (TGNU) was inaugurated on 17 June 1984 by Prime Minister P.W. Botha, in terms of Proclamation R.101. The proclamation was based primarily on principles on which unanimity had been reached in broad terms on 25 March in a so-called Cape Town Agreement. Afterwards there were differences of opinion about the stipulations and interpretation of this agreement. In compliance with Proclamation R.101, the National Assembly would consist of 62 members, of which 22 were awarded to the DTA and eight to each of the other five parties. In the Cabinet the DTA were assigned five members and each of the other parties one member. The chairmanship would rotate every two months, David Bezuidenhout being the first Chairman. I was assigned the portfolios of finance and governmental affairs. The DTA found itself, as was the case with the Multi-Party Conference, in a minority position.

Two weeks after the establishment of the TGNU, Adv. Louis Pienaar took over as Administrator General from Willie van Niekerk. Dr Gerrit Viljoen had established representative authorities, Dr Van Niekerk had instituted an interim central authority in accordance with P.W. Botha's requirements and now – although his powers were not the same as those of his predecessors – it was Adv. Pienaar's responsibility to keep an eye on the new rulers.

The belief that this short-sighted experiment would contribute in any way towards strengthening an anti-SWAPO front was subsequently proven to be wrong. The debates of the National Assembly were soon characterised by attempts by newcomers Moses Katjiuongua and Andreas Shipanga to have Proclamation AG. 8 – which made provision for representative authorities – revoked, with the National Party representative resisting strongly. While the DTA's viewpoint was that R.101 made such a course of action impossible, we were of the opinion that the powers and functions of these authorities should be limited to matters which affected population groups in particular, and that the unfair allocation of state income should be revised.

The method of dividing assets and sources of income was unjust and indefensible. While the white representative authority had millions in investments, and on top of this earned a large income from the personal tax the whites were paying, the other representative authorities had no reserves and only a minimal income, due mainly to the fact that members of their population groups fell into lower income brackets. The contribution made by these population groups to the economy of the country and the profits made by whites, was often underestimated. The argument that personal tax paid by whites should rightfully go to their Representative Authority did not hold water, neither did the perception that the benefits gained by individuals from tax money was proportionate to the tax they were paying. Individuals paying the lowest or no taxes, often benefit the most from tax income.

In the meantime we took cognisance of the fact that in South Africa important political changes were also taking place. As a result of international pressure and the internal demand a democratic political dispensation was also being sought there. In 1983, the National Party (NP) Government introduced an amendment to the South African Constitution to create a new structure of Parliament. The new Tricameral Parliament would consist of three Parliamentary chambers:

- The House of Assembly (white representatives)
- The House of Representatives (coloured representatives)
- The House of Delegates (Indian representatives)

Voters on separate ethnic voter's roles would elect the members of each chamber of Parliament. Each House would furthermore have jurisdiction over matters such as health and education, relevant to the community it represents. Under the new Constitution, a new presidential cabinet system would also be introduced. The most important criticism against the proposed Tricameral Parliament was that the black majority was excluded from the entire process. The NP Government argued that blacks did not qualify for representation in Parliament, because they already had political rights in their respective homelands, and that greater political rights were extended to coloured and Indian people because they did not have their own homelands in which to exercise such rights.

When this far-reaching bill was introduced I recalled the conversation I had with P.W. Botha in 1979 when he indicated that the coloured people might be placed back onto the common voters' roll and the question came up why did it take so long? To me it became more evident that P.W. Botha first wanted to experiment with constitutional models in South West Africa.

In South West Africa/Namibia Adv. Pienaar continually took issue with the impingement on the powers and competencies of the representative authorities, and attacked me personally. After Namibia had become independent, At van Wyk, author of *Reënmaker van die Namib*, through personal conversations with Adv. Pienaar and by delving into documents in the archives, came across letters and reports to President Botha in which I was depicted in a very bad light. I would probably never have known about these if it had not been for At van Wyk's research. I owe him a great deal for the insights they provided. Without them my book would not have told such a complete story. Adv. Pienaar had written in letters and reports to the President that I was unpopular in the DTA as a result of my "domineering style" and exceedingly "autocratic behaviour". He claimed that people were already talking about the "post-Mudge era" and about my "demagogic pronunciations" as "main beater of the popular drum" of independence.

A new "phenomenon" on the local scene, Gert Petzer of the Department of Foreign Affairs, warned the President that Jan Greebe, Executive Officer in the Administrator General's office, could favour the DTA and suggested that the Administrator General warn him accordingly. Petzer was one of several South African representatives who was sent to meddle in our local politics. On occasion he expressed the opinion that the ideal outcome of the forthcoming election would be for SWAPO to win, but not with a two-thirds majority. All of this indicated that Petzer and Pik Botha were playing an important role in polishing Peter Kalangula's image. It also emerged that bugging devices had been placed in my and other offices. The Administrator General had nothing positive to say about the DTA, writing that "the DTA wants to demonstrate its independence from South Africa like an adolescent child." He took this further by referring to my "Mudgian Logic" and "Mudgian confusing statements" on minorities and majorities.

One of the few achievements of the TGNU was establishing a Constitutional Committee under chairmanship of former Judge Victor Hiemstra. The DTA, which had been working on legislative models for the past ten years, was able to play a leading role. The final draft was approved by the Committee on 12 July 1987 with a majority vote. The National Party and Rehoboth Free Democratic Party, each with two members, voted against the draft. Because of the dominant role the DTA played in compiling it, the Alliance accepted the Hiemstra draft as its own. It was this draft that the DTA submitted as its proposal to the elected Legislative Assembly in November 1989. The draft constitution ditched ethnic second-tier authorities completely. This meant that the National Party found itself in a much weaker position as was the case under the previous government, which they wanted to get rid of at all costs. Adv. Pienaar advised President Botha to prevent the TGNU from publishing the Committee's draft constitution under the auspices of former Judge Hiemstra "because it did not make provision for the protection of minorities".

During the term of the TGNU, the Administrator General and I were at loggerheads regularly. On 29 April 1987, at the opening of a show in Grootfontein, he claimed that the TGNU was not representative of the population, since it had been instated through a process in which 70% of the population had not been involved. He should have addressed this to his Government, which had instated the TGNU in the first place. The Government that had been established on the strength of a one-person-one-vote election ten years earlier, had been dissolved by his Government on the basis that it was not representative. Adv. Pienaar was a fine one to talk about logic!

The TGNU attempted to have a new Public Holidays Act signed by the Administrator General. This attempt failed when P.W. Botha instructed him not to sign the bill before he himself had discussed it with the Namibian Cabinet. He added: "I think the South Westers will have to decide for themselves whether they still need the protective hand of the Republic of South Africa, or whether they want to find their own way to wherever this may be." According to At van Wyk these last words had been underlined in the document in pencil, with a side note in the margin: "Send them to ...?"

I was not privy to this background information, but on various occasions I criticised the South African Government severely for attempting to force their policy down our throats. The Administrator General replied that my behaviour was that of "an adolescent boy who wanted his father's car but didn't want to be told that he had to drive carefully". He continued, saying that the people of Namibia, "... in the final analysis, when the time has come to walk the home stretch to independence, will be at liberty to decide about their future themselves." This did not make sense. We were already in the home stretch towards an election in terms of Resolution 435, but were still expected to apply the South African policy of racial discrimination for the sake of the rightist elements in South Africa. Could we be expected to fight an election against SWAPO carrying this baggage? I was being challenged and pushed to the limit once again. According to Adv. Pienaar's letters to President Botha, he had learnt from Jan de Wet that my colleagues were worried about me eliciting a confrontation, which could lead to the Government being dissolved. I was expected to stay "out of the firing line". The TGNU's inflexibility motivated President Botha to play his last trump card. He cut South Africa's contribution to the Namibian budget by R200 million, causing even the AG to protest.

Meeting with Eben van Zijl again

Eben van Zijl in the meantime started crossing swords with the National Party. In 1987 he wrote a long letter to the National Party Congress detailing his dissatisfaction with the Party. He already implied in speeches that he was contemplating the possibility of a quick election in terms of Resolution 435. In addition, the moderate attitude he was taking towards certain discriminatory measures raised questions and suspicion from members of the National Party. He subsequently resigned as NP representative from the Cabinet of the TGNU, to be succeeded by Jan de Wet.

After his resignation from the National Party, he established an organisation under the name Aksie Nasionale Stigting (ANS) (Action National Foundation). He widened its base by forming an election front – the National Patriotic Front – with Moses Katjiuongua (SWANU) and the Caprivi African National Union (CANU), as he had attempted to do ten years before, following my resignation as a member of the National Party. He then indicated that the NPF would be prepared to merge with the DTA, on condition that the DTA give up its name, colours and symbols. This was really expecting too much. It was rather like the story of the butcher who made a chicken pie by using one chicken and one horse. The final election results with the NPF winning only one seat compared to the DTA's 21 proved that there was no market for Eben's chicken pie. Needless to say, his proposal was unacceptable to me as well as the DTA. It was often said that Eben and I would have made a formidable team, but Eben never was prepared to accept my seniority, which had already become apparent during the National Party Congress of 1969.

The beginning of the end of the National Party

Although my struggle with the National Party became ever less relevant as time went by and I no longer was a member of the white Legislative Assembly (where politics were still running riot), I never felt entirely distanced from it. In the Legislative Assembly, the Republican Party, of which I was leader, was the opposition, and what transpired there affected me personally. Time was catching up with the NP – South West Africa was unequivocally on a rollercoaster towards independence.

Right from the start of the Legislative Assembly session from 10 to 13 March 1987, it was perfectly clear that there were significant differences of opinion among the members of the National Party. Frequent reference was made to the caucus meetings of the previous day, confirming that party members were already on a collision course. The resignation of Eben van Zijl from the Party, and shortly afterwards that of his brother Frans from the Executive Committee (albeit not from the Party itself), were probably primary causes of the tension among National Party ranks. Frans van Zyl's resignation from the Executive Committee was no big surprise. I have already pointed to the fact that Frans was level-headed, and that in his speeches and actions he demonstrated a dislike of offensive, discriminatory measures. Several years before his resignation, he chaired a committee that made recommendations for the removal of unnecessary discriminating practices. Ironically enough, his brother Eben did not then agree with him.

The motions tabled during the session of the Legislative Assembly on 12 and 13 March and the ensuing debates, led to absolute consternation. Four members of the National Party – Koos Pretorius, Jan de Wet, Willem Odendaal and Frans van Zyl – each had their own story. Their speeches were all over the place, overlapping here and there and ending in an outright confrontation between Koos Pretorius and Frans van Zyl. The Republican Party members, especially Abraham Davids, Hans Staby and the obstreperous Paul Minnaar, did not make it any easier for them.

Koos was the first to present his motion. He expressed concern about certain attempts "to curb the democratic functioning of the representative authorities and especially the Legislative Assembly of the Whites ..."

Fanie Vilonel let the cat out of the bag in his first sentence by explaining that – following the discussions in the caucus – he would not take part in the discussion of Koos's motion because it could create the impression "that he would be breaking his word to the caucus". His short speech gave the impression of someone who had something to say but couldn't find the appropriate words. He declared: "The time has now come for us to try and reach consensus behind closed doors." Who the "us" were, nobody knew. It was clear that he was referring to the differences of opinion expressed in the caucus. He mentioned the amendments and efforts to clarify each other's beliefs; that "we" should not be unshakeable in our viewpoints; that this would not be in the interest of the whites in our country and would only make it more difficult to meet each other halfway; and that, to his mind, this would be wrong.

Koos's motion was approved by majority vote. Then Jan de Wet unexpectedly proposed a motion:

> ... that this Assembly reconciles itself with and commits itself to the previous agreements as set out in R.101 and the Charter of Fundamental Rights, as well as in the Constitutional Act that gave the necessary powers to and prescribed the procedures on how South West Africa would be governed by the TGNU and how to proceed with the constitutional process.

Jan de Wet's motion was an utter contradiction of Koos's motion. Koos was highly critical of R.101 and the TGNU, while Jan de Wet wanted the Legislative Assembly to accept it.

Frans van Zyl, who had resigned from the Executive Committee shortly before, proposed a motion that, due to its importance, I quote here in full:

> That this House takes cognisance of:
> (a) the Charter of Fundamental Rights as contained in Proclama-
>   tion R.101 of 1985 as well as the objective of this proclama-
>   tion in terms of which current legislation must be aligned
>   with the stipulations of said Charter; and
> (b) the understanding that member parties in the Government
>   of National Unity had reached as regards education, namely
>   that schools in the country would be open to any prospective
>   pupil in accordance with the terms of said Charter, regard-
>   less of race or colour.

The Legislative Assembly accepted Frans van Zyl's motion by major-ity vote. The seven members of the Republican Party – Davids, Greeff, Wolff, Staby, Frank, Schneider-Waterberg and Minnaar – agreed with Van Zyl, Blaauw and Vilonel on this motion. Pretorius, De Wet, Oden-daal, Potgieter, Brand, Schwartz and Verster voted for Koos's amend-ment. This was indeed an historic occasion. A bell tolled once again – this time announcing the funeral of the National Party.

The home stretch to independence

While we were haggling over short-term issues, important events were taking place on the international and military fronts. In spite of his involvement in the establishment of a transitional government, Presi-dent Botha announced that he still regarded himself as committed to the implementation of Resolution 435 – as soon as the Cuban troops had been withdrawn from Angola. While we were in the process of setting up a transitional government, the war in Angola escalated in intensity and extent as a result of ever-more sophisticated weaponry. We were aware of the unrelenting military operations carried out by the SADF in Angola, no doubt at great expense to South Africa, which was probably the reason why President Botha held us responsible for the burden on the South African taxpayers.

In the same year the American Senate revoked the Clark Amend-ment, which stopped South Africa's advance, assisted by the Ameri-cans, to Luanda. America could now take part in covert operations in Angola. This proved that South Africa wasn't the only country concerned about the presence of Cuban and Russian troops in Angola. Chester Crocker unremittedly continued to convince the countries involved of the necessity of the withdrawal of Cuban troops.

The change of policy in Russia under the leadership of Mikhail Gorbachev gave new momentum to Crocker's attempts to put an end to the Cuban presence in Angola. It was generally accepted that Gorbachev's political U-turn was the result of economic problems emanating from the failure of communism in his country. He could simply not ignore the financial burden Russia's involvement in Angola was putting on his country. The same problems were being faced by other countries involved. The price that Cuba was paying in terms of human lives and military expenses must have been considerable. Moreover, the Angolan Government could hardly afford to repay these countries for the aid they were providing. Once again, and probably as could be expected, our local leaders were not involved in these developments. Afterwards we heard for the first time through the media of the Geneva Protocol that had been signed on 5 August 1988 by America, Russia, Cuba and South Africa, whereby it was agreed in principle that the Cuban troops be withdrawn from Angola.

I was still faced with the problem that we had to prepare ourselves for an election while having no idea when this would take place. I often compared this to an athlete expecting to compete in a 100-metre race, but then having to run a marathon. The DTA had been preparing for an election campaign from as far back as the acceptance of the Western settlement plan, and having already spent a considerable part of our available funds, the DTA would possibly run out of funds before the race had even started. When the South African Government did actually speak to us, it was about broadening the base of interim governments and protecting minority rights as if there were no prospect of an election. We were prevented from making meaningful changes that could strengthen our chances in an election. Moreover, we didn't always know whether the South African Government intended allowing an election to take place at all.

The election is announced

On 22 December 1988, in terms of the New York Accord between South Africa, Angola and Cuba, it was finally agreed that Cuban troops would be withdrawn from Angola. This paved the way for the implementation of Resolution 435 and enabled the Security Council to announce on 16 January 1989 (my 61st birthday) that the implementation date would be 1 April. All the stumbling blocks had now been removed, allowing South Africa to dissolve the Transitional Government of National Unity (TGNU) on 1 March. In accordance with the agreement reached between South Africa and the Western countries the Administrator General, Louis Pienaar, took over all the governmental functions at national level and the supervision of the electoral process in cooperation with the UN Commissioner Martti Ahtisaari. Ahtisaari was instructed to make arrangements for implementing the envisaged ceasefire agreement. The dates on which the election of a Constituent Assembly would take place were set for 7 to 11 November 1989. The task of this Assembly would be to write and adopt a constitution for an independent Namibia and to determine a date for independence. In doing so, a winning post had finally been determined and the Western proposals, which had been accepted by South Africa and the internal parties no less than ten years ago, were implemented.

The last election for whites

One would expect that by now all parties concerned would be preparing themselves for the determining election. However, the Legislative Assembly for Whites had other plans. They wanted an election, or at least an extension of their term of office, which would have expired soon. What they wanted to achieve I will never comprehend. One can only guess.

On 1 March 1989, the TGNU was dissolved and on the same day a white Legislative Assembly was elected. My father would have asked: "To do what?" It would have been a relevant question at the time, since we were already involved in an election struggle with SWAPO. The National Party and the Administrator General still had an obsession with second-tier authorities and were determined to retain the discriminatory measures, including exclusively white schools until we had become independent.

The Republican Party, a member party of the DTA, did not participate in the white election. Consequently, the election struggle degenerated into a fight between the National Party and the Herstigte Nasionale Party (HNP). It was ridiculous in the extreme for two right-wing groups to be waging a political war against each other while an election against SWAPO was imminent. The Administrator's advice to the President that a strong white second-tier government could strengthen the National Party's chances in the election was nothing short of wishful thinking. At the same time Jan de Wet warned that second-tier authorities could not be dismantled without their support and cooperation. The naivety of Koos Pretorius and the National Party in their belief that a strong white pressure group – which they did not have – could have an influence on the pending election and writing of a constitution was beyond my comprehension. Administrator General Louis Pienaar, however, supported the National Party's viewpoint, maintaining his stance that the second-tier authorities would continue to exist, retaining all their powers and competencies until independence.

The establishment of UNTAG

The announcement that Resolution 435, concomitant with a ceasefire, would become operational on 1 April 1989 caught the internal parties, with the exception of the DTA, unawares. Apparently the organisers of the United Nations Transitional Assistance Group (UNTAG) were also not prepared for this. We had heard much about this strong and powerful UN peace force, but were surprised to see so few of them when having meetings in Owambo. Because we had been conducting our political campaigns in the operational area under circumstances that were unsafe for so long, we were looking forward to an appropriate management of the security situation. I was, as would subsequently be confirmed, on SWAPO's hit list and some of our leaders and members had already paid the highest price.

During talks with the Western Contact Group and Chester Crocker, we had learnt that UNTAG would consist of a military component of between 4000 and 5000 men, a police force of 500 and an administrative corps of 1200. The total cost of the operation would amount to over R2 billion. For an estimated population of some 1,5 million people, it was probably one of the most expensive elections per voter that had ever been held in Africa, if not the world. What it came down to was that one member of UNTAG would be present for every 100 voters. The question was often asked why a solution for the Namibian issue was so important to the international community that its members were prepared to splurge so much money and manpower to resolve it. One answer is probably that racism and communism could lead to war in Africa. Whether Namibia was the only threat in this respect is of course debatable.

The deployment of UNTAG took longer than had been expected. On D-Day only about 1000 members of UNTAG's military component were deployed in Namibia. Martti Ahtisaari, the Secretary General's Special Representative who would be heading UNTAG, arrived at Windhoek Airport – 35 km east of the capital where thousands of SWAPO and DTA supporters were waiting to welcome him – only shortly before the implementation date. It was crucial for the DTA to prove that Ahtisaari was not supposed to be a SWAPO ally. DTA supporters, coming from as far afield as Kaokoland, gathered in and around a large tent near the airport. The next morning the large number of hopeful enthusiasts took up their positions next to the entry road to the airport; SWAPO on one side of the road, and the DTA on the other. Colourfully decked out DTA supporters on horseback rode up and down the road waving flags. Some of my colleagues and I walked up and down between the two rows of supporters. I can still see Bokkie Kolver, a friend and someone on whom I could always rely, waving a large flag with a broad smile on his face. In the election campaign that followed, nothing was ever too much for him to take on.

I speak to Koevoet

I never involved myself in military matters and gained much of my information in this field only after independence. During the demobilisation of the South African forces, which included the demobilisation of local territorial units such as Koevoet, I received an unexpected call from the military headquarters in Oshakati asking me to come and assist them in solving a sensitive problem. I was surprised, because I wasn't used to the Defence Force asking advice from politicians. To be honest, the Defence Force, even at the highest levels, described the internal political struggle in South West Africa as "*boeresport*". I don't think they ever, or even wanted to, understood what it was all about. The local political initiatives ultimately played a decisive role in finding a political solution, but was neither acknowledged nor appreciated by Jannie Geldenhuys and Magnus Malan in the voluminous books they wrote on the topic afterwards. It was also not recognised by historians in South Africa. Were it not for Max du Preez and a few other media sources, few people in South Africa would have known what happened in the political arena locally.

I suppose we should accept that it was a great disappointment to the Defence Force when the war eventually, as my half-English grandfather Dick would have put it, ended in a draw. Could one articulate it in cricket terminology as having been suspended due to "poor light conditions"? I was and still am convinced that the Defence Force was in control of the match at that point. I repeat what I have already said several times, namely that I owe a great deal of gratitude to the SADF and the local military units for preventing our country from turning into a battlefield. If they had not done this, I might well not have been here to write this book. Seen in a different light, the battle front might have moved south to the Orange River, and Walvis Bay could have become a Russian-controlled harbour. What was described locally as "*boeresport*" probably also contributed to the political developments that took place in South Africa shortly afterwards. Unfortunately, as Frans van Zyl put it, the politicians in South Africa only started getting dressed when the church bell had already rung.

Back to the call from Oshakati. When I arrived there I was informed that the Defence Force was having problems with the demobilisation of the local units, especially Koevoet. These men had been trained as soldiers over many years and would find it difficult to adapt to life in a civil society. In addition, no one could predict what the new Government's attitude would be towards members of Koevoet. The townspeople at Oshakati wanted to know whether I could involve the Koevoet members in politics. I did not think it would be possible, but I was prepared to talk to them and a meeting was arranged.

When I arrived at the meeting the hall was packed – white and black intermingled. The expressions on their faces were bleak and the tension was palpable. Although this was not my responsibility, I explained to them why their unit was being disbanded and that we had to talk about the road ahead. They apparently understood, but there was another problem. The white members of Koevoet were the first to speak and were emotional. Their concern was that when they as South Africans returned to South Africa, they would have no idea what was to become of their black "buddies". One after the other they insisted that their "buddies" should be allowed to go back to South Africa with them. I found this moving and also impressive. Whatever and whoever were responsible for their involvement in the armed struggle, this group of men were not fighting against black people, but against a common enemy. This was how they saw it, whether I agreed with it or not. I could identify with their concerns but explained that I was not in a position to make any decisions. I could merely try to involve them locally in one way or another. I proposed that where until then they had fought against SWAPO as armed soldiers, they had to now rather participate peacefully in the approaching political struggle, and that I would help where I could. While the white members of the unit were noticeably unhappy about this, it did seem as if the rest of them accepted it.

My proposal was tested for the first time shortly after that. One of our organisers was murdered in Ovamboland and I travelled to the north to attend his funeral. We walked to the cemetery in a long procession, with the crowd behind us growing ever larger as we slowly moved forward. While we were walking, I became increasingly uneasy about the mood of the crowd behind me. At the graveside they quietened down and the service could proceed. After the pastor said "Amen" we heard loud explosions and saw clouds of smoke rising from a clump of trees in the middle of a mahangu field. In the meantime a police vehicle was driving from town towards the smoke, and that's when the problems started. When a large number of the funeral attendees began running in the direction of the smoke, I suspected that the people responsible for the explosions were former members of Koevoet. They were probably using hand grenades they'd not returned after being demobilised. I also realised that a large section of those attending the funeral were former members of Koevoet. The police only had time to pick up one of the people responsible for the explosion when they realised that the crowd was turning on them. In their attempt to pick up a second culprit, they were in such a hurry to get away that they dragged him behind the moving vehicle for some distance before they could haul him inside.

This was not the end of the story. While the police vehicle was racing off, two UNTAG members approached in a white Land Cruiser. The two unsuspecting "blue helmets" in the Land Cruiser became the crowd's next target. By that time I had caught up with the running horde of people, but they ignored my appeals to turn back. I was exhausted, I wasn't accustomed to running through a mahangu field dressed in a suit. I had to look on resignedly while they slashed the tyres of the vehicle using pangas. When the Land Cruiser took off, it was obvious that there was something wrong with its wheels. Although the supposition was that all weapons and ammunition were handed in and kept under control, some of the former Koevoet members had obviously kept hold of a supply of hand grenades. I then realised that it would not be easy to turn soldiers into political organisers.

An unnecessary human massacre on 1 April 1989

The ceasefire agreement was to be implemented on 1 April 1989. Demobilisation entailed that South African units would be limited to bases within the Territory and SWAPO forces to bases in Angola. Unarmed SWAPO expatriates and members of SWAPO's previously armed forces could return to Namibia. Early on the morning of 1 April, in total violation of all the conditions that had been agreed upon before the time, 1600 heavily armed SWAPO combatants crossed the border at various places. It was subsequently established from UNTAG sources that Sam Nujoma had instructed his military units to cross the border, having brought them under the impression that they would not meet with any resistance. It is possible that he actually believed there would be no resistance, since the South African Territorial Forces were restricted to their bases. It was abundantly clear, however, that Nujoma wanted to prove that SWAPO had achieved a military victory at all costs. His earlier insistence that his units be based at designated locations in Namibia before the election, made it obvious that SWAPO wanted to convince the uninformed population that the organisation had already had fixed bases in Namibia during the war, which was not the case.

In his last attempt to create the impression that SWAPO had achieved a military victory, Nujoma was sending his unsuspecting fighters to their graves. They walked into a police unit that was patrolling the border. The police unit was soon supported by a redeployment of Defence Force members. A total of 300 SWAPO fighters and 26 members of the Defence Force lost their lives in skirmishes that were fought over a period of more or less a week. The Security Council and Ahtisaari found themselves in a difficult position. Ahtisaari had no choice other than to allow the redeployment of the Defence Force units, which he did with the approval of the Secretary General of the UN. As can be expected, this elicited sharp criticism. What had come to pass also indicated that the slow deployment of UNTAG was the reason they were unable to take effective action. It was only after this tragedy that UN-TAG's numbers were increased to 8000, of which 6000 comprised the military component.

By coincidence, Margaret Thatcher, the then British Prime Minister, was in South Africa at the time. Chester Crocker described her presence on the scene as a "superbly appropriate coincidence". She had obviously come to Namibia to establish for herself what was happening at the border. There is no doubt that her presence strengthened Ahtisaari in his actions. SWAPO maintained consistently afterwards that it was not responsible for the slaughter. After the election, Theo-Ben Gurirab remarked to At van Wyk that it was a "Pik Botha fabrication" and that Pik was not exactly scrupulous when it came to the evidence in front of him. However, it was also clear that Gurirab was not exactly scrupulous about the truth either.

The Mount Etjo Conference

The violation of the ceasefire agreement by SWAPO brought the further implementation of Resolution 435 to a halt. The election process could only be put back on track after a Joint Committee, consisting of representatives from South Africa, the United States, Russia, Cuba and Angola had convened on Mount Etjo – a farm bordering ours – from 9 to 11 April 1989. The agreement reached determined that SWAPO fighters would have the choice to either return to bases in Angola or be restricted to camps in the north under UNTAG's supervision. Most of them chose to return to Angola. After that the Defence Force and Territorial Force were also to be confined to their bases.

During May 1989 peaceful circumstances were restored to such an extent that the election process could continue. I was able to lay my hands on a great deal of interesting information about the Conference, since it happened on our neighbouring farm. Apparently it wasn't all work, they took regular breaks to relax, some more so than others. About this, the less said the better.

How does one fight an election without funds?

The election campaign could now begin. Although the DTA had been politically active since its foundation, we had to spend a great deal of time and money to convince inflexible elements in our country that a

UN-supervised election was unavoidable. This time, however, we had to deal with our actual political opponent, SWAPO. If SWAPO were to win the election with more than two-thirds of the votes, it would for all practical purposes be in a position to force its constitutional proposals on us. While it would have been unrealistic of us to expect to defeat SWAPO, we had to win more than a third of the votes at all cost.

The fact that we had to take SWAPO on with a seriously divided opposition weakened our chances of reaching our goal. Ten parties registered to take part in the election, namely Aksie Christelik-Nasion-aal (ACN), Christian Democratic Action (CDA), Democratic Turnhalle Alliance of Namibia (DTA), Federal Convention of Namibia (FCN), Namibia National Democratic Party (NNDP), Namibia National Front (NNF), National Patriotic Front (NPF), SWAPO Democrats (SWAPO-D), South West Africa Peoples' Organisation of Namibia (SWAPO) and the United Democratic Front (UDF). The National Party conspicuously did not take part under its own name, but was registered as Aksie Christelik-Nasionaal. At a later stage Koos Pretorius tried to explain why, saying Jan de Wet believed the National Party would not do well under its existing name, and neither would they receive financial support. The name was changed to Aksie Christelik-Nasionaal. According to Pretorius it was decided that Jan de Wet would take over as leader until after the election when the leadership would revert to him. Not only was the opposition fractured; there was also division within the National Party itself. It was not the end of the feud between Pretorius and De Wet.

In the DTA our main problem was to obtain the necessary financial resources and infrastructure to fight an election against SWAPO. We knew that SWAPO would receive financial support from a large number of countries from all over the globe, something that we, due to our history, could not expect. The international community as represented by the UN still incorrectly regarded the DTA as a South African ally.

It became clear right from the outset that it was expected that I would be responsible for the fundraising. In the preceding decade, the DTA had been financially dependent on funds from the SWAMEX Trust, which I had founded during the Turnhalle Conference to propagate the Turnhalle message to the population. My two white colleagues at the time did not favour joint meetings with black people. SWAMEX Trust started the ball rolling with donations collected by two good friends of mine: Piet Malherbe (a partner in the local audit firm P.J. Malherbe & Co.) and A.P. du Preez (of Nuwe Westelike Beleggings – New Western Investments). With the approaching elections in mind, this was a mere drop in the ocean, but I will always remember these two friends for their moral and financial support.

By now finding funds for the election campaign had become a matter of urgency, so I decided to visit contacts I had made in South Africa in earlier years. Since I had broken away from the National Party and especially after the DTA was established, we had been given a fair amount of publicity by the South African media and, among other things, were invited to address South African chambers of commerce whose principals were interested in learning more about what we were doing here. I visited the capitals of all four provinces in South Africa to have talks with businessmen. The response was positive, but the contributions not much to speak of. They were used to the amounts normally donated to political parties in South Africa at a provincial level, and could probably not envisage the extent and importance of our election here.

A letter the Administrator General wrote to President P.W. Botha during the election campaign informing him that the DTA had hired vehicles and appointed organisers with a funding of R2 million, and in so doing set an example for others, bears testimony to the fact that we employed the funds we had at our disposal responsibly. What he didn't realise, however, was that the elections would have been easier and less expensive for the country if the DTA had been allowed to put its policy into practice during the period it was governing the country.

I then had an idea. We *could* ask the South African Government for funding, since after all was said and done, we had resolved a most serious and never-ending problem for them by accepting independence and an election. Had this not transpired, they would have been faced with a long-drawn-out war at the cost of human lives and money. Had we not been able to fend off a two-thirds majority in the election, it would have created even more problems for South Africa. I asked the previous Administrator General, Dr Willie van Niekerk, to arrange a meeting for me with representatives of the South African Government. At that stage he was the coordinator between South Africa and Namibia. The meeting took place at a military base near Cape Town. The South African representatives consisted primarily of senior military officers and other senior officials, many of them unknown to me. I gave them a breakdown of everything I had done so far to raise money and informed them that the funds in the SWAMEX Trust were not nearly enough to fight an election against SWAPO. It would have been political suicide to take on an election against SWAPO with such limited funds. I pointed out that SWAPO would have South Africa's enemies of many years on their side, with ample financial means at their disposal.

The Administrator General pointed out that even if the South African Government were to approve my request, it would not be able to support the DTA financially, since it would then also have to support all the other participating parties. Needless to say, I could not fault this. Aiming high, I asked for R100 million for these parties. I realised that this would seem exorbitantly high for those who had taken part only in white elections in the past, but those of us who had participated in the one-person-one-vote election in 1978 knew better. The impending elections could not be compared to the 1978 elections in which SWAPO did not participate. This time the future of our country was at stake.

A short while after the meeting, Van Niekerk informed me that financial support had been approved in principle for all the internal parties, without mentioning any amounts. He emphasised further that this assistance would be subject to certain conditions. Money would not be paid over directly to political parties, but only to bodies acting as mediators. In the case of the DTA, amounts were paid from time to time into the SWAMEX Trust, which was controlled jointly by the auditing firm P.J. Malherbe & Co. and the South African Treasury. The Trust could only disburse funds to the DTA when backed by budgets submitted to the Secretariat of the DTA on a monthly basis. Initially, I did not know to whom the funds for the other parties would be paid, but I heard later that a foundation, controlled by a general of the South African Security Police handled these contributions. Koos Pretorius and the leaders of other parties were probably not aware that I had negotiated this financial support for them. How much money the other parties received from South Africa I do not know. In the ensuing months the SWAMEX Trust received about R60 million, although not all of it came from South Africa.

The strict control over the financial support to the political parties referred to above was to be expected, since political parties do not have a good reputation when it comes to handling money and assets.

Large amounts were at stake, and I had to protect myself. For that reason I never accepted a salary from a political party in all the years I was involved. Neither was I given a vehicle by the DTA but used my own vehicle and aircraft without compensation whatsoever, while my DTA colleagues received vehicles and travel and accommodation allowances. SWAMEX Trust paid funds directly to the DTA Secretariat, which was managed by Johan de Waal. I had no signing powers and never handled any money. The donations that I had negotiated were paid into the SWAMEX Trust account without fail.

The reason for this detailed explanation will emerge as my story unfolds. The maxim that money is the root of all evil was borne out later by the activities within the DTA. I never disclosed the names of our donors – not even to my DTA colleagues – because sooner or later such details would most certainly have been leaked. I was also not sure how my colleagues would feel about so much of our funding coming from South Africa, and whether this could possibly have made them feel that they now had to dance to South Africa's tune. I knew I was running a great risk, but the fact that an auditor's firm was managing the Trust set my mind at rest. After all, no one really knew where SWAPO's money was coming from. In fact, I even wondered whether SWAPO wasn't also receiving financial support from the South African Government. This might sound far-fetched, but I knew from experience that there was no end to the schemes of the South African Government and especially Pik Botha. Surely they knew by then that SWAPO would in all probability become the ruler of their neighbouring country.

I already pointed out that the Republican Party had since the 1980 election for members of the white Legislative Assembly not taken part in elections under its own name, but as a member party of the DTA it had put its full weight behind the Alliance. However, the Republican Party did not cease to exist. The RP Executive decided that it should become dormant and left it to me to reactivate it, should this become necessary in the future. In the meantime my colleagues and I continued working for the DTA without remuneration, collecting donations for the Party from our members. The biggest contribution the RP made was through our newspaper, *Republikein*, which had been established entirely by the RP and was maintained as the mouthpiece of the DTA, thanks to great sacrifice and support by the Republican Party. It goes without saying that the company Republikein (Pty) Limited had to incur large expenses at the onset of the election campaign. The Republican Party was as entitled to financial support as the other member parties, especially when taking into consideration that Jan Spies, the then editor of the newspaper, was one of our most energetic fundraisers. Financial statements in my possession, however, shows that when it came to funding, the Party and the *Republikein* had to make do with the short end of the stick.

The election campaign and intimidation

The time came for the election campaign to start in all earnest and it was a real adventure. The DTA held meetings in virtually every place on the map – from the Orange River in the south to the Zambezi River in East Caprivi. The experience we had gained in the one-person-one-vote election in the 1978 stood us in good stead. The meetings were held in large tents, community halls and black towns; sometimes on open plains during rain and dust storms; and under trees in Owambo, Kavango and Caprivi where we had to contend with the threat of landmines. Colourful processions, T-shirts, flags and banners were part and parcel of the campaign. In Katutura my colleagues and I were privileged to address crowds of up to 20 000 people, mostly black. I tried to speak at as many of the meetings as I possibly could, and feel both humble and grateful for the way I was received, often being the only white face in a throng of black people.

My colleagues often wanted to know why so few whites attended the meetings. As was the case in 1978, my answer was that black and coloured people, for obvious reasons, attended meetings and funerals only over weekends, while white people preferred to do so during the week. Over weekends whites liked to do sport or spend time with their family and friends and relax. For this reason we had to have two meetings in each town. Another reason for whites not attending DTA meetings was that these get-togethers often lasted from two in the afternoon until dark, since every speech had to be interpreted into different languages. Since most of our supporters had no transport, we had to transport them to the meetings and take them back home after dark.

The DTA meetings were not always peaceful. At Gibeon the SWAPO and DTA supporters threw stones at one another and in Ovamboland a fracas broke out in which the "blue helmets" of UNTAG also became involved. On one occasion, when driving back from a meeting in north-ern Ovamboland, we had to drive past one of the camps where return-ing SWAPO fighters had been assembled under UNTAG's supervision. A bus full of DTA supporters was driving ahead, while the leaders were following in a smaller bus. Directly opposite the SWAPO camp we saw the bus coming to a standstill diagonally across the road where a scuffle was taking place between our supporters and the SWAPO returnees. I jumped out and was trying to get the passengers back into the bus when a pale little UNTAG soldier started yelling at me, accus-ing our supporters of having started the fight. I completely lost my temper, took him to one of the windows of the microbus, which had been broken by the SWAPO members, and knocked his head against the window shouting: "If you can't see, smell!" Afterwards I was criti-cised by my colleagues for behaving irresponsibly. They were probably right. Nevertheless, I did manage to get our supporters back onto the bus and we were able to continue our journey. This would not be the last incidence of violence, intimidation and murder. The assassination of Anton Lubowski came as a great shock to me. I failed to see how he could be regarded as an enemy by anyone. He was a kind and humble person who, in my opinion, was politically harmless.

SWAPO's election campaign was impressive; obviously having re-ceived massive support from many different sources. The smaller par-ties weren't all that visible. Aksie Christelik-Nasionaal (ACN) focused primarily on white voters. There was no indication that the policy of the ACN under leadership of Jan de Wet had changed in any way. Its principles were still based on the protection of group rights, and the protection of the fundamental rights of the individual previously described by Koos Pretorius as "humanistic" remained unacceptable to them. Under leadership of Hans Diergaardt, the FCN (Federal Con-vention of Namibia) supported this ACN principle vigorously. It was ironic, however, that Sam Nujoma and SWAPO also expressed their misgivings about the emphasis on fundamental individual rights, and rather had an inclination towards a social democracy. The DTA con-sistently emphasised the necessity of the protection of fundamental rights for the smallest conceivable minority, namely the individual. We favoured a democratic system and a free-market economy, linked to social responsibility. An unadulterated capitalist democracy does not exist anywhere in the world anymore.

As we progressed I discovered that motivating and informing the inhabitants politically was no easy task. Addressing the Bushmen and other traditional groups about constitutional and economic principles, for instance, did not make much of an impression. They didn't even have words in their own language for many of the terms. I'm not saying this to humiliate them in any way, but purely because, and this unfortunately was the reality, they had been left behind politically in the past. Some of the more literate groups understood these concepts and I approached them differently. It frequently struck me that some of my black colleagues who were informed and could speak Afrikaans and/or English well, spoke over their audience's heads, to the extent that even the interpreters could not keep up. I wondered occasionally what came out at the other end.

A show of strength played a big role in our elections, because no one wants to support a loser. The DTA fought to win, although the chances were slim. Our biggest problem was probably the fact that, due to the inflexibility of the Administration for Whites, some discriminating practices were still being upheld. It was not easy to explain why the DTA had been unable to change this during the period of the transitional government.

The hour of reckoning arrives

Early on the morning of 7 November 1989, long queues of voters began lining up at the various polling stations, positioned far and wide across the 824 000 square kilometres of Namibia. UNTAG personnel, media representatives and observers from all over the globe arrived to watch the 700 000 voters – which were probably less than the number of inhabitants of a largish town in South Africa – casting their votes.

This makes one wonder yet again: What made this election so important? For the world community it was important because it could lead to the solution of a long-standing international problem. Some countries saw it as the beginning of the end of Soviet imperialism in Africa; for the black voter in the long queues it was about independence, the end of apartheid and discrimination. Many of them, however, had unrealistic expectations and dreams of farms and houses and money.

The election extended over five days and drew to a close on 11 November. The entire process took place in a surprisingly peaceful atmosphere. While there were attempts to intimidate voters, these were very subtle and nothing could be done about it. We did all we could possibly do during the campaign to the best of our abilities. All that was left was to wait for the results.

Despite the long distances over which the ballot boxes had to be transported, the results of the southern constituencies were the first to be announced. South of the Red Line the DTA won an absolute majority in 14 of the constituencies, compared to SWAPO's six. The constituencies where SWAPO managed to gain an absolute majority were Lüderitz, Swakopmund, Tsumeb, Karibib, Maltahöhe and Windhoek. In five of these, large concentrations of Owambos were employed in the mining, fishing and other industries, and in the case of Maltahöhe, Hendrik Witbooi – at the time Chief of the Namas and Vice-President of SWAPO – had a major influence. In the Kavango Constituency SWAPO achieved only a small majority. The UDF gained the majority in Damaraland and Captain Hans Diergaardt fared well in the Rehoboth Constituency. Initially there was great excitement about the DTA's lead in the southern constituencies. However, at that stage the results already indicated that the voters had voted according to ethnicity. The voting pattern in the populous Owambo regions would be the decisive factor.

We had to wait a long time for the results of the Owambo Constituency which covered only a small area. I already knew what to expect, but what I did not foresee was that the DTA would receive a mere 9000 votes compared to SWAPO's 196 169 votes. We expected the Owambos and their families who had fought on the side of the security forces to vote for the DTA, and had estimated that this would be in the region of 30 000 votes. Many reservations were expressed afterwards about this result in the Owambo Constituency, and questions were asked. Why had there been a power cut that plunged the premises where the ballots were being counted into darkness for many hours? Was it sheer coincidence that the DTA gained exactly 9000 votes?

However, by that time questions like these were no longer relevant. Whether the minority vote was 30 000 or 9000, it made no significant difference in respect of the number of seats that would be allocated to the different parties. Seats in the Constituent Assembly were not allocated on the basis of constituencies but according to the percentage of the total number of votes that the participating parties had polled.

What it amounted to was that SWAPO, which had won 57% of the total votes cast, was allocated 41 seats, while the DTA was allocated 21, the UDF 4, the ACN 3 and the NPF, FCN and NNF one seat each. SWAPO had not achieved a two-thirds majority of the 72 members in the Constituent Assembly and could therefore not write a constitution without the participation of the opposition. The credit for this favourable election result must go primarily to the hard work, dedication and sacrifices made by the DTA – a process that started with the formation of the Republican Party 12 years earlier.

The outcome of the election proved unequivocally that each and every one of the political parties was ethnically based – which is the case to this day. According to analysts, SWAPO received 83% of its support in the election from Oshiwambo-speaking people. When the votes that SWAPO attained from the Kavango and Caprivi regions south of the Red Line are added, it received no more than 6% of the votes from other population groups. Although SWAPO has since consistently censured ethnicity, its supporters are to this day still the most ethnically bound group in the country.

CHAPTER 13

Writing the Constitution

A lost chapter in our history

The Namibian Constitution is being described as a model constitution by constitutional lawyers locally as well as abroad. I regard the writing of the Namibian Constitution as the highlight of my political career, and my participation in its drafting as a great honour and privilege. But after 25 years of independence the ignorance prevailing among a large section of the population regarding their rights and freedoms enshrined in the Constitution is unbelievable. In my opinion, it is also important that over and above being informed about the provisions of the Constitution, the leaders and citizens of Namibia should also take cognisance of the intentions of the founding fathers when they wrote the Constitution.

It is incomprehensible to me that the minutes of the Constituent Assembly, and especially those of the Standing Committee on Standing Rules and Orders (also known as the "Constituent Committee") have not been made public yet, 25 years after independence. I can see no reason why any member of the Committee would object to my summarising these minutes (16 volumes, 4800 pages) in my book. I hope that readers who are interested in what the intentions of the founding fathers were, will take the trouble to read this somewhat lengthy chapter.

It took the Committee 80 days to draft the most important law in Namibia. In a spirit of patriotism, avowed political opponents put the past behind them and placed the interests and future of our common fatherland first. They succeeded, despite initial widely divergent proposals, in reaching consensus on every one of the 148 Articles of the Constitution. This historical exercise can serve as an example that is worthy of emulation by political leaders of the future. No problem will be unsolvable if matters of public interest are elevated above personal and political concerns at all times. How did we do it? That is what this chapter is about.

The first meeting of the Constituent Assembly

On 21 November 1989, at the start of the first meeting of the elected Constituent Assembly, Hage Geingob was elected as Chairman. At the same time a committee – referred to as the Committee on Standing Rules and Orders and Internal Arrangements – was assigned to compile rules and procedures for the Assembly. The leaders of the participating parties were then given the opportunity to address the Assembly.

First to take the floor was the President of SWAPO, Sam Nujoma, who said:

> Through a cross-fertilisation of our diverse cultures we should be able to emerge with a national culture. As a nation we should work together to provide meaningful education to our young, and to provide proper hospitals and medical care to the sick. And yes, to provide security to all Namibian families, for as a human race we desire the same thing, namely proper shelter, proper clothing, security in our homes, and so on. We all want to see our children happy and having three meals a day … be it a family in Eros Park, in Katutura, in Khorixas, in Katima Mulilo, in Epukiro, in Ondangwa or in Keetmanshoop. Our noble task as founding fathers and mothers of the nation is to contribute constructively towards the adoption of a constitution and the formation of a government; and that we attempt to answer the many problems that beset our country and its people. I am confident that you, Honourable Members, will execute the mandate entrusted to you properly, and will not let our people down. For my part, I will do the best I can to realise the objectives that we have set for ourselves. May our proceedings be crowned with success.

Sam Nujoma's words came as a pleasant surprise to me and I trusted that he would live up to his aspirations. Unfortunately, as it turned out later, this did not happen.

In his contribution, the President of the DTA, Mishake Muyongo, declared that the DTA, who represented a wide spectrum of the population, was prepared to cooperate constructively on the basis of the 1982 principles. He explained the DTA's constitutional proposals in broad terms to the Assembly. As it subsequently turned out, this was not the best way to set the ball rolling. Acting on legal advice, the leader of the ACN, Jan de Wet, questioned certain stipulations of the election proclamation, saying they were prepared to live with it despite their reservations. He pointed out the importance of the 1982 principles, claiming that the ACN did not represent only whites. He said they were prepared to adapt to the new circumstances and would offer what they had at their disposal "in terms of experience, in terms of knowledge, and in terms of the abilities of the people of this country, provided we are accepted as part of this country". Moses Katjiuongua congratulated the Chairman on his election to this important position.

Nahas Angula argued that all the parties had been given the opportunity to set out their political and constitutional proposals in the past election campaign, and besides, the 1982 principles had already been accepted by the Constituent Assembly. Further discussion would therefore be superfluous, merely a delaying tactic by the opposition. Deliberations such as these had to take place in the right atmosphere under the right circumstances, and political showmanship for the benefit of the public media had to be avoided. Press conferences carried an inherent risk in so far as they could develop into talk shows and end up delaying the process. Angula then proposed that:

> Registered political parties represented in this Assembly submit their constitutional proposals or ideas, if any, to the Acting Secretary of the Assembly not later than 10:00 Wednesday 6 December 1989.
>
> 1. The Standing Committee be mandated and instructed to receive and consider with appropriate urgency the proposals and ideas from registered parties in the Assembly regarding the future constitution for Namibia; to identify and formulate working categories for a future constitution or areas of material dispute in the various proposals submitted by registered parties, appropriate regard having been given to paragraph 3.1 of the notice of motion by the Honourable Member, Mr Muyongo (regarding and accepting the Assembly as representative of the people of SWA/Namibia and vested with certain powers in the interests of the people of Namibia); to make proposals for establishing committees to deliberate and negotiate on matters referred to it in paragraph 1.2 above, and to suggest terms of reference and the method of operation of the committees.
>
> 2. The Standing Committee report back to the Assembly during its sitting on Monday 11 December 1989.

The Standing Committee drafts its procedure

Under the chairmanship of Hage Geingob of SWAPO, the Standing Committee became known as the Constituent Committee. It consisted of 21 members, with 11 representing SWAPO, five the DTA, and one each the ACN, UDF, NPF, FCN and NNF respectively. On 7 December 1989, after the parties had tabled their respective constitutional proposals at the first meeting of the Committee, the meeting was adjourned until the next day to give parties the opportunity to scrutinise the proposals and – as the Chairman put it – to not only identify the points of difference, but also those in agreement.

When the Committee met the following day – 8 December – the Chairman proposed that a member of any party who had done his homework and felt he could make a contribution, could set the ball rolling. Since my colleagues who represented the DTA on the Committee – Hans Staby, Andrew Matjila, Barney Barnes and John Gaseb – and I had spent many hours the previous day and night scrutinising the different concepts, we were in a position to identify the points of difference as well as those in agreement. A factor that stood us in good stead was the considerable time spent on studying constitutional models in previous years. I accepted the Chairman's invitation and argued that it would be an impossible task to look at and compare half a dozen constitutions at the same time. In our view there were only two comprehensive draft constitutions on the table, namely those compiled by SWAPO and the DTA. Both of them contained all the aspects usually provided for in a constitution. We also found that while there were fundamental differences between the two, there were also many similarities. I proposed that we use the SWAPO draft as a "working document" and refer to the DTA draft and the other proposals if necessary. I emphasised that it did not mean I accepted the SWAPO proposal.

Surprisingly enough it was Koos Pretorius who rose to his feet directly after I had spoken, making the following statement: "I just want to say I am also prepared to accept SWAPO's constitution as a basis for our discussion." As far as the DTA and the other parties were concerned, it was more than conceivable that the SWAPO proposal could be amended in such a way that it would become acceptable to them. I failed to see how Pretorius could bring about meaningful changes to the SWAPO draft. From SWAPO's side, Ben Amathila and Mosé Tjitendero confirmed that they also accepted the proposal. In my view Dr Tjitendero interpreted my proposal correctly:

> I was very much impressed by the approach that Mr Mudge took. I think it was beginning to show progress in that direction ... I think Mr Mudge made a very progressive move by saying that we must first adopt. In any conference you come to, you have a working document. You look for its shortcomings and its omissions, and then you try to fill that ... I thought the reason why Mr Mudge [has suggested] the adoption of a working document, was taking into account how conventionally it covers the areas that are covered by constitutions [...]

As it turned out, my proposal to use the SWAPO draft constitution as a working document opened doors for us throughout the deliberations of the Committee. The DTA was accepted as a co-writer of the Constitution and not as a political opponent. I could take part in the discussions of every Section in the Constitution with confidence, and did exactly that. When I differed from the SWAPO representatives – and this happened frequently – they accepted it as my democratic right. When I became apologetic at one point about the fact that I had so much to say and criticise, the Chairman's reaction was: "That is why we have you here." At the start of the Conference I took a seat at the bottom end of the conference table, but when the Chairman realised I was hard of hearing he invited me to sit next to him. This was the spirit in which we wrote a model Constitution for Namibia.

One of my fondest memories is the wonderful spirit of loyalty to our common fatherland in which former enemies had joined hands to reflect on our future together. The meetings of the Committee took place in camera and confidentiality, as we had agreed that each delegate should participate freely and without fear of repercussions. This decision was a good one. The fact that members of the same party sometimes expressed different viewpoints was especially gratifying.

The first round: Surveying the terrain

The first point of material dispute identified by the DTA was the "Preamble" in the SWAPO document. Different dictionaries interpreted this word as meaning: a beginning, commencement, introduction, exordium, opening remarks, preliminary fact or circumstances and more. The proposed Preamble read as follows:

> Whereas recognition of the inherent dignity and of the equal and inalienable rights of all members of the human family is indispensable for freedom, justice and peace;
>
> Whereas the said rights include the right of the individual to life, liberty and the pursuit of happiness, regardless of race, colour, ethnic origin, sex, religion, creed or social or economic status;
>
> Whereas the said rights are most effectively maintained and protected in a democratic society where the government is responsible to freely elected representatives of the people, operating under a sovereign constitution and a free and independent judiciary;
>
> Whereas these rights have for so long been denied the people of Namibia by colonialism, racism and apartheid;
>
> Whereas we, the people of Namibia, have finally emerged victorious in our struggle against colonialism, racism and apartheid; are determined to adopt a constitution which expresses for ourselves and our children our resolve to cherish and protect the gains of our long struggle; desire to promote amongst all of us the dignity of the individual and the unity and the integrity of the Namibian nation among and in association with the nations of the world; will strive to achieve national reconciliation and to foster peace, unity and a common loyalty to a single state; committed to these principles, have resolved to constitute the Republic of Namibia as a sovereign, secular, democratic and unitary State securing to all our citizens justice, liberty, equality and fraternity;
>
> Now, therefore, we, the people of Namibia, accept and adopt this Constitution as the fundamental law of our sovereign and independent Republic.

The white and black delegates responded differently to references to the past in the Preamble and a long debate followed. We came from different backgrounds and had completely different experiences and lived under different circumstances. The black delegates – also those who had not been part of the armed struggle – were proud of what had been achieved, and did not shy away from history. The white people on the other hand, including those of us who had fought against racial discrimination for many years, did not want to be reminded of the past. It was painful and we did not want to see it perpetuated in the Constitution. Right from the outset the acceptance or non-acceptance of this formulation would become a test for us three whites in the Committee. Staby of the DTA expressed himself on the SWAPO proposal as follows:

> Concerning the preamble, I think it is necessary that the various proposals be reconciled. So, one has to look carefully at the various proposals that have been tabled ... [U]nfortunately a preamble isn't a preamble in terms of a Bill of Rights, so I think the attitude is fairly divergent. In essence I think the preambles should be fairly easy to reconcile, because they say the same thing in different words. First of all our attitude should be that the preamble must be oriented to the future and not deal with the past. I think this is the first prerequisite. The second one is that we think the preamble must cover essentials only, and not embark on emotional matters, for which we obviously have understanding. There is for instance ... a reference to "apartheid, racism and colonialism." We have understanding for this; there can be no argument about it. But I would just like to point out – particularly in view of the fact that further on in the document there are various prohibitions against the practice of apartheid and racism with which we agree in essence – that we want to draw attention to the fact that there are other practices that are equally repugnant. Take fascism, for instance. If we mention one specifically, the question arises whether we do not condone the others. I think this is basically what we are saying with regard to ... a positive approach orientated at the future. I would like to draw attention to the fourth paragraph where it says: "Whereas these rights for the people of Namibia have been denied for so long by apartheid, racism and colonialism ...", is one way of formulating it. The other one – "Whereas the people of Namibia have finally achieved freedom" – would be a positive way of formulating it.

When the Chairman asked whether there were any more objections to the Preamble, Pretorius remarked: "I don't want to point out any differences, but I think in general I agree with Mr Staby that we must try to look to the future and not the past." Hartmut Ruppel of SWAPO reacted positively to Staby's proposal, but was of the opinion that we should, in fact, refer to the past, because we had not been born in a vacuum and could not ignore it. In his view it was possible to marry the differences.

I expressed my support of Staby's proposal, and added the following:

> Let me make our view very clear. A constitution is not written for one generation, it is written for generations to come, and let me repeat that we have understanding for SWAPO's sentiments. When you refer to apartheid, discrimination and colonialism, I really appreciate your strong feelings about it, but in two or three generations from now, I hope the people will not even know the word 'apartheid' anymore. I hope it will not be part of the vocabulary anymore. Do we want to write things into our Constitution which in two or three generations will not be understood? I don't have the answer, but we have identified a difference of approach that should be discussed.

Theo-Ben Gurirab of SWAPO thought that while we could overcome these problems, we could not deny the past. The Chairman concluded the discussion with the following: "[T]his kind of thing can be left to the experts … Some people are against apartheid; I don't think this can be mentioned differently. So, we can tell the experts: basically agreed but redraft so that it doesn't look like we are just attacking the past, dwelling on the past and not the future."

Already on the first day of the Committee's activities, this debate turned out to be a typical example of the spirit and goodwill in which former enemies made an effort to overcome their differences.

Points of material dispute

The following significant points of difference were then identified: the character of the State; the President's powers; the division of functions; a Second House of Parliament; the electoral system; and regional and local governments. Moses Katjiuongua added aspects such as amending the Constitution, fundamental rights, land reform, and the way in which the future government would be instated.

Next we discussed the SWAPO document chapter by chapter, especially with a view to identifying specific points of difference. Some of the differences were solved immediately, while others were referred to our legal advisers. We perused the working document at least three times over the next two months. For the purposes of my story, I have summarised the discussions and decisions on important "Articles" (as referred to in this specific document) briefly while spending less time on the less important points.

The President's powers and competencies

The authoritarian powers and competencies granted to the President in the SWAPO document was the first and probably most important point of difference we identified. Here the DTA proposals were poles apart from those of SWAPO, which favoured an executive president with extensive powers who would be assisted by a council of ministers. This council would serve only in an advisory capacity, and the President would not be obliged to take its advice. The DTA provided for a ceremonial President, whose role would be that of a unifying factor, and who would not be involved directly in politics. We did not want a repetition of the Zambian situation where the Central Committee of the governing party had a greater influence on the President than the ministers. The DTA, furthermore, favoured a cabinet system, to which we were accustomed, and in accordance with which ministers could also have original powers.

It was clear to me from the outset that the SWAPO delegates were not too happy about the subordinate position proposed for the council of ministers, but that they felt committed to give their leader, Sam Nujoma, the status he sought. They pointed out that there were already certain restrictions to the powers of the President in the working document, for example, that he could serve for only two terms, and that the National Assembly could impeach him. By reaching consensus that further checks and balances could be considered, we moved closer to each other. I proposed that we should not attach too much significance to the words "executive" or "ceremonial" but rather look at his powers, bearing in mind the principle of the separation of powers between the executive, legislative and judiciary. In the event of an executive President the Prime Minister would be nothing more than the chairman of an advisory council. Pretorius also had doubts on this count, but did not try particularly hard to have his viewpoints accepted.

I was surprised at the progress we had made and the considerable measure of consensus we had reached when the Committee adjourned after one day of discussions.

A row over private schools

While we, the three whites in the Committee, were having to measure up to the first test of our credibility, a local newspaper featured an article revealing that the Administrator General, Louis Pienaar, was planning to have 15 schools that were controlled by the white representative authority privatised and transferred to Cultura 2000. At the time this organisation was immersed in controversy as a result of assets that had been assigned to it by the white authority. The report gave rise to a highly emotional debate, the outcome of which was the appointment of a delegation consisting of Mosé Tjitendero (chairman), Hans Diergaardt, Koos Pretorius, Vekuii Rukoro and Andrew Matjila to discuss his unacceptable decision with the Administrator General. Public assets had to be disposed of once again to prevent a future government from laying its hands on them. There is no doubt that the Administrator General intended to donate the 15 schools to Cultura 2000, but the newspaper report and intervention by the Committee prevented him from doing it immediately.

On Monday 11 December, at the commencement of the Committee session, the Chairman informed us that a group of parents led by Rev. De Klerk of the Dutch Reformed Church (Koos Pretorius's brother-in-law) would like to meet the Committee in relation to the privatisation of schools controlled by the Administration for Whites. Tjitendero requested the approval of the Committee of the following points to be conveyed to the parents: Firstly, that the proposals in the working document did, in fact, make provision for private schools; secondly, that the AG should not continue privatising schools; thirdly, that the existing policy and rules would suffice until a new constitution had been implemented; fourthly, that the Committee was willing to meet the parents; and finally, that an announcement would be issued by the Committee. The members of the Committee had considerable understanding for the fears of the white parents, who were apprehensive that chaotic situations might develop a month later when the schools were scheduled to reopen. However, given that the existing regulations would be binding until the new Constitution came into force, such fears were unfounded. In conclusion, I proposed that the Constitution should also provide for mother-tongue education.

The discussion on the privatisation of the 15 schools was used by Pretorius to return to points of difference that had already been identified for discussion at a later stage, such as the reference to apartheid in the working document. Staby and I had discussed this point at length during the debate the previous day. Pretorius then asked the Committee's permission to inform his people that he did not agree with the proposal and that he would prefer to be left out of the delegation. In answer to the Chairman's question of whether his people actually still believed in apartheid, he replied that his people believed in differentiation, variety and minority rights. But he did not succeed in coming up with a workable solution.

Prompted by the attempt of the Administrator General to anticipate the Constitution and the resulting discussion requested by the group of parents under leadership of Rev. De Klerk, the Committee continued discussing the sensitive issue of private schools. While the working document did make provision for private schools, it was on condition that such schools would not be funded by the State. After a short discussion it was agreed that this condition be left out of the Constitution, and that it should be for the Government to decide as a policy matter in which cases private schools would be funded.

The working document suggested that when it came to the admission to schools of pupils and teachers: "... no restrictions of whatever nature may be imposed with respect to the admission of pupils or the recruitment of staff based on race, colour and creed." Pretorius had problems with this, arguing that a Catholic school, for example, should have the right to appoint teachers who belonged to that religious creed. The Chairman's response was that teachers were not appointed to promote a specific religion, but to teach subjects such as mathematics. However, Pretorius maintained that even mathematics could be taught against a specific philosophical background. He concluded by asking that the point be referred to a committee. My perspective on these matters was that although I wanted my language and faith to be protected, I did not subscribe to the way Pretorius thought this should be done. My attempt to reach a compromise, however, was unsuccessful.

As had happened so many times before, the Chairman treated Pretorius with endless patience and understanding. His conclusion of the debate impressed me deeply:

> This is a very emotional issue, and we are operating in a spirit of co-operation, brotherhood and reconciliation. It also refers to the educational forces. We will come to know one another and trust will be developed, so that fears of the unknown will also be removed. In this regard, maybe without changing anything in this paragraph, the Honourable Member is asking to discuss it later on. Maybe he wants to go and consult other members

of his group after having received his education here, and also having received our strong point of view. So, maybe it will be fair to allow you to go and talk to your people and say: "This is what they are saying, and they are not going to change," and then allow him to come back and we will face the same thing. It is a compromise and not just to say "we are not going to listen to you". He is a colleague; he has a big problem. Not that we are going to go back to apartheid, that is out, but allow him the chance to maybe go and explain to the others, then to come back and again discuss it, without changing anything here.

This satisfied Pretorius, and the matter was left there, bringing our discussion of sentimental and cultural matters to an end. We then had to contend with a long discussion on the structure of government and the powers and competencies of the different organs and officials.

On 12 December the Chairman reported to the full session of the Constituent Assembly on the progress that had been made regarding the discussions of a constitution for Namibia. The work done on Friday the 8th, Monday the 11th and the morning of Tuesday the 12th of December was reflected in his report, which dealt especially with the Preamble, the position of the President and the question of private schools. There was consensus that the leaders of the parties would express themselves positively and supportively regarding the progress. However, because he still had certain reservations, Pretorius also had problems with this. Giving him some leeway, the Chairman said he could express himself, "[a]s long as it does not spoil the spirit, the spirit of having the country's interests at heart".

It was apparent from the discussions up until that point that although there was still insufficient clarity in some instances, agreement had nonetheless been reached on several matters in the working document. There were also several points on which the parties differed, and for which considerable debate would be required before consensus could be reached. With a view to accessing further information and in anticipation of the appointment of legal advisers, it often happened that points were postponed for later deliberation. Examples of points to be explored and discussed further were Parts 3 and 4 of the working document, which contained proposals on state and economic policy.

The Committee requested Hans Staby and later on Vekuii Rukoro to make available their notes for the record and to keep the members informed. These notes would also be made available to the intended legal advisers.

Land reform

Land reform was never discussed by the Committee and the Constitution does not contain a section providing for land reform. It is true that the Herero-speaking members of the Committee on several occasions insisted that this issue should be discussed. It never happened. Land reform only came to the fore two years after independence when a Land Conference was called. It was obvious at the time that there were concerns in some circles about the Herero's claim for the restitution of ancestral land. The Conference decided against the restitution of ancestral land and in favour of a policy on land reform. Strictly speaking, land reform is not a constitutional matter but rather a matter of policy.

The character of the State

When the character of the State was again discussed, Pretorius pleaded that the word "secular" be deleted but he did not take the matter any further. He again had problems with this word when the description of the future state came up for discussion for the second time in the Preamble of the working document as "a sovereign, secular, democratic and unitary State". He articulated it as follows: "… because other parties, even the DTA, is referring to the 'Creator and Almighty God'. Can't we in the spirit of give and take, delete the word 'secular'?" However, with no further elaboration, he left it at that.

Principles for government policy

Provision was made for the Principles of State Policy in Part 3 of the working document. As a result of my protesting strongly against the inclusion of government policy in a constitution, it was decided that this chapter should be deferred for later discussion.

The President's powers

My next objection was to the requirement that the President had to approve the submission of all draft bills to the National Assembly and had to sign all laws made by the National Assembly. While I agreed that the President should sign laws, I differed from the majority on the question of what would happen if he were to refuse to do so. Also unacceptable to me was the provision that in such a case the National Assembly should be dissolved. To my mind Rukoro came closer to re-solving the matter with his proposal that the President could only refuse to sign an Act if it was incompatible with Chapter 1 providing for the protection of fundamental rights. In all other cases the Act had to be referred back to the National Assembly. As to what would happen if the President refused repeatedly to sign an Act, I said that this problem could be solved when we discuss the Second House of Parliament.

I repeated my objection to the appointment of six members of the National Assembly by the President on the grounds that this would not comply with democratic principles. The Chairman then decided that, for the sake of harmony in the Committee, the provision should be scrapped. The majority of the members were opposed to this; they were resolute that the President should be able to nominate additional members to the National Assembly on the basis of their knowledge and experience. The Chairman complied, saying that he wanted to maintain democratic principles and would therefore accept the majority position.

The National Assembly (NA)

We had already decided how members of the National Assembly were to be elected, namely by means of a system of proportional representation. While Pretorius mentioned the ACN's proposal that the National Assembly be compiled of representatives nominated by the representative authorities (ethnic authorities), he did not try to substantiate it appropriately at any stage.

The Cabinet

We also needed to look incisively at the powers and competencies of other organs of government, namely the Ministers' Council (Cabinet), the legislature and the judiciary, since the powers and competencies of the President could not be looked at in isolation. The DTA stood firmly by the principle of the separation of powers between the executive, legislative and judicial authorities and that the areas of jurisdiction had to be clearly defined. Needless to say, this led to an extremely drawn-out debate.

A Second House of Parliament

In addition to the National Assembly, the establishment of a Second House of Parliament elicited a lengthy discussion, especially apropos the way it would be set up. While nothing of this nature was contained in the SWAPO proposals, the DTA proposals provided for a Second House, or Senate, consisting of representatives of the different regions.

Fundamental rights

Articles 5 to 19 of the working document, under the heading "Fundamental Rights, Responsibilities, Guarantees", provided for the following fundamental rights and freedoms that had to be protected in the Constitution:

- The equality of all inhabitants, including freedom from discrimination.
- Freedom of speech, meeting, association and movement.
- Protection of life and personal freedom.
- Protection against arrest and imprisonment under certain circumstances.
- The right to privacy.
- The right to a fair trial.
- The right to administrative justice.
- The right to political activities.
- Cultural rights.
- The right to property.
- The right to education.
- The right to vote.
- Respect for human dignity.

As he had done in the past, Pretorius insisted that the stipulations should include fundamental responsibilities, but to this day he is yet to answer my question as to which responsibilities he regarded as fundamental. Protecting inhabitants against the impairment of their fundamental rights and repressive measures was precisely the objective of this provision in our Constitution.

Although the DTA supported affirmative action in principle, I objected vigorously to previously disadvantaged people being referred to as a "class of persons" in the Constitution. In addition, I pointed out that when it came to fundamental rights, no reference had been made to groups anywhere in the DTA proposal. When it comes to fundamental rights, I regard the individual as the smallest possible minority. Grouping people on the basis of race and colour ultimately led to reverse discrimination. I had often pointed out that when giving fundamental rights to groups, the fundamental rights of the members of that group would inevitably become impaired. My insistence that this aspect needed to be resolved in cooperation with the consultants ultimately gave rise to a heated argument between myself and one of the consultants.

There was also a difference of opinion on the fundamental right to life, which amounted to the abolishment of capital punishment. Since I had misgivings about this, I posed the question of whether taking a life was wrong if you could save ten lives in the process. At a later stage I conceded that we should provisionally entrench the right to life in the working document, leaving the final decision to the Constituent Assembly. As it turned out, this was not a good decision. If we were unable to reach consensus in a small committee of 21 attendees, how likely was it that we would achieve this in an assembly of 72?

Article 15 of the SWAPO draft providing for the right of every individual to enjoy, practise, profess, maintain and promote in his/her personal life any culture, language, tradition or religion subject to the terms of this Constitution was accepted on condition that this right would be applicable to individuals and not to groups. This did not prevent anyone from exercising his or her right in association with others.

The fundamental right to acquire, own, sell or bequeath property to your heirs was contained in Article 16. To align it with the 1982 principles, the proposal in the working document had to be amended.

So we had come to the end of the chapter on fundamental rights. To me the way in which former enemies were prepared to put the best interests of the country above those of the party was impressive. It was also remarkable how SWAPO proposals were often reconciled with DTA proposals and vice versa. The members of the Committee agreed that the rights entrenched in this chapter should be respected by Government. That we could reach consensus on these important principles was encouraging, to say the least. Moreover, it convinced me that we would also overcome other possible stumbling blocks. Differences about wording and interpretation could be ironed out with the assistance of our legal advisers.

Consolidation of our progress at the end of 1989

Ruppel's summary and proposals that had been finalised in the meantime served a twofold purpose: firstly, to serve as a basis for a discussion on the legal aspects of proposals by the Committee with the legal advisers we wanted to assign, and secondly, to serve as the basis of the Committee's report to the full Constituent Assembly. In the meantime, the Administrator General suggested that our decisions be passed on to him and that he would in cooperation with the jurists he had at his disposal finalise the proposals. However, the Committee decided on 12 December to appoint experts to assist in the formulation of constitutional concepts and correct articulation of the wording of decisions. Afterwards these legal advisers were often referred to jokingly as the "men from heaven". Hence, three South African jurists were identified, namely Arthur Chaskalson and Profs Marinus Wiechers and Gerhard Erasmus. Ruppel was tasked to go to South Africa to discuss with them his summary of the decisions on policy principles taken during the holiday season. Vekuii Rukoro would accompany him. As to be expected, Pretorius still needed to get something off his chest and asked for a turn to speak shortly before the adjournment on 18 December. He said the following:

> If you will allow me another minute, since I don't want there to be any misunderstanding about this. I have said in the past and I want to repeat it. It has been an honour for me to take part in this process, and we see ourselves as part and parcel of this effort, but I want to compare our position with Bavaria in West Germany. Bavaria was the only state that had not accepted West Germany's constitution to date, but they were prepared to live with it and to make a success of it. And that is why, because we have fundamental differences, I can't tell my people outside that I have now agreed to this, but I will tell them we accept it and that we will try to make a success of it, because that, in my opinion, is the best result of your proposals. So I hope you will see it against that background.

Koos's dilemma was understandable, and I sympathised with him. His Party's constitutional proposals never came up for discussion, and once he had accepted the SWAPO proposal as a working document, it was no longer relevant.

The role of Koos Pretorius during the deliberations

While Koos Pretorius had reservations about several aspects of the decisions taken by the Committee, he never made a concerted effort to have his viewpoints accepted, but consistently asked for permission to clarify his viewpoints with his caucus and to explain his viewpoints in an open session of the Constituent Assembly. While he didn't see his way clear to present his case in the Committee where the Constitution was being written, he did so to the news media and elsewhere, which at that stage was a futile exercise. When the Preamble to the Constitution and the issue of the appointment of teachers in private schools was under discussion, the Chairman referred to Pretorius's "standard position". His answer to my question of why he wasn't prepared to discuss his problem in the Committee was that since he had been out-voted before, he deemed it necessary to state his case publicly, upon which I accused him of wanting to speak for the gallery. To this he replied: "To the minority in the gallery." When we were discussing a future form of government, Pretorius's only contribution was to listen.

The second round: Meeting with our legal advisors

The legal advisers were requested to attend the discussions and to comment on the provisional draft when the Committee met again on 16 January 1990. Some members, especially Barney Barnes, criticised Hartmut Ruppel for having cleared certain points with me before departing for Johannesburg to discuss the amendments to the working paper with the legal advisers. As he had done so many times in the past, and continued doing in the future, Barnes could simply not resist the temptation to oppose me. Impartial as always, Rukoro regarded Barnes's objections as an infringement upon his and Ruppel's integrity, and asked that the matter be put on the agenda to be dealt with at a later stage.

After this unpleasant incident, Advocate Chaskalson explained the legal advisers' position as follows: "I think that we should also make it clear to you that in our work we saw our task not as devising a constitution for Namibia, but as trying to record the consensus as we understood it had been reached. That was the task we set ourselves to do." Since the decisions taken by the Committee amounted to decisions taken by politicians about principles, the task of the legal advisers was to formulate them in legal terminology.

The discussions we had with our legal advisors were basically a repetition of discussions in the Committee during the first round and what we were discussing now was in fact a revised version of the working paper with the emphasis on detail.

This is how Pretorius started the discussion:

> Mr Chairman, before you proceed, I just want to clarify my posi-
> tion, the ACN's position, because as you know, and I don't know
> whether the gentlemen know it, in some aspects we differ fun-
> damentally. So I couldn't contribute in detail then and we have
> now referred the concept to our lawyers for their comments. I
> am not a legal man myself. Will I perhaps have the opportunity
> to hand the comments over to the three gentlemen later? Other-
> wise it will take a lot of time for me to point out every difference.
> I don't think this is the idea, but rather that my lawyers try to
> criticise their legal wording in some respects.

The first one to express his surprise about Pretorius's request was Katjiuongua: "If there are members in this house whose documentation
is with somebody else at present, I think they should collect it, so that
when it comes to the Preamble, if they have anything to say from the
paper from their lawyers, they can make a contribution. Then we can
finish the Preamble and never come back to it again."

We had now reached the last phase of the Committee's activities.
The political decisions had already been made and three recognised
constitutional jurists were accessible to discuss the final formulisation
with us. There was now an element of urgency, because they had other
obligations and their time was limited. However, at this late stage of
the proceedings Pretorius wanted time to discuss fundamental differences with his legal adviser, which he then wanted to hand directly
to the consultants. This was how Prof. Wiechers commented on his
request: "We are now your servants. In other words, what you have
decided, we, to the best of our abilities, will draft and put into place.
We cannot at this stage … look at various inputs on our own. We cannot now start a mini-Constituent Committee amongst ourselves."

To conclude the discussion of Pretorius's request, the Chairman
said that we could not continue tabling new documents every day and
expect the Committee to start looking at them from scratch. It became
patently obvious to me once again that Koos was not up to the task he
had taken on himself. But then, in all fairness, I must concede that he
wasn't the only one.

The Preamble

The first item we discussed was the Preamble. Again the reference to
and emphasis on the past was raised, to which I reacted as follows: "In

our own way we have also struggled against apartheid and racism, whether you believe it or not. We have already said we are not going to fight about this one, so leave it as it is." To the statement by Pretorius that he reserved the right to put his case at a later stage and on a different occasion, the Chairman replied: "Your position is standard."

In response to my suggestion that the term "unitary state" be replaced with "single state" to which all its citizens should be loyal, the Chairman remarked that while they did not see it like this, he accepted my proposal: "Thank you, that is why we have you on that side." This was how one of my many proposals for amendments to the working document was accepted. It gave me reassurance and the belief that with an attitude like this, we would eventually have a perfect Constitution.

The next aspect, namely the description of Namibia as a secular state, was less straightforward. Here I will quote at length from the minutes, because so much has been said and written about this aspect since then. Because I was apprehensive about the possible incorrect interpretation of the description of Namibia as a secular state, I articulated it as follows:

> There could be different interpretations of the word "secular" but our lawyers brought to our attention that in some dictionaries "secular" is described as "sceptical of religious truth" or "opposed to religious education". I would not want to support the principle of a secular state should that be our interpretation (understanding) of the word secular.

Koos Pretorius concurred with this as follows: "I am glad to get some support about this word 'secular,' because it is still troubling me. It has various interpretations and it was not mentioned in the 1982 principles … I think we must leave it out." Somewhat more light was shed on the matter by Hidipo Hamutenya: "A new meaning is definitely being given to the word 'secular,' but this word appears in so many constitutions; it simply means that it is not a theocratic state. Simple, straightforward. We don't want another Iran here." Professor Wiechers, responding to a question by Eric Biwa, finally clarified the issue with the following: "In constitutional theory 'secular' is the division between church and state." With this explanation both Pretorius and I were satisfied.

When we reached the end of this debate, I was unable to drum up any support for my final plea that the Constitution should at least acknowledge God Almighty in a country where 90% of the population was religious. Prof. Erasmus clarified that there were countries where a particular church was recognised in the constitution as the official church of the State. I didn't have the slightest inkling then that former President Sam Nujoma would want to give preference to certain churches and exclude others at a later stage. He would have been able to do this had it not been for the fact that our Constitution provided for a secular state. Now, 25 years later, I would like to warn those individuals who are so determined to try and change the Constitution that they would do well not to go scratching where it's not itching. In SWAPO there are many radicals who would also like to amend the Constitution. In fact, they could have amended this stipulation with a mere majority and have one church or another declared as the state church.

By way of reassurance, Rukoro informed the meeting that in future if a dispute about the interpretation of this stipulation were to arise, the courts could consult the minutes of this Committee to establish what the intention of the writers of the Constitution had been. At the time I accepted that this was the case, but jurists informed me subsequently that courts were not influenced in their findings by debates that had taken place in legislative bodies.

The capital, national anthem, flag and national symbols

It was decided unanimously that Windhoek would be the capital of the Republic of Namibia, and that a committee would be appointed to make suggestions about a flag, anthem and national symbols.

Walvis Bay and the offshore islands

The interim government had discussed the ownership of the Walvis Bay enclave and the offshore islands on several occasions with the Administrator General, but the South African Government had stated unequivocally that ownership of the enclave and the islands was not negotiable. However, the Committee had decided that the enclave and islands should be described in our Constitution as part of Namibia, and that it would be up to the future government to continue negotiations with the South African government.

Official language

When language, culture and religion came up for discussion, the past counted against us whites. There was no way we could deny that in the past black children had no choice when it came to the medium of instruction, and that the National Party, and especially the Afrikaans churches, had been allies in the political struggle. Needless to say, Pretorius and I had a problem with the subordinate status of Afrikaans in the proposed future dispensation, especially when it came to education. In the course of the debate, the Chairman remarked that Pretorius apparently expected that after independence only English would be spoken in the country, and that Afrikaans would have no place. Geingob said that he was also proud of his language, but that the problem had been intercepted by the proposal on the table. "Nothing contained in this Constitution shall prohibit the use of any other language as a medium of instruction in private schools as well as schools financed or subsidised by the State, subject to proper compliance with such requirements as might be imposed by law." The Chairman asked Pretorius whether he was suggesting that he, Geingob, should be allowed to address the National Assembly in Damara. When Pretorius answered in the affirmative, the Chairman suggested that the clause in question be amended accordingly and that English be accepted as the official language, with the proviso that under certain circumstances the use of other indigenous languages could be authorised by legislation.

Citizenship

We spoke at length and in depth about the requirements and qualifications for citizenship. SWAPO delegates felt strongly that citizenship should not come cheap. They objected vehemently against awarding citizenship to the children of officials and members of the Defence Force and Police Service, proposing that a person had to have lived in Namibia ordinarily for ten years to qualify for citizenship by means of naturalisation. It was obvious to me that SWAPO was afraid that large numbers of South Africans would become Namibian citizens. It was no simple matter convincing them that former South African citizens and their children who had been living in Namibia before independence and who would otherwise qualify for citizenship should automatically be entitled to citizenship.

Fundamental rights and freedoms

A declaration of human rights, as accepted internationally, was invariably regarded with suspicion when the National Party was in power. It was regarded as interference in South Africa and South West Africa's domestic affairs, and as an attempt to give rights to the black inhabitants to which they were not entitled. The Party's position was that the black inhabitants could not simply lay claim to rights and that they also had to accept responsibilities. Although there cannot be an objection in principle to such a viewpoint, it must be seen against the background of the political system to which the black inhabitants of our country had been subjected for a century or longer. The argument was used purely to withhold fundamental rights, which they didn't have, from them. Somewhere I read that the highest form of freedom can be attained when you submit yourself to self-imposed laws. However, the black inhabitants of our country had to submit themselves to laws that had been made without them playing any role in their making. Earlier on I quoted Pretorius saying that to be free, the black inhabitants did not necessarily need the right to vote for the government that had been set up to rule over them.

The discussion in the Committee was first and foremost about fundamental rights. Protection had to be given to citizens against the Government's repressive rules and laws that impaired their fundamental rights. Therefore, a distinction had to be made between ordinary rights and fundamental rights. Let me illustrate by way of an example: Government can make a law that prohibits me from driving faster than 120 km per hour, or from shooting protected game without a permit, but it can never make a law that denies me the right to a fair trial, recognition of my human dignity, freedom of religion, the right to own property, the right to education and the right to practise my culture – to mention but a few.

Pretorius was adamant yet again that there had to be the necessary balance between rights and responsibilities. In this respect, he maintained, he could not differ from the charter of a Communist country such as Cuba. That he had not grasped what this was about, was becoming increasingly clear to me. Evidently he was still under the impression that the stipulations over fundamental rights were there only for the benefit of the black inhabitants. It was beyond my comprehension that he wanted to give our Government the right to place responsibilities on Namibians, as was done in Communist Cuba.

To my mind the necessity to protect fundamental rights was summarised accurately by Prof. Wiechers: "The State is very powerful, the individual powerless. The whole philosophy behind human rights is to protect the individual against abuse of power by the State. All the various laws that Parliament will make and pass, thousands of them, and all the executive actions that are being taken by the executive, contain obligations for the individual." It was still not clear to me which fundamental obligations Pretorius wanted to place on the individual. Katjiuongua expressed the fear that under certain circumstances the Government could impinge on fundamental rights or could deviate from them – as would indeed happen subsequently with the implementation of affirmative action. The Chairman concluded this part of the debate stating: "I have a problem also with giving with the one hand and taking it away with the other."

Henceforth the fundamental rights provided for in the draft in front of us were discussed sequentially, starting with the right to life. Pretorius reserved his Party's position on capital punishment, saying that it was a matter of policy and not a fundamental right. The proponents of capital punishment did not realise that to leave it to a government to decide for which crimes people could be executed would under prevailing circumstances have been unwise.

During the discussions with our legal advisors Adv. Chaskalson was becoming prescriptive, especially when stating that the discussions should be about principles. As far as he was concerned," we were now bickering about small matters such as language and stylish formulation. At the end of the day, a court breathes life into a constitution ... Is this debate on small matters really worth that?" Although this reprimand was actually aimed at Barnes, who often tried to be clever, I didn't identify with the advocate's viewpoint, so I decided to spell out that we also had the right to criticise the wording of the advisers' draft:

> I don't know who is going to decide whether a matter is a small matter or not. As far as I am concerned, I will take that decision myself. I am only writing a constitution once. For us this is a very serious occasion and I did not ask the permission of the Committee to delay the process. I haven't done so thus far. All I want to say is that it need not be a waste of time if we go through the Articles at a steady pace, giving us just time enough to consult our papers.

We continued our discussion of the legal advisers' document on 17 January. In the meantime the advisers had made the amendments that had been proposed in the draft the previous day. I expressed my reservations about the provision that all fundamental freedoms would be subject to the laws of the country, cautioning that this could lead to the infringement of fundamental rights and freedoms. Adv. Chaskalson explained that freedom of speech, to mention one example, must sometimes be restricted to limiting incitement of violence or indecent acts. He then referred to a provision that had already been accepted, "… that any limitation … shall not negate the essential content of any freedom and shall not be aimed at any particular individual …" While I accepted his explanation, I stuck to my position that fundamental freedoms could not be exercised in such a way that other persons were harmed in the process. Chairman Hage Geingob enquired why this phrase could not be added, reminding us that he had stated earlier that this point was fully covered in the DTA's constitution. This illustrates yet again that the Chairman was always prepared to take cognisance of the proposals made by the DTA, and that the DTA's draft completely covered all aspects of the Constitution. Since the meeting remained divided on this provision, Adv. Chaskalson undertook to have another look at its formulation.

Freedom of association

There was scant discussion on the right of freedom of association. Conversely, Pretorius stated that to him this was the most important freedom. It was clear to all of us that this was an attempt to promote his customary policy of separateness or differentiation. Katjiuongua asked justifiably whether this also meant that people would have the right of dissociation. There was no further discussion on the matter.

The right to own property

Hans Staby criticised the proposal giving the right to the State to expropriate property "as parliament may enact, regard being had to the resources and the requirements of the expropriating authorities to the public interest and to what is fair in all circumstances to the expropriatee." To my mind this proposal deviated from the 1982 principles providing for "fair and just compensation" and in it there was no reference to the sources and the needs of the State. Adv. Chaskalson admitted that it was a mistake and that the Article will have to be reformulated after which the Chairman proposed that all the words after "parliament may enact" be deleted. I strongly objected to his proposal and the Chairman agreed that the words "fair and just compensation" should remain in the provision.

It was becoming increasingly clear to me that SWAPO delegates were concerned that land would be too expensive and that the State would not have sufficient funds to settle the black farmers. I pointed out that we were not currently discussing affirmative action, but expropriation when in the public interest. "[W]e are talking about property which might be expropriated to construct a road or to construct a building. We are not talking about white farms being expropriated now."

The right to political activity

In my view the right to create a political party or to belong to one was essential. Nevertheless, I proposed that it should be qualified to apply only to parties "having and pursuing a democratic object". This led to a long discussion, after which my proposal was accepted.

Administrative justice

The important provision relating to administrative justice in our Constitution is known to only a small number of people. In short, it provides that when making decisions and executing their duties, organs of the State (including officials) should act reasonably and fairly at all times, and that persons aggrieved by the exercise of such acts and decisions shall have the right to seek redress before a competent Tribunal. This provision was accepted by all parties.

Cultural rights

When the fundamental right of people to own, protect and promote their cultural rights and freedoms was raised, Pretorius once again threw the cat among the pigeons. Earlier on this right had been accepted unanimously, but he asked that the stipulation be expanded to entitle every person to exercise this right on his own or in association with other people. This was completely unnecessary because there was nothing that prevented a person from exercising his right of association with others. While everyone present immediately agreed with this, in their minds they once again linked the proposed inclusion of the words "in association with others" with division, separateness and ethnicity.

The discussion was concluded when Vekuii Rukoro and Hartmut Ruppel, both jurists who had played an important role all along, supported me. Rukoro worded it as follows: "Mr Mudge settled this question when he said that the right of everyone to do these things freely in association with others is not ruled out by the present formulation, and that the problem of including this formulation ... is going to create all kinds of false expectations ...". A long and emotional debate followed, after which Pretorius agreed to accept the original formulation. The debate was closed by the Chairman saying in his usual diplomatic way: "[I]t seems that Mr Pretorius does it for the record; that is what I understood. That is why I gave him the right to speak, so that he could say, 'I fought for you, I never gave up'."

The right to education

During the discussion of the fundamental right to education it was patently obvious once again that some of the members did not understand that although all their objectives – in the form of election promises – could not be written into a constitution and should be seen as matters of policy and legislation. While everyone agreed that the right to education was a fundamental right, we had to decide until which stage education should be free and obligatory. Nahas Angula responded to my proposal that the Constitution should stipulate only that education was a fundamental right. He cautioned that determining until which stage it would apply and in which cases it would be free should be left to the legislators, and that we should tread carefully, since the newspapers were already writing about it. This proved yet again that SWAPO had probably made certain promises to the voters. My proposal was accepted by the Chairman.

There was no dispute from the outset about the right to establish private schools, but that as far as the admittance of pupils and appointment of teachers were concerned, there would be no restriction on the basis of race, colour or creed. On the question of the appointment of teachers, Pretorius repeated his objection to the inclusion of the word "creed". To this the members of the Committee displayed considerable understanding, and decided to omit the word "creed".

Affirmative action

A lengthy discussion followed when the question of affirmative action was raised again. It was pointed out correctly by Pretorius that although he did not oppose the concept in principle, it did not belong in the chapter on fundamental rights, since according to the proposal it was going to be phased out after 25 years. I raised an objection to the new Article proposed by the legal advisers in which former disadvantaged people were again referred to as a "class of persons", proposing that they simply be called "persons who had been disadvantaged". Adv. Chaskalson had a problem with the argument that for historical reasons it might be necessary to give preference to, for example, black applicants when appointing medical doctors, although he admitted that it would be exceedingly difficult to formulate such a provision.

It was only with great difficulty that I managed to control myself. Cosmetic changes had never appealed to me. I believed that we as drafters of the Constitution had to be practical and realistic. Fortunately, by pointing out that we criticised Pretorius because he referred to groups and now we ourselves wanted to create a group – a class of persons – on the basis of colour, Katjiuongua came to my rescue. Nevertheless, after hours of deliberations, I finally managed to get my point across. Expressing the hope that something that fell somewhere between what they had in mind and what I had proposed could be formulated, Angula and Katjiuongua requested that my proposals be perused meticulously by the legal advisers.

The discussion on the period within which affirmative action had to be concluded was raised, and it was decided that the original proposal of 25 years should be scrapped. I thought the period was too long; 25 years seemed like a lifetime. The Committee decided that a specific period should not be mentioned, but that the process should be completed within a shorter period of time. In my view this was an error of judgement. Now, 25 years after independence, affirmative action is still being applied in a discriminatory way. Hopefully the leaders of our country will eventually come to realise that affirmative action also has its disadvantages, and that in some cases, for example in the government service and for children born after independence, it had already achieved its objective. The Chairman made arrangements for this matter to be dealt with elsewhere in the Constitution, and that it be reformulated "bringing in Mr Mudge's contribution and not to create a situation where it is going to be exploited by opportunists, if not abused by some people who are not poor, who did not suffer, who happen to be black, like Nahas and myself, and benefited from that."

Election and powers of the President

I anticipated that when it came to the formulation of this Article by our legal advisors there would be significant differences of opinion. In fact, this was exactly what happened, with tempers flaring up regularly. In response to passages read from previous minutes, it was even alleged that the minutes did not reflect the actual decisions. This resulted in friction rising between the Chairman and myself for the first time since the Committee had commenced its deliberations. The most serious differences of opinion were on the following issues: whether it had been decided initially that the President should be elected directly by the voters or by the legislative body; whether he or she would be an executive President; if so, to whom he should be accountable for his actions; and whether he should attend National Assembly meetings or not.

An earlier decision that there would not be an election for a government immediately following the acceptance of the Constitution, but that the Constituent Assembly would be transformed into a National Assembly and that the leader of the majority party would be the President for the first term, complicated matters even further. Once again there were serious differences of opinion on whether the President would be elected directly by the voters or by the National Assembly in the next election. I reminded the Committee that during the initial discussions I had pointed out that since the first President would be elected by the National Assembly, the Constitution should provide for that and that alone, and that during the first term we could consider whether we wanted to amend the Constitution to provide for a President being elected directly. The SWAPO members of the Committee objected to this, insisting that the Constitution should provide only for a directly elected President.

The same arguments were being repeated by different speakers, causing the debate to run around in circles. What did emerge, however, was that SWAPO favoured an executive President who had comprehensive powers. In their view he should be accountable to the voters and the voters alone, and should not attend meetings of the National Assembly. While the minority parties had favoured a ceremonial

President from the outset, I proposed that we not argue about what we called him. I conceded that for the purposes of the Constitution, we were prepared to refer to him as an executive President, but not to give him unlimited powers. To this Dr Ngarikutuke Tjiriange objected as follows: "If you look at the documents we had earlier, our president was very strong. In the process so many teeth have been pulled that we are left with a president without teeth ... The president has to get his mandate from the people." However, the opposition parties were set on extracting even more teeth. When Rukoro said: "We don't want a runaway president," he was speaking on our behalf.

In answer to my question of what the previous viewpoint of the Committee had been in this regard, the Chairman quoted from the minutes of 15 December 1989, alleging that all we had decided then was that the first President would be elected by the National Assembly, and that in further elections the method of election would be left open. Left open until when? Did this mean that during the first term a decision had to be taken in this connection, and that the Constitution could then, if necessary, be amended as I had suggested? Or conversely, had we decided that the Constitution should determine that the next President was to be appointed by means of a direct election? For some reason SWAPO members felt strongly that the President should not be a member of the National Assembly and would not be required to report to the National Assembly.

So an exceedingly difficult day came to an end. With the following closing thoughts I tried to link the election of the President with the powers and abilities he would have:

> The question I will ask tomorrow is whether it is only a matter of deciding on the different ways of elections or whether this is going to have an effect on all the other provisions of the constitution. Will it have an effect on the powers of the President? Will it be making him a runaway president? When we discussed the rest of the Constitution, we always kept the way in which the President would be elected in mind and the fact that he was accountable to Parliament. If we change that, then we have to reconsider the whole constitution.

In conclusion, the Chairman reminded us that SWAPO was prepared to compromise in the hope that there would not be a Second House in Parliament. He then adjourned the meeting until the next day without the Committee having reached agreement on any of the points discussed.

When the Committee resumed its activities on 18 January, a request by Pretorius that the ACN's legal advisers be allowed to attend the discussions as observers was turned down. Koos stated in response: "(We) were prepared to settle if the executive power is in the President in consultation with his Cabinet, and he should not necessarily be a member of the Cabinet. We are also prepared to accept the idea of a president elected by the people."

The transitional period

The Committee then focused on the situation during the transitional period – that is the first term of government. Staby repeated our viewpoint that the decisions had to remain within the framework of the 1982 principles, or else the entire process would have to start from scratch and an election be held for a future government. The Chairman then read a section from the proposal I had made in December, upon which I objected to his not having quoted me in full. To prevent this episode from resulting in a crisis, if not an impasse, I reiterated my position I had taken in December a year ago:

> We have already agreed that this body [Constituent Assembly] will become the Government for the first five years. As far as the President is concerned, I pointed out that it [the election of the President] is of no practical significance right now, whatever the position might be in future. The first President will be elected by Parliament and because of that practical situation we must provide in the constitution for the President being elected by Parliament, not as a temporary measure, but as a provision in the Constitution. Should we during the five years come to the conclusion that this is not really what we want, we can amend the Constitution by a two-thirds majority. I did not suggest that this must be a temporary measure.

In response to my contention that he had misquoted me, the Chairman defended himself as follows: "I never had any intention to misquote anybody. I was reading the minutes. If you say I left out some part, that is a point, but don't say I misquoted you because I was reading." He had pinpointed my problem exactly, which was that he had left out the relevant part of my proposal. The result of this unfortunate incident was that several members questioned the correctness of the minutes, in spite of the fact that the personnel of the transcription service were experienced, professional people.

At this point it was abundantly clear that we were heading for a confrontation. To Rukoro's suggestion that we have no further discussion on what we had agreed or not agreed, the Chairman's response was to put the issue to the vote. Rukoro pointed out that we had decided not to vote about matters. This led to the discussions becoming unmanageable, and the Chairman threatening to adjourn the meeting indefinitely.

In the end we took the obvious route, namely to put the presidency in its entirety under scrutiny once again. The relationship between the President and the legislative body was the main problem area. SWAPO wanted him to be elected directly by the nation and did not want him to be accountable to the National Assembly, with minimum control such as, for example, the right to impeach him. The Cabinet should only be an advisory body to the President. On the other hand, we were aware of the risk of abuse of power and unbridled discretion; in other words, of a runaway President. It was therefore essential to first gain clarity on the President's powers before decisions could be made on how he would be appointed.

Valid points that in effect corresponded with what I had proposed initially were raised by Angula and Ruppel, such as Angula saying: "[W]hatever president we are going to have will have to be accountable to Parliament in one way or another … So there are many ways to control the President. But I have no difficulty with what Mr Mudge is saying. Why don't we go Article by Article?" Referring to the terms of office of the National Assembly and the President, Ruppel elaborated on this aspect as follows: "That is one of the problems which, I think, Mr Mudge raised legitimately. There are consequences flowing from a different mode of election and we have to look at them." Yet again Angula proved that he was a level-headed and independent thinker. When he differed from me, he was consistently outspoken, but on the other hand he had no qualms about agreeing with me. He brought our viewpoints closer together to some extent when he continued: "I don't think that the President should be part of the Assembly, to be honest. This President should be above party politics, especially in our country … He should represent the interests of the country as a whole." My response to Angula was that I agreed with him, but that I had a problem with reconciling a President who was above politics with one who had executive powers and had to exercise those powers in accordance with a constitution, but who would be dictated to by his party. I also asked whether the Cabinet would be part of the executive authority, because the stipulation in the proposal that the Cabinet had to be consulted did not imply that the Cabinet forms part of the executive authority.

The same arguments were repeated over and over again for hours on end without us, the Committee, being able to reach consensus. As a last option, the Chairman proposed that in spite of our agreement not to refer Committee disputes to the Constituent Assembly of 72 members, in this case it would be advisable to do so. However, I still suspected that not everyone in SWAPO felt the same about this matter. Angula and Ruppel continued looking for common ground between my viewpoint and that of the SWAPO spokesmen. Ruppel, being a jurist, was less influenced by political considerations. Like Rukoro, he invariably attempted to find a balance between political expectations and that which, from a legal point of view, would be the right decision. He pointed out that there was no dispute about the principle that we would have an executive President. The decision that needed to be taken was how this person would be elected. In his view we had not reached an impasse. In SWAPO's view it was a *fait accompli* that an executive President had to be elected directly and that he would then be controlled by various checks and balances. Ruppel continued:

> I think Mr Mudge this morning, in all fairness, before there was any ruling, asked what the consequences of a direct election would be with a view to the remaining provisions in the Constitution which we have already discussed, the checks and balances; what will it mean with the different mode of election now, from the indirect one by Parliament to a direct one? Would that have drastic effects on his powers vis-à-vis the other organs of state? Those were his questions.

According to Ruppel, these questions could be answered by the jurists. It became apparent that the SWAPO members had not reached agreement on the President's powers among themselves. The three advisers then attempted to answer the questions I had posed that morning. They were in agreement that the method of electing the President, his powers and responsibilities and his accountability, had to be spelt out clearly in the Constitution. There was no response to my question what the influence of a directly elected President would be on his powers, responsibilities and accountability. Prof. Wiechers then explained that a directly elected President would be a much stronger President due to the manner of his election, and would not be that easy to keep in check. To me this raised the question regarding the sequence in which the three points should be discussed and settled. I would agree to the President being elected directly, provided I could rely on SWAPO's cooperation when it came to deciding on his powers, competencies and accountability. As long as we could be confident there would be no abuse of power, we would be able to reach an agreement. My proviso was that if we could not agree on the President's powers, competencies and accountability, we could return to this point. The bottom line here was that I was determined to avoid the possibility of a "runaway" president.

Since no objections were raised regarding the oath of office the President would take, it was accepted without further discussion. Questions were asked about the extent of the immunity the President would have, upon which the Chairman referred to the common perception that most African presidents were reluctant to relinquish their positions, which led to their staying on for life. He asked about the expediency of making retirement attractive by means of generous pensions and other benefits. On this note the discussion was concluded.

Although we had made some progress in the discussion of the President's position, we again spent time discussing the President's functions, powers and duties on the afternoon of 18 January. By then the members were exhausted, and the Chairman had to call them to order from time to time and it was agreed that the President would uphold the Constitution and all the President's actions should take place in consultation with the Cabinet. I then asked what his position would be if, for some reason or another, he were to dissolve Government, and on what grounds he could dissolve Government. Prof. Wiechers maintained that a directly elected President could not dissolve Government; Hidipo Hamutnetya agreed. This again elicited a long discussion, after which I proposed that the advisers formulate in such a way that in the case of Parliament being dissolved, the President would have to be elected again. To my surprise it was accepted like this. It was clear that the Committee did not grasp the implications of this decision.

It was also decided that the executive authority (the President and the Cabinet) could negotiate when it came to the conclusion of international and bilateral treaties, but that these should be ratified by Parliament and signed by the President. While this would be necessary in certain cases, in my view it was an impractical proposal. When Ruppel said that we should not use Parliament to ratify every single action taken by the executive authority, he had made a valid point.

I agreed with Katjiuongua that the appointment of senior officials and judges should not be left solely to the President and that the National Assembly should not become involved. I suggested that a Public Service Commission be established consisting of competent and impartial individuals who would not be lackeys of the President. We had lengthy arguments about the appointment of the Attorney General, ambassadors and the Director of Planning, during which questions were asked whether these positions could be regarded as political appointments. It emerged once again that SWAPO delegates wanted to avoid too much interference with the President's powers. We were unable to reach unanimity on any of these issues, so the Chairman suggested that we adjourn to go and reflect on these matters.

The powers and competencies of the Cabinet

On 19 January 1990, when the Committee assembled again, I pointed out that the powers and competencies of the President and Cabinet were so interlinked that they could not be discussed separately. I started with the method in which the President would be elected, asserting that this would most definitely have an influence on the compilation and activities of the executive authority. It would determine whether the President would have a seat in the National Assembly and would therefore be accountable to the Assembly, or whether this would be the ministers' responsibility.

During the last two sessions Pretorius was noticeably more actively involved in the discussions. It was obvious that he had consulted with his Party's legal adviser about the various points under discussion. In his view there would not be much scope for a Prime Minister if the President had executive powers. Consequently, he proposed that the Cabinet consist of the President and such Ministers as he might appoint from Parliament. The President could then nominate a Prime Minister from the members of Parliament. Being an independent thinker, Angula differed on the role of the Prime Minister:

> We are saying for the sake of nation building that we need a President who should be above party politics. So you need a leader of a government as a prime minister who can say something about how his or her party are responding to the views of the people in terms of the policies of that party. So the need for a prime minister to be there as the leader of Government in Parliament to be daily answerable to the Parliament … is very, very critical … if you want an effective government and an effective executive that is answerable to the National Assembly.

At the end of an exceedingly long discussion, it was decided that the President would be chairman of the Cabinet, and that he would have the right to appoint his Cabinet from members of Parliament. However, the arguments regarding the limitation of the powers of the President would still not go away. SWAPO insisted that action should be taken against him only when he oversteps his powers and acts unconstitutionally. Katjiuongua once again presented the viewpoint of the opposition, referring to how in Africa having a president rule a country had so often led to a concentration of power. He was strongly opposed to the National Assembly being merely a rubber stamp, especially during the first term and until such time as we had a Second House of Parliament. While agreeing with him that we should guard against having a centralisation of power, I was opposed to the National Assembly, a legislative body, being able to control the President, unless, of course, the Constitution stipulated that the President be elected by Parliament. Once again Rukoro, as we had come to know him, presented a very logical case on the disadvantages and dangers of a directly elected President.

We were heading for yet another impasse. Nevertheless, I was equally convinced that it would lead to a confusion of Babel-like proportions to refer the matter back to the Constituent Assembly of 72 members. If this were to happen, we would have to replay the entire match, and this in full view of the media. In conclusion, I referred to the 1982 principles, which stipulated that the President would be accountable to the legislative authority. I wanted to find out from the legal advisers whether they were satisfied that we had adhered to the principles of 1982 in the decisions we had taken so far. I felt satisfied that my earlier question had been answered: "The way in which the

President is elected will in no way influence his powers, because ... he derives his powers from the Constitution and not from the people."

Given that the ACN was opposed to the principle of general suffrage, it did not acknowledge a difference between a President who had been directly elected and one who had been appointed by the National Assembly, as the voters' corps was the same for both. Once again the Chairman wanted to put the matter to vote. However, Rukoro suggested that, since the majority of members were in favour of a directly elected President, we accept it, and that the reservations of the members who opposed it be recorded in the minutes. This is how the Chairman summarised the decision: "So, it is decided the President will be elected by direct vote by the masses, but he is accountable to Parliament." To my mind this was a good compromise.

Our being able to step off this point and move on to discussing the legislative authority came as a great relief to me.

The legislative authority

Our next decision to be taken was whether the Second House of Parliament should be regarded as part of the legislative authority and what it should be called. We accepted Katjiuongua's proposal that the Second House be called the National Council, since it would represent the different geographical regions of the country. There were different views on when the National Council should be instituted. We were reminded by the Chairman that I had proposed earlier that this should transpire only after five years, since a great deal of preparation still needed to be done, such as holding a census to determine the population distribution, the demarcation of the regions, the provision of accommodation, and so on. Moreover, no one felt like having a second election so soon after the previous one.

Since SWAPO members still regarded the principle of a Second House with suspicion, the cart was again put in front of the horses and we continued talking about it before discussing the legislative authority — that is the National Assembly. We decided that a demarcation commission should be appointed as soon as possible. This was followed by an unnecessary debate on the difference between regional and municipal councils. Adv. Chaskalson recommended that setting up regional and municipal councils should be done through an Act of Parliament.

When the functions of the National Council – often referred to as a "House of Review" – were discussed, Staby in my absence presented our position and requested Prof. Wiechers to explain the British system, in terms of which legislation was accepted by a legislative body (the House of Commons) and then scrutinised by the House of Lords. If the House of Lords were to have problems with legislation, they could refer it back to the legislative body with their comments. In our case, therefore, the National Council would not be able to reject or block legislation. This brought to light that the formulation by the legal advisers that the National Assembly could approve or reject legislation was not correct. Prof. Wiechers clarified that the National Assembly had the last word. Katjiuongua said he would like to see the regional councils having teeth through the National Assembly. In response, Ruppel quoted from the minutes, which indicated that during various discussions on the functions of the National Council, I had confirmed that the Council did not have a veto right.

I could see from the demeanour of my SWAPO colleagues that they were not happy, for which I had understanding, since they had no former experience of a parliamentary system. They feared that the National Council, due to the way it was set up, could block the decisions taken by the National Assembly, upon which I pointed out that all the parties would be represented in both Houses and that the regions would not necessarily represent ethnic groups, but the total population of the regions. In addition, the discussions in the National Council would create an opportunity for further public debate and criticism of the decisions of the legislative authority. In this way the voters would be informed and reassured that decisions by the Government were being considered thoroughly. Once again I emphasised that the National Council would not have the authority to veto laws, but only to refer laws back to the National Assembly for reconsideration.

On 20 January, after dealing with the Second House of Parliament, the Committee returned to a discussion of the First House – the National Assembly. The Committee was reminded by the Chairman that the National Assembly and virtually everything relating to it had been discussed earlier, and that accordingly it was not necessary to spend too much time on it.

Responding to a question by Pretorius, Ruppel explained that the election of members of the National Assembly shall be on party lists and in accordance with the principles of proportional representation. In terms of the system of proportional representation, parties and not individual candidates are voted for. The total number of votes brought out in the election is then divided by 72, the fixed number of members in the National Assembly. This is how the number of votes a party must gain to obtain a seat in the National Assembly is determined. In most cases it so happens that once seats have been assigned to them, parties have a surplus of votes, but not enough for a seat. The surplus votes of all the parties are then added together and awarded to the party or parties in sequence of the highest surplus.

It was agreed that public servants, state corporations and parastatals could not be members of Parliament. The circumstances under which such officials could make themselves available for election, and whether they could return to their original positions should they not be successful, was left to the Government and Public Service Commission to determine.

There were no lengthy discussions on the powers and competencies of the National Assembly as formulated by the legal advisers, since their proposal reflected the usual stipulations typical of all democratic constitutions. The only exception was the circumstances under which the President could refuse to sign laws, about which there was a difference of opinion, or rather a lack of understanding. The Committee reached consensus that the President could only refuse to sign a law if the relevant law was incompatible with the Constitution, in which case he could refer it back to the National Assembly. If an agreement could not be reached, the only remaining option would be to refer the matter to the courts.

Having consulted the constitutions of several democratic countries, I realised that a constitution could not be a static document, and that, in the light of changing circumstances, it might be necessary to amend it. According to the 1982 principles, our Constitution could be amended either by means of a parliamentary decision or by means of a referendum. While I was not too happy about the idea of a referendum, I accepted it for the sake of cooperation. The Committee agreed with the 1982 provision, but the majority that would be required in both instances elicited a long discussion. The matter was complicated further by the fact that there would also be a National Council. We ultimately reached consensus, deciding that an amendment to the Constitution should be approved separately by the National Assembly and the National Council by a two-thirds majority. Our earlier decision that the chapter on fundamental rights should be entrenched in the Constitution did not prejudice this regulation. In my view one of the most significant decisions we had to make up to that point was to make amendments to the Constitution subject to rigorous limitations.

Regional and municipal councils

Because this matter would have a direct bearing on the composition of the National Council, I expected it to be especially tough to deal with. From previous discussions it had emerged clearly that SWAPO was afraid that regional councils would be seen as ethnic authorities. I was pleasantly surprised when the Chairman suggested that the proposals my party had compiled on this topic be given to the legal advisers for proper formulation. The proposals could then be scrutinised by the Committee to determine whether there were remaining points of difference that had to be discussed. Unfortunately, I then made the mistake of informing the Committee briefly about the DTA's proposals, immediately evoking a debate on the following points contained in the DTA proposal that:

- Every regional council shall consist of nine members elected by enfranchised voters in the region on the basis of proportional representation.
- Regional councils shall be elected simultaneously for a period of five years, the first election to take place on a date determined by the president by proclamation, but not later than one year after the date of independence.
- Every Namibian citizen over the age of 18 years, ordinarily resident in a particular region, but subject to the same disqualifications applicable to voters in national elections, should be entitled to vote for the election of members of the regional council for the region in which he is so resident.
- Every person entitled to vote in a particular region shall be entitled to be elected as a member of the regional council for that particular region.
- Provision should be made for the powers of regional councils, which powers should, inter alia, include the power to form part of an electoral college or form an electoral college to elect representatives to the National Council; to exercise on a regional basis all the executive powers and perform the duties

> connected thereto as may be delegated to the regional council by an act of parliament.
> • Provision should be made for the chairman and executive members to be elected.
> • Provision should be made in the constitution for the delimitation of Namibia into an agreed number of regions.

In addition, I informed the Committee that we also had a few ideas concerning municipal councils that I would hand to the legal advisers for formulation.

Both Katjiuongua and I insisted that we would like to refrain from discussing the details at that stage, but rather wait until the legal advisers had formulated the proposal correctly. However, some of the SWAPO members were not prepared to wait. They immediately started asking questions and making comments. This stood to reason, since provision had not been made for regional councils in the SWAPO proposal we were using as a working document.

The most important reservations were about the demarcation of constituencies and the question of whether these should be multi-member or single-member constituencies. On this the Chairman and I differed. His interpretation was that a "single-member" constituency meant that there would only be one candidate from each participating party and that only one would be elected as the representative of the constituency, in other words, that it would be a "winner-takes-all" situation. This was a departure from the previous decision, when the principle of proportional representation had been accepted. To clarify this I explained that a multi-party constituency was one that would have more than one representative on the regional council and that the seats would be allocated to participating parties on the basis of proportional representation. To this I added that he could differ from me on which of the two alternatives was the best, but that he should not argue with me about terminology!

The Chairman and other representatives of SWAPO took a strong stand in favour of a single-member system. I explained that the regional councils would only have delegated powers and that this was the only way in which the population could be involved in governing the country. I added that in the past our experiences with regard to centralisation and being governed from Windhoek had not been good and that there were matters that could be managed more effectively by local authorities. Eventually the Chairman managed to convince the Committee that we should wait for the legal advisers to give us their written formulation of my proposal.

Katjiuongua's proposal that the Constitution provide for a House of Chiefs, as was the case in for example Botswana, concluded the proceedings in respect of local authorities. SWAPO was opposed to this, while Katjiuongua himself was clearly not that committed to it either. He pointed out that he had made certain promises to the headmen for the sake of votes. It was noticeable that Pretorius did not participate in the discussion. A proposal was tabled by Rukoro that the Constitution contains a provision empowering Parliament to create a statutory body for traditional leaders. That there was a significant difference of opinion on this was abundantly clear, and the point was provisionally held over. I was convinced that the existence and influence of traditional leaders should neither be denied nor ignored.

The judiciary

We continued discussing the judiciary on the basis of the document that had been prepared by the advisers. Although a layman in this field, I nevertheless picked up a technical error in Article 73 of Part Six of the draft, which had been taken verbatim from the SWAPO document. It read as follows: "The judicial power shall be vested in judges or other judicial officers who shall be independent and subject only to the Constitution and the law." My question was whether it would not be more correct to replace it with the following: "The judicial power shall be vested in the Supreme Court of Namibia, which court shall be the guardian of the rights, liberties and freedoms of all persons in Namibia." Adv. Chaskalson did not agree with me, saying that it would make no difference. I pointed out that in the case of the National Assembly we had not stipulated that the legislative authorities would be vested in the members of the Assembly but in the National Assembly. The Chairman agreed with me, as did Angula, the latter pointing out that the legislative authority should rest with an institution and not with individuals. Adv. Chaskalson then proposed that the authority should be vested in the courts, which was accepted accordingly.

Long arguments ensued on the different divisions of the courts. The members with legal backgrounds – Ruppel, Rukoro and Tjiriange –

participated actively. As always, Angula came up with logical suggestions and demonstrated understanding for our proposal that there
should also be a constitutional court or division. Eventually, it was
proposed that the judiciary should be composed of a Supreme Court,
which would also have jurisdiction over constitutional matters; a
Higher Court for all cases, which would also determine which cases
concerned constitutional matters; and Magistrate's and Lower Courts.
Our proposal, summarised by Rukoro, was then approved.

A proposal by Andrew Matjila was also accepted by the Committee.
It was an addition to the draft concerning the qualifications of judges
and read as follows:

> No person shall be eligible for appointment as a judge unless
> such person –
> (a) possesses legal qualifications which would entitle him to
>   practise in all the divisions of the Supreme Court of Namibia
>   and is practising as such;
> (b) is by virtue of his experience in practice, conscientiousness
>   and integrity a fit and proper person to be entrusted with the
>   responsibilities of the office of judge.

Dr Tjiriange proposed that the qualifications of judges be stipulated in a
separate Article. The Chairman once again demonstrated his impartiality by ruling the acceptance of both Matjila's proposal and Tjiriange's
amendment. That SWAPO delegates were seldom prepared to look at
their or our proposals objectively was conspicuous throughout. They
consistently tried to thwart amendments to their original proposals.
Angula, Ruppel and Hamutenya were the exceptions.

In the next Article it was stipulated that the first judges to be signed
up following independence should be appointed for no longer than
five years, while those appointed after that could serve until they had
reached the age of 65. This age limit could be increased to 70 by the
President. To this I protested vehemently. While I knew that for some
reason or another there were probably reservations about the serving
judges, I pointed out that there already was a shortage of judges in the
country. Should this provision apply, I foresaw that some of the current judges could decide to accept an appointment elsewhere instead
of waiting for five years to see whether they would be reappointed, in
which case they would be five years older and unable to secure an appointment anywhere else.

Reacting to my objection and with reference to the 1982 principles and the call for balanced restructuring of the public service, Angula conceded that the objective of the proposal was to accommodate the "holy cow". I appreciated his honesty, but suspected his reason for this concession. At my request Ruppel informed the meeting that there were only five judges in the country, while we actually needed ten. I followed up by contending that to achieve this goal five more judges could therefore be appointed. However, the Chairman ruled that the original provision should stand, although some individuals had reservations. This I found disturbing, and said that I would prefer to wait for the final proposal.

The Chairman becomes impatient

It gradually became evident that the Chairman was becoming impatient. We started racing through certain aspects of the Constitution, some of which were important. Sections with a bearing on the Judicial Service Commission, Public Service Commission, Defence Force, the Police and Prison Services, and the Ombudsman and Auditor General were dealt with at such speed that I wasn't always sure whether we had accepted or rejected a provision, and whether it coincided with former decisions. That we would argue over the same points again when it came to the final document I knew full well.

We dealt with the important provisions on finance in record time, approving Articles that had not been discussed, and referring decisions to the legal advisers, or postponing them. It was clear that the members were somewhat out of their depth. When we came to the provision on the financial year, Dr Tjiriange wanted to know where the Government would find money to function while waiting for the budget to be approved. The Chairman referred this question to me and I explained it as follows: In the past there had always been legislation empowering the executive authority to incur expenses during the first four months of the financial year on the basis of the previous year's budget.

When we came to the chapter dealing with the arrangements during the transitional period to independence and what the situation in relation to existing legislation would be, we decided without further discussion that the Constituent Assembly would be converted into a National Assembly and that, subsequent to independence, the powers and competencies of the State President of South Africa prior to independence would be handed over to the President of Namibia. We also decided that all decisions taken by the South African Government, including the provisions of any existing laws that could still be applied in Namibia, would be regarded as having been passed by the Namibian Cabinet. I proposed that, since this matter was extensive and technical in essence, the legal advisers, assisted by other experts, should determine exactly what had to be handed over and what not.

The position of the current bureaucracy

An emotional debate followed when the position of the existing appointments in the public service were discussed. The Chairman read the proposed section: "Subject to the provisions of this Constitution, all laws which were in force immediately before independence shall remain in force until repealed or amended." Adv. Chaskalson said this could cause practical problems, since it amounted to serving officials being reappointed unless they resigned, in which case they would be dealt with according to existing legislation. In response the Chairman pointed out that if a person appointed under a contract were to resign, he would be entitled to certain benefits. While I fully agreed that practical problems could materialise if this were to happen, it was becoming ever more clear to me that SWAPO had reservations about existing officials. They wanted to clear the way towards the appointment of people who had been previously disadvantaged by means of the provisions of the Article on affirmative action; more specifically, the provision for a balanced restructuring or reorganisation of the public service.

I often said that the public servants of the time paid the highest price as a result of affirmative action. They were professional people who had been trained to perform their duties, regardless of the government in power. For the vast majority of them, especially those in senior positions, being white was their major disadvantage. Some members of the Committee were under the false impression that these officials were South Africans. It had to be pointed out to them that South West Africa/Namibia had adopted its own Public Service Act during the period of interim government, and that, with a few exceptions, all seconded South African public servants had returned to South Africa. It was an indisputable fact that in accordance with the provisions of affirmative action the new Government would gradually replace white public servants with black ones. We only had to decide whether they would be entitled to the pension benefits as specified in their service agreements. Some SWAPO members objected to this, since they were not prepared to take over the agreements and obligations of the previous regime.

I cautioned that if we were to default on our obligations by following Zimbabwe's example, we would be causing serious harm to Namibia's international image. Katjiuongua, Rukoro and Barnes took strong views on these matters. Astute and sometimes even scathing, Katjiuongua was never afraid of stating his case. He could afford to do this, because he was black. As a counter-balance, Rukoro was calm, controlled and logical. People listened to him because he spoke sense.

However, once a debate was over, it was the Chairman's task to take the lead, to make peace and to reconcile the differences. In this case he did so as follows: We have exhausted this topic. The problem is, whatever happens, all the political parties represented here have requested the citizens of this country to remain here and reconcile, and we have a 1982 holy cow which also tells us to restructure; to have balanced structure. This is going to be our major task, since the people are here. If we restructure, we will have to see what we can do with them. So this clause, even if – as somebody said – we have to "remove some people", you will need a legal basis to do so and this binds us to keep people and not to fire them. It also allows you to do some things, and besides that … we must honour existing laws. So, really, we can express our indignation about this, but we can't do anything to resolve it. This is why we have started the process of seeing how we can restructure the public service. We are talking to the civil servants themselves, and we have some experts who are here to help us … Thus we are ending on this very, very serious note …

Do principles of government policy belong in the Constitution?

On the evening of Friday 20 January, Part 4 of the working paper under the heading "Principles of State Policy" came up for discussion as the last important point in the Constitution that had to be dealt with. While we'd had a long day behind us, I was determined to dig in my heels against a chapter that provided for government policy. To my mind this did not belong in a constitution, since policy could change from government to government. I suggested that we postpone the debate until Monday. The Chairman made a few snide remarks about my viewpoint, probably thinking that they would be able to steam-roller through the chapter. Nevertheless, he asked for the Committee to reassemble on Monday.

He was on the point of adjourning the meeting when Ruppel enquired who would preside at the swearing in of the members of the National Assembly, and whether it had to be the current Chief Justice, Hans Berker. Once again he had thrown the cat among the pigeons. Attempts were made to rule out Judge Berker, such as proposing that it could be someone else, or even that the new Chief Justice should be identified and appointed before the time. But by whom? In the end it was decided that it would be Judge Berker after all. In answer to the question on which date the country would officially become independent and when the swearing-in ceremonies would take place, the Chairman replied: "It will be the international day of the Elimination of Apartheid: the 21st of March."

There were still important matters of principle to be dealt with, although we had already discussed the institution of the new Government. Among other things there were the chapter on government policy and the question of affirmative action, about which we had yet to reach consensus.

On Monday morning, before we could resume the discussion on principles of government policy, Pretorius said we were going too fast for his legal advisers, who were in the process of putting something together on communal land and cultural organisations. He asked permission to give the document, once completed, to our legal advisers to see if it was in any way at odds with the proposals by the Committee. In answer to my question of whether he wanted the legal advisers' opinion purely for the record, he replied that he also wanted it for future use. I must admit that I, as well as the other members, failed to understand what he had in mind. I think I was correct in saying that he wanted it for the record.

We then returned to the chapter on "Principles of State Policy", which took up the greater part of the day. Our point of view that this chapter did not appear in the constitutions of other countries, was supported by Katjiuongua. To this Angula responded that we didn't want to be "copycats", and that our Constitution had to be unique. I reminded him that in SWAPO's document this chapter had been taken verbatim from the Indian Constitution, so in this respect it was SWAPO being a "copycat". I had certainly caught him off guard with this observation. In fact, part of the Preamble had also been copied from the Indian Constitution, of which I was also aware. It was common knowledge at the time that Judge Mohamed, the compiler of SWAPO's proposals, was of Indian origin, and I had scrutinised, among others, the Indian Constitution.

The members of the minority parties were all opposed to provisions in the Constitution that prescribed policy, which can change from time to time. Hence Parliament, in which the opposition was represented, could also influence policy. What was more, the chapter in question also contained provisions that had already been covered in other Articles. The fact that the provisions in the proposed chapter were not enforceable indicates that they were merely promises made to satisfy the population. Once the information pertaining to the Indian Constitution was revealed, the fat was in the fire. The opposition refused to agree when SWAPO members insisted that the chapter be discussed point by point. This would amount to our accepting the inclusion of the chapter in the Constitution in principle. When Hamutenya stated that he had problems with discussing the chapter paragraph by paragraph since some of the clauses had already been covered in the draft constitution, I was taken by surprise. Then again, when the Chairman adjourned the meeting for the tea break directly after Hamutenya had expressed his reservation, I was not surprised.

I did not know what happened during the tea break, but when we resumed, the Chairman presented the Articles one after the other with a view to taking out the principles that had already been covered in the Constitution. Rukoro remarked that we were now playing a cat-and-mouse game, and suggested that we adjourn to enable those members who had problems with the chapter to come up with a unanimous proposal. He instructed them to also reflect in principle on the Article relating to affirmative action, about which they were yet to reach unanimity. Taking it further, the Chairman suggested that a committee be appointed to formulate the proposal. Staby, Hamutenya, Rukoro, Mudge and Katjiuongua were nominated to do this.

At this point Pretorius wanted to know whether the Constituent Assembly could once again discuss the draft constitution clause by clause when it had to be approved. A more chaotic state of affairs was hard to imagine. To expect the 72 members of the Constituent Assembly, who had not heard all the arguments during the sessions of the Standing Committee, to discuss the draft clause by clause would amount to our having to replay the entire game, but this time with even more players. My assumption had been that the delegations had kept their caucuses informed at all times, and could still do so. It was understandable that there were members like Pretorius who wanted to impress how hard they had fought by making their mark on the Constitution in the presence of members of the press, or by explaining why they had not done so or had not succeeded in doing so. Nonetheless, I felt that the discussions in the Constituent Assembly should be kept to the minimum, with the understanding that the parties would be given the opportunity to make short speeches.

To give the members of the designated committee the opportunity to execute the instructions they had been tasked with, the meeting was then adjourned. When the discussions were resumed, Rukoro presented their proposals. The recommendations were met with general approval. The DTA agreed to accept the proposal in spite of our reservations about the inclusion of such a chapter in the Constitution. But I wanted to make sure once and for all that we were interpreting the Article on the sovereign ownership of natural resources correctly. Since I was expecting there to be a lot more discussion about it, this was crucial. In the SWAPO document the original stipulation read: "... that the ownership and control of material resources of the community are so distributed as best to serve the common good." It was stipulated in the new proposal that only natural assets that could not otherwise be legally owned by persons or corporations would belong to the State. I enquired whether this meant that all land that was not legally owned by persons or corporations would belong to the State, and how the words "sovereign ownership" should be interpreted. I was aware that landownership was a highly sensitive matter and was furthermore concerned about the utilisation of natural resources. I was satisfied when Ruppel suggested that the words "persons and corporations" be left out, since there could also be other forms of legal ownership. How important this was, was confirmed by subsequent events.

At this stage Adv. Chaskalson informed the Committee that he and Prof. Wiechers had to return to South Africa, but that Prof. Erasmus would stay on to assist us further. The legal advisers' final document, which contained all the proposed amendments, was being typed and would soon be made available to the Committee. He stated that it had been a privilege for them to be part of this historical procedure, after which the committee members were suitably thanked by the Chairman, and the meeting was adjourned until 24 January 1990.

The third round: Resolving differences

How to report back

When the Committee assembled on 24 January 1990 the Chairman informed us that we now had the complete document, as prepared by the legal advisers, to work on. After expressing his appreciation to the legal advisers, he stated that it was our task to establish whether all the points we had discussed were contained in it, and to finalise it for submission to the Constituent Assembly. The contents had already been leaked to the press, so it was vital that the Constituent Assembly be informed accordingly. With this I agreed wholeheartedly, but suggested that we immediately make copies available to the party caucuses. In doing so, all the members of the Constituent Assembly would be fully informed. While Katjiuongua agreed that we should discuss the document to establish whether it contained all our decisions, he added that it would be a waste of time to discuss the points on which he reserved his position. My response to this was that to reach consensus we should, for example, discuss the stipulations concerning the President. Once again Pretorius wanted to know which procedure the Constituent Assembly would pursue when the draft was submitted to them. If it were done by means of a motion, all the ACN members would want to participate in the ensuing discussion. In general terms Katjiuongua agreed with him, but asked that it be borne in mind that he was the only representative of his Party in the Constituent Assembly.

In SWAPO's view we needed to submit a unanimous proposal to the Constituent Assembly. They contended that parties should be allowed to participate in the discussions, and to say, for instance, that in the spirit of cooperation and reconciliation, in the spirit of give and take, and in spite of doubts and reservations, the Constitution had been accepted by consensus. Pretorius, on the other hand, argued that this was not possible since he had already announced that while he could live with the Constitution, he was not prepared to approve it. I believed that if the caucuses of the parties approved the draft, the Constituent Assembly could, for instance, ratify it not necessarily Article by Article but page by page.

However, the general public and especially the media were becoming impatient. They had to rely on leaks, which focused primarily on points of difference. To my mind it was imperative for the Committee to sort out such differences. In the Constituent Assembly discussions had to be limited to one or two members of each party, and should be aimed primarily at informing the public and demonstrating unity and trust in the Constitution. Besides, this was our opportunity to boast a little with our achievement of writing a model constitution in record time. It did not mean that I was prepared to repeat the process in public and give everyone who did not have their way the opportunity to complain and show off their oratorical prowess.

At that point Moses Katjiuongua took the floor again. As mentioned before, I was always impressed with the way Katjiuongua stated his case – logically and without mincing his words. However, this time he went too far when he insisted that he wanted to present his entire case in the Constituent Assembly and propose his amendments there. What follows is partly how he vented his feelings:

> I never understood that this Committee was actually a smoke-screen for deals behind doors, more or less to take what might appear as final decisions and more or less to present a *fait accompli* to the Assembly … I thought this Committee was to convert the different statements presented in the Assembly into some kind of a common document or common approach and hopefully try to get understanding, agreement, consensus, whatever the case may be. But it was certainly not an opportunity through the backdoor to try to isolate ourselves from public opinion, to try to suffocate a genuine, authentic public debate in the House about matters where we might have differences of opinion … There is talk about people wanting to impress the gallery, the people and such things. In the first place we must honestly admit that no one in this House has not attempted to talk to the gallery in that hall … If that is what you call trying to impress the public, then everybody has an equal opportunity … I don't agree in any case on some kind of secrecy and some kind of artificiality in dealing with these matters in public.

That Katjiuongua wanted a public debate about the stipulations on which there were fundamental differences was clear. Earlier on Pretorius had also indicated that he preferred a public debate. Addressing me directly, Katjiuongua said that any attempt to try and resolve the differences within the Committee would be a waste of time. How he could think that it would be easier to accomplish this in a meeting attended by 72 members was beyond me. It was becoming ever more evident that we were talking at cross-purposes. In reality not one of us had objected to the members of the Constituent Assembly and the public being informed. We disagreed on whether we shouldn't first try everything possible to reach a compromise in the Committee. The objective here was to prevent us from provoking a dogfight on sensitive matters in an attempt to score points for our various parties in public. On earlier occasions when we reached an impasse we had managed to resolve it through debate and compromise. Katjiuongua had lost sight of the fact that all the representatives in the Committee were supposed to seek advice from their caucuses on a regular basis, thereby gaining their support for decisions in the Committee. Hence, there could be no question of our wanting to present the members of the Constituent Assembly with an unassailable fact. It goes without saying that the public had to be properly informed through the media. The question was centred purely on how to accomplish this. There was no objection to party representatives being entitled to state their reservations and affirm what they had fought for hard and long, but also important was that they had eventually found one another and were proud of what had been achieved. It was precisely this that would reflect the spirit shown in the Committee throughout.

The SWAPO representatives were frequently prepared to make concessions regarding points they felt strongly about, such as the Second House of Parliament, the powers of the President, proportional representation and regional councils, among others. They were prepared to look at the merits of every matter and often did not allow party-political considerations to influence them. The result was that SWAPO did not insist that their reservations be recorded and that they wanted to argue about them again in the Constituent Assembly. Since I appreciated their approach, I insisted that we iron out the points on which we were unable to reach consensus in the Committee. From the DTA's perspective, the most important point of difference was the way

in which the President was to be elected. In his long speech Katjiuongua referred as follows to those matters about which he still sought
clarity:

> I feel sincerely that we should go through these documents ...
> there are certain things here which I think should be corrected,
> and there are certain things which have been omitted, for ex-
> ample there is nothing like a House of Traditional Leadership
> and a number of other things ... when you come to the vot-
> ing concerning the Second House and the First House, there is
> a fundamental misunderstanding. I am not clear on this and I
> need an explanation. I think those things should be dealt with
> this morning ... I appeal to Mr Mudge that there is no point in
> repeating the points on which we have reserved our positions
> ... and the points on which we differ should be left to the sense
> of responsibility of the people concerned how and in what fash-
> ion, and in what manner they will raise those questions in the
> Assembly without detracting from the fact that the essence of
> this document is a common product.

It was Pretorius's contention that although SWAPO members reserved
their position regarding the Second House of Parliament, they were
prepared to discuss the details. And he wanted to be free to do the
same. This would mean that in his caucus he could vote against the
Constitution in principle or abstain from voting, but that his Party, as
in the case of Bavaria in West Germany, would cooperate when it came
to the details. He contended that he surely did not need the Committee's permission to do so, thereby reminding us of how, on two prior
occasions, he had presented his case in the Constituent Assembly in
great detail and without permission. This serves to demonstrate that
presenting viewpoints in the Constituent Assembly was never ruled
out of order, and that Pretorius had never been prevented from im-
parting his point of view in public. This brings to bear another aspect I
could never fathom, namely that he regularly insisted that he wanted
to put his viewpoint forward "elsewhere", while at this point he was
prepared to take part in the discussion of the details. Yet he had not
once expanded at length on his viewpoint in the Committee and had
seldom attempted to have his views put into practice.

To the point and logical as always, Angula stated that no one could
be barred from presenting his view in the Committee or in the Constituent Assembly. He said that all of us had reservations and that we
could express them in the Assembly, but this could reflect on us as par-

ties, and a debate there could lead to all sorts of consequences: "I have fundamental difficulties also with certain provisions, but I accepted them because I wanted progress." He concluded astutely: "If you want to do that, well and good, let it be … Let us go and talk and talk, destroy this document if you want and at the end of it adopt it. I don't know what that will serve us in any case."

Then Andrew Matjila of the DTA took the floor, saying that we had arrived at the meeting late that morning because our caucus had worked through the document methodically and had found errors that needed correcting. We had been under the impression that we would have the opportunity to bring such errors to the attention of the Committee members. We were now on the wrong track, he cautioned, and needed to do everything in our power to iron out the difficulties. This would enable us to defend the draft when we submitted it in the Constituent Assembly. He asked whether the Committee could not take the same course as our caucus, namely to work through the document. I then suggested we accept his proposal. Still, I couldn't resist the temptation of reminding SWAPO that when we had differed fundamentally on the election of the President, SWAPO members had made threats that the issue should be referred to the Constituent Assembly.

Affirmative action on the table again

The Chairman arranged that we discuss the document page by page after the tea break. Different suggestions, especially in terms of wording, were brought to Prof. Gerhard Erasmus's attention. We raced through the pages, but were brought to a standstill by the provisions relating to affirmative action.

From this point on it was me against the rest, and I fought a lone battle. Pretorius refrained from commenting, although he had said earlier that he wanted to state his case when the details were being discussed, which was precisely what the disagreement was about. We had already accepted the principle. All that we still needed to decide was where it should be placed in the Constitution and how it should be worded. It was a battle to convince the Committee. My point of departure was that we were all in agreement that affirmative action would encroach on the fundamental principle of equality and freedom from discrimination. Initially, I proposed that it should be provided for in a separate clause, but the clause drawn up by the legal advisers was unacceptable to me. It read that no provision in the Constitution could prevent the Government from implementing affirmative action. Not only did this mean that the fundamental right of freedom from discrimination would be impaired, but also other rights, including the right of ownership. When it came to affirmative action, I could not endorse that the entire Constitution would be assailable. I wanted to see it confirmed in the Constitution that affirmative action was an impairment of fundamental rights, and that to include it was intended solely to promote the position of those who had been previously disadvantaged.

In making my point, I informed the Committee that programmes had been implemented in the past to support previously disadvantaged people in our country as well as elsewhere. I mentioned that discounts on school and hostel fees were available for less affluent parents, and that loans to purchase land and animals were awarded to novice farmers. In the past, professional people and businessmen had not had access to Land Bank (the agricultural bank) loans, and this had never been regarded as discrimination. However, to ensure that court cases would not develop at a later stage as a result of "discriminatory regulations", I agreed, suggesting that in the clause on freedom from discrimination it should be stated clearly that such programmes would not be interpreted as an infringement on this fundamental right. Consequently, I proposed that in the Article providing for freedom from discrimination it should also be stipulated that this would not preclude measures for improving the position of formerly disadvantaged people. The proposal that had been suggested covered an issue that was too wide.

My proposal resulted in a lengthy debate. Still, although I gained the impression that the SWAPO members had appreciation for my viewpoint, it was also abundantly clear that they were suspicious that when it came to the implementation of this principle I wanted to limit the future government. In spite of this, my proposal was eventually accepted. However, except for Angula saying that they had no intention of taking anything away from anybody to give to someone else, the issue of land reform was never raised during the debate, which is interesting and worth knowing. This observation was repeated by Mosé Tjitendero.

The President once again

The next point, and this kept us busy for the rest of the day, concerned the way in which the President should be elected. It was clear to me from the outset that on this point we differed fundamentally. Threats came from both sides that this contentious issue had to be referred to the Constituent Assembly. Tempers flared unnecessarily in response to what members had to say. At a later stage, when Vekuii Rukoro announced that his caucus had decided he must accept a directly elected President, it was only the DTA and Moses Katjiuongua who still had reservations. Even Katjiuongua and I differed on this point. While he was adamant that a further discussion in the Committee would be a waste of time and insisted that the matter be referred to the Constituent Assembly, I persevered, maintaining that we could and should find a solution. I cautioned yet again that if we were unable to find a solution in the Committee, we would be even less likely to find one in the full Assembly.

Participating in a public debate did not interest me in the least. This stood to ruin the Constitution over which we had laboured so intensively and in such a wonderful spirit. Once again, I insisted that we should resolve our points of difference within the Committee. This would enable all of us to defend the Constitution in the Assembly and, should there be questions, provide answers.

Angula's approach was yet again logical and open-minded, and not shying away from expressing his opinion, he remarked: "I want to come back to what Mr Mudge has proposed. I tend to also see things from his perspective, namely that there are a few issues people are asking about and I feel that we should discuss them at least, not just say we don't want to." At that point Hidipo Hamutenya interrupted him, asking what the procedure would be when electing the President. This put the spotlight on Katjiuongua, who remained resolute in his stance on the election of the President. I responded with a suggestion that we stop threatening each other through public statements. Once again Angula tried to encourage a positive discussion. The Chairman expressed his agreement that we needed to determine procedure on the subject of the President. He asked whether we had not reached consensus on enough matters yet, but Katjiuongua prevented me from replying, and turned it into a long story.

I was simply not in the mood for a continuation of unnecessary arguments between Katjiuongua and the SWAPO members. These exchanges had reached the stage where they were becoming personal. I pointed out that we would not be the only country in the world with a directly elected president. Prof. Erasmus could study other constitutions and put a document together that we could discuss later. Katjiuongua agreed with the compilation of such a document, but retained his position that it should then be discussed in the Assembly. Since we had already decided that the elected Assembly would be converted into the first National Assembly, this meant that during the first term there would not be a separate and direct election of a President, and that the President of SWAPO, who was one of the elected members, would probably be the first President of the country. He would have to step down as member of the National Assembly, but would nonetheless be accountable to the National Assembly. What the procedure would be when electing the President for the second term was therefore the main issue that needed resolving.

Then an uncalled for and unnecessary remark by Barnes caused tempers to flare up again, pressing the Chairman to comment on rumours being spread and suspicions being roused. He referred specifically to speculation on what Sam Nujoma would do if he were to become President. I once again made a plea for letting the election of the President stand over until the legal advisers had had the opportunity to make a study of the different constitutions and the ways in which presidents were elected in other countries. To me the answer was already clear, but for the sake of consensus I was prepared to wait for the feedback from the legal advisers. I was not in favour of an adjournment until this point had been dealt with and suggested that we return to the rest of the working document.

I don't know whether it had to do with petulance, but the Chairman and other SWAPO members announced that they still had matters (ones on which we had already decided) they wanted to add to the remaining points. Matters were now really going haywire. In an attempt to deflect this, I made a lengthy and emotional attempt to bring about conciliation. Angula came to my assistance once again: "We must have the political will and courage to do things. If we come together and deliberate on matters that will have no consequences for the drafting procedure, we will get nowhere. So, if you don't have that political will and courage, then we mustn't deceive the public that we are doing things."

The following discussion then followed:

CHAIRMAN: [W]hat are we reporting tomorrow?

DR TJITENDERO: You can report that we agreed, we engaged lawyers to do the technical work, we went back to the document, reopened issues, we disagreed and there are even minutes … and the whole thing is open. Let's open the entire thing. Let's not lie tomorrow; let's tell the truth.

CHAIRMAN: Yes, we don't lie two or three times. Our credibility is at stake …

MR MUDGE: Mr Chairman, give me one good reason why you will have to explain that to the public? Because you have a difference of opinion on Article 27, you have stopped the deliberations.

CHAIRMAN: Because it is simply a waste of time; because it is the third time we are doing it.

MR RUPPEL: You had a chance to discuss this very Article with your caucus how many times. Why don't you come back to us and say what the position of the caucus is?

MR MUDGE: I have done this and I want to discuss it now. I have agreed to accommodate Mr Katjiuongua the way I have accommodated other people, that we get an addendum on the election of the President, the procedure. That is what he wanted. Let him do that; maybe he can improve on the present one. It is not going to make that much of a difference. That is all; the principle is accepted. This is the minimum that is in here; about the rest we want to know. Now we go on with the rest, and we discuss it. I can't see any reason why not. Why not?

Despite my having great understanding and appreciation for Katjiuongua's strong viewpoint, I realised that we were running the risk of reaching stalemate. I suggested that the problem could be resolved if we put the question of election aside for the time being to reflect on the position of the President in its entirety. It was clear to me that the closer we came to the next day's open session of the Constituent Assembly, the less SWAPO and also Katjiuongua would be prepared to compromise. The only party that was not afraid to be engaged in a public debate was the DTA, the reason being that we were happy with what we had achieved. Fortunately, the situation was salvaged by Prof. Erasmus proposing that the meeting adjourn for half an hour for him to discuss Katjiuongua's problems with him. I was hoping this might help us surmount the stumbling block of Article 28. After the adjournment Prof. Erasmus informed the meeting that Katjiuongua had accepted the direct election of the President in principle, including the way in which candidates would be nominated.

The SWAPO members continued asking questions and expressing their misgivings about the President's relationship with the legislative authority. I became increasingly convinced that they did not fully understand the meaning of the term "accountability". Not even the fact that the 1982 principles stipulated that the executive authority must be accountable to the legislative authority convinced them. The Chairman was also not unhappy with my formal proposal that the President deal with his own budgetary appropriation in the National Assembly. It became ever more evident in the ensuing discussion that they did not want their President in the National Assembly. They repeatedly raised the question of whether it would not be expedient for one of the ministers to act on his behalf in the Assembly. Hamutenya said, among other things: "I have listened carefully to Mr Mudge and to Mr Barnes, and neither of them have convinced me. As far as I am concerned the arguments they are advancing have no adequate contribution to offer. The question of accountability does not necessarily mean that he must appear in person." In response to this, Katjiuongua commented:

> I don't understand why some friends are so eager to isolate the President and keep him away from the centre of public life, but maybe we will know that in the future ... [W]hat is important to me is the constitutional controls of the powers of the President and the Assembly, how they interplay ... But I cannot agree to a system where the President will be seen practically only by those around him, while the rest of us have no contact with our President.

The Chairman posed the question whether the wording could not be changed in such a way that, when requested, the President could attend the meetings. In my view this amounted to an insult to the President. It was also unacceptable to me in other ways. A practical solution would be to have a special occasion for this every year, enabling him to slot it into his programme and prepare himself for it. To this end I submitted the following proposal for consideration: "In terms of the responsibility of the President towards the Legislature, the President shall attend Parliament during the annual discussion of the budget to inform members on the state of the nation and on policies which the Government intends to pursue and to report on the activities of the Government over the past financial year." While Angula agreed in principle that the President should be accountable to the National Assembly, he could not grasp that there would be any sense in him appearing in Parliament to talk about the budget. The impression that Sam Nujoma had to be kept out of Parliament for some or other obscure reason had reared its head yet again.

It was interesting how the debate around the President's relationship with Parliament kept making these strange twists and turns. Hamutenya indicated that he would support my proposal, but suggested that we go back and change Article 24 to stipulate that the executive authority would be vested in the President. Since this was clearly intended as a threat, it was obviously not acceptable. He was, however, supported by Tjitendero, who argued that if the executive power were to be vested only in the President, the exact meaning of the function would become clear when making reference to the executive authority. When it was pointed out to them that in this case they would no longer need a cabinet, Tjitendero said this was exactly what he was proposing. This was seconded by his colleague, Tjiriange.

I found such a statement difficult to believe, coming from two future ministers who could have original powers but preferred to vest all the executive powers in a President. They were possibly using it merely as an argument to support the notion of not exposing the President to the legislative authority and especially not to the opposition and to public opinion.

In an attempt to accommodate the views and questions I proposed the following:

> In accordance with the executive's responsibility to the legislature, the President and his Cabinet shall attend the session of Parliament during the consideration of the budget to report to Parliament on the activities and performance of his Government during the past year and to inform Parliament on its plans and policies for the future, and to be available to respond to matters raised by members.

We had succeeded in convincing the Chairman and he decided that the proposal would be accepted like this. We had achieved our goal, although there were still questions on why the President would be required to be present only at the discussion of the budget. All that was still required was for the legal advisers to take care of the final formulation.

Next on the agenda were the other duties and responsibilities that normally were vested in the President of a country. These were the dissolution of Parliament under certain circumstances; the appointment of judges, the Ombudsman, Attorney General, head of the Defence Force and other senior officials; the creation of different commissions and ministries; and the appointment of Ministers. Once again Katjiuongua became stubborn, wanting the National Assembly to approve certain appointments. While I had understanding for his viewpoint, I did not agree that such powers should be given to a legislative body. This was also now becoming a pattern. Each time Katjiuongua was opposed, he threatened to go and present his case in the Constituent Assembly. It goes without saying that this instigated SWAPO members to follow suit, which led to unnecessary tension. It was already late in the night, and I was in no mood to play along. Saying that he needed sleep, Tjitendero asked for an adjournment until the next morning.

However, the Committee's discussions could not be wound up until we had worked through the entire draft constitution. We made some progress when Pendukeni Ithana quoted another Article:

> Subject to the provisions of this Constitution and save where this Constitution provides otherwise, any action taken by the President pursuant to any power vested in the President by the terms of this Article shall be capable of being reviewed, reversed and corrected on such terms as deemed expedient and proper if there be a resolution proposed by at least one-third of the members of the National Assembly and passed by a two-thirds majority.

In all probability the members of the Committee did not all understand the many implications contained in the quoted Article, but they were all prepared to accept that the President could make the appointments.

Prof. Erasmus reminded the Committee that it had been decided in principle to create a representative body for traditional leaders, but that it did not yet feature in the Constitution. Although SWAPO didn't like it, Moses felt strongly about it. Prompted by a suggestion by Prof. Erasmus, the following provision was eventually accepted: "There shall be an advisory council of traditional leaders established in terms of an Act of Parliament."

Judicial authority

When we reached the next point, Pretorius came with "a friendly request", asking whether he could give the many questions he had about the wording and technical aspects to the legal adviser rather than raise them in the Committee. Since these questions were not about principles, the legal adviser could save a great deal of time by using his discretion. For some reason or another, Pretorius did not want to give the Committee a breakdown of the document his own legal advisers had compiled for him. On the other hand, such a procedure would have caused confusion, since at this late stage the Committee's most important task was about formulation and wording. This sometimes led to long-drawn-out discussions and serious differences of opinion. In most cases the differences about the wording and technical aspects were resolved speedily, so we progressed fast.

By this time the members were becoming sleepy and irritable. However, we still had to jump a few significant hurdles, the first being Article 77: The Administration of Justice. In the original working document the provision that the first judges (mainly serving judges) should be appointed for only five years had already been amended. Once again it was proposed that all the judges already appointed on Independence Day could serve until the age of 65. On Ruppel's suggestion the matter was discussed with the serving judges, and the proposed age limit was increased.

Regarding the appointment of the Attorney General and Ombudsman; the formulation of the legal advisers was approved. However, it became apparent during the discussion that the SWAPO members were very sceptical about existing appointments, even in the case of the Ombudsman.

Outstanding points are settled

The formulation of the provision for the creation of regional and municipal councils had initially elicited a long debate. I heaved a sigh of relief when it was accepted without much discussion.

When I asked in terms of which provision in the Constitution permanent secretaries would be appointed, I again evoked a hefty reaction. It was common knowledge that people had already been identified for these positions, and I wanted to find out whether they would be public servants and whether they would be subject to the same provisions as other officials. It was no simple matter to get a clear answer. Answers like I "had to accept that we would have a different dispensation now" did not satisfy me. I had accepted the new dispensation, and also had no problem with the appointment of permanent secretaries. However, I wanted to know whether they would be ordinary public servants, or political appointments (the term "political animals" was often used) as in the case of the Attorney General. With his legal background Ruppel put my mind at ease by comparing permanent secretaries with the way in which the Attorney General had been appointed in the past, namely "subject to the laws relating to the public service". However, what he did not say was that under the previous dispensation the position had a different function to the one it would have under the new dispensation, which would undeniably make him/her a "political animal".

We had virtually come to the end of the document formulated by the legal advisers. Prof. Erasmus revisited the President's responsibility to the National Assembly for the last time. He had been instructed to draw up a final formulation, which read: "Each year during the consideration of the official budget, the President and his/her Cabinet shall attend Parliament. During such a session, the President shall address Parliament on the state of the nation, on the policies of the Government, and shall be available to respond to questions."

This did not satisfy me, and I reacted as follows: "The words missing refer to the executive's responsibility to the legislature and reporting on the activities of the Government during the past financial year. I cannot understand why we are avoiding the responsibility and the report in this way."

By then the Chairman was probably also tired, so he ruled that what I had asked for be added. The final provision as it now appears in the Constitution reads:

> In accordance with the responsibility of the executive branch of Government to the legislative branch, the President and the Cabinet shall each year during the consideration of the official budget attend Parliament. During such a session the President shall address Parliament on the state of the nation and on the future policies of the Government, shall report on the policies of the previous year and shall be available to respond to questions.

In conclusion the Chairman thanked the members of the Committee and the legal advisers for their forbearance with the torture to which they had been subjected. It was clear that he was no longer in a particularly good mood, and to be honest, neither was I. It had been a long day and it was late.

However, the last hurdle still lay ahead. The Constituent Assembly of 72 members elected in the 1989 election still had to approve and accept the concept drafted by the Standing Committee. Hence, before we could adjourn, we had to decide on how the Committee would report to the Constituent Assembly. I was under the impression that the caucuses of all the parties had already been fully informed as regards the contents of the final draft and that acceptance would be a mere formality. Likewise I accepted that we would be expected to inform the public on the contents of the Constitution in this open meeting, which would be attended by the press. Although the members of the Committee could not be prevented from participating in the debate, I was hoping that members of the Committee would not use the opportunity to depart from the decisions they had taken and the concessions they had made. The impression should not be created that the Constitution was subject to reservations. The ACN according to Pretorius had considered abstaining from voting. Although he frequently referred to his Party and caucus, few people probably knew who the actual leader was. I gained the impression in the Constituent Assembly that Jan de Wet was the leader, while Koos Pretorius acted with the authority of a leader in the Committee.

Did we reach consensus?

This was how we managed to write a draft constitution for an independent Namibia within 80 days. It was possible because we began the process with two complete draft constitutions on the table, namely those of SWAPO and the DTA. Although our concept was the product of more than ten years' study, research and deliberations within own ranks, we were prepared to make concessions, as were SWAPO and the other parties. It took a concerted effort, and there can be no doubt that the draft constitution was debated and accepted Article by Article. The only exception was Aksie Christelik-Nasionaal (ACN), which differed on the basic principles of the draft. Nevertheless, the ACN representative indicated that he was prepared to subject himself and his Party to the Constitution. Pretorius encapsulated it as follows: "Consensus means not voting against something, but unanimous means something different." There would still be much argumentation about what the concept "consensus" meant. The fact that Pretorius differed fundamentally from the other members of the Committee on the basic principles reflected in the Constitution could be used to argue that we had never at any stage reached consensus on the principles contained in the draft.

The Constituent Assembly considers the concept

On 25 January 1990, the Committee submitted its product to the full Constituent Assembly. The session started with the Chairman informing the Assembly that he had received a letter from Pretorius in his capacity as Chairman of the ACN stating that Jan de Wet's membership of the Constituent Assembly had been revoked. However, he had also received a letter from De Wet stating that he, De Wet, still represented the ACN and was not planning to vacate his seat. The Chairman distanced himself from this dispute, appealing to the two colleagues to resolve their differences themselves.

Since the participating parties were to approve the final draft constitution Article by Article, this information surfaced at a critical stage. Which of the two leaders was going to speak on behalf of the ACN in this process? Why did Pretorius want to terminate the membership of his colleague, Jan de Wet, in the Constituent Assembly? Had Jan de Wet been kept informed on the position his colleague had taken in the Committee over the past months? While I was waiting for them to be given the floor, these questions kept whirling through my mind. Many years later, when I was making notes for my manuscript, I reflected on this incident again. I telephoned Koos and asked him what had happened between him and Jan at the time. I was given the following brief account: Before the 1989 election Jan de Wet had expressed the opinion that they would not do well at the polls under the name "National Party". Moreover, this would make raising funds for the election campaign difficult. Jan suggested that they participate in the election under a different name and under his leadership. Jan maintained that this would only be a temporary arrangement. After the election, Koos would again resume the leadership. This was how Aksie Christelik-Nasionaal (ACN) came into being and was registered as a participating party in the election with Jan de Wet as leader. After the election a dispute developed between the two about who was actually the party leader, and dissatisfaction on Koos's part about a salary that he had not received. Apparently these were the reasons why Koos wanted to terminate Jan's membership of the Constituent Assembly. In this bid, however, he was unsuccessful.

Tjiriange of SWAPO described the draft as "the product of a job well done". In his view "the final draft now before you reflects the agreements on all principle issues correctly." He thanked the members of the Committee for the spirit of reconciliation in which the discussions had taken place, stating that SWAPO saw its way clear to live with the proposed Constitution. He went on to describe it as a compromise that reflected the aspirations of all sections of our society. He said that he, without detracting from SWAPO's commitment to this compromise, wanted to point out that in the process SWAPO had been prepared to make compromises in respect of specific aspects, among which were elections on the basis of constituencies instead of proportional representation, a one-house Parliament, rules against apartheid (which in his opinion had been watered down) and powers and competencies of the President, which had been reduced drastically.

Mishake Muyongo thanked the Chairman and the Committee on behalf of the DTA for the work they had done, adding that other countries having problems with their constitutions should feel free to approach the Committee for assistance. But, he offered, he was concerned that the Constitution contained nothing pertaining to the question of communal land. This was a concern I shared. He put it as follows:

> Another matter that I want to make reference to is the fact that very important matters – to me at least – were left out, one being the issue of communal land. In this Constitution there is no reference to it, other than to customary and common law which, to my mind, don't tie in with the important issue of communal land. We have our people living in these areas, the land belongs to them, but our Constitution has not made reference to it. So, Mr Chairman, I wish to ask that a few of these issues be tackled again by our very able committee under your very able chairmanship, so that we can allay the fears of our people, wherever they may be, so that nothing that belongs to them is forgotten, and nothing that belongs to them in terms of land is going to be snatched away in a dubious manner.

Muyongo was virtually pleading. This was not the first time in his political career that friction had arisen between Muyongo and SWAPO
over communal landownership in the Caprivi. He stated that he was
not asking for secession or independence for the communal areas; he
was only asking for some or other form of security of tenure. It would
be appropriate to ask to what extent the denial of this added to the
clash among the inhabitants of the different communal areas, or more
specifically, to what subsequently happened in the Caprivi. Ten years
later this issue was still the subject of a long-drawn-out court case.

Two years after independence, Muyongo made the same point during the Land Conference. While no one could approve of what had
happened a decade earlier in the Caprivi when he wanted to lead a secession movement, could this not have been avoided with a little more
insight? This is purely conjecture on my part. When I raised the problem in the Committee at the time, there was little understanding for
it. In the past 30 years or so in my discussions with members of other
groups, reference was often made to Owambo imperialism. However,
we must not lose sight of the fact that at the time the Owambo people,
who represent more than half of the population in the country, were
limited to a mere 6% of Namibia's surface area, and that they were
previously allowed in the southern part of the country only as contract
labourers. This led to the establishment of the Ovamboland People's
Organisation (which later became SWAPO).

While Muyongo welcomed the protection of fundamental rights
in the Constitution, he expressed the hope that discrimination would
never resurface in a different form. The final product compiled by the
Committee was also welcomed by Justus //Garoëb of the Damara people. Now, he said, we could announce to the inhabitants of the country
and the entire world that we had crossed the Rubicon.

I wondered how Pretorius was going to wriggle out of the dilemma
in which his Party found themselves. When it was his turn to speak,
he made no mention of the internal issue between himself and Jan de
Wet. Instead he indicated that he would abide by the decision of the
majority on the basis of the biblical teaching as reflected in Romans 13.
He stated:

> We are prepared to accept realities, but we prefer to stand firm
> on our principles. We cannot agree to the principles, but we ac-
> cept the challenges as far as the reality is concerned. We believe

> that the function of an opposition party, especially a small op-
> position party, is primarily to convince more than merely to op-
> pose. Deviating from your principles just to try and be popular
> will hamper much in the fulfilment of your responsibilities and
> task.

He made reference again to the provisions pertaining to a secular state, the protection of minority groups and the balance between fundamental rights and responsibilities. Other than reserving his position regularly, he'd had little to say on any of these principles when they were discussed in the Committee. He substantiated this by saying that he found it unnecessary to state his reservations on every Article, since his "standard position" was known, and he only wanted to refer to a few of them. I must acknowledge that he stated his case clearly and comprehensively. I have yet to fathom why he hadn't presented his case in the Committee where the Constitution had been drafted. When I needed his support, he remained silent.

He again referred to the provisions on fundamental rights and the fact that provision had not been made for responsibilities. He referred to the Ten Commandments maintaining that they were actually a "Charter of Responsibilities". Surely no one would object to God placing responsibilities on us, but to now give Sam Nujoma and the SWAPO government the right to, above and beyond the limitations and obligations laid on us by laws, burden us with other "fundamental" responsibilities was and remains unacceptable to me. Earlier on Pretorius had already tried to substantiate his argument by pointing out that Cuba and Russia also made provision for responsibilities in their constitutions. What strange bedfellows these two turned out to be! There was no doubt whatsoever that the entrenchment of fundamental rights in our Constitution was the best protection possible against irresponsible governments in future. How Pretorius (or the ACN) could be opposed to this, was beyond me.

Pretorius concluded his speech as follows:

> The ACN and my integrity, reliability and trustworthiness are at
> stake. Nobody will believe us ever again if we vote in principle
> for this Constitution as a whole … therefore we will abstain from
> voting because we cannot agree to the principles that form the
> basis of this Constitution. As democrats and as a minority we
> will, however, accept the challenge to help make the best of this
> Constitution.

He neglected to say what the basic principles in the Constitution were with which he did not agree, although we all knew. In the election campaign it was emphasised by the ACN that Pretorius was adhering unyieldingly to the basic principles of the Turnhalle Constitution, which provided for an ethnically based government. I was curious to hear what the position of his colleague, Jan de Wet, would be vis-à-vis the acceptance of the final document.

When the Chairman appealed to De Wet and Pretorius to resolve their mutual differences, Jan responded as follows: "[I]n the first instance those brotherly remarks made by the brother Chairman were accepted in a brotherly way." He then thanked the Committee for the important document that would secure the future of the country and the generations to come. He said that the coordination of the proposals of the different political parties to the satisfaction of all concerned so that consensus could be reached had initially seemed like an impossible task to him. It was clear to me that the two colleagues interpreted the concept of consensus differently. It was also obvious that Jan de Wet accepted the draft in principle, with the exception of a few Articles. About the principles that had fallen by the wayside he said nothing. Which one of them spoke on behalf of their caucus, and whether the caucus and Jan de Wet had ever been informed about what transpired in the Committee remains a mystery to me.

After the speeches by party leaders, the different clauses of the draft were presented one by one. While some clauses were only commented upon, the Committee was requested to consider amendments to others. I fully agreed with Jan de Wet when he mentioned certain requirements of a constitution. Among others, he referred to technical errors and asked whether the legal adviser of the ACN could assist our consultants in correcting these. Another suggestion was that the Constitution, as in the case of all laws, should have a "long title". His comments about the Preamble were mostly the same as those Staby had proposed in the Committee. He mentioned the time when he was Commissioner General of the Indigenous Peoples, and pointed out what he had achieved. Whether the Assembly regarded him as one of the people who had established apartheid in this country had obviously become a sensitive issue to him. I don't think it is necessary for me to comment on this any further.

Quoting Prof. Joseph Diescho and various other people in substantiating his point, Pretorius expanded on mother-tongue education, and said he would leave the matter to the Assembly. The Chairman read out the clause in the draft that already provided for this aspect and it was accepted. Next to speak was Jan de Wet, who contended that insufficient provision had been made in the draft constitution for ethnic groups to protect their language, culture, traditions and religion. Here also the Chairman read the provision in the draft, which provided adequately for this aspect.

The provision on detention without trial elicited a lengthy discussion. My view was that it was occasionally required in the interests of the State. However, some members expressed serious misgivings on the issue, especially in terms of the negative reaction it could elicit at an international level.

A subcommittee hones the final product

The final approval of the Constitution was scheduled to take place on 9 February 1990. The Constituent Assembly abided by the comments it had made at the meeting of 25 January, and requested that a smaller subcommittee in the meantime have a final look at the formulation and technical aspects of the draft constitution to ensure that the document corresponded to the decisions taken. The meeting of the subcommittee on 6 February also took place under considerable pressure, since the final document had to be available for the important final meeting of the Constituent Assembly.

The previous day, in an explanatory memorandum to the Constituent Assembly, Chairman Hage Geingob pointed out the following:

> ... that the final editing of the whole Draft should be undertaken to ensure consistency of style and punctuation. It is important that in the final editing particular attention be paid to the internal references to other provisions of the Constitution that may now have become changed as a result of the renumbering process ... [A] very careful job needs to be done on all the existing legislation to decide what should be repealed and what should be left in place. We are not in the position to undertake the task.

At the beginning of the meeting of the subcommittee Staby pointed out that there were certain matters that could not possibly be finalised before 9 February but needed to be included in the Constitution. However, Prof. Erasmus did not find the problem that serious, and said it had in fact already been taken into consideration.

Yet to be resolved was how exactly the draft would be presented in the Constituent Assembly and whether final approval would be gained by majority vote, unanimously or with consensus. In addition, we had not taken into consideration that although the purpose of this last meeting was to ensure that the final technical attention to detail and editing by the legal team did not deviate from the decisions of the Committee, amendments to the draft would be suggested again. Nonetheless, the Chairman was determined to conclude the debate as quickly as possible, and I did my best to assist him.

The formulation of the provisions on citizenship, more specifically on the position of former members of the Defence Force and Police, by the legal team presented me with a problem. I thought that the provisions failed to reflect our decision accurately. The SWAPO members were still not keen on giving such people citizenship on the basis of birth and did not want to concede that many of them had been living in Namibia long before independence, that they were still living here, and that their children – who had been born here – were entitled to citizenship on the basis of birth. Removing the baseless suspicions of SWAPO members was no simple task. My suggestion was eventually accepted. This meant that when Namibia became independent in 1990, the children of former members of the Defence Force and Police who had been living in the country for at least five years were entitled to citizenship on the basis of where they had been born. The parents of such children could obtain citizenship through registration, as was the case with all other persons who did not qualify by birth.

Another provision about which I had serious reservations was detention without trial. We had initially decided that in the interests of State security, a person could be held in detention without trial for 48 hours. At an earlier stage Adv. Chaskalson had pointed out that when a large number of people were being detained, it would be impossible to stand trial within 48 hours. By then, however, it was already clear, according to the media, that members of the public were opposed to detention without trial. The Chairman pointed out that we were being praised throughout the world because we subjected detention without trial to strict conditions.

I found the proposal that it should be left to Parliament to provide for detention without trial by means of legislation unacceptable. I strenuously objected, and quoted from the original provision, which stated unequivocally "… that no law shall provide for preventative detention unless such detention is reasonably necessary to provide against what is reasonably apprehended, and constitutes a clear and present danger to the security of the State."

I elaborated further:

> Now we leave it to Parliament to make a law providing how this must be done. Personally I would have preferred to retain the whole paragraph. At least it made clear provision for the procedures to be followed. Now we want to give carte blanche to a Parliament to detain people without trial, without dictating to them precisely how it should be done. Gentlemen, you have taken a decision and you must now live with the consequences of that decision. There is no way you can come in by the back door with just a carte blanche to Parliament to detain people and then violate the principle contained in this paragraph. Then I will insist that the original paragraph be brought back.

Prof. Erasmus contended that if his proposal in this regard was not accepted, an emergency situation would have to be declared. The original provision, which had been brought back at my request, did actually provide for preventative detention, on condition that the detainee would be tried within 48 hours. In Article 11 in the final Constitution the stipulation reads as follows:

1. No persons shall be subject to arbitrary arrest or detention.
2. No persons who are arrested shall be detained in custody without being informed promptly in a language they understand of the grounds for such arrest.
3. All persons who are arrested and detained in custody shall be brought before the nearest Magistrate or other judicial officer within a period of forty-eight (48) hours of their arrest or, if this is not reasonably possible, as soon as possible thereafter, and no such persons shall be detained in custody beyond such period without the authority of a Magistrate or other judicial officer.

The only other provision in the draft constitution providing for detention without trial (subject to strict conditions) was the section pertaining to an emergency situation.

The dust would not settle on the interpretation of the concepts "public interest" and "just compensation" in the case of expropriation of movable and immovable property. Even today, more than two decades later, this is still the case. Gurirab articulated it as follows: "You should be in a position to quantify what just compensation would be. Unless you do that by an Act of Parliament, how else would you do it?" Needless to say, this was not acceptable to me. It was obvious that my SWAPO colleagues had only the expropriation of land in mind, while the 1982 principles referred to immovable as well as movable property. As far as I was concerned, leaving it to the legislative body to determine what would be paid for a farm, house, cattle or a vehicle in the case of expropriation was not negotiable. The only internationally acceptable interpretation of the concept "just compensation" was market price, in other words that which another buyer would also be prepared to pay. "Public interest" can be interpreted only as meaning that property could not be expropriated in the interests of a minority and at the expense of the majority of the population.

The formulation of the sections dealing with academic freedom, freedom of the press, declaring war, the nomination of candidates for elections, the appointment of officials and the necessity of a public service commission was accepted. The Article on circumstances under which Parliament could be dissolved if the country were to become ungovernable was discussed at length, and then left to the legal advisers to reformulate.

Establishing a Council of Traditional Leaders did not elicit discussion again, although I did have a problem with the uncertainty regarding the status, control and utilisation of communal land, and questioned the proposed provision. It read: "… the ownership of communal land … and control over such land, which vested in the executive committees of the Representative Authorities, shall vest in the Government of Namibia." When communal land came under discussion, SWAPO members were generally sceptical, especially since they saw it as confirmation of the old homeland system. It was my opinion that while provision had been made in the chapter on the protection of fundamental rights for the protection of all other forms of property rights, this did not include the protection of communal landownership. I voiced my viewpoint as follows:

> Mr Chairman … you have shown a lot of understanding for the property rights of many people in this country and I very much appreciate that. I think everybody is impressed by the respect and regard you have for the cultural and material assets of people in this country. I think it would be wrong to ignore the rights of those people who do not own land individually.

It was noticeable that it was exclusively Herero-speaking members of the Committee who participated in the debate that followed. Rukoro attempted to reach a compromise by proposing that the regulation and utilisation of communal land should be managed by Government in consultation with the Council of Traditional Leaders. Since the envisaged Council would comprise all the headmen of all the different regions and they, when land was discussed, would possibly be competing against one another, I did not think this could not work. The reluctance to discuss the matter was possibly because some of the members wanted the entire issue of ownership of and control over communal land to be postponed until the issue of land reform had been discussed.

We had to tread carefully because land reform was a crucially important and sensitive matter. Until this late stage it had only been referred to in passing, but not discussed in detail. It became increasingly clear that the participants in the debate would prefer to postpone the entire land matter, albeit for different reasons. Dr Tjiriange did not agree and remarked: "You can rest assured that this question, if we simply end the discussion like this, will create a problem within our own caucus. The members feel very strongly about the land issue. Communal land problems should not be dealt with as if they are the only problem, because they are not the only problem; the problem is the land problem all over the country, across the board." He apparently had no problems with regions such as Owambo, Kavango and Caprivi, but he did have problems with "reserved areas" where traditional leaders were not in the same position as those in other areas. In those reserves they just don't have the right on any land." He was clearly not favourably disposed towards the Herero leaders, and so did not want to give them any authority over that land. He was set on keeping it for the Central Government, of which he would be part.

Here the Chairman joined in, asking why there should be a council of chiefs, "… because our people are questioning who are the chiefs". Riruako responded: "I think the reality of the situation is that in a free, independent Namibia, free of colonialism, we are going to have areas which will have to be defined objectively as being communal, over which some of these chiefs and their councils and traditional authorities, not all of them, will have control functions delegated by the Central Government." Certain areas were left out again, without stating which areas. Riruako concluded the discussion by proposing that the matter stand over and that the future government should decide on this by means of legislation. The non-Herero-speaking delegates still refrained from commenting. It was obvious that I was fighting a losing battle. The outcome was that the entire issue of landownership remained hanging until two years after independence, when a representative Land Conference reached consensus on the subject of a future land-reform policy. And so the claims of the Herero nation to ancestral land died a quick death. On this I will elaborate later.

We had reached the end of the draft constitution as formulated by the legal advisers in the subcommittee, and all the Articles were approved. However, I had one last point to raise. During the election for independence, some irregularities had taken place. It was therefore crucial to prevent a repetition of such irregularities in future elections. To this end I proposed a last amendment, namely that the political parties should be involved not only in the counting of votes, but in the election process in its entirety. Ruppel reacted positively to my proposal, and Point 4 of Schedule 5 of the Constitution was accordingly worded as follows: "Provision shall be made by an Act of Parliament for all parties participating in an election of members of the National Assembly to be represented at all material stages of the election process and to be afforded a reasonable opportunity for scrutinising the votes cast in such election."

The Constitution is officially ratified on 9 February 1990

We had finally crossed the finishing line following two and a half months of intensive deliberations. The 72 members of the Constituent Assembly took their positions on the steps in front of the Tintenpalast to ratify the Constitution formally in the presence of a large number of dignitaries, including Martti Ahtisaari (the Special Representative of the Secretary General of the UN) and foreign diplomats, as well as a large number of Namibians. It was an intensely emotional experience for me. While we were waiting for the ceremony to commence, I couldn't help but reflect on the long and winding road we'd had to walk from South West Africa to Namibia. It had certainly not been easy, but was definitely worth the effort. The delegates gathered around me reminded me of a team photograph taken on the playing field after winning a match. Rather than winning a war, peace and democracy had won. I felt immensely privileged to have been part of it.

The proceedings were opened by Hage Geingob as follows:

> This is indeed a historic day, the day on which we are gathered here to discuss and, hopefully, adopt the basic law for this nation. Your elected representatives have been working day and night like a good architect drawing a plan for a beautiful house. For a house to be long-lasting, well built and liked by the owner, the foundation and design must be carefully considered and the builders' work properly supervised by the architect. Likewise, to run a modern democratic state, a well-written constitution is a *sine qua non*. This is what your Constituent Assembly has been doing over the past three months. The foundation for a new Namibia has been laid with the completion of the draft fundamental law. The framers recognised the inherent dignity, equal and inalienable rights of the human family that is indispensable for freedom, justice and peace. They pointed out that these rights include the right of an individual to life, liberty and the pursuit of happiness regardless of race, colour, ethnic origin, sex, religion, creed, social or economic status. The above-mentioned rights are most effectively maintained and protected in a democratic society where the government is responsible to freely elected representatives of the people, operating under a sovereign constitution and a free and independent judiciary.

Mishake Muyongo accepted the draft constitution on behalf of the DTA, but not without expressing his disappointment that the National Council (or Second House of Parliament) could not institute regional and municipal councils until such time as the necessary legislation had been accepted. He cautioned against unrealistic expectations and an opposition that might be negative and destructive. Then he thanked the four of us who had served on the Committee for our contribution in drawing up the Constitution. Moses //Garoëb of the UDF said that reaching this historical milestone had seemed impossible a few months ago, but he and his party were now committed to the draft.

Acting as leader of the ACN, Jan de Wet said that it had been a privilege for him to participate in the preparation of the Constitution, and that Aksie Christelik-Nasionaal had played a positive and constructive role in drawing up the draft. This caused me to wonder once again whether he had been properly informed on what had transpired in the Committee. He referred again to certain reservations that his Party had in respect of the Preamble, and to assurances regarding the protection of the traditions, culture, language and religion of the many different groups within the population. He contended that the section in question did not offer sufficient protection for the collective rights of those groups. He also had problems with affirmative action being linked to colour, and expressed his concern over the fact that the National Council could not be instituted immediately. Of the many other objections in relation to principles that his colleague in the Committee had raised, he made no mention. He then stated emphatically that if the Constitution were accepted through consensus, it did not mean that it had been accepted unanimously. If this were the case, it would surely mean that the ACN was not prepared to vote for the Constitution, but only to submit to it. In conclusion he made the following undertaking: "The ACN hereby solemnly affirms to uphold the Constitution and the laws of the Republic of Namibia to the best of its ability. God bless our country." Whether the ACN accepted the fundamental principles of the Constitution or only regarded itself as being subject to them is something that will be disputed for many years to come.

After the other smaller parties had also expressed their support of the draft, the Chairman announced that the Constitution had been accepted by consensus. Chairman Hage Geingob and I embraced each other. There was no talk of a winner or loser. Peace and democracy had won. This, to me, was the highlight of my long political career. I was totally convinced that the reconciliation that had been attained in the previous months and the friendships that had been forged would be permanent, and that the new Government would maintain this attitude.

It is my belief that this story of the drafting of a Constitution for Namibia proves that what we achieved was not the product of only one party or one group. I would like to stress that the perception that the country is currently being governed by a SWAPO Constitution is false. Over a period of some three decades, many parties, bodies and individuals were involved in this historical process. The outcome was ultimately the work of political leaders, international organisations, freedom fighters, knowledgeable people and ordinary Namibians who represented a wide range of beliefs and aspirations. On the home stretch it was especially the contributions of the South West Africa Peoples' Organisation (SWAPO) and the Democratic Turnhalle Alliance

(DTA) that gave the Constitution of an independent Namibia form and substance. The end result is a constitution established by a multi-party democracy that protects the fundamental rights and freedoms of every person in Namibia and that contains a mission aimed at promoting the welfare of the people of the country, with special emphasis on less privileged and disadvantaged people.

CHAPTER 14

Independence and afterwards

The first National Assembly

As recommended by the Standing Committee, the Constituent Assembly decided that Namibia would become independent on 21 March 1990, and that the elected Assembly would be transformed into a National Assembly. Therefore, there would not be an election for a government as had originally been intended because the parties agreed that they could not foresee that the outcome of another election would differ from the outcome of the previous election. Why then should we repeat the arduous processes necessitated by the previous election? This also meant that the first President would be appointed by the National Assembly and not by the voters in a separate election.

The Republic of Namibia came into being on 21 March 1990 in a ceremony that took place in the presence of President F.W. de Klerk of South Africa, United Nations dignitaries and a number of visiting heads of state. The occasion was so momentous and my mind so preoccupied with my personal thoughts, that once the South African flag was lowered and the Namibian flag raised for the first time, I registered very little of what was being said. As I wrote in the opening chapters of this book, I had to put much of my sentiments, dating back to my childhood, behind me. While I had no doubt whatsoever that what was happening was positive and as it should be, I realised that my life and political career would never be the same again.

Since we were moving into a new era and a new generation would be rising to face new challenges, I had informed my colleagues at an early stage that I did not want to serve in the new Government. Apart from anything else, I was tired of conflict and strife. My wish was to withdraw and enjoy the rest of my life with Stienie and our children. Yet I allowed myself to be dissuaded and agreed to serve as a member of the National Assembly for one term. My SWAPO colleagues in the Standing Committee even encouraged me to assist in the implementation of the Constitution we had drawn up together. To the members of the National Assembly the colour of my skin was never a problem, as it had never been among the members of the Committee. Some diplomats were even instrumental in my being asked whether I would be prepared to serve in a SWAPO cabinet. This, however, was an eventuality I would never consider.

To this day I regret having allowed myself to be swayed to serve in the National Assembly for one term. This was a mistake I should never have made.

My three years in the National Assembly

Before the first session of the National Assembly in the newly independent Namibia, the DTA Caucus appointed members to act as spokespeople for the different portfolios. I was tasked with Finance, and Dr Otto Herrigel became the first Minister of Finance. He and I clashed regularly, albeit not on the basis of colour, since we were both white.

When I took the floor in the Assembly for the first time, I appealed to my DTA colleagues to make positive contributions by coming forward with constructive suggestions. It soon emerged that the SWAPO members who had come to know me in the Standing Committee were completely opposed to my fulfilling a similar role in these open meetings to the one I had played in the closed meetings of the Standing Committee. It would have been naïve of me not to have expected this.

That SWAPO was trying to exploit the susceptibility of the DTA when it came to cooperating with, or depending on whites, was gradually becoming apparent. Some of the SWAPO members who had served with me in the Standing Committee even accused my DTA colleagues of allowing me to take them for a ride. Coming from people who had often expressed their appreciation for the leading role I had played in the Committee, I found these remarks particularly disappointing. Likewise, the behaviour of my DTA colleagues came as a shock. The embarrassment on their faces was evident each time they were reminded of the fact that they were mere puppets on the string of a white leader. Earlier on there had been complaints, especially from Muyongo and some of his colleagues, that I was too prominent and should maintain a lower profile. I had ignored such comments in the past, since I knew that this attitude was confined to the leadership of the DTA. But I was well aware that while the leaders of the Party accepted and trusted me, they did not take kindly to my invariably being in greater demand to speak at meetings than they were.

By then I knew how to handle these undercurrents, so I did not find them difficult to deal with at the time. However, this was in the belief that colour no longer played a role. Accordingly it came as a shock to me that it was still an issue and remained a convenient political weapon. The reality is that in my years with the DTA I had never found it embarrassing to serve under a black president. When I was branded a *"kafferboetie"* (negrophile), I treated the accusations with the contempt they deserved. On the other hand, after everything I had done for the DTA, I couldn't simply ignore these problems, and in so doing become a burden to the Party. I believed that I had fulfilled my role and was reluctant to serve in the National Assembly. With its 21 seats, the DTA was well equipped to continue the struggle on its own.

After serving as a Member of Parliament for three years, I announced that I intended stepping down. I said that I had been active in politics for over 30 years and felt I had played my role. Without making a fuss, I took leave of the members on both sides of the House as you would part company with friends and colleagues.

In response, the Speaker of the National Assembly, Mosé Tjitendero, arranged a farewell dinner for me to which he invited all the political leaders. That evening he expressed his sincere appreciation for the role I had played in the politics of the country. Moses//Garoëb of SWAPO, whom I had always regarded as an extremist, addressed us. I was surprised by the many compliments he paid me, among other things that when he and his colleagues were still abroad, they had followed my career with interest, and had much appreciation for what I was doing. That the president of the DTA, Mishake Muyongo, refrained from saying anything did not surprise me.

The next day President Nujoma invited me and my wife to join him for lunch at State House. We had a pleasant conversation in a friendly atmosphere, during which no mention was made of politics. Neither did we exchange any compliments. In all probability he was expecting me to broach the subject of my retirement, but I chose not to.

Afterwards there was speculation that this gesture had been made with ulterior motives, but I doubt it very much. SWAPO members knew me better than to attempt anything like this.

Party politics after independence

Since I was no longer playing a leading role in the government of the country, it stood to reason that I should reconsider my position in the political organisations I had established and with which I was associated for over 25 years. I was still Chairman of the DTA (not the leader), although the status and responsibilities of the chairperson had been scaled down to give the President, Mishake Muyongo, and the Vice-President, Katuutire Kaura, additional status. I had no problem with this, as it often caused them embarrassment when we were abroad and I was referred to as the leader of the DTA. In fact, it embarrassed me as well. I was also still leader of the Republican Party, a member party of the DTA. But by then the RP had been dormant for some years in terms of a decision taken by its Executive to enable its members to devote more of their time and energy to strengthen the Democratic Turnhalle Alliance. As leader of the Party I had been given the mandate to, should this become necessary, call a meeting of the RP members to decide whether this arrangement should continue or not.

The Republican Party resurges

Once again, as had happened several times in the past, I had to make a decision that could have far-reaching consequences on my personal life. In my long political career I had invariably spent too little time at home with my family. The time had come for me to consider my own as well as their interests. By then, I must admit, I was tired, as well as physically and financially depleted. In the entire course of my political life I had never received a salary, a motorcar or any other fringe benefits from a political party. Conversely, I invariably made sure that my DTA colleagues received such benefits and that members of the secretariat were paid liberal retirement packages.

I was in charge of fundraising for the Republican Party from the time it was founded in 1977. It was primarily due to my efforts that we had sufficient money and equipment to manage an impressive election campaign in 1989. But the election was over, and the DTA had secured 21 seats in the National Assembly. As the official opposition, it would continue to play an important role. However, substantial funding was required to accomplish this, and was no longer available.

After the election I was fully aware that the DTA's monthly expense budget still peaked at a staggering N$400 000. In my mind I needed clarity on whether I could leave the Party high and dry at this crucial stage. This was not a decision I could make straight away. As it turned out, it took the best part of a decade before I was finally able to retire altogether.

Nine years after independence, in terms of the mandate given to me by the Executive of the RP, I convened a meeting to reflect on the future of the Party. This took place in August 1998, on which occasion I informed those present that I was finding my current position untenable and was no longer prepared to shoulder the interests of the Party and its supporters on my own. I said I wished to withdraw from party politics and requested the members to decide whether they were in favour of the RP being resurged. If they decided that it still had a role to fulfil, they should arrange a congress, during which I intended relinquishing my leadership and handing it over to the new management. A committee was chosen under the chairmanship of Johan de Waal, after which I took my leave.

The new committee was faced with a daunting task. First Johan de Waal and then Pieter Boltman arranged meetings in different areas. On 22 June 2002, Boltman was elected chairman of a reactivation committee. There was a good measure of support for the revival of the Republican Party, among others by former supporters of the National Party and its successors. However, they were no longer interested in further cooperation with the DTA. This prospect came as a major shock and disillusionment to me, since I found the continued existence of the RP without being linked to the DTA unacceptable.

The financial difficulties experienced by the DTA in 1997 had resulted in antagonism towards the Party. It was alleged by some of the DTA leaders that the Trust had misappropriated DTA funds to benefit the Republican Party and Republican (Pty) Ltd (the publisher of the *Republikein* newspaper) to the detriment of the DTA, an accusation that was unfounded. As substantiated by audited statements, in the period from the 1989 election until 1997, a total of N$9 621 476 had been paid to the DTA. This was double the surplus left after the election. That same year the National Assembly decided to support the political parties financially, and the *Republikein* was able to cease its contribution to the DTA.

My concerted efforts to unite the RP and DTA were unsuccessful. Pieter Boltman was elected leader of the RP on 12 April 2003. Three months later he resigned as leader and as member. The other white members of the Executive Committee followed suit. After this the RP continued as a primarily black party under the leadership of my oldest son, Henk Mudge. At present, it has one seat in the National Assembly. Whether the two parties that had brought me so much happiness on the one hand but also heartbreak on the other still have a role to play, only time will tell.

CHAPTER 15

Reflection

Since our independence, South Africans have shown a keen interest in developments in Namibia. Almost invariably visitors to our country speak with admiration about the sound human relations prevailing here and the friendly way they are received and treated by both white and black Namibians.

My belief that a political and constitutional solution could be found only if the people of our country respected one another's human dignity sustained me throughout my political career, and I maintained this approach throughout. In the DTA, well before we achieved independence, white and black fought together against common political opponents. We cooperated by holding meetings and taking part in mixed marches together. We celebrated our accomplishments together, and when our colleagues were murdered, we cried together.

Namibia is one of Africa's jewels. I can state this with conviction, since I have visited many countries on the continent. Accompanied by my children and travelling as far north as Uganda, I have driven some 25 000 kilometres through Africa, visiting countries that have been independent for more than 50 years. We have the good fortune of never having fought a civil war in Namibia, and the new Government has the privilege of not having inherited a country destroyed by war. The armed struggle ran its course, with white and black combatants risking their lives in our neighbouring country Angola. In the process the infrastructure in Namibia remained intact. All the newly instated Government had to do was maintain and develop it further, which they did in a highly commendable manner. While there certainly were doubts to start with, the people of Namibia slowly but surely regained confidence in their country.

The armed struggle of many years was brought to an end by independence. Former enemies joined hands and wrote a democratic Constitution, one that guarantees the fundamental rights of all the inhabitants in the country unambiguously. Our country is no longer the controversial territory it was in the days when it was being administered by South Africa, during which a policy of racial discrimination was enforced on its inhabitants. Achieving independence put an end to this, as a result of which both Namibia and South Africa gained economically and financially. All over the country – even in the most remote corners – new enterprises mushroomed. Donations were made to Namibia from all over the world in the shape of large sums of money for development aid and expertise, changing the lives of Namibian citizens for the better. In a process that was set in motion several years before independence, Namibians grew to know and understand each other better. One of the advantages is that we have a relatively small population, unlike South Africa where the considerably larger population makes this process significantly more difficult.

The inevitable question that arises is whether the independent Namibia has fully shed its problems of the past. Unfortunately, the reality in 2016 is that we are still struggling with the aftermath of problems that plagued us in former years, some of which in all likelihood will continue to test us in the future. When writing the Constitution we did our best to create opportunities for addressing challenges such as unemployment, poverty and landownership. In this endeavour the concept of affirmative action was our most important tool. At this point in time certain conclusions can be drawn from our experiences of the past two and a half decades.

The new Government, in terms of the provisions of the Constitution, immediately implemented programmes to improve the lives of previously disadvantaged people. One of these was making the former predominantly white public service more balanced in terms of race. Since it provided a livelihood for a large number of black and coloured Namibians, the restructuring of the bureaucracy provided more favourable prospects for the previously disadvantaged. While I wholeheartedly supported this principle when it was written into the Constitution, I was fully aware that once implemented, white public servants would have to pay a price. I had great understanding and sympathy for them, since they would be the first white Namibians who would have to do this. There was no other option. While this process could be implemented swiftly, it goes without saying that only skilled people would benefit from it. An indication that most members of the new bureaucracy have been schooled and educated in their professions in Namibia is the fact that the majority of them can speak Afrikaans. In my view those who accuse them of incompetence and poor service are not being fair. Senior officials must be held responsible for the exceptions, especially in some departments.

Needless to say, the senior positions in the government service were kept for loyal SWAPO supporters. To further attain this goal, a plethora of parastatal institutions was created. The President set the example by appointing an unrealistically large executive authority. Apart from a few exceptions, members of SWAPO were appointed as Ministers and Deputy Ministers. This came as a surprise to me, since when we discussed the size of the Cabinet in the Standing Committee, Theo-Ben Gurirab of SWAPO put his viewpoint across as follows: "... the other controlling reality that will soon face us is money. A proliferation of ministries would not serve us well; they are very expensive. Some of you have experience in this. I don't, and the mere creation of ministries would not serve the President's interests ... if he were to go on creating ministries to pay back his political friends, it would become a costly business." It seems that Gurirab did not stick to his guns, as what he feared has come to pass. Besides, these friends were also well looked after in terms of salaries and fringe benefits. In the process a new elite was created in the country, maintaining a standard of living that is accepted as an ideal by the underprivileged section of the population.

In my view we have now reached the stage where we can ask with justification whether the public service is not already sufficiently balanced. Gaining clarity on this would be in the public interest, since this type of "affirmative" action cannot be practised indefinitely. This notion was accepted by SWAPO in its original proposal for a constitution, which stated that the process should be completed within the next 25 years. The members of the Standing Committee, however, stated unanimously that a period of 25 years was too long, and that the process of affirmative action should be concluded sooner. They posed the following questions: When, how and by whom would the decision be made whether a balance had been reached in the public sector? How do you determine whether a previously disadvantaged person has been sufficiently promoted and is no longer entitled to privileged treatment? It stands to reason that such a person cannot be promoted indefinitely. The harsh reality is that many of our inhabitants are worse off today than they were before independence.

During the independence process, great and unrealistic expectations were created, as a result of which the wider public were looking forward to a better future and a dramatic improvement in their standard of living. Since the writers of the Constitution, of which I was one, emphasised the welfare of the people as an ultimate goal throughout the process, they had every reason to expect this. While the Constitution does not spell out a redistribution of wealth in so many words, it does allude to this. Moreover, it states that previously disadvantaged people would only be sharing in the welfare, or wealth, of the country if they gained a stake in our natural resources. How can the difference between wealth and welfare be explained to ordinary people if the political leaders do not even have clarity on the subject themselves?

It is understandable that people who did not own land or share in the exploitation of our natural resources in earlier years would want to do so now. However, it needs to be accomplished in such a way that it is in the national interest and benefits the people in their totality. Namibia's main natural resources are its minerals, fish and land; especially agricultural land. These resources are not human-made; they are scarce and in most cases irreplaceable. The goose that lays the golden egg will be destroyed if these resources are not utilised responsibly and productively. Examples where this has already taken place are legion in the mining and fishing industry. By peddling with mineral concessions or fishing quotas, the individuals or small groups who gained them became rich, and in certain cases – as a result of mismanagement – the workers and population as a whole did not reap any benefits. This reality is generally not recognised. While previously disadvantaged people saw affirmative action as the answer to their prayers, many of them are still waiting to benefit.

Following the introduction of land reform, the ownership and utilisation of land – neither of which the Constitution provides for specifically – became matters that were highly controversial and emotional. Expectations in this regard were raised both before and during the election campaign. Why the redistribution of agricultural land was so important to the wider population was initially difficult to comprehend. As I see it, the answer is historical. In pre-colonial times the indigenous population consisted primarily of subsistence farmers who regarded the entire country as their grazing and hunting ground. In these times there were major collisions between the Hereros and the Namas about land. Traditionally, the Hereros maintained that land on which their cattle had left tracks belonged to them. The Namas, on the other hand, laid claim to land where their hunters had left their tracks.

Natural resources such as minerals and fish played a subordinate role with the Herero and Nama people. This explains why, after they had been defeated by the Germans, the Hereros persevered in their attempts to have their conquered land returned to them.

In the wake of independence, most of Namibia's black inhabitants were still communal farmers or farm labourers and therefore dependent on agriculture for their livelihood. But they were not landowners. The SWAPO government referred to them as "landless" and pledged that millions of hectares of commercial agricultural land would be bought for them or given to them through land expropriation. This created such unrealistic expectations that even people who were not dependent on agriculture for their living laid claims to land. A scheme was created by Agribank to give loans to individuals at low interest rates and under easy repayment conditions, enabling them to purchase farms. A relatively large number of farms were bought under this scheme. I had serious doubts about this from the outset, since it enabled ministers, senior officials and affluent businesspeople who were not bona fide farmers – and therefore not dependent on farming for their livelihood – to acquire farms. Since these people do not need the income from farming to make a living, this means that they are not putting the land to its optimal use. It is unnecessary for me to elaborate any further on the consequences of this underutilisation of a valuable natural resource. I also had my doubts as to whether the communal farmers who bought these farms would be able to repay the large loans they were being granted.

Nevertheless, a fair number of the emergent farmers – especially those who had stockpiled large herds of cattle or had other sources of income – became successful farmers. I am proud of them, since it proves that my black countrymen have what it takes. Especially noteworthy is the fact that the farmers who bought land through Agribank gained property rights and could therefore benefit from land appreciation. This not only influenced the ratio of debt versus assets favourably, but put them in a position to sell these farms for a large profit should conditions necessitate this. Commercial farmers can testify to the fact that increasing land values have helped them out of difficult circumstances.

Unfortunately, I cannot say the same for the Government's resettlement scheme, which did not remotely live up to the expectations created. To pacify a large section of the population which has yet to benefit from affirmative action – and to whom it is still an unrealised dream – it is announced regularly that millions of hectares of agricultural land are still going to be bought or expropriated for resettlement. Yet it is claimed equally regularly that this process is being delayed because white commercial farmers refuse to make their land available, or that they are expecting too much for their land. This claim is not valid. The price of land is determined by supply and demand, and the Government's policy that should a farmer want to sell his land, he first has to offer it to the Government has disrupted the ratio between supply and demand. Moreover, this temporary withdrawal of farms from the open market until such time as the Government decides whether it wants to exercise its right of first refusal or not has resulted in the number of farms available to private buyers becoming limited, and the market value of land to rise dramatically. Introducing the right of first refusal to the Government when it comes to selling farms was therefore short-sighted.

Referring to farmers on settlement farms as beginner or upcoming farmers would not be correct, as it was and still is a cul-de-sac for most of them. They have no assets they can offer as security when applying for loans from financial institutions, since they have no form of security of tenure on such farms. Moreover, they can also not benefit from the escalation of land prices. The farms – which are small and distributed throughout the country – are nothing more than communal land. This makes supervision, control and coordinated marketing difficult if not impossible. In my opinion this scheme is no different from the Odendaal Plan of many decades ago, when South Africa's National Party Government expropriated over 400 farms for settlement by black inhabitants. In both cases the schemes were politically motivated in so far as no consideration was given to economic and practical factors. The main objective was political, and in the case of SWAPO, election promises that had to be honoured. Even if all the commercial farms in Namibia were acquired for resettlement purposes, no more than 300 000 people could be accommodated on this land, while approximately the same number of people (farm labourers and their dependants) living on such farms would have to be settled elsewhere, if not reduced to wandering around the country looking for an alternative way to survive. However, other than pointing fingers at the occasional commercial farmer who wants squatters removed from his land due to special circumstances, nothing is ever said.

The farms that were purchased now belong to the Government. Farmers resettled on such farms have no property rights whatsoever. All they are entitled to is living there and grazing their livestock on the land. They were never selected appropriately and not all of them are bona fide farmers. The Government therefore finds itself in a checkmate position, having resettled as many landless people as possible in great haste, without giving the necessary thought to the correct way of implementing the resettlement scheme.

The news media informs us almost daily about some or other case of crime and corruption. I'm well aware that the Government is making attempts to combat crime and corruption by means of disciplinary measures and law enforcement, but in the long run there is no "quick fix" for illegal behaviour. A great deal more than merely applying the law and disciplinary measures is required. When we travelled through Africa we regularly saw posters bearing the message "Zero tolerance for corruption!" on the borders of countries that have long been independent. The bottom line – above and beyond being firm, especially with government officials – is that educating Namibians to respect the law of the land must start on the school benches. However, I hasten to add that I do not have all the answers.

The authorities identified unemployment, poverty and housing as issues that should receive immediate attention and much has already been done to alleviate the problems. However, due to the accelerated tempo at which our population is increasing, the shortfall remains substantial and stands to become even greater. The only way to solve these problems is by mutual deliberation and planning. We will achieve nothing through opportunistic politicking and negative criticism. By all accounts, however, the rulers of the country already realise that they had made mistakes for the sake of gaining popularity and votes, and that this has to be rectified. Experience has always been the best taskmaster.

That the Constitution might be changed to their detriment is still feared by many white Namibians. Since constitutions are not rigid, this is obviously a possibility. Nevertheless, it is stated clearly in our Constitution that any infringement of the entrenched fundamental rights will be unconstitutional.

Epilogue

During my long involvement in politics, I often pondered on and wondered about the meaning of life. What is the significance or non-significance of one generation in the history of humankind? I have attempted to compare the life of man and his achievements with one of the most impressive feats in the architectural heritage of our globe – the building of the Great Wall of China.

The question of what contributions were made by previous generations to make our country a better place for all its inhabitants is one that gives rise to much speculation and many arguments. In this book I have tried to present a broad outline of the events of the past 130 years. The narrative bears witness to the greed and hunger for power that started in pre-colonial times already; it dwells on land distribution and the territorial domain for which the inhabitants and ultimately the rulers of Namibia were prepared to go to war; and culminates in the achievement of independence and its aftermath, ending with a few thoughts on where Namibia finds itself today.

The struggle is over, and while I am the last person to begrudge inhabitants of Namibia the privilege of commemorating their past, this must be done in such a way that others are not hurt and that what we want to achieve in future is not hampered. To prove who won the war is no longer important. It was peace that triumphed, putting an end to the war before there could be a victor.

The responsibility of creating a better future for our country and its people rests on the shoulders of a new generation of leaders. Every inhabitant of this country will have to contribute – politically, socially and economically – to build the Namibian "wall". It must be a wall that protects what we Namibians have achieved with so much sacrifice and dedication; it must be strong enough to resist every assault of whatever nature; and it may never be a wall of separation. We must appreciate that not all the problems in our country will be solved during our lifetime. We need to recognise that each and every one of us must play our part in building the wall, setting an example to our children and future generations that will inspire them to continue laying the bricks.

Many years ago a friend of mine, Oom Ernst Kallweit of Keetmanshoop, spoke wise words when he said you can plant a tree
even when you are 80 years old.

I ask myself whether I will still be granted the privilege "to plant a
tree" before I finally leave this earth.

I continued being the First Trustee of Democratic Media Trust and
Chairman of the Board of Democratic Media Holdings (DMH), which
owned our newspaper and printing company after I had withdrawn
from active politics.

In 1994 my daughter Chrisna Greeff was appointed Managing Director of DMH, and over the next 18 years she developed the company
into the media giant it is today. DMH managed a modern printing
house and three independent daily newspapers – *Republikein*, *Allgemeine Zeitung* and *Namibian Sun*. It was therefore logical that Chrisna
would succeed me when I resigned as Chairman and member of the
Board of Directors.

We were in agreement that the Democratic Media Trust of Namibia
had made its contribution towards establishing a free press in the
country. However, we never had the necessary funding for the other
lofty goals we would have liked to promote. To achieve these, we were
faced with a difficult decision. We came to the conclusion that the only
practical means of gaining access to the required funding would be by
selling part, if not all, our shares in DMH and applying the proceeds
to promote the interests of the people of Namibia as envisaged in the
Deed of Trust. Reaching this decision was no easy matter. However,
by then I was already well versed in making weighty decisions. We
decided to sell 50% of the shares in DMH to Media24, which we did
in 2008, donating the proceeds to the Polytechnic of Namibia for the
construction of a media centre. Following discussions with the Polytechnic, however, we reached agreement that the funds could be utilised more advantageously by building a hotel school. In August 2012
the remaining 50% of the shares were sold to a private empowerment
group, Stimulus (Pty) Ltd, with Monica Kalondo as Chairperson of
the Board of Directors. Once this last sales transaction had been finalised, I decided – as founder and First Trustee of this important institution – to disengage myself from it. I appointed my daughter Chrisna
Greeff as First Trustee and Dr Zedekia Ngavirue and Albie Basson as
Co-Trustees. The new trustees invested the funds of Democratic Media
Holdings in a new trust, the Dirk Mudge Trust. The main objective of

this Trust is to promote education for underprivileged black children in remote areas of the country.

Expanding the Uahekua Herunga Primary School by adding two classrooms and a small kitchen was the first project in which the Trust became involved. This small school is located near Ruacana in the Omusati Region of Owambo and serves the Otjorute community. Local men and women participated in the building operations with great enthusiasm and excitement, supervised by two experienced bricklayers. A second school is currently being built at Etunda at a cost of over N$20 million. The Dirk Mudge Trust will also finance the running costs of this school.

Several other projects are currently being considered and planned. As and when the Trust can handle and afford it, additional projects will be considered in the rest of the country. In future the remaining yield from the sale of the DMH shares will be applied to empower the people of Namibia, whether through education, training or development.

While I helped plant the tree, I will probably not be afforded the time to see it reach maturity. Nonetheless, I feel privileged to be part of an enterprise that has the interests of my country and its people at its core.

That this enterprise has been eminently worthwhile was manifested when I had the opportunity to visit the first project and an elderly gentleman from the community presented me with a watermelon. To me this gift was worth more than a gold medal.

So ends the story of my involvement in the constitutional and political process in Namibia; the end of the journey from South West Africa to Namibia that began on 17 March 1961. Since then 54 years have come and gone, and on 16 January 2016 I turned 88.

Since I have now relinquished my last public obligations to the Dirk Mudge Trust, I am looking forward to spending the time I have left with my wife and soul mate Stienie, our children, grandchildren and great-grandchildren. In all probability the past will be discussed a great deal, and many questions will be asked, especially by our grandchildren who were not involved at the time. There are also bound to be speculations about the future, which now belongs to the younger generation, in whom I have great trust.

It will be their task to continue building Namibia's wall.

Official documents

Debates of the Legislative Assembly 1961–1980
Minutes of the Committee (Where to? Committee) on self-determination 1974
Minutes of the Turnhalle Conference 1975–1976
Debates of the Constituent Assembly 1979
Debates of the National Assembly 1979–1982
Documents of the Multi-Party Conference (MPC) 1983–1984
Debates of the National Assembly of the Government of National Unity 1984–1989
Minutes of the Constituent Assembly 1989–1990
Minutes of the Constituent Committee 1989–1990
Debates of the National Assembly of the Republic of Namibia 1990–1993
Ethiopia and Liberia versus South Africa. 1967. Johannesburg: Department of Information
South West Africa Survey 1967. 1967. Pretoria: Department of Foreign Affairs
South West Africa Advisory Opinion 1971. 1972. Pretoria: Department of Foreign Affairs
South West Africa Basic Documents. 1979. Pretoria: Department of Foreign Affairs

Books

Bosl, Anton, Horn, Nico & Du Pisani, André. 2010. *Constitutional Democracy in Namibia.* Windhoek: Macmillan Education.
Bothma, L.J. 2006. *Die buffel struikel.* Bloemfontein: L.J. Bothma.
Crocker, Chester. 1994. *High Noon in Southern Africa.* New York: Jonathan Ball Publishers.
Du Preez, Max. 2003. *Pale Native.* Cape Town: Zebra Press.
Geldenhuys, Jannie. 1993. *Dié wat gewen het.* Kaap en Transvaal Boekdrukkers.
Gewald, Jan-Bart. 1999. *Herero Heroes.* London: James Currey.
Leys, Colin & Saul, John S. 1995. *Namibia's Liberation Struggle: The two-edged sword.* London: James Currey.
Namibia 1990: An Africa Institute Country Survey. 1991. Johannesburg: Africa Institute of South Africa.
Ngavirue, Z. 1997. *Political Parties and Interest Groups in South West Africa (Namibia).* Switzerland: P Schlettwein Publishing.
O'Linn, Bryan. 1974. *Die toekoms van Suidwes-Afrika gebou op die werklikheid.* Windhoek: Verenigde Pers.
Papenfus, Theresa. 2010. *Pik Botha en sy tyd.* Pretoria: Litera Uitgewers.
Pool, Gerhard. 1991. *Samual Maharero.* Windhoek: Gamsberg Macmillan.
Potgieter, De Wet. 2007. *Totale aanslag.* Kaapstad: Zebra Press.
Sanders, James. 1999. *Apartheid's Friends.* London: John Murray Publishers.
Sarkin, Jeremy. 2010. *Germany's Genocide of the Herero.* Cape Town: UCT Press.

Scholtz, Leopold. 2013. The SADF in the Border War, 1966–1989. Cape Town: Tafelberg.

Spies, F.J. du Toit. 1989. *Operasie Savannah, 1975–1976*. Johannesburg: Perskor.

Stals, E.L.P. (Ed). 1991. *The Commissions of Palgrave*. Cape Town: Van Riebeeck Society.

Thomas, Antony. 1996. *Rhodes, The Race for Africa*. Johannesburg: Jonathan Ball Publishers.

Thomas, Wolfgang H. 1978. *Economic Development in Namibia*. München: Chr Kaiser Verlag.

Van Wyk, At. 1999. *Reënmaker van die Namib*. Pretoria: J.L. van Schaik Uitgewers.

1982 principles 362, 404, 405, 418, 422, 427, 433, 438, 441, 446, 448, 461, 475

Abrahams, Ottilie 299
Action Front for the Retention of the Turnhalle Principles *see* AKTUR
Advisory Board 35, 137, 138, 140–141
affirmative action 417, 426, 428, 430–431, 447, 449, 450, 456–457, 479, 488, 489, 490, 492
Africa, Ben 168, 201, 213, 245, 282, 291, 323
Afrikaner Broederbond (*see* Broederbond)
Afrikaners 18, 19, 25, 31, 32, 36, 40, 51, 52, 56, 59, 72, 271, 335, 349, 372
agricultural land 237, 309, 490, 491, 492
Ahtisaari, Martti 267, 270, 280, 283–284, 292, 298, 299, 302, 387, 389, 392, 393, 477
Aksie Christelik-Nasionaal (ACN) 394, 399, 466, 467, 479
Aksie Nasionale Stigting (ANS) 386
AKTUR 201, 257, 266, 282, 285, 286, 288, 291, 296, 298, 304, 305, 309, 310, 311–313, 317, 318, 320–322, 323, 336, 337, 338, 341, 342, 344, 347, 360, 372
Allgemeine Zeitung 110, 228, 495
Amadhila, Libertine 376
Amathila, Ben 406
Amin, Idi 126
Anamulenge Catholic School 212, 227
Andalusia Internment Camp 37
Anglo-Boer War 25, 30, 31, 54
Angola 19, 21, 71, 111, 112, 114, 155–157, 166–167, 175, 187–188, 227, 249, 263, 279, 302, 317, 319, 355–356, 360–362, 364, 373, 385–386, 392, 393, 487
Angra Pequena 30
Angula, Nahas 405, 429, 430, 434, 435, 438, 444–445, 446, 449, 455, 457, 458, 459, 461
Anthonissen, Dina 232

apartheid 18, 29, 67, 89, 92, 103, 104, 110, 117, 123, 131, 139, 140, 154, 159, 163, 165, 287, 288, 315, 321, 322, 326, 330, 339, 343, 400, 408, 409, 410, 412, 413, 414, 422, 449, 468, 471
Arden-Clarke, C. 136
Arp, Heinrich 43
Arp, Helene Ferendine (Ouma Lyna) 40, 43, 45
Ashford, Nicholas 280–281
Association International Organisation 200
Augustinium Training School 96
Australia 32
Austria 119
Avis Dam 45, 48

Barnard, Dr Chris 132–133
Barnes, Barney 243, 363, 406, 420
Basson, Albie 495
Becker, Caswell 57
Becker, Sarel 282, 297, 305, 336, 337, 339
Beeld 367, 368
Berlin 178
Berlin Conference 28
Beyers, General 31
Bezuidenhout, David 378
Biwa, Eric 422
Blaauw, Commandant 113, 385
Blatt, Arnfried 213
Blatt, Cathy 213
Bloemhof Girl's School 58
Böhme, Kurt 235–236
Boltman, Pieter 22, 485, 486
Border War 19, 111, 113, 114, 155–156, 373
Boskop (farm) 47–48, 51, 63, 64
Botha, Bertie 26, 161, 205, 206, 216, 229, 236, 252
Botha, Elize 238
Botha, General Louis 31, 40, 44
Botha, M.C. 144, 147, 149, 225
Botha, Ouboet 46

Botha, Pik 20, 110, 111, 136, 142, 143, 147, 177, 213, 214, 222, 223, 229, 238, 239, 262, 263, 268–269, 270, 271, 277, 282, 285, 289, 298, 300, 301, 302, 317, 327, 354–355, 361, 366, 367, 368–370, 375, 377, 380, 393, 397

Botha, P.W. 19, 20, 123, 155, 156, 157, 222–223, 229, 238–240, 275, 276, 277, 278, 279, 280–281, 282, 283, 289, 290, 292, 299, 302, 304, 310, 314, 316, 217, 343–347, 348, 354, 355–356, 359–362, 363, 364, 368, 368, 370, 371, 373–374, 277–278, 380, 381, 395

Bothma, L.J. 111

Botma, Boet 332

Botswana 74, 115, 302, 317, 444

Brand, Coen 240, 241

Brandt, J.W. (Grammie) 89, 90, 98, 101, 105, 241

Brinkman, Adolf 129, 162, 225, 226

Britain 29, 31, 32, 52, 72, 133, 177, 211, 267, 278, 284

Britz, Johan 246

Broederbond 65, 66, 67, 192, 333, 374

Brown, Susan 112, 114

Brückner, Albi 230

Brunette, Hennie 56

Buren Hilfsfonds 32

Bushmen 28, 153, 178, 366, 400

Bynadaar (farm) 63

C-mandate (territories) 33, 165

Caetano, Marcelo 155

Calueque 155, 158

Cameroon 32

Cape Fria 28, 118

Cape Town 29, 52–54, 60, 147, 151, 152, 161, 177, 192, 212, 213–215, 219, 239, 240, 261, 282, 343, 352, 354, 376, 395

Cape Town Agreement 378

Caprivi 171, 183, 186, 251, 398, 402, 469, 476

Caprivi African National Union (CANU) 383

Caprivians 152, 153, 171

Carpio, V 113, 136

Cassinga 263–264, 270

Cato Manor 70

Celliers, Miss 51

Centenary of 1938 51–52

Central Administrative Authority 214

Central Government 182, 221, 312, 368, 476

Charter of Fundamental Rights 139, 171, 384, 385

Chaskalson, Arthur 419, 420, 426, 427, 430, 439, 444, 447, 451, 473

China 112, 494

Christian Democratic Action (CDA) 361, 394

Christy, Engelhardt 313, 323

citizenship 295, 305, 424, 473

Clark Amendment 279, 385

Coetzee, Susanna Johanna Maria 43

Committee on Standing Rules and Orders and Internal Arrangements 17, 173, 174, 180, 182, 183, 184, 186, 201, 203, 205, 207, 208, 213, 219, 221, 222, 226, 237, 242, 243, 244, 250, 272, 403, 404, 405, 406–407, 451, 466, 481, 482, 489

concentration camps 29, 31, 52, 299, 438

Concordia College 352

Consolidate Diamond Mines (CDM) 352

Constituent Assembly 17, 18, 218, 231, 289–304, 306, 307, 309–315, 318, 323, 324, 326, 331, 335, 343, 353, 362, 387, 401, 402, 403, 404–405, 414, 418, 419, 420, 431, 433, 435, 438, 446, 450–456, 458, 460, 463, 466, 467–473, 477, 478, 481

Constituent Committee *see* Committee on Standing Rules and Orders and Internal Arrangements

Constitutional Committee 75, 381

Constitutional Conference 171, 172, 175, 198, 207, 209, 218, 220, 224, 244, 267, 345

Council of Performing Arts (SWAPAC) 169

Council of Traditional Leaders 475, 476

Credentials Committee 141, 171

Crocker, Chester 13, 356, 360, 361, 375, 376, 386, 388, 393

Cuban presence 155, 156, 227, 269, 278–280, 290, 356, 360–362, 364, 386, 393

Cultura 2000 349, 412

Dahlmann, Kurt 110, 228

Dairy Board 100

Damaraland 183, 308, 401

Damaras 27, 78, 140, 152, 153–154, 195, 341, 424, 469

Davids, Abraham 384, 385

Day of the Covenant 52, 371

De Alva, S.M. 113, 136

De Bruyn, Jurie 50

De Jager, Christo 217, 256

De Klerk, F.W. 14, 18, 481

De Klerk, Wimpie 334

De la Rey, General 31

De Lange, Piet 56

De Lange, Willem 56

De Spínola, António 155

De Waal, Johan 199, 397, 485

De Wet, Blok 64, 66, 70, 232

De Wet, Jan 57, 64, 69, 90, 91, 92, 125, 136, 137, 138, 140, 144, 147, 148, 149, 150, 151, 190, 222, 223, 242, 243, 282, 296, 297, 312, 321, 322, 323, 336, 338, 341, 353, 361, 382, 384, 388, 394, 399, 405, 466, 467–468, 469, 471, 472, 478

Declaration of Intent 172, 173, 174, 175, 220

democracy 15, 19, 166, 204, 217, 247, 316, 341, 399, 478, 479, 480

Democratic Media Holdings 495

Democratic Media Trust 495

Democratic Turnhalle Alliance 20, 24, 75, 233, 244–245, 249, 261, 285, 294, 313, 328, 381, 394, 397, 479, 484

Denmark 44

Depression, the 45–46

Der Burenfreund 32

Der Internationalen Burenliga 32

detention without trial 472–474

Deutsch-Südwestafrika 28, 39, 40

Deutsche Afrikanische Partei 37

Deutsche Bund 35, 36

Die Buffel Struikel 111

Die Burger 368

Die Fontein (farm) 49

Die Hervormer 331, 332

Die Oosterlig 238

Die Suidwes-Afrikaner 104, 106, 115, 116, 130, 203, 246

Die Suidwester 197, 215, 228, 241, 246, 250, 251, 257, 262

Diergaardt, Hans 282, 286, 305, 313, 322, 338, 363, 399, 401, 412

Diergaardt, Pieter 305, 322

Diescho, Joseph 472

Dié wat gewen het 111, 252, 260, 300

Dirk Mudge Trust 495–496

discrimination 18, 140, 171, 174, 214, 274, 280, 287, 297, 306, 321, 322, 323, 326, 327, 335, 336, 337, 338, 339, 340, 432, 343, 346, 363, 382, 400, 408, 410, 417, 456, 457, 469

Doll, Paolo 334

drought 45, 48, 77–78, 80, 95, 99, 106, 116, 119, 121, 132

Du Plessis, A.H. 26, 56, 71, 84, 87, 89, 102, 103, 105, 107, 108, 123, 124, 125, 127, 131, 135, 137, 147, 149, 152, 159, 174, 176, 177, 185, 193, 199, 213, 215, 222, 225, 226, 240, 244, 265, 266, 282, 296, 306, 326, 337, 341

Du Plessis, Wennie 85, 87, 123, 127

Du Preez, A.P. 186, 395

Du Preez, Max 389

Du Toit, Bettie 49

Du Toit, Rev. Paul 333, 334

Dutch Reformed Church 39, 43, 65, 67, 100, 171, 332, 333, 334, 412

Dutch, the 103

Eendekuil 39, 57

Egypt 112

Elandsvreuge (farm) 60, 61, 63
Elisenheim (farm) 56, 57
Eloff, Zacharias 58
Elundu 300
Emma Hoogenhout Primary School 58
Engelbrecht, Angel 104, 117, 322
England 30, 32, 41, 42, 53
Erasmus, Gerhard 419, 423, 451, 456, 459, 460, 463, 465, 473, 474
Erasmus, Tienie 87
Eros 62, 404
Eros Airport 222, 223, 347, 354
Eros Mountains 56
Escher, Alfred 134, 136–138, 141, 195
Ethiopia 23, 94, 110, 112, 120
Eyadéma, President 376

Farmers' Assistance Board 78, 95, 97, 121, 127
Federal Convention of Namibia (FCN) 313, 394, 399, 402, 406
Federal Party (FP) 159, 161, 163, 189, 190, 193, 216, 217
Finnish Missionary Society 100
First Committee 174
First World War 29, 31, 32, 40, 57, 108
first-tier government 347, 367
FNLA 155, 167, 279
foot-and-mouth disease 77–78, 81, 119, 121
Fort Namutoni 30
Fourie, Brand 137, 285
Fourie, Jopie 31
Fourie, Mr (of the De Riet farm) 87
Fourth Committee 174
France 133, 211, 267, 279, 284, 373
Frank, Simmy 56
Free State 29, 56, 65, 90, 255
Frey, Carl H. 195
Friesland 43
fundamental rights 236, 307, 309, 316, 353, 384, 385, 399, 410, 416, 417–418, 425–430, 442, 457, 469, 470, 475, 480, 487, 493

Gabon 376
Gang of Five 365, 373
//Garoëb, Justus 152, 153, 154, 363, 373, 469
//Garoëb, Moses 187, 478, 483
Geingob, Hage 18, 404, 406, 424, 427, 472, 478, 479
Geneva Conference 356–358
Geneva Protocol 386
Genscher, Hans-Dietrich 359, 376
George, Lloyd 34
German East Africa 32
German Evangelical Lutheran Church (GELC) 334
Germany 25, 28, 30, 31, 32, 34, 36, 38, 44, 54, 99, 177, 211, 255, 267, 284, 287, 376, 419, 455
Getzen, Eric 74
Gobabis 45, 90, 117, 156, 231, 241, 242, 250, 251
Gobbs, Simon 154
Good Offices Committee 136
Gorbachev, Mikhail 386
Gorges, Howard 35
Great Britain 32, 177, 211, 278
Greebe, Jan 380
Greeff, Chrisna (née Mudge) 64, 495
Greeff, Niel 206, 385
Gresse, Daan 333
Grootfontein 45, 47, 48, 67, 90, 95, 167, 240, 241, 250, 381
Gurirab, Theo-Ben 353, 358, 393, 410, 475, 489

Hälbich, Thea 334
Halenke, Herbert 230
Hamaambo, Dimo 264
Hamutenya, Hidipo 422, 436, 458
Hansa Hotel 62
Hansard 26, 79, 87, 88, 117
Haraseb, Max 313, 323
Hardap Dam 81, 86, 137
Hardap Rest Camp 137
Henning, Piet 49, 51, 208
Henties Bay 119

Hereros 25, 29, 30, 48, 73, 74, 75, 140,
141, 142, 145, 148, 152, 153, 158, 171,
265, 340, 490, 491
Hermanus 251
Heroes' Day 114
Herrigel, Otto 482
Hertzog, General 31, 36, 72
Hiemstra, Victor 381
Hisleiti, one 336
hit list 253, 254, 255, 388
Hitlerjugend 37
Hochland congregation 333
Hofmeyer, Gys R. 35
Hoogenhout P.I. (Administrator) 72
Horabe Block 95
Hough, Danie 353–355, 357, 369, 370,
374
Houphouët-Boigny, President 376
House of Commons 440
House of Lords 440
House of Review 440
Hulme, Bill 247
humanism 126, 138, 170
Hurter, Koot and Anna 62

Illuminati 251
Indian Constitution 450
Interessengemeinschaft Deutschsprachiger Südwester (IG) 230
interim government 172, 183, 184, 186,
207, 209, 211, 212, 214, 216, 219, 259,
307, 309, 312, 320, 321, 323–327, 343,
346, 347, 348, 350, 362, 371–372, 373,
375–378, 386, 423, 447
International Court 23, 74, 94, 109, 110,
112, 120, 132, 133, 187, 301
Iraq 33
Ithana, Pendukeni 463
Ivory Coast 376

Jagger, Jermia 323
Jansen, Nico 161, 256
Japan 32, 373
Jooste, Anna 56
Jooste, Frikkie 36, 72

Jooste, Marius 247
Joubert, Jan 223, 232
Junius, Joey 336

Kalangula, Peter 20, 177, 178, 355, 358,
361, 362, 365, 367, 368, 373, 380
Kalkfeld 41, 47, 49, 64, 252
Kallweit, Ernst 495
Kalondo, Monica 495
Kamanjab 67, 205, 206, 211
Kamanjab speech 205
Kamburona, Rudolph 241
Kaokoland 81, 246, 389
Kapuuo, Clemens 18, 21, 25, 75, 140,
141, 142, 145, 148, 149, 152, 153, 161,
171, 178, 179, 188, 189, 190, 198, 201,
245, 252, 253, 254, 255, 264, 265, 336
Karasburg 115, 119, 215
Karibib 119, 334, 401
Karuaera, Rev. 75
Karuaihe, Johannes 141, 178
Kashe, Bushman representative 176,
366
Katima Mulilo 240, 251, 404
Katjiuongua, Moses 375, 379, 382, 405,
410, 421, 426, 427, 430, 436, 437, 438,
440, 443, 444, 448, 449, 450, 452, 453,
454, 455, 458–460, 461, 463
Katutura 70, 75, 79, 127, 140, 252, 254,
376, 398, 404
Kaunda, President 156, 376
Kaura, Katuutire 484
Kavango 99, 100, 119, 178, 183, 251, 308,
398, 401, 402, 476
Kavangos 152, 153, 157
Keetmanshoop 39, 40, 57, 119, 256, 404,
495
Kemp, General 31
Kerina, Mburumba 74, 75, 76, 254
Khorab 32
Khorixas 404
Kilian, Mr 51
Kirkpatrick, Ian 282
Kirkpatrick, Jeane 355
Kissinger, Henry 13, 202, 279

Klopper, Henning 51, 72
Kloppers, Andrew 305, 322, 336, 338, 372
Koekenaap 53
Koevoet 389–392
Kohl, Helmut 376
Kolver, Bokkie 389
Kongwa 111
Korsten, Gé 286
Kozonguizi, Fanuel 74, 75, 149, 243, 357
Kuhlmann, Ernst 339
Kunene River 86, 193
Kunene Scheme 119, 158
Kutako, Hosea 73, 74, 75, 142, 145
Kwando 111
Kwanyama tribal area 28

Labuschagne, Faan 206
Land Bank 63, 121, 338, 339, 457
land reform 82, 107, 237, 410, 415, 457, 476, 477, 490
Langenhoven, C.J. 22, 77, 248, 266
Laubscher, Maritz 69
Lazy Spade (farm) 63, 64, 67, 77, 91, 95, 333
Le Clus, Willem 49
Le Roux, P.A.S. 89, 90
Lebanon 33
Legislative Assembly 23, 24, 35, 36, 37, 56, 67–68, 70, 71, 73, 75, 79–81, 83, 84, 85, 87–93, 95, 98–99, 101, 103, 104, 105, 108, 115, 116, 117, 118, 121, 122, 124, 126, 127, 128, 129, 132, 138, 144, 145, 149, 152, 157, 159, 160, 162, 164, 166, 168, 169, 174, 175, 176, 177, 185, 186, 188, 193, 196, 202, 205, 208, 211, 215, 216, 218, 219, 223, 229, 230, 235, 237, 245, 249, 256, 257, 260, 264, 265, 272, 306, 319, 322, 325, 326, 327, 328, 329, 330, 346, 350, 351, 352, 381, 383, 384, 385, 387, 397
Lemmer, Nico 67
Leuvenink, Inno 57
Liberation Front 282, 286, 305, 322
Liberia 23, 94, 110, 112, 120, 156

Lilienthal, Conrad 230, 235
Lombard, Koos 101
London 37, 119, 178, 307, 376
London Times 280
Louw, Appie 26, 222, 225, 229, 232, 234, 236, 242, 245, 250, 293, 296, 297, 336
Louw, Bokkie 250
Louw, Eric 109
Louw, M.S. 65
Louw, W.P. 250
Lubowski, Anton 399
Lüderitzbucht 30
Luipert, Daniel 249, 323, 341
Lusaka 111, 295, 301, 375, 376

Maasdorp, Willie 207, 323, 336
MacDonald, Bobby 88
Macmillan, Harold 70
Maharero, Frederick 29, 74
Maharero, Samuel 74
Maitland 53
Majavero, Alfons 178
majority rule 21, 254, 328
Malan, D.F. 33, 72
Malan, Magnus 354, 355, 369, 370, 389
Malan, Stefaans 26, 229, 236
Malherbe & Kiesewetter 62
Malherbe, Piet 186, 395
Maltahöhe 206, 246, 401
Mamili, Chief 171
mandate agreement 24, 32, 35, 39, 79, 82, 110
mandatory 33, 34, 145
Mandela, Nelson 18
Mangetti Quarantine Station 119
Marais, Billy 138, 140, 141, 153, 181, 200, 252, 259, 314, 339, 358, 359
Marais, Charl 78
Marais, Willem 49, 50
Maree, Marius 200
Mariental 214, 215, 315
Maritz, Engela 70
Maritz, Manie 31
Maskamberg 39, 53
Matjila, Andrew 406, 412, 445, 456

Maxuilili, Nathaniel 114

Mbanderus 152

McHenry, Donald F. 212, 359

Media24 495

Mey, Theo 199–200, 363, 366

Meyer, E.T. 125, 129, 229, 334, 351, 352

Meyer, Gertjie 63, 64, 67, 68, 69, 101

Meyer, Michael 242, 245

Meyerton 63, 64

Minnaar, Paul 26, 229, 236, 384, 385

Mohamed, Judge 450

Mootseng, Sylvester 178

Moraliswani, Chief 171

Mostert, Eddie 49

mother-tongue education 351, 412, 472

Mount Etjo 49, 77, 393

Mount Etjo Conference 393

Mouton, Chris 56, 225, 226

Mouton, Johanna 56

Mozambique 167, 302, 317, 319

MPLA (Movimento Popular de
    Libertação de Angola) 71, 155, 156,
    167, 279, 319

Mudge & Sons 63, 64

Mudge Brothers 61

Mudge, Chrisna 64, 495

Mudge, Dirk Frederik 49

Mudge, Dirk Frederik (Oupa Dick) 35,
    39, 43

Mudge, Dorothea Wilhelmina 40, 43

Mudge, Helene 40

Mudge, Henry Ferdinand (Hendrik)
    42, 43

Mudge, Henry Ferdinand (Henk) 42,
    63

Mudge, Jane 41, 43

Mudge, Mary 41, 43

Mudge, Richard Henry (Harry) 41, 42,
    43

Mudge, Riéth 247

Mudge, Sannie 50, 53, 54, 63

Mudge, Stienie (née Jacobs) 26, 58, 61,
    62, 63, 64, 65, 66, 69, 92, 252, 282, 481,
    496

Mudge, Susan 41, 43

Mudge, Thomas 42

Muller, Hilgard 137, 141, 142, 151

Multi-Party Conference 375, 378

Munjuku 152

Mutenga, Mrs 154

Muundjua, John 75

Muyongo, Mishake 357, 404, 406,
    468–469, 478, 482, 483, 484

Mynhardt, Mr 65, 66

Nankudu, Johny Otto (John ya Otto)
    111, 114

Namas 25, 30, 73, 140, 152, 153, 158,
    168, 195, 249, 341, 401, 490, 491

Namibia Christian Democratic Party
    (NCDP) 282, 286

Namibia United Democratic Organisa-
    tion (NUDO) 75

Namibia's Liberation Struggle 22, 111, 112

national anthem 423

National Assembly (NA) 312, 323, 324,
    325, 326, 327, 328, 330–331, 335, 336,
    342, 343, 344, 348, 349, 350–353, 354,
    360–361, 364, 365, 366, 367, 371, 372,
    373, 378, 379, 411, 415, 416, 424, 431–
    432, 434, 437, 438–441, 442, 444, 446,
    449, 459, 461, 462, 463, 465, 477, 481,
    482–483, 484, 485, 486

National Executive 98, 369

National Party (of South West Africa)
    18, 21, 23, 24, 25, 26, 35, 36, 66, 67, 70,
    71, 72–73, 79, 80, 82, 84, 87, 90–91, 92,
    96, 97, 102–106, 109, 111, 115–118,
    122, 123, 124, 126, 128, 129, 130, 132,
    133, 139, 140, 150, 152, 154, 159, 160,
    161, 163, 168, 169, 170, 171, 173, 175–
    176, 185, 190, 192, 193–199, 200, 201,
    203, 204, 205, 206, 211, 216–219, 220,
    222, 223, 224, 225, 226, 227, 228–230,
    231, 232, 233, 235, 236, 237, 238, 239,
    240, 241, 242, 243, 244, 246, 249, 250,
    251, 255, 256, 257, 259, 260, 261, 262,
    265, 267, 272, 273, 276, 285, 286, 287,
    291, 297, 304–307, 309, 313, 315, 319,

320, 321, 322, 326, 327–330, 331, 332, 333, 334, 335, 337, 338, 341, 344, 345, 346, 347, 348, 349, 351, 352, 353, 354, 359, 360, 362, 369, 372, 374, 381, 382, 383–385, 387, 388, 394, 395 424, 425, 427, 485

National Party (of South Africa) 31, 33, 38, 54, 72, 94, 103, 117, 130, 149, 163, 200, 201, 202, 223, 243, 246, 346, 356, 361, 379, 492

National Party Congress 26, 210, 231, 233, 249, 250, 382, 383

National Patriotic Front (NPF) 382, 394

National-Sozialistische Deutscher Arbeiter Party (NSDAP) 36–37

natural resources 107, 130, 287, 451, 490, 491

Naudé, Piet and Fanie 56

Naute 119

Ndjoba, Cornelius 21, 245, 253, 254, 264, 323, 325

Neef, Werner 20, 26, 228, 229, 234, 236, 298, 361

Netherlands, The 43–44

New Guinea 32

New Western Investments 395

New York 138, 142, 143, 147, 148, 178, 285, 292, 317

New York Accord 386

New Zealand 32

Ngavirue, Zedekia 17, 73, 495

Niehaus, Percy 79, 80, 81, 89, 92, 93, 96, 97, 98, 100, 102, 103, 104, 105, 109, 159, 202, 215, 266, 296, 297, 321, 322, 336

Nieuwoudt, Thys 334

Nkongo base 300

Noordoewer 240

Nortjé, Mr 49

NPP 435 161

Nujoma, Sam 21, 75–76, 111, 164, 205, 263, 299, 301, 302, 358, 376, 392, 399, 404, 411, 423, 459, 462, 470, 483

O'Linn, Bryan 104, 122, 159, 161, 189, 190

Oberholzer, Johanna 56

Oberholzers from Outjo 56

Observatory (in Pretoria) 363

Odendaal Commission 83, 85, 93, 97, 268

Odendaal farms 100, 106, 116

Odendaal Plan 23, 24, 86, 94, 103, 106, 116, 276, 308, 492

Odendaal Report 81–84, 86, 87, 88, 92, 93, 100, 115, 118, 128, 158

Odendaal, F.H. (Fox) 81

Odendaal, Willem 218, 384

official language 157, 424

Okahandja 45, 56, 119, 130, 227, 254

Okahao (farm) 252

Okatana (Oshakati) 81, 85

Okavango River 193

Omaruru 85, 119

Omatjenne Dam 45, 46, 48

Omatjenne North (farm) 39, 40, 45

Ombalantu 252

Omingonde (farm) 49

Ongulumbashe 111–114, 157

Ongwediva 96

Oosthuizen, Louis 238

Operasie Savannah 111

Opperman, Danie 334

Opperman, Duimpie 247

Opperman, Jurie 240

Oranjemund 137

Organisation of African Unity (OAU) 112, 135

Ossewa Brandwag movement 56, 239

Oshikango 112, 167

Oslo (farm) 46

Otavi 32, 45, 47, 63, 95, 119

Otjenga (farm) 63

Otjiwarongo 36, 39, 40, 41, 44, 45, 46, 47, 48, 49, 50, 51, 52, 54, 57, 61, 63, 64, 68, 100, 126, 137

Otjiwarongo Constituency 68, 70

Ottoman Empire 32, 33

Outjo 45, 49, 50, 56, 63, 64, 65, 66, 67, 68, 69, 84, 85, 95, 98, 100, 159, 242, 293, 333, 334

Outjo Constituency 67
Ovamboland 28, 81, 82, 86, 99, 100, 111, 119, 122, 128, 158, 183, 189, 190, 212, 251, 252, 253, 254, 255, 282, 299, 363, 391, 398, 399
Ovamboland People's Organisation (OPO) 75, 76, 469
Owambos 28, 50, 75, 76, 79, 122, 148, 149, 152, 153, 157, 177, 198, 252, 253, 362, 401, 469

Palace of Nations 358
Palestine 33
Papenfus, Theresa 143
Paternoster 53
People's Liberation Army of Namibia (PLAN) 114, 115, 302
Pérez de Cuéllar, Javier 376
petty apartheid 103, 104, 123, 326
Petzer, Gert 380
Philipp, General 283
Pienaar, Louis 378, 380, 381, 382, 387, 388, 411
Pik Botha en sy tyd 143
Piketberg 53
Pionierspark 242
P.J. Malherbe & Co 395, 396
PLAN *see* People's Liberation Army of Namibia
Platveld 47
Political Parties and Interest Groups in South Africa 17
"Politik in meinem Leben" 37
Polytech of Namibia 495
Port Elizabeth 238, 239, 283
Portugal 28, 114, 155, 167
Potgieter, Tom 84
poverty 488, 493
powers of the President 411, 431, 432, 438, 454, 461
Pratt, David 70
Preamble 407, 408, 409, 414, 415, 420, 421, 450, 471, 479
Pretoria 51, 113, 114, 136, 137, 238, 272, 282, 284, 354, 363, 366

Pretorius, J.W.F. (Koos) 68, 89, 90, 92, 96, 105, 117, 121, 127, 133, 138, 165, 170, 179, 185, 188, 193, 202, 217, 218, 219, 224, 225, 231, 241, 258, 262, 288, 306, 308, 309, 322, 328, 332, 350, 352, 353, 354, 363, 372, 384, 388, 394, 396, 399, 406, 412, 419, 421, 422, 433, 466, 467, 468
Pretorius, Pieter 68
Prinsloo, Boebie 56
Prinsloo, Daan 200
private schools 121, 411–414, 420, 424, 429
Proclamation 12 248
Proclamation AG 8 349, 379
Proclamation AG 21 330, 331
Proclamation AG 24 335
Proclamation AG 63 293, 296
Proclamation R. 101 368, 378, 379, 384, 385
Proclamation R. 429 234

raised-hands referendum 84
Rapport 190, 205, 367
Rapportryers 65, 66, 67, 333, 374
Rebellion of 1914 31
Reconstituted National Party (Herstigte Nasionale Party [HNP]) 129, 192, 217, 240, 251, 286, 387
Reënmaker van die Namib 354, 368, 380
Rehoboth 169, 183, 249, 322
Rehoboth Constituency 401
Rehoboth Free Democratic Party 381
Renosterkloof 49
representative authority 35, 182, 183, 220, 221, 258, 309, 321, 349, 350, 361, 379, 412
Republican Party (RP) 22, 24, 56, 233, 234, 235, 236, 237, 240, 241, 242, 245, 246, 247, 248, 249, 250, 255, 256, 260, 261, 263, 264, 272, 276, 286, 306, 307, 308, 309, 313, 327, 333, 349, 350, 352, 353, 383, 384, 385, 387, 397, 398, 402, 484–485, 486

Republikein 246, 247, 248, 249, 250, 251, 397, 398, 485, 495

Resolution 385 187, 212, 265, 270

Resolution 435 161, 277, 281, 284, 285, 290, 291, 292, 293, 295, 296, 297, 298, 299, 305, 311, 312, 314, 317, 324, 328, 356, 361, 362, 382, 385, 387, 388, 393

Resolution 439 284

Resolution 447 317

Rhenish Mission Society 100

Rhodes, Cecil John 29, 30

Rhodes, the Race for Africa 29

Rhodesia 74, 167, 187, 275, 318

Richard, Dirk 246

Rietfontein 63

Riruako, Kuaima 144, 255, 323, 340, 376, 477

Robben Island 114

Robberts, Paul 206

Robberts, Rob 206

Rodenwoldt, Volker 230

Röhr, Hans 305

Roux, Piet 125, 208

Rowse, A.L. 28

Ruacana 113, 496

Ruacana Hydroelectric Scheme 82

Ruacana Project 158, 336

Rukoro, Vekuii 282, 412, 414, 419, 429, 458

Rundu 99, 251

Ruppel, Hartmut 409, 419, 420, 429, 434, 435, 437, 440, 444, 445, 446, 449, 451, 460, 465, 477

Russian forces 155, 156, 269, 278, 279, 280, 386

Rusthof (farm) 40, 45–46, 47, 50

Samoa 32

Sarusas Development Corporation 118

Sauer, Paul 223

Schaaf, Gernot 240, 241

Schneider-Waterberg 385

Schneider, Herbert 77

Schoeman, Hendrik 115

Scholtz, Leopold 111, 114, 156

Schülerheim 100

Schultz, George 376

Schumann, Prof. 60

Schwartz, Stuart 172

Schwarzenfels (farm) 49, 50

Scott, Michael 74

Second Committee 174

Second House of Parliament 410, 416, 438, 439, 440, 454, 455, 478

Second World War 54, 58, 72, 73, 108, 236

second-tier authority 181, 183, 207, 224, 249, 326, 328, 347, 348, 381, 387, 388

Security Council 122, 132, 134, 136, 147, 158, 186, 187, 188, 218, 261, 263, 267, 268, 269, 270, 271, 273, 274, 277, 283–285, 290, 291, 296, 297, 302, 310, 312, 314, 315, 316, 318, 324, 325, 336, 345, 359, 362, 387, 392

Security Police 206, 396

separate development 24, 83, 89, 92, 117, 123, 126, 140, 158, 162, 163, 165, 168, 170

Sharpeville 23, 70

Shipanga, Andreas 282, 375, 376, 377, 379

Shiyagaya, Toivo 21, 252, 256, 336

Silas, headman 336

Simasiku, Siseho 357

Siseho, Gabriel 323

Skietkommando 66

Skrywer, Johannes 289, 293, 336

Slabbert, Frederik van Zyl 192

Smit, B.J. 36

Smit, Paul 26, 161, 217, 229, 236

Smuts, General J.C. 31, 32, 34, 35, 36, 44, 72, 73, 81, 109, 165

South West Africa issue 109, 132, 138, 200, 283, 310, 311, 332, 344

South West Africa National Union (SWANU) 75, 76, 112, 375, 382

South West Africa People's Organisation (SWAPO) 14, 20, 21, 23, 25, 75, 76, 111, 112–114, 126, 142, 143, 145, 149, 152, 153, 156, 157, 177, 178, 185,

186, 187, 189, 190, 192, 196, 197, 198, 202, 203, 204, 205, 212, 216, 227, 232, 234, 249, 251, 252, 253, 254, 255, 257, 259, 260, 261–264, 267, 268, 269, 270, 272, 273, 274, 275, 277, 280, 281, 284, 286–288, 290, 291, 292, 295, 296, 297, 299–300, 302–304, 305, 310, 311, 313, 314, 315–316, 317, 319, 320, 323, 324, 334, 335–336, 337–338, 340, 343, 345, 352, 357–358, 361, 362, 367, 368, 375, 376, 378, 380, 382, 387, 388, 389, 391, 392–393, 394, 396, 397–398, 399, 401– 402, 404, 406–407, 409, 410–411, 417, 418, 419, 423, 424, 428, 428, 431, 432, 434, 435, 436, 437, 438, 439, 440, 442, 443, 444, 445, 447, 448, 450, 451, 452, 454, 455, 456, 457, 459, 461, 462, 464, 466, 468, 469, 470, 473, 475, 479, 481, 482–483, 489, 491, 492; SWAPO Democrats (SWAPO-D) 282, 375, 394; SWAPO document 406, 407, 410, 411, 444, 451

South West Africa Survey 1967   119, 143, 166, 170, 344

Soviet Block 112

Spies, F.J. du Toit 111

Spies, Jan 22, 246, 247, 248, 249, 339, 398

Staby, Hans 384, 385, 406, 409–410, 412, 414, 427, 433, 440, 450, 471, 472

Stals, Ernst 26, 28

Standing Committee on Standing Rules and Orders and Internal Arrangements *see* Committee on Standing Rules and Orders and Internal Arrangements

Steenkamp, A.P. 208

Steenkamp, Jannie 56

Steenkamp, Stony 129

Stellenbosch 43, 57, 58, 59, 192, 240

Steyn, A.P. 129

Steyn, Jan 206

Steyn, M.T. 231, 234, 243, 254, 335, 346, 347

Strauss, Franz Josef 255

Strydom, Florrie 58

Strydom, Jan 58

Südwestafrika Gruppe 36

Summerhayes, David 42

Sunday Express 367, 368

Sunday Times 151, 367, 368

Swakop Dam 119

Swakopmund 54, 58, 69, 156, 261, 321, 349, 356, 357, 371, 401

SWAMEX Trust 186, 394, 396, 397

SWANU *see* South West Africa National Union

Switzerland 357

Syria 33

Tanganyika 32

Tanzania 111, 302, 317

Tawse, Mrs 57

Terblanche, Sampie 192

terrorism 23, 112, 114, 131, 156, 188, 227, 270, 314, 317, 321, 322

Thatcher, Margaret 393

The Citizen 368

The Hague 23, 93, 110

The SADF and the Border War 114, 390

The Star 368

Theunissen, Coeries 67

Third Committee 174

Thomas, Antony 29

Thompson, Brian 69

three-tier government system 181, 182

Tibinyane, Gregor 178, 201, 323, 336

Tjingaete, Elifas 323

Tjingaete, Fanuel 338

Tjiriange, Ngarikutuke 432, 444, 445, 446, 462, 468, 476

Tjirimuje, Erwin 75

Tjitindero, Mosé 406, 412, 457, 483

Togo 32, 376

Toivo ya Toivo, Herman Andimba 75, 111, 114

Tokarev pistols 111

Tondern, Schleswig-Holstein 43

total onslaught 19, 155, 279, 290, 338, 360, 373

Totthill, David 147

Transvaal 29, 40, 41, 56, 70, 81
Tromp, Jan and Wiks 56
Tsumeb 85, 401
TUFEK 219
Tuhadeleni, Eliaser 114
Tuhandele, Eliazer 111
Turnhalle Conference 19, 152–154, 157, 171, 174, 176, 177, 185, 189, 191–193, 195, 199, 205, 207–208, 218, 219, 221, 227, 237, 242, 244, 272, 308, 313, 336, 337, 341, 345–346, 348, 394
Turnhalle Constitution 183, 184, 190, 209, 211, 212, 215, 216, 217, 219, 227, 249, 257, 367, 297, 309, 312, 313, 321, 328, 341, 348, 371
Turnhalle model 328

Uahekua Herunga Primary School 496
Uganda 126, 487
unemployment 488, 493
Union Party (subsequently South West Party) 35
UNITA 155, 167, 279
United National South West Party (UNSWP) 36, 37, 54, 66, 69, 71, 72, 79, 82, 88, 92, 93, 96, 104, 109, 115, 116, 117, 118, 126, 130, 159, 266, 322
United Nations (UN) 19, 20, 25, 33, 74, 83, 94, 108, 113, 116, 132, 133, 134, 135, 138, 142, 186, 187, 189, 237, 259, 261, 263, 264–265, 267, 268–269, 271, 273, 274, 276, 281, 284, 297, 301, 355, 374, 388, 481
United Nations Transition Assistance Group (UNTAG) 268, 269, 270, 272, 292, 298, 304, 310, 324, 388–389, 391, 392, 393, 398, 399, 400
United Party 33, 44, 72, 109, 130, 145, 189, 321
United States of America (USA) 110, 156, 173, 177, 187, 211, 212, 267, 279, 317, 355, 359, 360, 376, 393
Urquhart, Brian 357
USA see United States of America
Usakos 54

Van den Bergh, Hendrik 147, 149, 157, 276
Van den Bergh, Kerneels 115
Van der Merwe, Banie 51
Van der Merwe, Gert 50
Van der Merwe, Paul 199, 223, 224, 225, 227, 230, 242
Van der Walt, Ben 135, 147
Van der Walt, Tjaart 188, 191, 334
Van der Wath, J.G.H. (Johannes) 89, 123, 124, 127, 132, 135
Van Eck Power Station 158
Van Jaarsveld, Rev. 101
Van Lills 56
Van Niekerk, Boesman 56
Van Niekerk, Willie 374, 377, 378, 395, 396
Van Rooyen, Rit 208
Van Schalkwyk, Paul 247
Van Tonder brothers 40
Van Tonder family 43, 44
Van Tonder, C.J. (Cornelius) 36, 41
Van Tonder, Magrieta Cornelia 40, 45
Van Tonder, Petrus Stefanus (Oupa Piet) 35, 39, 41, 44, 45, 49
Van Tondern, Andreas Corneliz 43
Van Waterberg, Phillipus 73
Van Wyk, At 354, 368, 380, 382, 393
Van Wyngaarden, Louise 235
Van Zijl, Eben 89, 90, 105, 124, 125, 127, 137, 140, 151, 152, 153, 162, 163, 165, 168, 169, 170, 172, 173, 174, 175, 176, 177, 179–180, 183, 184, 191, 199, 200, 202, 203, 206, 208, 209, 210, 219, 220, 221, 222, 224, 225, 226, 229, 231, 240, 243, 244, 249, 250, 251, 259–260, 291, 296, 298, 307, 311–312, 314, 323, 326, 328, 333, 336, 338, 341, 346, 376, 382, 383
Van Zyl, Ben 56
Van Zyl, Frans 168, 176, 188, 384, 385, 390
Van Zyl, Joos 87
Vance, Cyrus 317